ultimate G[...]

BASS BONANZA

50 GREAT ROCK BASS TRANSCRIPTIONS IN NOTES AND TAB

ISBN 978-1-4584-1813-5

HAL•LEONARD®
CORPORATION

7777 W. Bluemound Rd. P.O. Box 13819 Milwaukee, WI 53213

Visit Hal Leonard Online at
www.halleonard.com

CONTENTS

Ain't No Mountain High Enough

Words and Music by Nickolas Ashford and Valerie Simpson

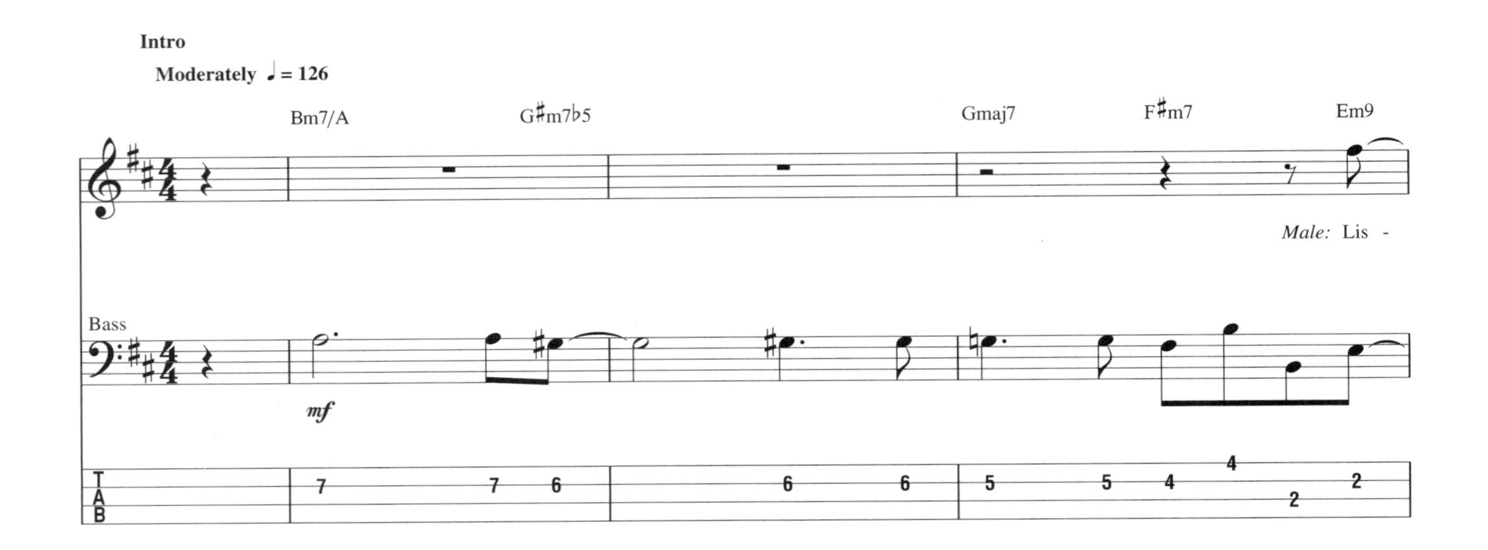
Intro
Moderately ♩ = 126
Bm7/A
G♯m7♭5
Gmaj7
F♯m7
Em9
Male: Lis -
Bass
mf

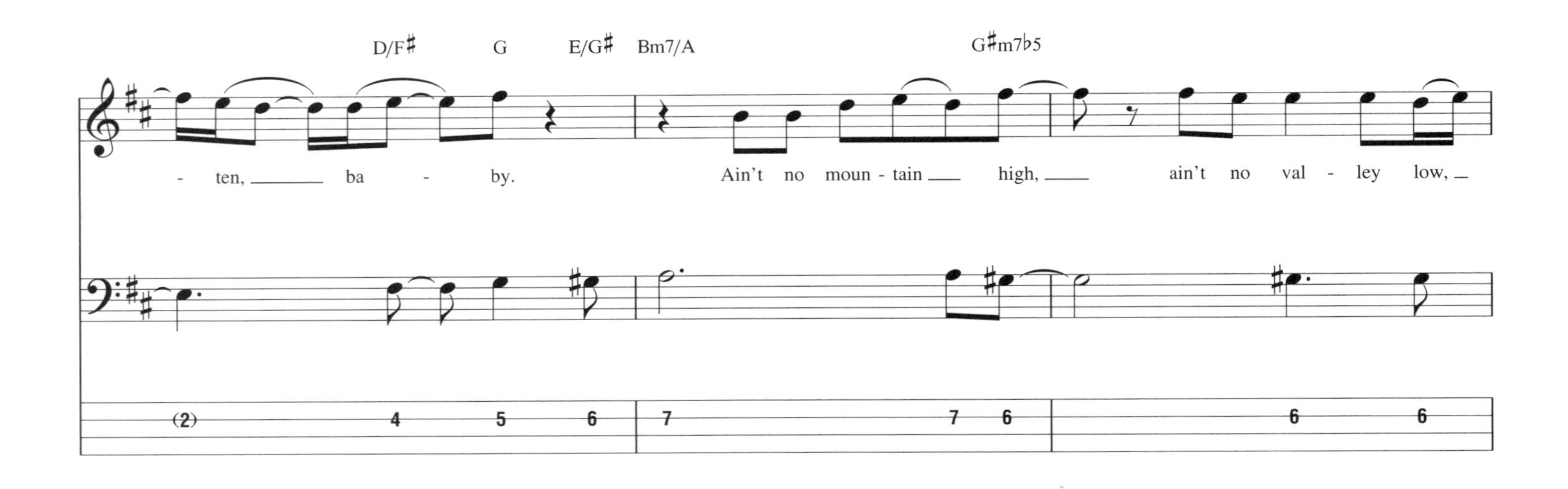
D/F♯
G
E/G♯
Bm7/A
G♯m7♭5
- ten, ba - by.
Ain't no moun - tain high,
ain't no val - ley low,

Gmaj7
F♯m7
Em9
D/F♯
G
E/G♯
Verse
Bm7/A
G♯m7♭5
ain't no riv - er wide e - nough, ba - by.
Female: 1. If you need me, call

Gmaj7 F#m7 Em9 D/F# G E/G#
me no mat - ter where you are, no mat - ter how far.
Male: Don't wor - ry, ba -
Bm7/A G#m7b5 Gmaj7 F#m7 Em7
Just call my name, I'll be there in a hur - ry. You don't have to wor -
- by.
Chorus
F#m7 Gmaj7 Em9 F#m7 Bm
- ry, 'cause, ba - by, there
Oh, ba - by, there
ain't no moun - tain high e - nough,
Gmaj7 Em9 F#m7 Bm Gmaj7 Em9 F#m7
ain't no val - ley low e - nough, ain't no riv - er wide

Bm
Esus4
E
D/F♯
G
e - nough to keep me from get - tin' to you, babe. Male: 2. Re - mem - ber the day
Verse
Bm7/A
G♯m7♭5
Gmaj7
F♯m7
Em9
I set you free? I told you you could al - ways count on me,
D/F♯
G
E/G♯
Bm7/A
G♯m7♭5
dar - lin'. From that day on, I made a vow. I'll be there when you want
Gmaj7
F♯m7
Em7
F♯m7
Chorus
Gmaj7
Em9
F♯m7
me, some way, some - how.
Female: 'Cause ba - by, there
Male: Oh, ba - by, now,
ain't no moun - tain high

Bm
Gmaj7
Em9
F♯m7
Bm
e - nough,
ain't no val - ley low
e - nough,
Gmaj7
Em9
F♯m7
Bm
Esus4
E
D/F♯
G
ain't no riv - er wide
e - nough
to keep me from get - tin' to you,
A7sus4
babe.
Male: Oh, no, dar - lin'.
Female: No
Bridge
A/G
F♯sus4
F♯
wind, no rain, or win - ter's cold

B7sus4
B7
Gmaj7
A/G
can stop me, ba - by,
No, no, ba - by.
'cause you are my
If you're
Bm/A
A
Bm/A
A
Bm/A
Cm/B♭
B♭
Fm
goal.
ev - er in trou - ble, I'll be there on the dou - ble. Just send for me, oh, ba -
Oh, ba -
Verse
E♭/G
Fm7♭5/C♭
Cm7/B♭
Am7♭5
- by. Ha!
- by. Ha!
3. My love is a - live way down in my heart,
Whoo!
A♭maj7
Gm7
Fm9
E♭/G
A♭
F7/A
Cm7/B♭
Am7♭5
al - though we are miles a - part.
Ev - er need a help - ing hand,
If you ev - er need a help - ing hand,

A♭maj7
Gm7
Fm7
Gm7
I'll be there on the dou - ble as fast as I can.
Don't you know that there
I'll be there on the dou - ble just as fast as I can.
Don't you know that there
Chorus
A♭maj7
Fm9
Gm7
Cm
ain't no moun - tain high e - nough,
ain't no val - ley low
e - nough,
Female: ain't no riv - er wide e - nough to
Male: ain't no riv - er wide e - nough.
Fsus4
F
A♭9
keep me from get - tin' to you, babe? Don't you know that there
There
ain't no moun - tain high

Cm
Abmaj7
Fm9
Gm7
Cm
e - nough,
ain't no val - ley low
e - nough,

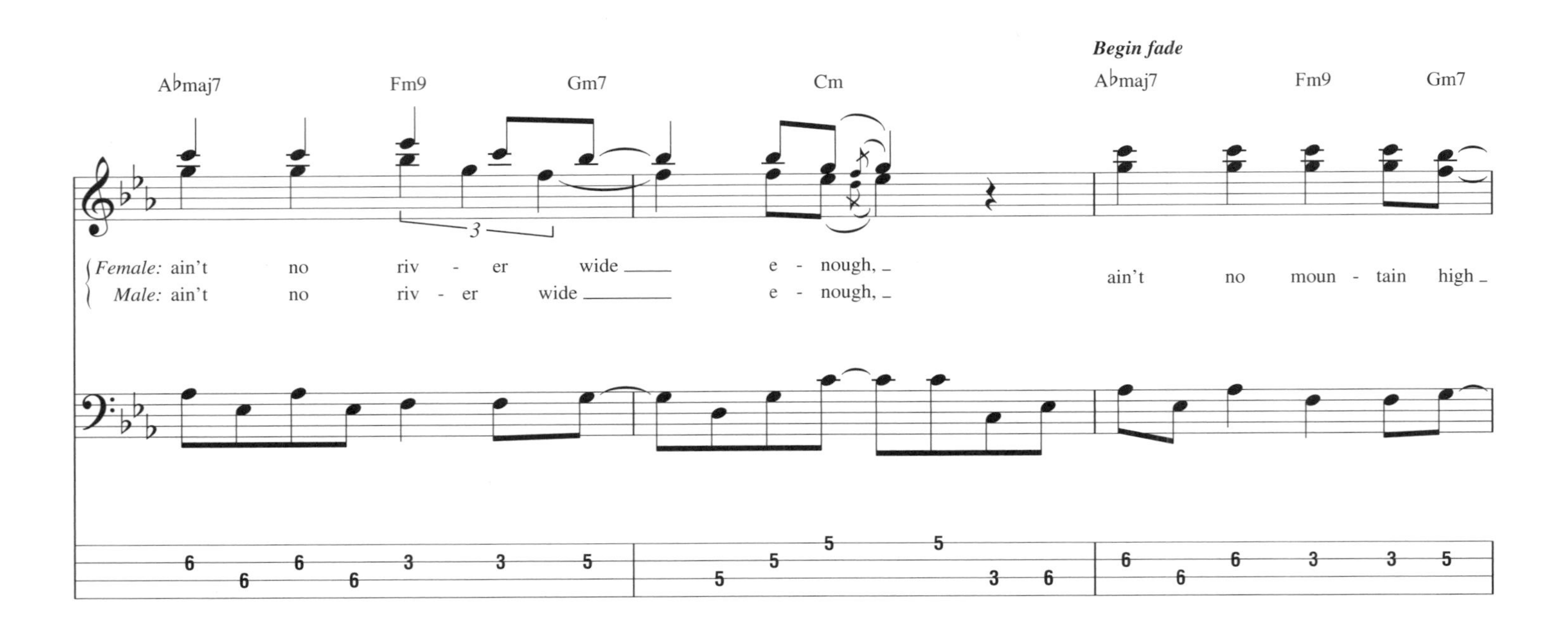
Begin fade
Abmaj7
Fm9
Gm7
Cm
Abmaj7
Fm9
Gm7
Female: ain't no riv - er wide
e - nough,
Male: ain't no riv - er wide
e - nough,
ain't no moun - tain high

Fade out
Cm
Abmaj7
Fm9
Gm7
Cm
e - nough,
ain't no val - ley low
e - nough...

All the Small Things

Words and Music by Tom De Longe and Mark Hoppus

Intro
Moderately fast Rock ♩ = 148
G5 F5
C5
F5/C
G5
N.C.
F5
f
Verse
C5
G5
F5
G5
1. All the small things. True care, truth brings.
I'll take one lift. Your ride, best trip.
Al - ways, I know you'll be at my show.

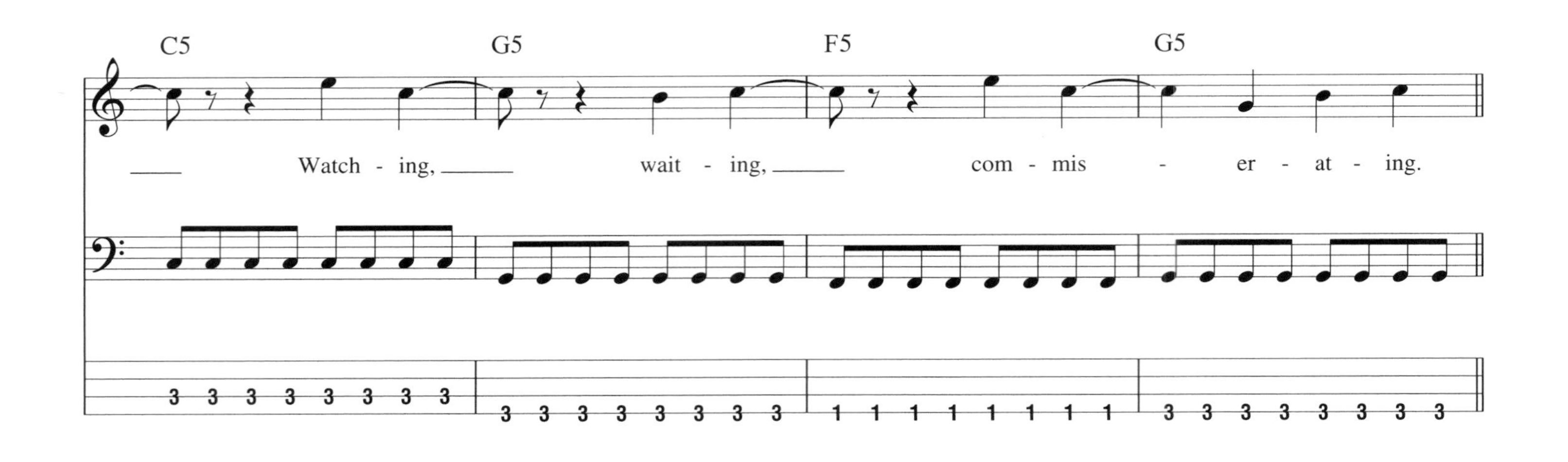
C5
G5
F5
G5
Watch - ing,
wait - ing,
com - mis - er - at - ing.
3 3 3 3 3 3 3 3
3 3 3 3 3 3 3 3
1 1 1 1 1 1 1 1
3 3 3 3 3 3 3 3

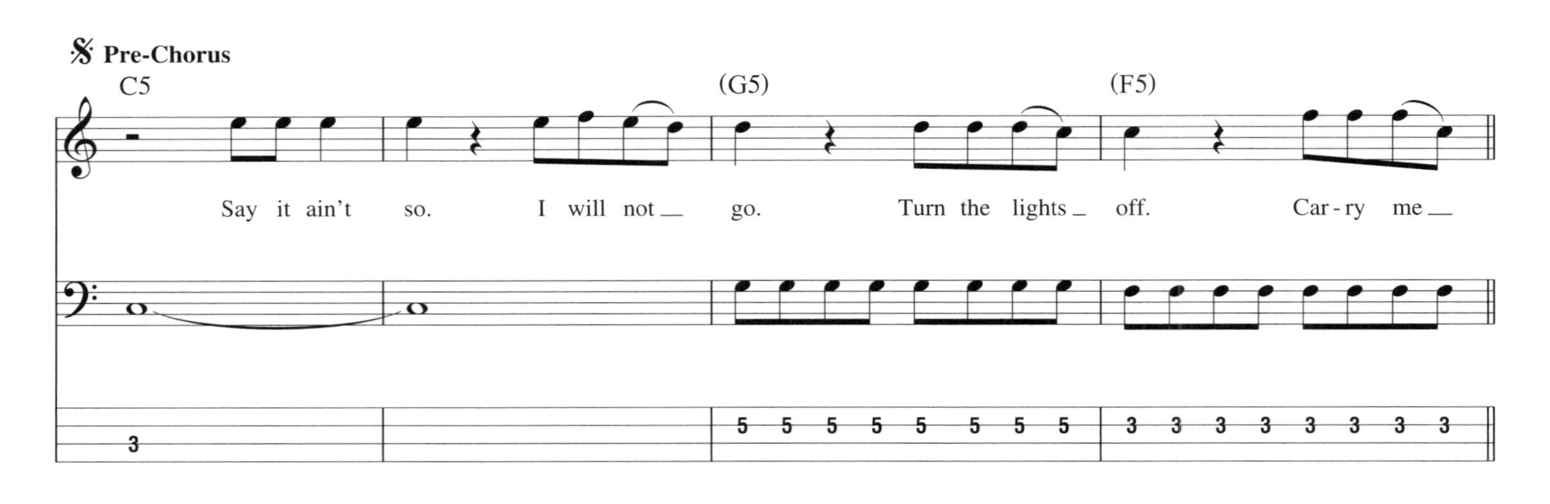
Pre-Chorus
C5
(G5)
(F5)
Say it ain't so. I will not go. Turn the lights off. Car - ry me
3
5 5 5 5 5 5 5 5
3 3 3 3 3 3 3 3

Chorus
C5
G5
F5
home.
Na, na, na, na, na, na, na, na, na, na. Na, na, na, na, na, na, na, na, na, na.
3 3 3 3 3 3 3 3
3 3 3 3 3 3 3 3
5 5 5 5 5 5 5 5
3 3 3 3 3 3 3 3

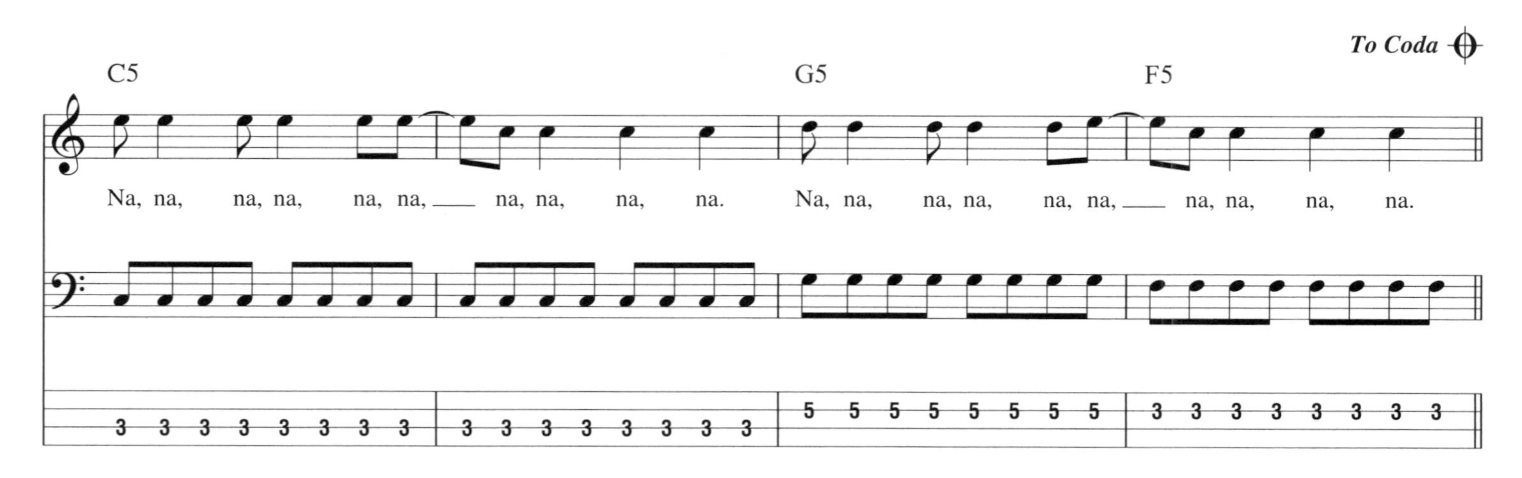
To Coda
C5
G5
F5
Na, na, na, na, na, na, na, na, na, na. Na, na, na, na, na, na, na, na, na, na.
3 3 3 3 3 3 3 3
3 3 3 3 3 3 3 3
5 5 5 5 5 5 5 5
3 3 3 3 3 3 3 3

Interlude
C5
F5/C
G5
N.C.
F5
Verse
C5
G5
F5
G5
2. Late night, come home. Work sucks, I know.
D.S. al Coda
C5
G5
F5
G5
She left me ros - es by the stairs. Sur - pris - es let me know she cares.
Coda
Interlude
C
F5
G5
Play 3 times
C5
F5
G5

Outro
C5 G5 F5
Say it ain't so. I will not go. Turn the lights off. Car-ry me
C5 G5 F5
home. Keep your head still. I'll be your thrill. The night will go on, my lit-tle wind-
C5 G5 F5
mill. Say it ain't so. I will not go. Turn the lights off. Car-ry me
C5 G5
home. Keep your head still. I'll be your thrill. The night will go
F5 C5
on, the night will go on, my lit-tle wind-mill.

Animal I Have Become

Words and Music by Neil Sanderson, Adam Gontier, Brad Walst, Gavin Brown and Barry Stock

Drop D tuning, down 1 step:
(low to high) C-G-C-F

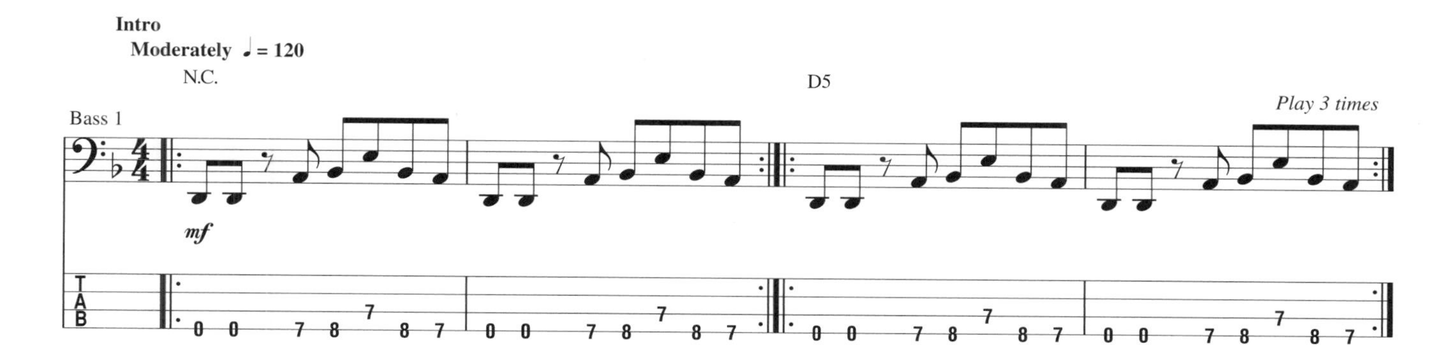
Intro
Moderately ♩ = 120
N.C.
D5
Play 3 times
Bass 1
mf
T
A
B

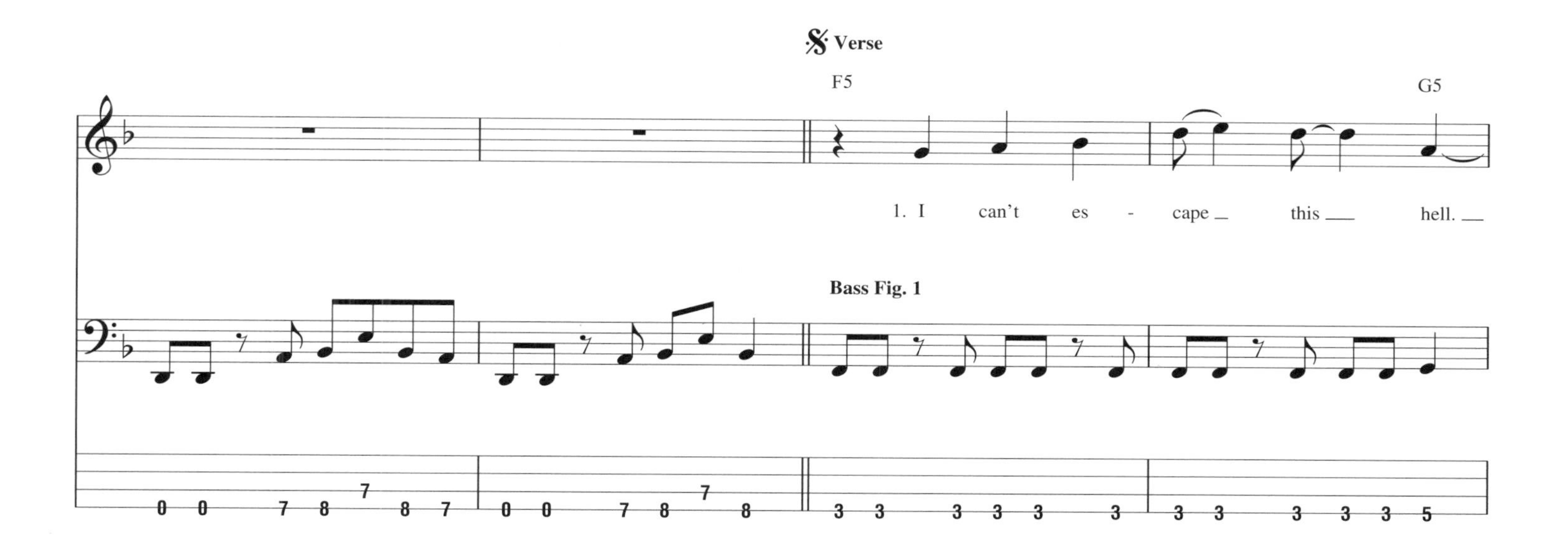
Verse
F5
G5
1. I can't es - cape this hell.
Bass Fig. 1

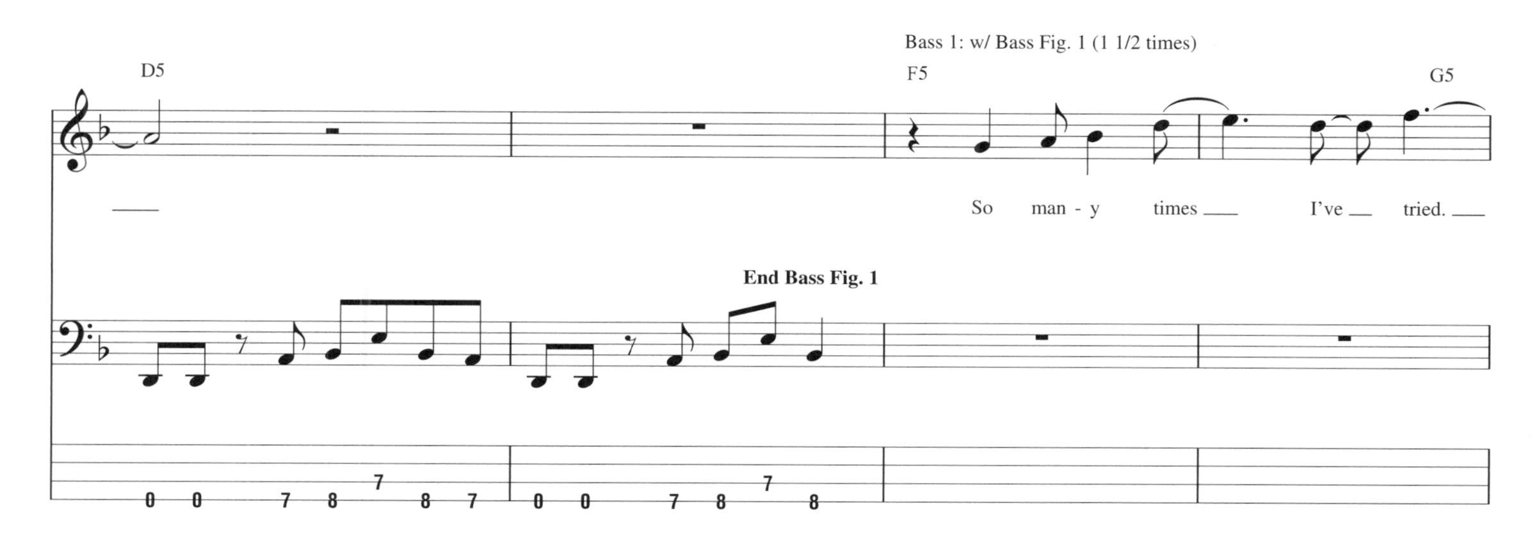
D5
Bass 1: w/ Bass Fig. 1 (1 1/2 times)
F5
G5
So man - y times I've tried.
End Bass Fig. 1

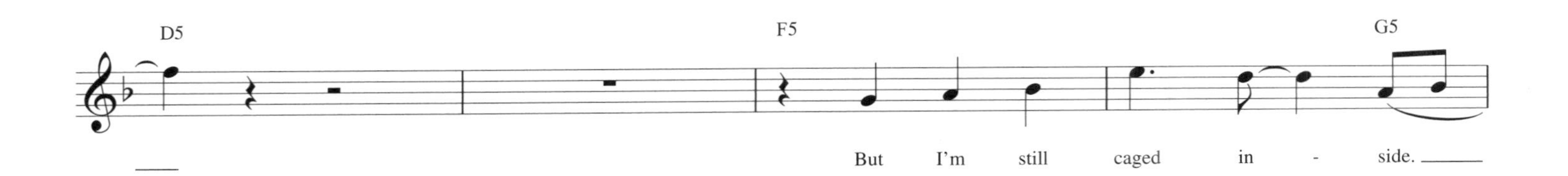
D5
F5
G5
But I'm still caged in - side.

D5
F5
Some-bod - y get me through this night - mare,
Bass 1
0 0 7 8 7 8 7
0 0 7 8 7 8
3 3 3 3 3 3
3 3 3 3 3 3

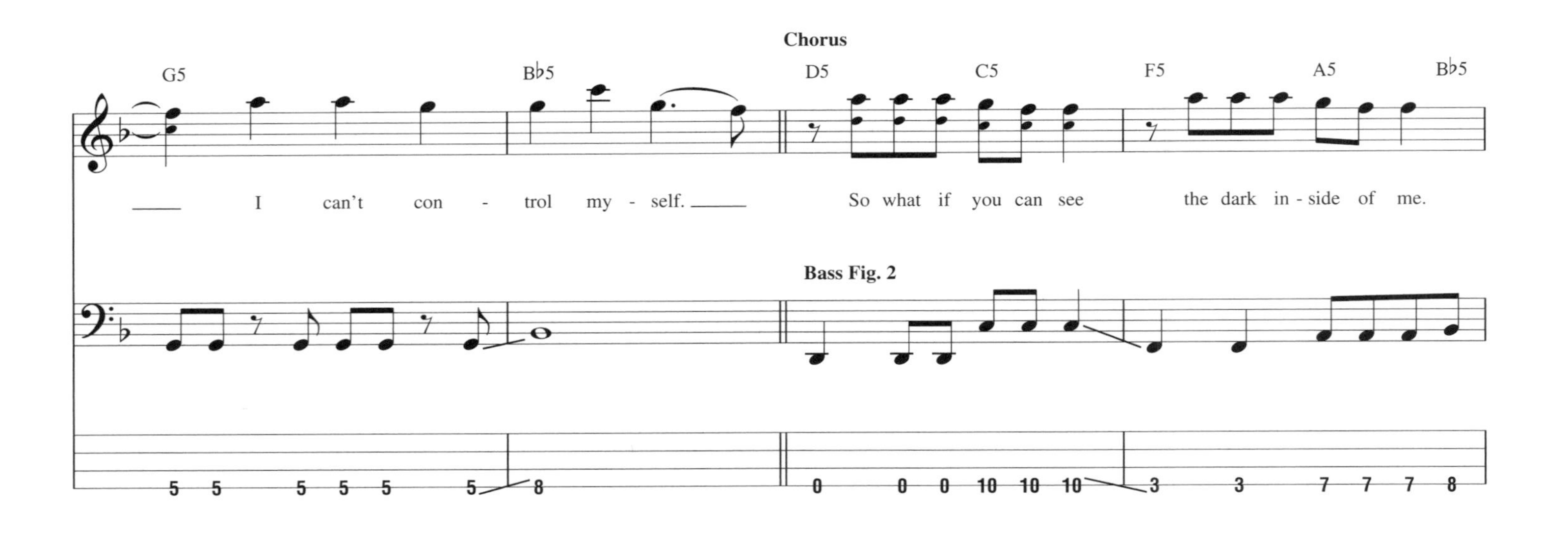
Chorus
G5
B♭5
D5
C5
F5
A5
B♭5
I can't con - trol my - self.
So what if you can see the dark in - side of me.
Bass Fig. 2
5 5 5 5 5 5 8
0 0 0 10 10 10
3 3 7 7 7 8

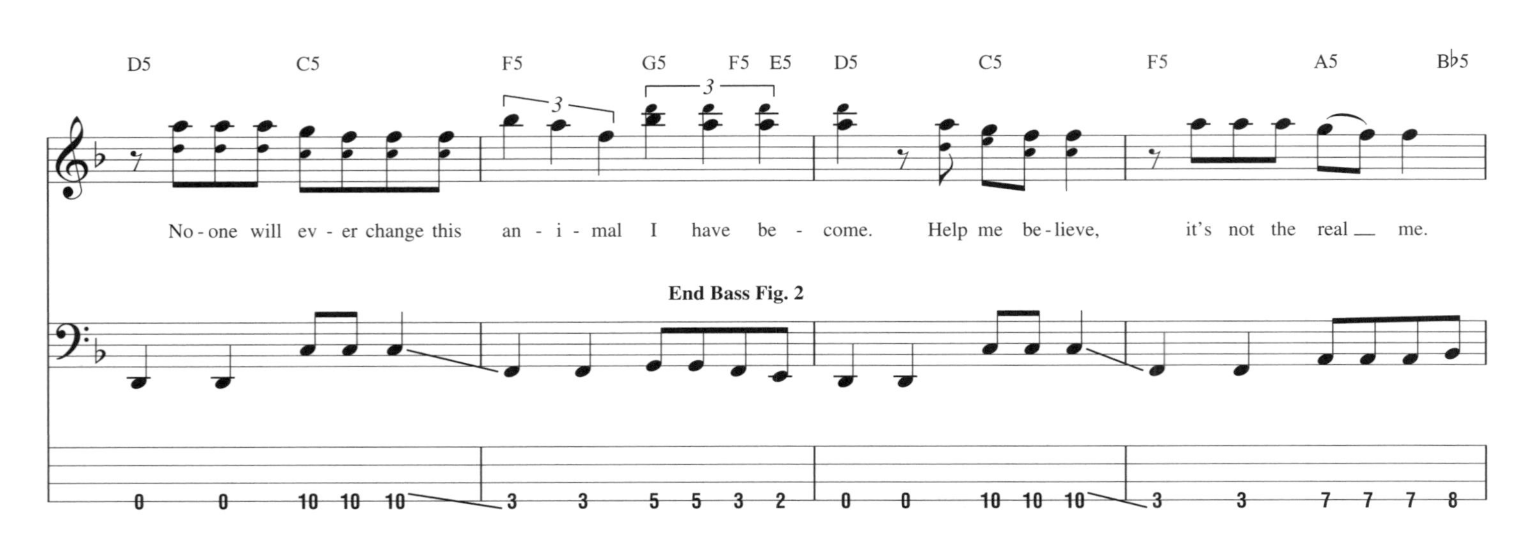
D5
C5
F5
G5
F5
E5
D5
C5
F5
A5
B♭5
No - one will ev - er change this an - i - mal I have be - come. Help me be - lieve, it's not the real me.
End Bass Fig. 2
0 0 10 10 10
3 3 5 5 3 2
0 0 10 10 10
3 3 7 7 7 8

D5 C5 F5 G5 F5 E5 D5
Some-bod - y help me tame this an - i - mal.
This an - i - mal, this an - i - mal.

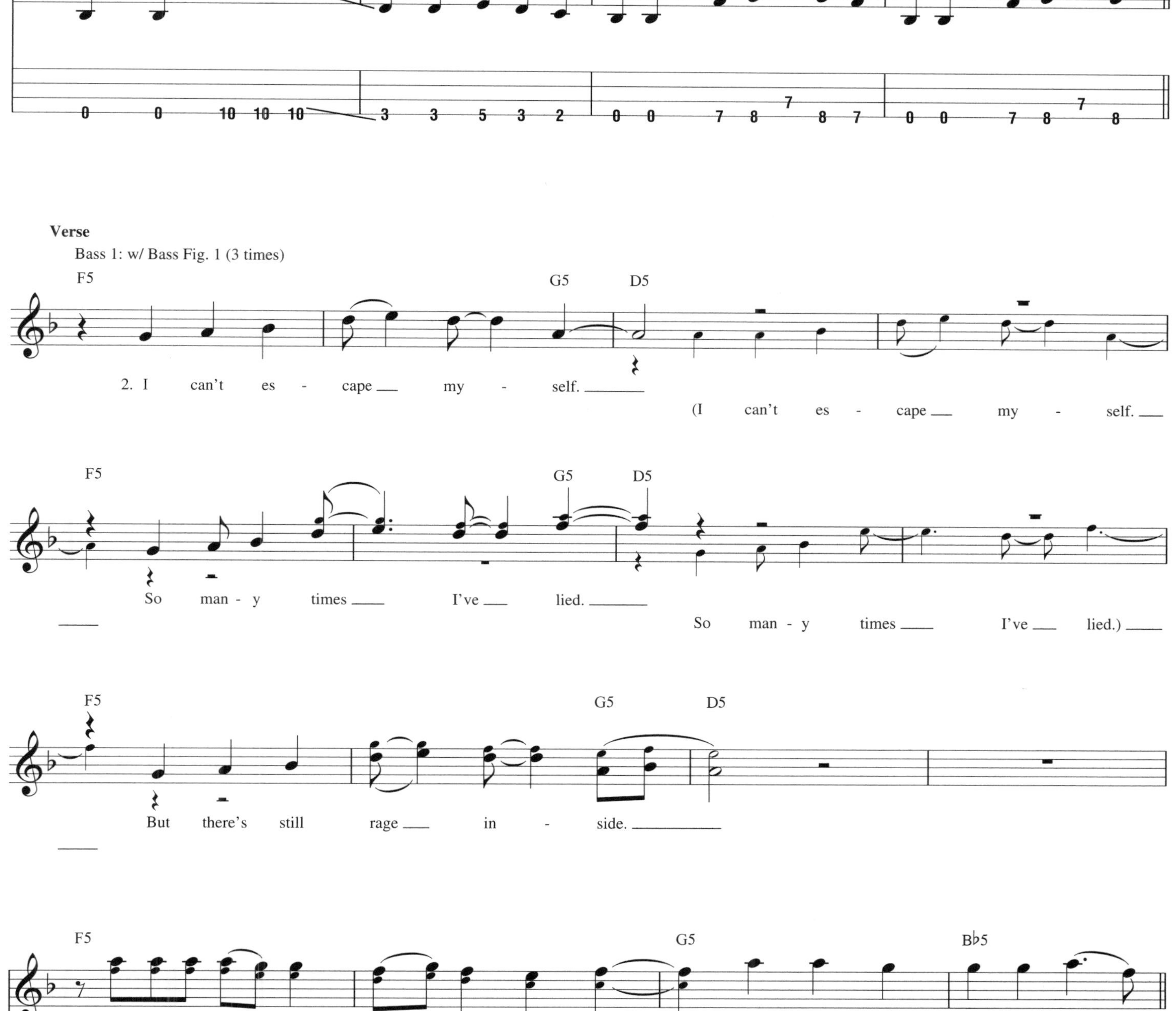
Verse
Bass 1: w/ Bass Fig. 1 (3 times)
F5 G5 D5
2. I can't es - cape my - self.
(I can't es - cape my - self.
F5 G5 D5
So man - y times I've lied.
So man - y times I've lied.)
F5 G5 D5
But there's still rage in - side.

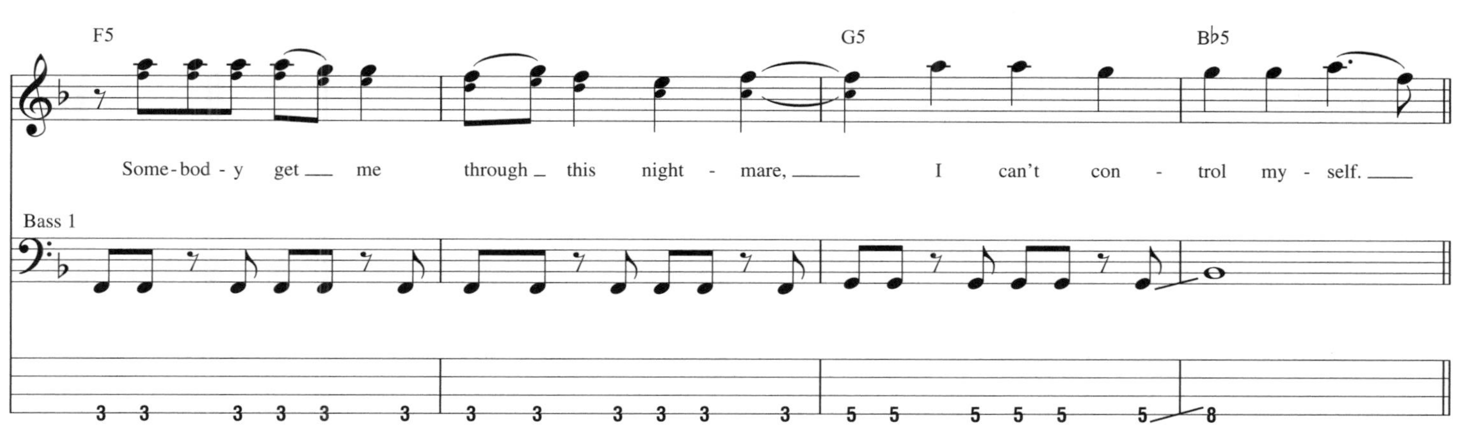
F5 G5 B♭5
Some-bod - y get me through this night - mare, I can't con - trol my - self.
Bass 1

Chorus
Bass 1: w/ Bass Fig. 2 (2 times)
D5 C5 F5 A5 B♭5 D5 C5 F5 G5 F5 E5
So what if you can see the dark in - side of me. No one will ev - er change this an - i - mal I have be -
D5 C5 F5 A5 B♭5 D5 C5 F5 G5 F5 E5
come. Help me be - lieve, it's not the real __ me. Some - bod - y help me tame this an - i - mal I have be -
D5 C5 F5 A5 B♭5 D5 C5 F5 G5 F5 E5
come. Help me be - lieve, it's not the real __ me. Some - bod - y help me tame this an - i -
Bass 1
0 0 10 10 10 3 3 7 7 7 8 0 0 10 10 10 3 3 5 3 2
Bridge
D5 B♭5 D5
mal. Some - bod - y help me through __ this night - mare. I can't con -
0 0 7 8 7 8 7 8 8 8 8 8 8 5 5 5 8 7 8 7 0 0 0 0 0 0
F5 B♭5 G5 D5
trol my - self. Some - bod - y wake me from __ this night - mare. Well, I can't __ es -
(Some - bod - y wake me from __ this night - mare.)
3 3 3 3 3 3 8 8 8 8 8 8 5 5 5 8 7 8 7 0 0 0 0 0 0

Interlude
F5
B♭5
N.C.
D5
cape this hell.
This an - i - mal,
3
this an - i - mal.
This an - i - mal,
this an - i - mal.
1., 2.
3.
Chorus
N.C.
Bass 1 tacet
So what if you can see the dark in - side of me.
No one will ev - er change this an - i - mal I have be -
*Bass 2
Bass 2
Bass 1
divisi
*Keyboard arr. for bass, played mf.
Bass 2 tacet
D5
C5
F5
A5
B♭5
G5
E5
come. Help me be - lieve it's not the real me.
Some - bod - y help me tame this an - i - mal I have be -
Bass 1

D5
C5
F5
A5
B♭5
D5
C5
F5
G5
F5
E5
come. Help me be-lieve it's not the real me. Some-bod-y help me tame this an - i -
mal,
(...mal.)
al,
al,
This an - i - mal I have be -
Outro
N.C.
al,
al.
come.

Another One Bites the Dust

Words and Music by John Deacon

Tune up 1/2 step:
(low to high) F-B♭-E♭-A♭

Intro

Moderate Rock ♩ = 110

N.C. (Em) (Am)

mf

T
A
B

5 3 | 0 0 0 0 | 0 0 3 0 5 5 3

(Em) (Am)

Play 3 times

0 0 0 0 | 0 0 3 0 5

(Em) (Am)

Ooh, let's go!

0 0 0 0 | 0 0 3 0 5

Verse

N.C. (Em) (Am)

1. Steve walks war - i - ly down _ the street, with the brim pulled way down low. _

0 0 0 0 | 0 0 3 0 5

(Em)
(Am)
Ain't no sound but the sound of his feet, ma - chine guns read - y to go. Are you
(C5)
(G5)
(C5)
(G5)
read - y? Hey! Are you read - y for this? Are you hang- in' on the edge of your seat?
(C5)
(G5)
(A5)
(B5)
Out of the door - way the bul - lets rip to the sound of the beat, yeah.
Chorus
N.C. (Em)
(A5)
(Em)
An - oth - er one bites the dust. An-

(Am)
(Em)
oth - er one bites the dust. _ And an - oth - er one gone, and an - oth - er one gone. An -
0 0 3 0 5
0 0 0 0
(Am)
(F♯5)
(A5)
oth - er one bites the dust, _ yeah. Hey, I'm gon - na get you too. An -
0 0 3 0 5
2 7 6 5 5 5
(F♯5)
(F♯m7)
G5
N.C. (Em)
oth - er one bites the dust. _
2 3
0 0 0 0
(Am)
(Em)
(Am)
0 0 3 0 5
0 0 0 0
0 0 3 0 5 5 3

Verse
Em
Am
2. How do you think I'm gon - na get a - long with - out you when you're gone? You
Em
Am
took me for ev - 'ry - thing that I had and kicked me out on my own. Are you
N.C. (C5)
(G5)
(C5)
(G5)
hap - py? Are you sat - is - fied? How long can you stand the heat?
(C5)
(G5)
(A5)
B5
G5
Out of the door - way the bul - lets rip, ah, to the sound of the beat. Look out!

Chorus
N.C. (Em)
(Am)
(Em)
An - oth - er one bites the dust. _
An -
oth - er one bites the dust. _
And an - oth - er one gone, and an - oth - er one gone. An -
(Am)
(F♯5)
A5
oth - er one bites the dust. _
Hey, I'm gon - na get you too. An -
Interlude
N.C. (F♯5)
(F♯m7)
G5
N.C. (E5)
oth - er one bites the dust. _
Hey!

3
Ah, take it! Bite the dust! Bite the dust,

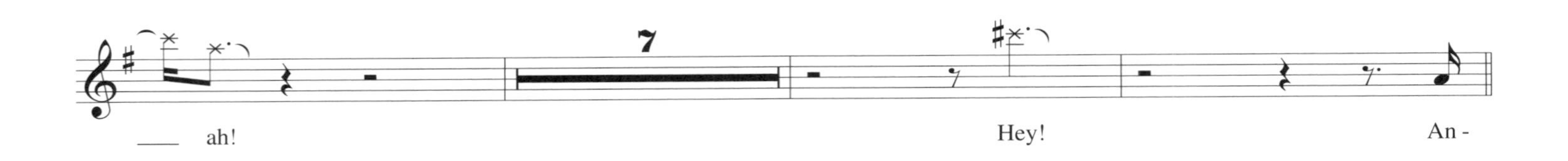
7
ah! Hey! An-

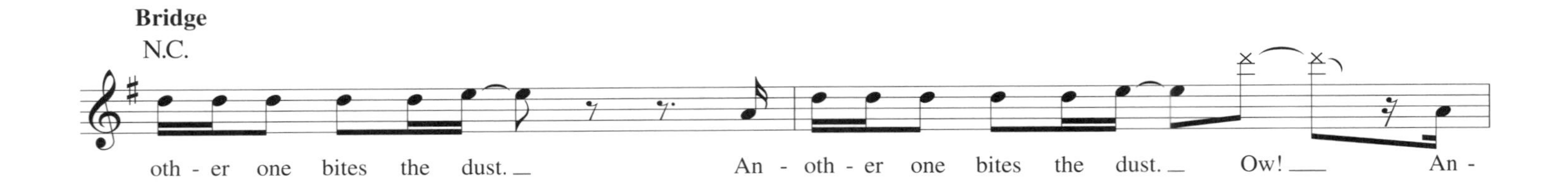
Bridge
N.C.
oth - er one bites the dust. An - oth - er one bites the dust. Ow! An -

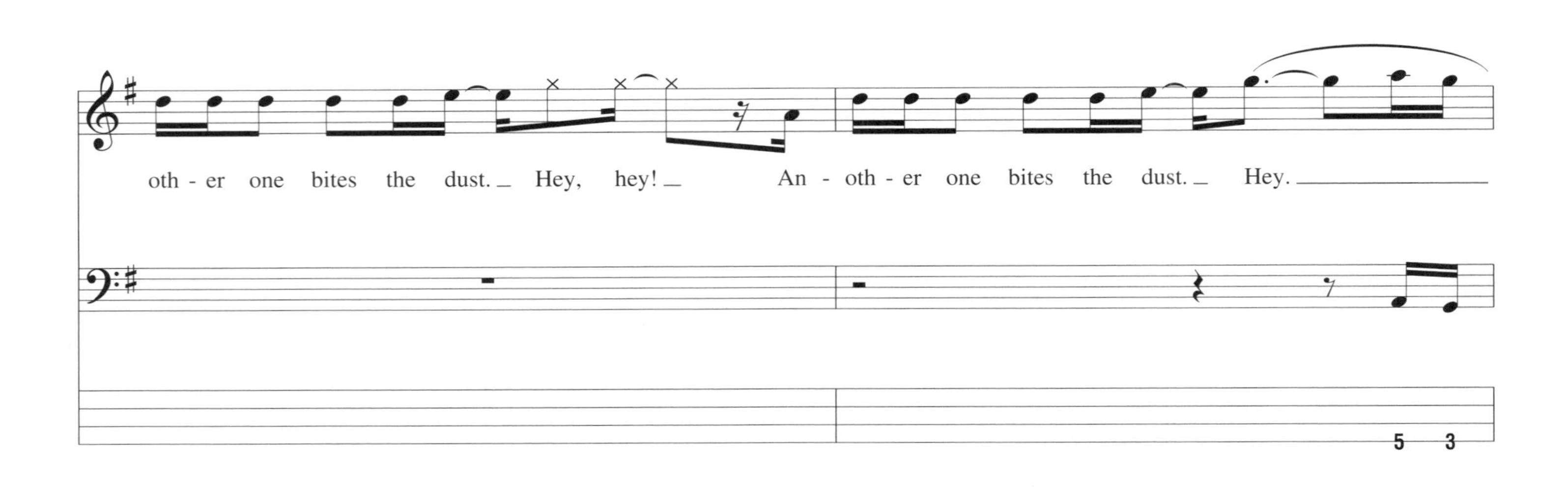
oth - er one bites the dust. Hey, hey! An - oth - er one bites the dust. Hey.
5 3

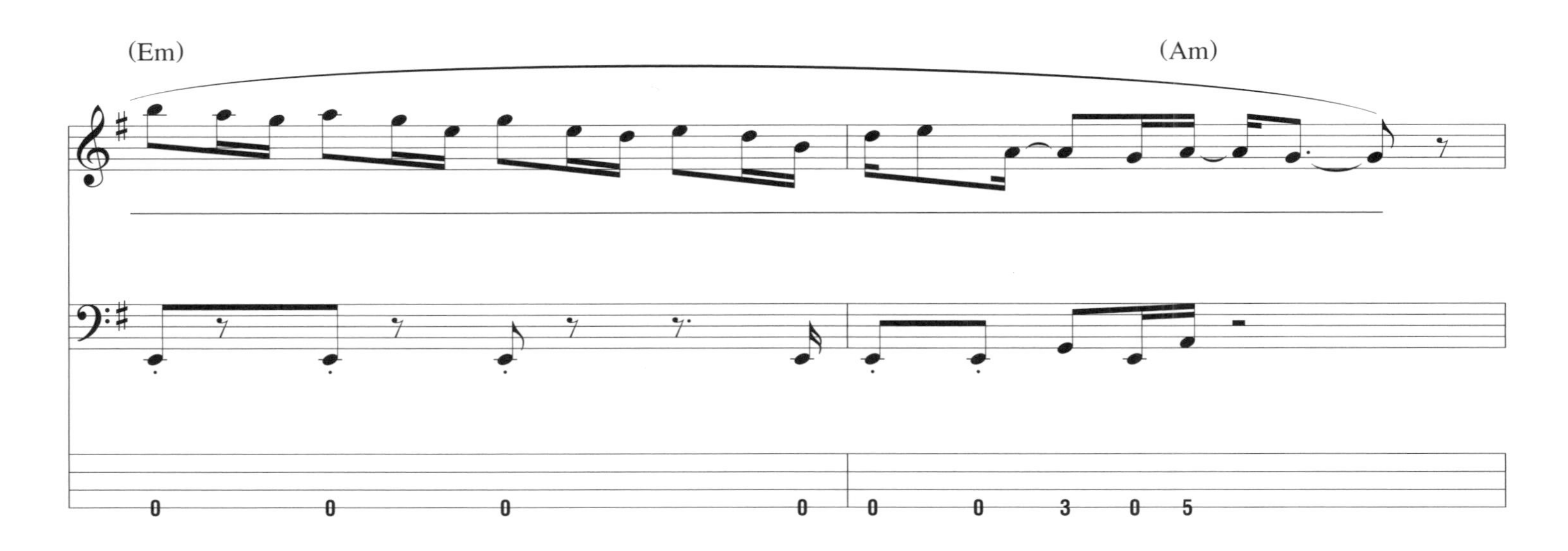
(Em)
(Am)
0 0 0 0 0 0 3 0 5

(Em)
(Am)
Ooh, shot! 3. There are
Verse
Em
Am
plen - ty of ways that you can hurt a man and bring him to the ground. You can
Em
Am
beat him, you can cheat him, you can treat him bad, and then leave him when he's down, yeah. But I'm
N.C. (C5)
(G5)
(C5)
(G5)
read - y. Yes, I'm read - y for you. I'm stand- in' on my own two feet.

(C5)
(G5)
(A5)
(B5)
G5
Out of the door - way the bul-lets rip, re - peat-ing to the sound of the beat. Oh,
Chorus
N.C. (Em)
(Am)
yeah. An - oth - er one bites the dust.
(Em)
(Am)
An - oth - er one bites the dust. And an -
(Em)
(Am)
oth - er one gone, and an - oth - er one gone. An - oth - er one bites the dust.
(Yeah.)

(F♯5)
A5
N.C. (F♯5)
G5
Hey, I'm gon - na get you too. An - oth - er one bites the dust.
Outro
Em
Am
Shoot - out!
Ay.
Em
Am
N.C. (C5)
(G5)
Al - right.
(C5)
(G5)
(C5)
(G5)
(A5)
(B5)
N.C.

Are You Gonna Be My Girl

Words and Music by Cameron Muncey and Nicholas Cester

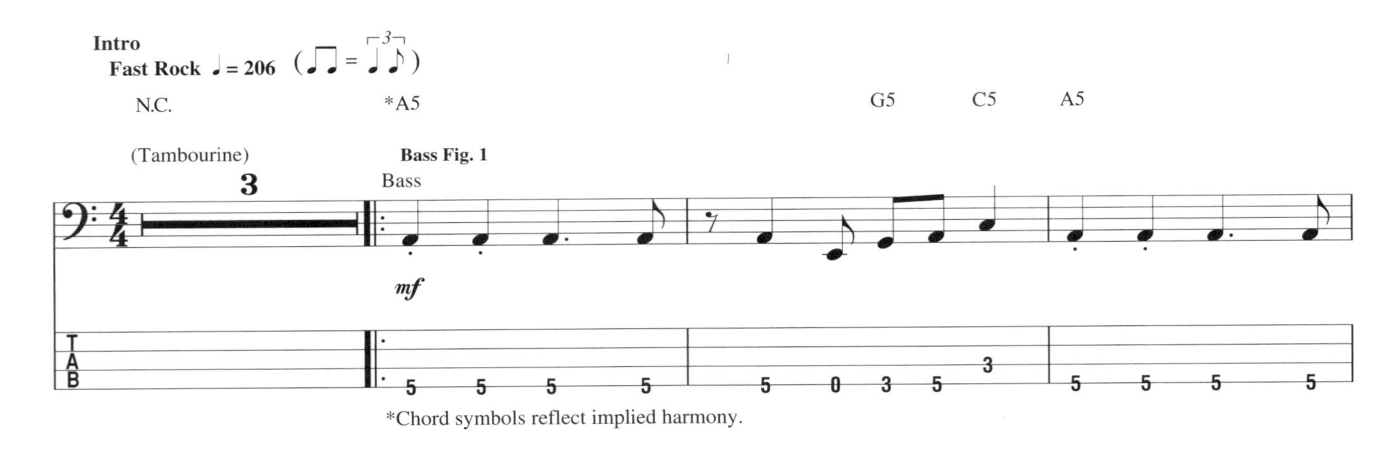

Intro
Fast Rock ♩ = 206
N.C.
*A5
G5
C5
A5
(Tambourine)
3
Bass Fig. 1
Bass
mf
5 5 5 5
5 0 3 5 3
5 5 5 5

*Chord symbols reflect implied harmony.

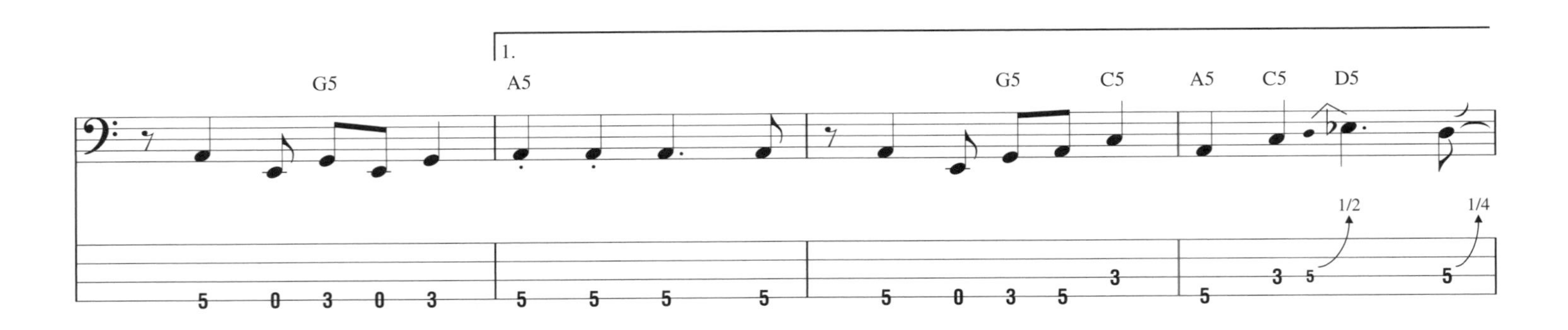

1.
G5
A5
G5
C5
A5
C5
D5
5 0 3 0 3
5 5 5 5
5 0 3 5 3
5 3 5 5
1/2
1/4

2.
A5
G5
End Bass Fig. 1
A5
G5
A5
N.C.
(5) 3 5 5 3
5 5 5 5
5 0 3 0 3
5

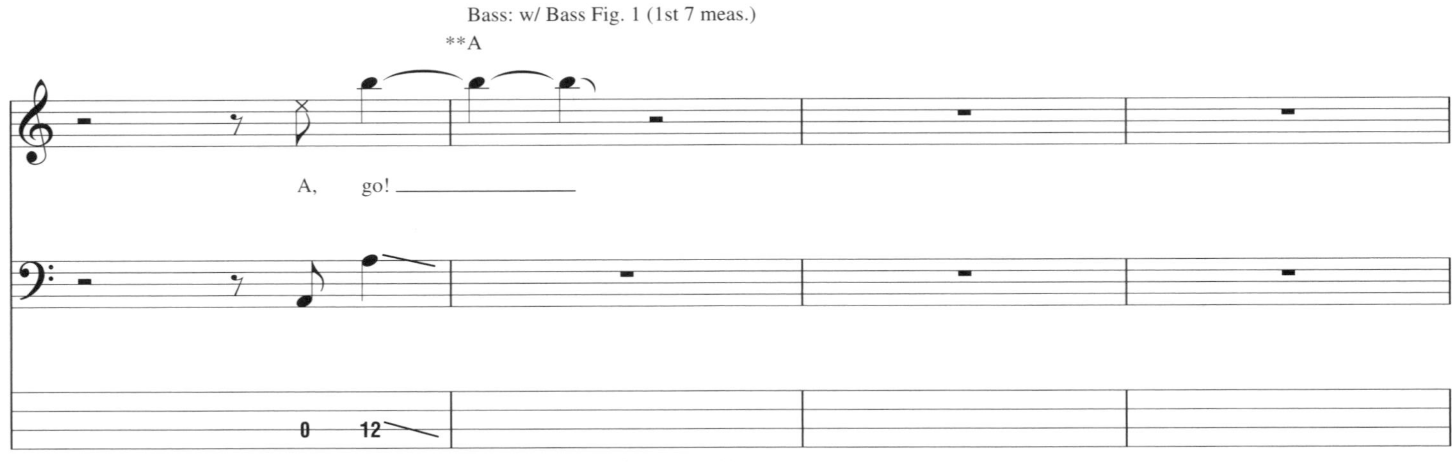

Bass: w/ Bass Fig. 1 (1st 7 meas.)
**A
A, go!
0 12

**Chord symbols reflect overall harmony.

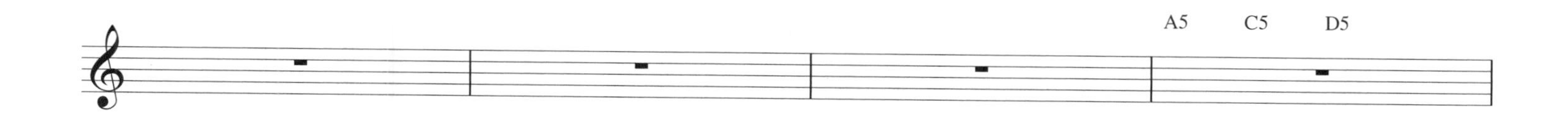
A5 C5 D5

A5 G5
Verse
A N.C.
1. So, one, two, three, take my hand and come with me be-cause you look so fine that I
(5) 3 5 5 3 5

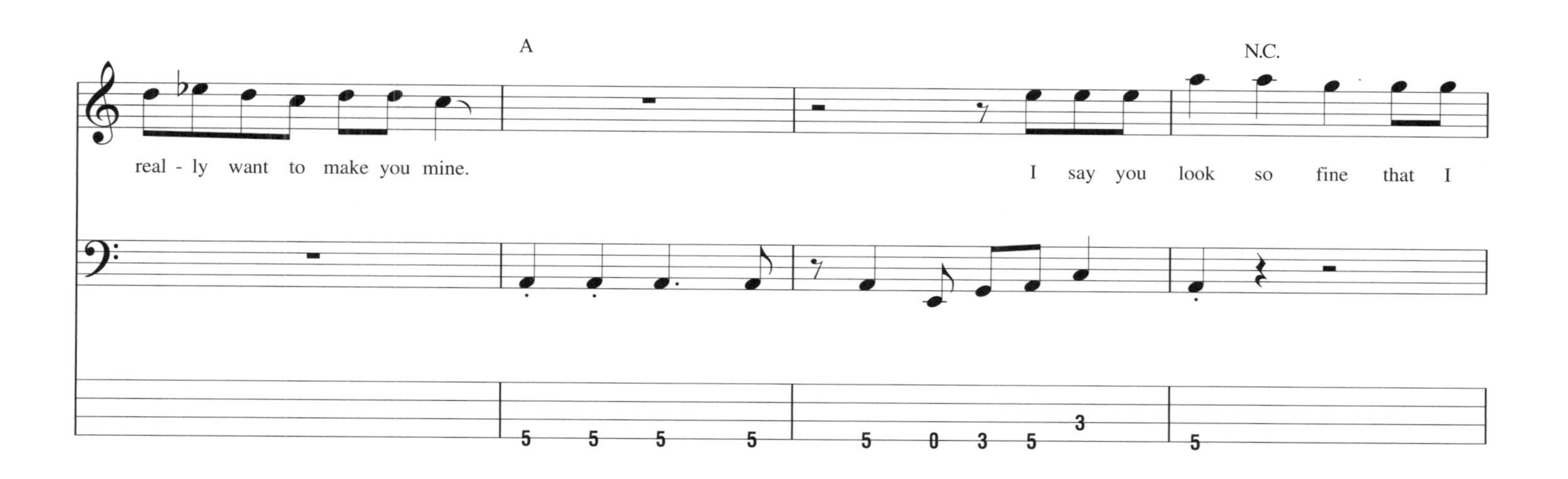
A
N.C.
real - ly want to make you mine.
I say you look so fine that I
5 5 5 5 5 0 3 5 3 5

A
N.C.
real - ly want to make you mine.
Well, four, five, six, come on
5 5 5 5 5 0 3 5 3 5

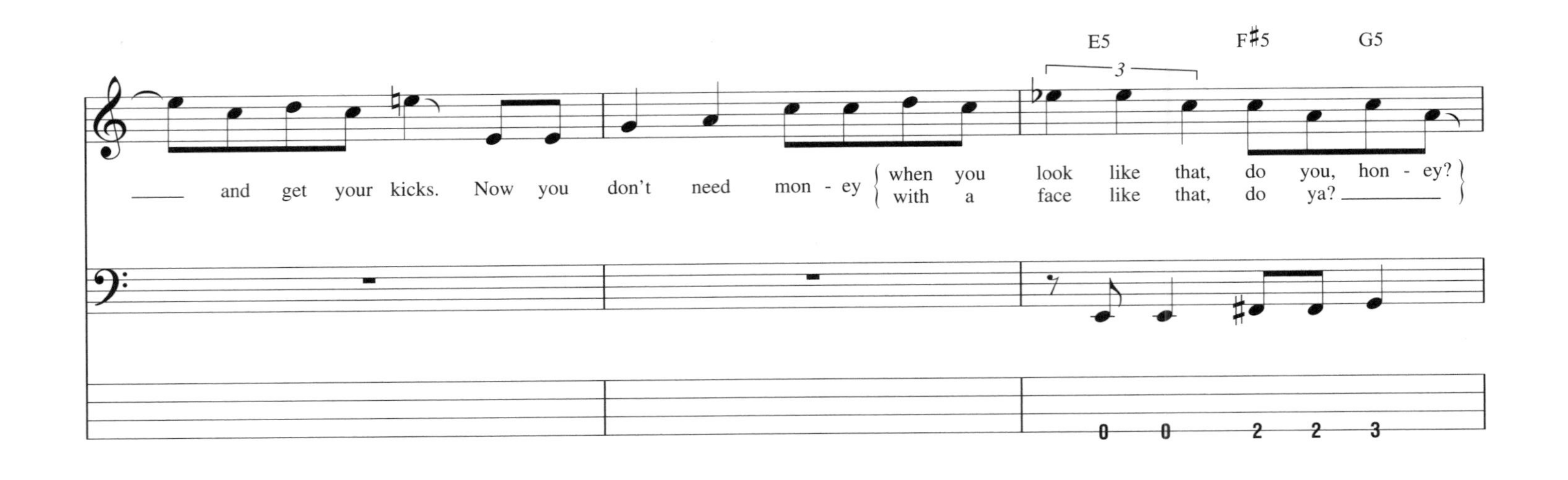
E5
F♯5
G5
3
and get your kicks. Now you don't need mon - ey
when you look like that, do you, hon - ey?
with a face like that, do ya?
0 0 2 2 3

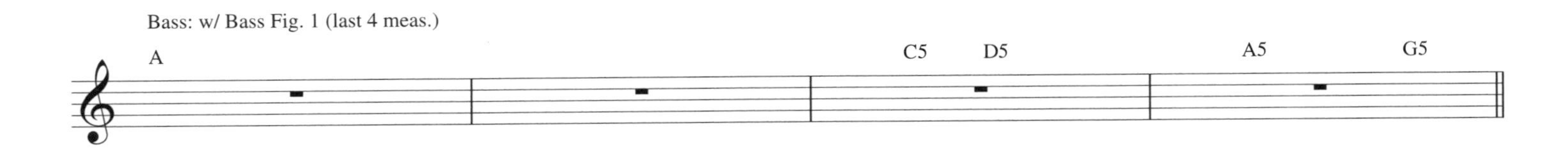
Bass: w/ Bass Fig. 1 (last 4 meas.)
A
C5
D5
A5
G5

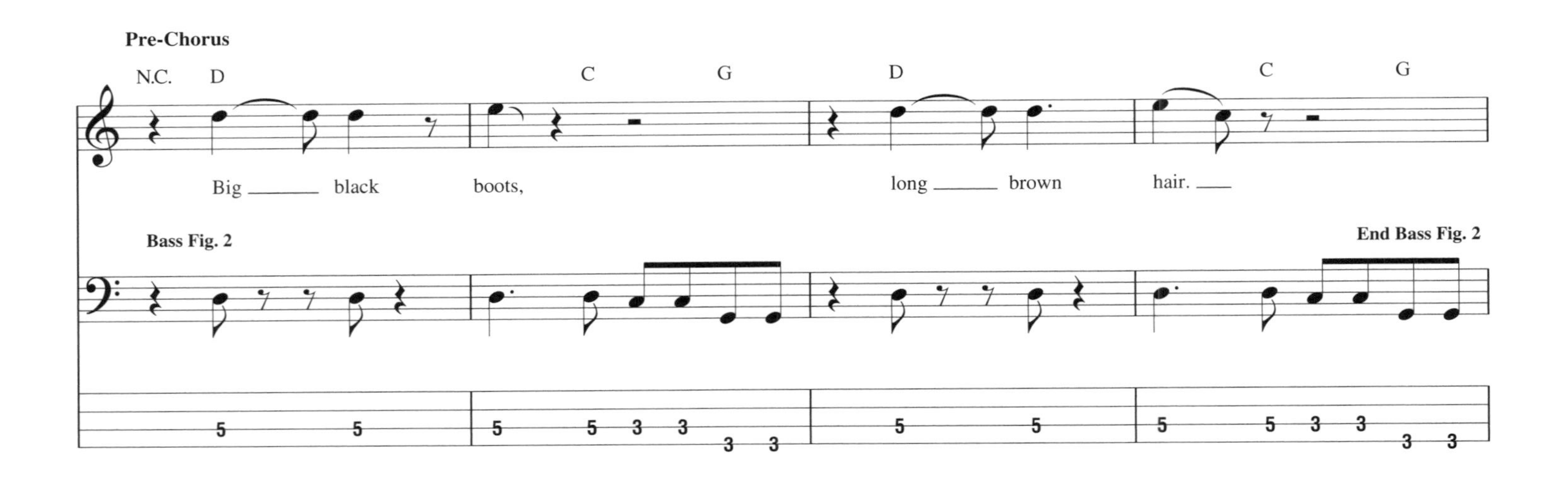
Pre-Chorus
N.C.
D
C
G
D
C
G
Big black boots,
long brown hair.
Bass Fig. 2
End Bass Fig. 2
5 5
5 5 3 3 3 3
5 5
5 5 3 3 3 3

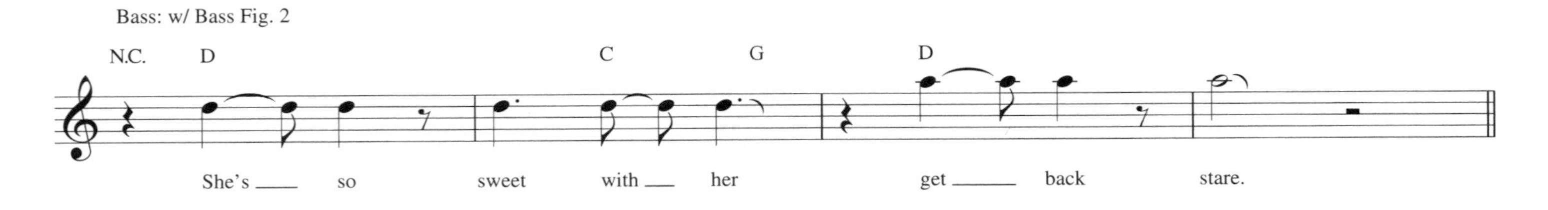
Bass: w/ Bass Fig. 2
N.C.
D
C
G
D
She's so sweet with her get back stare.

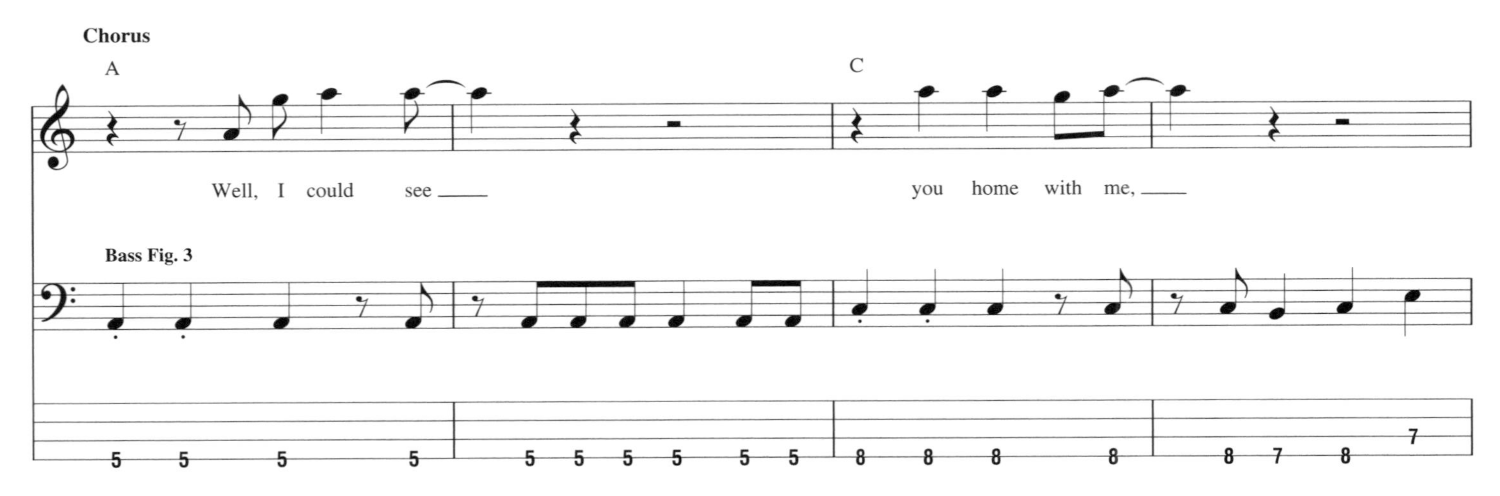
Chorus
A
C
Well, I could see
you home with me,
Bass Fig. 3
5 5 5 5
5 5 5 5 5 5
8 8 8 8
8 7 8 7

D
A
but you were with an - oth - er man, yeah.
End Bass Fig. 3
Bass: w/ Bass Fig. 3
C
I know we ain't got much to say
D
A
be - fore I let you get a - way, yeah.
To Coda
N.C. E
G
N.C.
I said, "Are you gon - na be
Interlude
Bass: w/ Bass Fig. 1
A
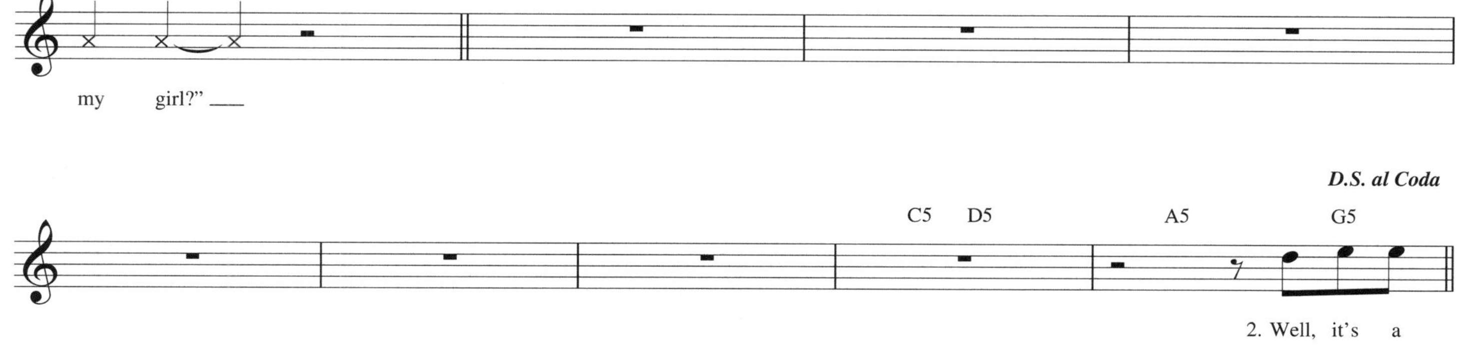
my girl?"
D.S. al Coda
C5 D5
A5
G5
2. Well, it's a

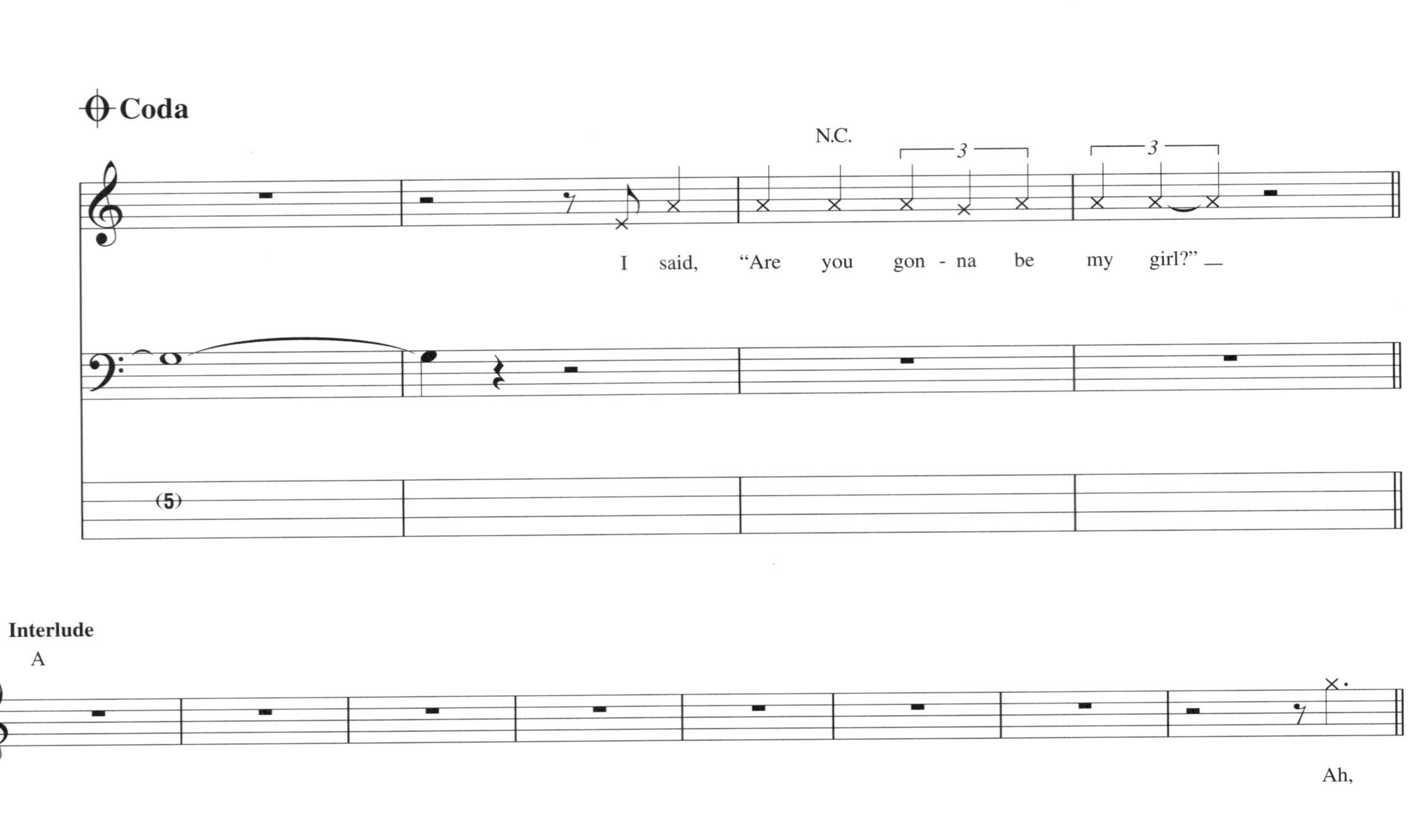
Coda
N.C.
I said, "Are you gon - na be my girl?"

Interlude

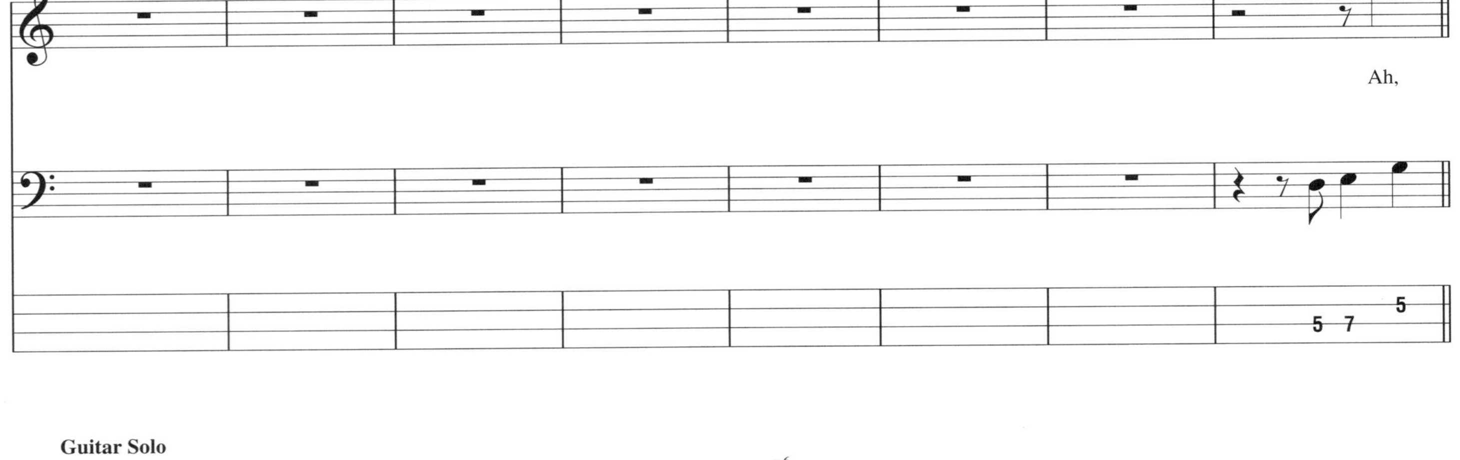
A
Ah,

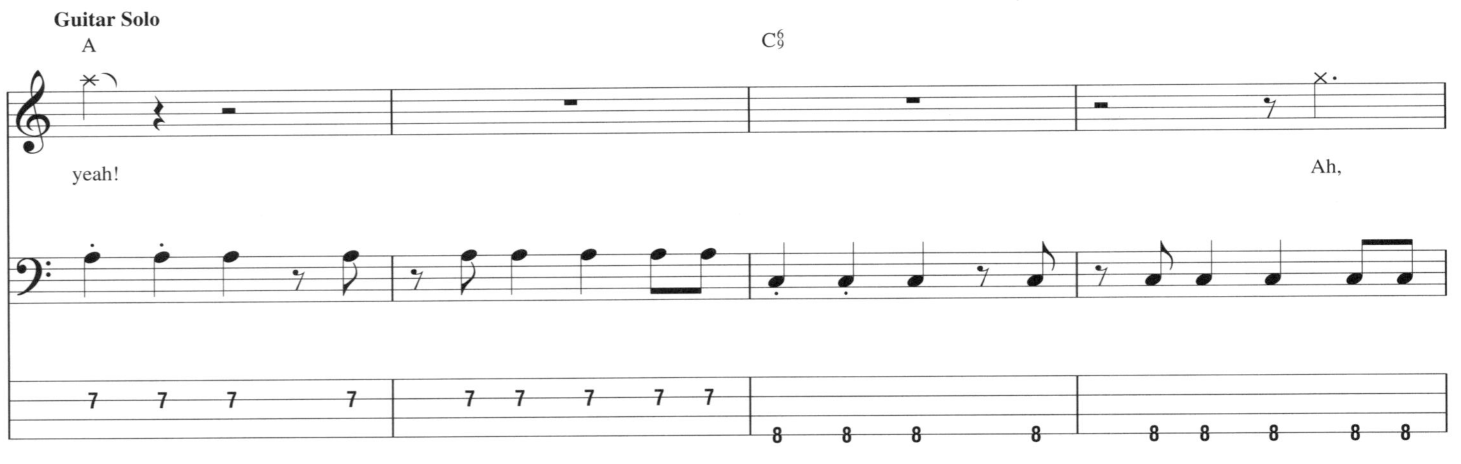
Guitar Solo
A
C6/9
yeah!
Ah,

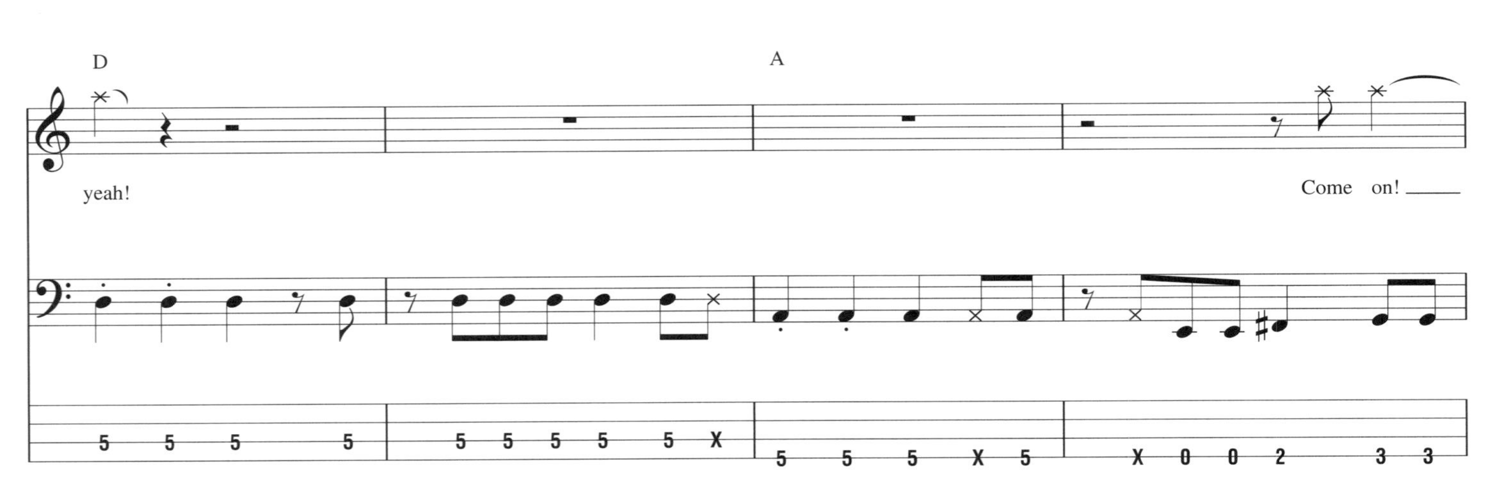
D
A
yeah!
Come on!

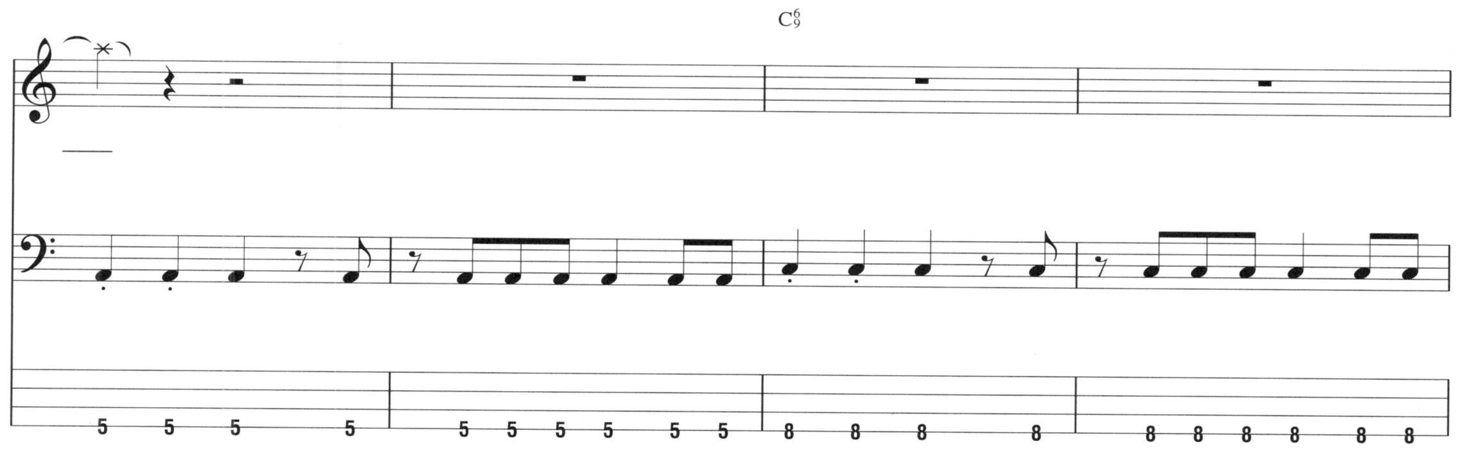
C6/9

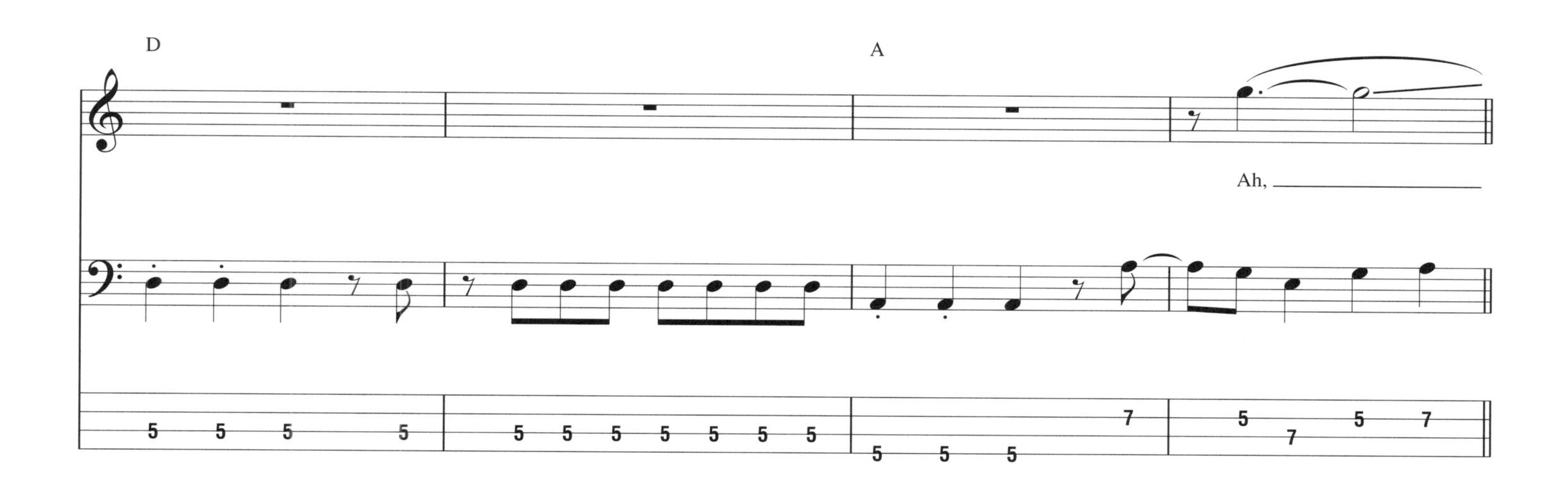
D
A
Ah,

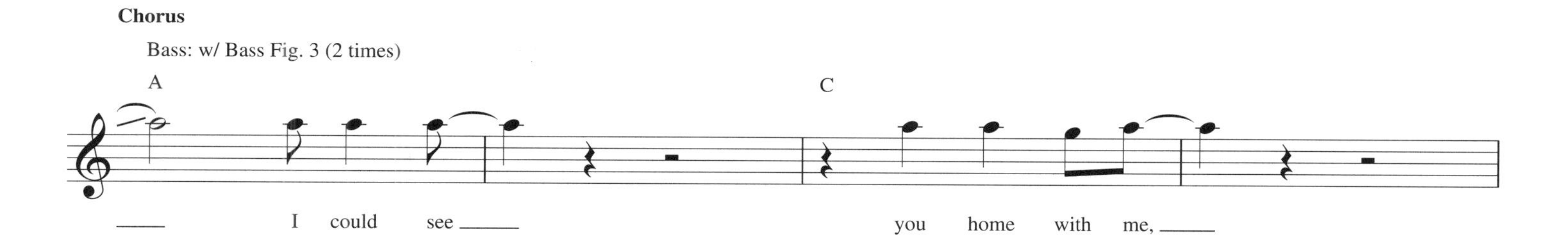
Chorus
Bass: w/ Bass Fig. 3 (2 times)
A
C
I could see you home with me,

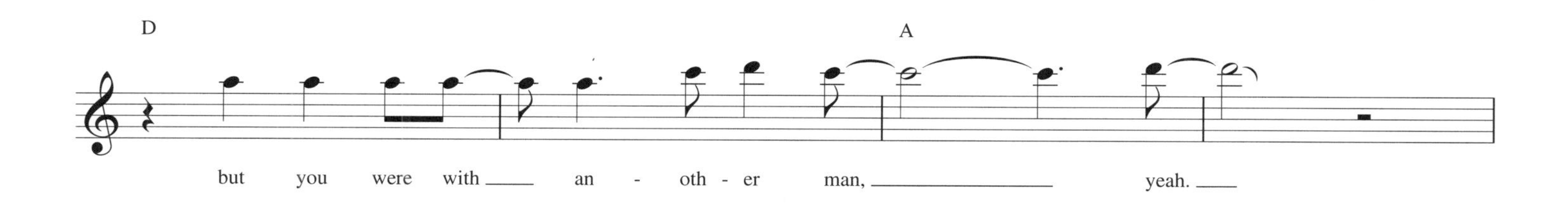
D
A
but you were with an - oth - er man, yeah.

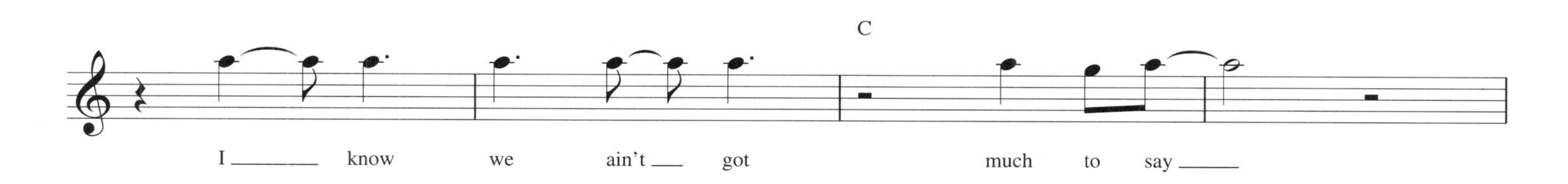
C
I know we ain't got much to say

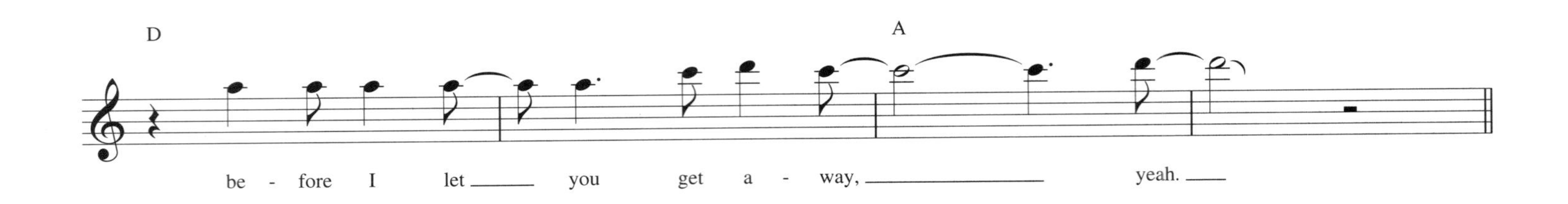
D
A
be - fore I let you get a - way,
yeah.

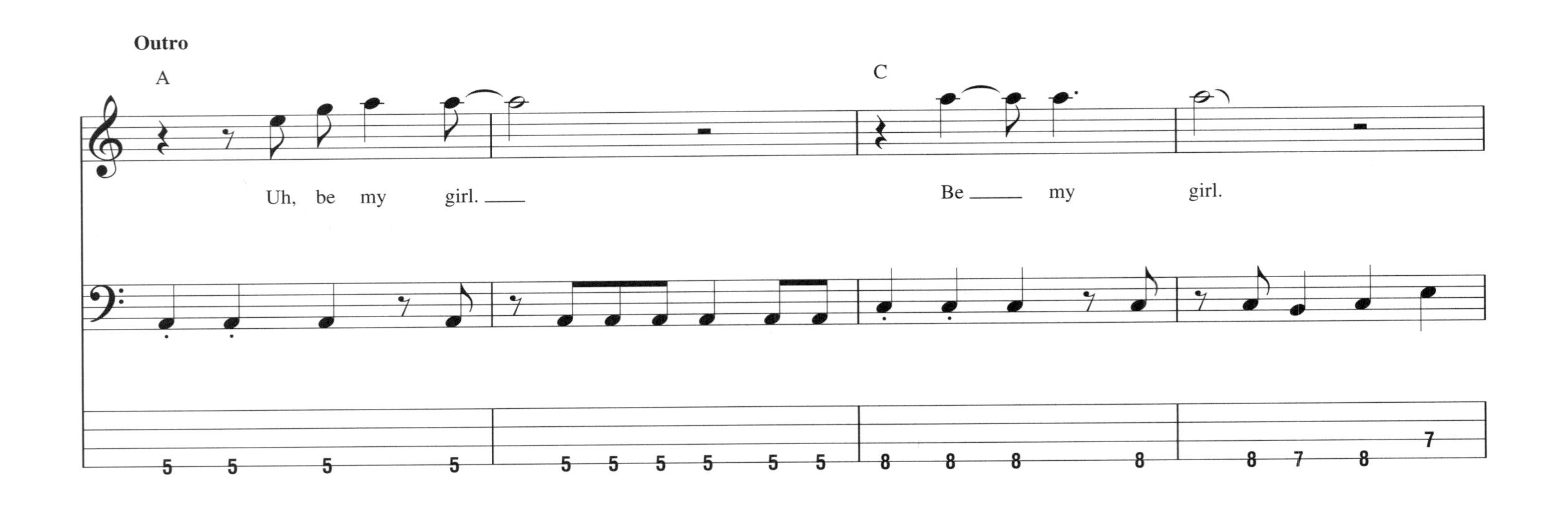
Outro
A
C
Uh, be my girl.
Be my girl.

D
A
Are you gon - na be my girl?

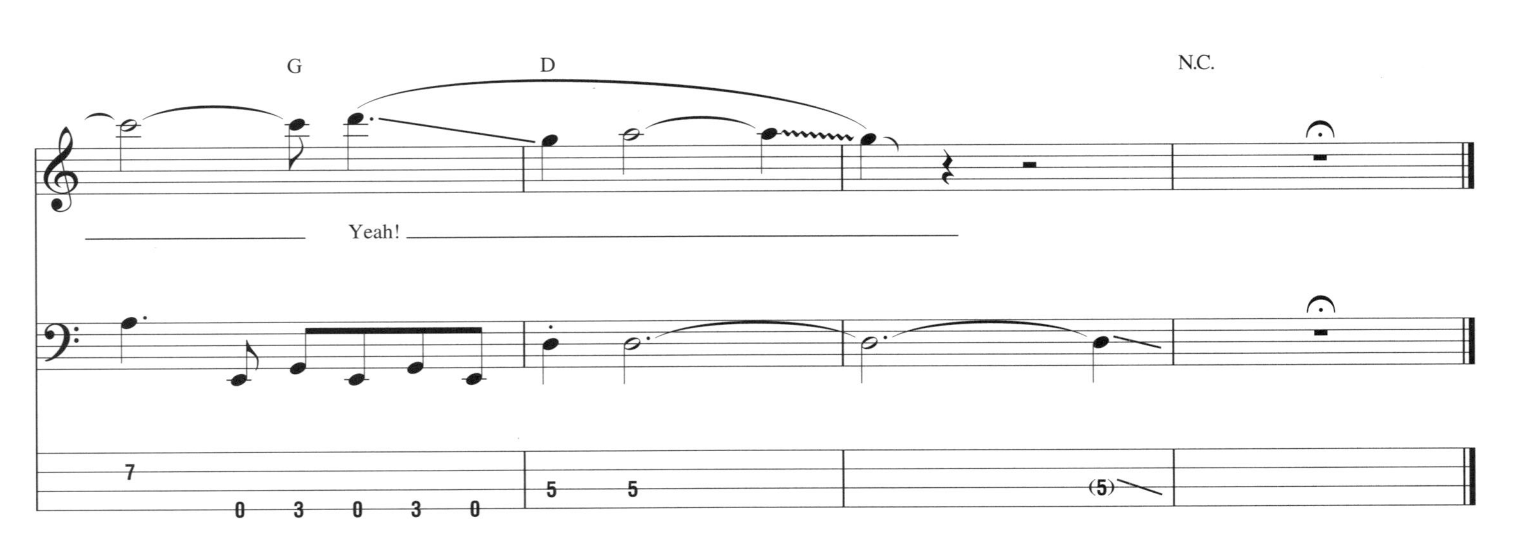
G
D
N.C.
Yeah!

Badge

Words and Music by Eric Clapton and George Harrison

Intro
Moderately slow Rock ♩ = 106
Am
D
Am
D
mf

Verse
Am
D
Em
1. Think- in' 'bout the times you drove _ in my car. ____

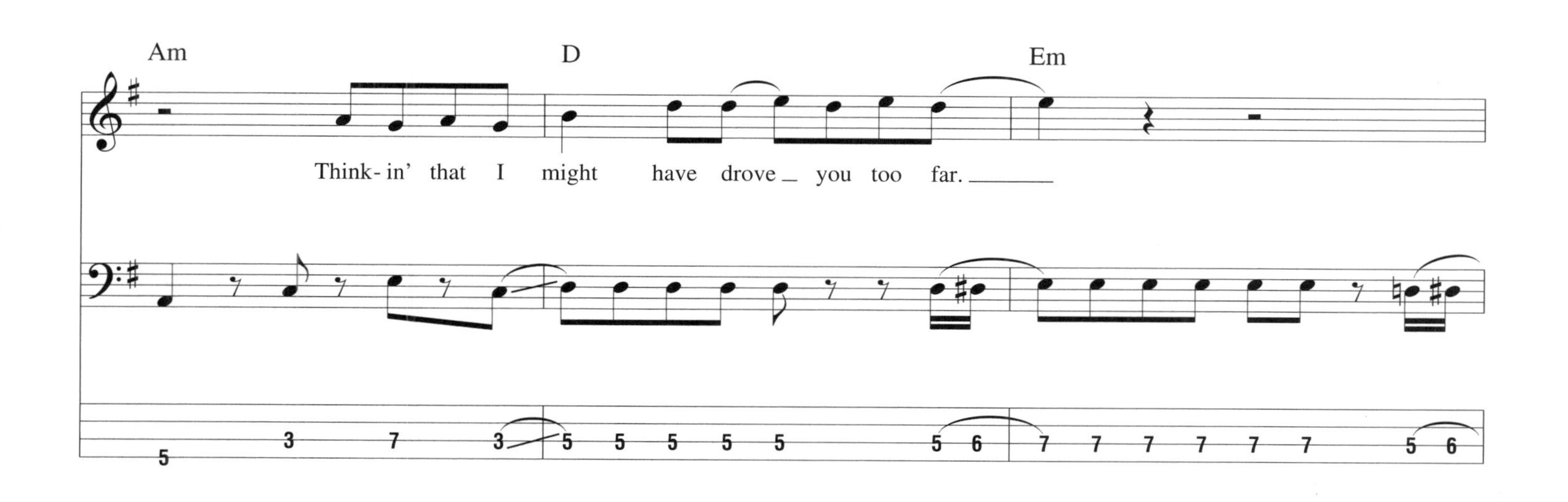

Am
D
Em
Think- in' that I might have drove _ you too far. ______

C
Am
Bm
And I'm think - in' 'bout the love that you laid on my ta - ble.
Am (add9)
Verse
Am
D
2. I told you not to wan - der 'round in the dark.
Em
Am
D
I told you 'bout the swans, that they live in the park.
Em
C
Then I told you 'bout our

Am
Bm
Am(add9)
D
Cmaj7
kid, now he's mar-ried to Ma - ble.
Bridge
G/B
G
D
Cmaj7
G/B
G
D
Cmaj7
Yes, I told
you that the light goes up and down. Don't you no - tice how the wheel goes
'round? And you bet - ter pick your-self up from the ground before

G/B G D Cmaj7 G/B G
they bring the cur - tain down.
Yes, be - fore they bring the cur - tain down.
Guitar Solo
D C G/B G D Cmaj7 G/B G
D Cmaj7 G/B G D Cmaj7 G/B G
D Cmaj7 G/B G D Cmaj7
G/B G D Cmaj7 G/B G D

Verse
Am
D
Em
3. Talk - in' 'bout a girl that looks quite like you.
Am
D
She did - n't have the time to wait in the queue.
Em
C
She cried a - way her
Am
Bm
Am (add9)
life since she fell off the cra - dle.

The Boys Are Back in Town

Words and Music by Philip Parris Lynott

Tune down 1/2 step:
(low to high) E♭-A♭-D♭-G♭

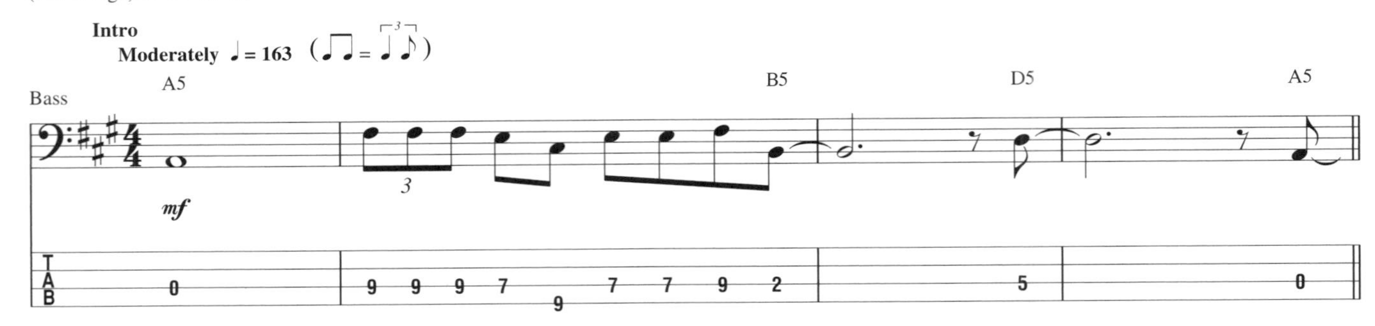

Intro
Moderately ♩ = 163
Bass
A5
B5
D5
A5
mf
T
A
B

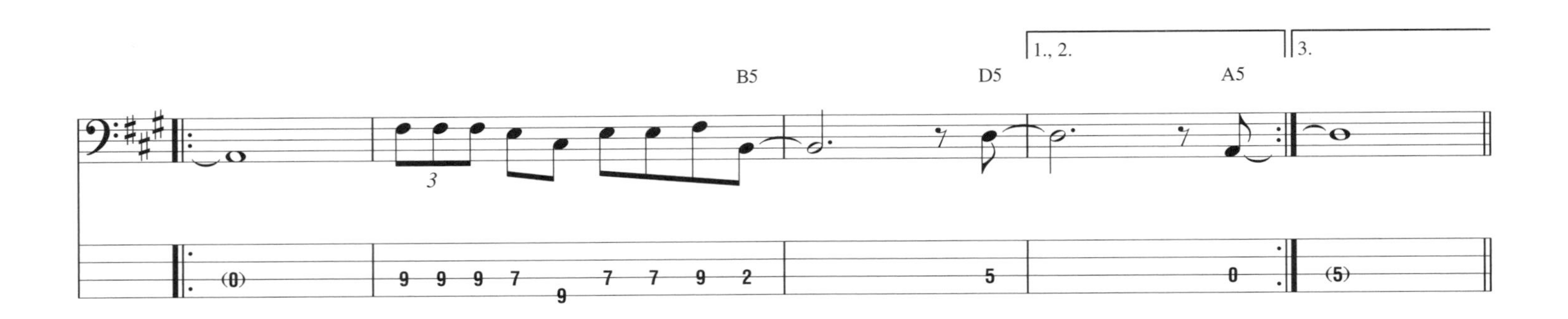

1., 2.
3.
B5
D5
A5

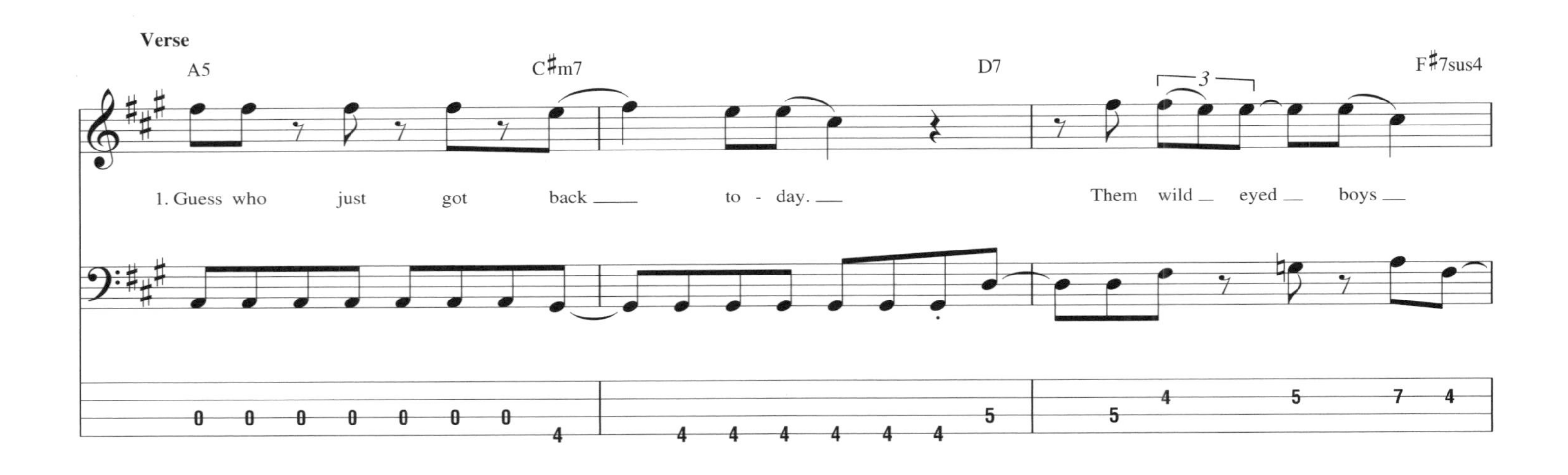

Verse
A5
C♯m7
D7
F♯7sus4
1. Guess who just got back to - day.
Them wild eyed boys

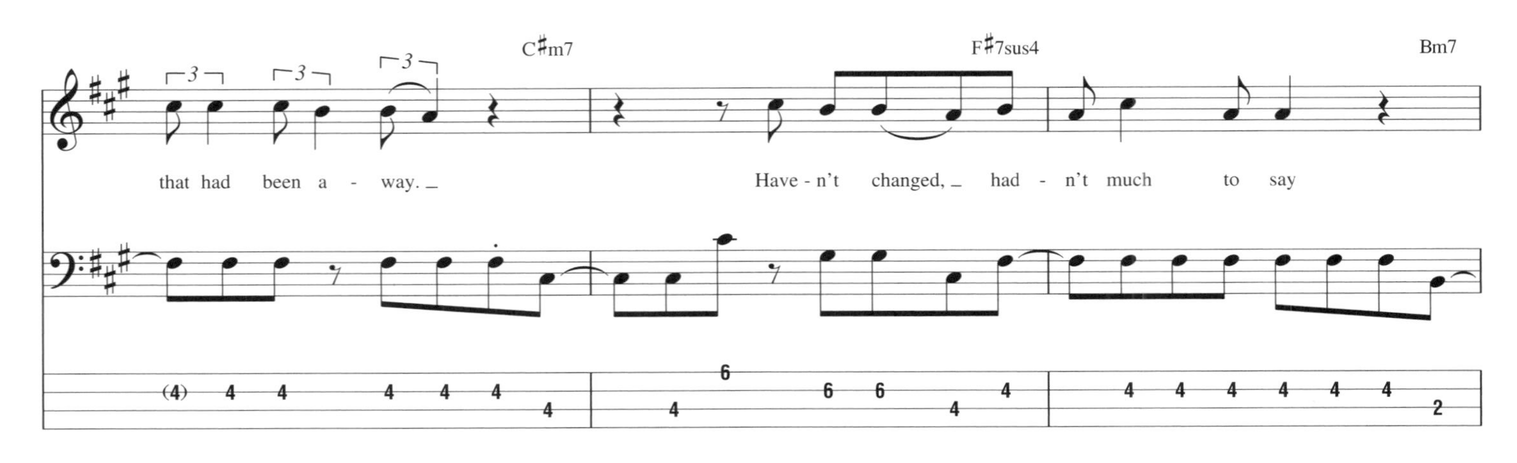

C♯m7
F♯7sus4
Bm7
that had been a - way.
Have - n't changed, had - n't much to say

E9sus4
A
C♯m7
but, man, I still think them cats are cra - zy.
They were ask - in' if you
D
F
C♯m7
were a - round,
how you was, where you could be found.
*Sung as even eighth-notes.
F♯7sus4
Bm7
E9sus4
I told them you were liv - ing down - town,
driv - ing all the old men
Chorus
A5
B5
cra - zy.
The boys are back in town.
The boys are back in town.

D5
A5
I said, the boys are back in town.
B5
D5
A5
The boys are back in town.
The
boys are back in town.
B5
D5
The boys are back in town.
The boys are back in town.
The boys
A
A/B
are back in town.
(2) 2 2 2 2 2 2 5
5 5 5 5 7 7 0
0 0 0 0 0 0
0 0 0 0 0 0 0 2
2 2 2 2 2 2 5
5 5 5 5 5 0
(0) 0 0 0 0 0 0 0 0
0 0 0 0 0 0 0 2
2 2 2 2 7 5
(5) 5 5
0 0 0 0 0 0 0 0
2 2 2 2 2 2 2 2

C♯m7
E9sus4
A

A/B
C♯m7
E9sus4

Verse
A5
C♯m7
D
2. You know that chick that used to dance a lot?
3. Fri - day night they'll be dressed to kill

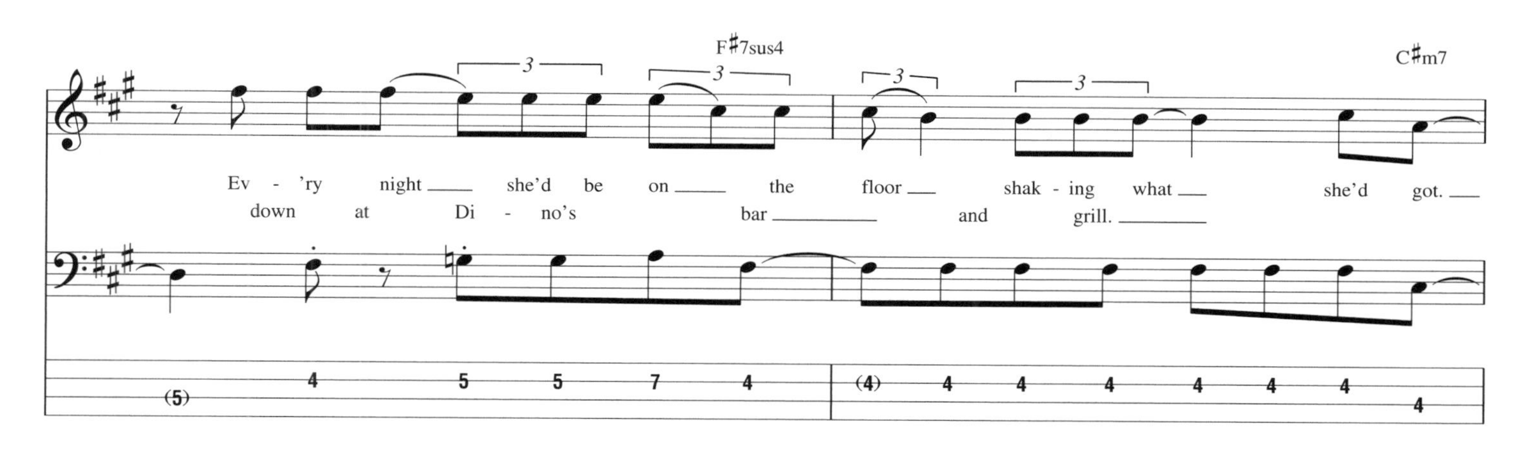
F♯7sus4
C♯m7
Ev - 'ry night she'd be on the floor shak - ing what she'd got.
down at Di - no's bar and grill.

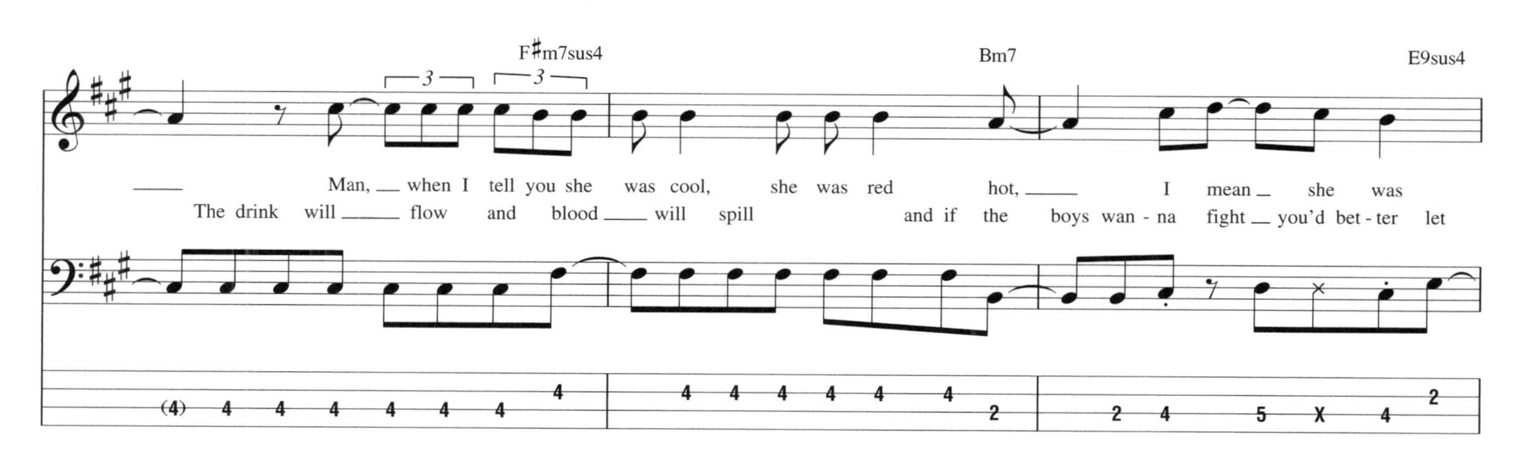
F♯m7sus4
Bm7
E9sus4
Man, when I tell you she was cool, she was red hot, I mean she was
The drink will flow and blood will spill and if the boys wan - na fight you'd bet - ter let

A
C#m7
D
steam - in'.
'em.
And that time o - ver at John-ny's place,
That juke - box in the corn - er blast - ing out my fa - v'rite song.

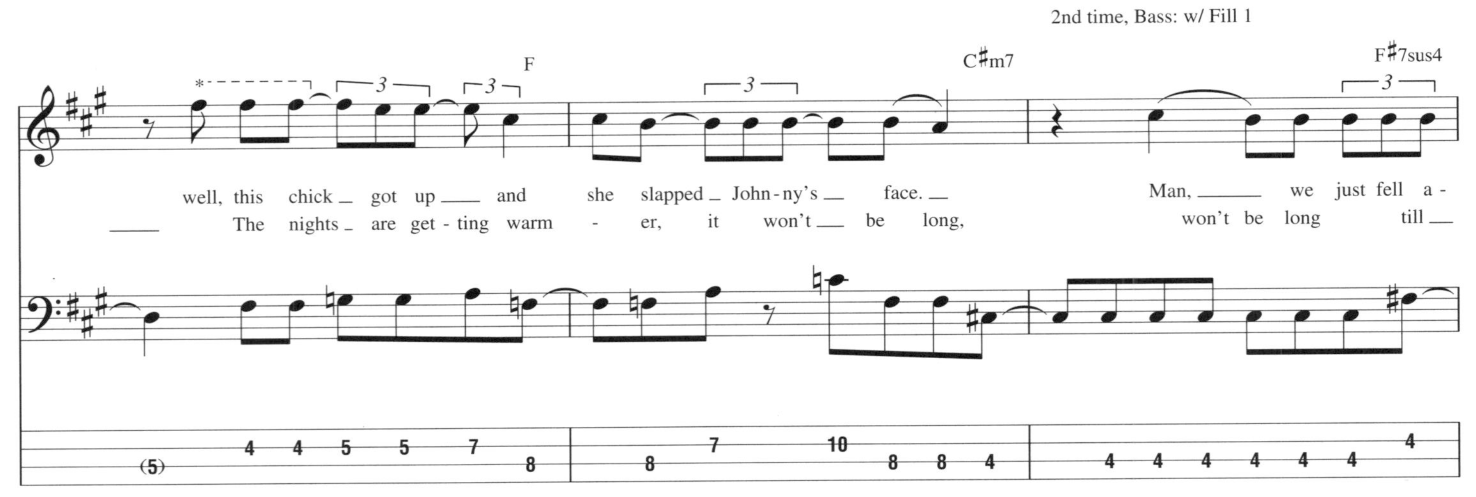
2nd time, Bass: w/ Fill 1
F
C#m7
F#7sus4
well, this chick got up and she slapped John-ny's face. Man, we just fell a -
The nights are get - ting warm - er, it won't be long, won't be long till

*Sung as even eighth-notes.

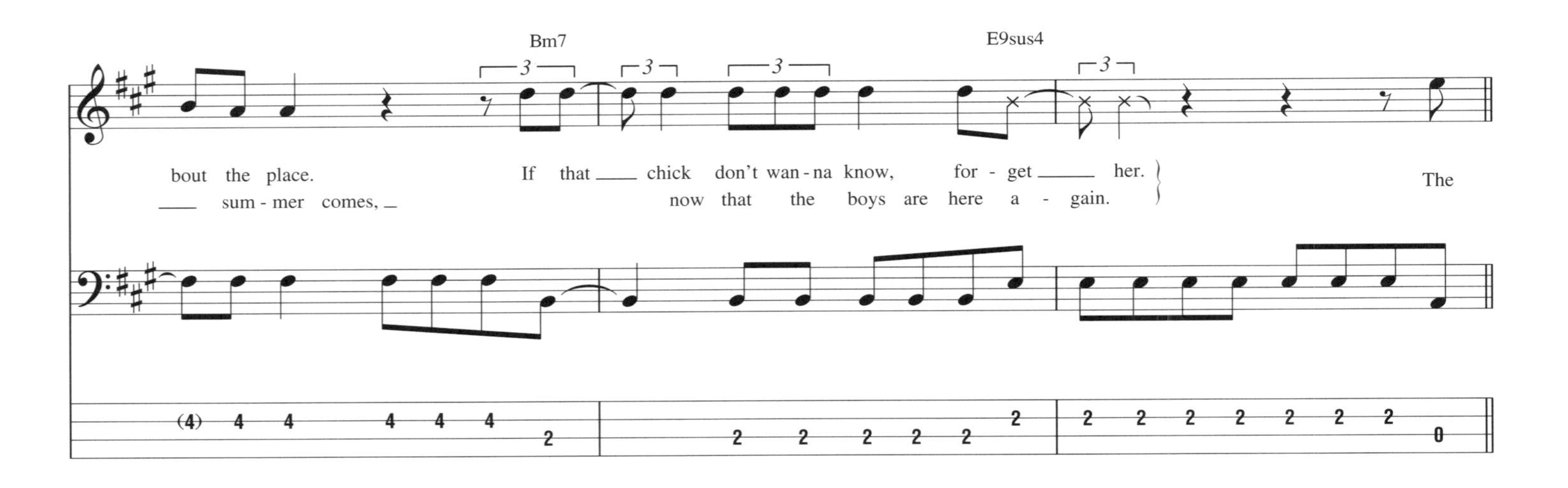
Bm7
E9sus4
bout the place. If that chick don't wan-na know, for - get her.
sum - mer comes, now that the boys are here a - gain.
The

Fill 1
Bass

Chorus
A5
B5
D5
boys _ are back in town. _
The boys _ are back in town. _
A5
B5
I said, the boys _ are back in town. ___
The
To Coda
D5
A5
boys _ are back in town. _
The boys _ are back in town. _
The
B5
D5
boys _ are back in town. _
The boys _ are back in town. _
The boys ___ are back in town. _

Interlude
A
A/B
C#m7
E9sus4

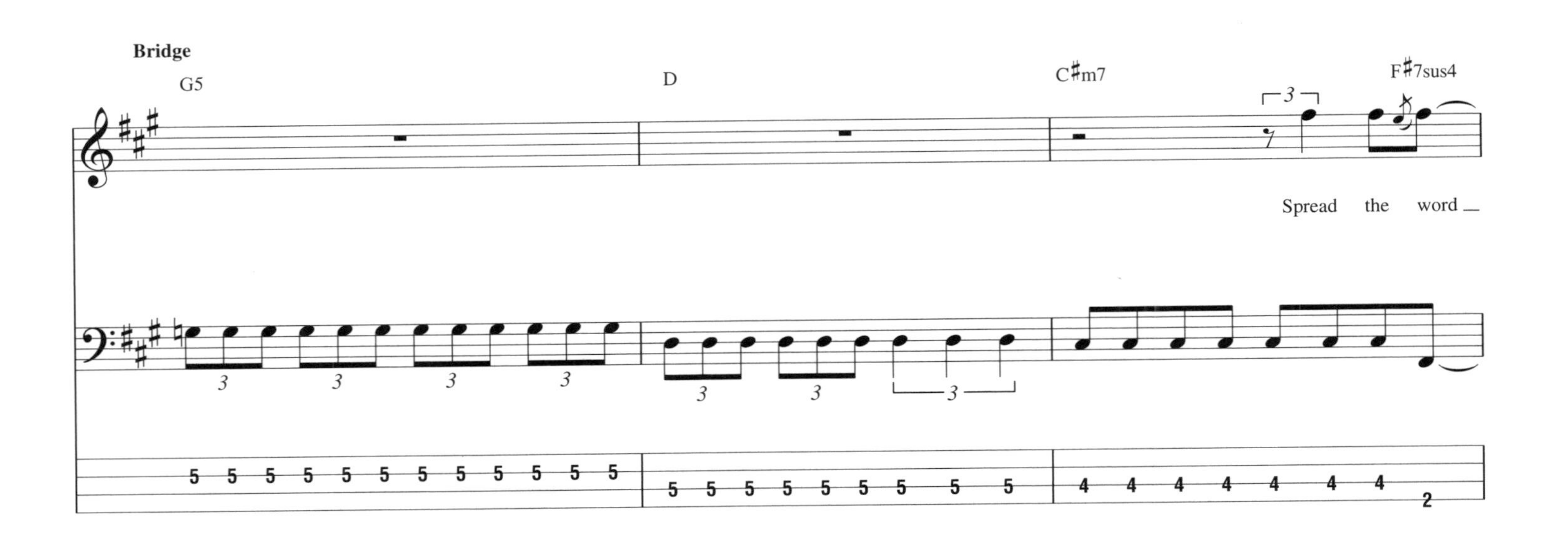
Bridge
G5
D
C#m7
F#7sus4
Spread the word

Bm7
E9sus4
F#7sus4
a - round,
guess who's back in town.

G5

D
C#m7
F#7sus4
Bm7
You spread the word a - round.

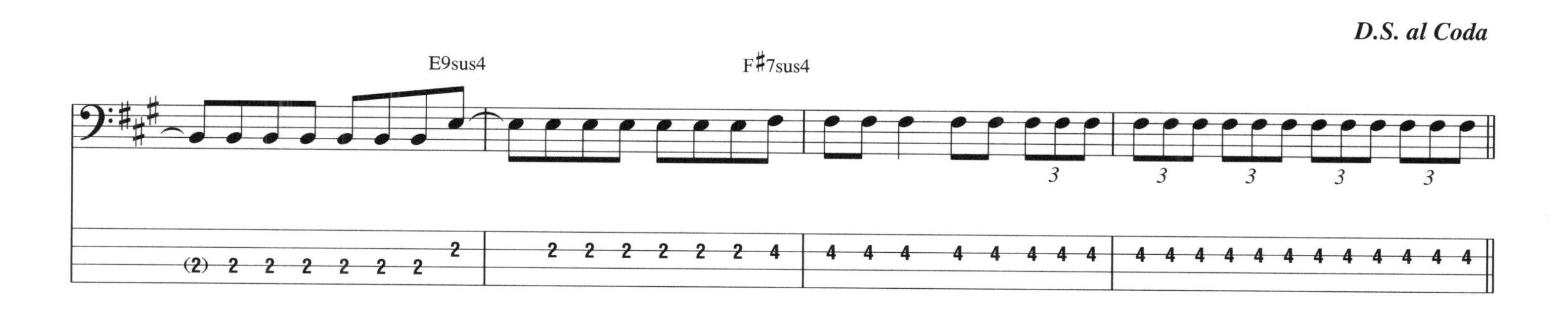
D.S. al Coda
E9sus4
F#7sus4

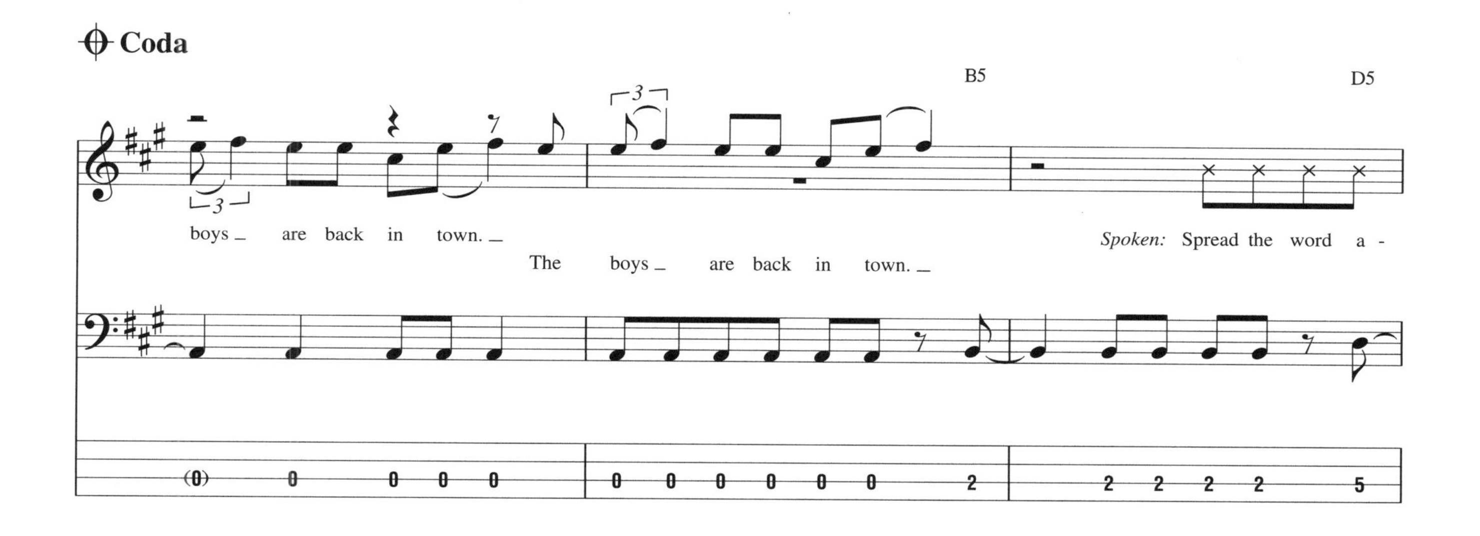
Coda
B5
D5
boys are back in town.
The boys are back in town.
Spoken: Spread the word a -

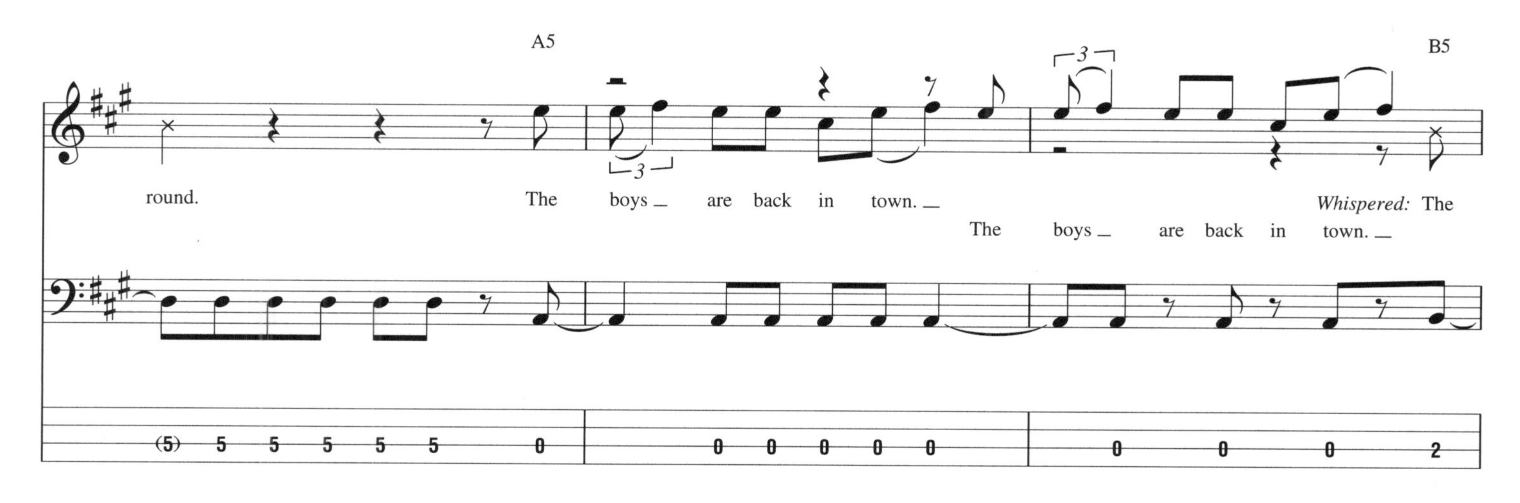
A5
B5
round.
The boys are back in town.
The boys are back in town.
Whispered: The

Interlude
D5
A
boys are back, the boys are back.

A/G
F♯m
A/G

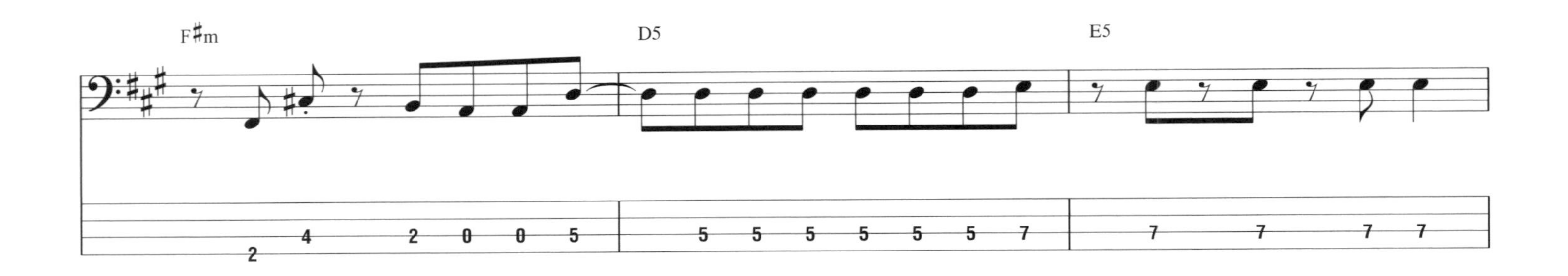
F♯m
D5
E5

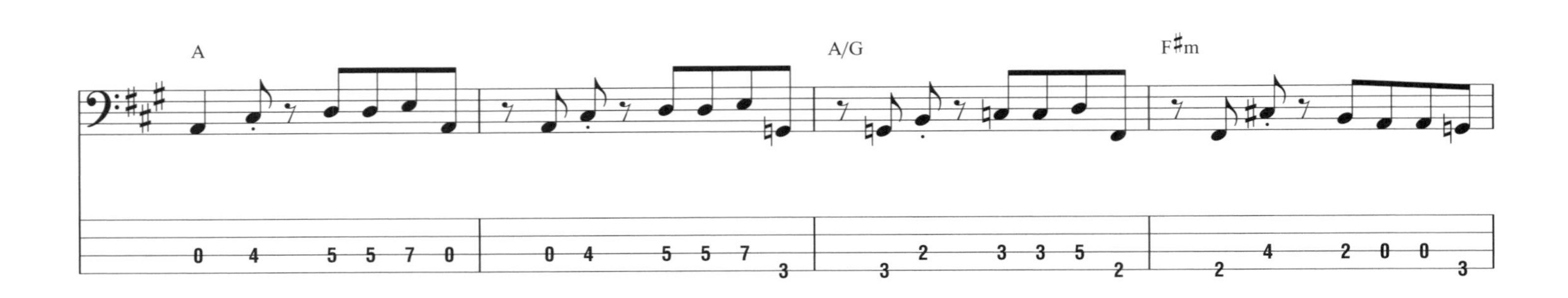
A
A/G
F♯m

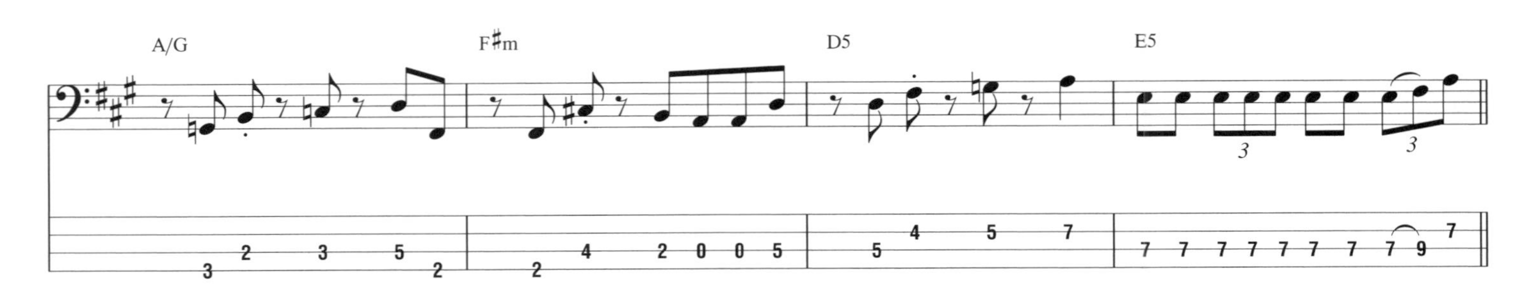
A/G
F♯m
D5
E5

Outro

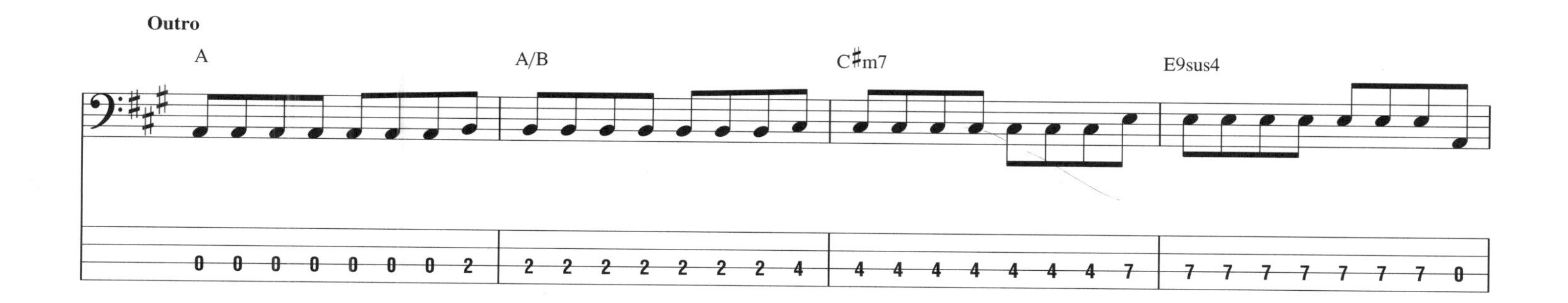
A
A/B
C♯m7
E9sus4
0 0 0 0 0 0 0 2
2 2 2 2 2 2 2 4
4 4 4 4 4 4 4 7
7 7 7 7 7 7 7 0

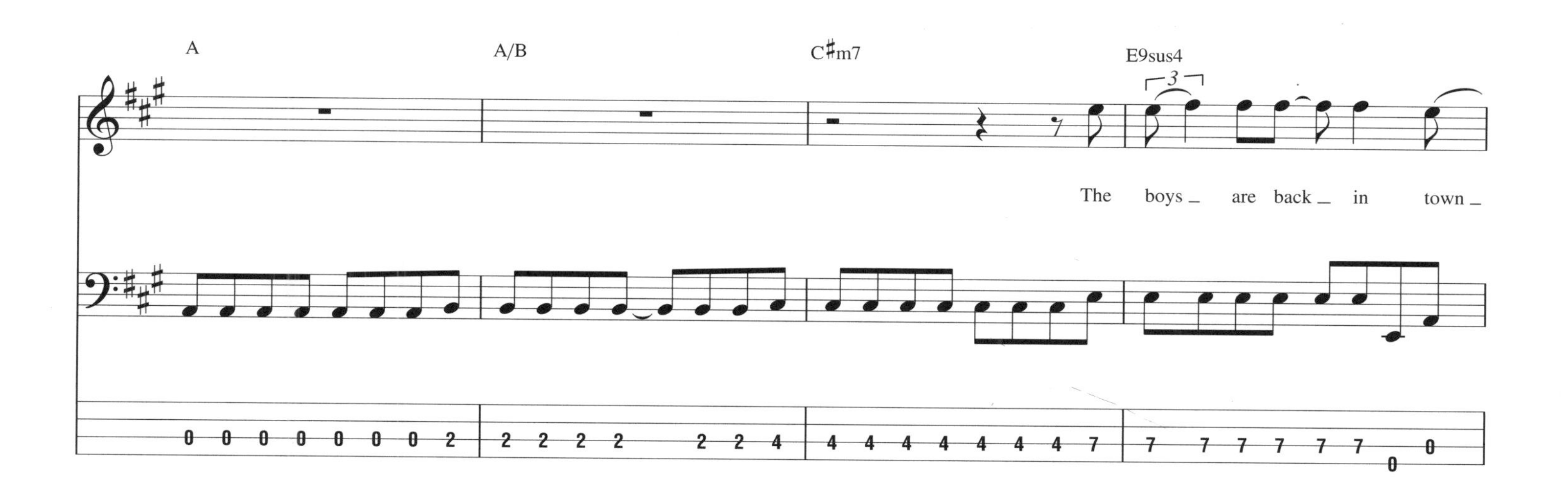
A
A/B
C♯m7
E9sus4
3
The boys are back in town
0 0 0 0 0 0 0 2
2 2 2 2 2 2 4
4 4 4 4 4 4 4 7
7 7 7 7 7 7 0 0

A
A/B
C♯m7
a - gain.
0 0 0 0 0 0 0
2 2 2 2 2 2 4
4 4 4 4 4 4 7

E9sus4
A
A/B
3
Been hang - in' down at Di - no's.
7 7 0 7 7 7 7
0 0 0 0 0 0
2 2 2 2 2 2 4

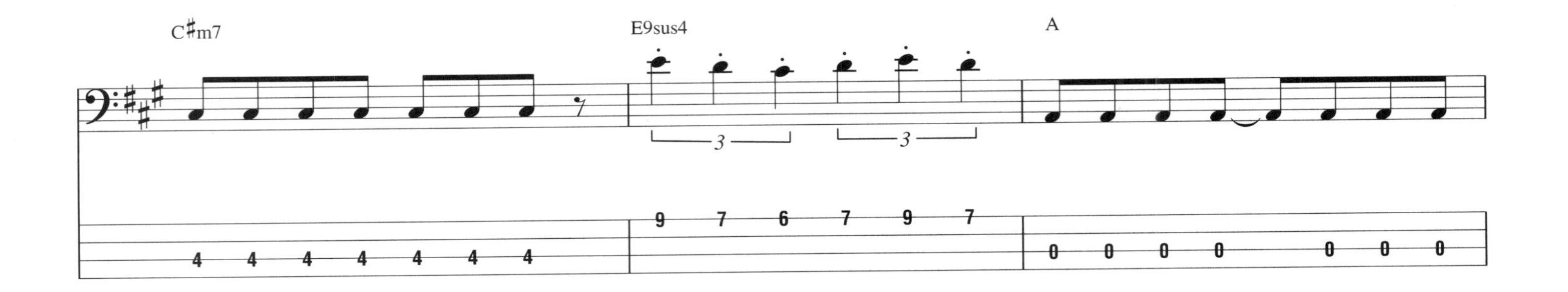
C♯m7
E9sus4
A
3
3

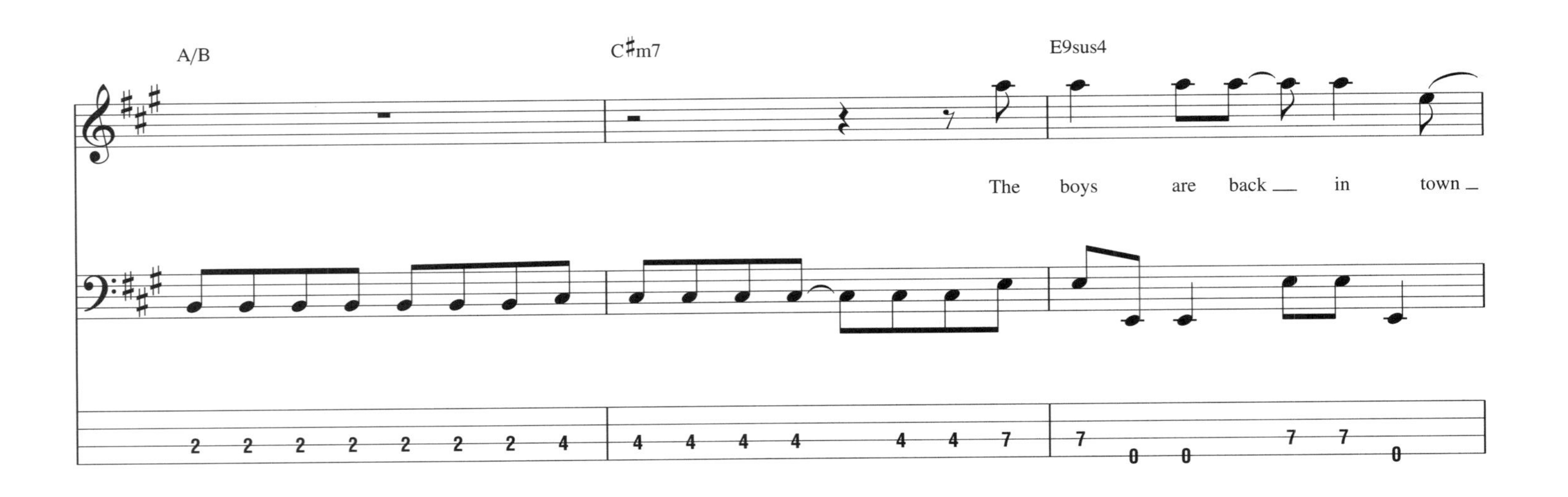
A/B
C♯m7
E9sus4
The boys are back in town

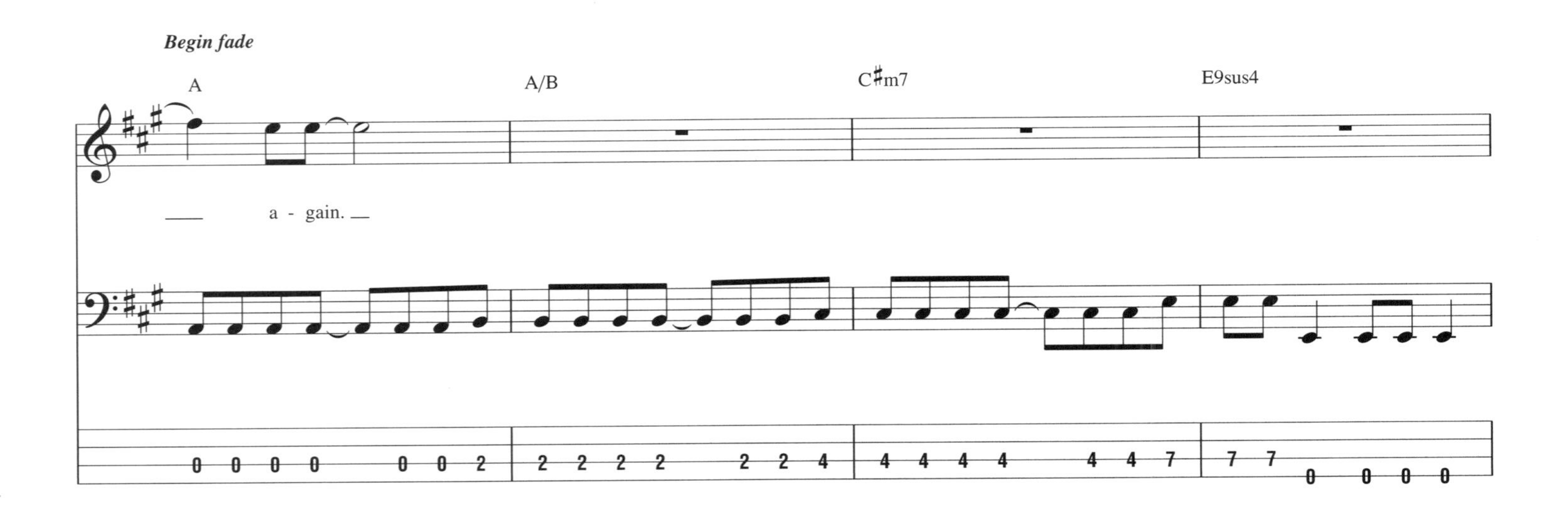
Begin fade
A
A/B
C♯m7
E9sus4
a - gain.

Fade out
A
A/B
C♯m7
E9sus4
3
3

Brick House

Words and Music by Lionel Richie, Ronald LaPread, Walter Orange,
Milan Williams, Thomas McClary and William King

Intro
Moderately ♩ = 102
Am
* (Drums)
Uh.
Bass
mf
P
P
T
A
B
*Key signature denotes A Dorian.

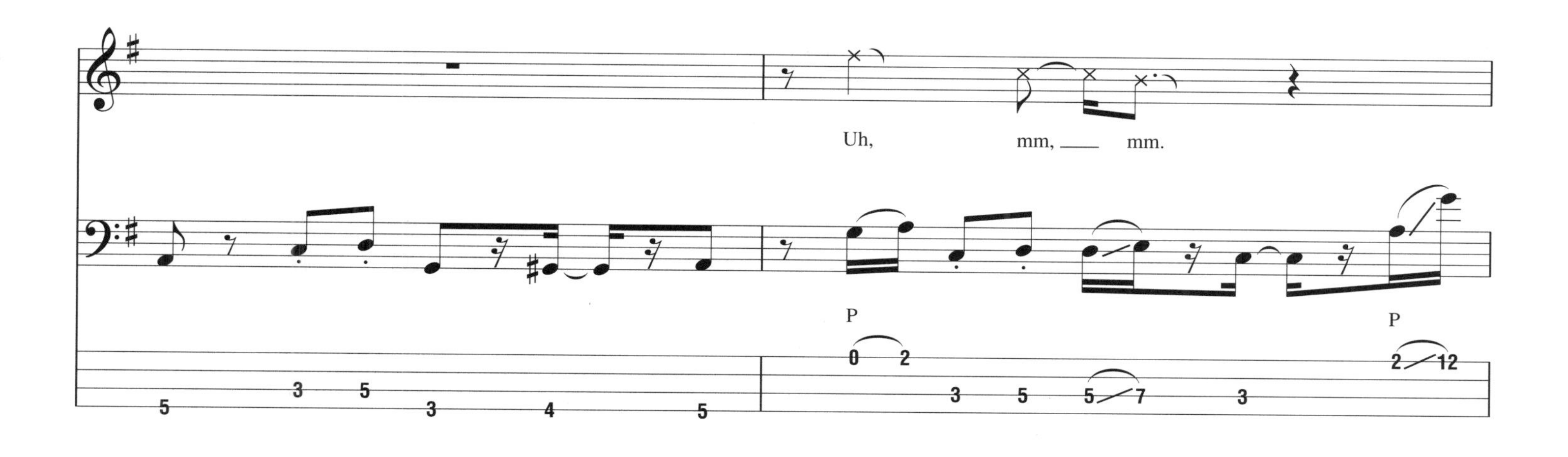
Uh,
mm, ___
mm.
P
P

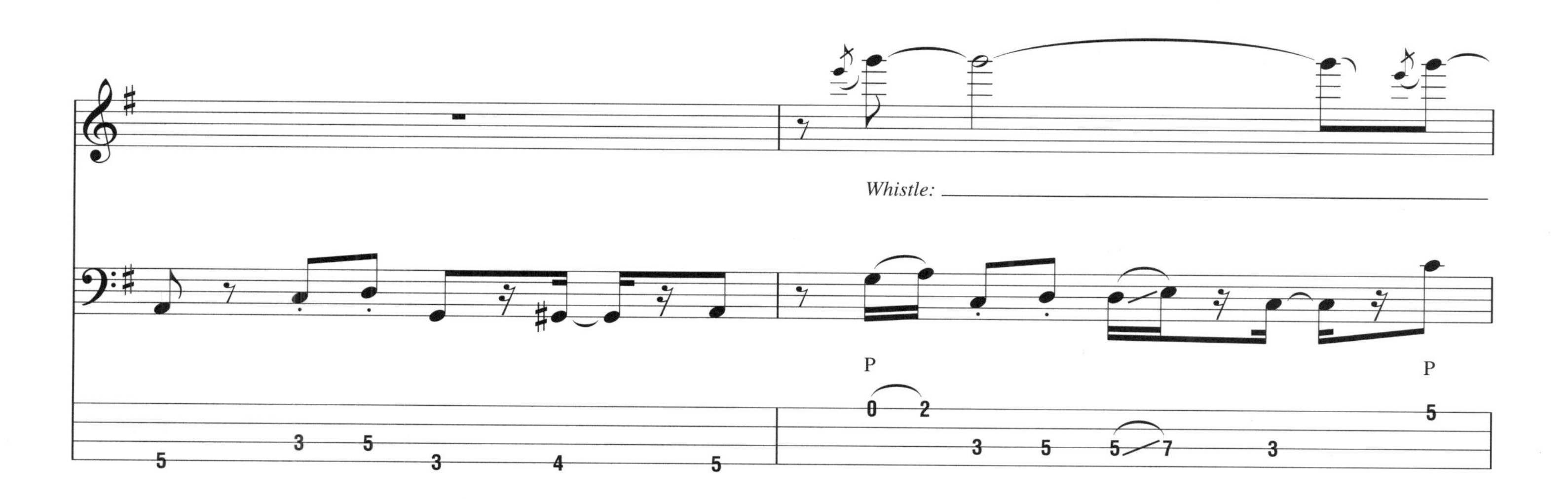
Whistle:
P
P

Ow, she's a
P P T P P
0 5 4 2 0 4 4
X
5 3 5 3 4 5

Chorus

*Am
brick
house.
Bass Fig. 1
P
P

*Chord symbols reflect basic harmony.

She's mighty - y, might - y just let - tin' it all hang out. Ah, she's a
P

brick
house.
I like
P
P

la - dies stacked _ and that's a fact. ___ Ain't hold - in' noth - in' back. _ Ow, she's a
P

brick house. ____ Well,
P

we're to - geth - er, ev - 'ry - bod - y knows _ this is how the sto - ry goes. __
End Bass Fig. 1
P

Verse
Am7
1. She knows she's got ev - 'ry - thing. ____________ Mm, that a wom - an

needs to get a man. Yeah, yeah. How can she lose with the
5 5 5 5 5 5 5 5 0 5 0 5 5 5 5

stuff she use? Thir - ty - six, twen - ty - four, thir - ty - six.
5 5 5 5 0 5 0 5 5 5 5

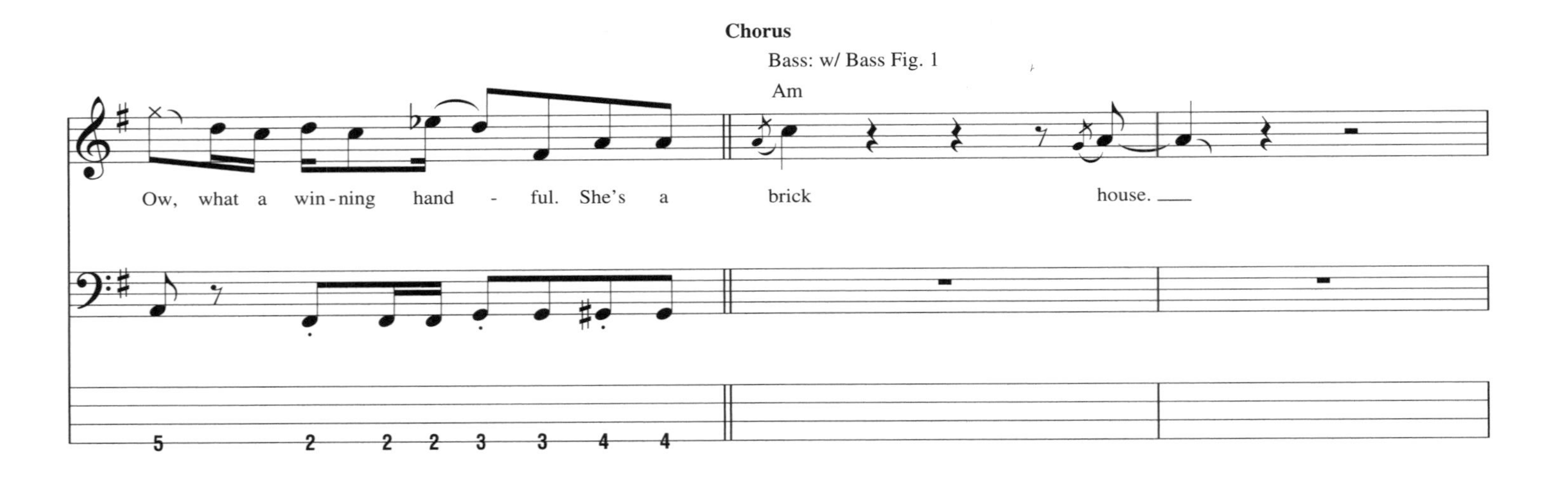
Chorus
Bass: w/ Bass Fig. 1
Am
Ow, what a win-ning hand - ful. She's a brick house.
5 2 2 2 3 3 4 4

She's might - y, might - y just let - tin' it all hang out. Ah, she's a

brick house. Oh, I like la - dies stacked and that's a fact.

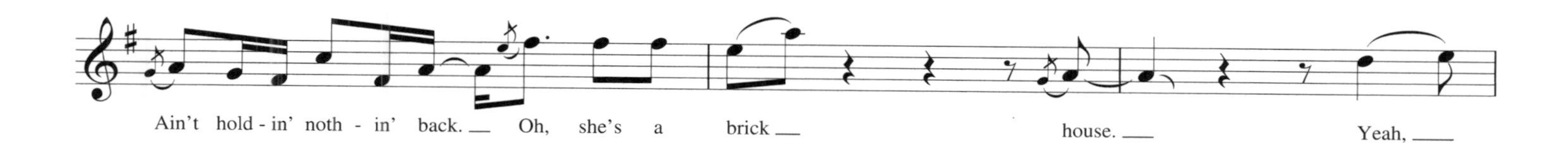
Ain't hold-in' noth-in' back. Oh, she's a brick house. Yeah,

she's the one, the on-ly one built like an Am-a-zon. 2. Mm,

Verse
Am7
the clothes she wear, her sex-y ways make an old man wish for
Bass

young-er days, yeah, yeah. She knows she's built and knows how to please.
P P

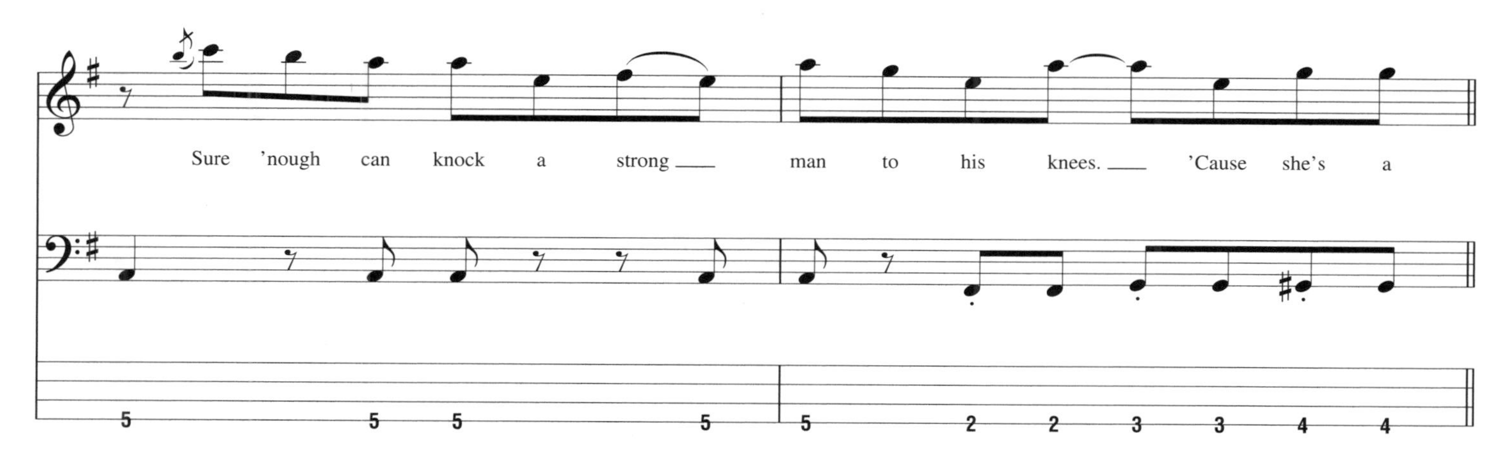
Sure 'nough can knock a strong man to his knees. 'Cause she's a

Chorus
Am
brick house. Yeah,
she's might - y, might - y just let - tin' it all hang out. Hey,

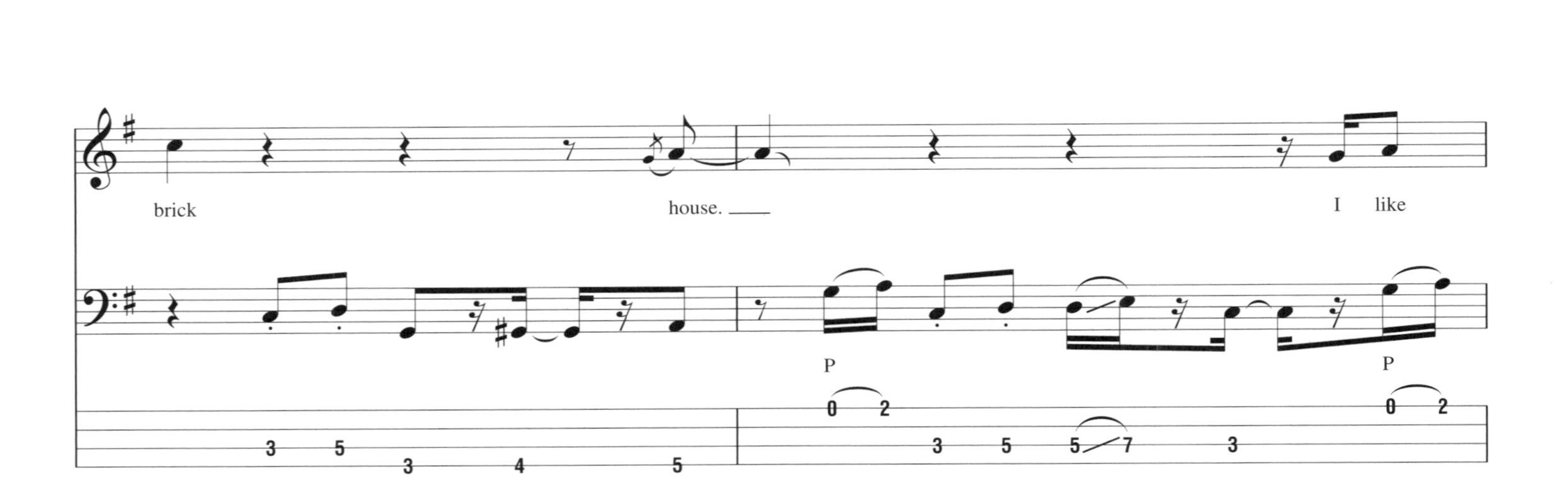
brick house. I like

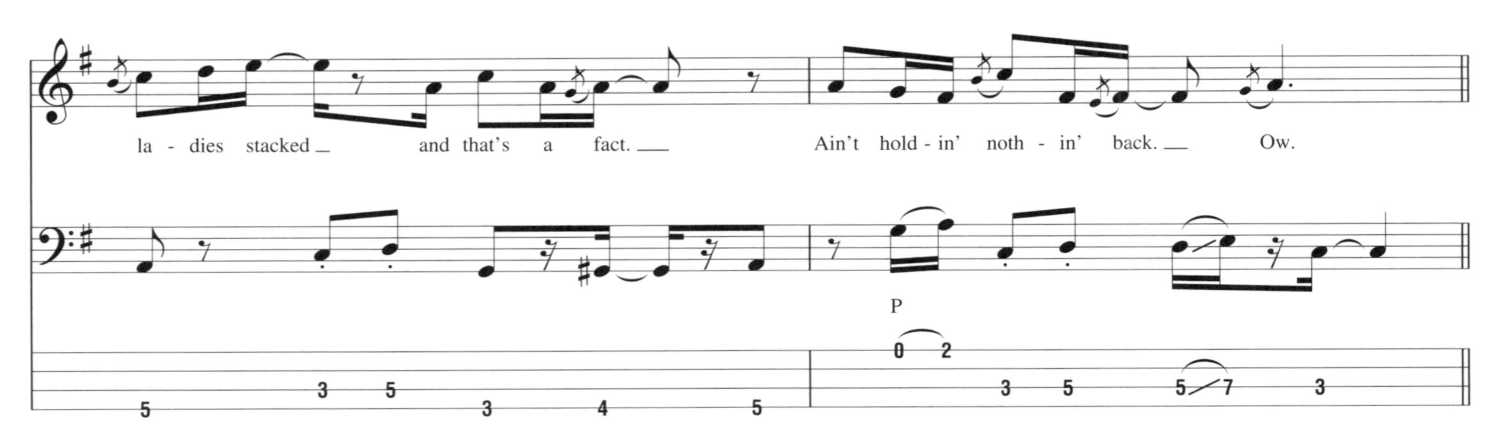
la - dies stacked and that's a fact. Ain't hold - in' noth - in' back. Ow.

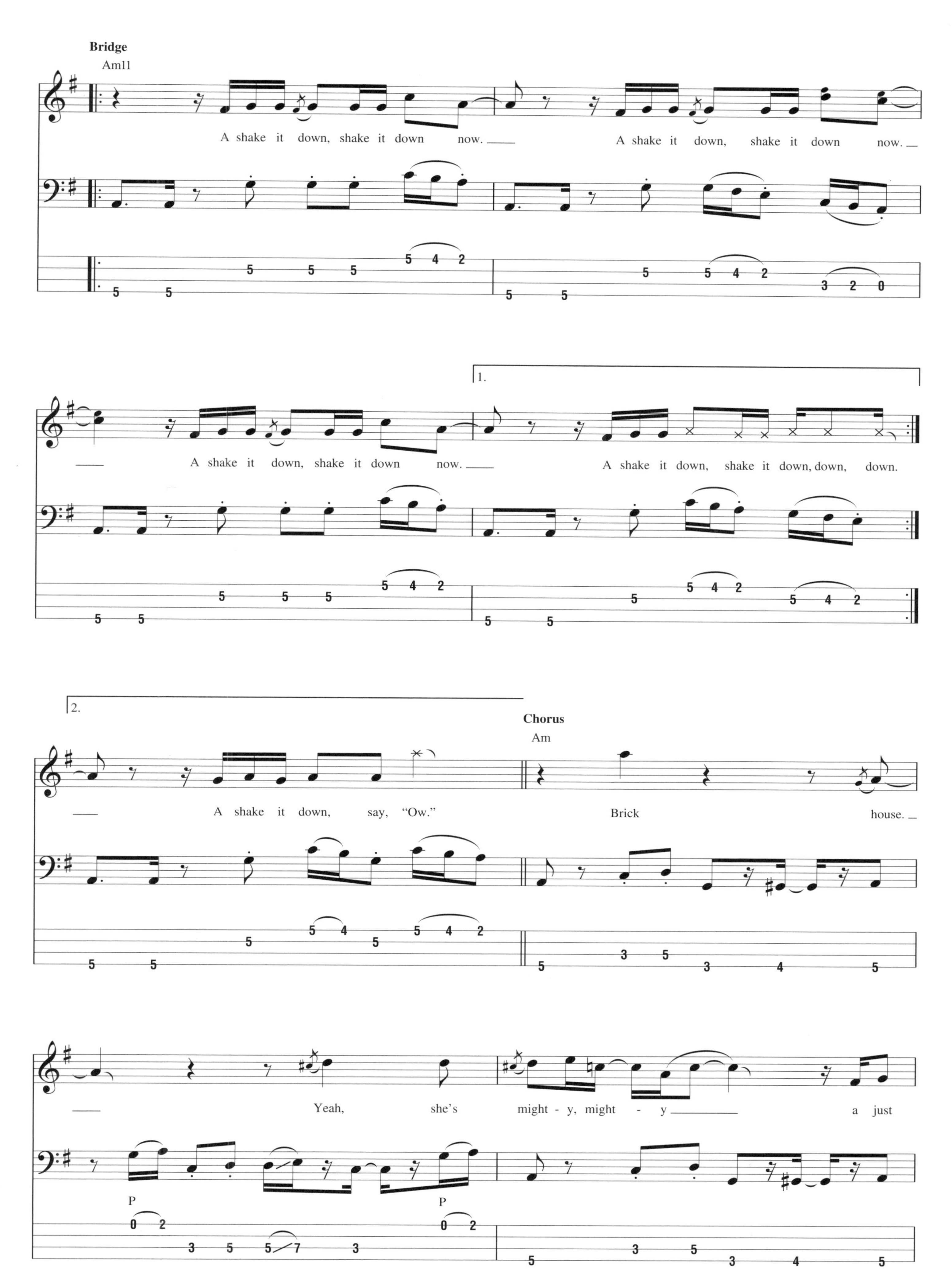
Bridge
Am11
A shake it down, shake it down now. A shake it down, shake it down now.
A shake it down, shake it down now.
1.
A shake it down, shake it down, down, down.
2.
Chorus
Am
A shake it down, say, "Ow." Brick house.
Yeah, she's might - y, might - y a just
P
P

let - tin' it all hang out. Ow, a brick house.
P P

Yeah she's the one, the on - ly one
P P

Bridge
Am
built like an Am - a - zon. Yeah. Shake it down, shake it down, shake it now, now.
P P P P

Shake it down, shake it down, shake it now, now. Shake it down, shake it down, shake it now, now.
P

1.
2.
Shake it down, shake it down, shake it, shake it.
Shake it down, shake it down. Shake it.
P
P
P
P
P
P
0 2
3 5 5 7 3
5
0 2 5 4 2 5 7

Interlude

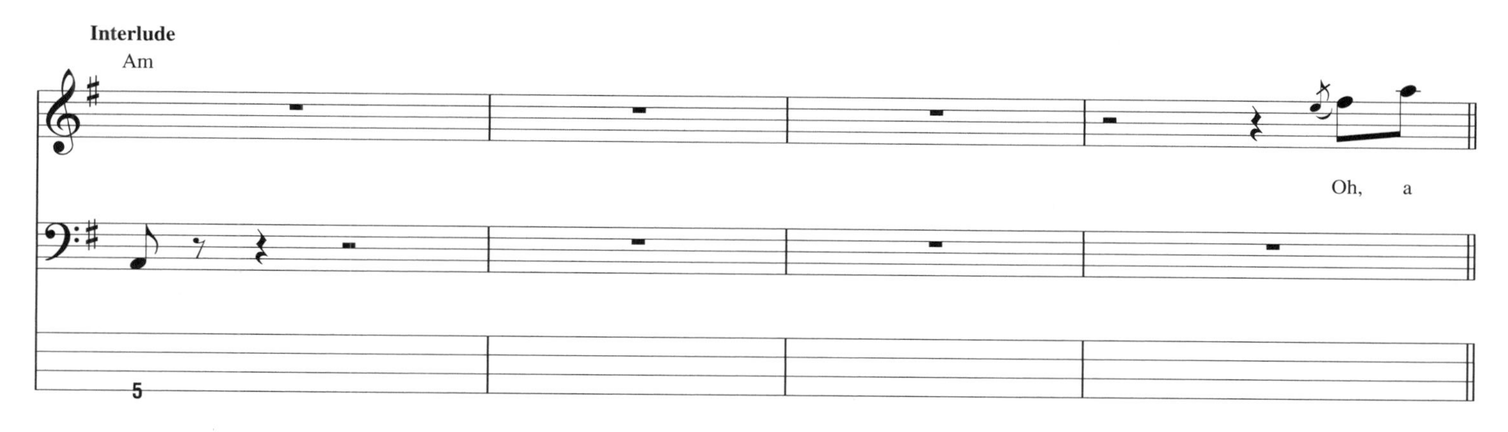
Am
Oh, a
5

Outro

Am
Begin fade
brick
house.
P
P
0 2
0 2
5 3 5 3 4 5
3 5 5 7 3

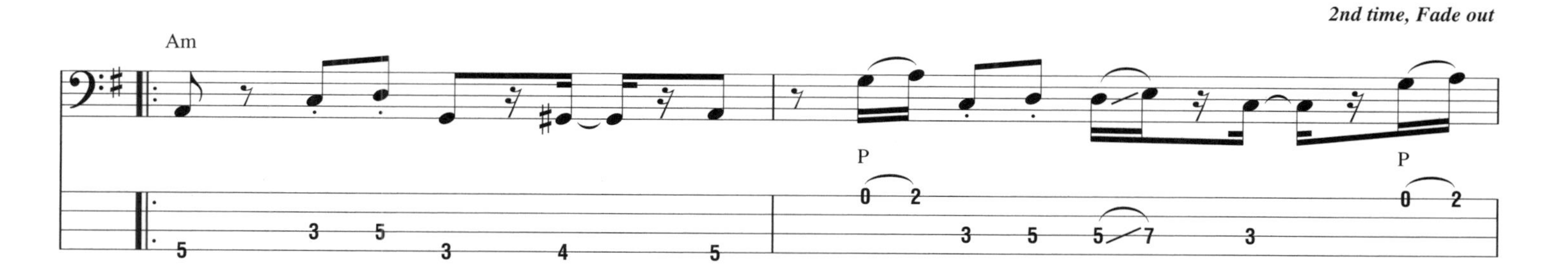
Am
2nd time, Fade out
P
P
0 2
0 2
5 3 5 3 4 5
3 5 5 7 3

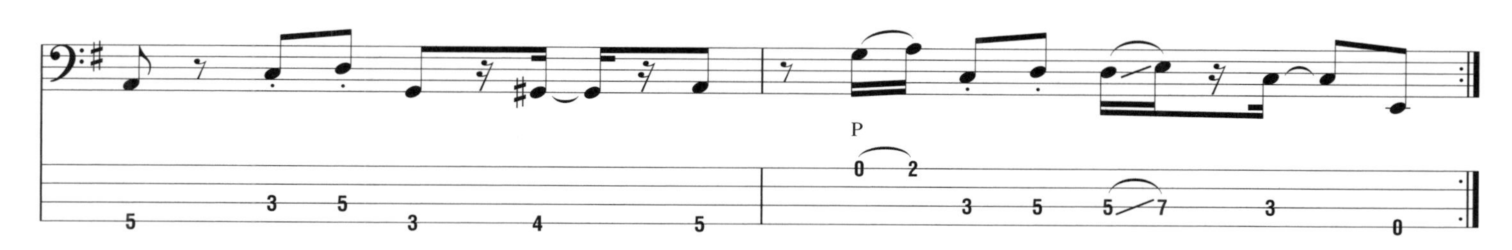
P
0 2
5 3 5 3 4 5
3 5 5 7 3 0

Carry On Wayward Son

Words and Music by Kerry Livgren

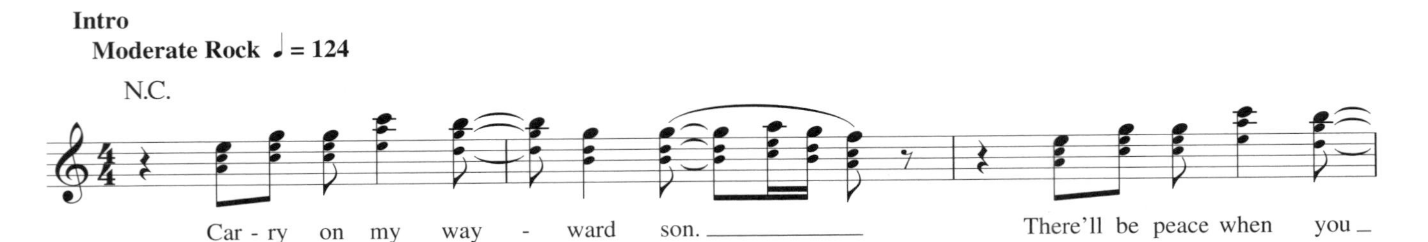
Intro
Moderate Rock ♩ = 124
N.C.
Car - ry on my way - ward son.
There'll be peace when you

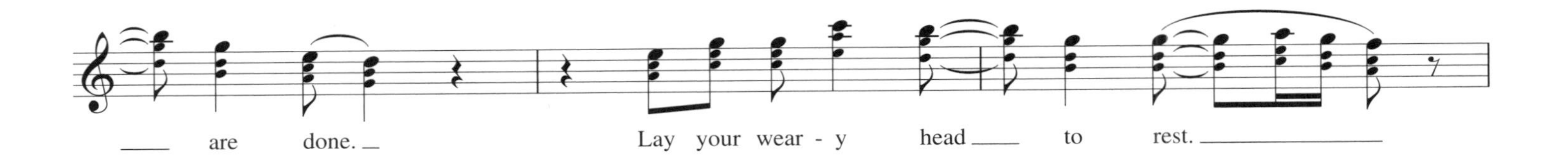
are done.
Lay your wear - y head to rest.

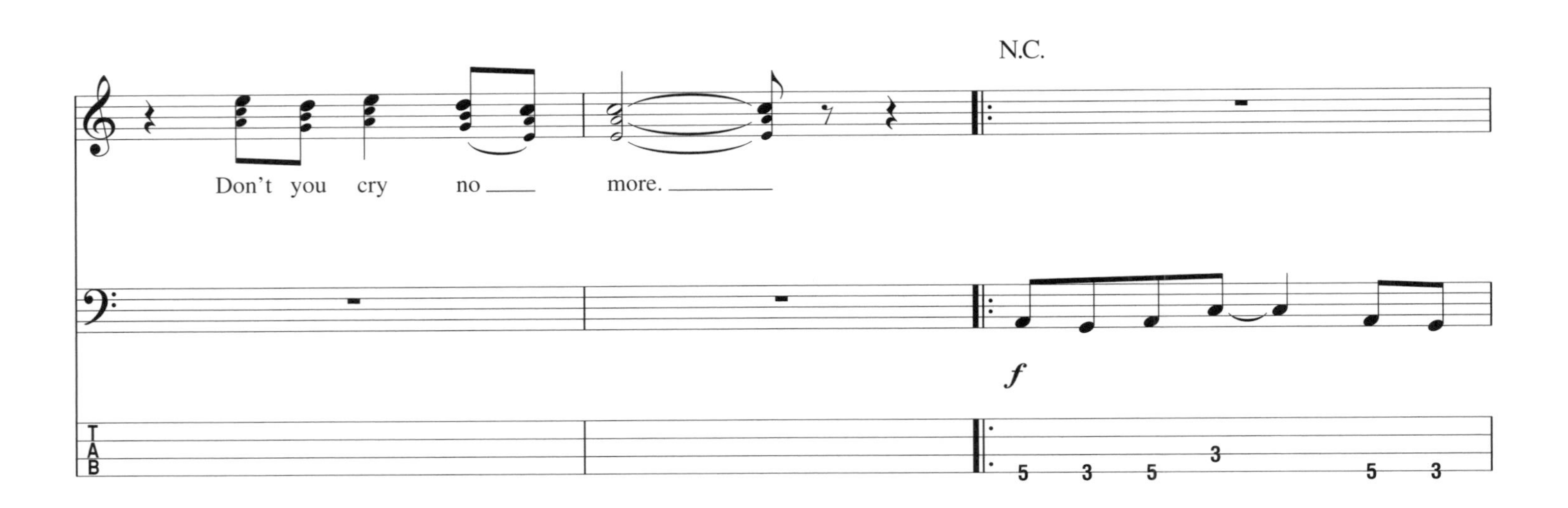
N.C.
Don't you cry no more.
f

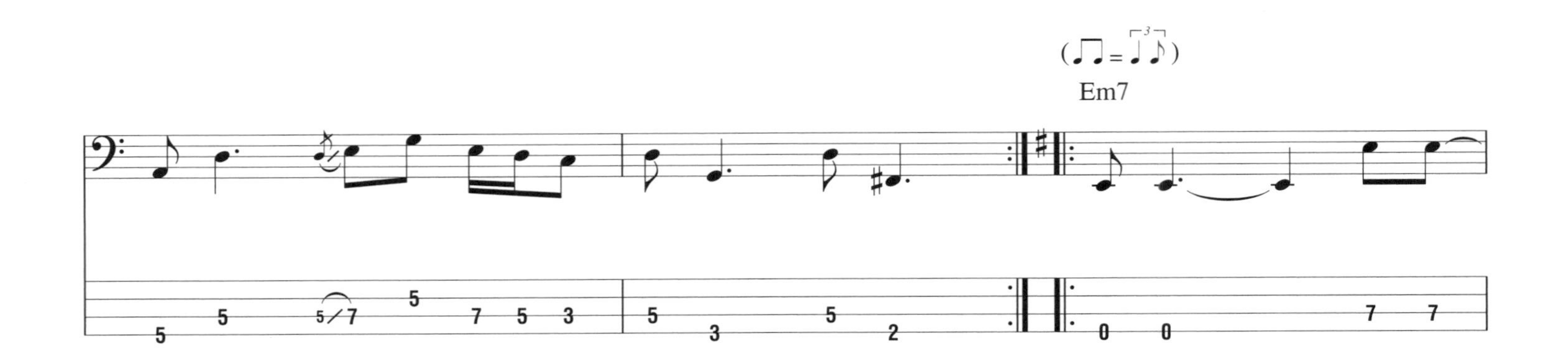
Em7

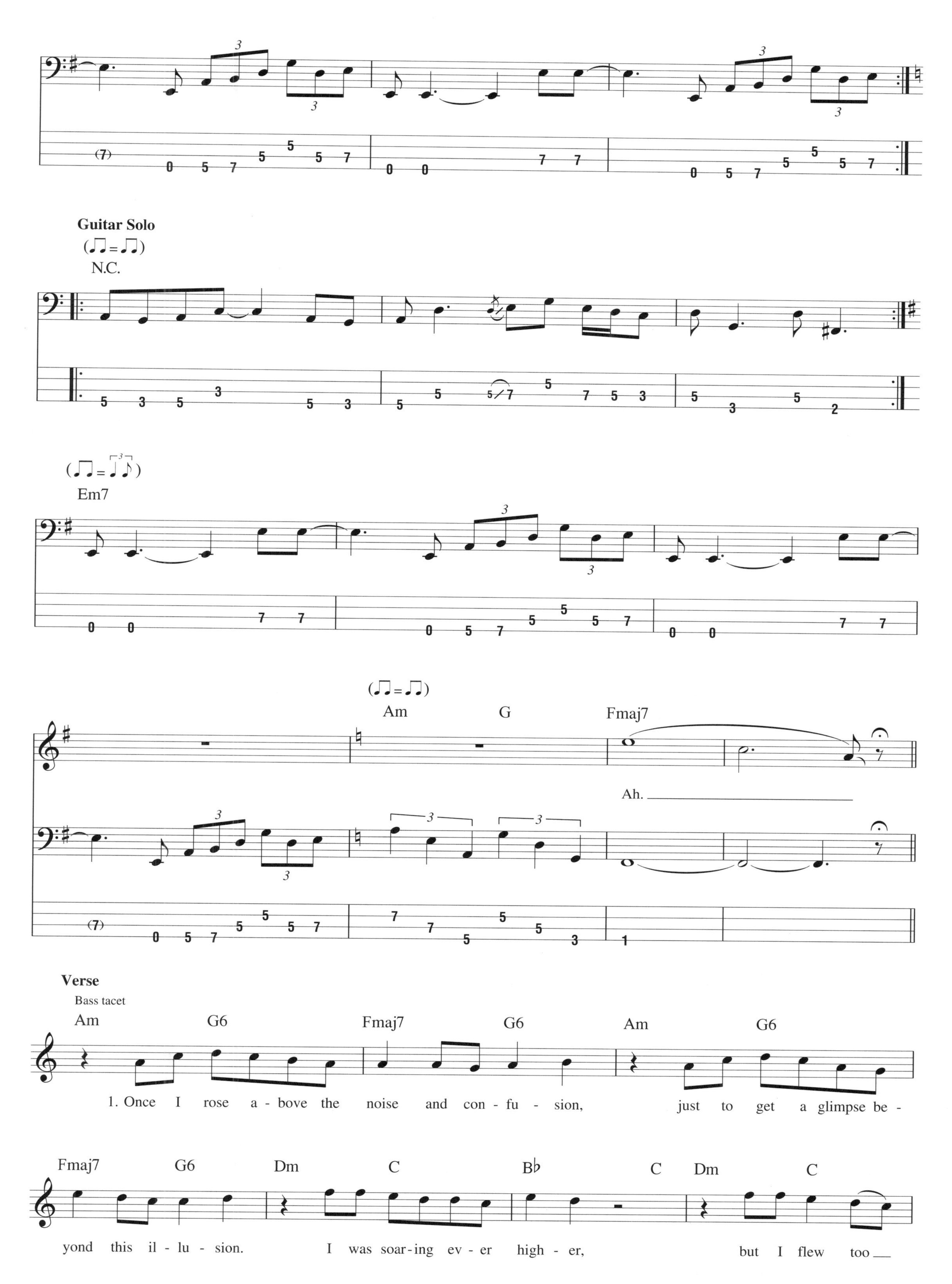

Guitar Solo
N.C.
Em7
Am
G
Fmaj7
Ah.
Verse
Bass tacet
Am
G6
Fmaj7
G6
Am
G6
1. Once I rose a - bove the noise and con - fu - sion, just to get a glimpse be -
Fmaj7
G6
Dm
C
B♭
C
Dm
C
yond this il - lu - sion. I was soar - ing ev - er high - er, but I flew too

G
Am
G6
Fmaj7
G6
high.
'Though my eyes could see, I still was a blind man.
mf
5
7
5
3
3
3

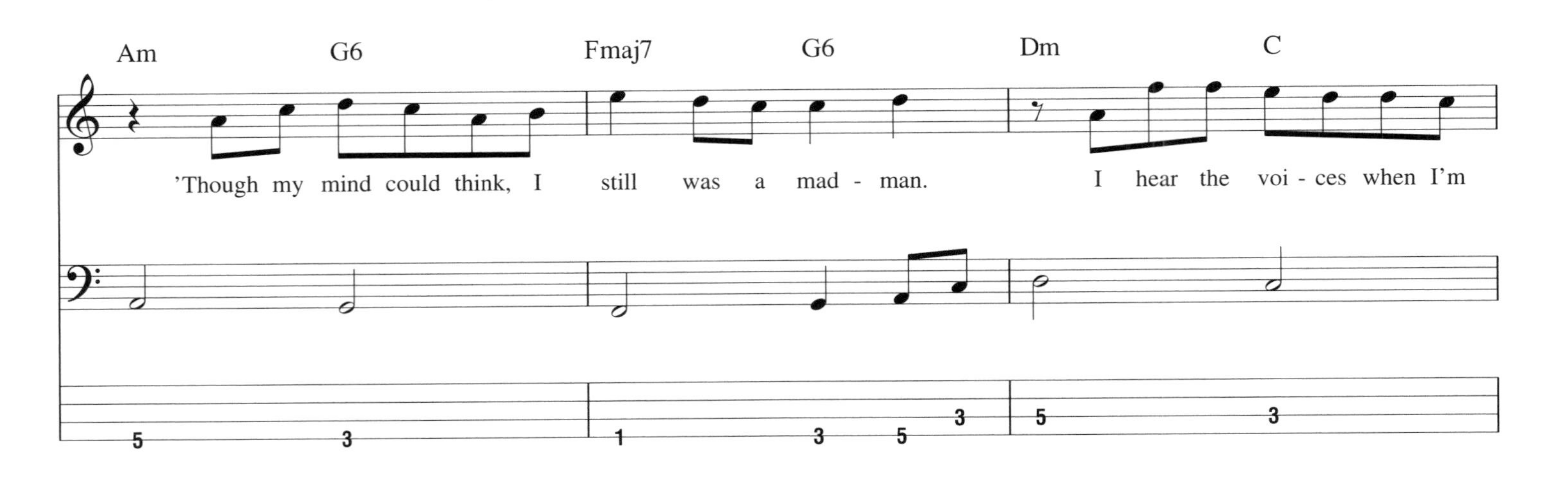
Am
G6
Fmaj7
G6
Dm
C
'Though my mind could think, I still was a mad - man.
I hear the voi - ces when I'm
5
3
1
3
5
3
5
3

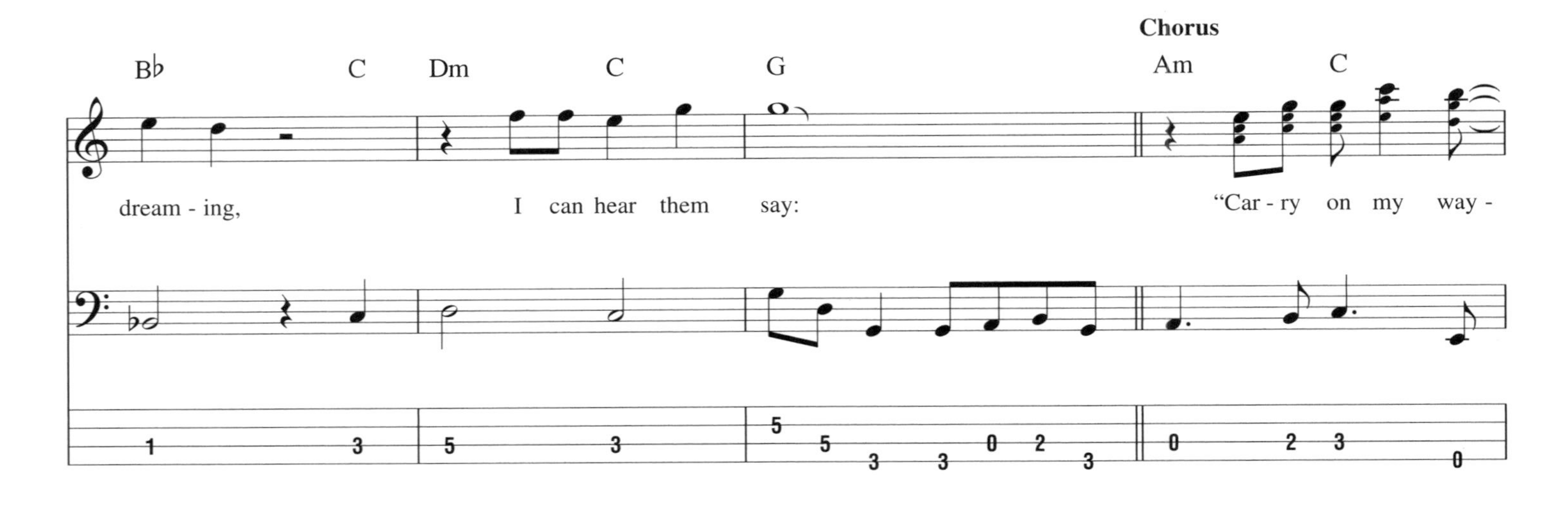
Chorus
B♭
C
Dm
C
G
Am
C
dream - ing,
I can hear them say:
"Car - ry on my way -
1
3
5
3
5
5
3
3
0
2
3
0
2
3
0

G
F
Am
C
G
- ward son.
There'll be peace when you are done.
3
3
1
3
0
2
3
0
3
3
0
3

Am
C
G
F
N.C.
Lay your wear - y head to rest.
Don't you cry no

more."

Verse

Am
G6
Fmaj7
G6
Am
G6
2. Mas - quer - ad - ing as a man with a rea - son. My cha - rade is the e -

Fmaj7
G6
Dm
C
B♭
C
vent of the sea - son.
And if I claim to be a wise man, ah,
Dm
C
G
Am
G6
it sure - ly means that I don't know.
On a storm - y sea of
Fmaj7
G6
Am
G6
Fmaj7
G6
mov - ing e - mo - tion.
Tossed a - bout, I'm like a ship on the o - cean.
Dm
C
B♭
C
Dm
C
G
I set a course for winds of for - tune.
But I hear the voi - ces say:

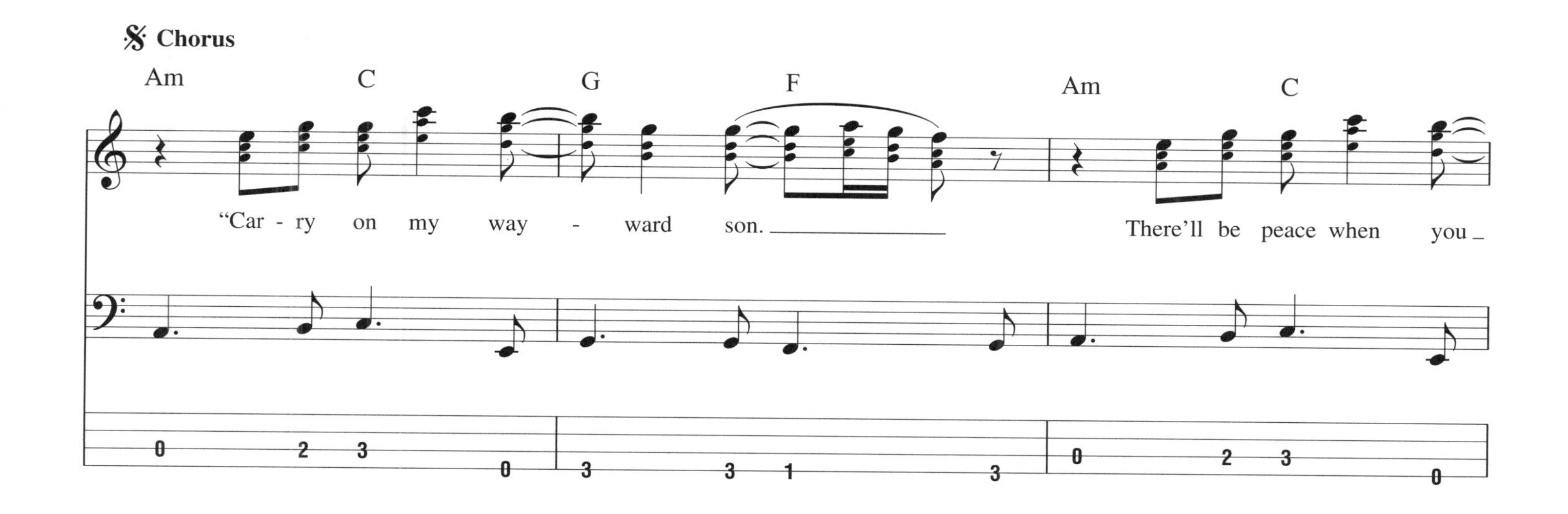
Chorus
Am C G F Am C
"Car - ry on my way - ward son.
There'll be peace when you

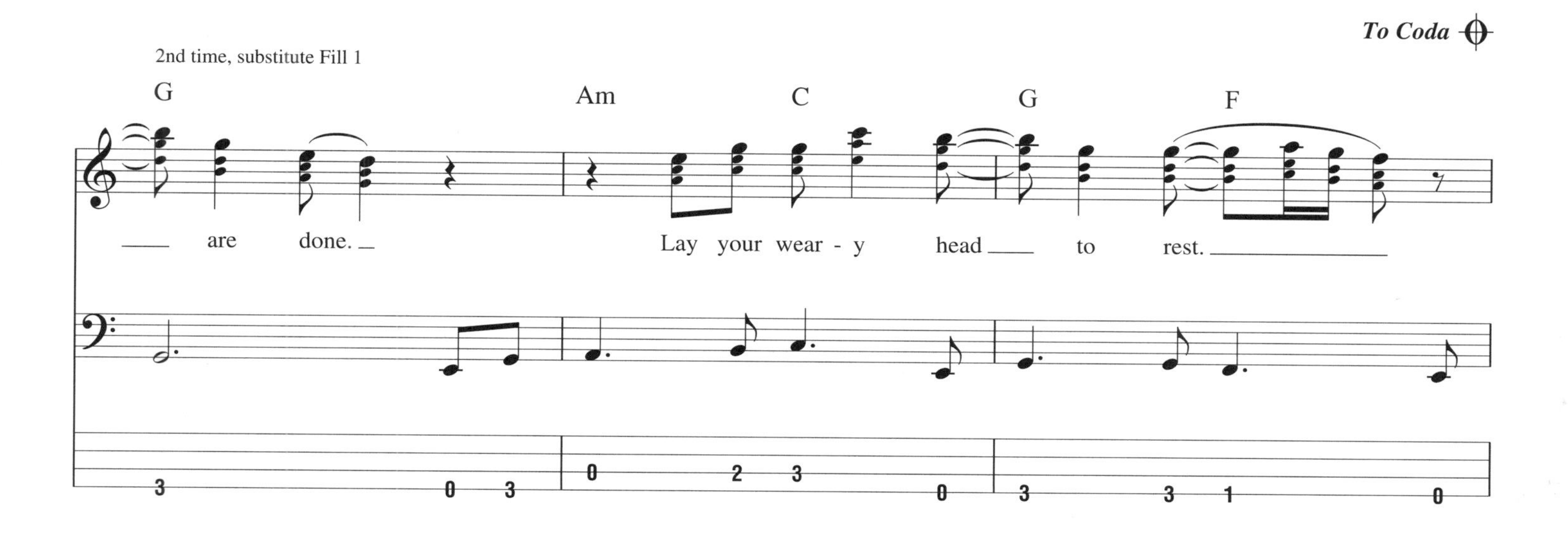
To Coda
2nd time, substitute Fill 1
G Am C G F
are done.
Lay your wear - y head to rest.

Interlude
N.C.
N.C. (Am)
D5 C5
Don't you cry no more. No!

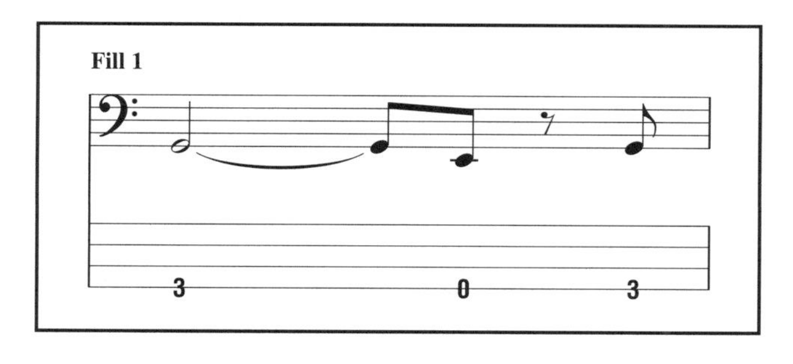
Fill 1

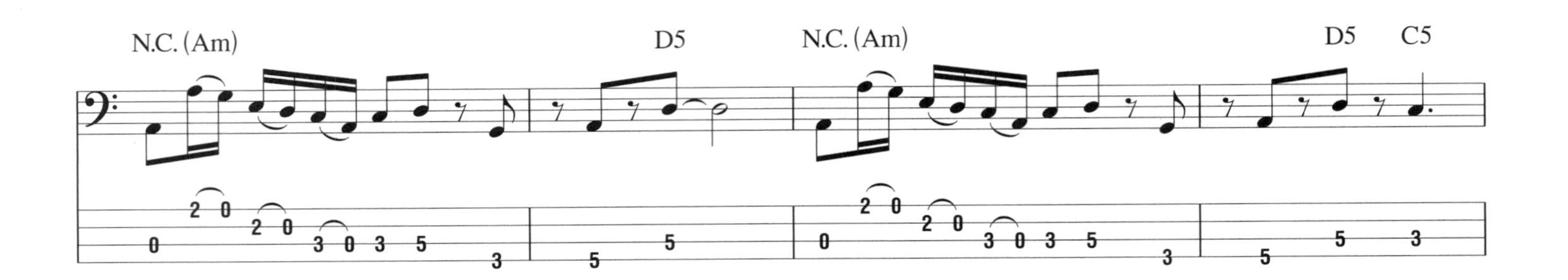
N.C. (Am)
D5
N.C. (Am)
D5
C5

Organ-Guitar Solo

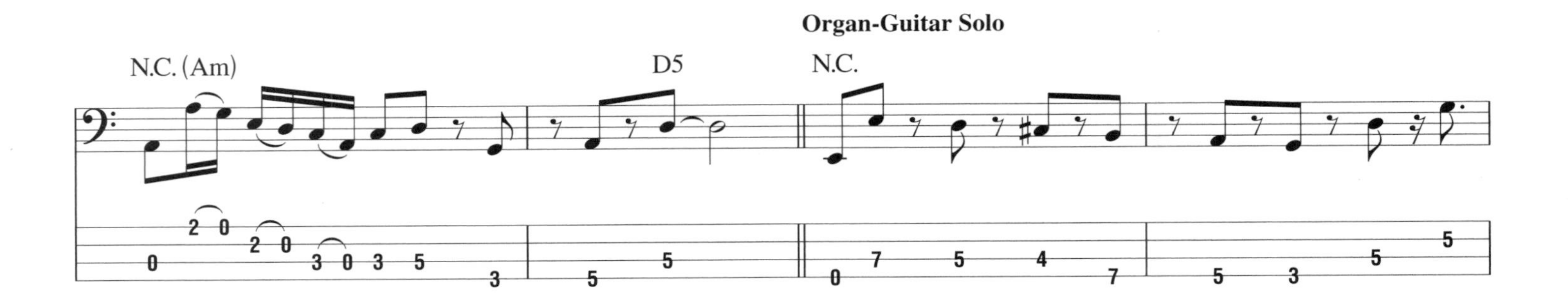
N.C. (Am)
D5
N.C.

Interlude

N.C.

Bridge

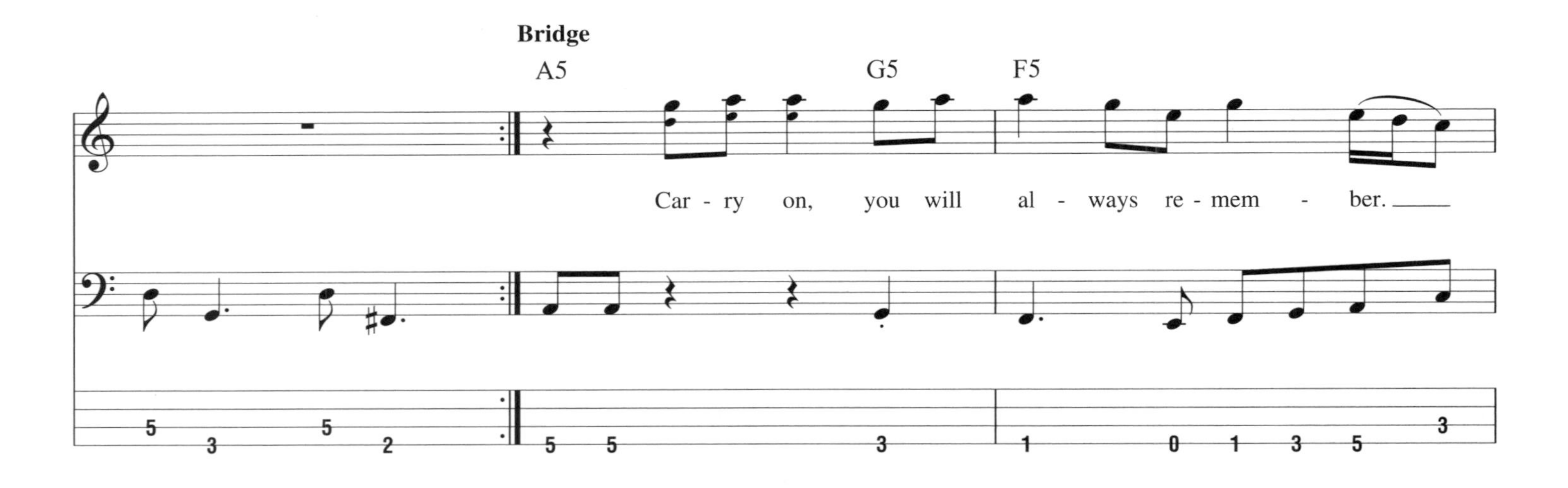
A5
G5
F5
Car - ry on, you will al - ways re - mem - ber.

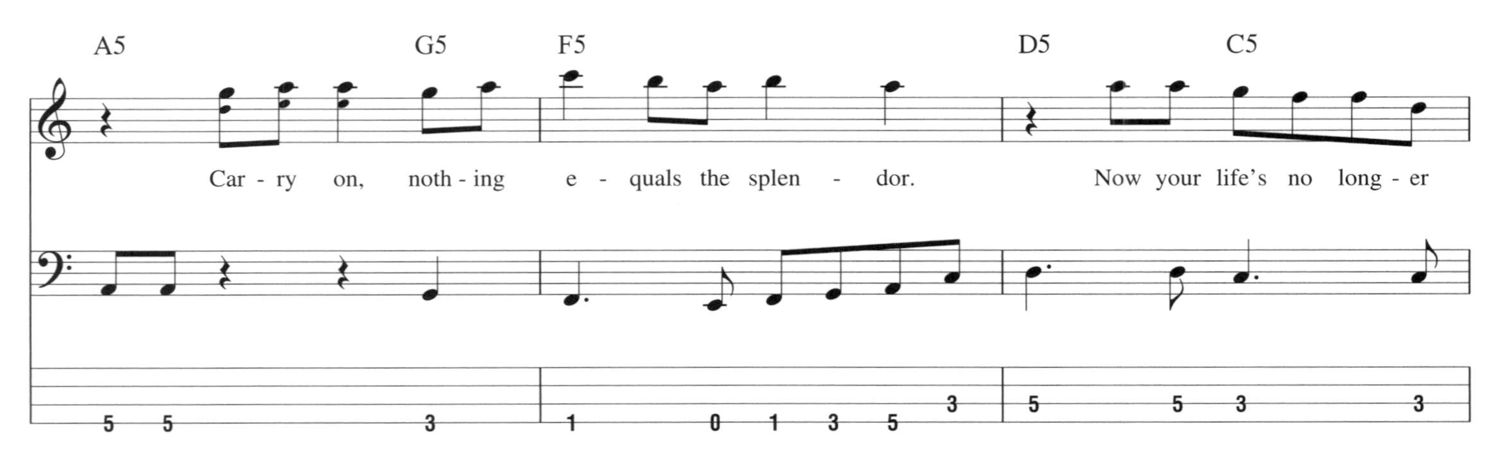
A5
G5
F5
D5
C5
Car - ry on, noth - ing e - quals the splen - dor. Now your life's no long - er

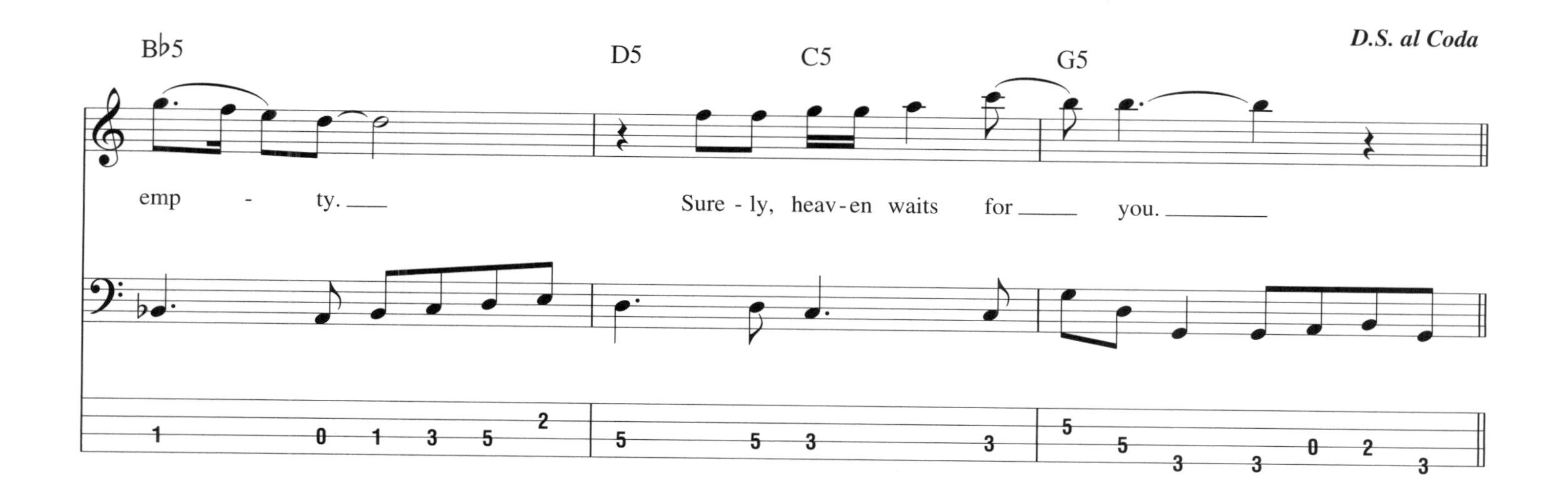

D.S. al Coda
B♭5
D5
C5
G5
emp - ty.
Sure - ly, heav-en waits for you.

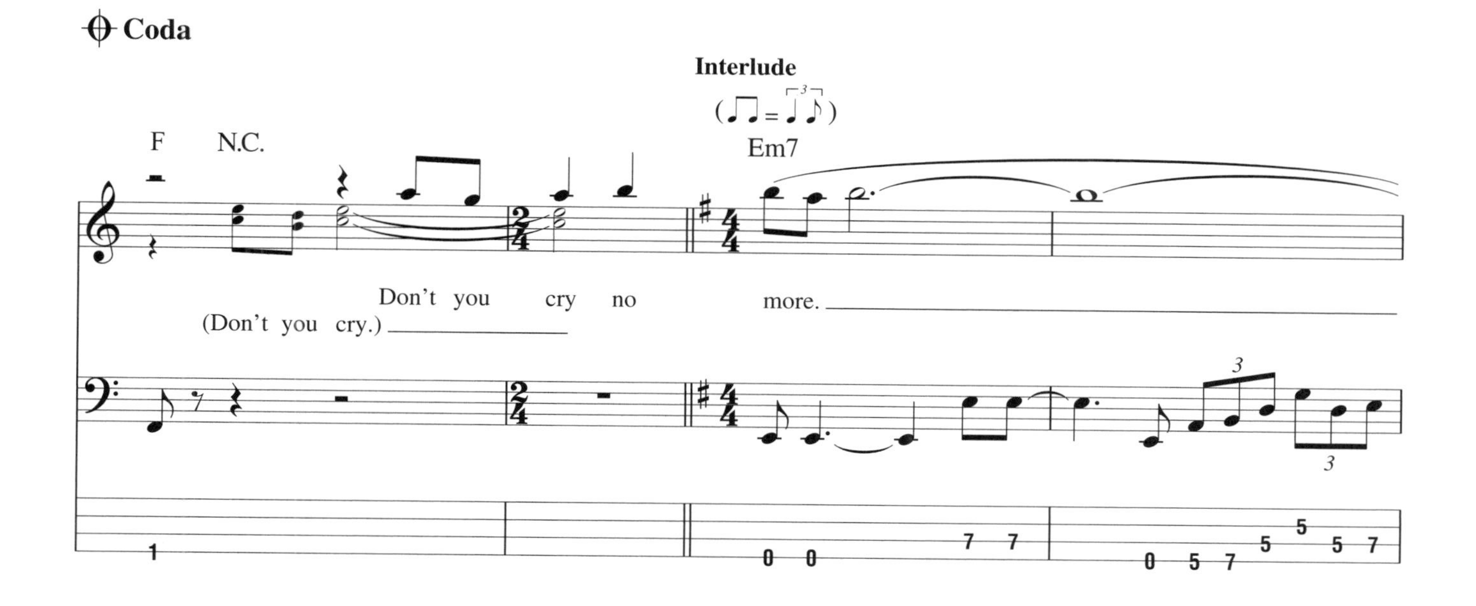

Coda
Interlude
F N.C.
Em7
Don't you cry no more.
(Don't you cry.)

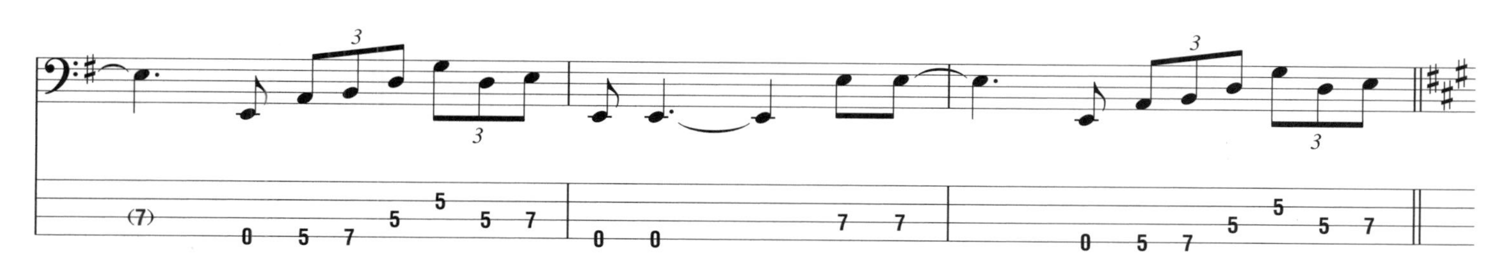

Outro-Guitar Solo

N.C. (F♯m7)
A5
E5
Play 3 times
N.C. (F♯m7)
A5

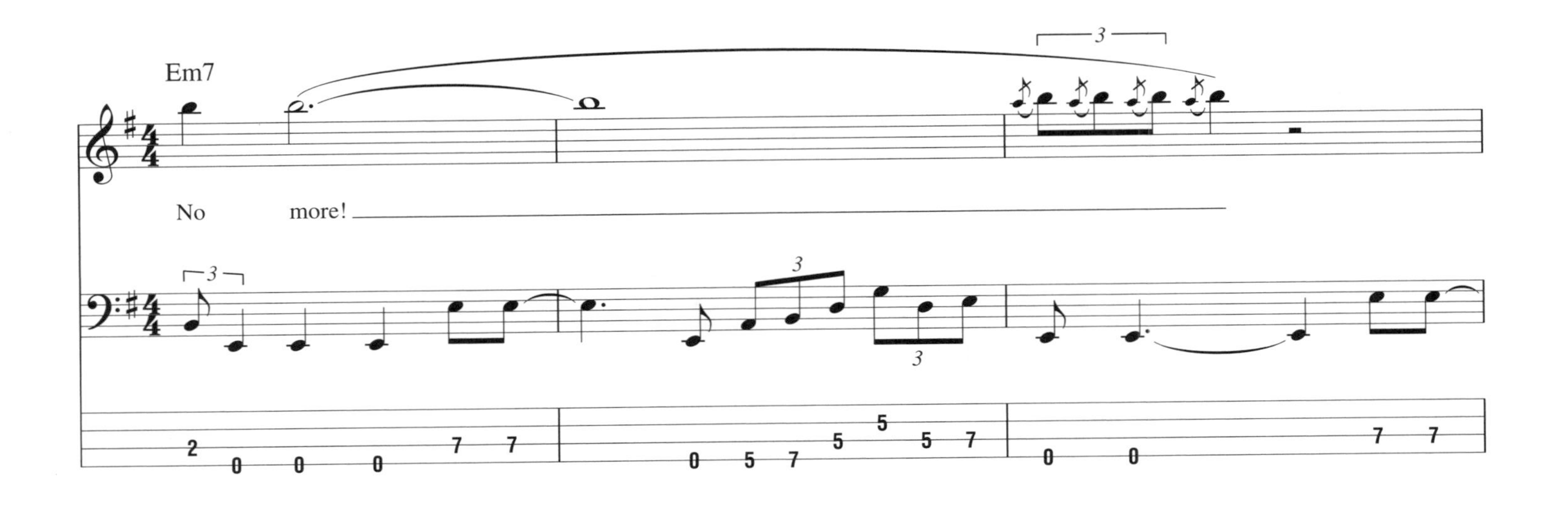
Em7
No more!

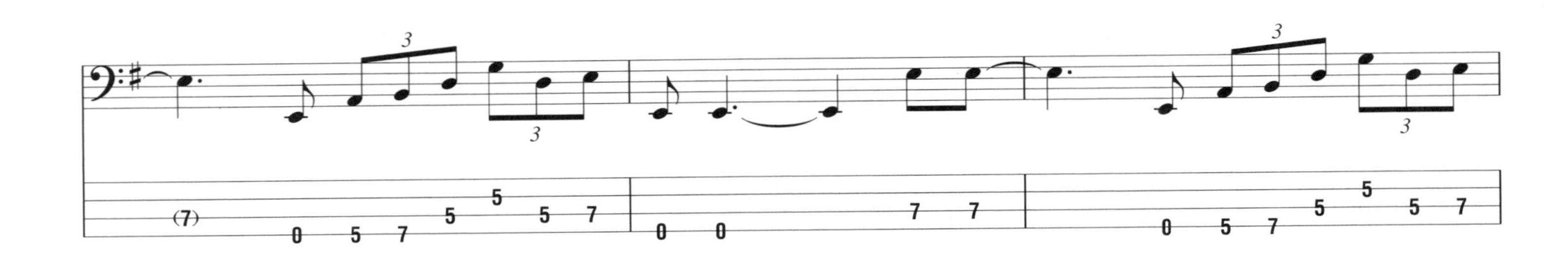

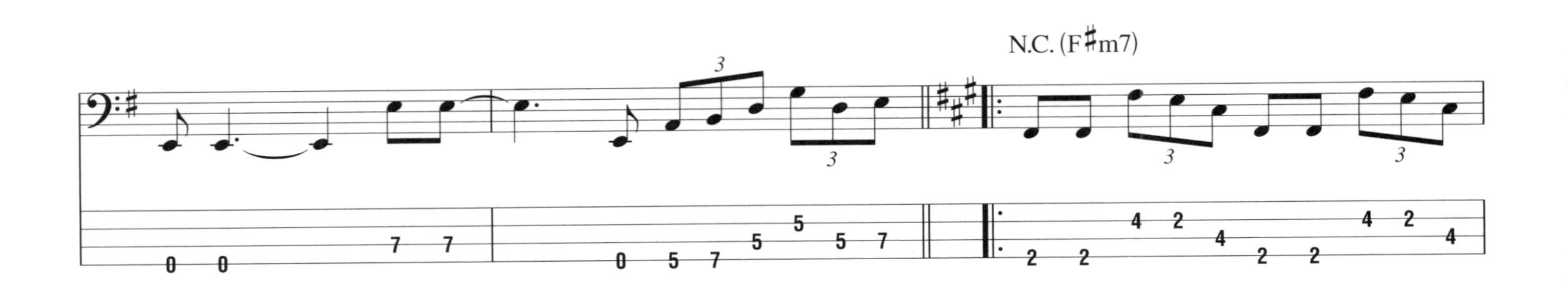
N.C. (F♯m7)

A5
E5
Play 4 times
Am
G
Fmaj7

The Chain

Words and Music by Stevie Nicks, Christine McVie, Lindsey Buckingham, Mick Fleetwood and John McVie

Intro
Moderately ♩ = 80
* Esus2
(Gtr.)
8
Verse
E5
A5
1. Lis - ten to the wind blow, watch the sun
*Chord symbols reflect overall harmony.
D
C
E5
rise.
Run in the shad - ows,
A5
D
C
E5
damn your love, damn your lies.
And if
Chorus
Am
you don't love me now, you will nev - er love me a - gain. I can
Bass
mf
Em
C
D
still hear you say - ing you would nev - er break the chain. And if
(Nev - er break the chain.

Am
you don't love me now, you will nev - er love me a - gain. I can
You don't love me now.)
0 0 0 0 0 0 0 0 5

Interlude
Bass tacet
Em C D E5
still hear you say - ing you would nev - er break the chain.
(Nev - er break the chain.)
(Still hear you say - ing.)
7 7 5 3 3 3 3 5 5 5 5 5 5 5 5 5 5

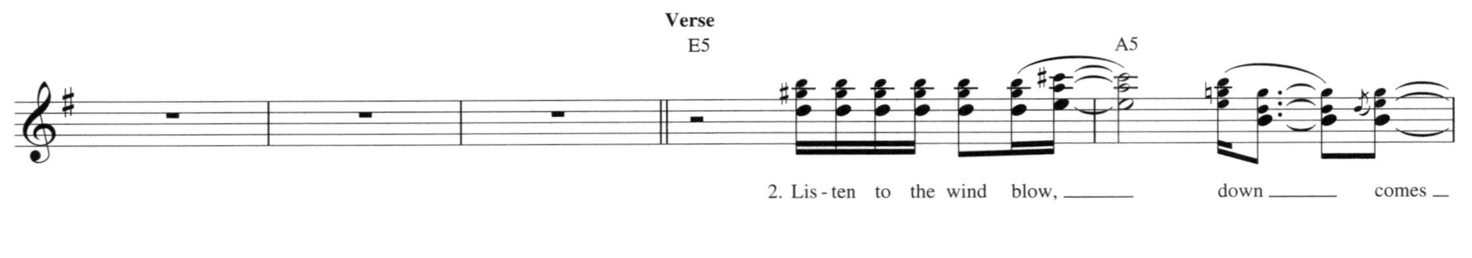
Verse
E5 A5
2. Lis - ten to the wind blow, down comes

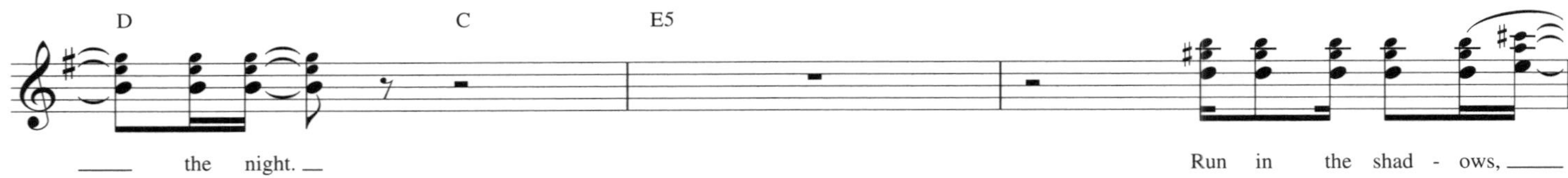
D C E5
the night. Run in the shad - ows,

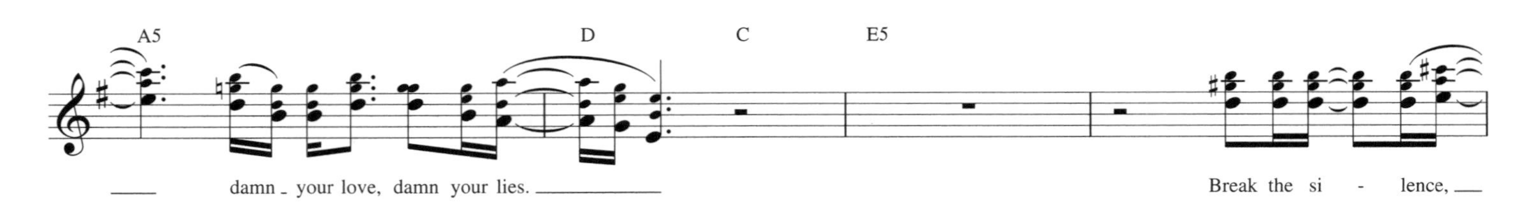
A5 D C E5
damn your love, damn your lies. Break the si - lence,

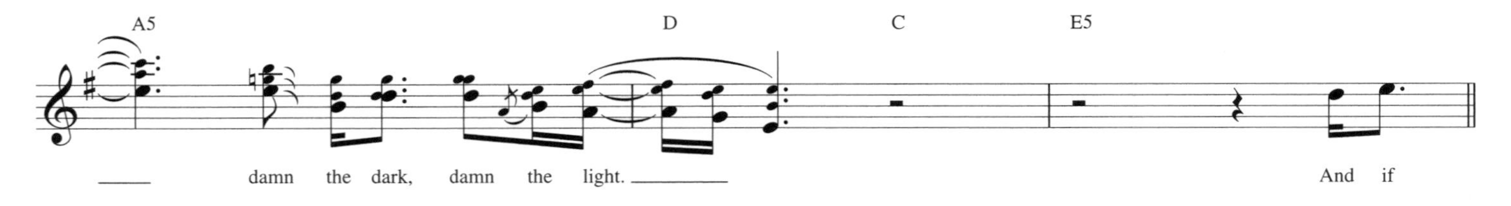
A5 D C E5
damn the dark, damn the light. And if

Chorus

Am
you don't love me now, you will nev - er love me a - gain. I can
Bass
0 0 0 0 0 0 0 0 3

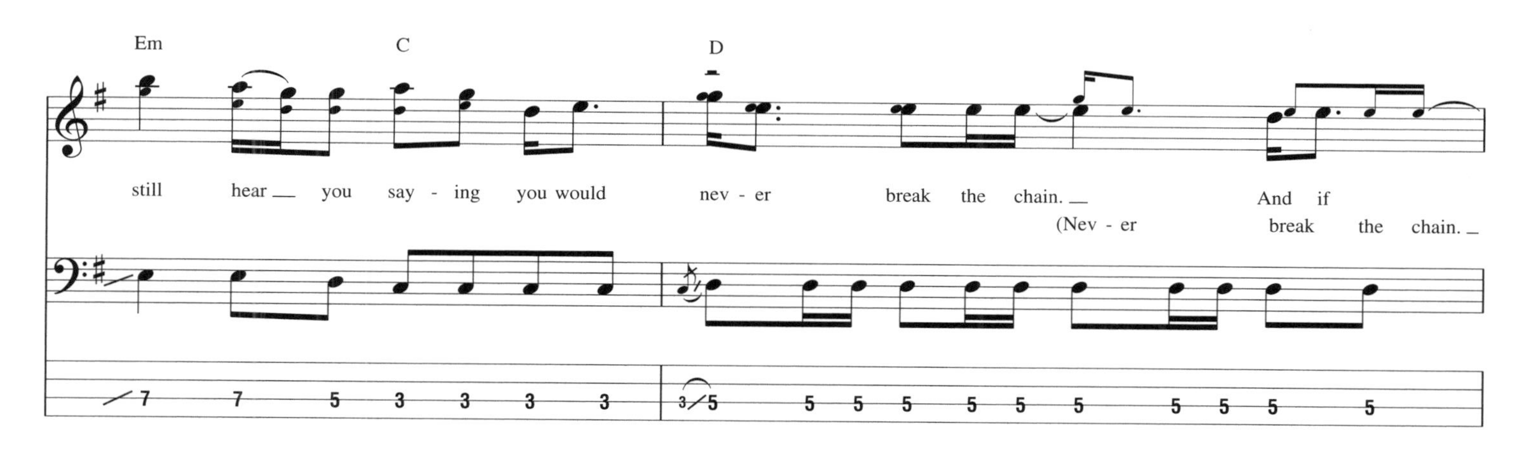
Em C D
still hear you say - ing you would nev - er break the chain. And if
(Nev - er break the chain.
7 7 5 3 3 3 3 3 5 5 5 5 5 5 5 5 5 5 5

Am
you don't love me now, you will nev - er love me a - gain. I can
You don't love me now.)
0 0 0 3 0 0 0 3 0 0 0 3 0 0 3

Em C D
still hear you say - ing you would nev - er break the chain. And if
(Nev - er break the chain.
(Still hear you say - ing.)
7 7 7 5 3 3 3 3 5 5 5 5 5 5 5 5 5 5

Am
you don't love me now, you will nev - er love me a - gain. I can
You don't love me now.)

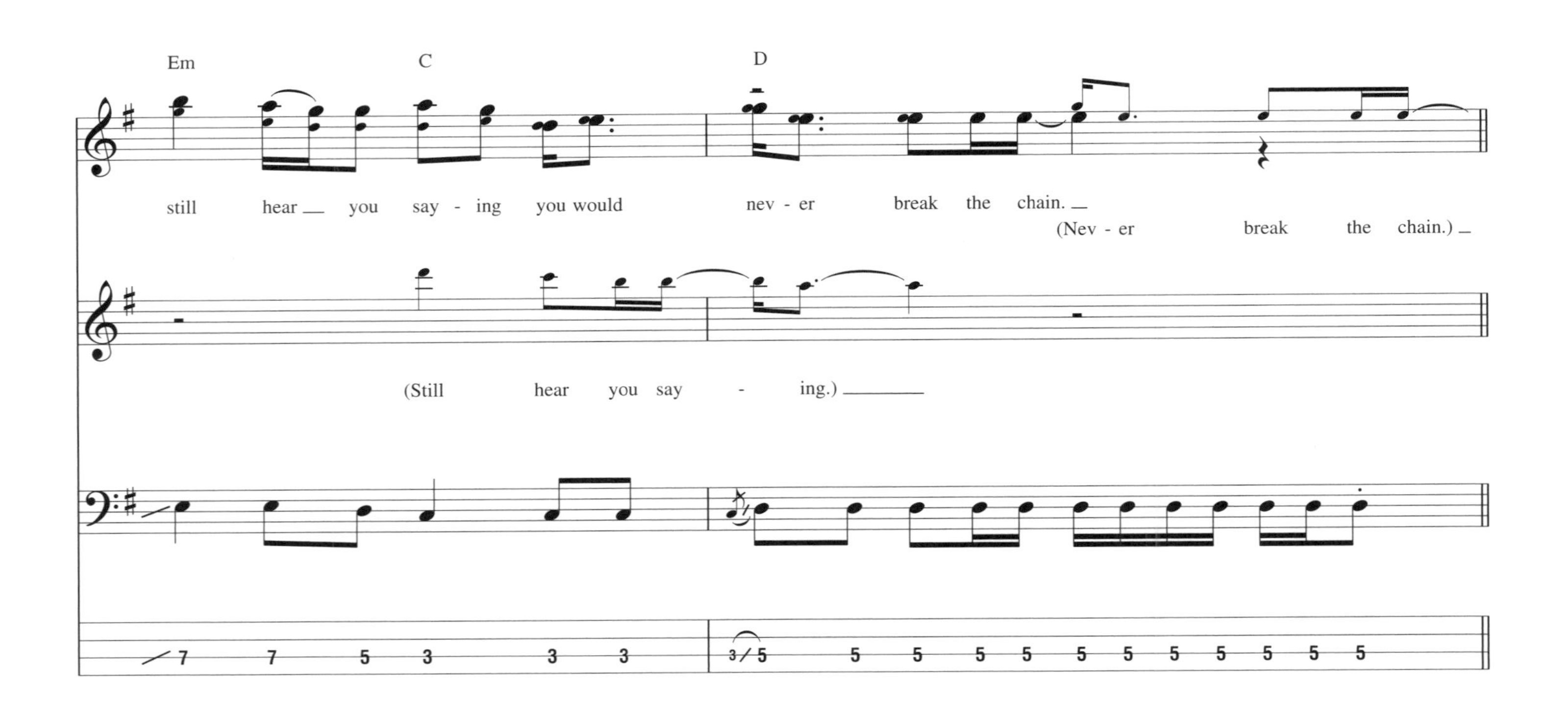
Em
C
D
still hear you say - ing you would nev - er break the chain.
(Nev - er break the chain.)
(Still hear you say - ing.)

Interlude

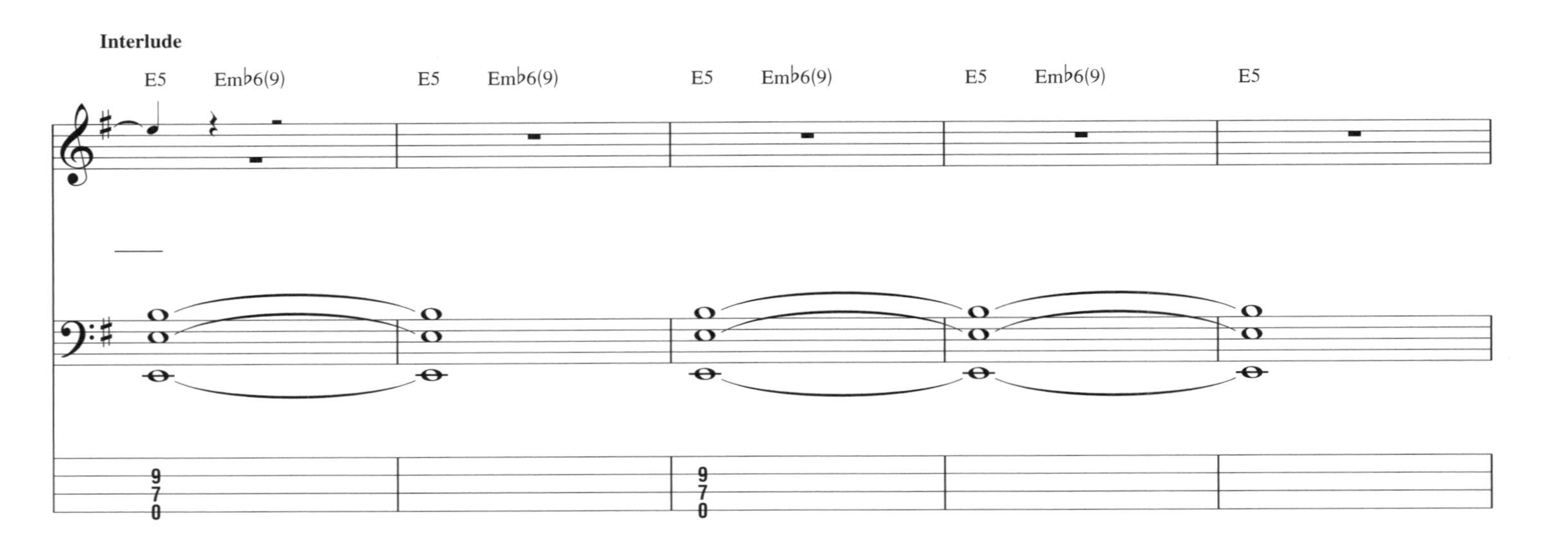
E5
Em♭6(9)
E5
Em♭6(9)
E5
Em♭6(9)
E5
Em♭6(9)
E5

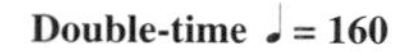
Double-time ♩ = 160

N.C.

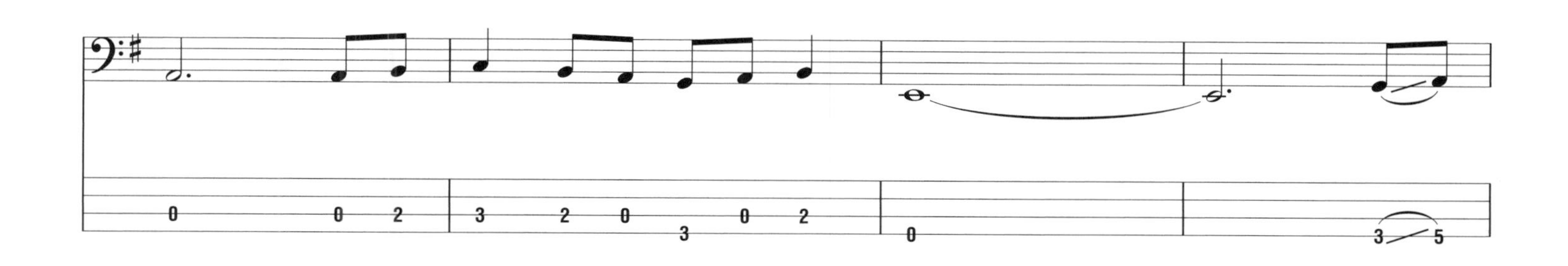

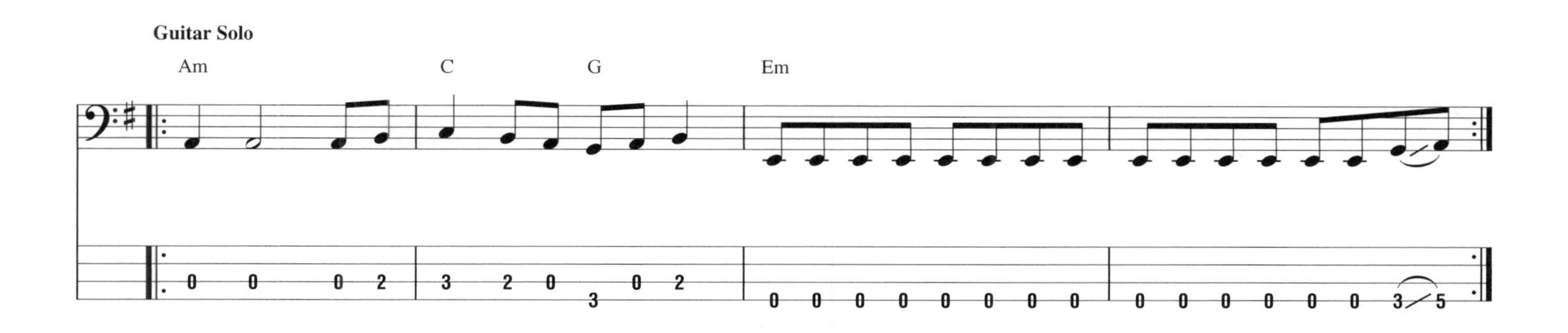
Guitar Solo
Am
C
G
Em

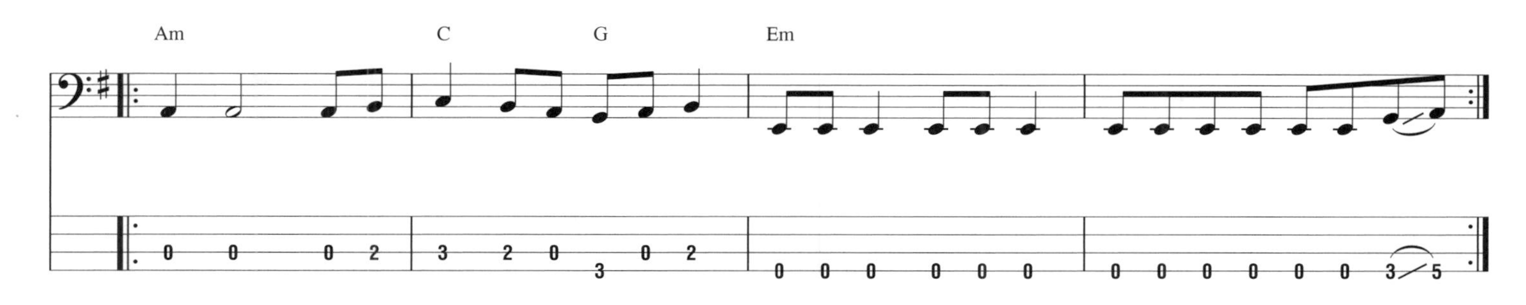
Am
C
G
Em

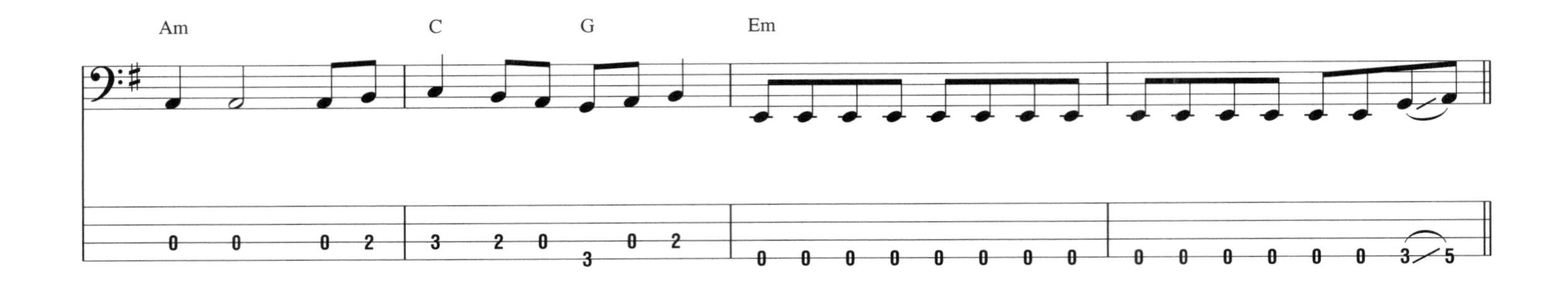
Am
C
G
Em

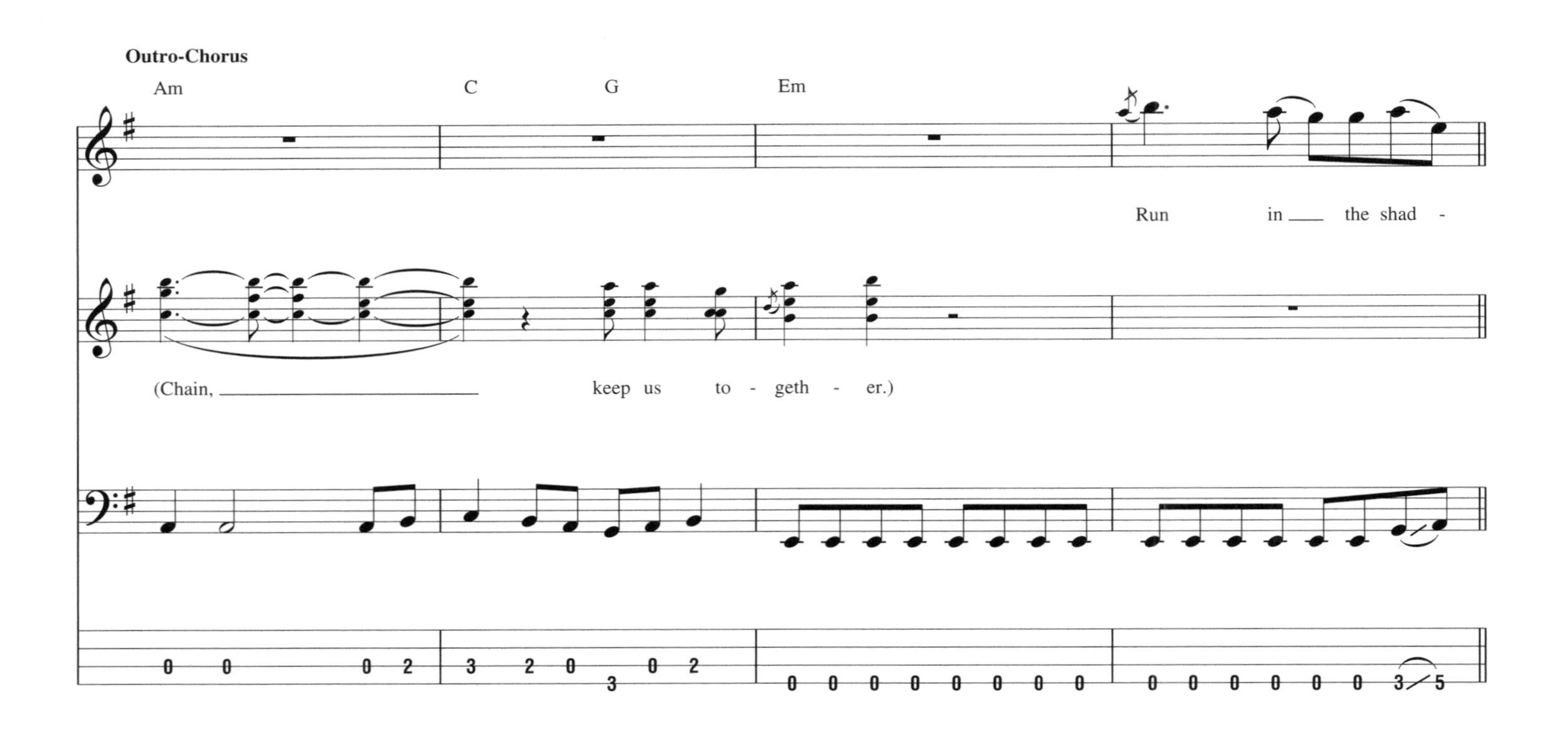
Outro-Chorus
Am
C
G
Em
Run in the shad -
(Chain, keep us to - geth - er.)

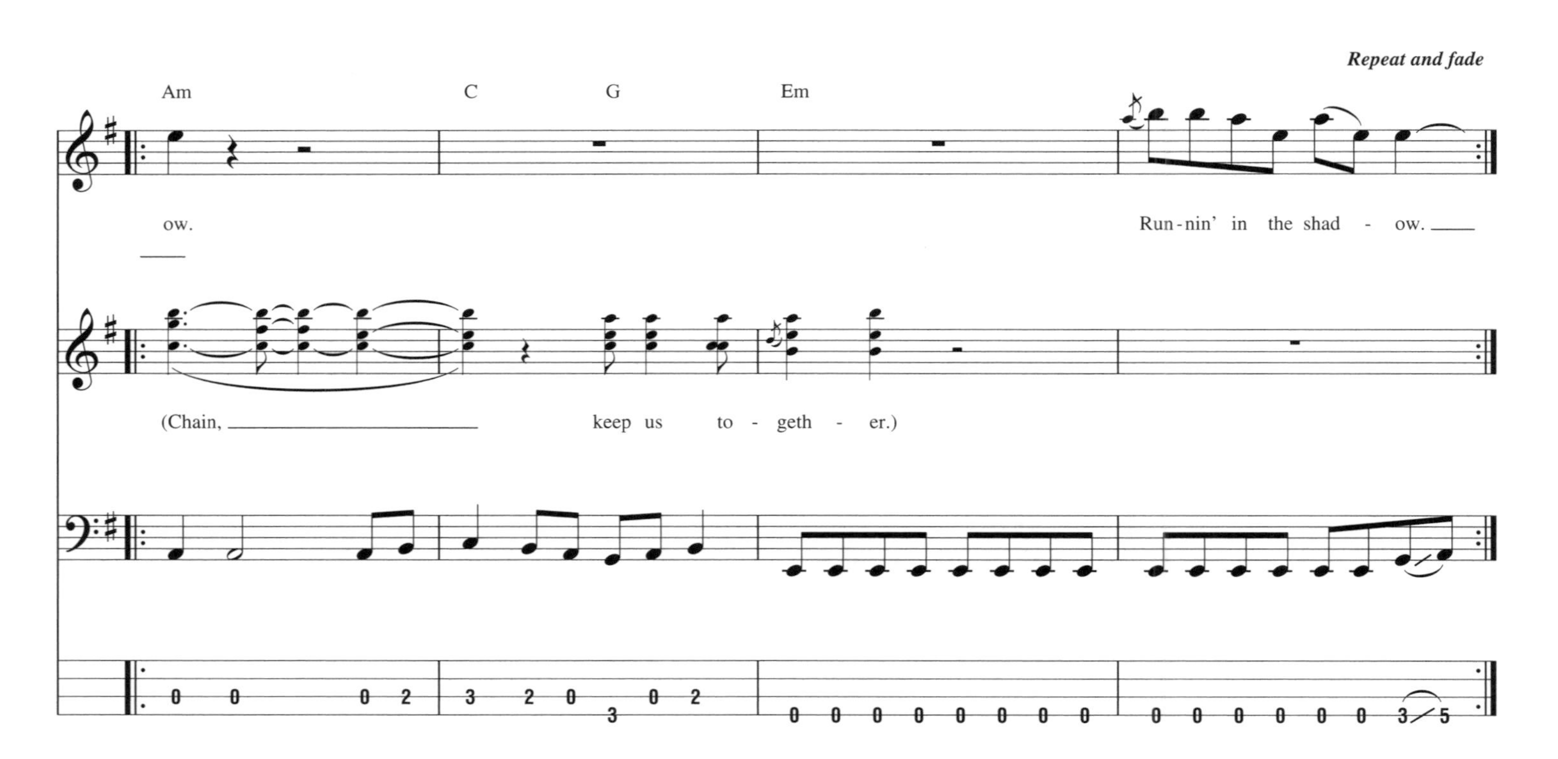
Repeat and fade
Am
C
G
Em
ow.
Run-nin' in the shad - ow.
(Chain, keep us to - geth - er.)

Chop Suey!

Words and Music by Daron Malakian and Serj Tankian

Drop D tuning, down 1 step:
(low to high) C-G-C-F

Intro

Moderately ♩ = 128

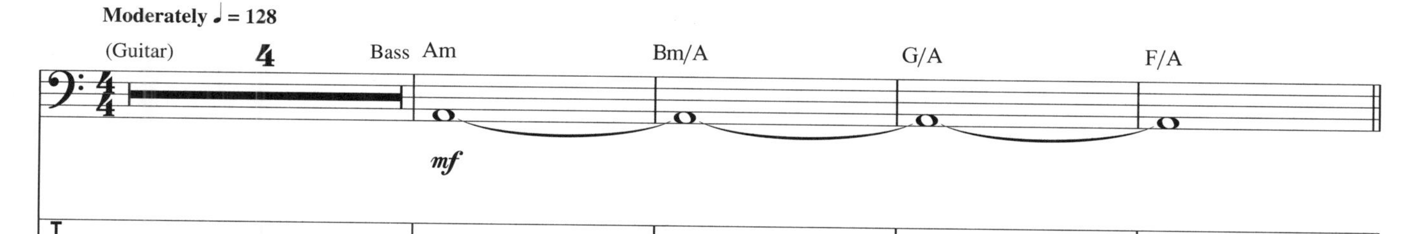
(Guitar)
4
Bass
Am
Bm/A
G/A
F/A
mf

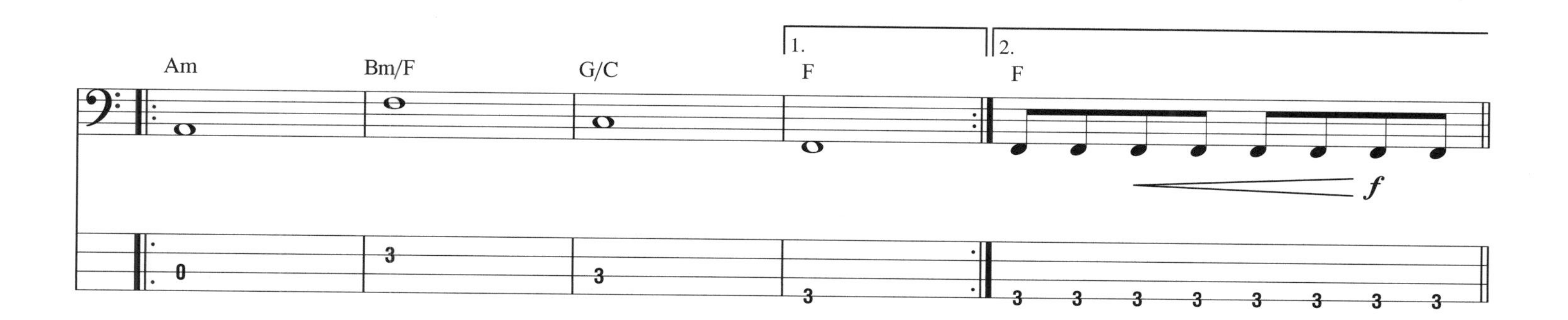
Am
Bm/F
G/C
1.
F
2.
F
f

B♭5 A5 B♭5 A5 B♭5 A5 B♭5 A5
G♯5 A5 G♯5 A5 G♯5 A5 G♯5
C5 B5 C5 B5 C5 B5 C5 B5 D5 C5 D5 C5 D5 C5 D5 C5
Bass Fig. 1
End Bass Fig. 1

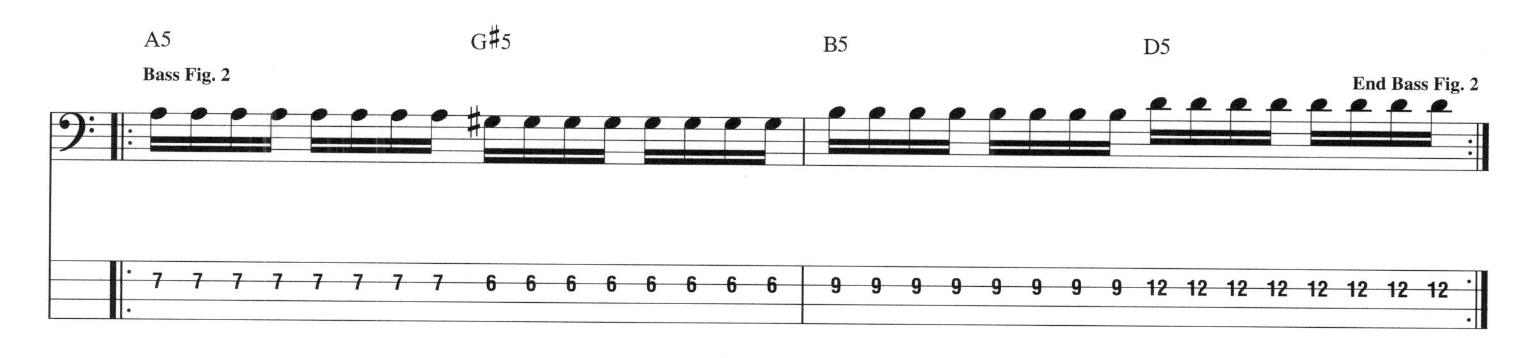
A5
G♯5
B5
D5
Bass Fig. 2
End Bass Fig. 2

Verse
A♭5 A5 N.C. B♭5 A5 B♭5 A5 B♭5 A5 B♭5 A5 G♯5 N.C. A5 G♯5 A5 G♯5 A5 G♯5 A5 G♯5
1., 2. Wake up, grab a brush and put a lit - tle make - up. Hide the scars to fade a - way the
Whispered: (Wake up.
Bass Fig. 3
End Bass Fig. 3
8 7 8 7 8 7 8 7 8 7 7 6 7 6 7 6 7 6 7 6

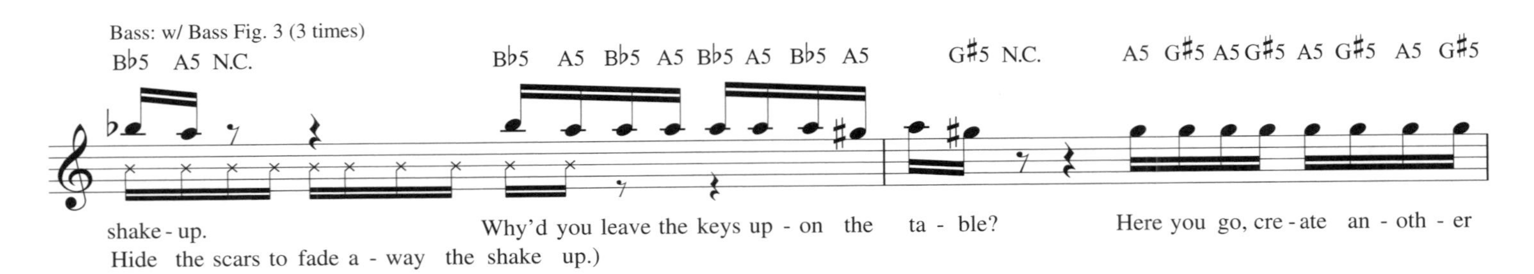
Bass: w/ Bass Fig. 3 (3 times)
B♭5 A5 N.C. B♭5 A5 B♭5 A5 B♭5 A5 B♭5 A5 G♯5 N.C. A5 G♯5 A5 G♯5 A5 G♯5 A5 G♯5
shake - up. Why'd you leave the keys up - on the ta - ble? Here you go, cre - ate an - oth - er
Hide the scars to fade a - way the shake up.)

B♭5 A5 N.C. B♭5 A5 B♭5 A5 B♭5 A5 B♭5 A5 G♯5 N.C. A5 G♯5 A5 G♯5 A5 G♯5 A5 G♯5
fa - ble, you want - ed to. Grab a brush and put a lit - tle make - up, you want - ed to. Hide the scars to fade a - way the

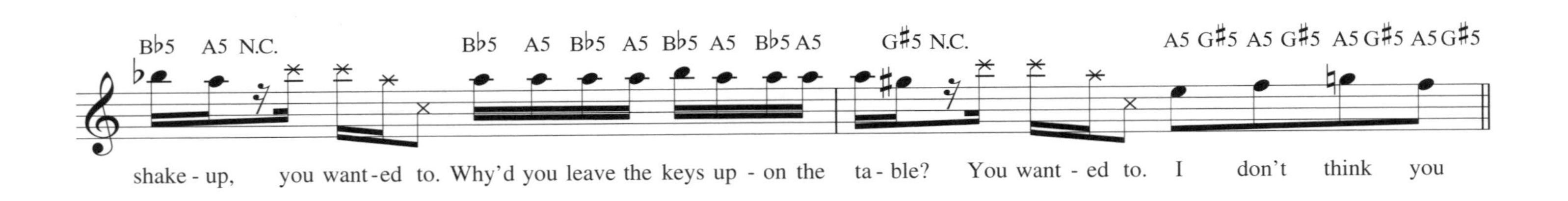
B♭5 A5 N.C. B♭5 A5 B♭5 A5 B♭5 A5 B♭5 A5 G♯5 N.C. A5 G♯5 A5 G♯5 A5 G♯5 A5 G♯5
shake - up, you want - ed to. Why'd you leave the keys up - on the ta - ble? You want - ed to. I don't think you

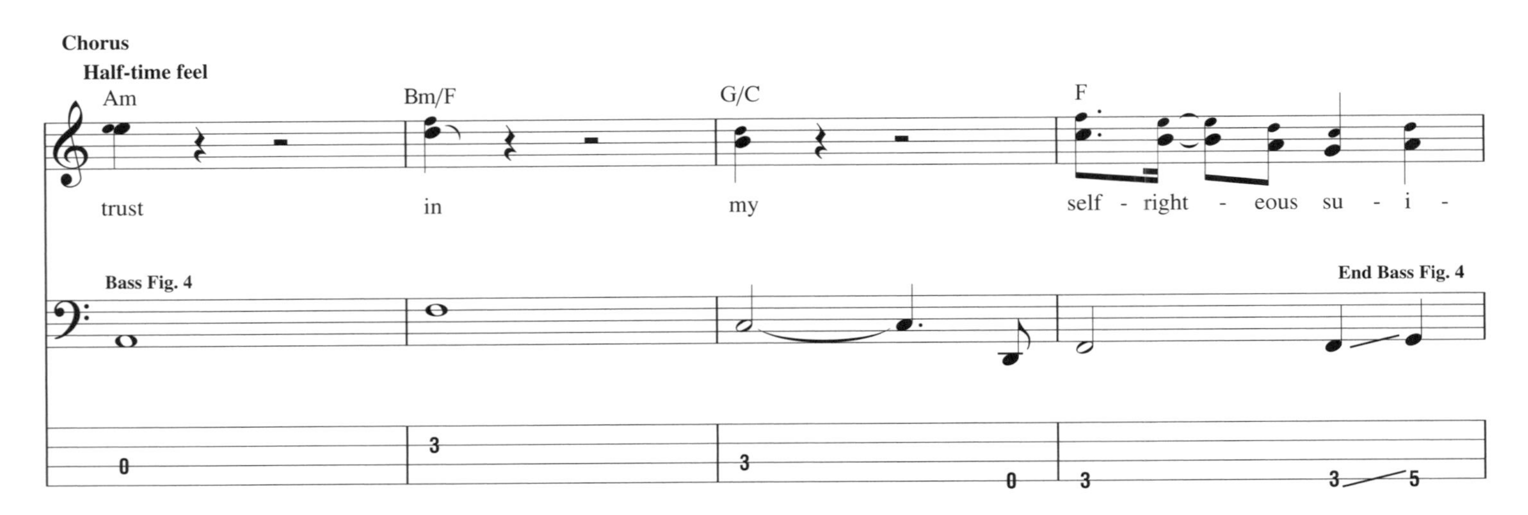
Chorus
Half-time feel
Am Bm/F G/C F
trust in my self - right - eous su - i -
Bass Fig. 4
End Bass Fig. 4
0 3 3 0 3 3 5

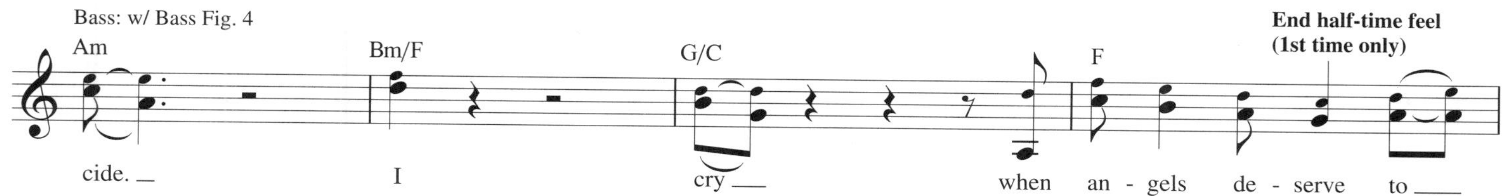
Bass: w/ Bass Fig. 4
Am
Bm/F
G/C
F
End half-time feel
(1st time only)
cide. I cry when an - gels de - serve to

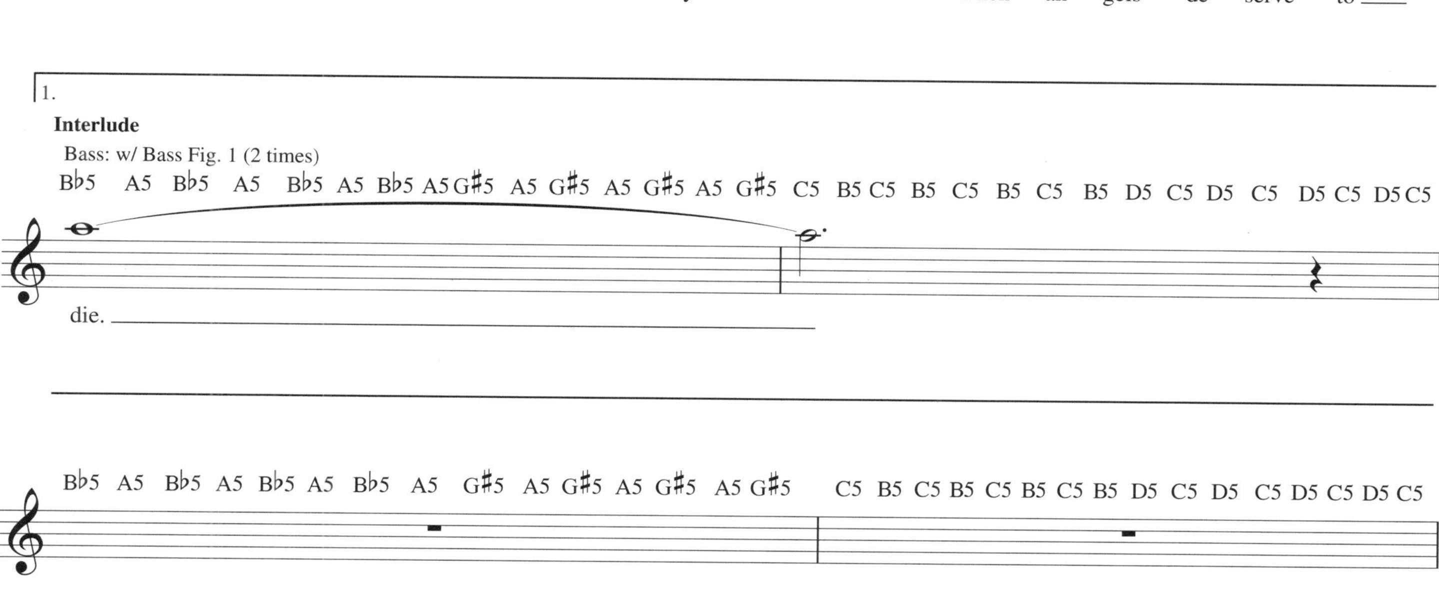
1.
Interlude
Bass: w/ Bass Fig. 1 (2 times)
B♭5 A5 B♭5 A5 B♭5 A5 B♭5 A5 G♯5 A5 G♯5 A5 G♯5 A5 G♯5 C5 B5 C5 B5 C5 B5 C5 B5 D5 C5 D5 C5 D5 C5 D5 C5
die.
B♭5 A5 B♭5 A5 B♭5 A5 B♭5 A5 G♯5 A5 G♯5 A5 G♯5 A5 G♯5 C5 B5 C5 B5 C5 B5 C5 B5 D5 C5 D5 C5 D5 C5 D5 C5

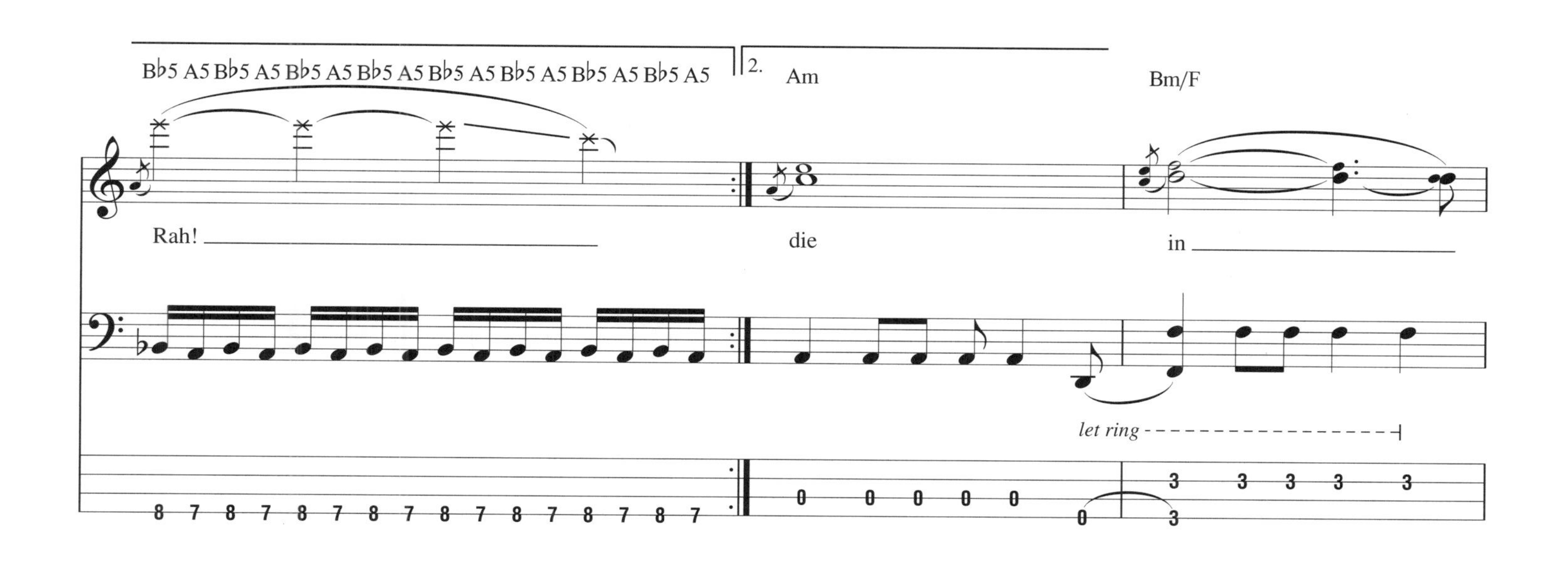
B♭5 A5 B♭5 A5 B♭5 A5 B♭5 A5 B♭5 A5 B♭5 A5 B♭5 A5 B♭5 A5
2.
Am
Bm/F
Rah!
die
in
let ring

G/C
F
Am
my self - right - eous su - i - cide.

End half-time feel
Bm/F
G/C
F
I
cry
when an - gels de - serve to die.
let ring

Bridge

Double-time feel

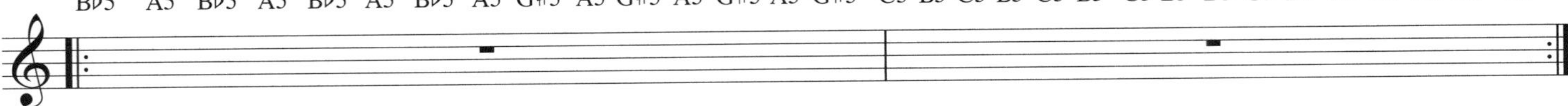
Bass: w/ Bass Fig. 1 (4 times)
2nd time, End double-time feel
Bb5 A5 Bb5 A5 Bb5 A5 Bb5 A5 G#5 A5 G#5 A5 G#5 A5 G#5 C5 B5 C5 B5 C5 B5 C5 B5 D5 C5 D5 C5 D5 C5 D5 C5

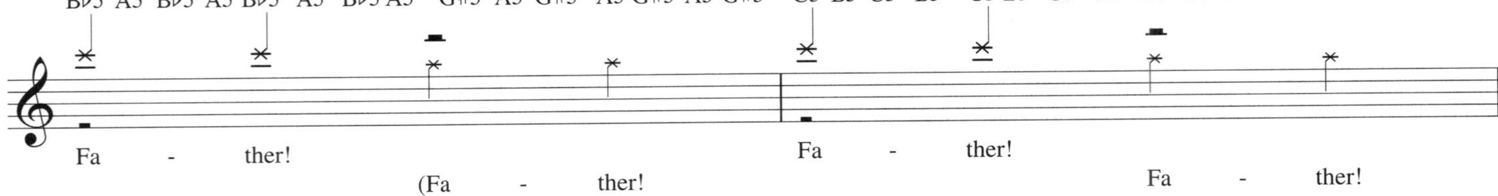
Bb5 A5 Bb5 A5 Bb5 A5 Bb5 A5 G#5 A5 G#5 A5 G#5 A5 G#5 C5 B5 C5 B5 C5 B5 C5 B5 D5 C5 D5 C5 D5 C5 D5 C5
Fa - ther! Fa - ther!
(Fa - ther! Fa - ther!

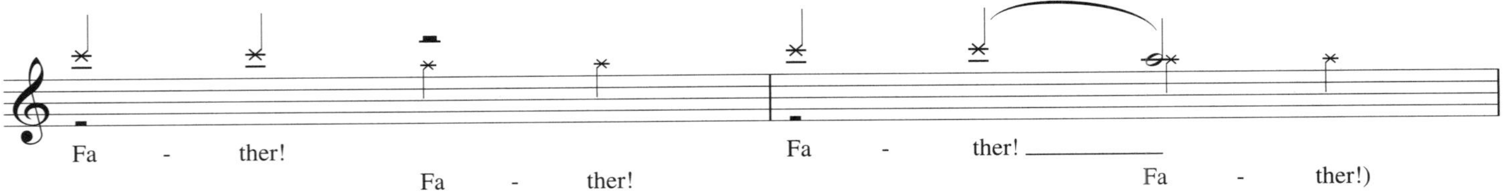
Bb5 A5 Bb5 A5 Bb5 A5 Bb5 A5 G#5 A5 G#5 A5 G#5 A5 G#5 C5 B5 C5 B5 C5 B5 C5 B5 D5 C5 D5 C5 D5 C5 D5 C5
Fa - ther! Fa - ther!
Fa - ther! Fa - ther!)

Bass: w/ Bass Fig. 2 (2 times)
A5 G#5 B5 D5 A5 G#5 B5 D5
Fa - ther in - to your hands, I com - mend my spir - it. Fa - ther in - to your hands, why have you for

Outro

Half-time feel

A5 F5 C5 F5
sak - en me in your eyes? For - sak - en me in your thoughts? For -

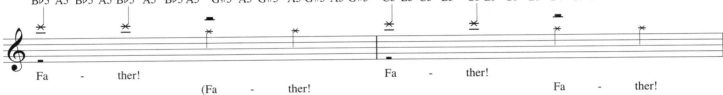

A5
F5
C5
F5
sak - en me in your heart? For - sak - en me. I'll
A5
F5
C5
F5
trust in my self - right - eous su - i - cide.
Bass Fig. 5
End Bass Fig. 5
Bass: w/ Bass Fig. 5 (2 1/2 times)
A5
F5
C5
F5
A5
I cry when an - gels de - serve to die
F5
C5
F5
A5
F5
in my self - right - eous su - i - cide. I
C5
F5
A5
cry when an - gels de - serve to die.

Come Together

Words and Music by John Lennon and Paul McCartney

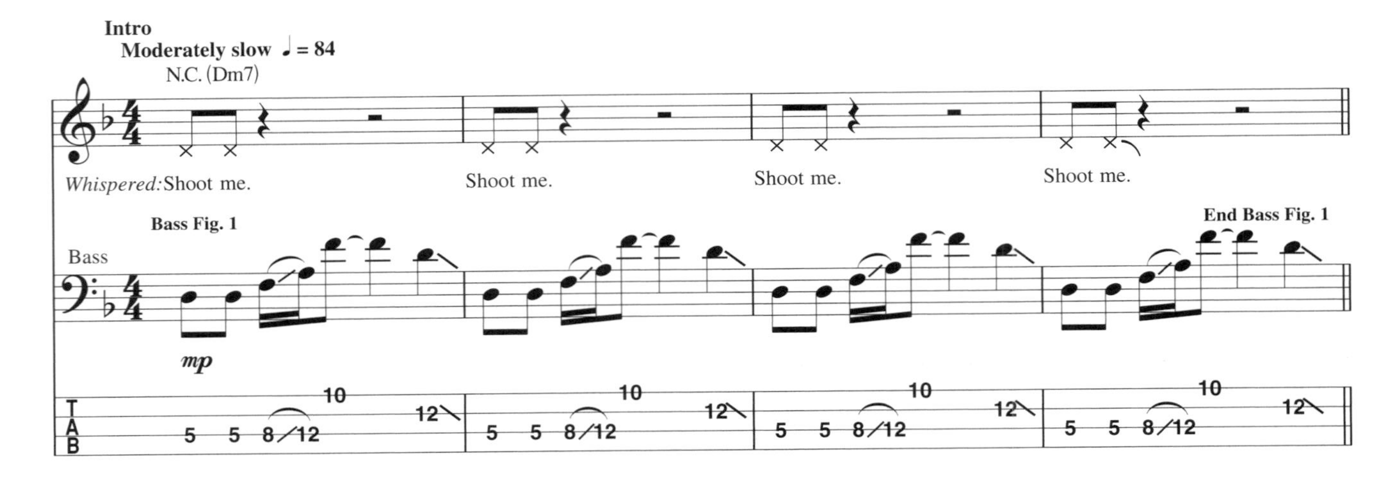
Intro
Moderately slow ♩ = 84
N.C. (Dm7)
Whispered: Shoot me.
Shoot me.
Shoot me.
Shoot me.
Bass Fig. 1
End Bass Fig. 1
Bass
mp

Verse
N.C. (Dm7)
1. Here come ol' flat - top, he come groov - in' up slow - ly. He got Joo Joo eye - ball, he one
Bass Fig. 2
mf

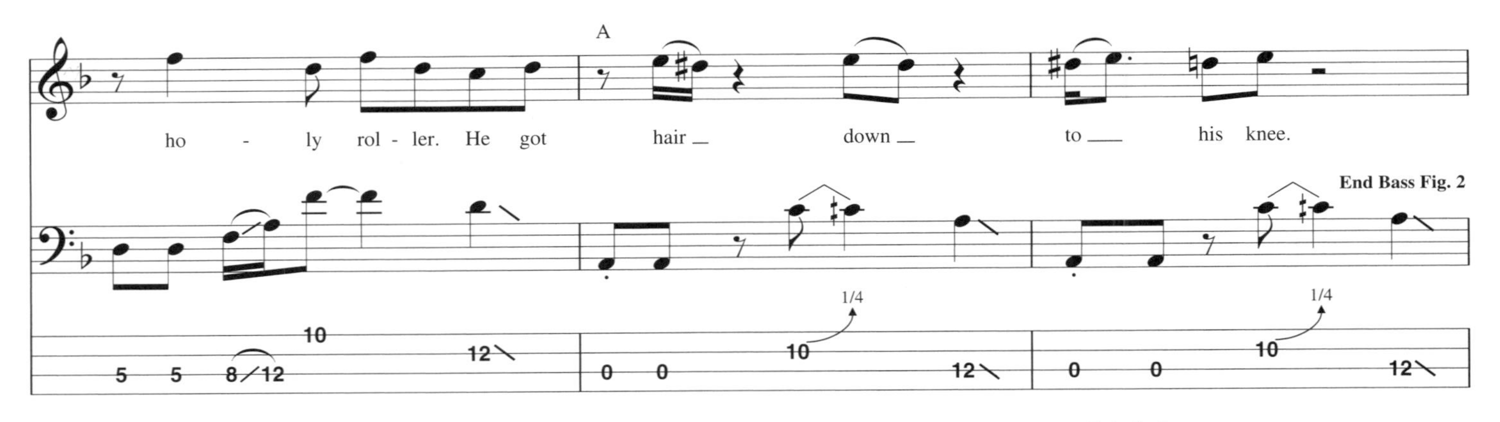
A
ho - ly rol - ler. He got hair _ down _ to ___ his knee.
End Bass Fig. 2
1/4
1/4

G
N.C.
Interlude
Bass: w/ Bass Fig. 1
N.C. (Dm7)
Got to be a jok - er he just do what he please. _
Whispered: Shoot me.

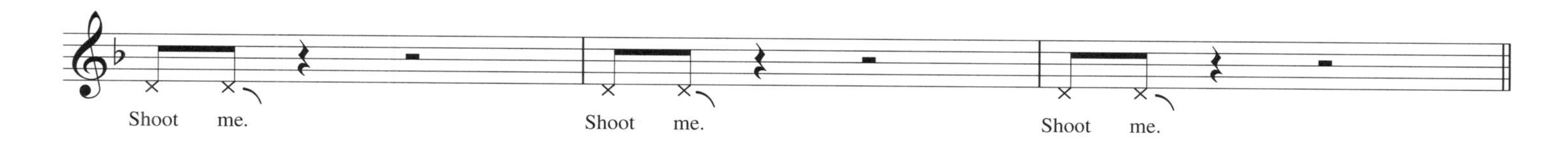
Shoot me.
Shoot me.
Shoot me.

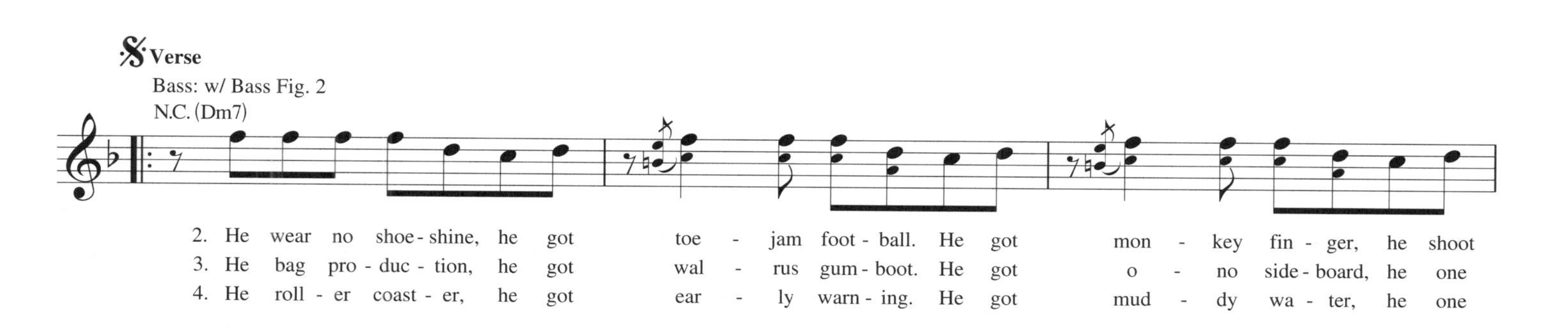
Verse
Bass: w/ Bass Fig. 2
N.C. (Dm7)
2. He wear no shoe-shine, he got toe - jam foot-ball. He got mon - key fin - ger, he shoot
3. He bag pro-duc-tion, he got wal - rus gum-boot. He got o - no side-board, he one
4. He roll-er coast-er, he got ear - ly warn-ing. He got mud - dy wa - ter, he one

A
Co - ca Co - la. He say, "I know you, you know me."
spi - nal crack - er. He got feet down be - low his knee.
Mo - jo fil - ter, He say, "One and one and one is three."

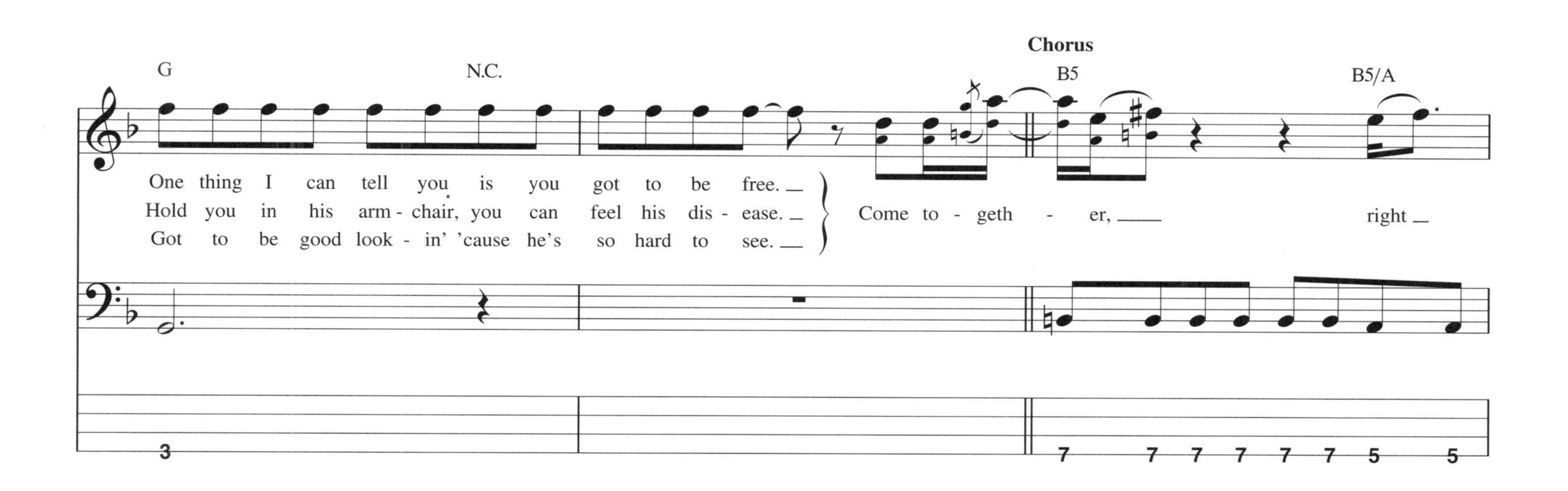
G
N.C.
Chorus
B5
B5/A
One thing I can tell you is you got to be free.
Hold you in his arm-chair, you can feel his dis-ease.
Got to be good look-in' 'cause he's so hard to see.
Come to - geth - er, right
3
7 7 7 7 7 7 5 5

To Coda
1.
Interlude
G5
A5 N.C.
N.C. (Dm7)
now, o - ver me.
Whispered: Shoot me.
Shoot me.
3 3 3 3 5
5 5 8/12 10 12
5 5 8/12 10 12
5 5 8/12 10 12

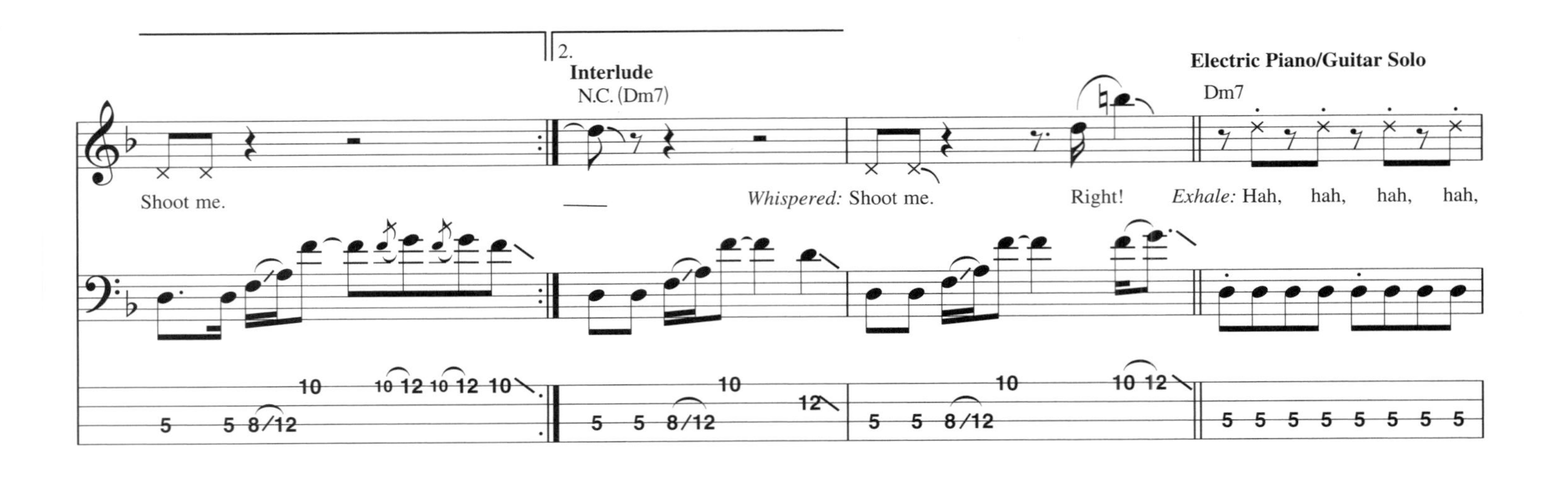
2.
Interlude
N.C. (Dm7)
Electric Piano/Guitar Solo
Dm7
Shoot me.
Whispered: Shoot me.
Right!
Exhale: Hah, hah, hah, hah,

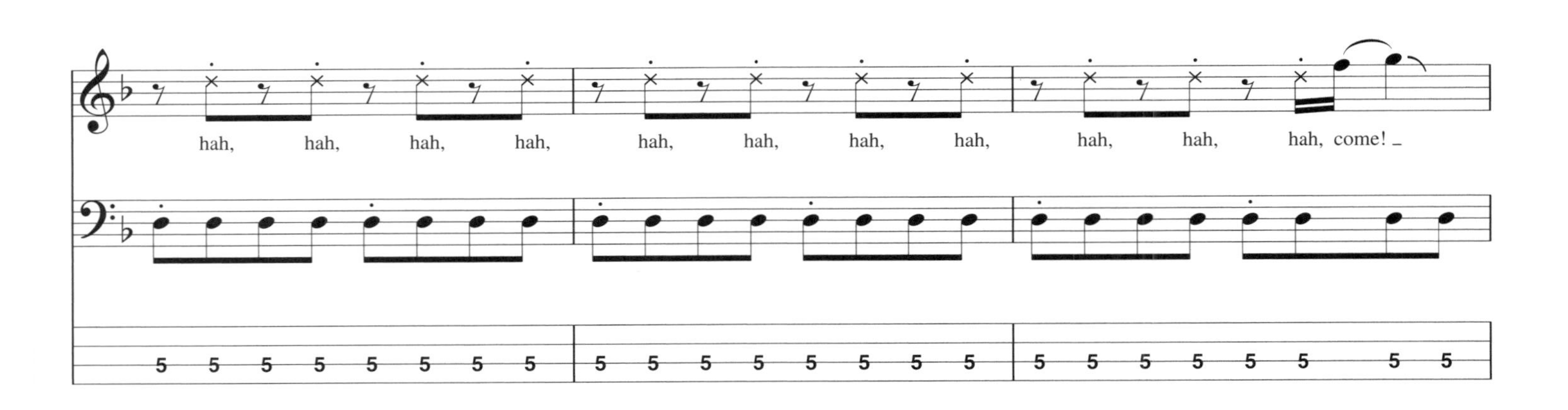
hah, hah, hah, hah, hah, hah, hah, hah, hah, hah, hah, come!

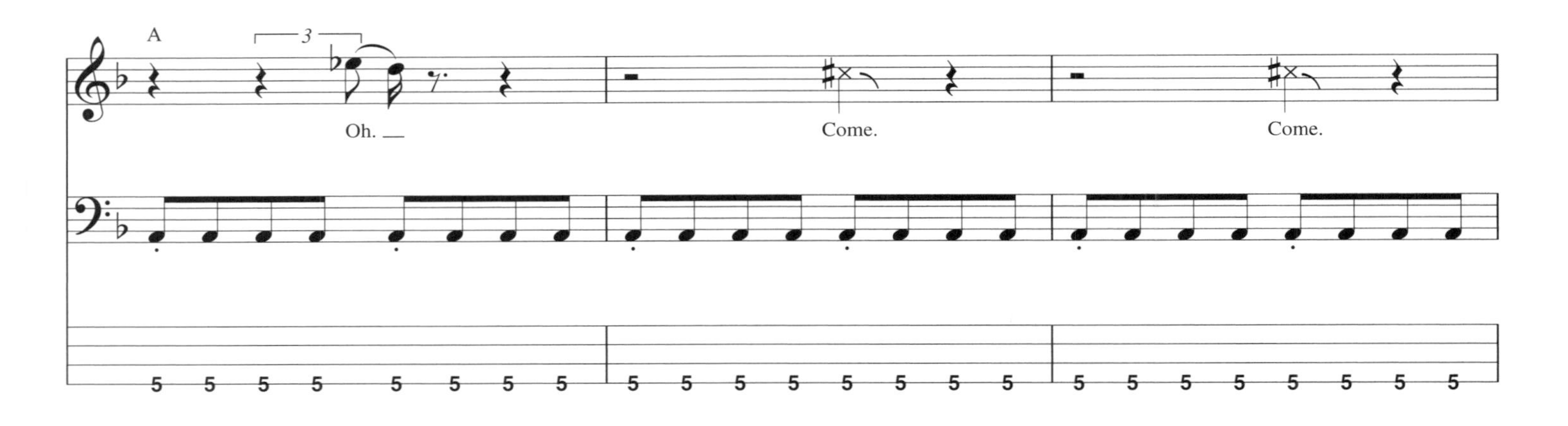
A
Oh.
Come.
Come.

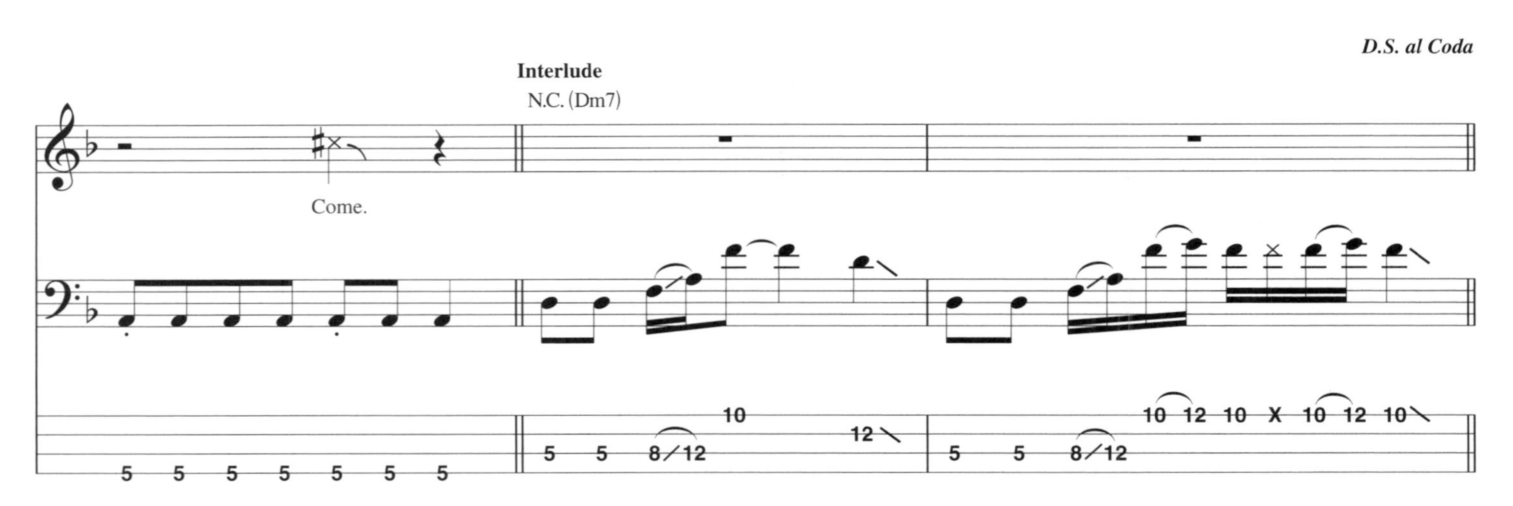
D.S. al Coda
Interlude
N.C. (Dm7)
Come.

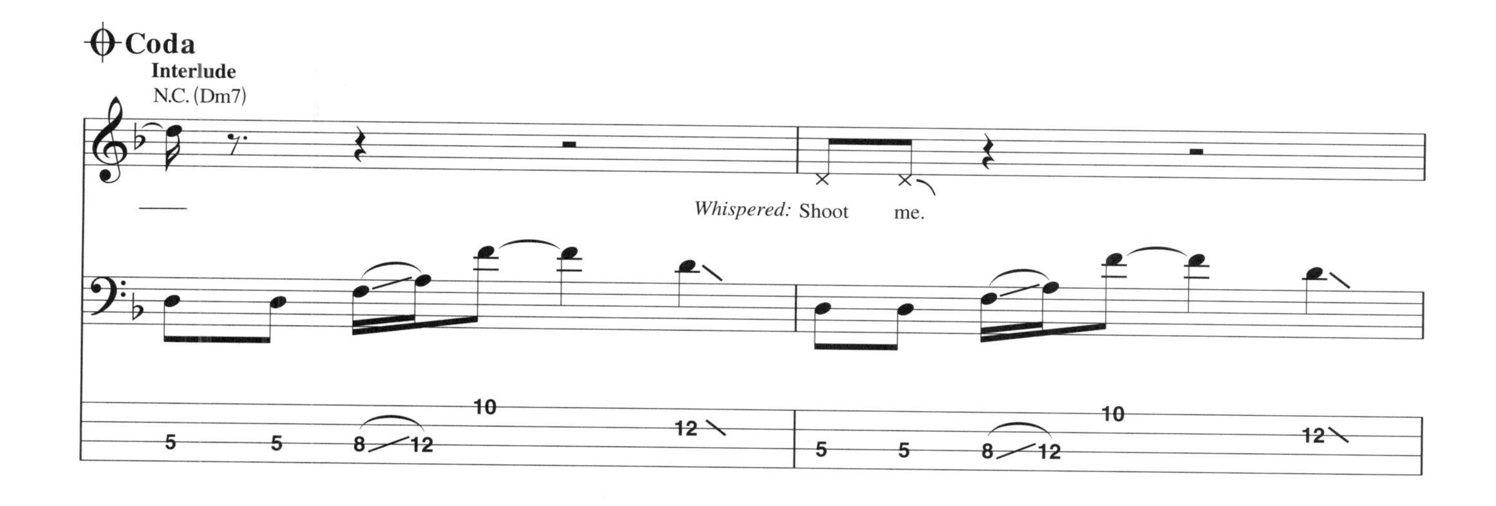
Coda
Interlude
N.C. (Dm7)
Whispered: Shoot me.
5 5 8 12 10 12
5 5 8 12 10 12

Outro
N.C. (Dm7)
Shoot me.
Shoot me.
Oh!
Bass Fig. 3
5 5 8 12 10 12
5 5 8 12 10 12 10 12
5 5 5 5 5 5 5 5

Come to-geth - er,
yeah.
End Bass Fig. 3

Bass: w/ Bass Fig. 3 (3 times)
Come to-geth - er,
yeah.
Come to-geth - er,

yeah.
Come to-geth - er,
yeah.

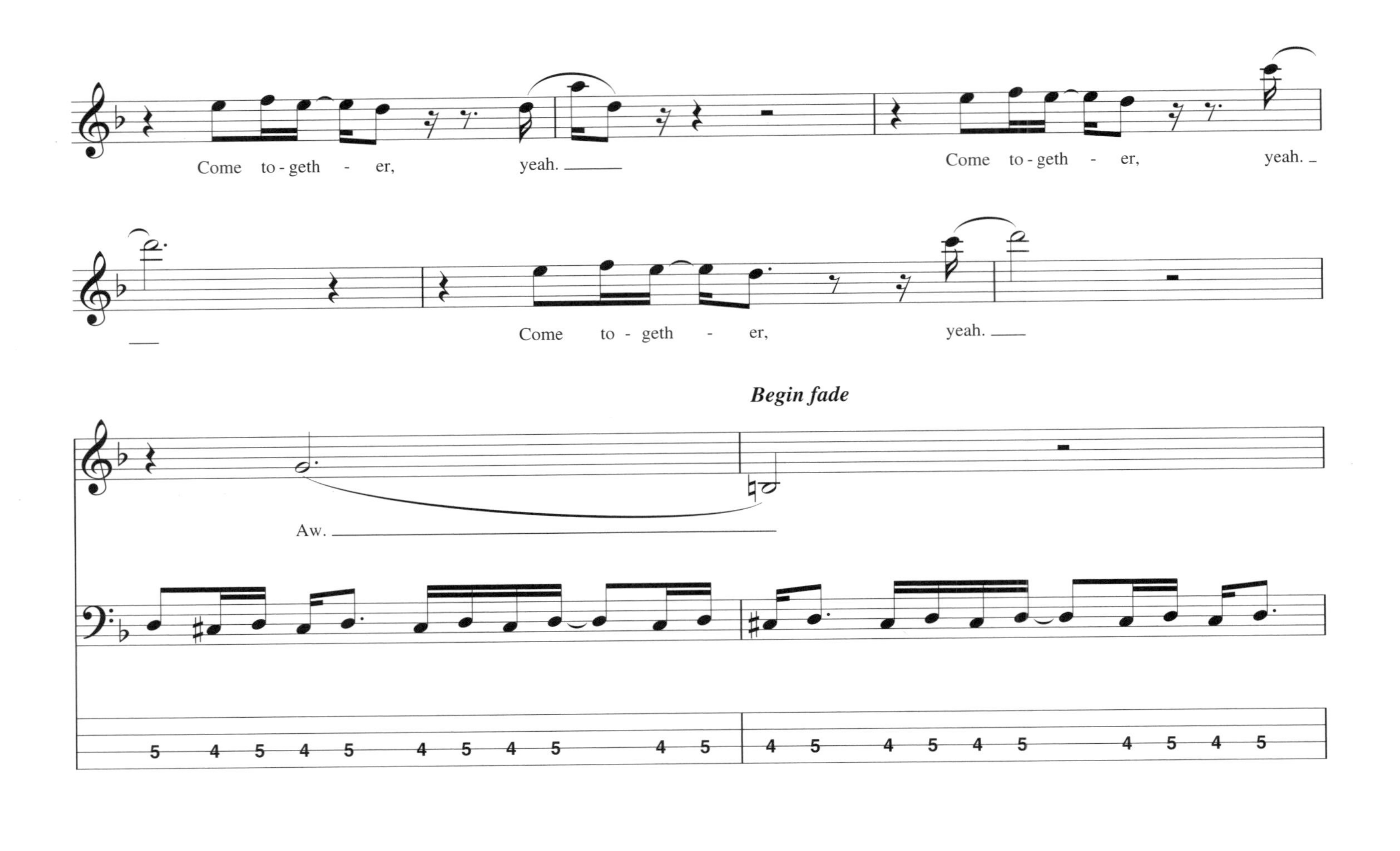
Come to-geth - er, yeah.
Come to-geth - er, yeah.
Come to-geth - er, yeah.
Begin fade
Aw.
5 4 5 4 5 4 5 4 5 4 5
4 5 4 5 4 5 4 5 4 5

Come to-geth - er yeah.
4 5 4 5 4 5 4 5 4 5 4 5
10
12
8 12 12 5 5 5 12 10

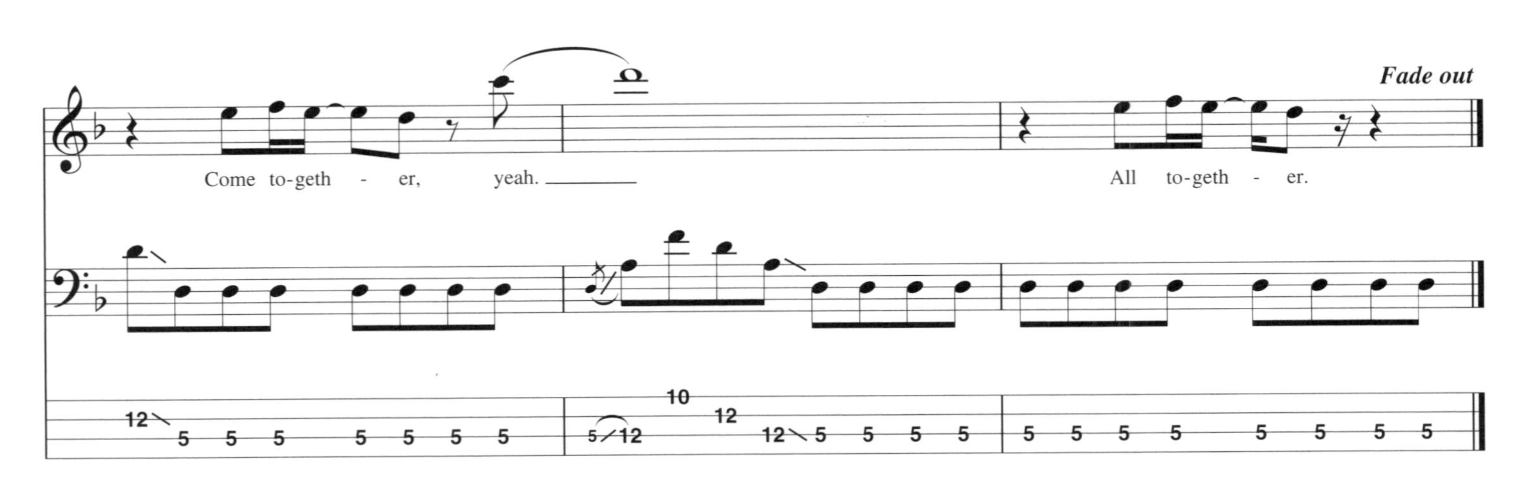
Fade out
Come to-geth - er, yeah.
All to-geth - er.
12 5 5 5 5 5 5 5
10
12
5 12 12 5 5 5 5
5 5 5 5 5 5 5 5

Creep

Words and Music by Albert Hammond, Mike Hazlewood, Thomas Yorke, Richard Greenwood,
Philip Selway, Colin Greenwood and Edward O'Brian

Intro
Moderately ♩ = 80
*G
Bass
B
mf
T
A
B

*Chord symbols reflect overall harmony.

C

Cm
Verse
G
1. When you were here before,

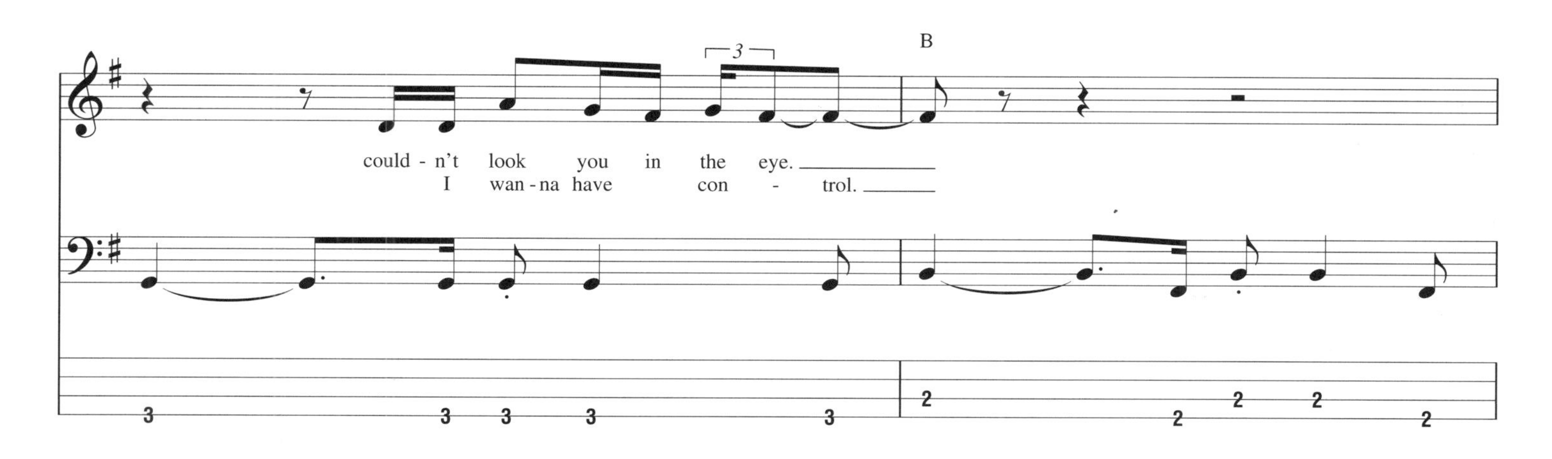
B
couldn't look you in the eye.
I wanna have control.

C
You're just like an an - gel.
I want a per - fect bod - y.
(Your) skin makes me cry.
I want a per - fect soul.
Cm
G
You float like a feath - er
I want you to no - tice
B
in a beau - ti - ful world.
when I'm not a - round.
C
I wish I was spe - cial.
You're so fuck - ing spe - cial.

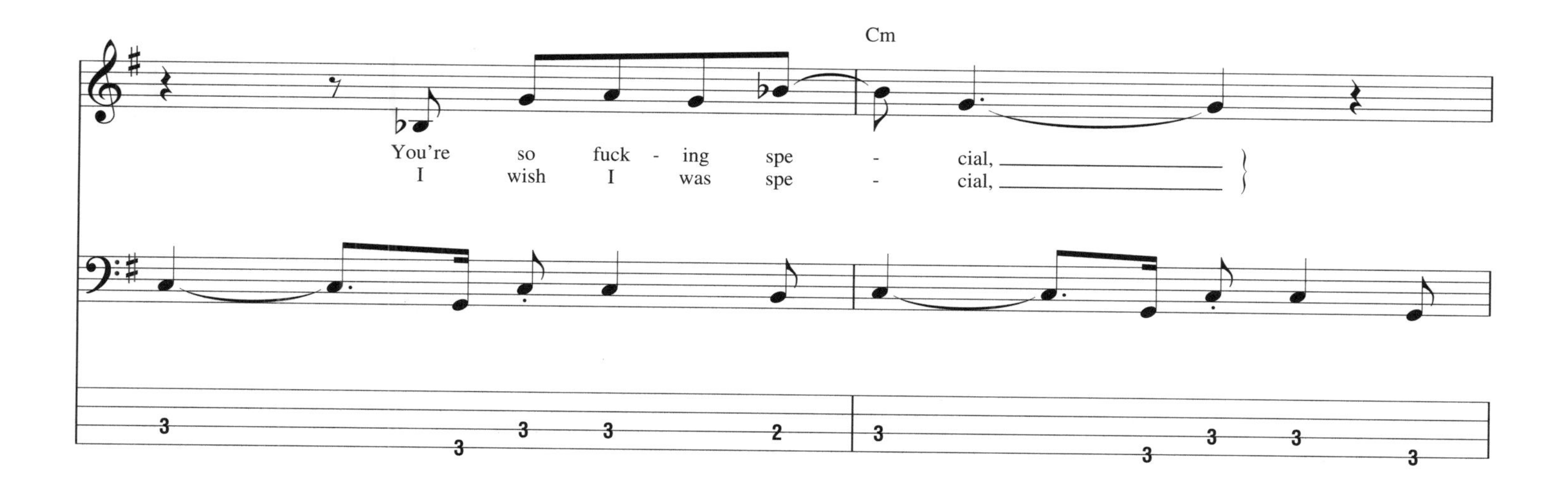

Cm
You're so fuck - ing spe - cial,
I wish I was spe - cial,

Chorus
2nd time, Bass: w/ Bass Fill 1
G
but I'm a creep.
I'm a weird -

B
- o.
What the hell am I do - ing here?

Bass Fill 1

C
1.
Cm
I don't be - long here.
2.
Cm
2. I don't care if it hurts, here.
Oh. Oh.
Bridge
G
She's run - ning out a - gain.
B
C
She's run - ning out. She

Cm
G
run,
run,
run,
run.
B
C
Cm
Run.
Verse
G
B
3. What-ev - er makes you hap - py.
What-ev - er you want.

C
Cm
You're so fuck - ing spe - cial.
I wish I was spe - cial,
2
3 3 3
3 3

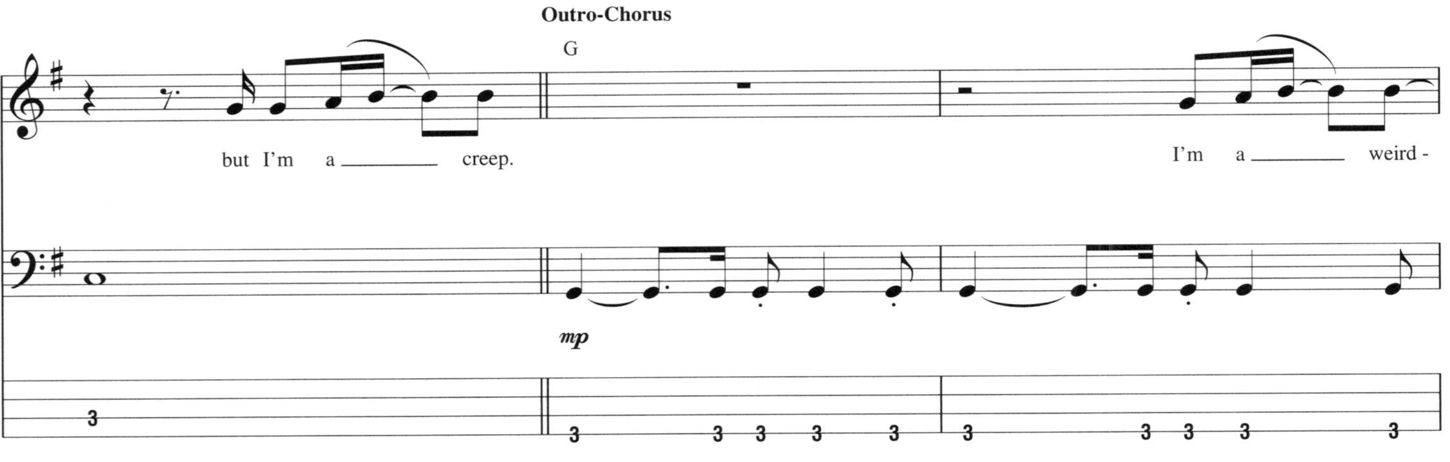
Outro-Chorus
G
but I'm a creep.
I'm a weird -
mp
3
3 3 3 3 3
3 3 3 3 3

B
C
- o.
What the hell am I do - ing here?
2 2 2 2 2 2
2 2 2 2 2
3 3

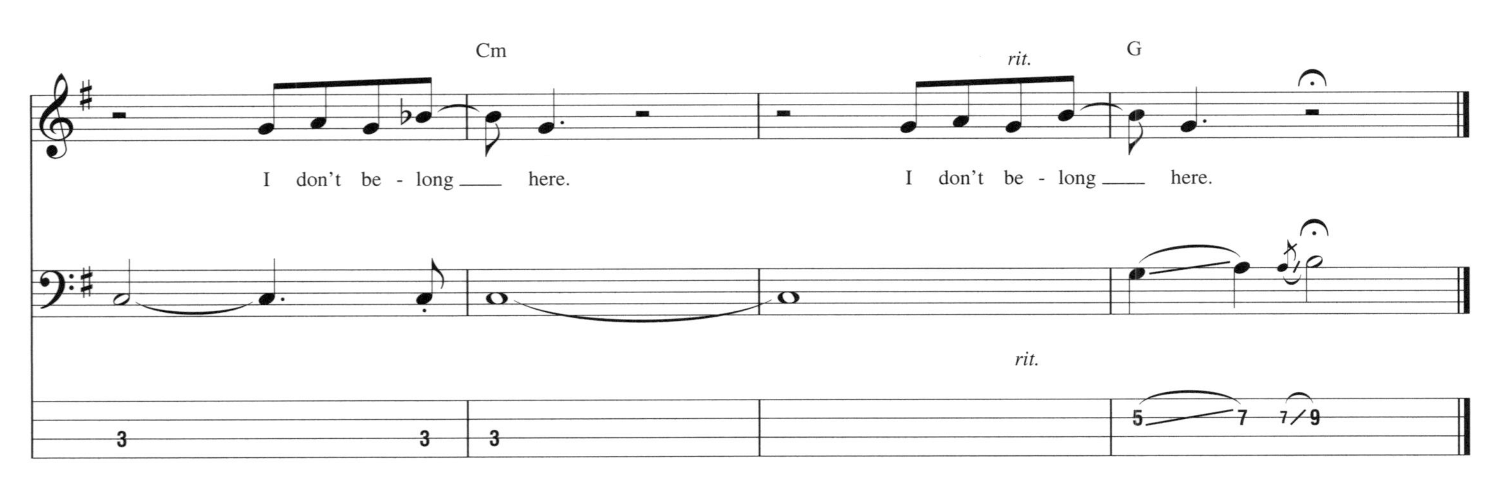
Cm
rit.
G
I don't be - long here.
I don't be - long here.
rit.
3 3 3
5 7 7 9

Dance, Dance

Words and Music by Patrick Stumph, Peter Wentz, Andrew Hurley and Joseph Trohman

Intro
Very fast ♩ = 230
*B5 D5 A5 G5 D5 A5
Bass Fig. 1
End Bass Fig. 1
(Drums)
Bass
mf
*Chord symbols reflect implied harmony.
Verse
Bass: w/ Bass Fig. 1 (4 times)
1. She says she's no good with words, but I'm worse.
Bare - ly stut - tered out, "A joke of a ro - man - tic," or stuck to my tongue.
Weighed down with words too o - ver - dra - mat - ic.
To - night it's "It can't get much worse" ver - sus "No one should ev - er feel like..."
Pre-Chorus
B5 C#5 D5 F#5 E5 F#5 B5 C#5 D5 F#5 E5 F#5 B5
I'm two quar - ters and a heart down, and I don't wan - na for - get how your voice sounds. Be - cause words
Bass Fig. 2
End Bass Fig. 2
Bass

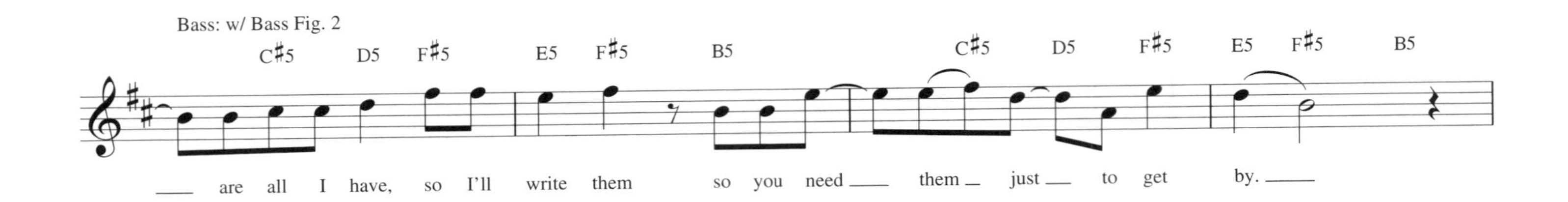
Bass: w/ Bass Fig. 2
C♯5
D5
F♯5
E5
F♯5
B5
C♯5
D5
F♯5
E5
F♯5
B5
are all I have, so I'll write them so you need them just to get by.
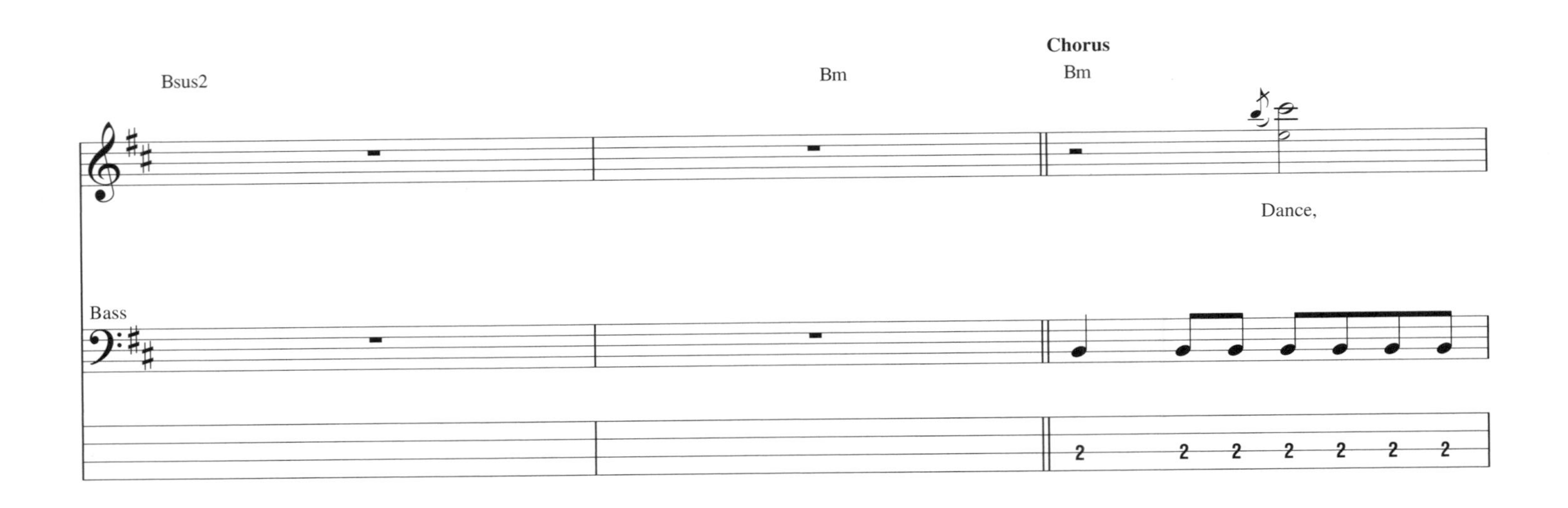
Chorus
Bsus2
Bm
Bm
Dance,
Bass
2 2 2 2 2 2 2
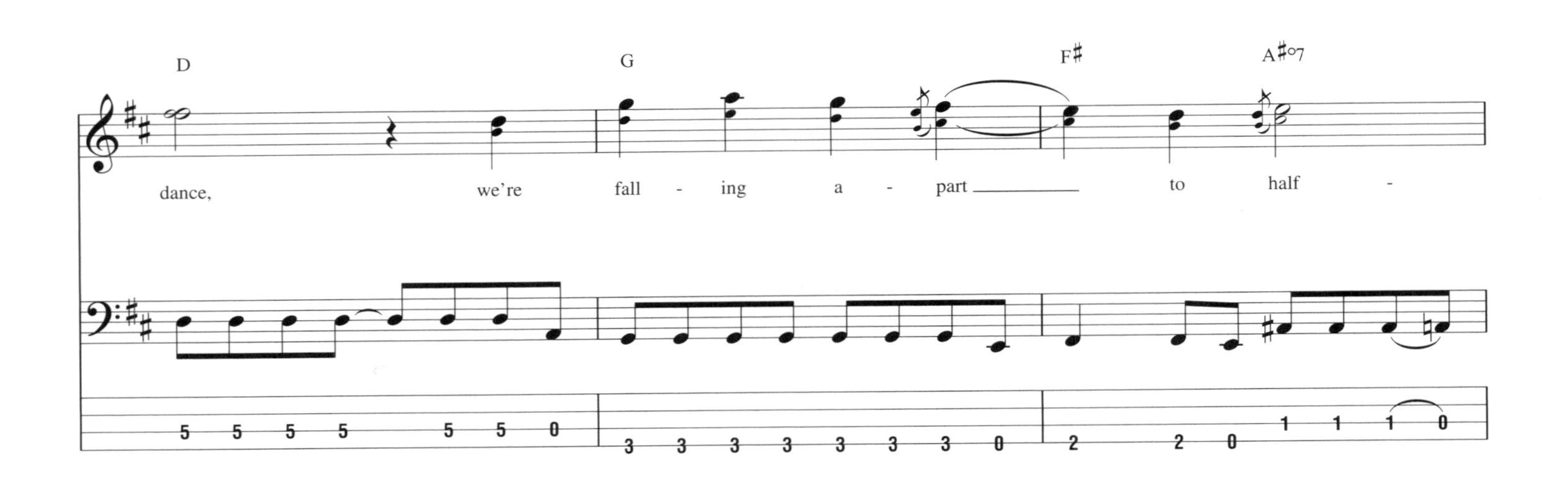
D
G
F♯
A♯°7
dance, we're fall - ing a - part to half -
5 5 5 5 5 5 0
3 3 3 3 3 3 3 0
2 2 0 1 1 1 0
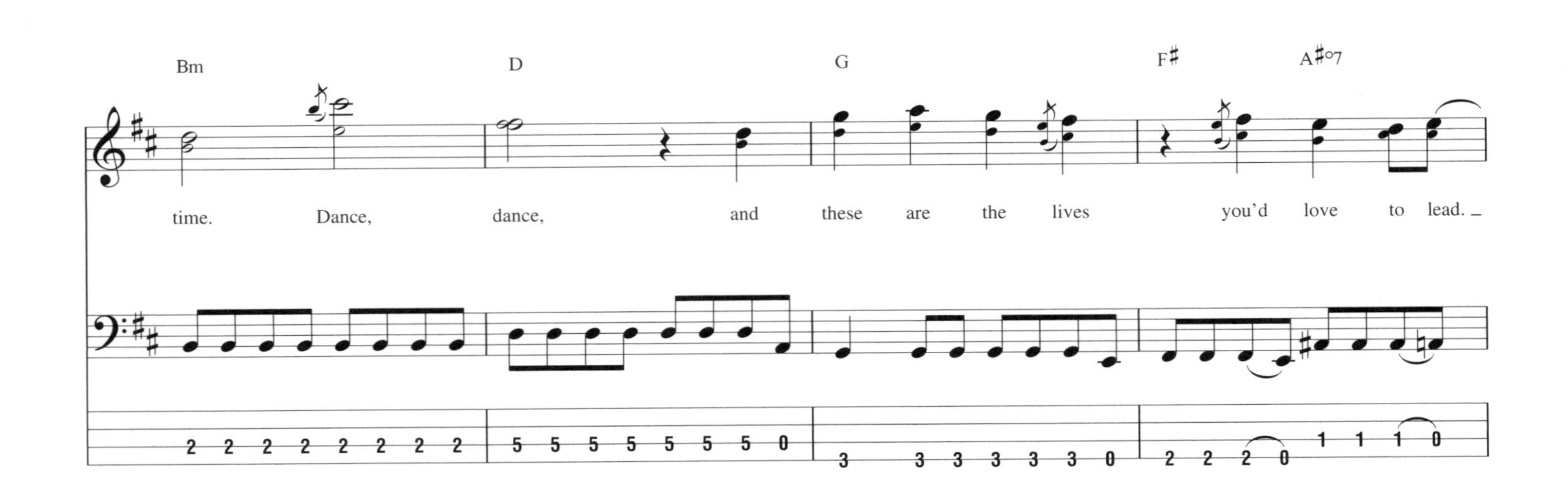
Bm
D
G
F♯
A♯°7
time. Dance, dance, and these are the lives you'd love to lead.
2 2 2 2 2 2 2 2
5 5 5 5 5 5 5 0
3 3 3 3 3 3 0
2 2 2 0 1 1 1 0

Bm
D
G
F♯
A♯o7
Dance. This is the way they'd love if they knew

Bm
D
G
F♯
A♯o7
how mis - er - y loved me.

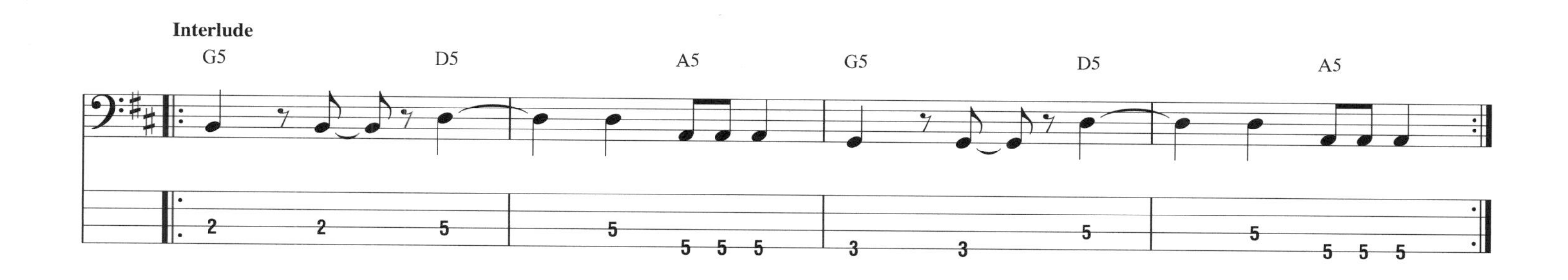
Interlude
G5
D5
A5
G5
D5
A5

Verse
B5
N.C.
B5
G5
D5
A5
2. You al - ways fold just be - fore you're found out.

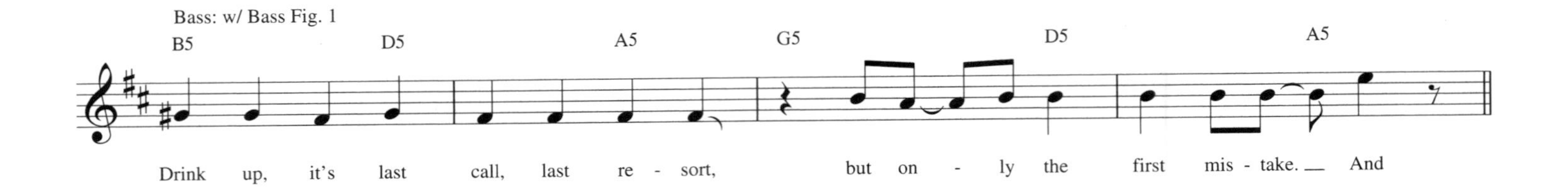
Bass: w/ Bass Fig. 1
B5 D5 A5 G5 D5 A5
Drink up, it's last call, last re - sort, but on - ly the first mis - take. And

Pre-Chorus
Bass: w/ Bass Fig. 2 (2 times)
B5 C♯5 D5 F♯5 E5 F♯5 B5 C♯5 D5 F♯5 E5 F♯5 B5
I'm two quar-ters and a heart down, and I don't wan-na for-get how your voice sounds. Be-cause words

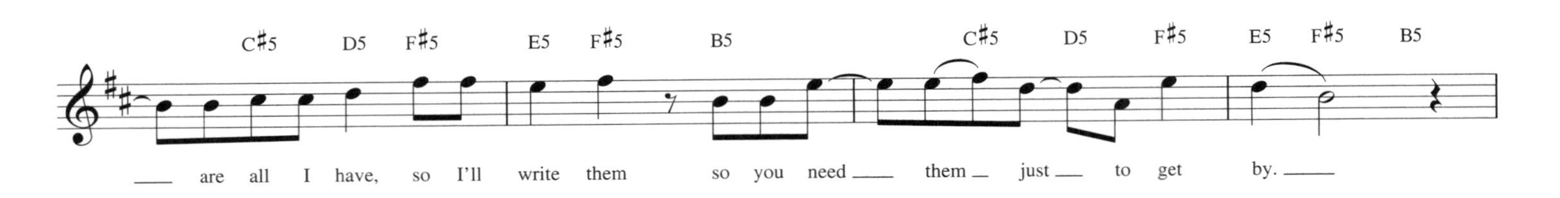
C♯5 D5 F♯5 E5 F♯5 B5 C♯5 D5 F♯5 E5 F♯5 B5
are all I have, so I'll write them so you need them just to get by.

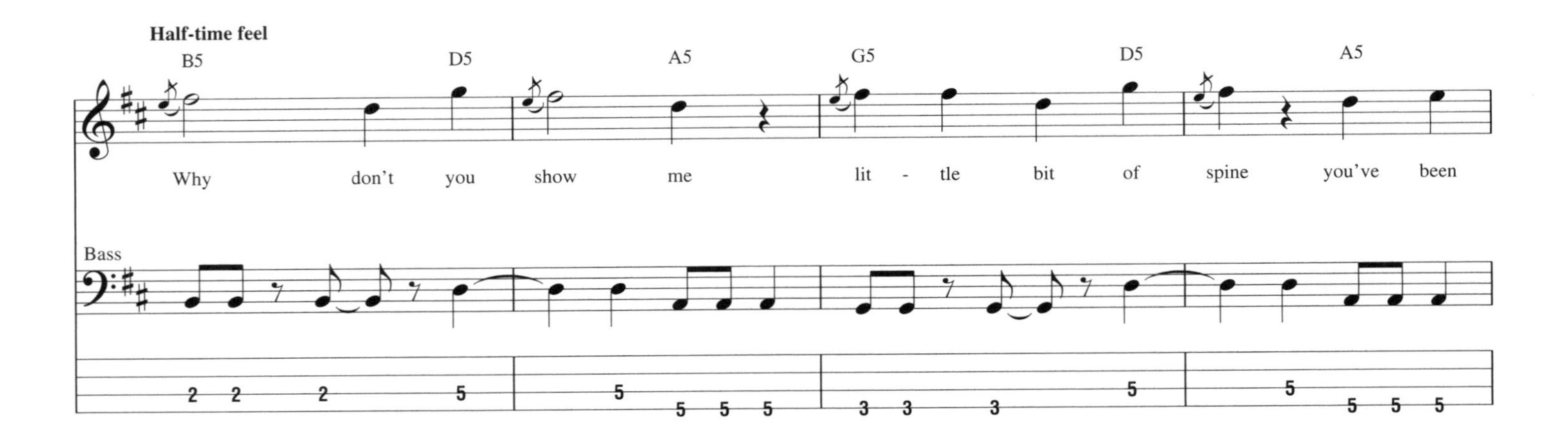
Half-time feel
B5 D5 A5 G5 D5 A5
Why don't you show me lit - tle bit of spine you've been
Bass

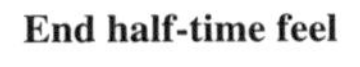
End half-time feel

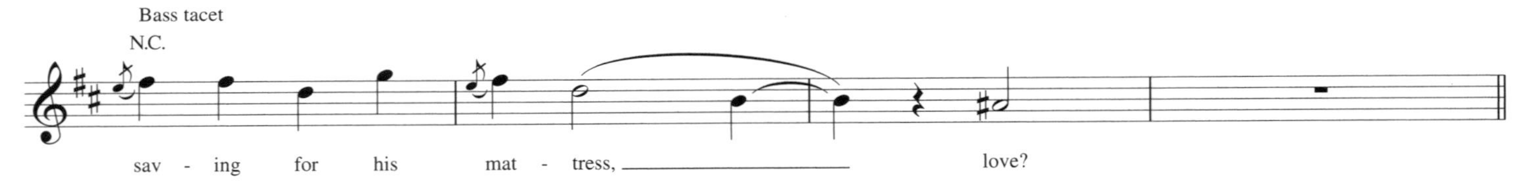
Bass tacet
N.C.
sav - ing for his mat - tress, love?

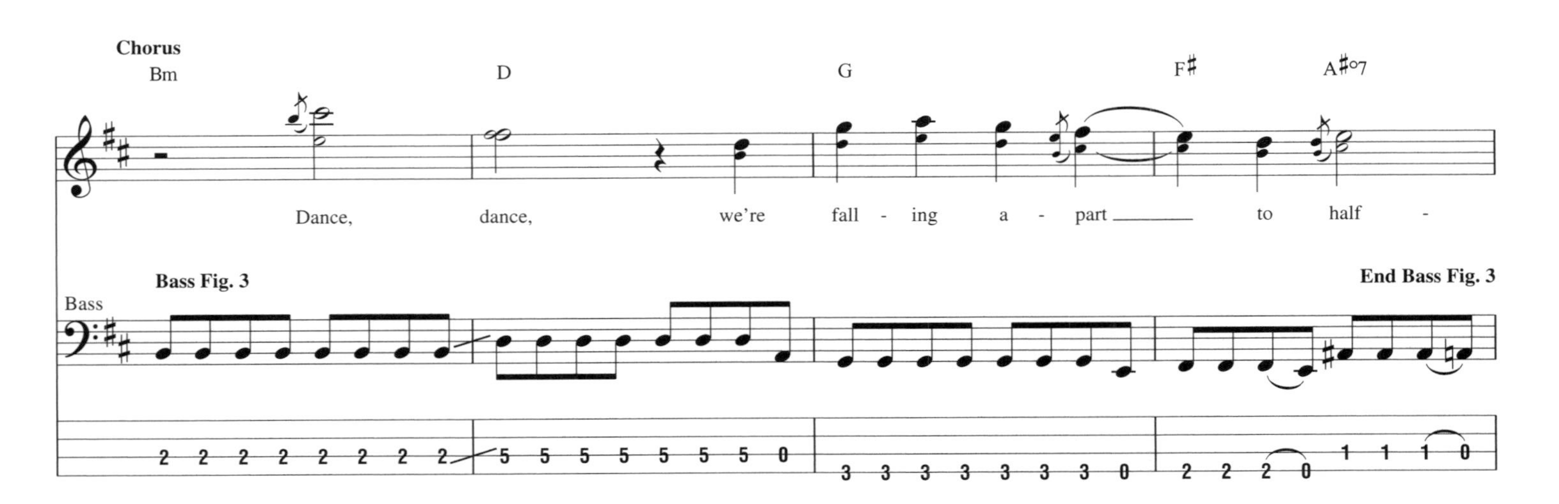
Chorus
Bm D G F♯ A♯°7
Dance, dance, we're fall - ing a - part to half -
Bass Fig. 3
End Bass Fig. 3
Bass

Bass: w/ Bass Fig. 3 (3 times)
Bm
D
G
F♯
A♯°7
time. Dance, dance, and these are the lives you'd love to lead.
Dance. This is the way they'd love if they knew
how mis - er - y loved me.
Interlude
B5
Bass Fig. 4
Bass
B5/A
D/F♯
G5
End Bass Fig. 4
Bridge
Quarter-time feel
Bass: w/ Bass Fig. 4 (1 1/2 times)
Why don't you show me the lit - tle bit of spine you've been
sav - ing for his mat - tress? (Mat - tress.)
(Mat - tress.)

B5
B5/A
I only - ly want sym - pa - thy in the form of you
End quarter-time feel
D/F♯
G5
crawl - ing in - to bed with me.
Bass
2 2 2 2 2 2 2 2 3 3 3 3 7 4
F♯5
B5/F♯
9
Chorus
Bass: w/ Bass Fig. 3 (6 times)
Bm D G F♯ A♯o7
Dance, dance, we're fall - ing a - part to half -
Bm D G F♯ A♯o7
time. Dance, dance, and these are the lives you'd love to lead.
Bm D G F♯ A♯o7
Dance. This is the way they'd love.
(Way they'd love.
Bm D G F♯ A♯o7
Dance. This is the way they'd love.
Way they'd love.)

Bm
D
G
F♯
A♯°7
Dance. This is the way they'd love if they knew
Bm
D
G
F♯
A♯°7
how mis - er - y loved me.
Interlude
Bass
G5
D5
A5
G5
D5
A5
2 2 5 5 5 5 5 3 3 5 5 5 5 5
Outro
B5
D5
A5
G5
D5
A5
Dance, dance. Dance, dance.
2 2 5 5 5 5 5 3 3 5 5 5 5 5
B5
D5
A5
G5
D5
A5
N.C.
Dance, dance. Dance, dance.
2 2 5 5 5 5 5 3 3 5 5 5 5

Dani California

Words and Music by Anthony Kiedis, Flea, John Frusciante and Chad Smith

Intro
Moderately ♩ = 96
N.C.
(Drums)
Am
G
Bass
mf
Dm
Am
G
Dm
Am
Verse
Am
G
Dm
Am
1. Get-ting born in the state of Mis-sis-sip-pi, pa - pa was a cop-per and her ma-ma was a hip-pie.
G
Dm
Am
In Al-a-bam-a, she would swing a ham-mer. Price you got-ta pay when you break the pan-o-ra-ma.

G
Dm
Am
She nev - er knew that there was an - y - thing more ___ than poor.
G
Dm
Am
What in the world does your com - pa - ny take ___ me for?
Verse
Am
G
Dm
Am
2. Black ban - dan - na, sweet ___ Lou - i - si - an - a, rob - bin' on a bank ___ in the state of In - di - an - a.
G
Dm
Am
She's a run - ner, reb - el, and a stun - ner, on her mer - ry way, ___ say - in', "Ba - by, what - cha gon - na?"

G Dm Am
Look - ing down the bar - rel of a hot met - al for - ty - five.
G Dm D5 E
Just an - oth - er way to sur - vive. Cal - i - for -
Chorus
F5 C5 D5 G5
- nia, rest in peace. Si - mul - ta -
Bass Fig. 1
End Bass Fig. 1
Bass: w/ Bass Fig. 1 (2 1/2 times)
F5 C5 D5 G5
- ne - ous re - lease. Cal - i - for -
F5 C5 D5 G5 F5 C5
- nia, show your teeth. She's my priest - ess, I'm your priest,

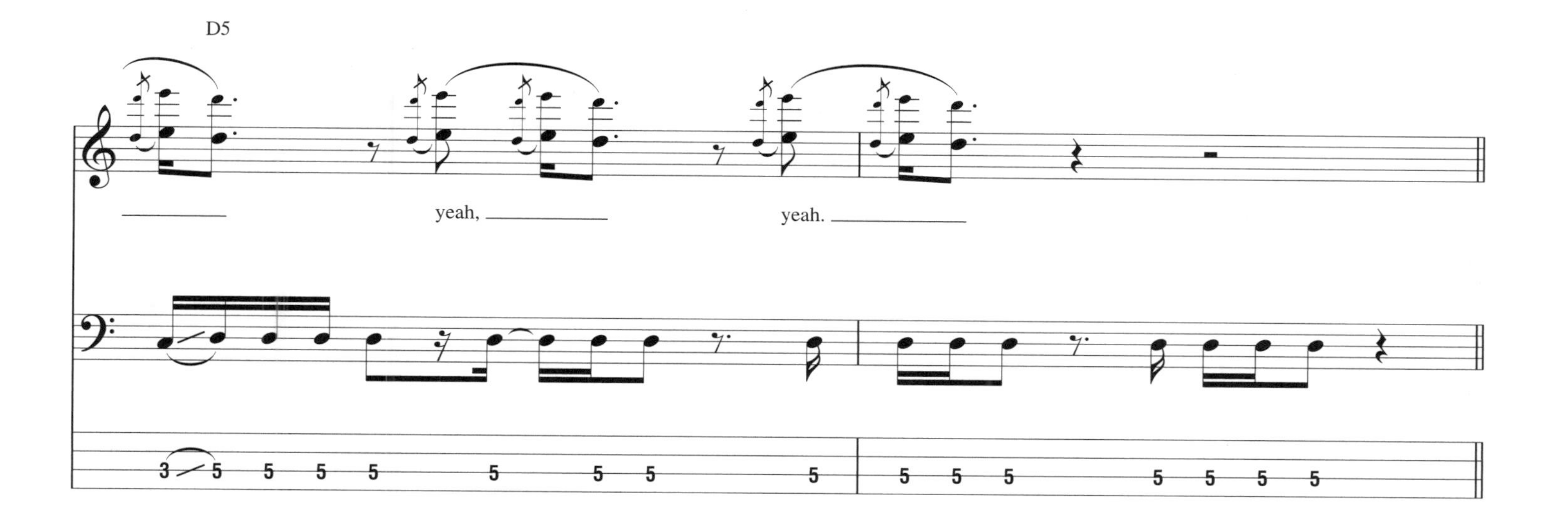
D5
yeah,
yeah.

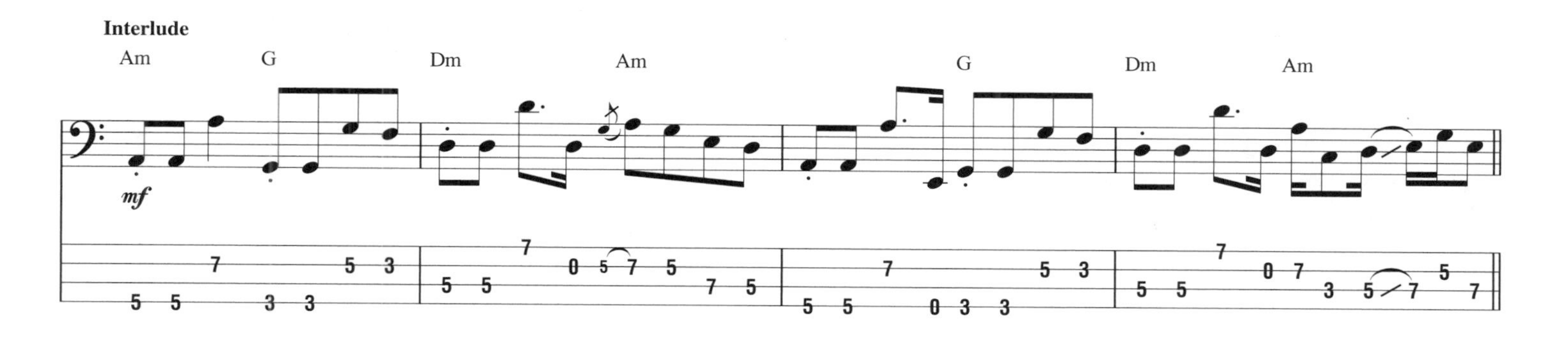
Interlude
Am G Dm Am G Dm Am
mf

Verse
Am G Dm Am
3. She's a lov - er, ba - by, and a fight - er. Should - a seen her com - in' when it got a lit - tle bright - er.

G Dm Am
With a name like Dan - i Cal - i - for - nia, (the) day was gon - na come when I was gon - na mourne ya.

G
Dm
Am
A lit - tle load - ed, she was steal - in' an - oth - er breath.
G
Dm
I love my ba - by to death.
Cal - i - for -
f
Chorus
Bass: w/ Bass Fig. 1 (3 1/2 times)
F5
C5
D5
G5
- nia, rest in peace. Si - mul - ta - ne - ous re - lease. Cal - i - for -
- nia, show your teeth. She's my priest - ess, I'm your priest,
D5
yeah, yeah.

Bridge
Bm
G
D/F♯
F♯5/C♯
Who knew the oth - er side of you?
mf
Bm
G
D/F♯
F♯5/C♯
Who know what oth - ers died to prove?
Bm
G
D/F♯
F♯5/C♯
Too true to say good - bye to you.
Bm
Too true to say, say, say...
3

Verse
Am
G
Dm
Am
4. Push the fad - er, gift - ed an - i - ma - tor one for the now and e - lev - en for the lat - er.
G
Dm
Am
Nev - er made it up to Min - ne - so - ta, North Da - ko - ta man was a gun - nin' for the quo - ta.
1/2
G
Dm
Am
Down in the Bad - lands, she was sav - in' the best for last.
G
Dm
D
Dm
It on - ly hurts when I laugh.

D
Dm
E7♭9
Gone too fast.
Cal - i - for -
f
Chorus
Bass: w/ Bass Fig. 1 (3 1/2 times)
F5
C5
D5
G5
- nia, rest in peace. Si - mul - ta - ne - ous re - lease. Cal - i - for -
- nia, show your teeth. She's my priest - ess, I'm your priest,
yeah, yeah. Cal - i - for -
Bass: w/ Bass Fig. 1 (3 1/2 times)
- nia, rest in peace. Si - mul - ta -
(Dum, de, dum, da.
- ne - ous re - lease. Cal - i - for -
Cal - i - for - nia.

F5
C5
D5
G5
F5
C5
A
- nia, show ___ your teeth. ___ She's ___ my priest - ess, I'm ___ your priest, ___
Dum, de, dum, ___ da.)

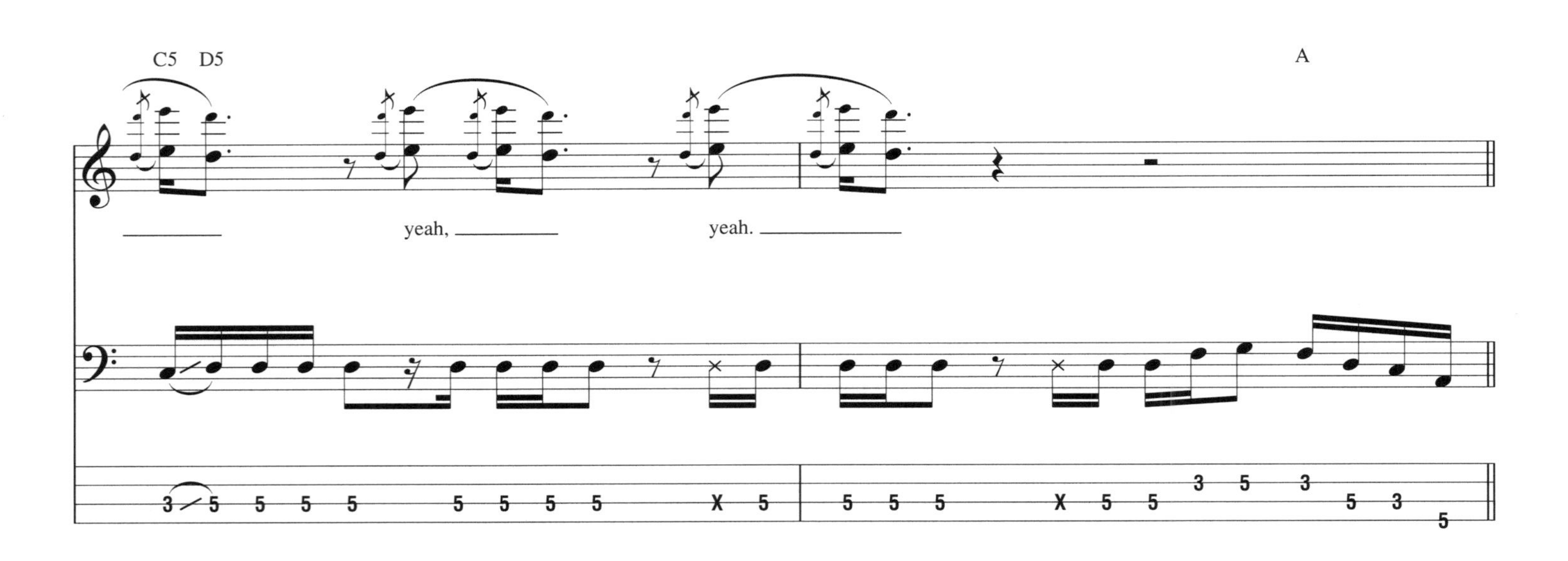
C5 D5
A
yeah, ___ yeah. ___

Outro-Guitar Solo

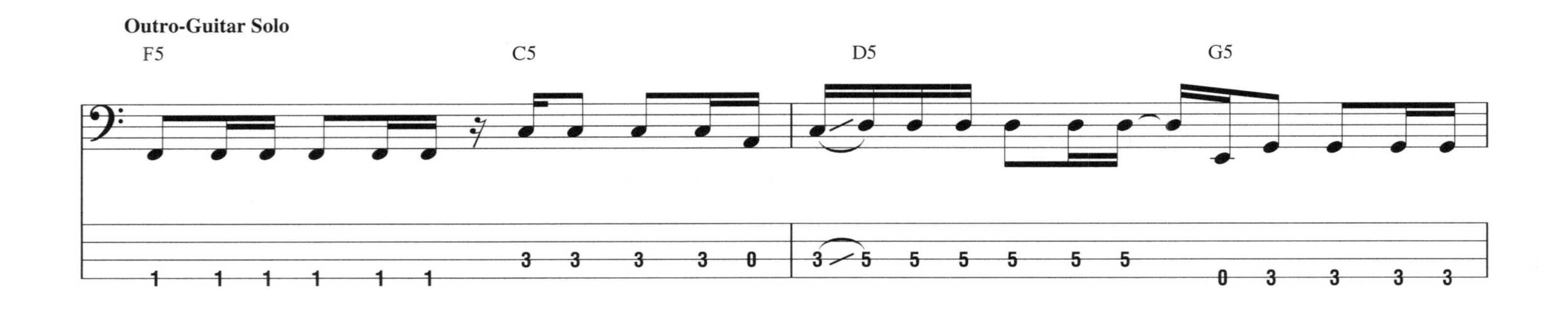
F5
C5
D5
G5

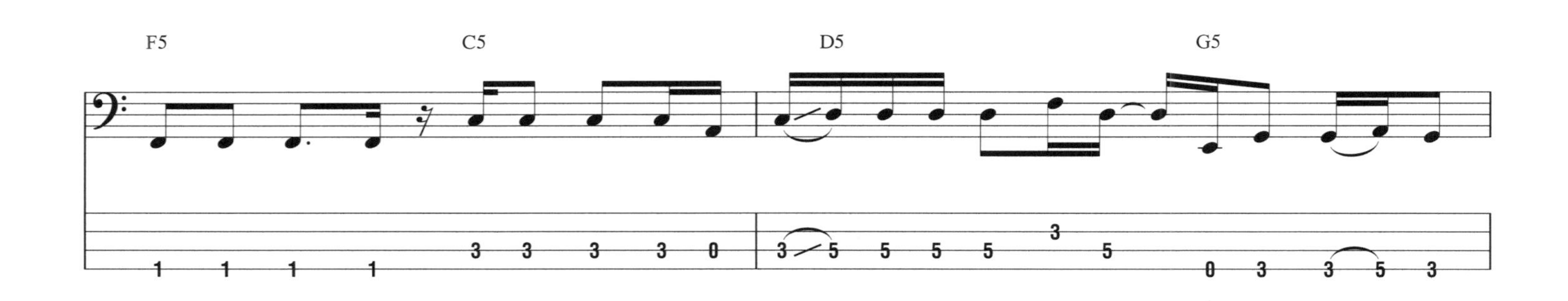
F5
C5
D5
G5

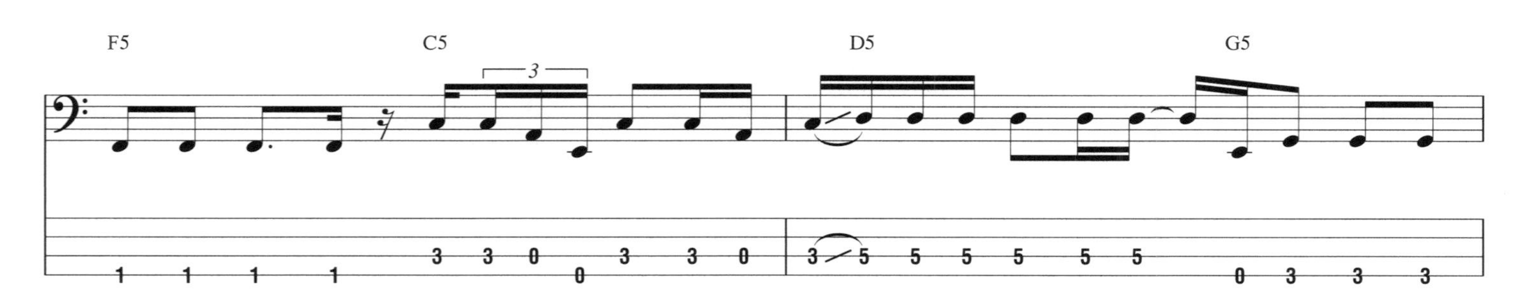
F5
C5
D5
G5

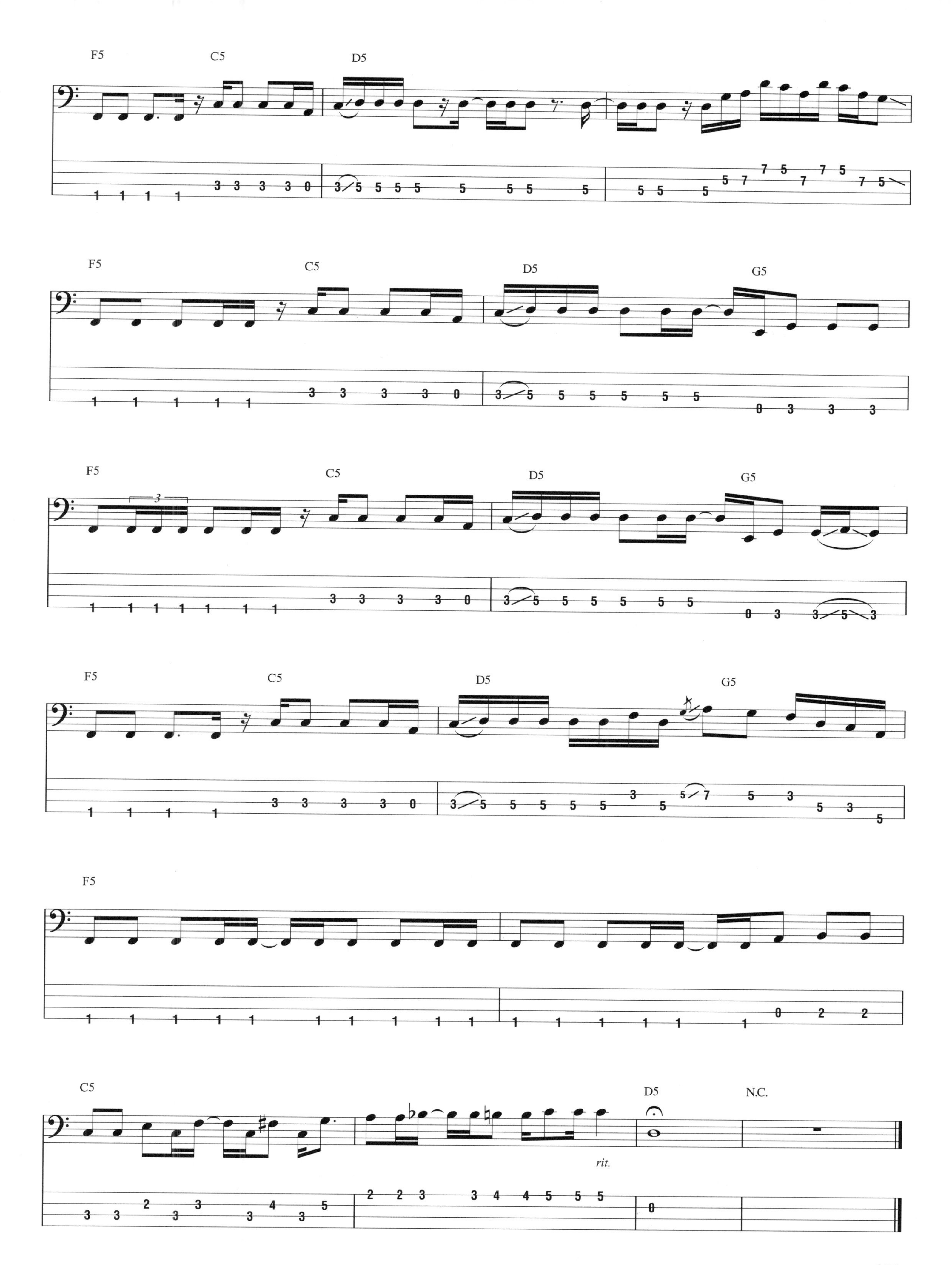

F5
C5
D5
F5
C5
D5
G5
F5
C5
D5
G5
F5
C5
D5
G5
F5
C5
D5
N.C.
rit.

Devils Haircut

Words and Music by John King, Michael Simpson, Beck Hansen, James Brown, Philip Coulter and Tommy Scott

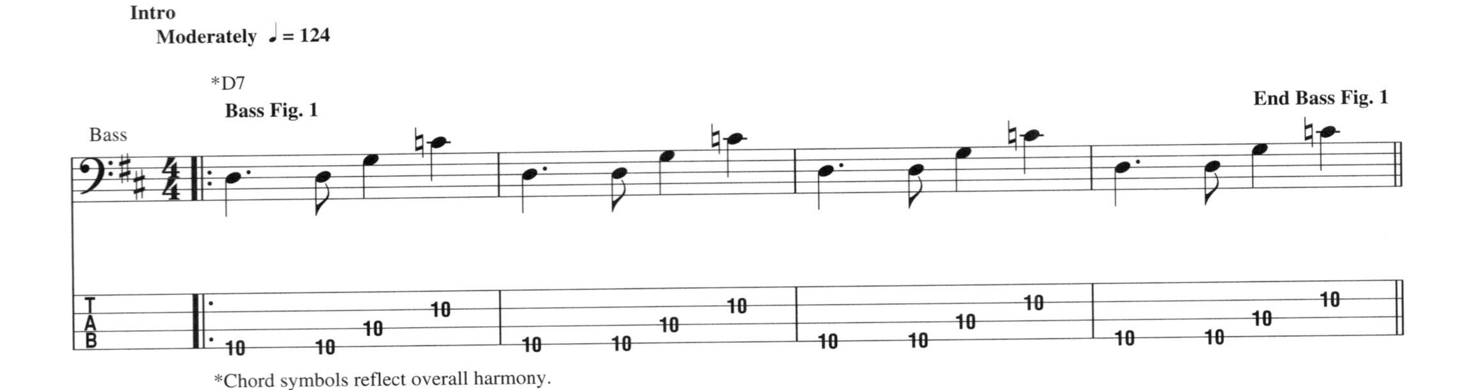
Intro
Moderately ♩ = 124
*D7
Bass Fig. 1
End Bass Fig. 1
Bass
T
A
B
*Chord symbols reflect overall harmony.

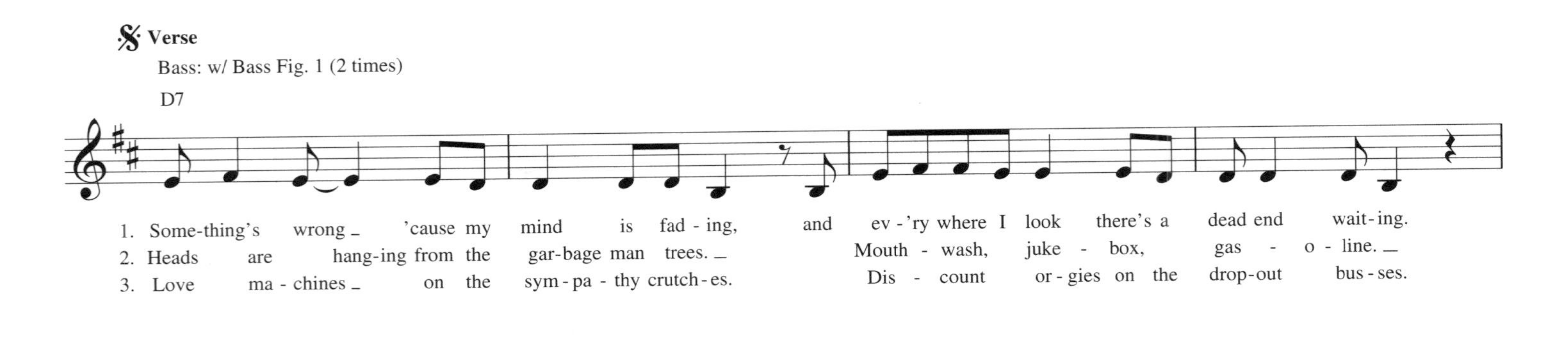
Verse
Bass: w/ Bass Fig. 1 (2 times)
D7
1. Some-thing's wrong 'cause my mind is fad - ing, and ev - 'ry where I look there's a dead end wait - ing.
2. Heads are hang-ing from the gar-bage man trees. Mouth - wash, juke - box, gas - o - line.
3. Love ma - chines on the sym - pa - thy crutch - es. Dis - count or - gies on the drop-out bus - ses.

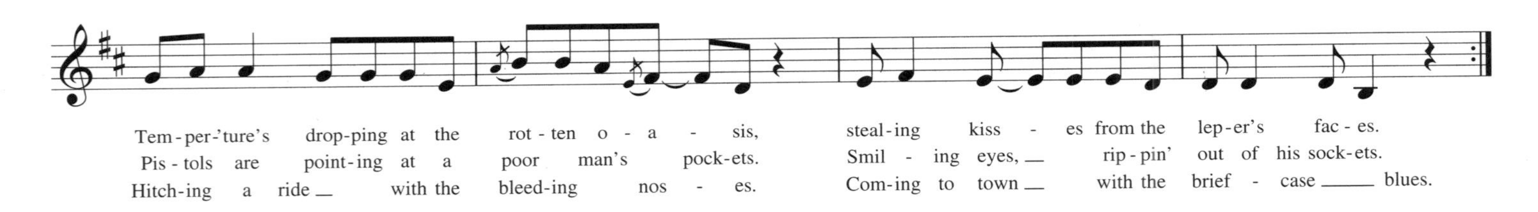
Tem - per - 'ture's drop-ping at the rot - ten o - a - sis, steal - ing kiss - es from the lep - er's fac - es.
Pis - tols are point-ing at a poor man's pock - ets. Smil - ing eyes, rip - pin' out of his sock - ets.
Hitch-ing a ride with the bleed-ing nos - es. Com - ing to town with the brief - case blues.

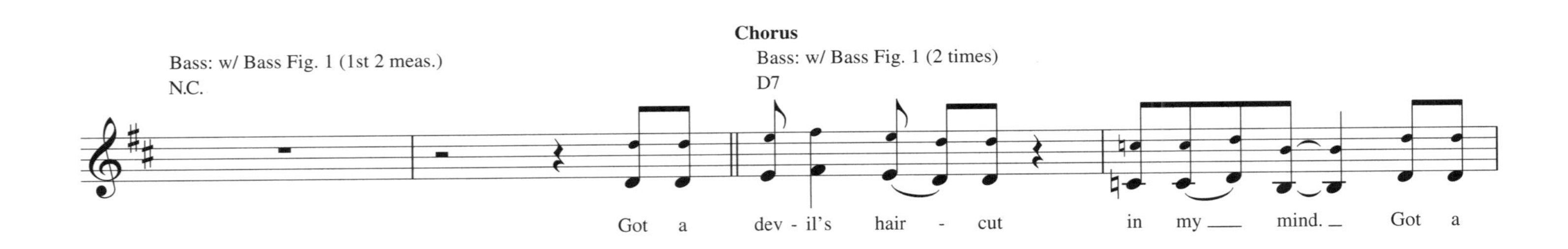
Bass: w/ Bass Fig. 1 (1st 2 meas.)
N.C.
Chorus
Bass: w/ Bass Fig. 1 (2 times)
D7
Got a dev - il's hair - cut in my mind. Got a

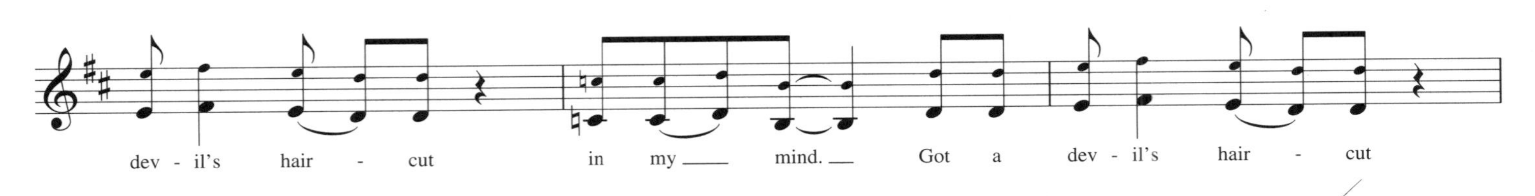
dev - il's hair - cut in my mind. Got a dev - il's hair - cut

To Coda 𝄌

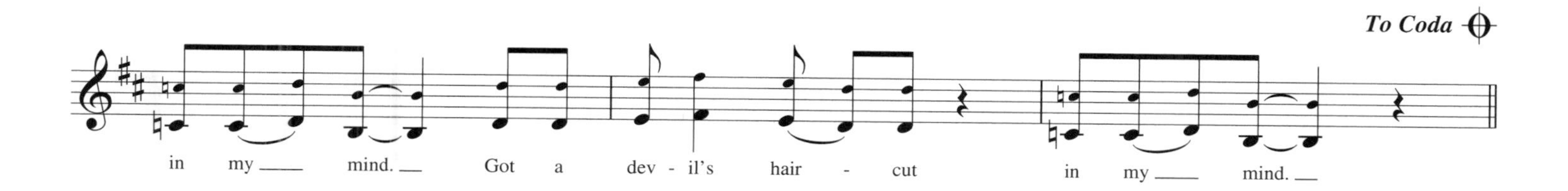

in my mind. Got a dev - il's hair - cut in my mind.

Interlude

Bass tacet

N.C.

D.S. al Coda (no repeat)

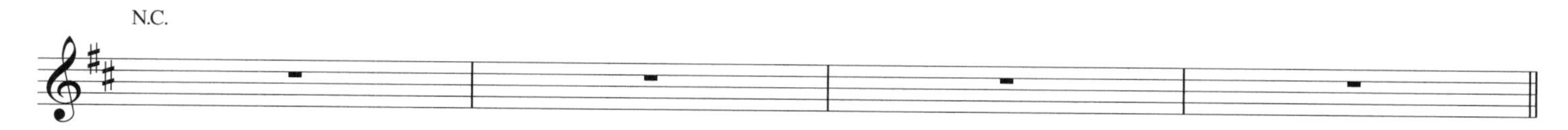

𝄌 Coda

Interlude

Bass

F

8 8

Verse

Bass: w/ Bass Fig. 1 (3 times)

D7

4. Some - thing's wrong 'cause my mind is fad - ing. Ghet - to blast - ing, dis -

in - te - grat - ing. Rock 'n' roll, know what I'm say - in'? And

ev - 'ry - where I look there's a dev - il la - dy.

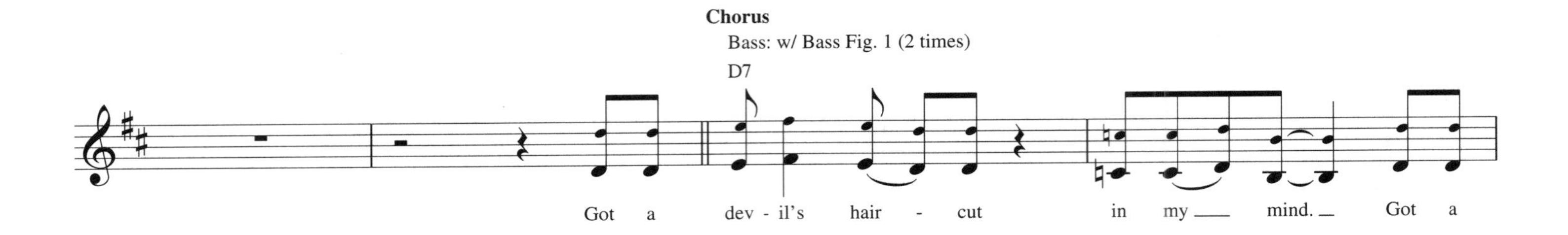
Chorus
Bass: w/ Bass Fig. 1 (2 times)
D7
Got a dev - il's hair - cut in my mind. Got a

dev - il's hair - cut in my mind. Got a dev - il's hair - cut

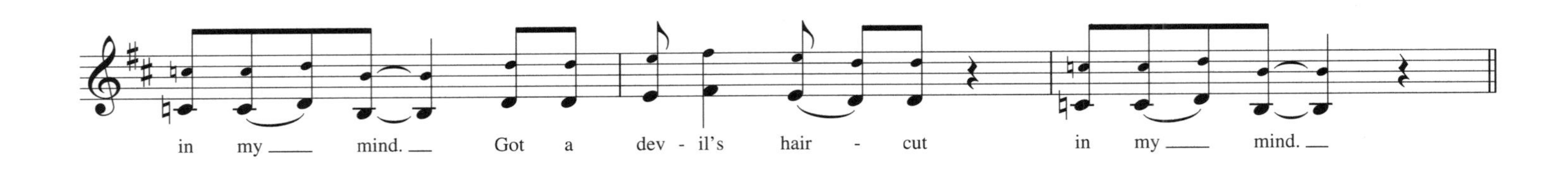
in my mind. Got a dev - il's hair - cut in my mind.

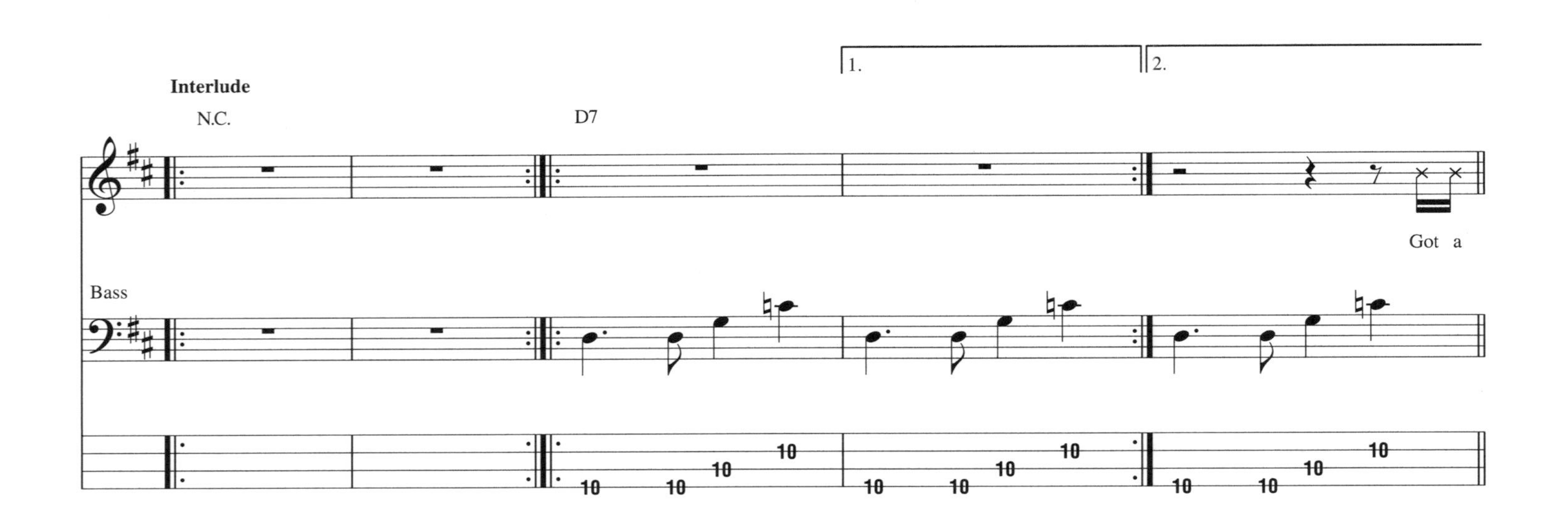
1.
2.
Interlude
N.C.
D7
Got a
Bass
10 10 10 10
10 10 10 10
10 10 10 10

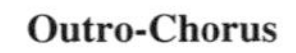
Outro-Chorus

Bass: w/ Bass Fig. 1 (1 1/2 times)

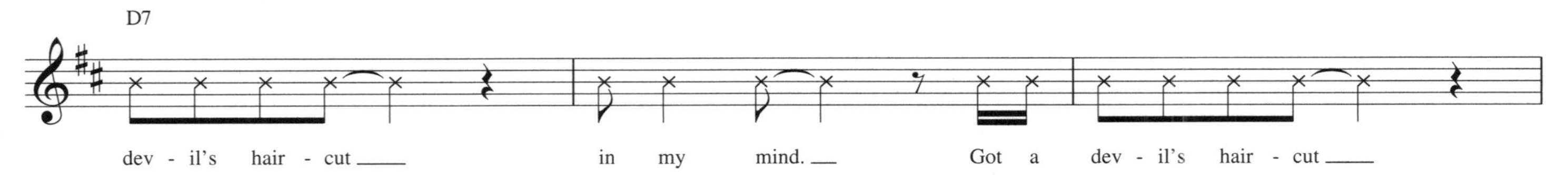
D7
dev - il's hair - cut in my mind. Got a dev - il's hair - cut

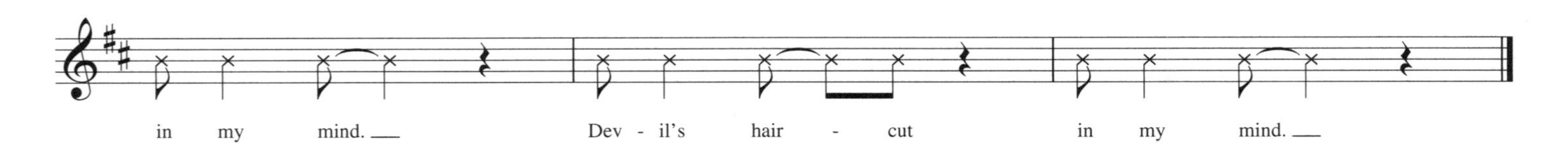
in my mind. Dev - il's hair - cut in my mind.

Feel Good Inc.

Words and Music by Damon Albarn, Jamie Hewlett, Brian Burton and De La Soul

Tune down 1/2 step:
(low to high) E♭-A♭-D♭-G♭

Intro
Moderately fast ♩ = 138
N.C.
E5
Voc. Fig. 1
Bm7
Am7
End Voc. Fig. 1
Feel good. (Shake it, shake it, shake it.) Feel good.
Bass
Bass Fig. 1
f
T
A
B

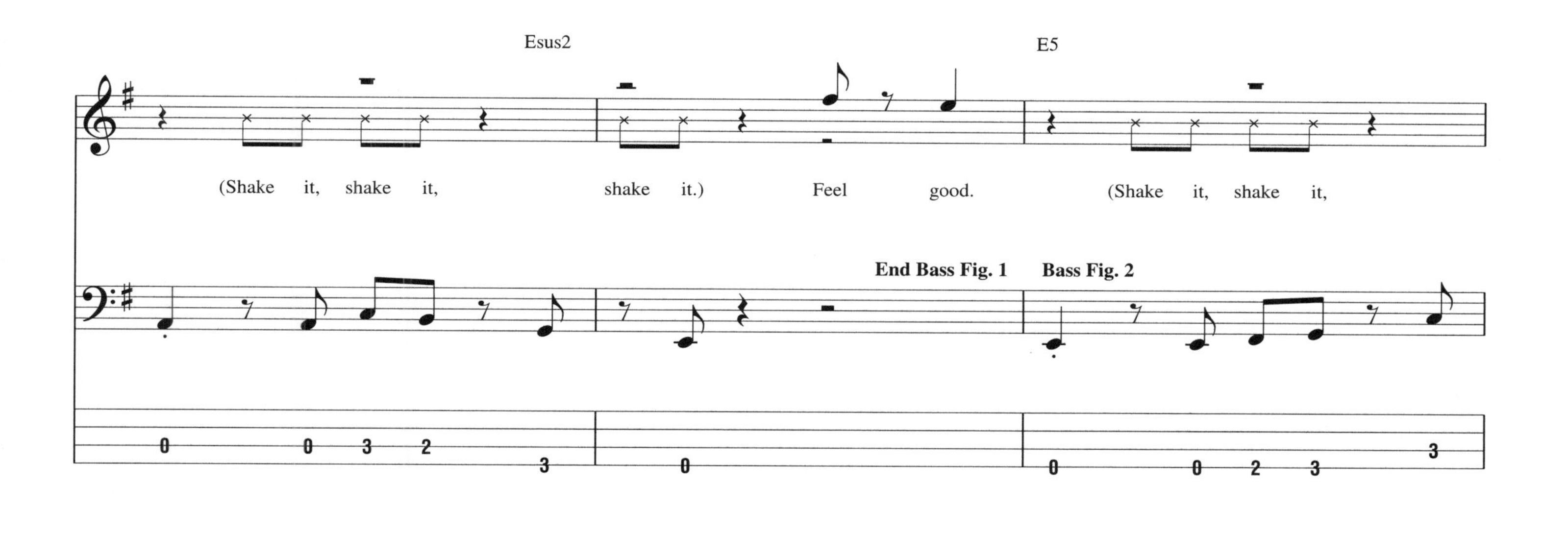

Esus2
E5
(Shake it, shake it, shake it.) Feel good. (Shake it, shake it,
End Bass Fig. 1
Bass Fig. 2

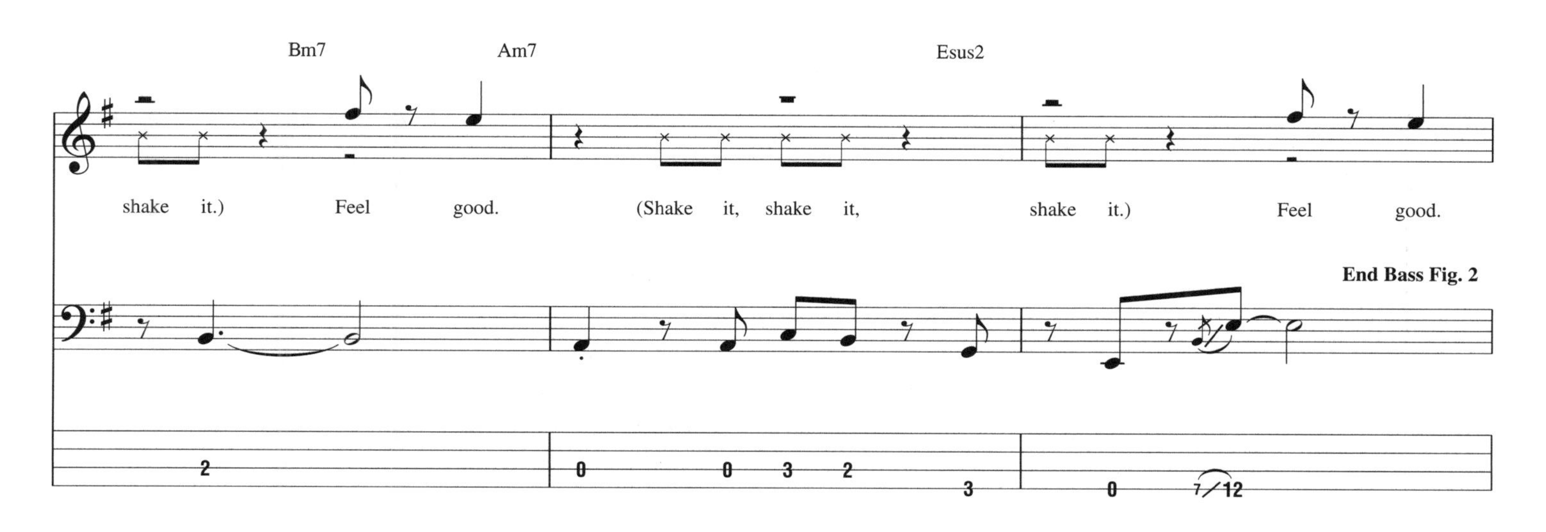

Bm7
Am7
Esus2
shake it.) Feel good. (Shake it, shake it, shake it.) Feel good.
End Bass Fig. 2

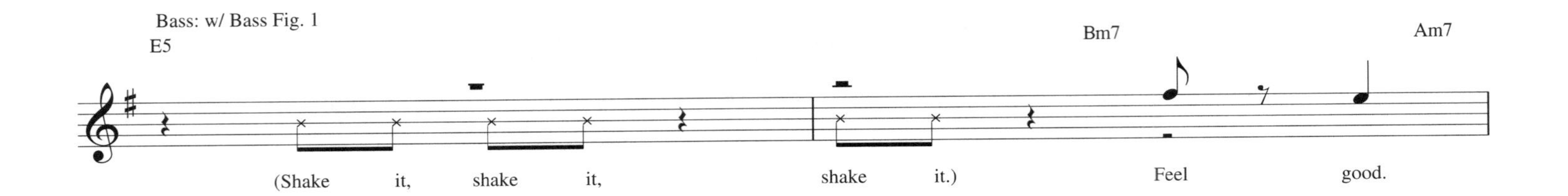
Bass: w/ Bass Fig. 1
E5
Bm7
Am7
(Shake it, shake it, shake it.) Feel good.

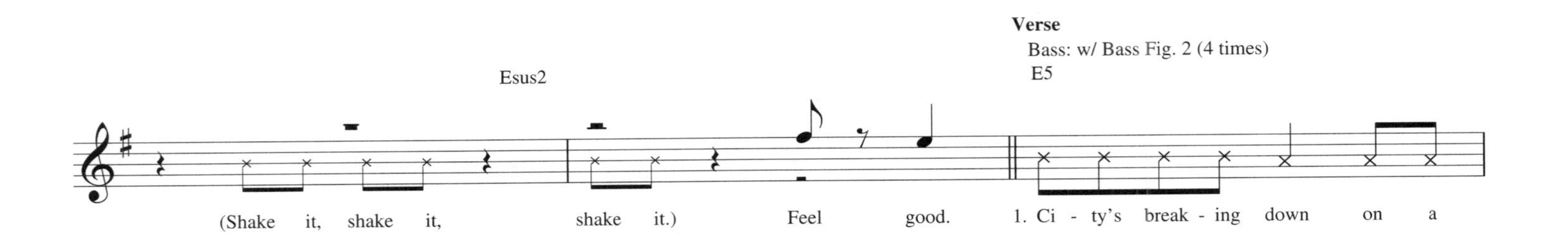
Esus2
Verse
Bass: w/ Bass Fig. 2 (4 times)
E5
(Shake it, shake it, shake it.) Feel good. 1. Ci - ty's break - ing down on a

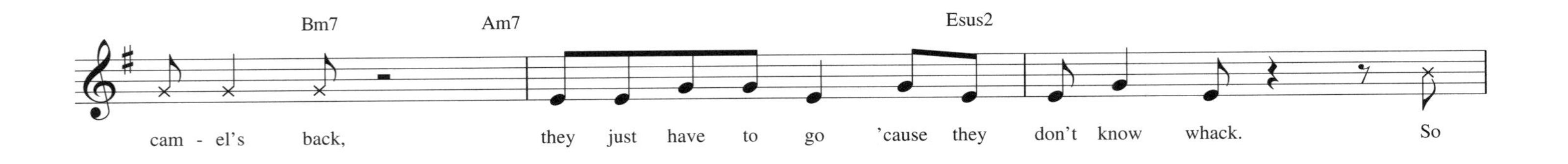
Bm7
Am7
Esus2
cam - el's back, they just have to go 'cause they don't know whack. So

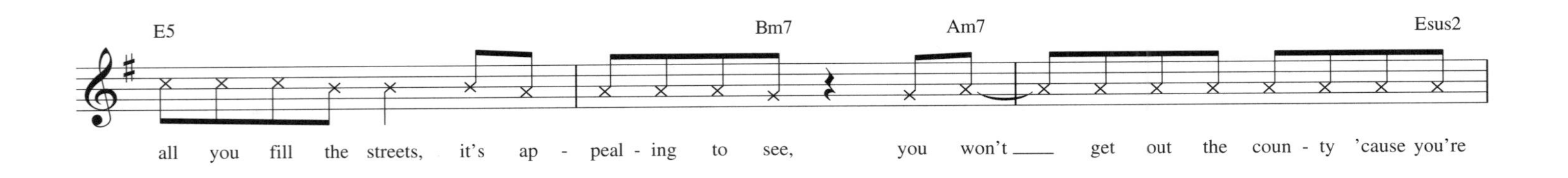
E5
Bm7
Am7
Esus2
all you fill the streets, it's ap - peal - ing to see, you won't get out the coun - ty 'cause you're

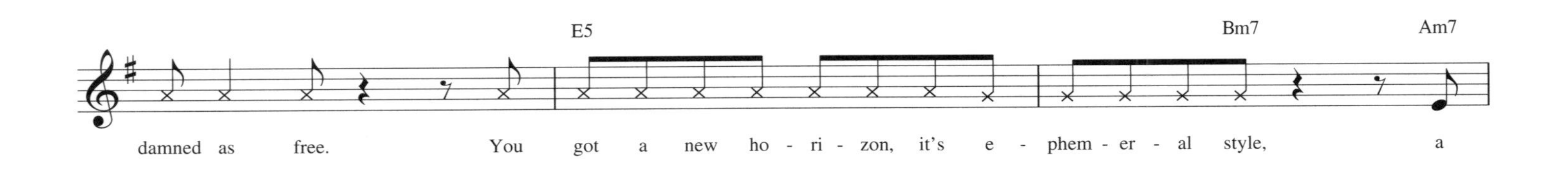
E5
Bm7
Am7
damned as free. You got a new ho - ri - zon, it's e - phem - er - al style, a

Esus2
E5
mel - an - cho - ly town where we nev - er smile. And all I wan - na hear is the

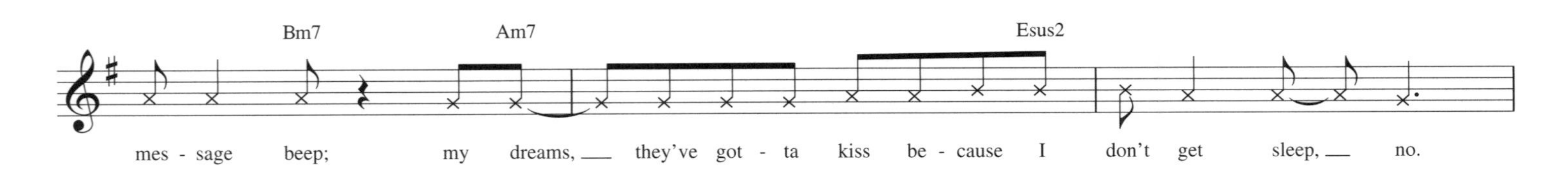
Bm7
Am7
Esus2
mes - sage beep; my dreams, they've got - ta kiss be - cause I don't get sleep, no.

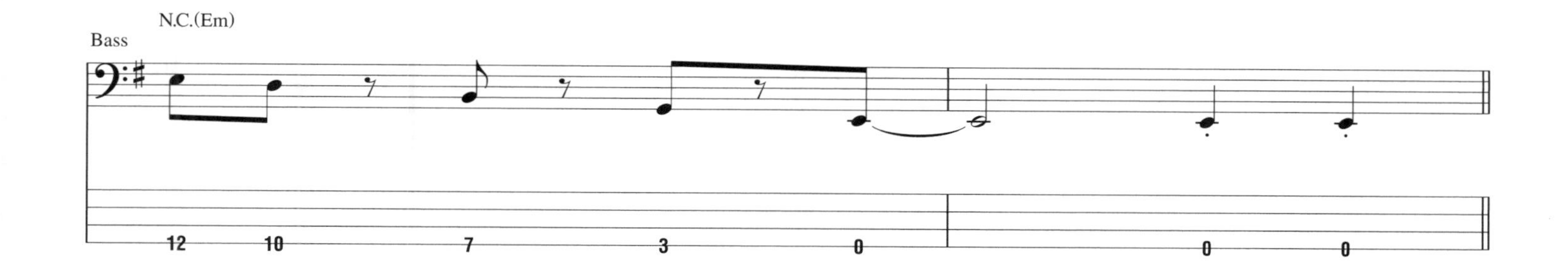
N.C.(Em)
Bass
12 10 7 3 0
0 0

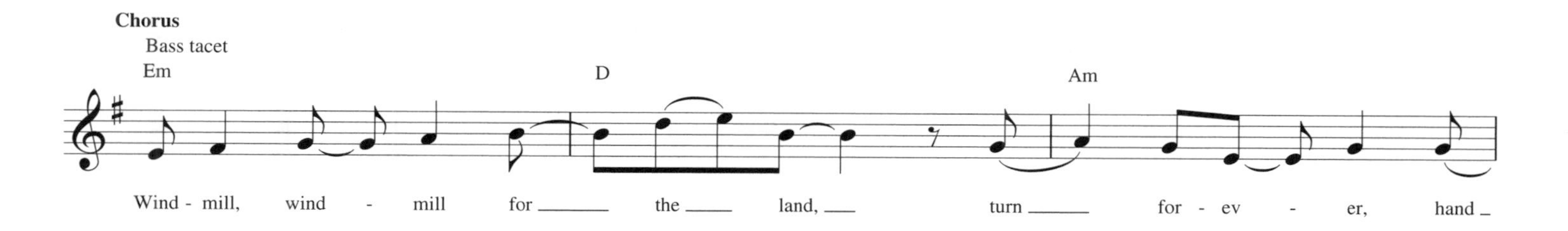
Chorus
Bass tacet
Em
D
Am
Wind - mill, wind - mill for the land, turn for - ev - er, hand

Bm
Em
D
in hand. Take it all in on your stride,

Am
Bm
Em
it is tick - ing fall - ing down. Love for - ev - er, love

D
Am
Bm
is free, lets turn for - ev - er, you and me.

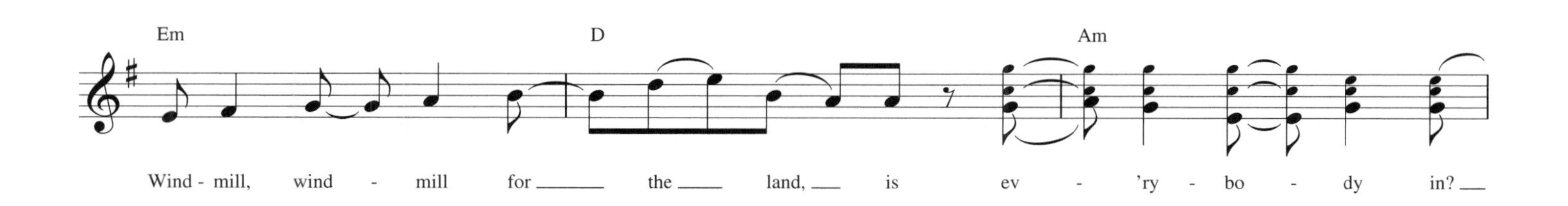
Em
D
Am
Wind - mill, wind - mill for the land, is ev - 'ry - bo - dy in?

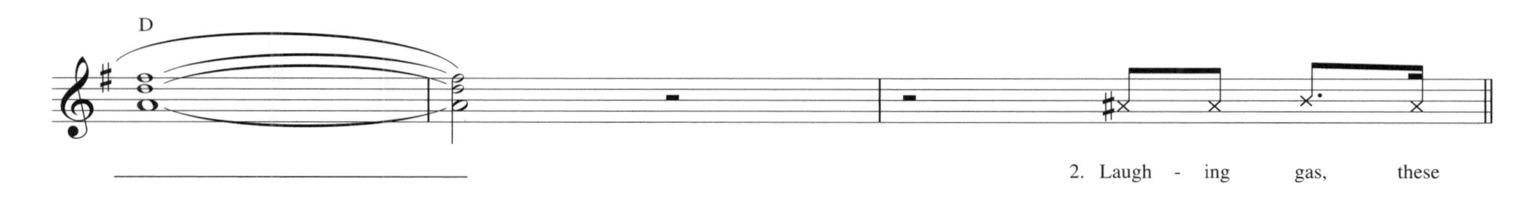
D
2. Laugh - ing gas, these

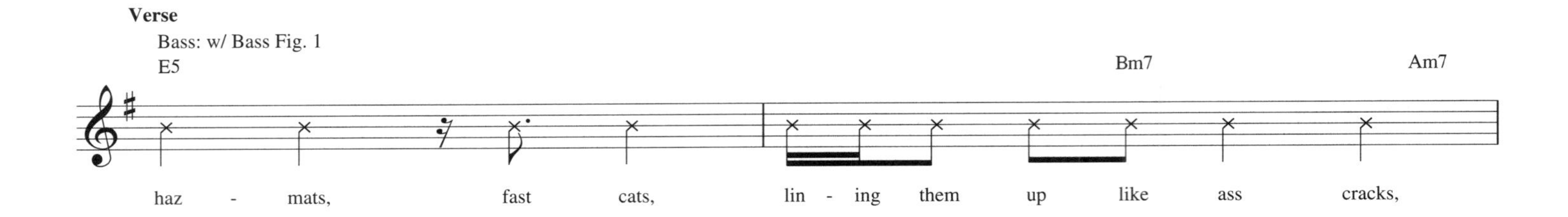
Verse
Bass: w/ Bass Fig. 1
E5
Bm7
Am7
haz - mats, fast cats, lin - ing them up like ass cracks,

Esus2
la - dies, po - nies at the track, it's my choc - o - late at - tack.

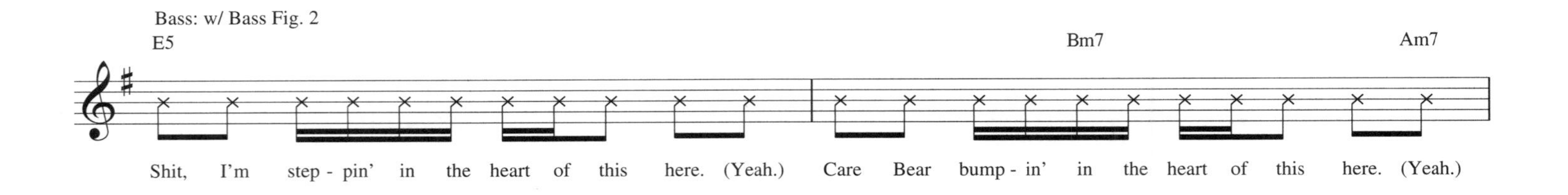
Bass: w/ Bass Fig. 2
E5
Bm7
Am7
Shit, I'm step - pin' in the heart of this here. (Yeah.) Care Bear bump - in' in the heart of this here. (Yeah.)

Esus2
Watch me as I grav - i - tate, ha - ha - ha - ha - ha. Yo, we go - in'

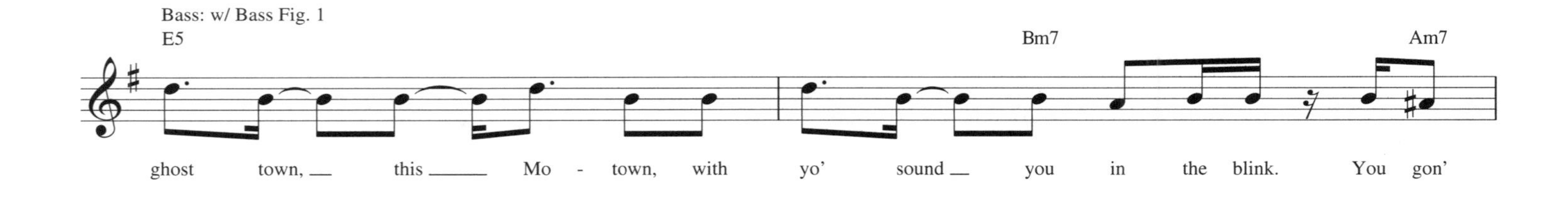
Bass: w/ Bass Fig. 1
E5
Bm7
Am7
ghost town, this Mo - town, with yo' sound you in the blink. You gon'

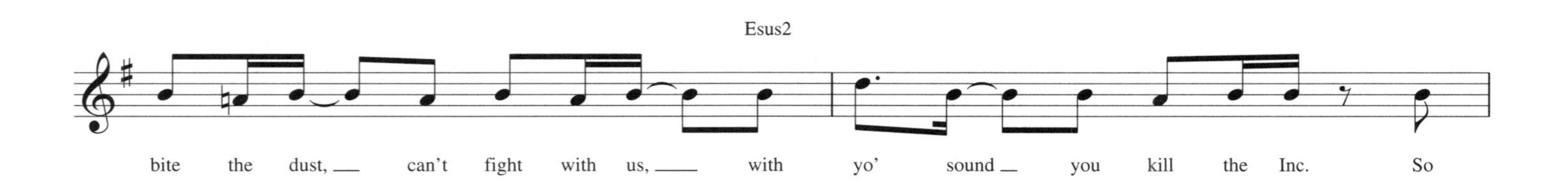
Esus2
bite the dust, can't fight with us, with yo' sound you kill the Inc. So

Bass: w/ Bass Fig. 2 (1 1/2 times)
E5
Bm7
Am7
Esus2
don't stop, get it, get it, un - til you jet a - head. Yo, watch the way I nav - i - gate, ha -

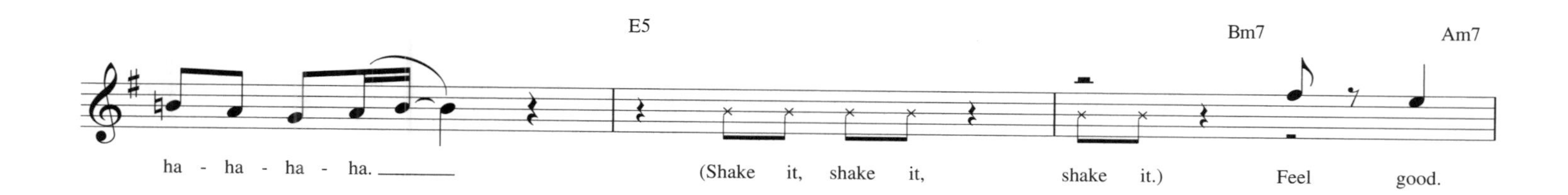
E5
Bm7
Am7
ha - ha - ha - ha.
(Shake it, shake it, shake it.) Feel good.

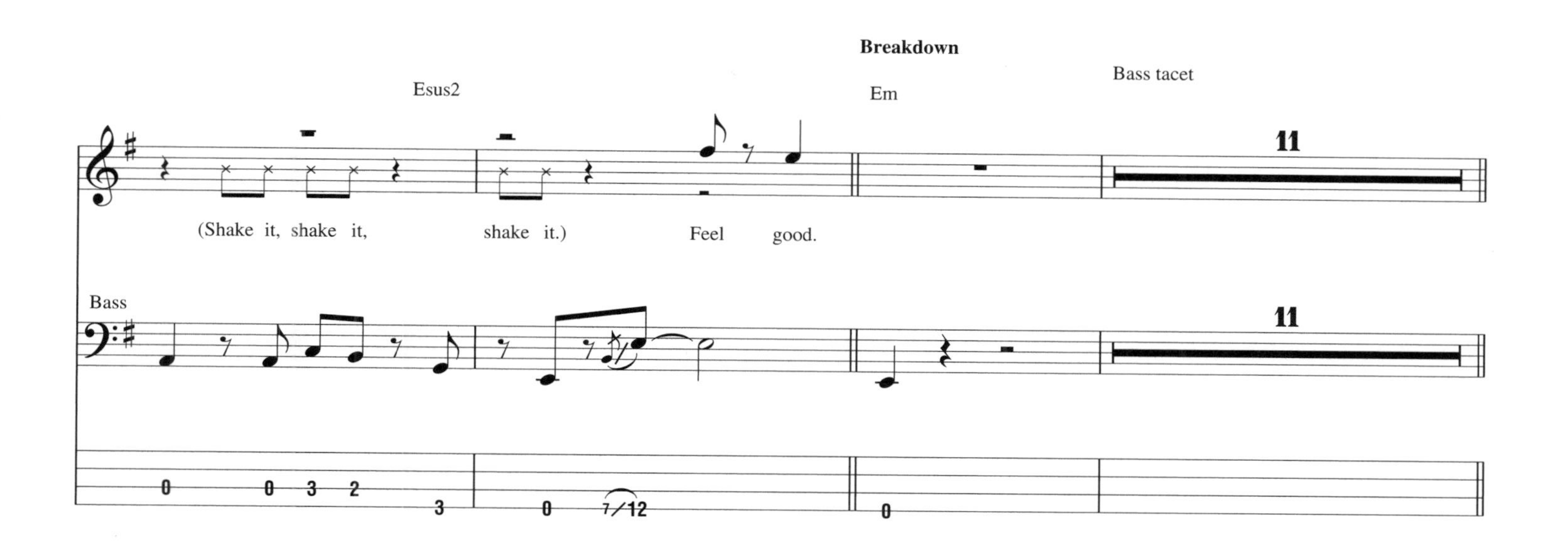
Breakdown
Esus2
Em
Bass tacet
11
(Shake it, shake it, shake it.) Feel good.
Bass
0 0 3 2 3 0 7 12 0

Chorus
Em
D
Wind - mill, wind - mill for the land, turn

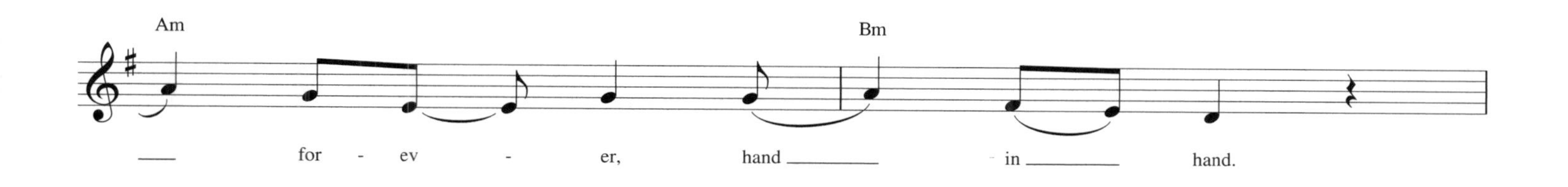
Am
Bm
for - ev - er, hand in hand.

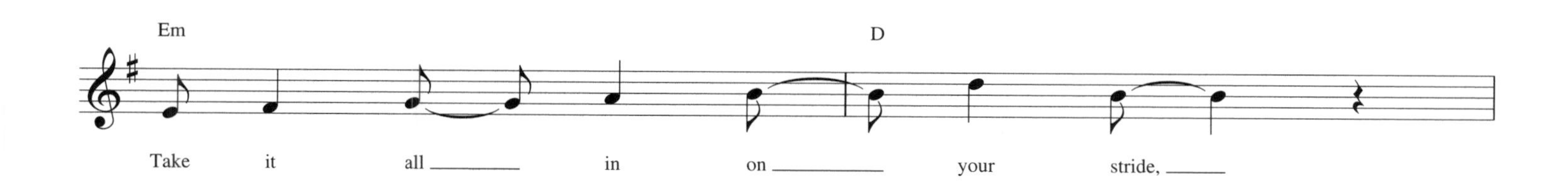
Em
D
Take it all in on your stride,

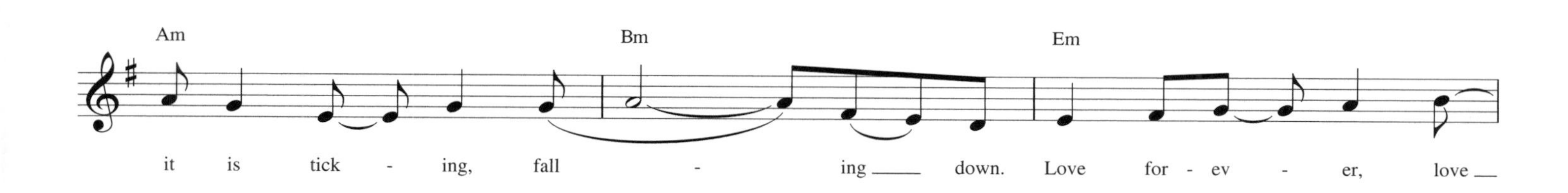
Am
Bm
Em
it is tick - ing, fall - ing down. Love for - ev - er, love

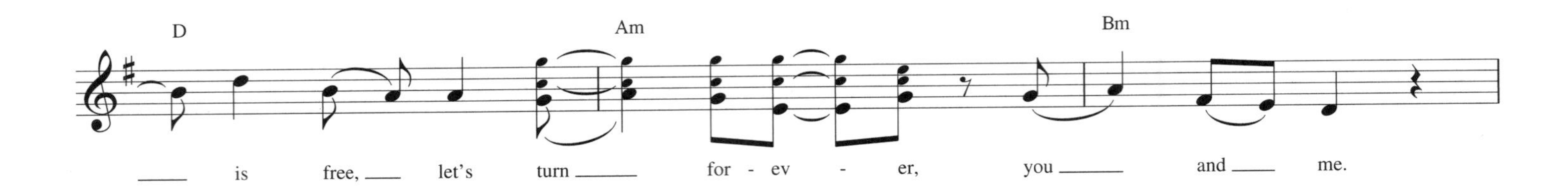
D
Am
Bm
is free, let's turn for - ev - er, you and me.

Em
D
Am
Wind - mill, wind - mill for the land, is ev - 'ry - bod - y in?

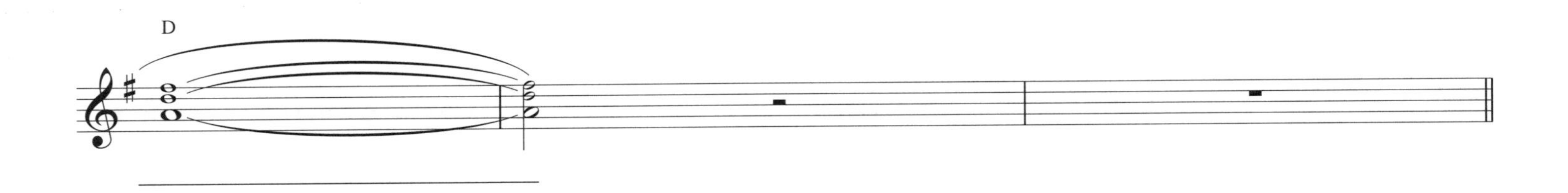
D

Verse
Voc.: w/ Voc. Fig. 1 (4 times)
1st time, Bass: w/ Bass Fig. 2
2nd time, Bass: w/ Bass Fig. 1
E5
Bm7
Am7
3. Don't stop, get it, get it, we are your cap - tains in it.

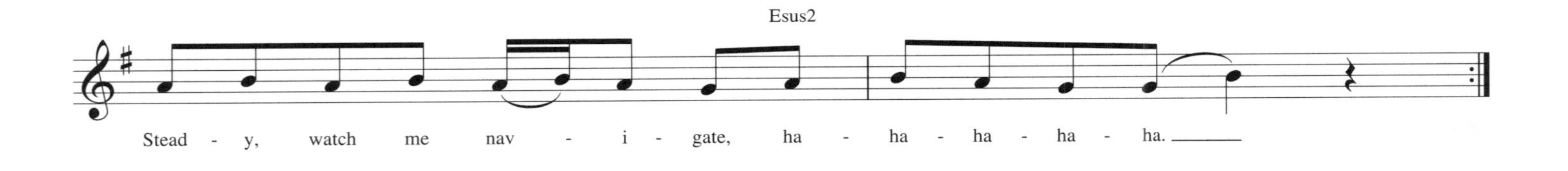
Esus2
Stead - y, watch me nav - i - gate, ha - ha - ha - ha - ha.

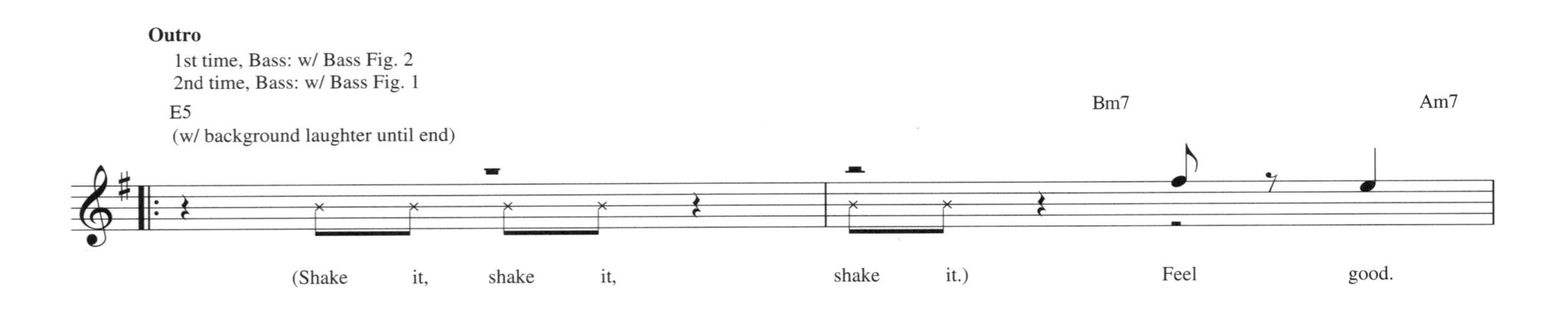
Outro
1st time, Bass: w/ Bass Fig. 2
2nd time, Bass: w/ Bass Fig. 1
E5
(w/ background laughter until end)
Bm7
Am7
(Shake it, shake it, shake it.) Feel good.

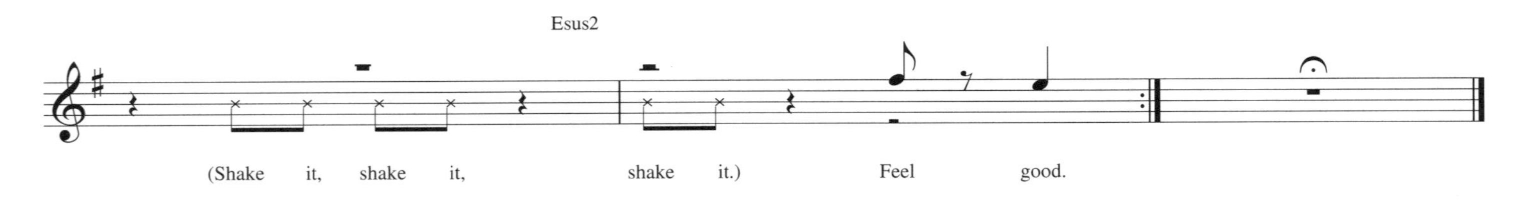
Esus2
(Shake it, shake it, shake it.) Feel good.

Free Ride

Words and Music by Dan Hartman

Intro
Moderately fast ♩ = 128
A G D
G D A
D A G D
4
f
0
0 0
0

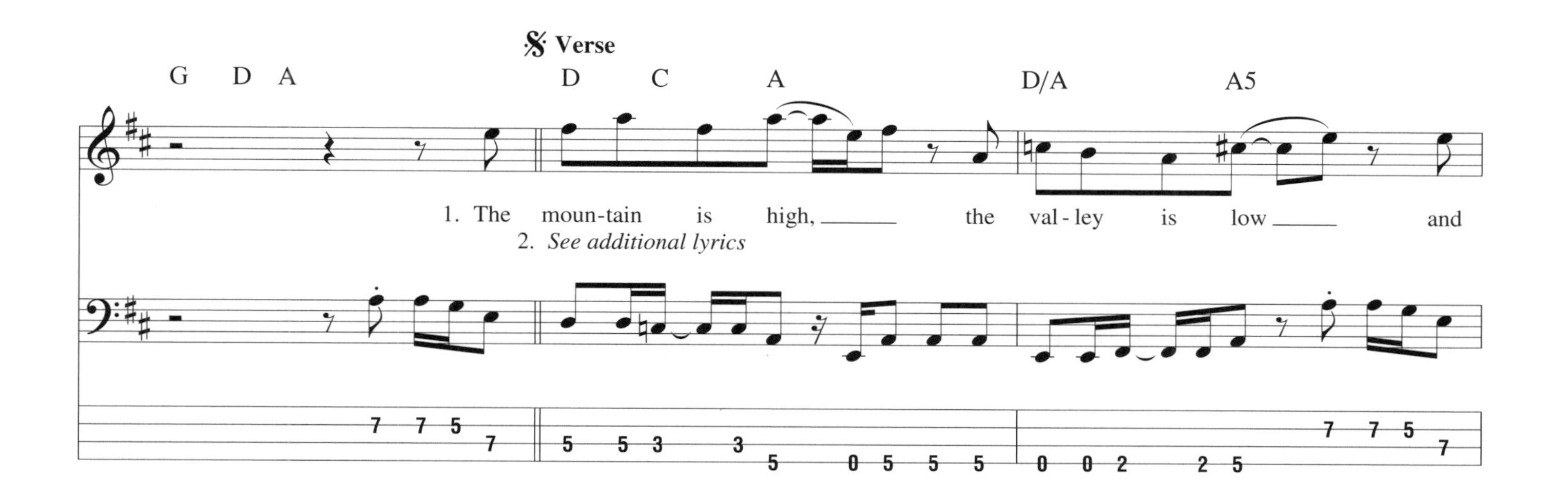

Verse
G D A
D C A
D/A
A5
1. The mountain is high, the valley is low and
2. See additional lyrics

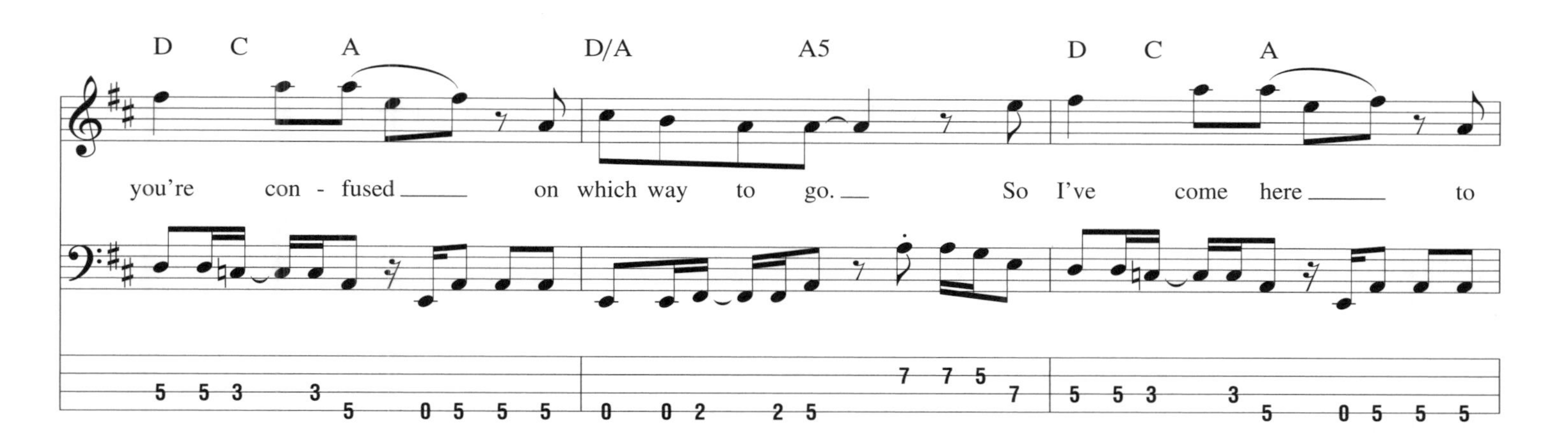

D C A
D/A
A5
D C A
you're confused on which way to go. So I've come here to

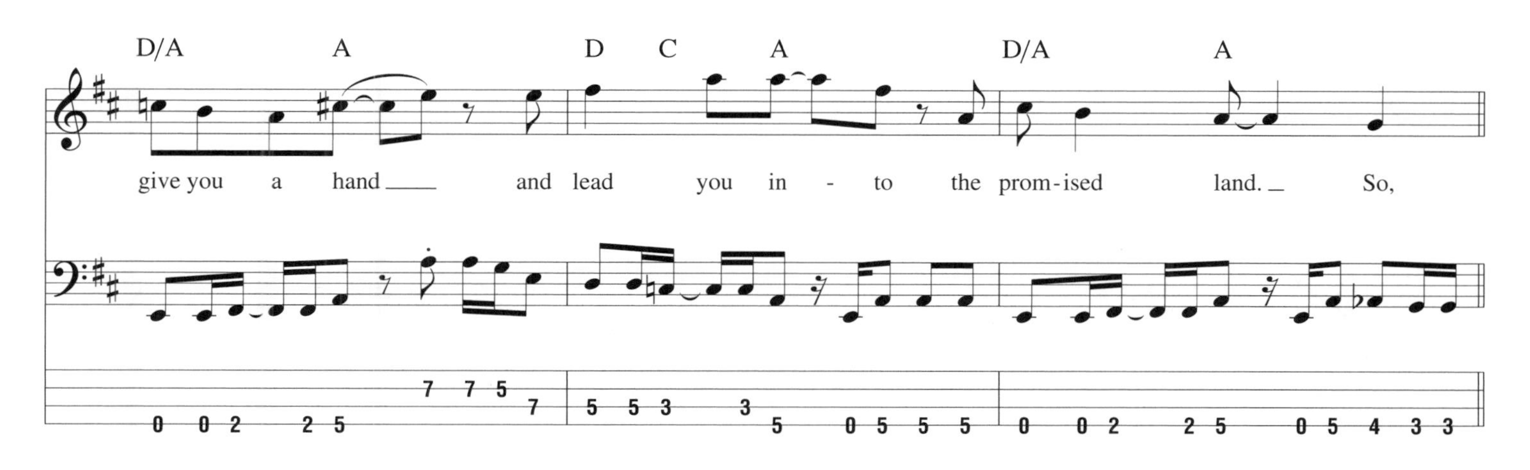

D/A
A
D C A
D/A
A
give you a hand and lead you into the promised land. So,

Chorus
F♯m G A F♯m G
come on ___ and take a free ride. _ Come on ___ and stand here

To Coda
D F♯m G D
by my side. ___ Come on ___ and take a free ride.

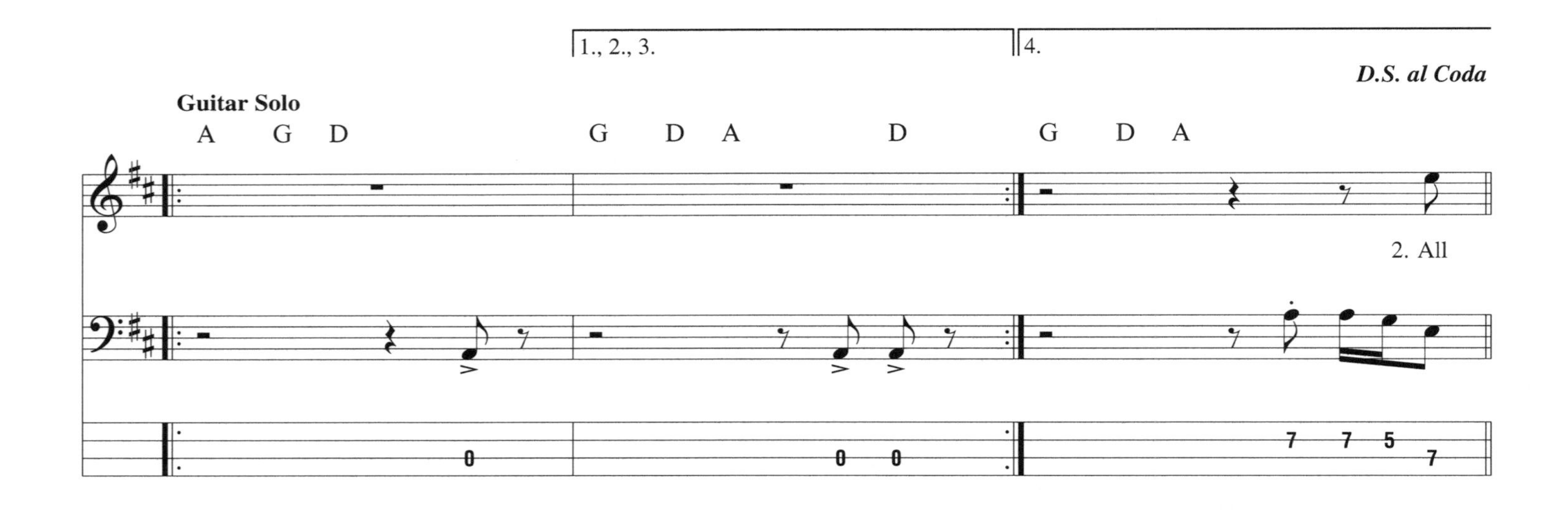
1., 2., 3.
4.
D.S. al Coda
Guitar Solo
A G D G D A D G D A
2. All

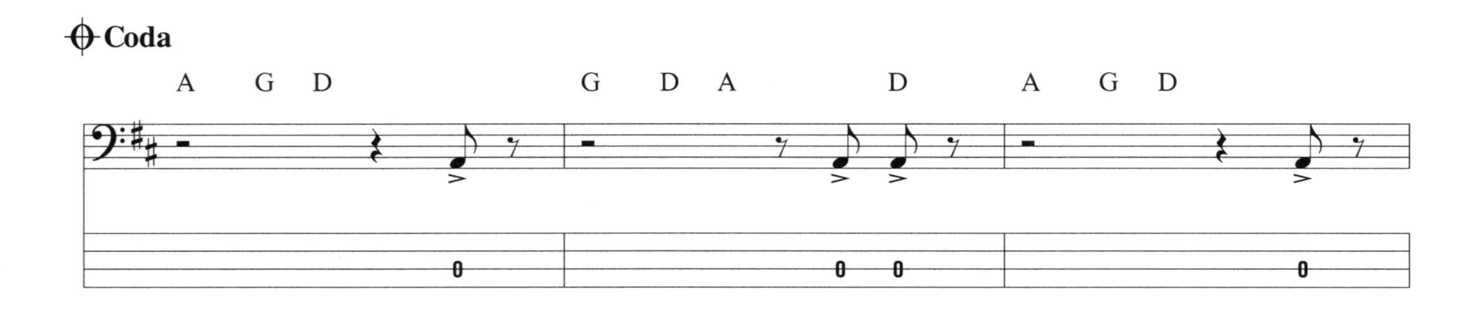
Coda
A G D G D A D A G D

Guitar Solo
1., 2., 3.
G D A D
D C A
D/A A5
Yeah, yeah, yeah, yeah.
4.
D/A A
F♯m G A
(Ooh.
F♯m G D
F♯m G D
Ooh.
Ooh.
Free ride.)
Interlude
N.C.
Play 4 times
Outro
w/ Voc. ad lib.
A G D
G D A D
Come on and take a free ride.

A G D G D A D A G D G D A D
Yeah, yeah, yeah, yeah.
5 2 3 3 4 5 4 5 3 4 5 4 5 3 4 5 4 5 3 4

1., 2., 3.
A G D G D A D A G D G D A D
5 2 3 3 4 5 4 5 0 3 4 5 2 3 X 0 3 4 5 4 5 X 0 3 4

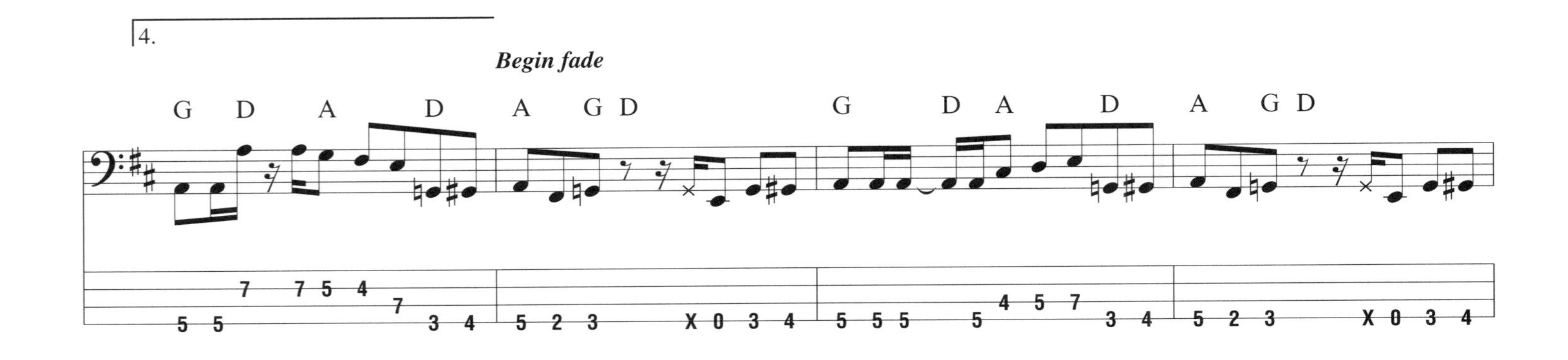
4.
Begin fade
G D A D A G D G D A D A G D

Fade out
G D A D A G D G D A D

Additional Lyrics

2. All over the country I've seen it the same,
   Nobody's winning at this kind of game.
   We've gotta do better, it's time to begin.
   You know all the answers must come from within.

I Want You Back

Words and Music by Freddie Perren, Alphonso Mizell, Berry Gordy and Deke Richards

Intro
Moderate Soul ♩ = 100
Bass
A♭
D♭
Fm
A♭maj7/C
D♭
A♭
mf
1.
2.
B♭m7
E♭
A♭
B♭m7
E♭
A♭
E♭/G
Fm7
E♭
Uh, huh, huh, huh.
D♭
D♭/C
B♭m7
E♭
Fm7
Cm7
D♭
A♭
Just let me tell you now. Huh, huh.
(Uh, huh, huh. Uh, huh, huh. Uh, huh, huh. Uh, huh, huh.
B♭m7
D♭/E♭
A♭
Woo, hoo, hoo.)
Verse
A♭
D♭
1. When I had you to my - self, I
2. Try - in' to live without your love is

Fm7 A♭maj7/C D♭ A♭
did - n't want you a - round. __ Those pret - ty fac - es al - ways make _ you
one long sleep-less night. __ Let me show _ you, girl, that
B♭m7 E♭ A♭ D♭
stand out in a crowd. ___ But some - one picked you from _ the bunch _ when a
I know wrong from right. ___ Ev - 'ry street you walk _ on, ___ I leave
Fm7 A♭maj7/C D♭ A♭
glance was all it took. __ But now _ it's much too late _ for me ___ to
tear stains on the ground. _ Fol - low - in' the girl _ I didn't
Chorus
B♭m7 D♭/E♭ A♭ A♭ E♭/G Fm7 E♭
take a sec - ond look. _ Oh, ___ ba - by, give _ me one _ more chance... _
e - ven want a - round. __ Let me tell you now. Oh, ___ ba - by, all __ I need _ is one ___

2nd time, Bass: w/ Bass Fill 1
D♭
D♭/C
B♭m7
E♭
Fm7
Cm7
D♭
A♭
more chance.
(To show you that I love you.)
Won't you please let
B♭m7
D♭/E♭
A♭
E♭/G
Fm7
E♭
me back in your heart.
Oh, dar - lin', I was blind to
To Coda
D♭
D♭/C
B♭m7
E♭
Fm7
Cm7
D♭
A♭
B♭m7 D♭/E♭
A♭
let you go,
(Let you go, ba - by.)
but now since I've seen you in his arms,...
Oh,
(... I want you back!
Bass Fill 1

I do, now.
I want you back!
Ooh, ooh, ba - by.
I want you back!
Yeah,
yeah, yeah, yeah.
I want you back!)
Na, na, na, na.
D.S. al Coda
Coda
Fm7 Cm7 D♭ A♭
Bridge
N.C.
now since I've seen you
in his arms.
Uh, huh.
(Ba, ba, bum, bum, ba, bum, ba, bum, bum.)
*Voc. Fig. 1
End Voc. Fig. 1
*Down stemmed part only.
Bkgd. Voc.: w/ Voc. Fig. 1 (7 times)
Voc. Fig. 2
End Voc. Fig. 2
(Ba, ba, bum, ba, bum, ba, bum, ba, bum, bum. Ba, bum,)

Bkgd. Voc.: w/ Voc. Fig. 2
Voc. Fig. 3
End Voc. Fig. 3
Bkgd. Voc.: w/ Voc. Fig. 3 (4 times)
(Ba, ba, bum, bum, bum.)
Uh, ba, bum, bum, bum. All I want.
Ba, ba, bum, bum, bum. All I need.
Ba, ba, bum, bum, bum. All I want!
Chorus
Ab Eb/G Fm7 Eb
Uh, ba, bum, bum, bum. All I need!
ba, bum, ba, bum, ba, bum, bum.
Oo, just one more
Db Db/C Bbm7 Eb
Fm7 Cm7 Db Ab
chance. Let me show you that I love you.
Ba - by! Ba - by!
Ba - by! Ba - by! Ba -

B♭m7
E♭
A♭
Ba - by!
by!
Ha!
I want you back!
For - get what hap - pened then,
and
E♭/G
Fm7
E♭
D♭
D♭/C
B♭m7
E♭
Oh, ba - by, I was blind to let you go!
But
let me live a - gain!
Fm7
Cm7
D♭
A♭
B♭m7
D♭/E♭
A♭
now I'm say - in' I, I've seen you in his arms.
I want you back!
Chu, ha!
Spare me of this cost,
For - get a - bout what I lost!

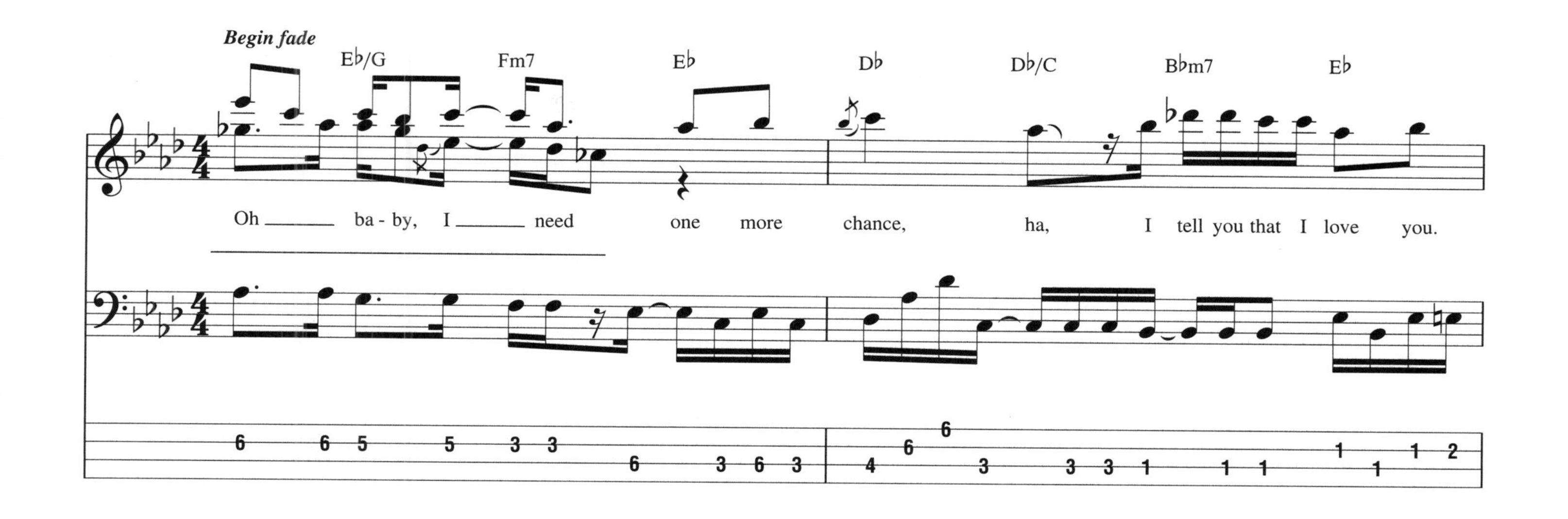
Begin fade
Eb/G Fm7 Eb Db Db/C Bbm7 Eb
Oh ba - by, I need one more chance, ha, I tell you that I love you.

Fm7 Cm7 Db Ab Bbm7 Db/Eb Ab
Ow! Ow! Ow! I want you back!
Ba - by! Ba - by! Ba - by! I want you back! For -

Fade out
Eb/G Fm7 Eb
Ha! Heh! I want you back! Oh. I want you back!
get what hap-pened then, and let me live a - gain!

I Want You
(She's So Heavy)

Words and Music by John Lennon and Paul McCartney

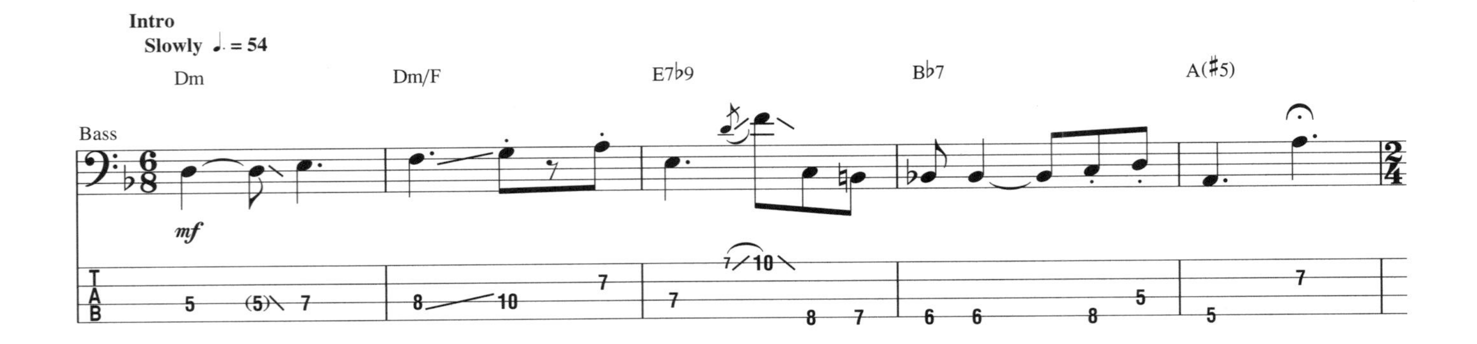
Intro
Slowly ♩. = 54
Dm
Dm/F
E7♭9
B♭7
A(♯5)
Bass
mf
5 (5) 7
8 10 7
7 7 10 8 7
6 6 8 5
5 7

Faster ♩ = 114
Half-time feel
Verse
N.C.
N.C.
Am7
N.C.
1. I want
you.
I want you so
bad.
5 5 5

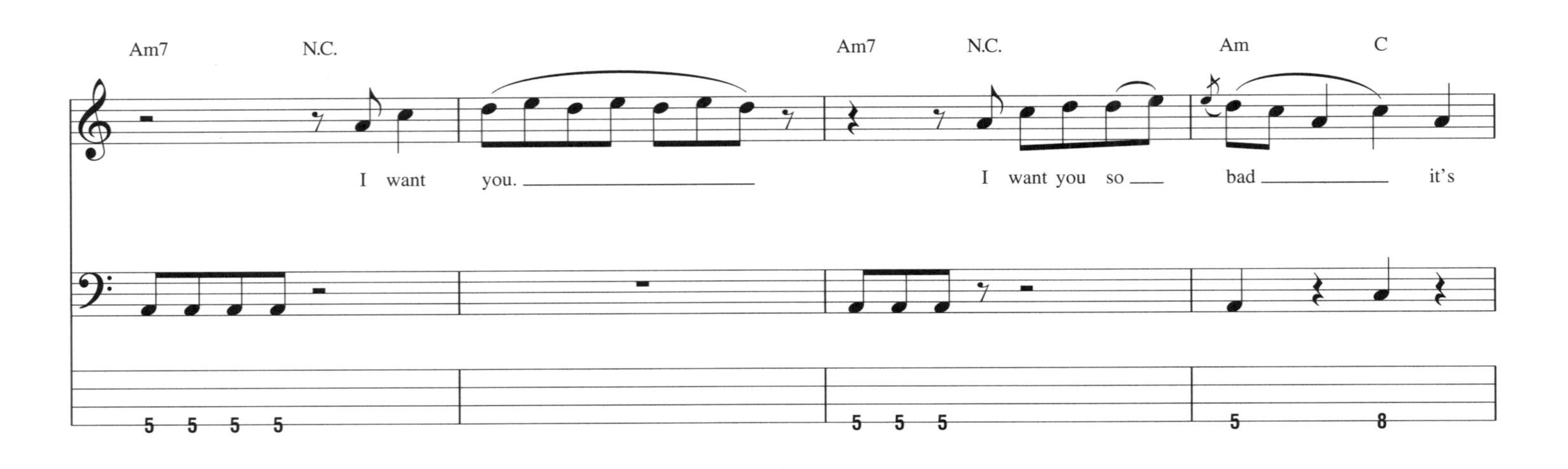
Am7
N.C.
Am7
N.C.
Am
C
I want
you.
I want you so
bad
it's
5 5 5 5
5 5 5
5 8

Dm F G Am7
driv - ing me mad, it's driv - ing me mad. I want

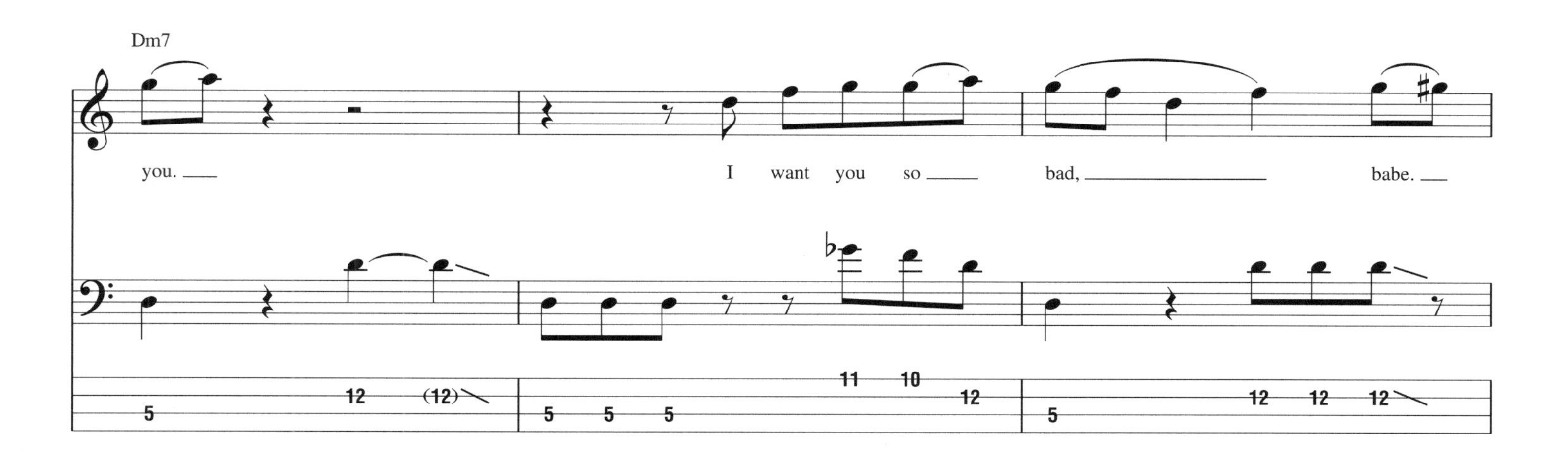
Dm7
you. I want you so bad, babe.

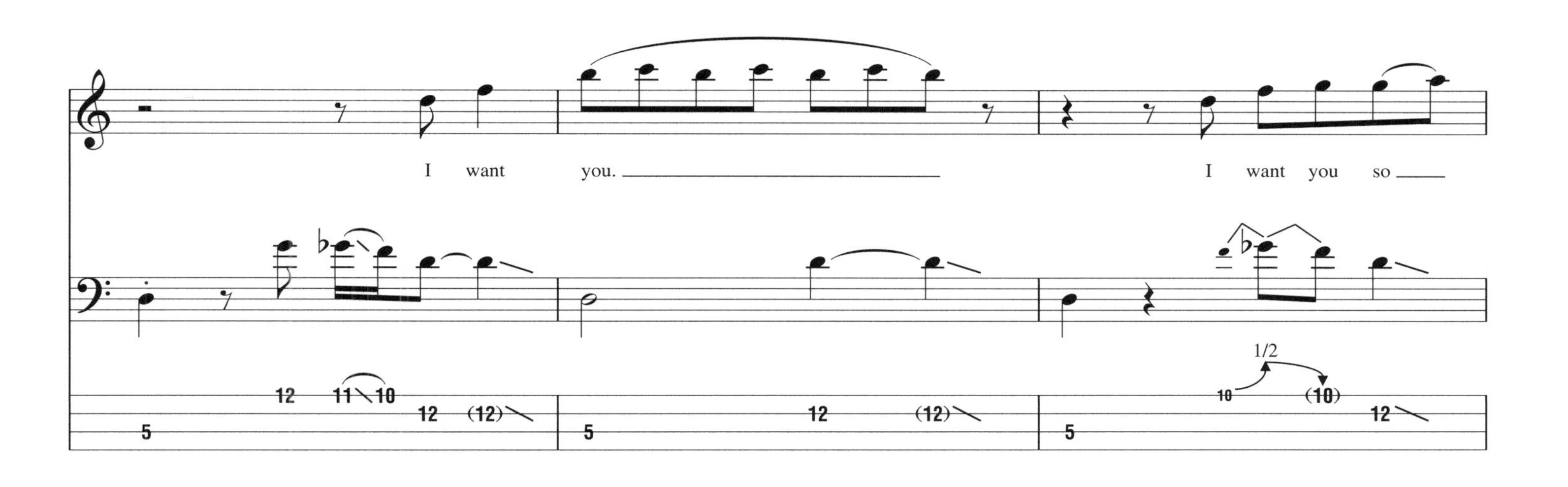
I want you. I want you so
1/2

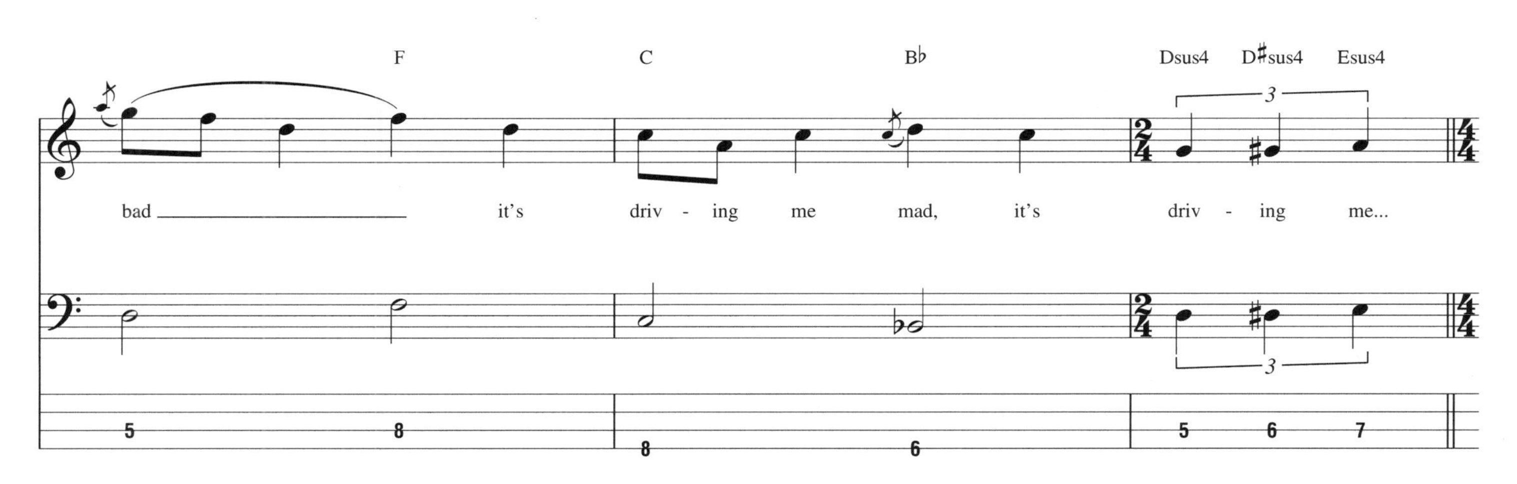
F C B♭ Dsus4 D♯sus4 Esus4
bad it's driv - ing me mad, it's driv - ing me...

Interlude
E7♭9
N.C.
E7♭9

N.C.
E7♭9
N.C.
2. I want

Verse
Am7
you.
I want you so
bad,
babe.

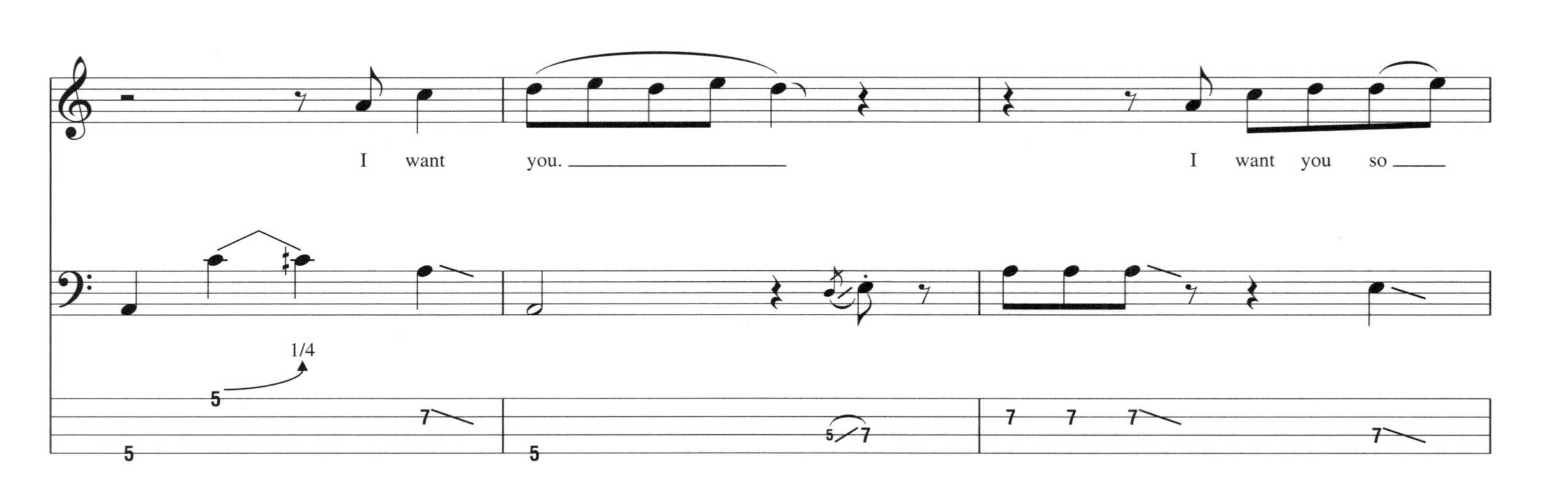

I want
you.
I want you so
1/4

Am
C
Dm
F
G
bad
it's
driv - ing
me
mad,
it's
driv - ing
me
Am7
Dm7
mad.
I
want
you.
I
want
you
so
bad.
I
want
you.
I
want
you
so
bad
it's
F

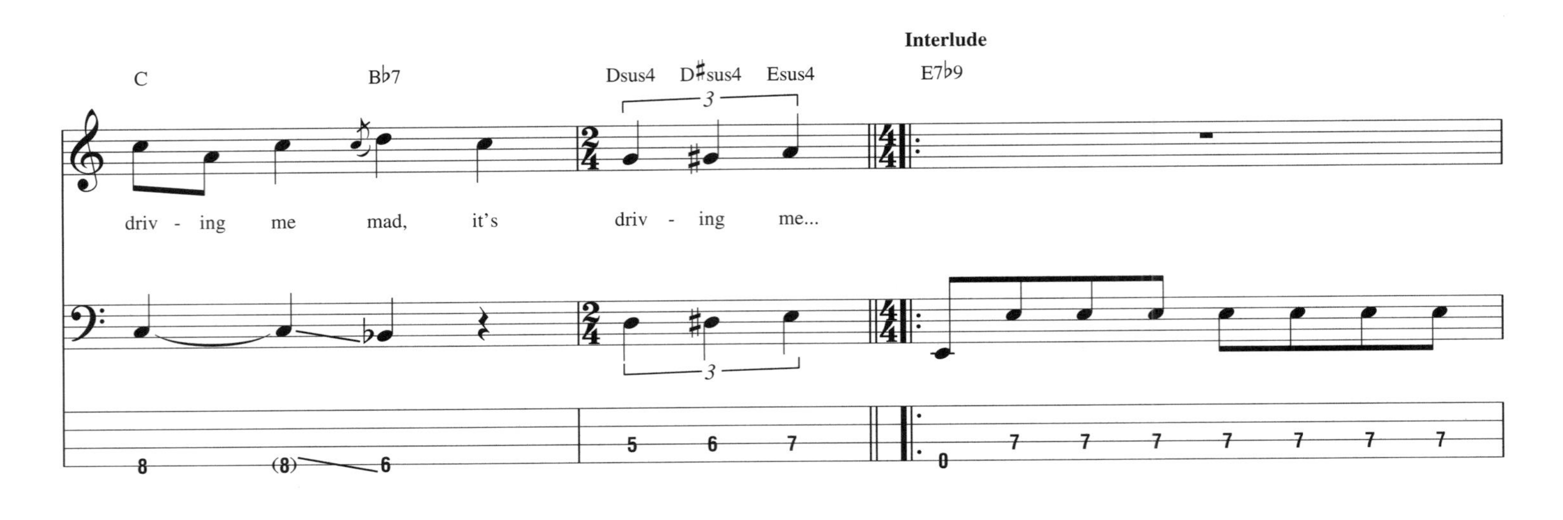
Interlude
C
B♭7
Dsus4
D♯sus4
Esus4
E7♭9
driv - ing me mad, it's driv - ing me...
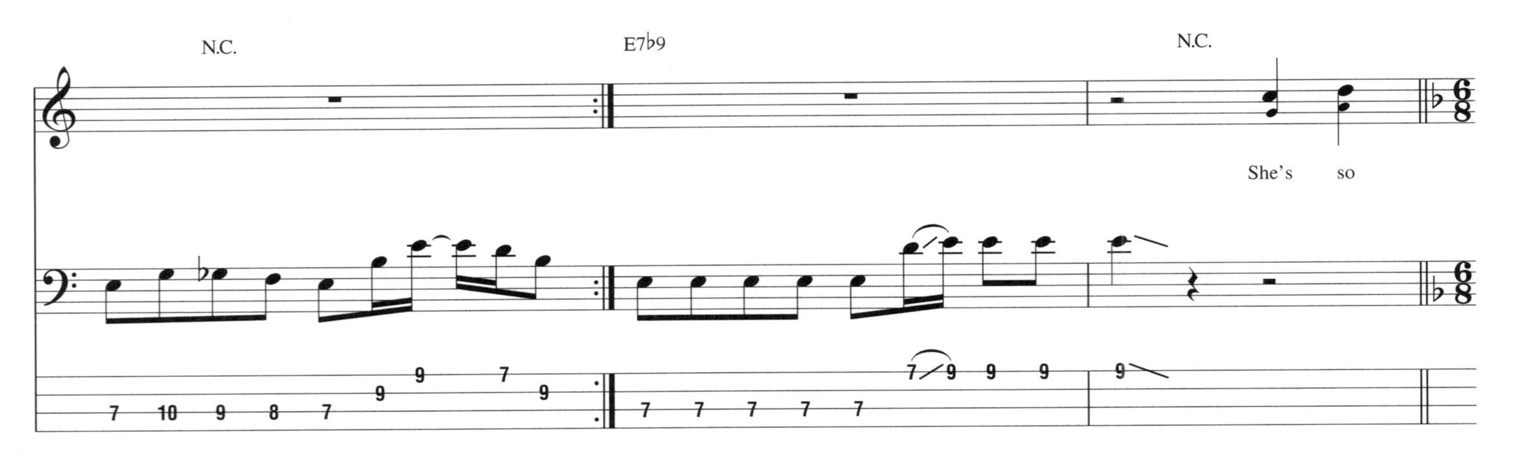
N.C.
E7♭9
N.C.
She's so
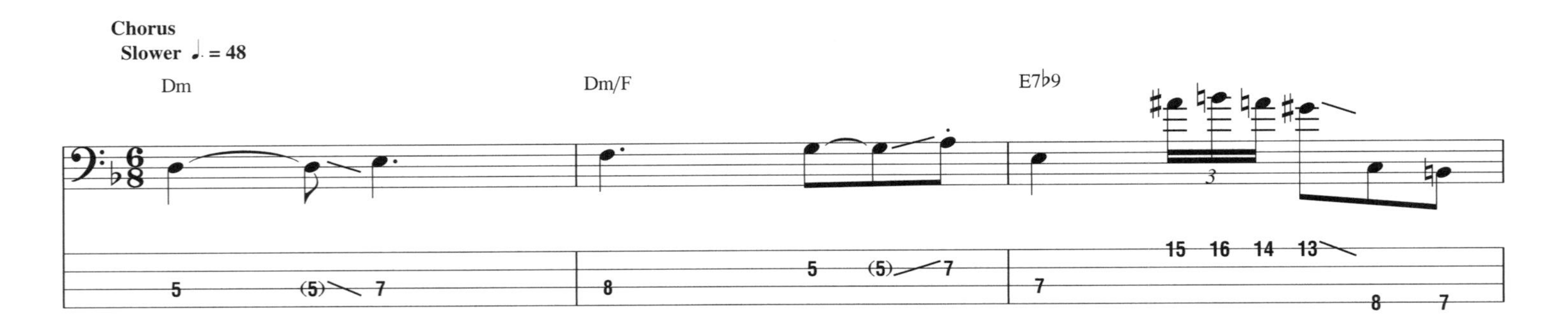
Chorus
Slower ♩. = 48
Dm
Dm/F
E7♭9
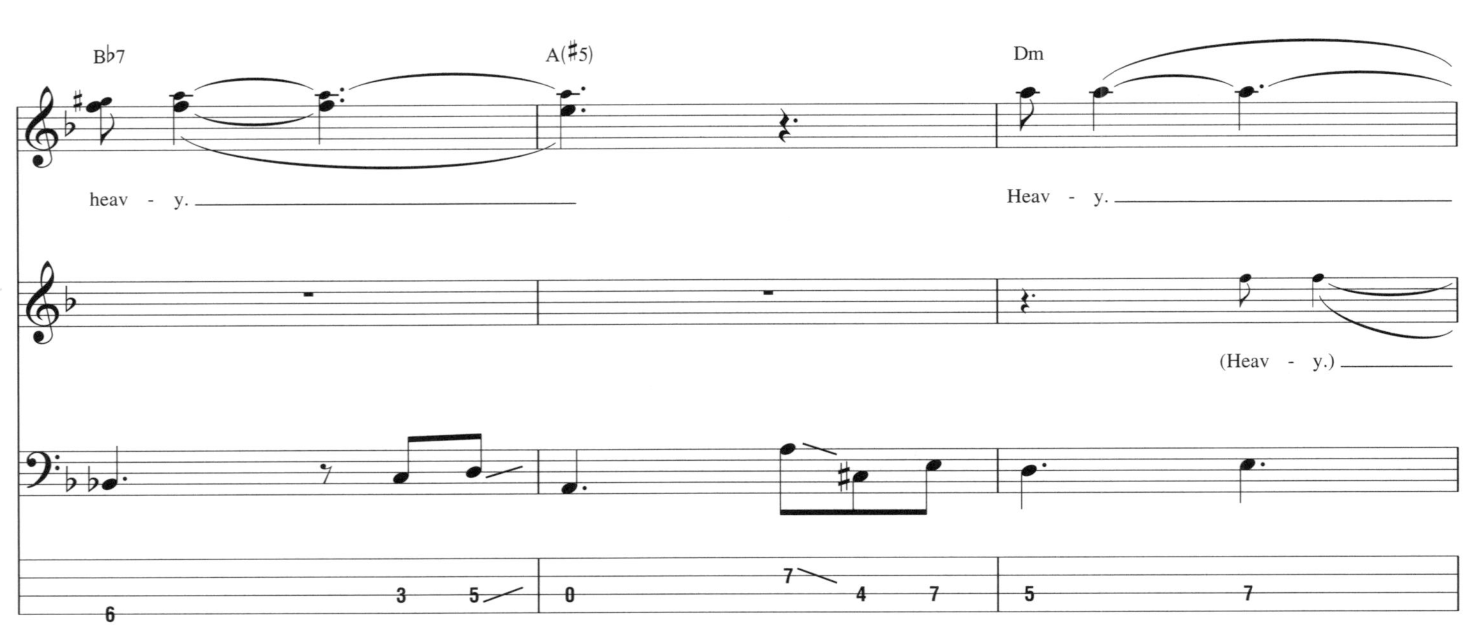
B♭7
A(♯5)
Dm
heav - y.
Heav - y.
(Heav - y.)

Dm/F
E7♭9
B♭7
(Heav - y.)
8va
loco
3
A(♯5)
Faster ♩ = 110
N.C.
Guitar Solo
Am7
C
Dm
F
G
Am7

Dm7

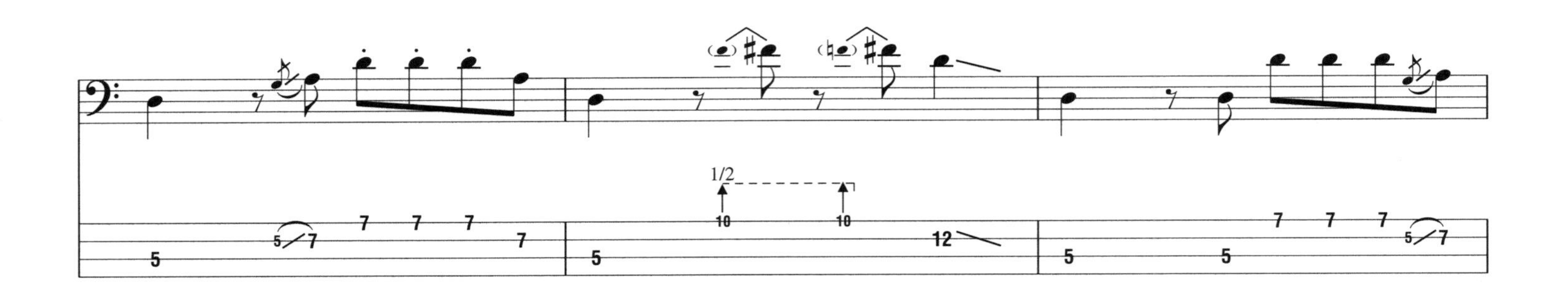
1/2

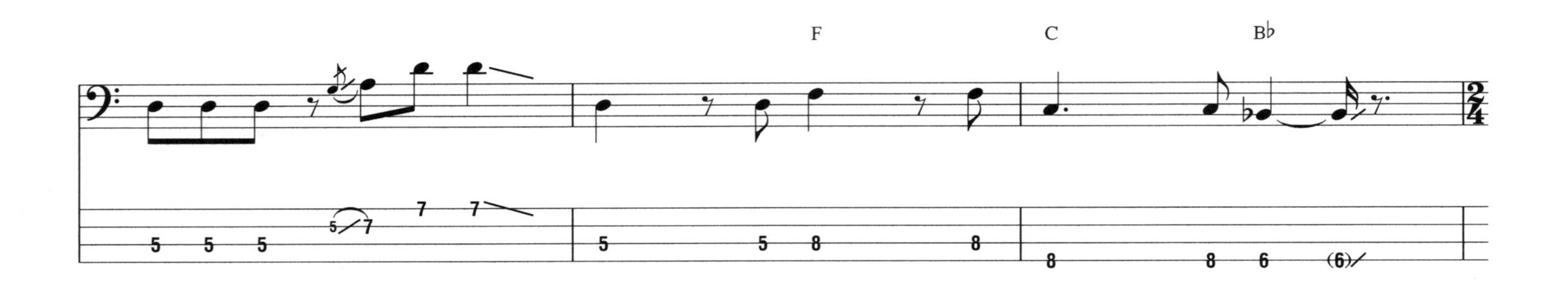
F
C
B♭

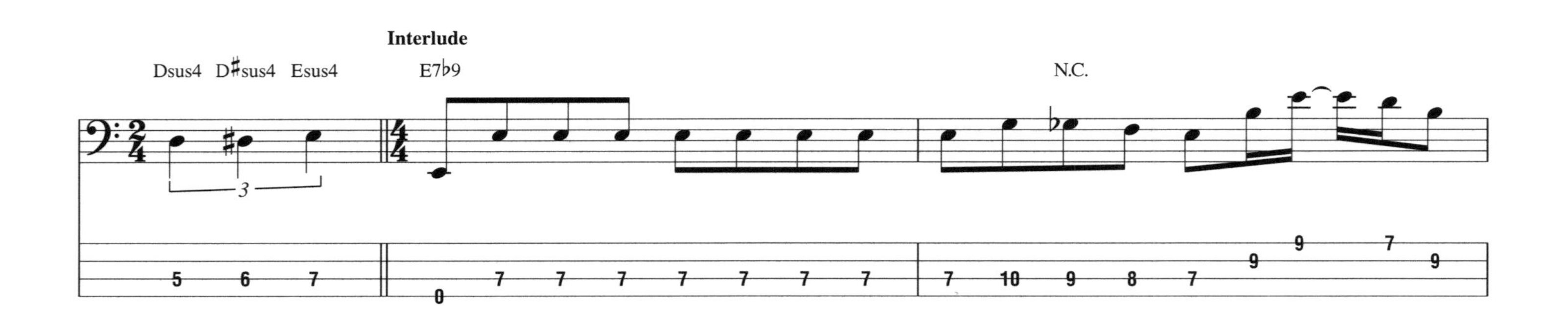
Interlude
Dsus4 D♯sus4 Esus4
E7♭9
N.C.

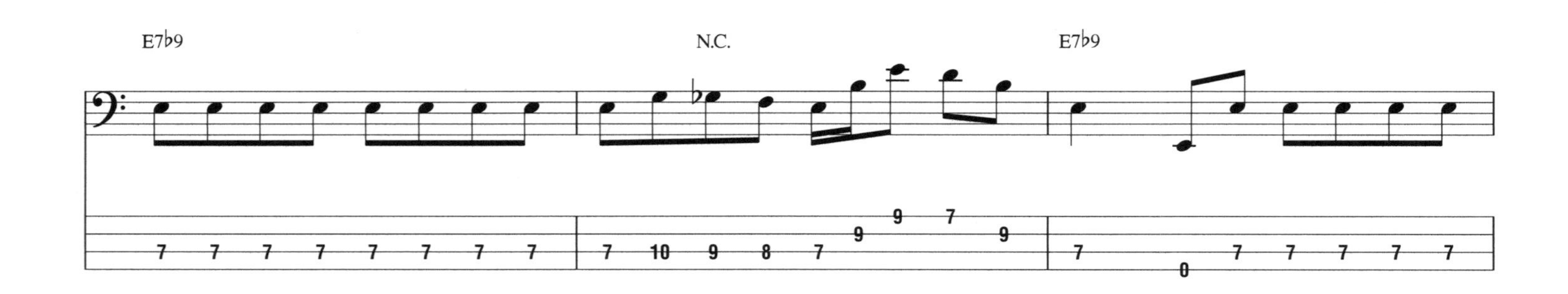
E7♭9
N.C.
E7♭9

Chorus
Slower ♩. = 48
N.C.
Dm
Dm/F
She's
so

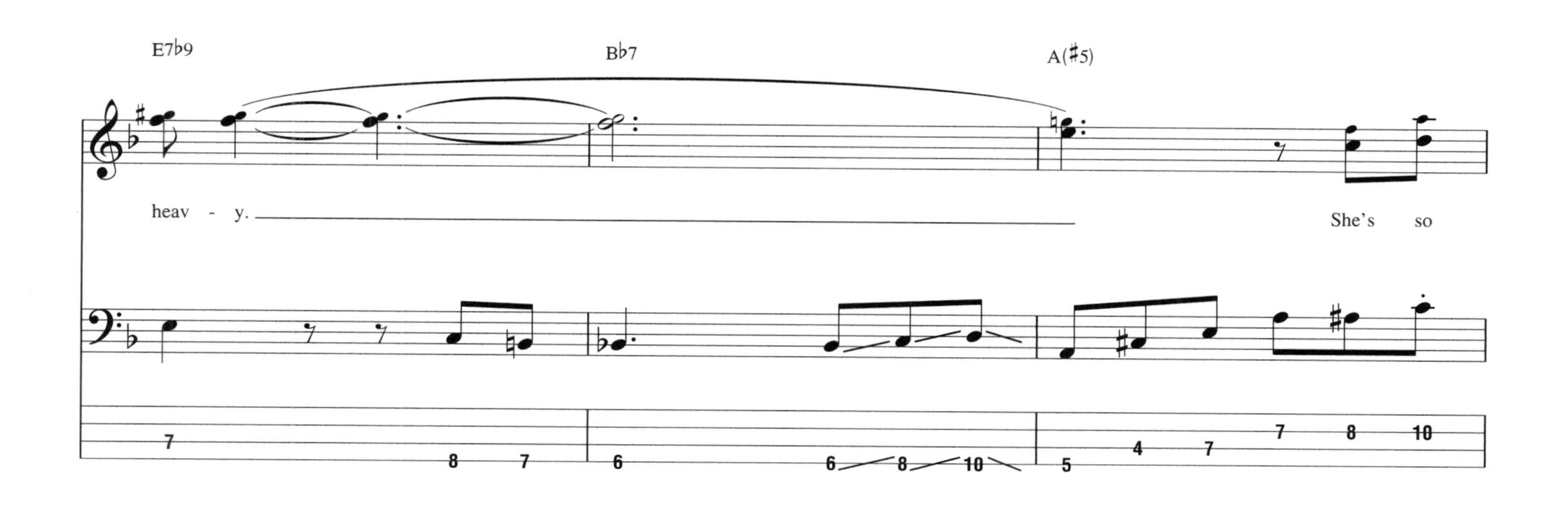
E7♭9
B♭7
A(♯5)
heav - y.
She's
so

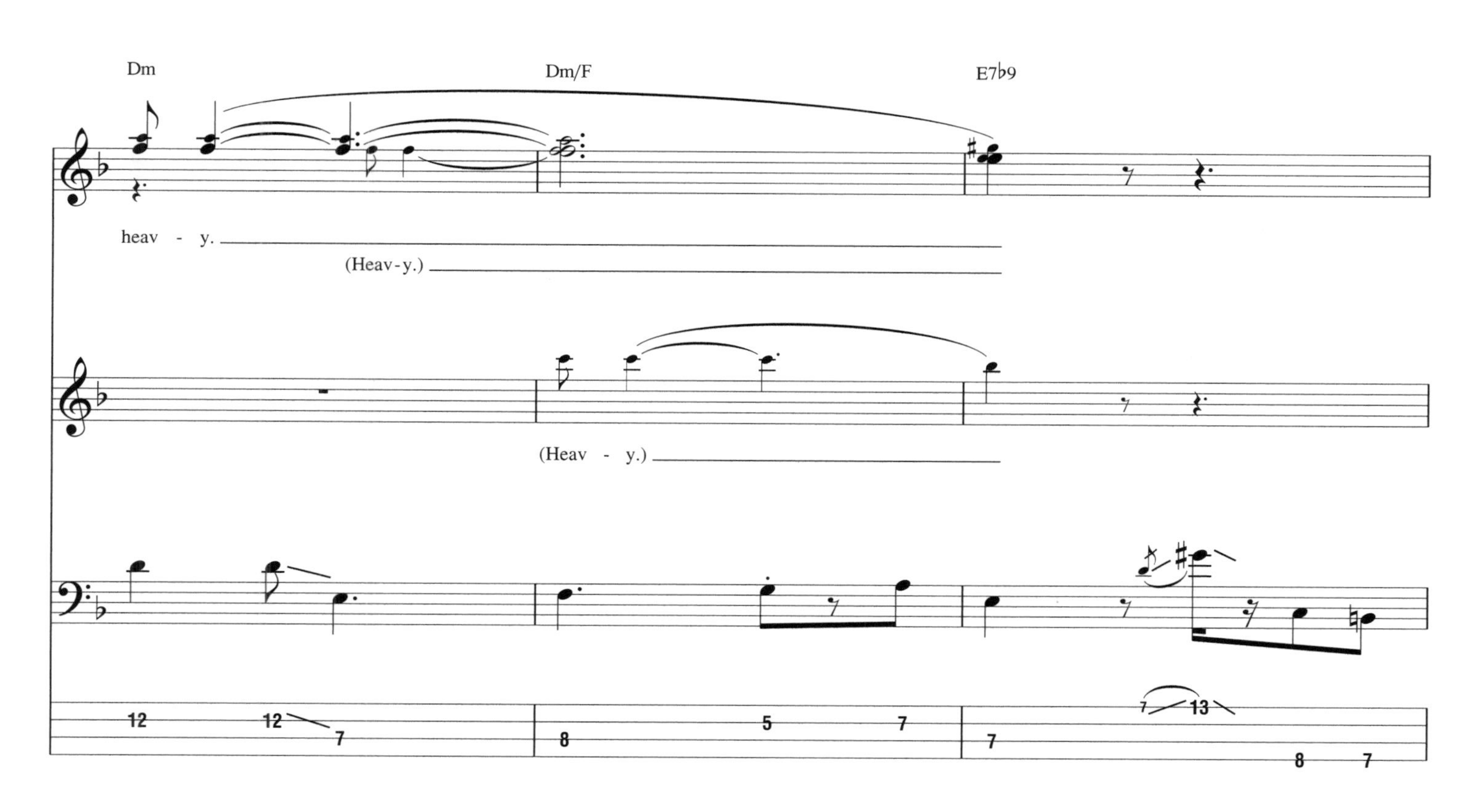
Dm
Dm/F
E7♭9
heav - y.
(Heav-y.)
(Heav - y.)

Faster ♩ = 116
B♭7
A(♯5)
N.C.
3. I want
Verse
Am7
you.
I want you so
bad.
I want
you.
I want you so

C
Dm
F
G
bad
it's
driv - ing me
mad,
it's
driv - ing me
1/2

Am7
mad.
I want
let ring
15 14 13 12 11 11 10 9 8 7 6 5 3 2
5 5 5 7 5 5 5 7
0

Dm7
you.
You know I want you so
bad,
babe.

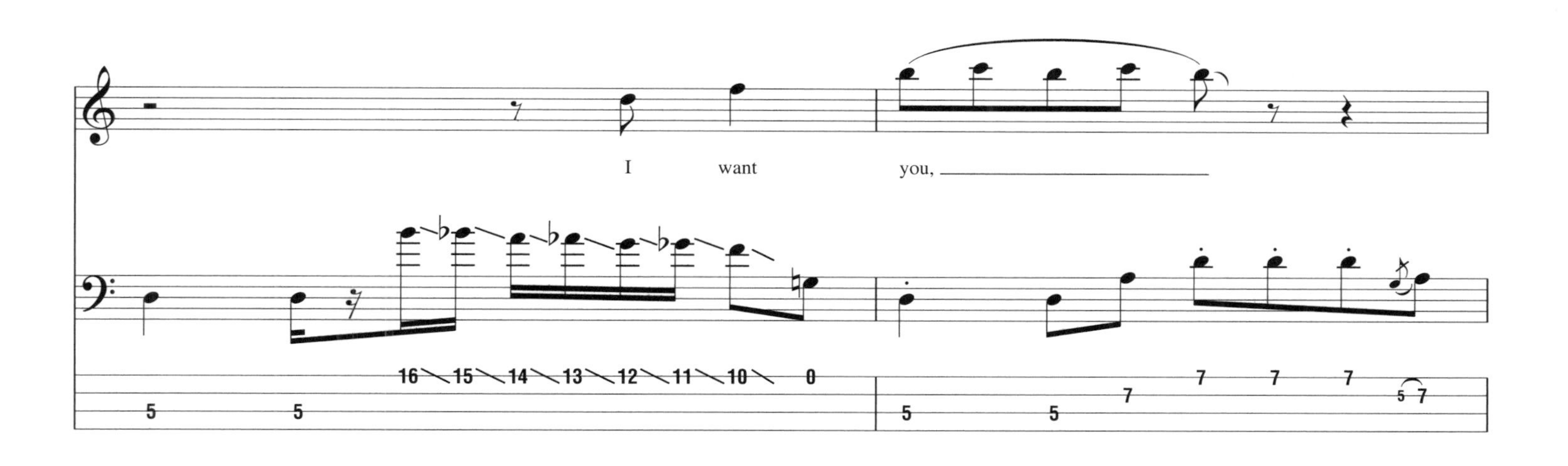
I want you,
16 15 14 13 12 11 10 0

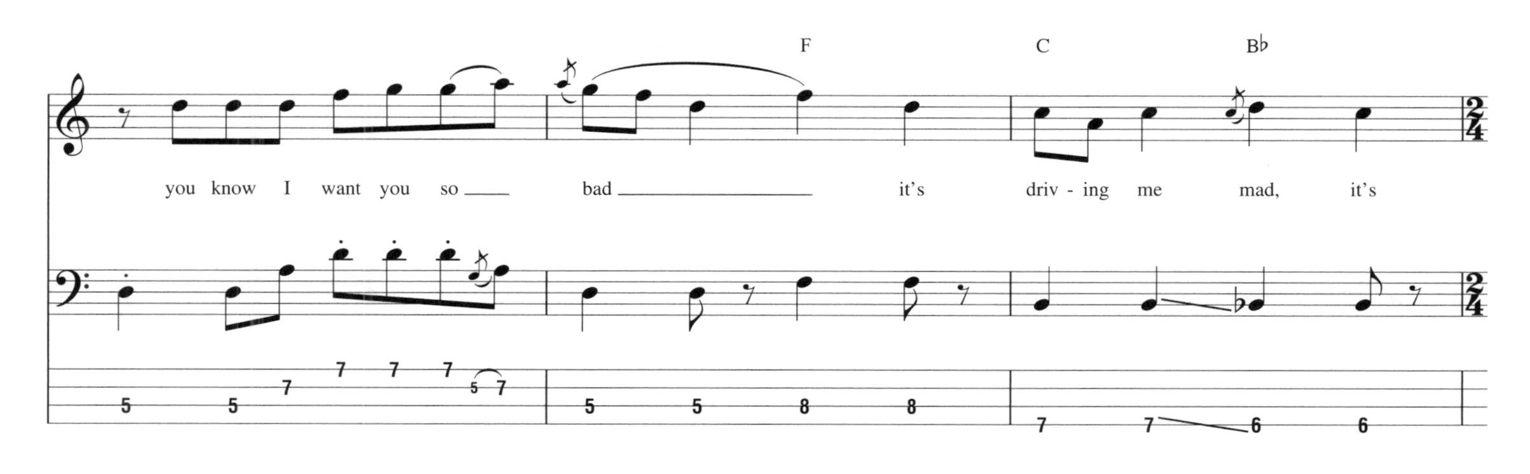
F C B♭
you know I want you so
bad
it's driv - ing me mad, it's

Interlude
Dsus4 D♯sus4 Esus4
E7♭9
N.C.
driv - ing me mad.
Yeah!
She's so...
Outro
Slower ♩. = 48
Dm
Dm/F
B♭7
A(♯5)
steady gliss.

A(♯5)
Dm
steady gliss.
Dm/F
E7♭9
B♭7
A(♯5)
Dm
Dm/F
E7♭9
B♭7
A(♯5)
Dm
Dm/F
E7♭9
B♭7
A(♯5)
8va
loco
Dm
Dm/F
E7♭9
B♭7

A(♯5)
Dm
Dm/F
E7♭9
B♭7
A(♯5)
Dm
Dm/F
E7♭9
B♭7
A(♯5)
Dm
Dm/F
E7♭9
B♭7
A(♯5)
Dm
Dm/F
E7♭9
B♭7
steady gliss.
A(♯5)
steady gliss.
Dm
Dm/F

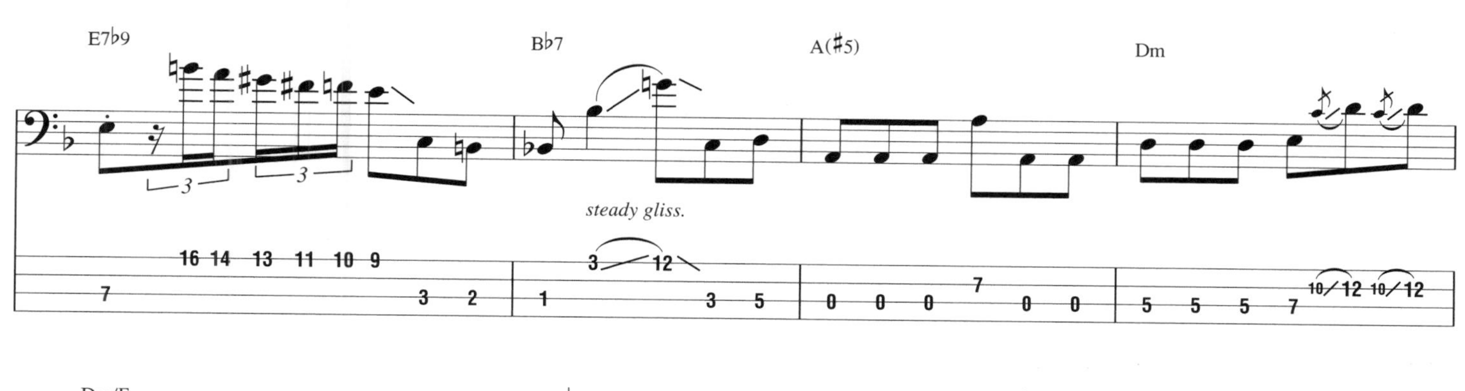
E7♭9
B♭7
A(♯5)
Dm
steady gliss.

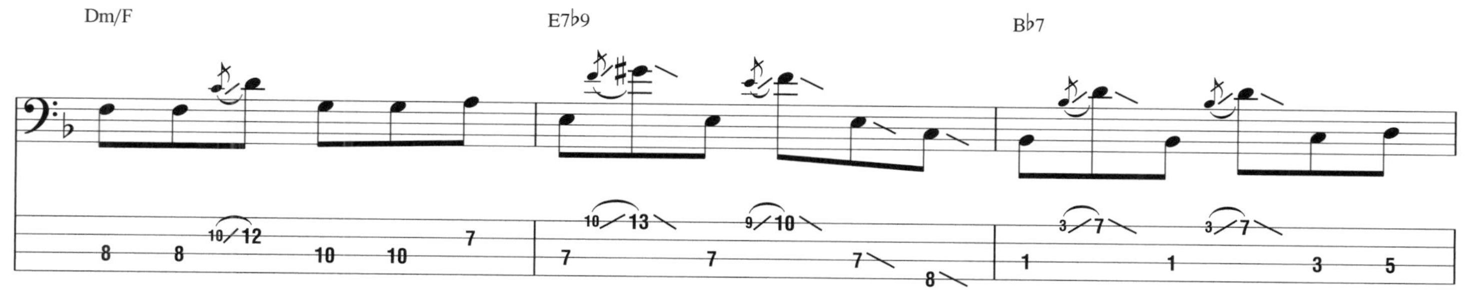
Dm/F
E7♭9
B♭7

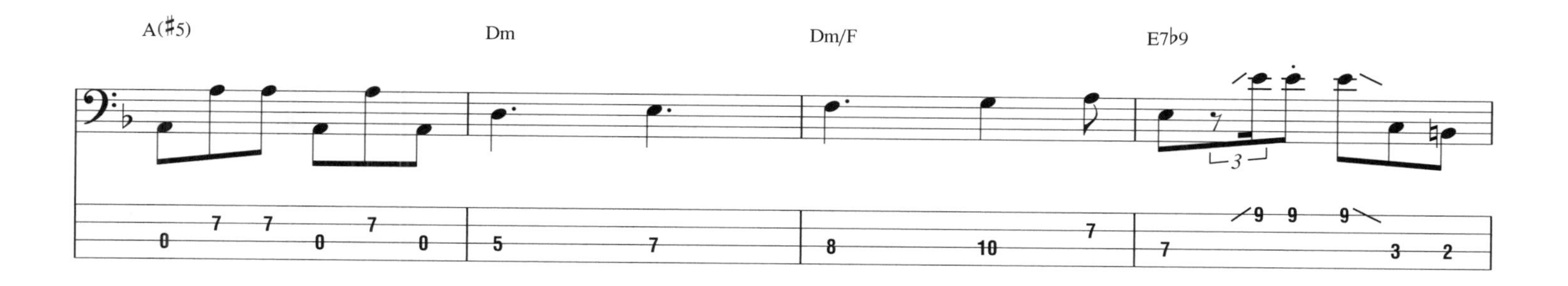
A(♯5)
Dm
Dm/F
E7♭9

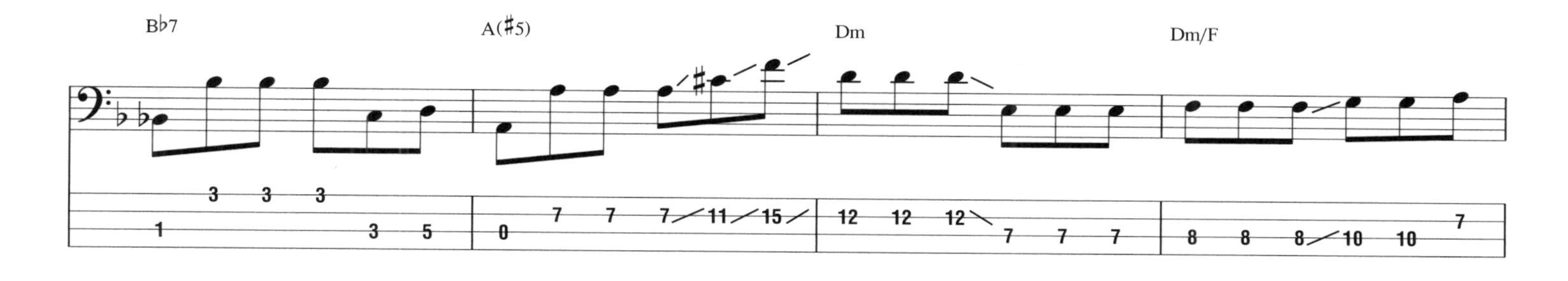
B♭7
A(♯5)
Dm
Dm/F

E7♭9
B♭7
A(♯5)

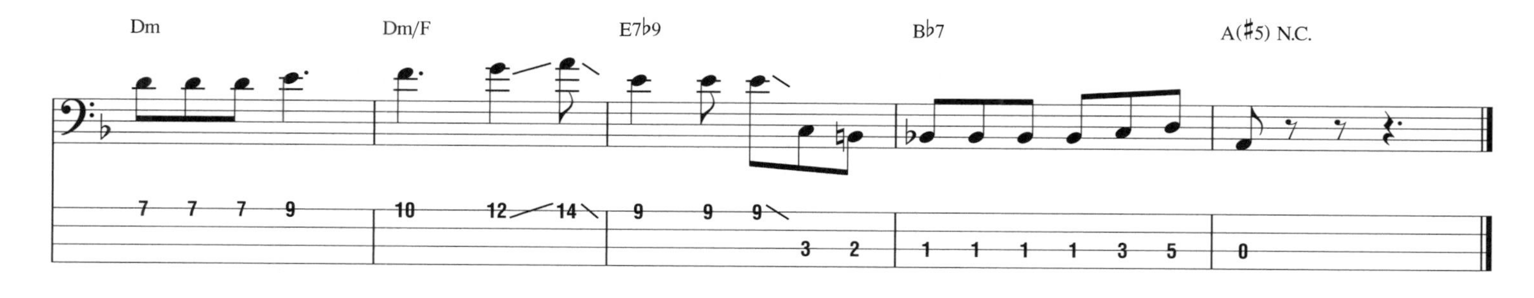
Dm
Dm/F
E7♭9
B♭7
A(♯5) N.C.

Just Got Paid

Words and Music by Billy F Gibbons and Bill Ham

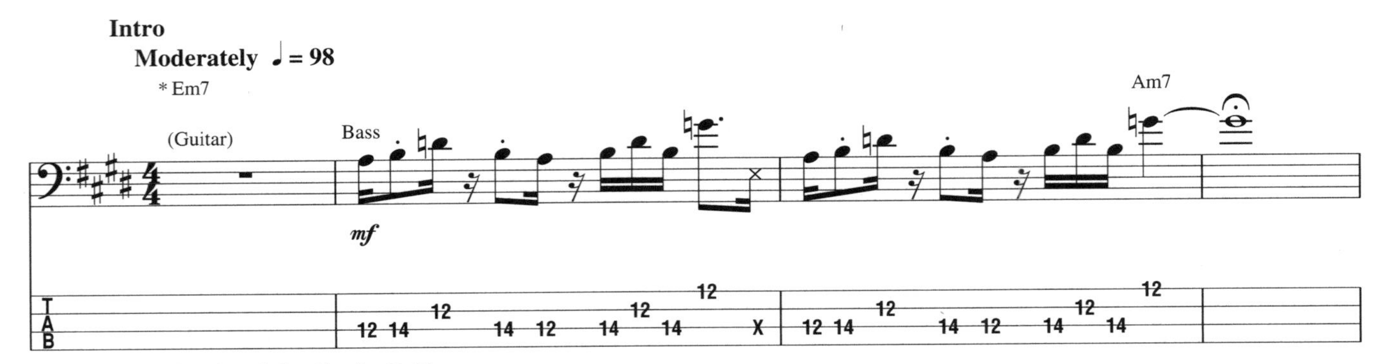
Intro
Moderately ♩ = 98
* Em7
(Guitar)
Bass
Am7
mf
T
A
B
12 14 12 14 12 14 12 14 12 X
12 14 12 14 12 14 12 14 12

*Chord symbols reflect implied harmony.

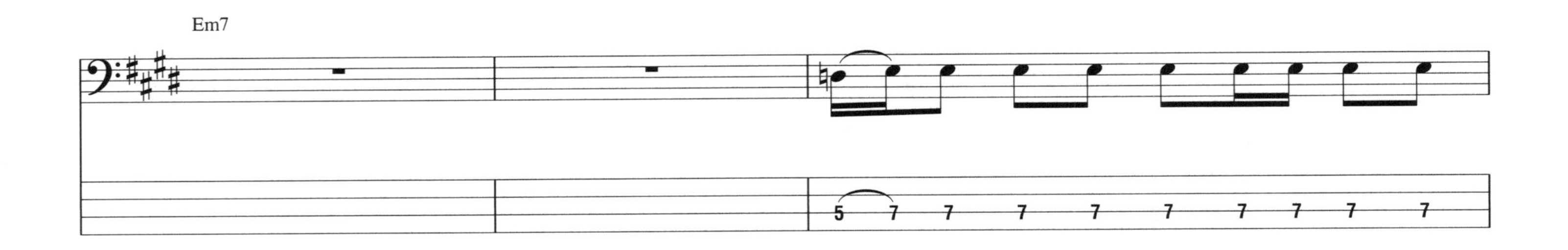
Em7
5 7 7 7 7 7 7 7 7 7

5 7 7 7 7 7 7 7 7 7
5 7 7 7 7 7 7 7 7 7
5 7 7 7 7 7 7 7 7 7

Verse
E
D
Em7
1. Just got paid to - day, got me a pock - et full of change.
Bass Fig. 1
7 7 7 7 7 7 7 7 7 7 7 7 7 7 7 7 7
5 5 5 5 5 5 5 5 5 5 5 5 5 5 5
5 7 7 7 7 7 7 7 7 7

E
D
Said I just got paid to - day, got me a pock - et full
Em7
G5
of change.
If you be - lieve like work - in' hard all day, just
A5
Em7
step on my shoes and take my pay.
End Bass Fig. 1
Verse
Bass: w/ Bass Fig. 1
E
D
Em7
2. I was born my pa - pa's son, when I hit the ground, I was on the run.
E
D
Had one glad hand and the oth - er be - hind. You can have yours, just give me mine.
Em7
G5
When the hound dog bark in the black of a night, stick my

A5
Em7
hand in my pock - et, ev - 'ry - thing's all right.
Bass
A5
Guitar Solo
A
E7
A
E7
A
E7
A
E7
Play 11 times
D
A7
D
A7
D
A7
D
A7
Interlude
E
mp
B5
ff

Em7
3. I

Verse
Bass: w/ Bass Fig. 1
E
D
Em7
just got paid to-day, got me a pock-et full of change. Said,

E
D
Em7
"Black sheep, black, do you got some wool?" "Yes, I do, man, my bag is full." It's the

G5
A5
Em7
root of e - vil and you know the rest, but it's way a - head of what's sec - ond best.

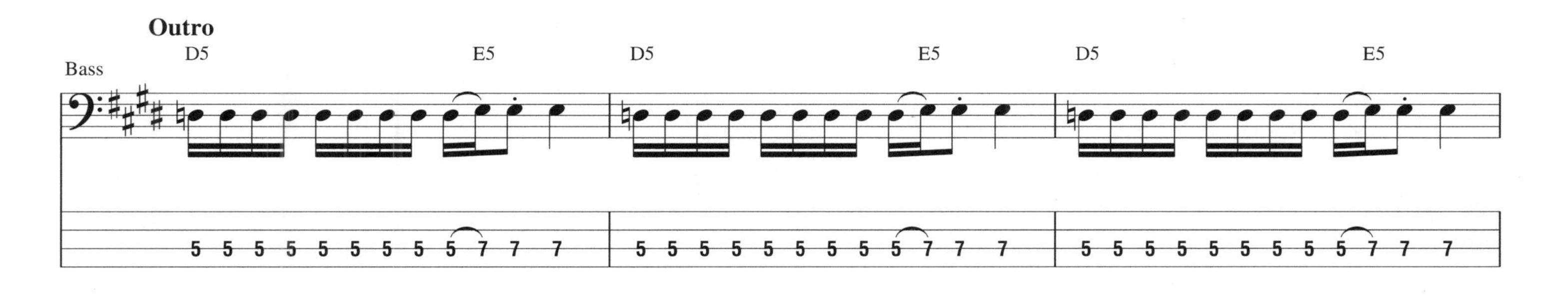

Outro
Bass
D5
E5
D5
E5
D5
E5

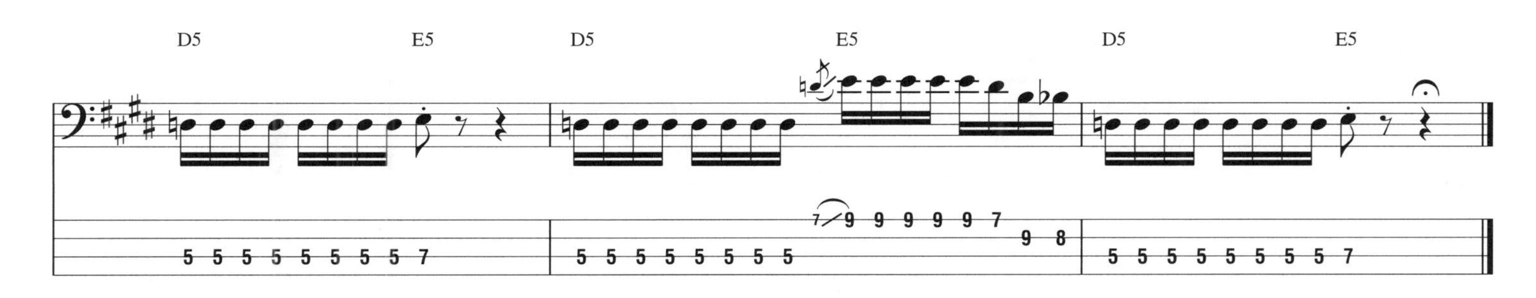

D5
E5
D5
E5
D5
E5

The Lemon Song

Words and Music by Chester Burnett, John Bonham, Jimmy Page, Robert Plant and John Paul Jones

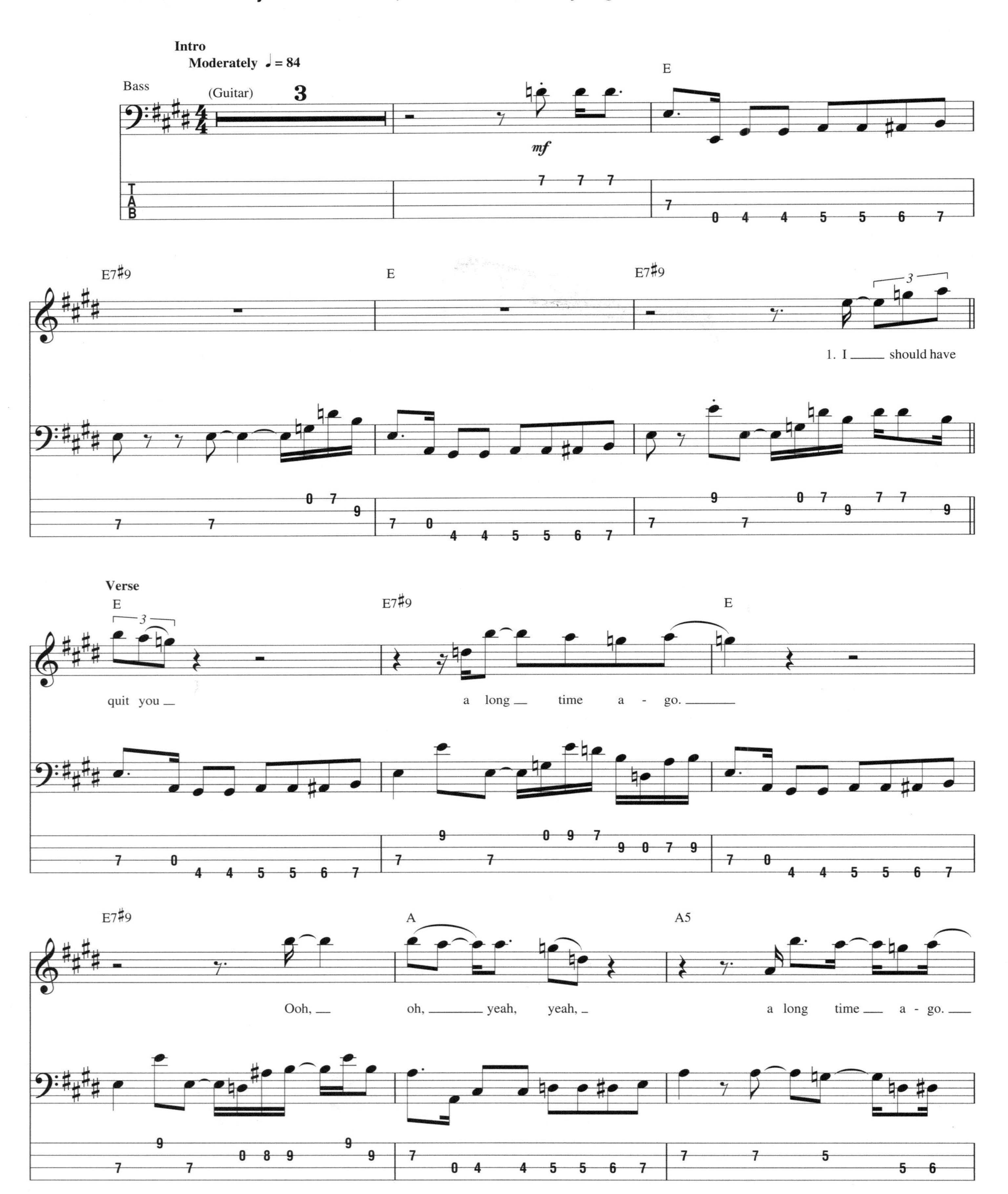

Intro
Moderately ♩ = 84
Bass
(Guitar)
3
mf
E
E7♯9
E
E7♯9
1. I should have
Verse
E
E7♯9
E
quit you
a long time a - go.
E7♯9
A
A5
Ooh,
oh, yeah, yeah,
a long time a - go.

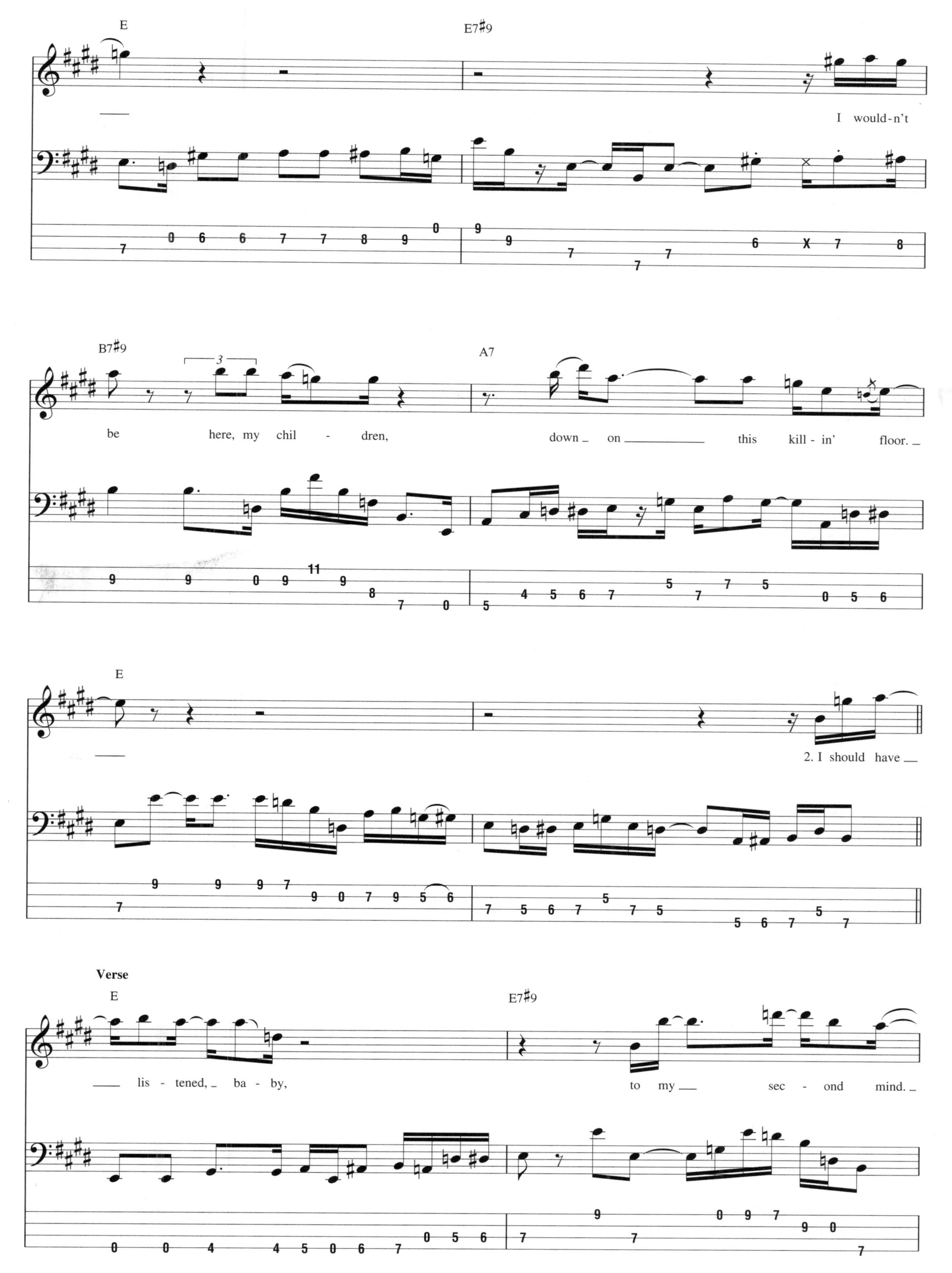
E
E7♯9
I would-n't
B7♯9
be here, my chil - dren,
A7
down on this kill - in' floor.
E
2. I should have
Verse
E
lis - tened, ba - by,
E7♯9
to my sec - ond mind.

E
E7#9
A
Oh.
I should have lis - tened, ba - by,
A5
E
E7#9
to my sec - ond mind.
B7#9
A7
Ev - 'ry time I go a - way and leave you, dar - lin',
you send me the blues way
E
Faster ♩ = 150
down the line.
No.

Guitar Solo
Double-time feel

E

A

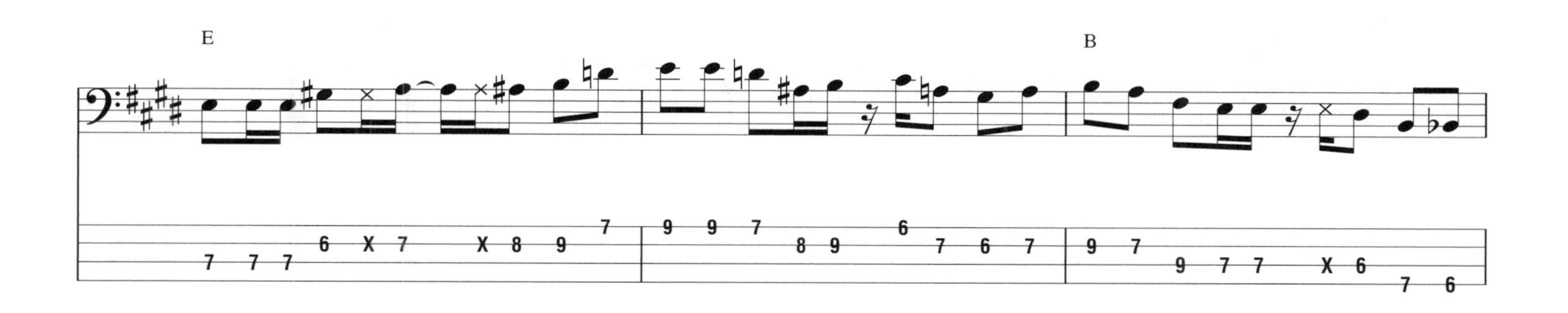
E
B

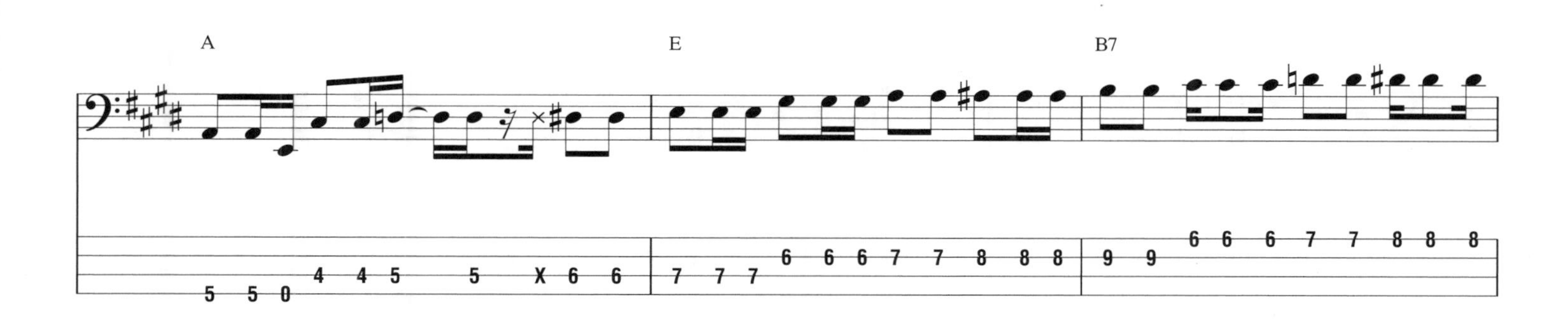
A
E
B7

E

A

E
B

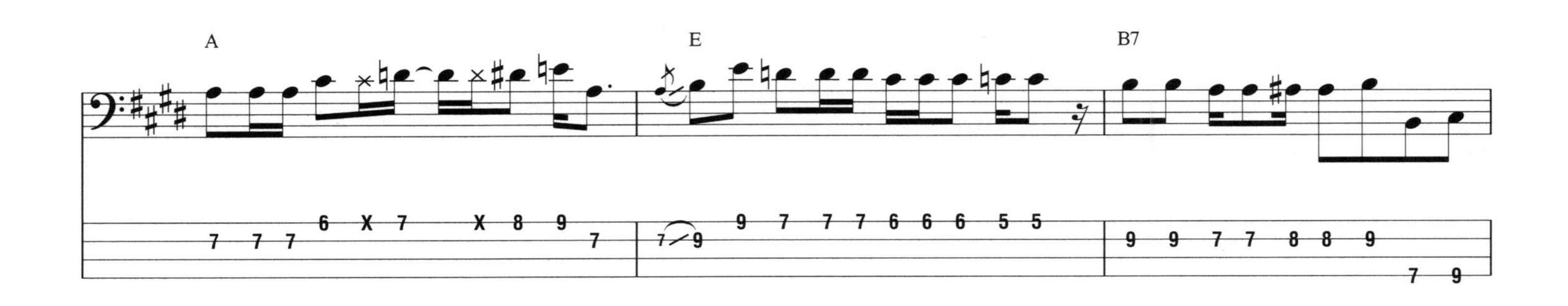
A
E
B7

E

A

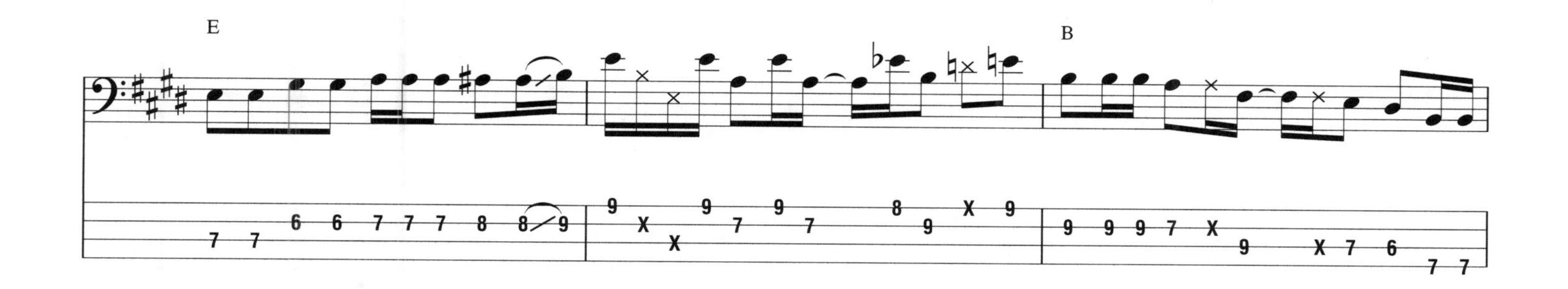
E
B

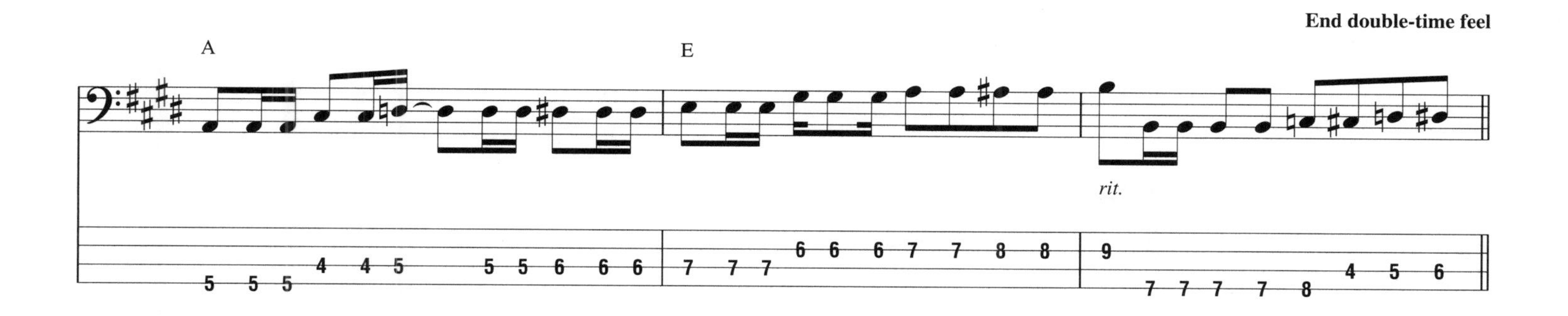
End double-time feel
A
E
rit.

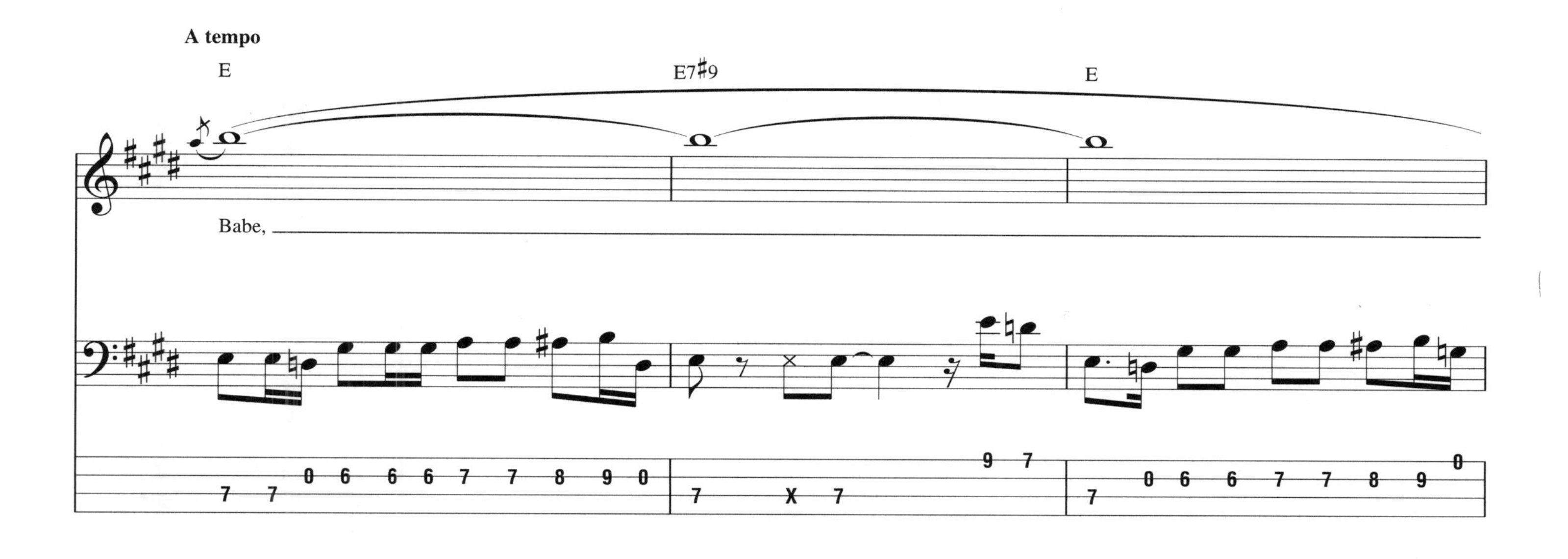
A tempo
E
E7#9
E
Babe,

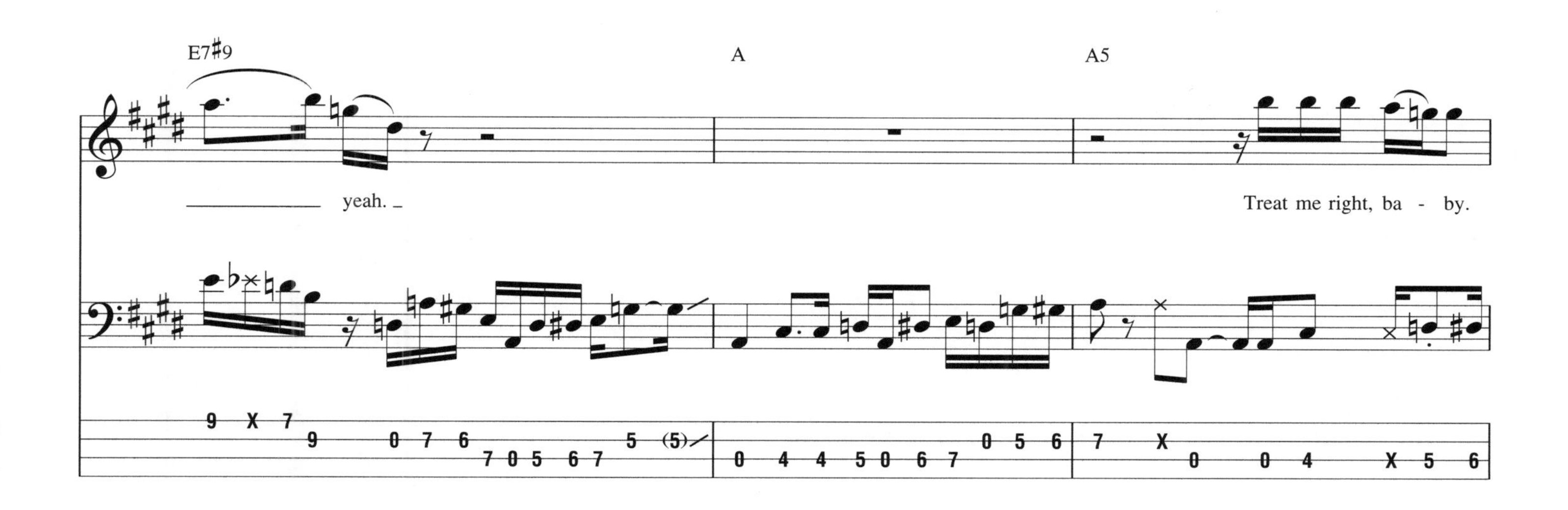
E7#9
A
A5
yeah.
Treat me right, ba - by.

E
E7♯9
B7♯9
Oh, oh, oh.
A7
E
My, my, my, my.
Spoken: Alright, take it down a little bit.
Verse
E
3. People tell me, baby, can't be satisfied.
Try to worry me, baby, but I never get you in my eyes, and...

A
People wor-ry, ba - by,
can't keep you sat - is -
E
fied.
Huh, let me tell ya,
B
babe,
oh, you ain't noth - in' but a, mm,
A
two - bit, no good
E
jive.

Verse
E
4. I went to sleep last night.
I worked as hard as I can.
I bring home my money, you take my money, give it to an-oth-er man.
I
A
should-'ve quit you, ba - by,
oh, such a long time
E
a - go,
oh.

B
A
I would-n't be here with all my trou-bles,
down on this kill-in'
E
floor.
Verse
E
5. Squeeze me, babe,
till the juice runs
down my leg.
Ooh.

A
Squeeze, squeeze me ba - by,
till the juice runs down my
E
leg.
B
The way you squeeze my lem - on, I,
A
I'm gon - na fall right out of bed,
E
bed, bed, bed.

Guitar Solo

E

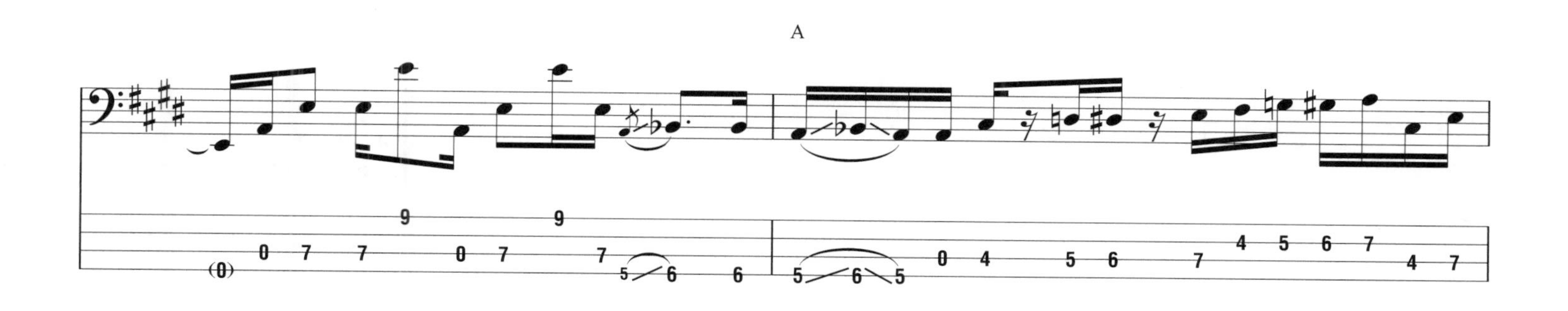
A

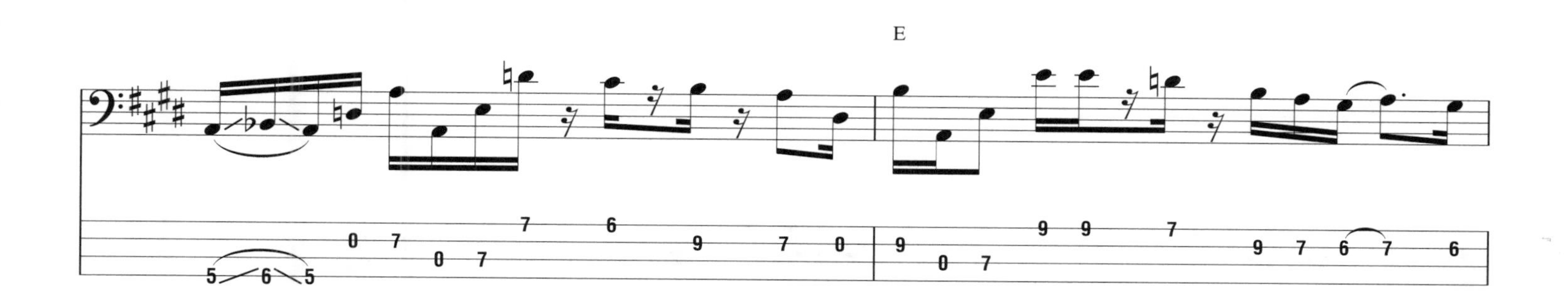
E

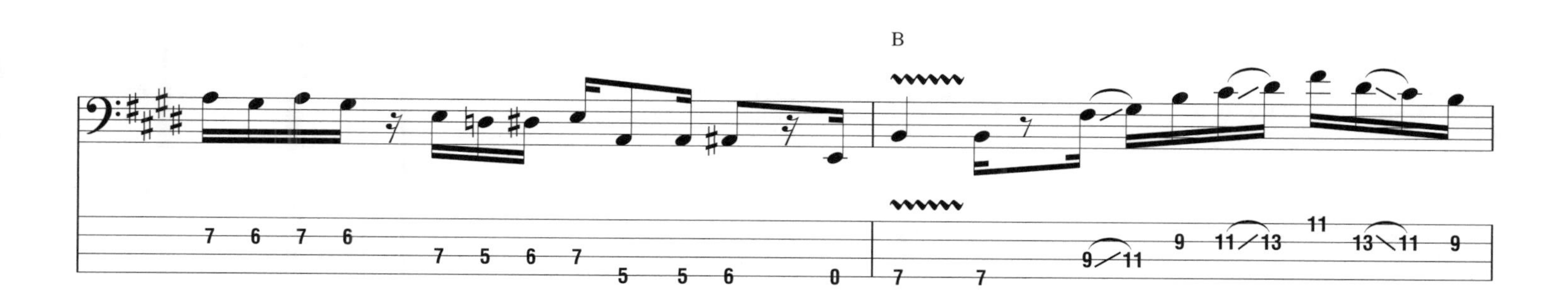
B

A
E

Hey.
Hey.
Hey,
hey.
Hey,
hey,
hey,
hey,
A
do.
Ba - by, ba - by, ba -
E
by, ba - by, ba - by, ba - by, ba - by, ba - by, ba - by, ba - by, ba - by.
B
Hey,
hey.
Oh,
hey,

A
E
Faster ♩ = 150
hey.
Uh,
oh.
Guitar Solo
Double-time feel
E
A
E
B
A
E
B7

E
2 2 0 0 2 0 3 2 1
0 0 0 4 4 4 5 5 5 6 7
7 7 6 X 7 X 8 9 7

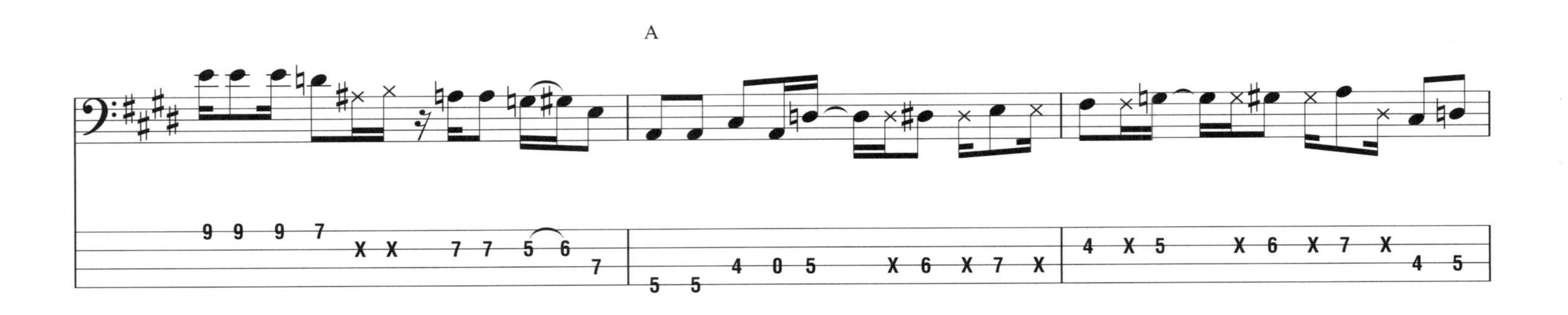
A
9 9 9 7 X X 7 7 5 6 7
5 5 4 0 5 X 6 X 7 X
4 X 5 X 6 X 7 X 4 5

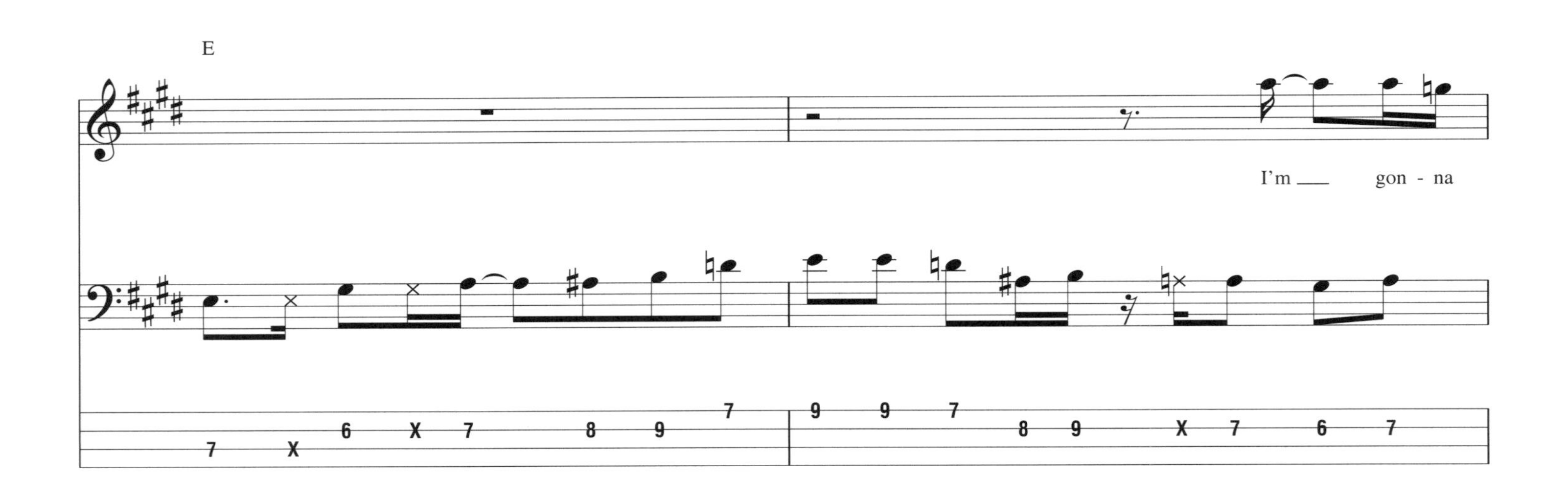
E
I'm gon - na
7 X 6 X 7 8 9 7
9 9 7 8 9 X 7 6 7

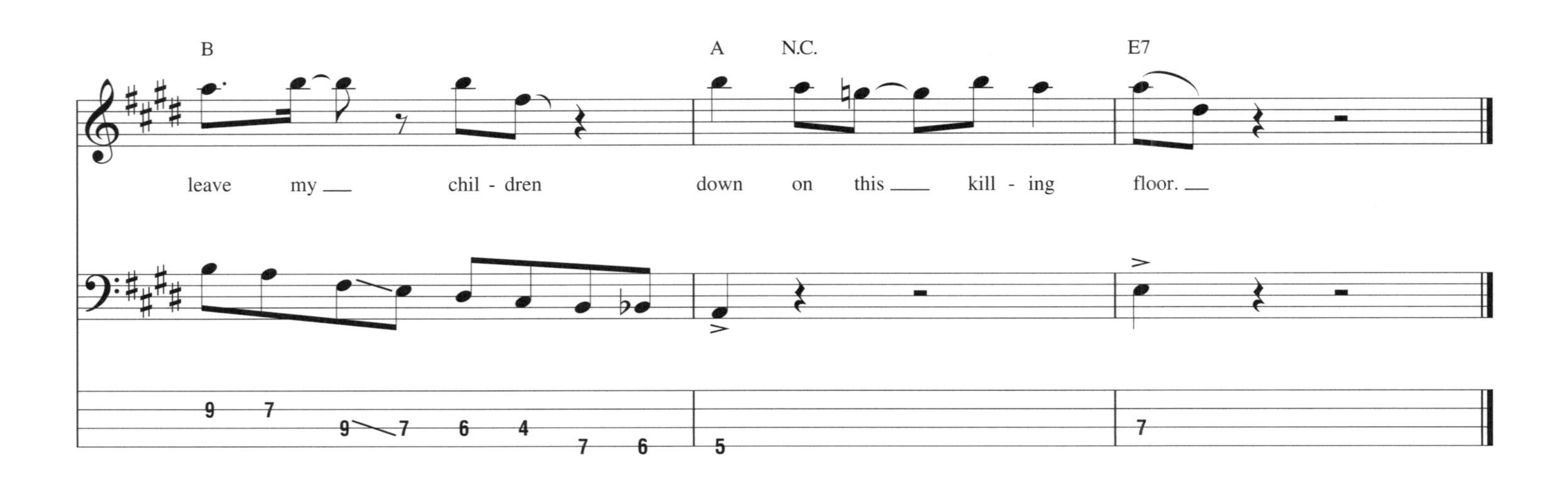
B
A N.C.
E7
leave my chil - dren down on this kill - ing floor.
9 7 9 7 6 4 7 6
5
7

Livin' on a Prayer

Words and Music by Jon Bon Jovi, Desmond Child and Richie Sambora

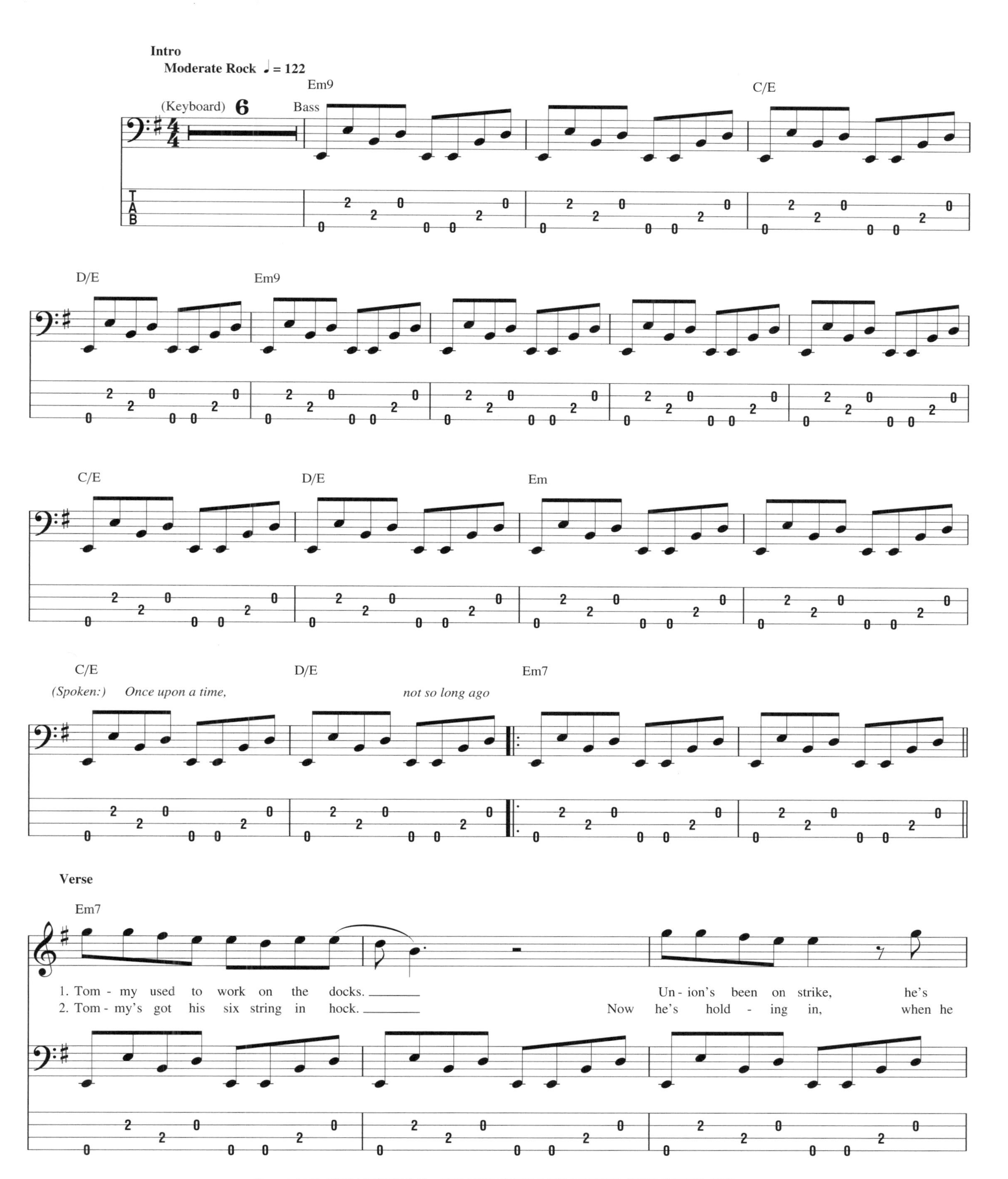

Intro
Moderate Rock ♩ = 122
Em9
(Keyboard) 6
Bass
C/E
D/E
Em9
C/E
D/E
Em
C/E
D/E
Em7
(Spoken:) Once upon a time,
not so long ago
Verse
Em7
1. Tom - my used to work on the docks.
Un - ion's been on strike, he's
2. Tom - my's got his six string in hock.
Now he's hold - ing in, when he

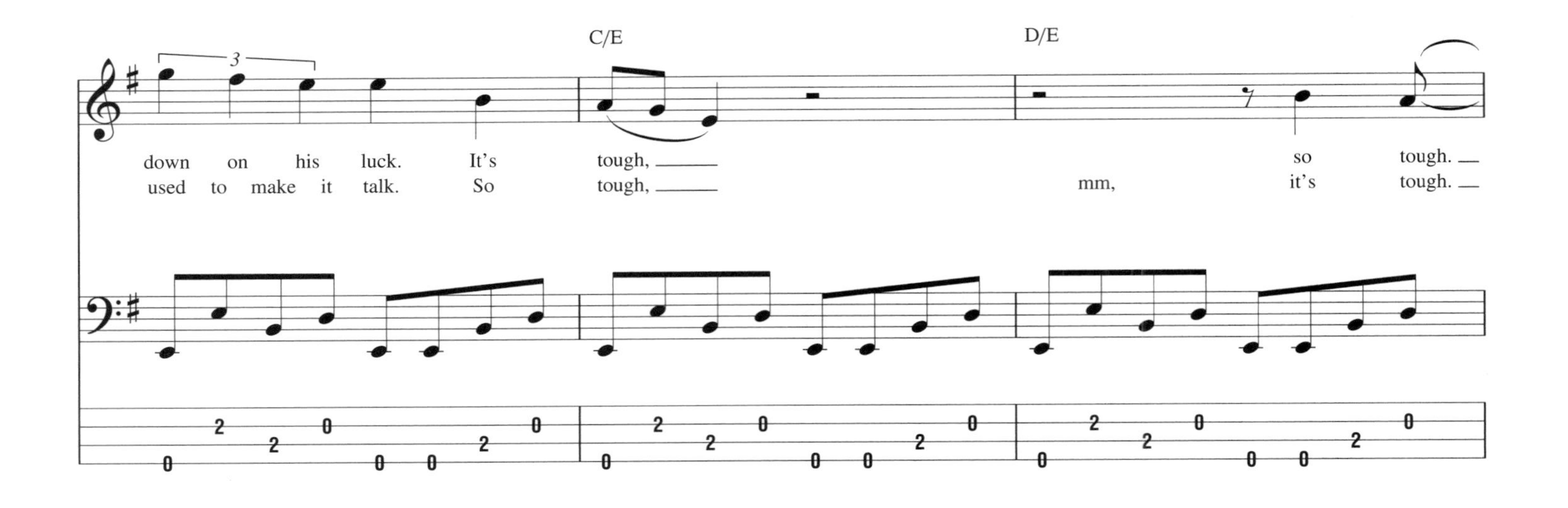
C/E
D/E
down on his luck. It's tough, so tough.
used to make it talk. So tough, mm, it's tough.

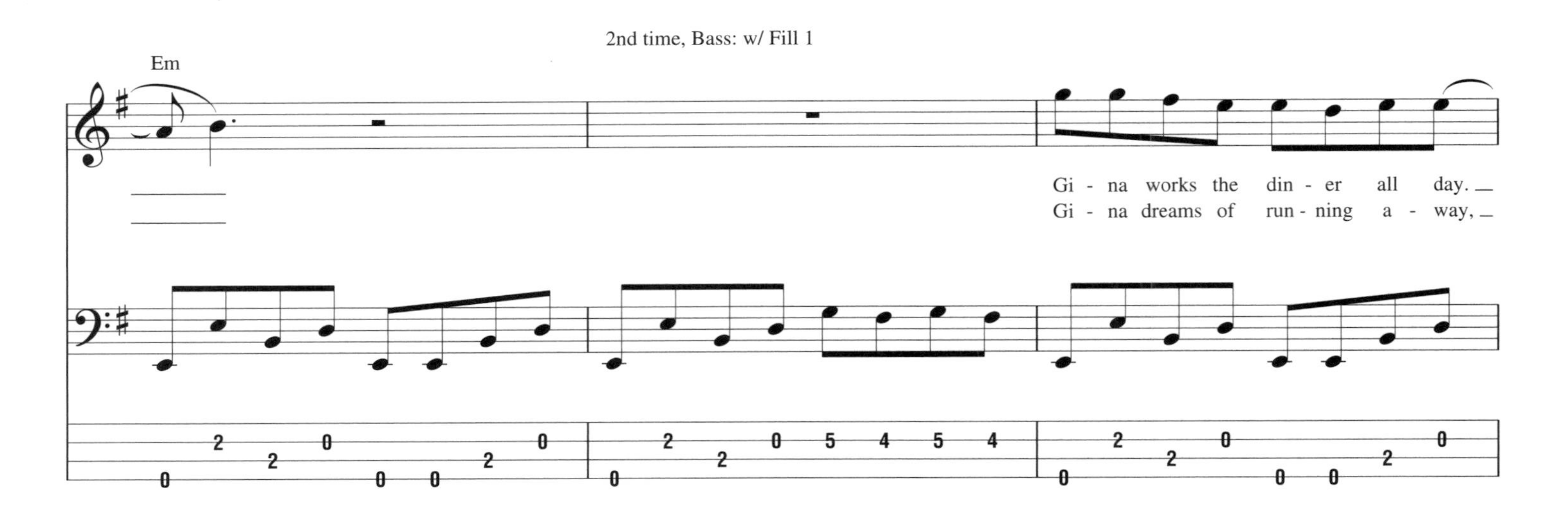
Em
2nd time, Bass: w/ Fill 1
Gi - na works the din - er all day.
Gi - na dreams of run - ning a - way,

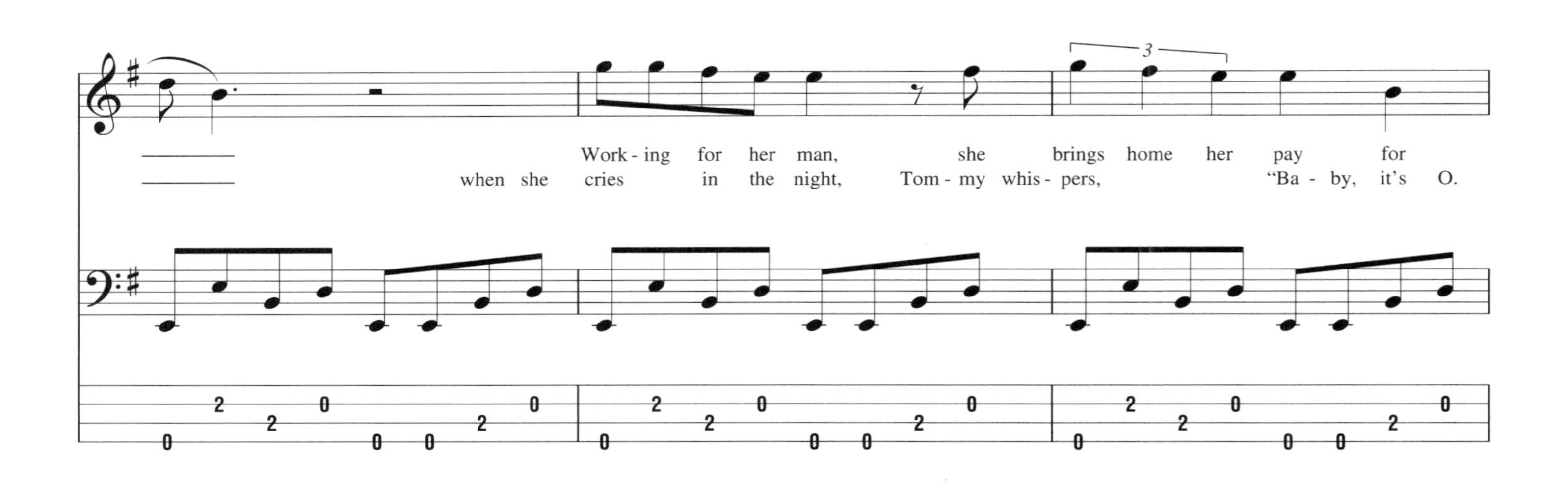
Work - ing for her man, she brings home her pay for
when she cries in the night, Tom - my whis - pers, "Ba - by, it's O.

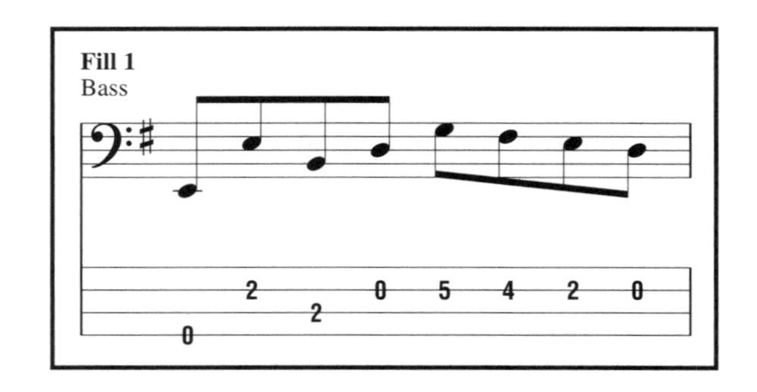
Fill 1
Bass

C/E
D/E
(Em)
love,
K.
mm,
for
love.
some
-
day."
Pre-Chorus
C5
D5
E5
She says, "We've got to
"We've got to
hold
on
to
what
we
got.
It
C5
D5
E5
C5
D5
does - n't make a dif - f'rence if we make it or not. We've got each oth - er and
E5
D5
C5
D5
that's a lot for love. We'll give it a shot."

Chorus

E5 C5 D5 G5 C5 D5
Whoa, we're half - way there. Whoa, liv - in' on a prayer.

2nd time, Bass: w/ Fill 2

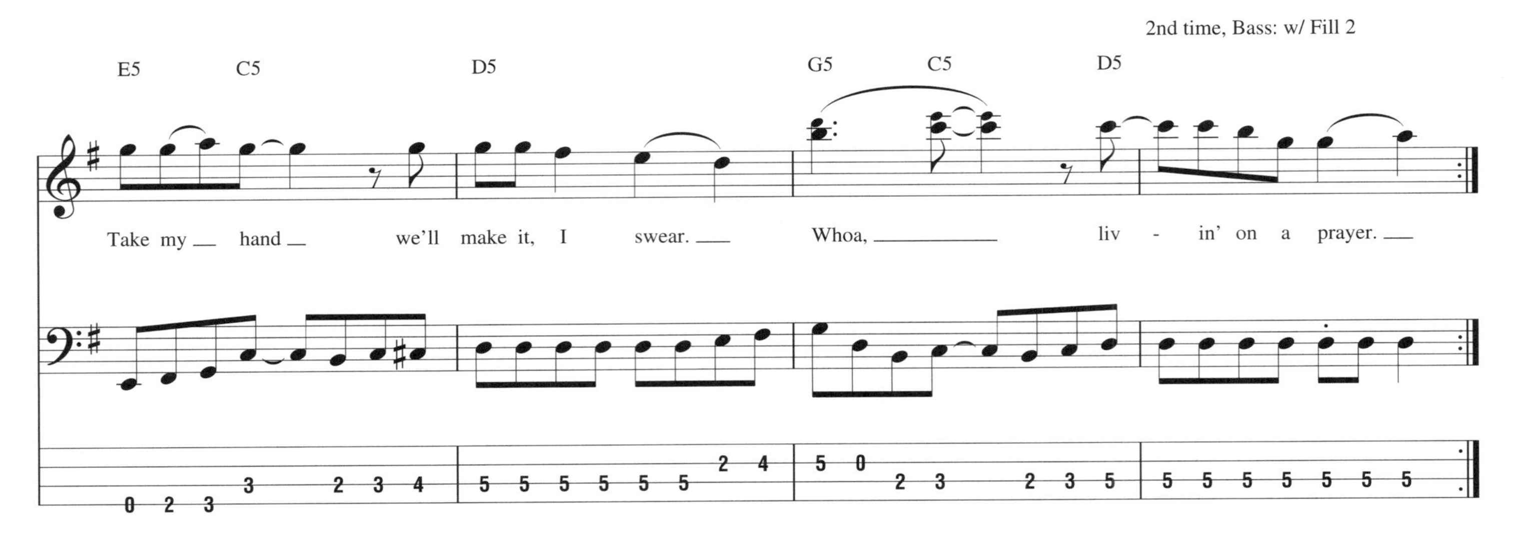
E5 C5 D5 G5 C5 D5
Take my hand we'll make it, I swear. Whoa, liv - in' on a prayer.

Guitar Solo

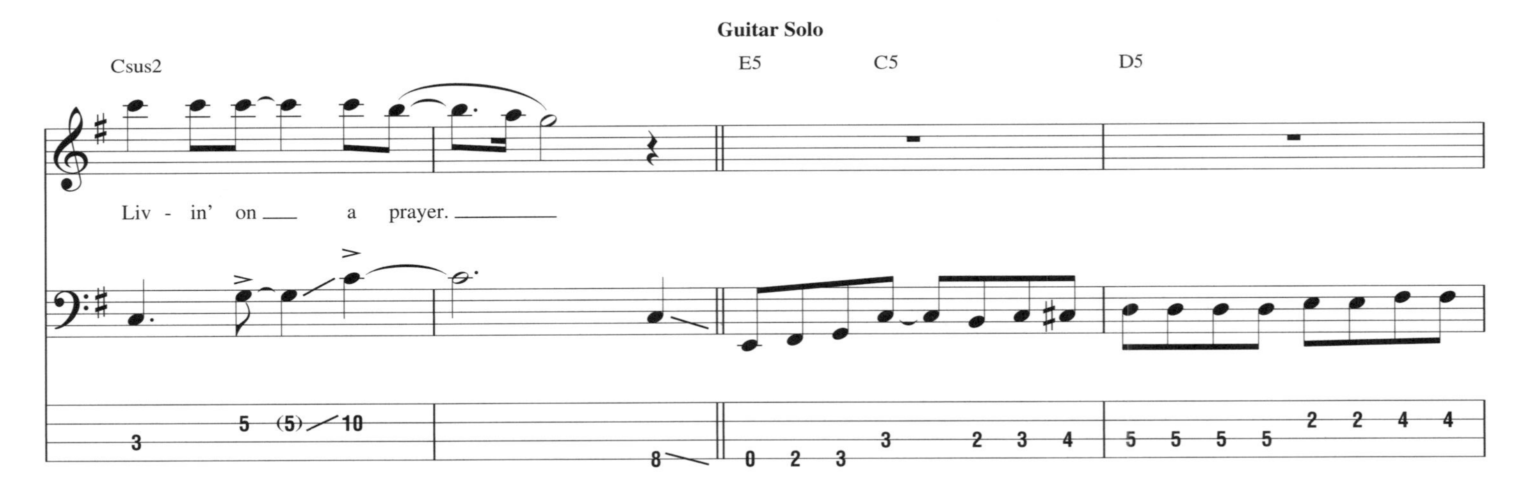
Csus2 E5 C5 D5
Liv - in' on a prayer.

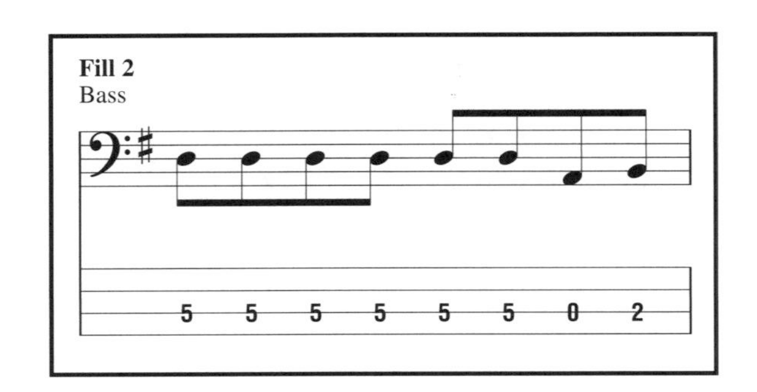
Fill 2
Bass

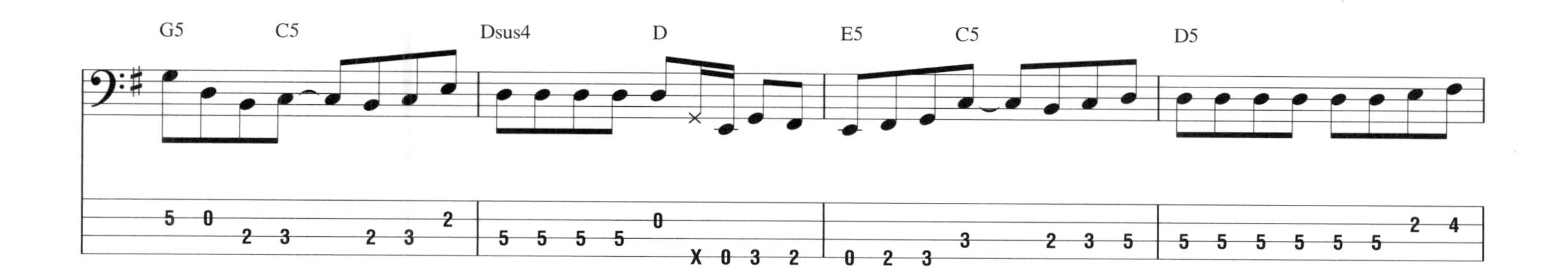
G5 C5 Dsus4 D E5 C5 D5

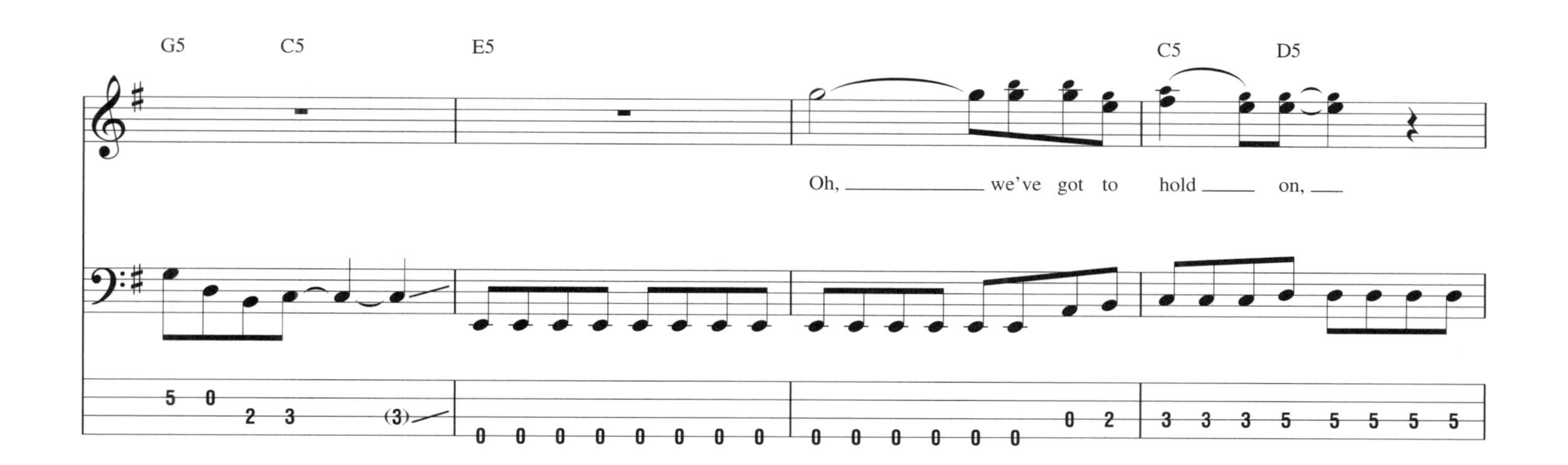
G5 C5 E5 C5 D5
Oh, we've got to hold on,

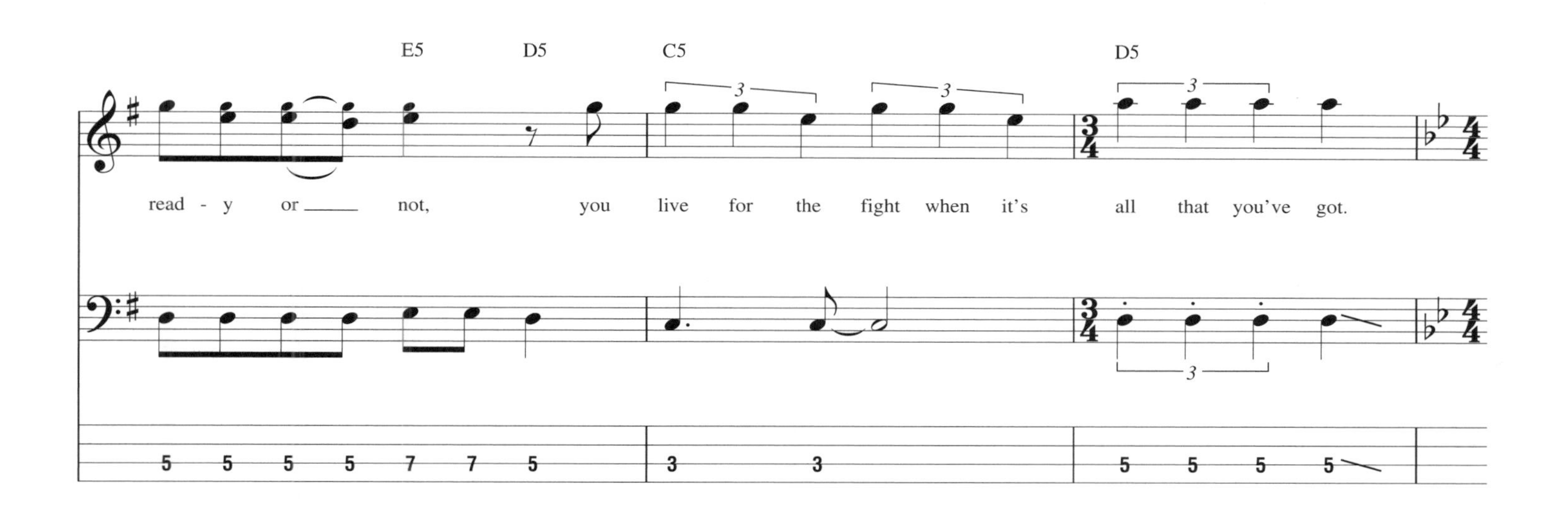
E5 D5 C5 D5
read - y or not, you live for the fight when it's all that you've got.

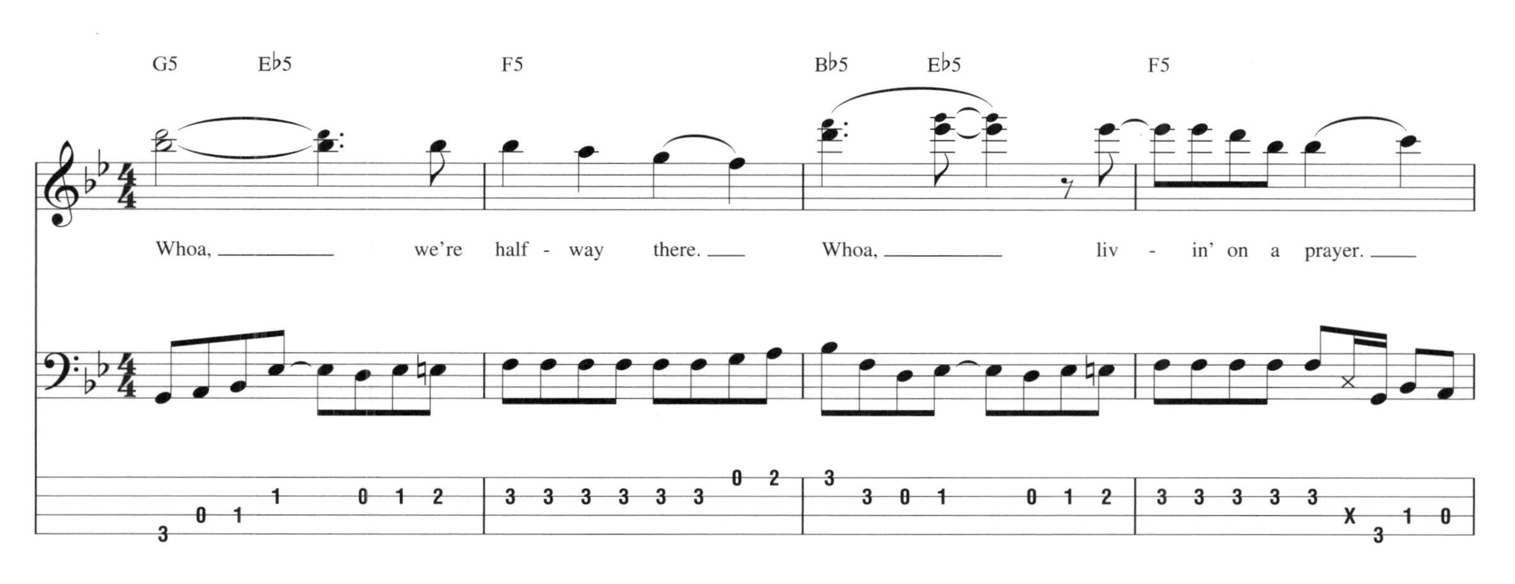
G5 E♭5 F5 B♭5 E♭5 F5
Whoa, we're half - way there. Whoa, liv - in' on a prayer.

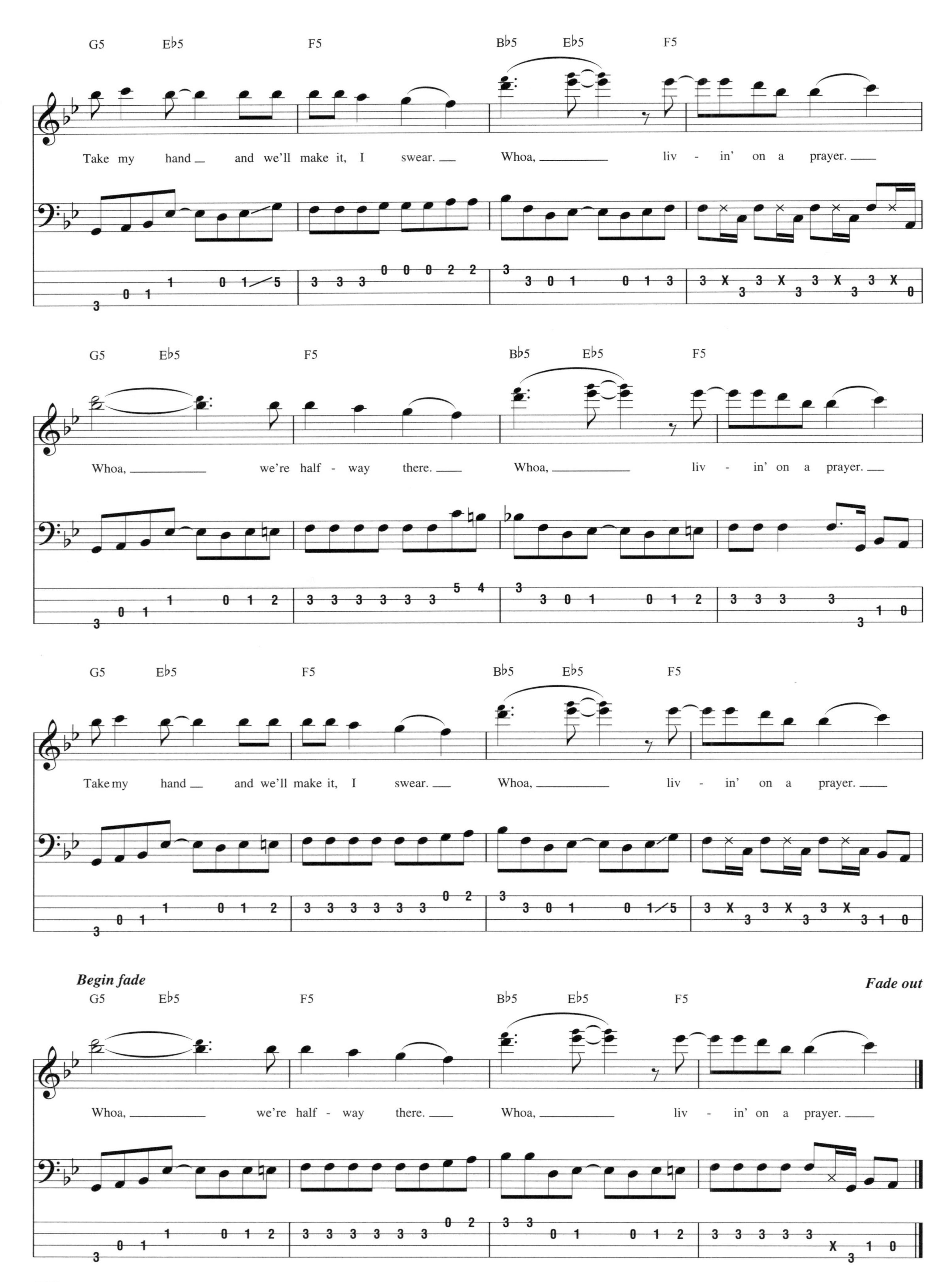
G5 E♭5 F5 B♭5 E♭5 F5
Take my hand and we'll make it, I swear. Whoa, liv - in' on a prayer.
G5 E♭5 F5 B♭5 E♭5 F5
Whoa, we're half - way there. Whoa, liv - in' on a prayer.
G5 E♭5 F5 B♭5 E♭5 F5
Take my hand and we'll make it, I swear. Whoa, liv - in' on a prayer.
Begin fade
Fade out
G5 E♭5 F5 B♭5 E♭5 F5
Whoa, we're half - way there. Whoa, liv - in' on a prayer.

Long Time

Words and Music by Tom Scholz

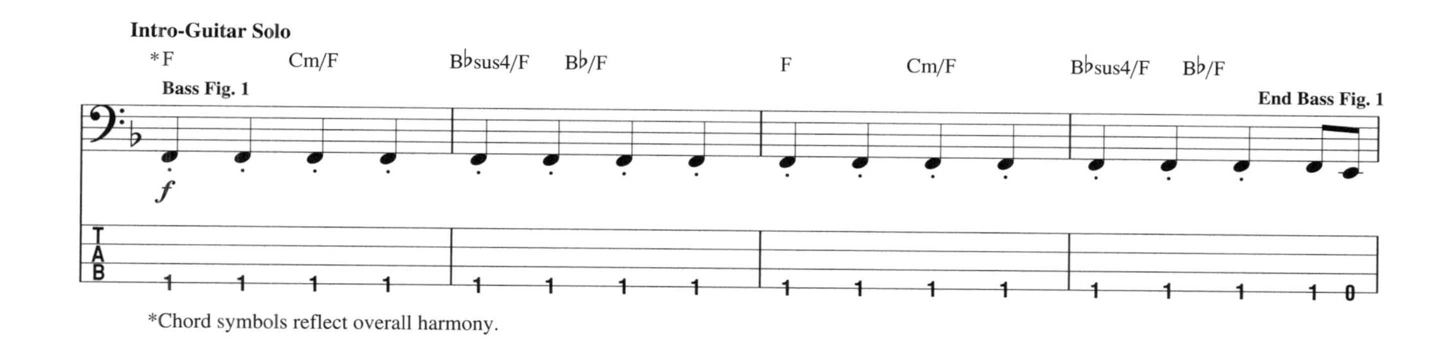

Intro-Guitar Solo
*F
Cm/F
B♭sus4/F
B♭/F
F
Cm/F
B♭sus4/F
B♭/F
Bass Fig. 1
End Bass Fig. 1
f
T
A
B
1 1 1 1 1 1 1 1 1 1 1 1 1 1 1 1 0

*Chord symbols reflect overall harmony.

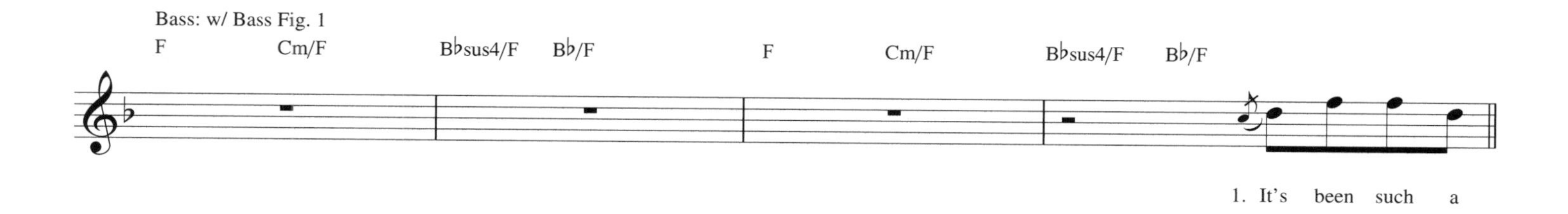

Bass: w/ Bass Fig. 1
F
Cm/F
B♭sus4/F
B♭/F
F
Cm/F
B♭sus4/F
B♭/F
1. It's been such a

Verse
F
Cm/F
B♭sus4/F
B♭/F
F
Cm/F
B♭sus4/F
B♭/F
long time, I think I should be go - in', yeah. And
1 1 1 1 1 1 1 1 0 1 1 1 1 1 1 1 1 0

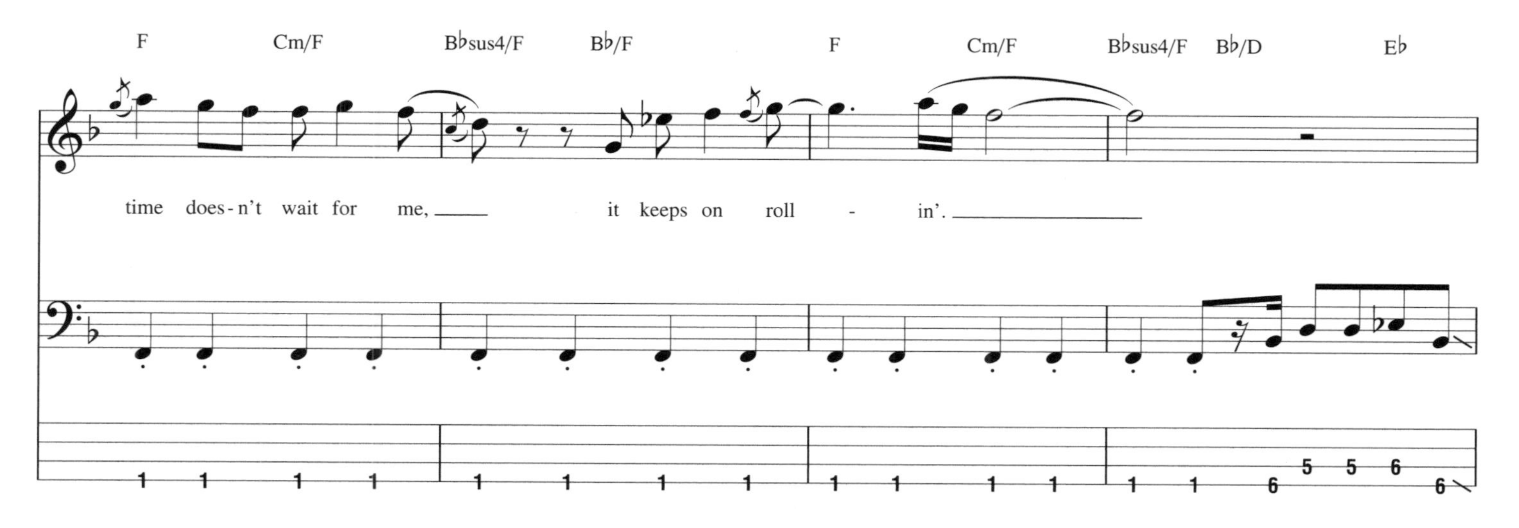

F
Cm/F
B♭sus4/F
B♭/F
F
Cm/F
B♭sus4/F
B♭/D
E♭
time does-n't wait for me, it keeps on roll - in'.
1 1 1 1 1 1 1 1 1 1 1 1 1 1 6 5 5 6 6

F Cm/F B♭sus4/F B♭/F F Cm/F B♭sus4/F B♭/D E♭
Sail on, on a dis - tant high - way, yeah. I've got to
(Sail on.)
F Cm/F B♭sus4/F B♭/F C5
keep on chas - in' a dream, I've got - ta be on my way.
F5/C C5 B♭5
Wish there was some - thing I could say.
Interlude
Bass tacet
F/C E♭/B♭ B♭ F/C E♭/B♭
*2nd time, vocal tacet on beat 1.

Chorus
B♭
F/C
E♭/B♭
B♭
I'm just, a, mov - in' on.
(Well, I'm tak - in' my time,

F/C
E♭/B♭
B♭
F/C
E♭/B♭
You'll for - get a - bout me af - ter I've been gone.
I don't
And I take what I find.

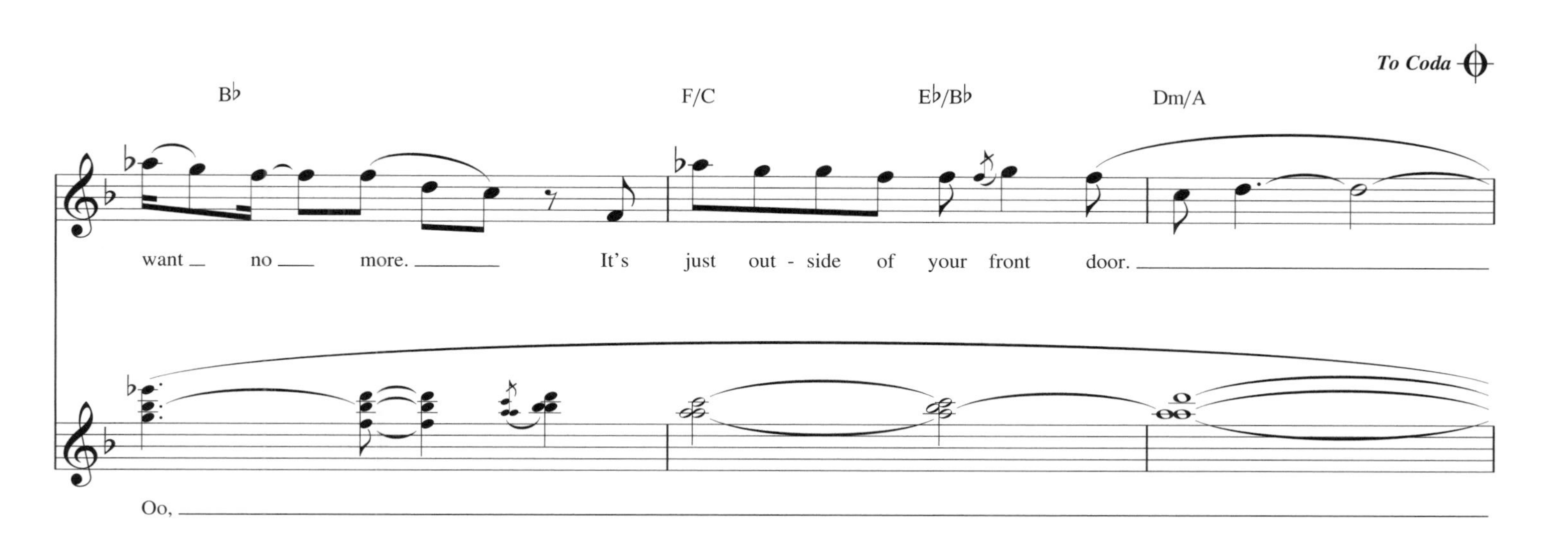
To Coda
B♭
F/C
E♭/B♭
Dm/A
want no more. It's just out - side of your front door.
Oo,

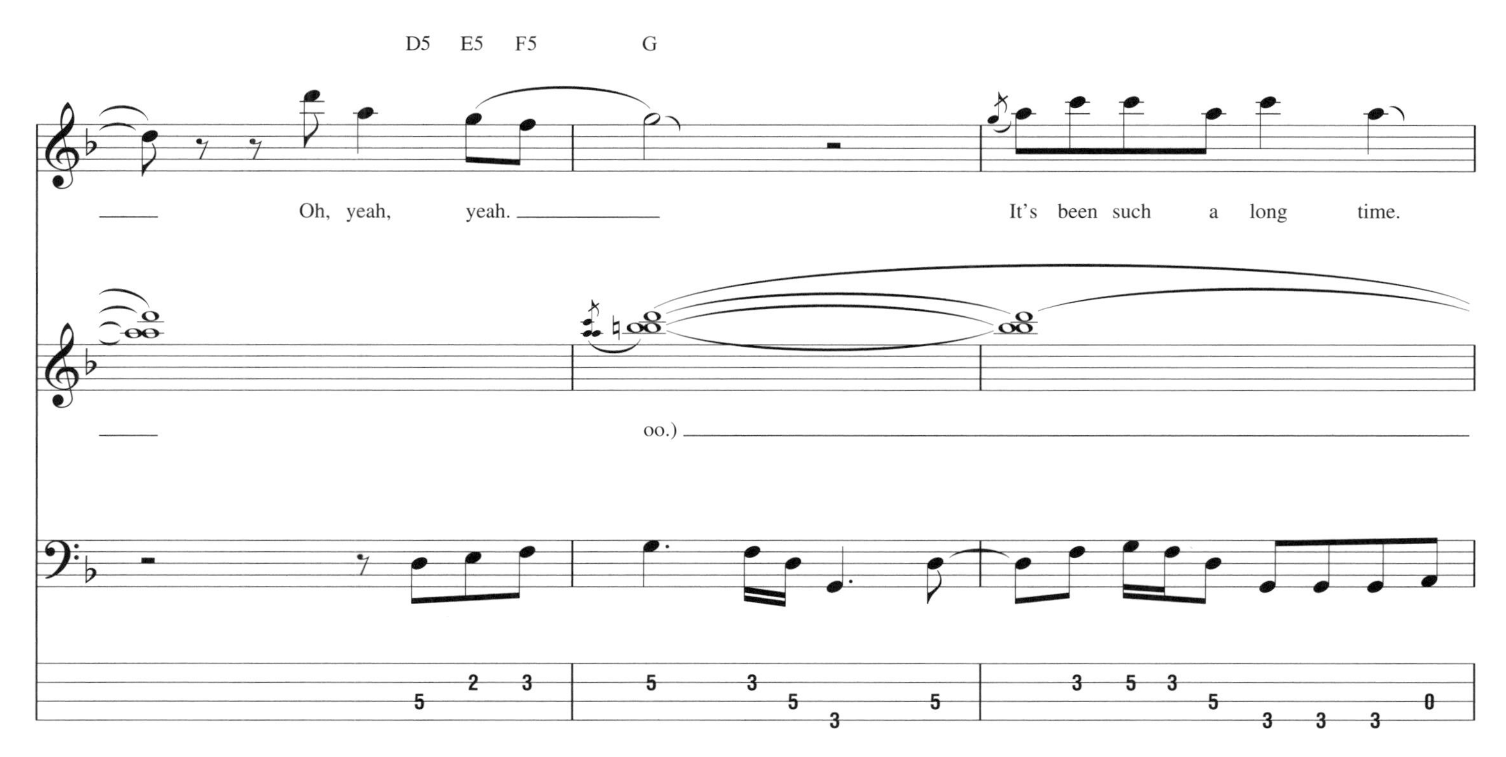
D5 E5 F5
G
Oh, yeah, yeah.
It's been such a long time.
oo.)

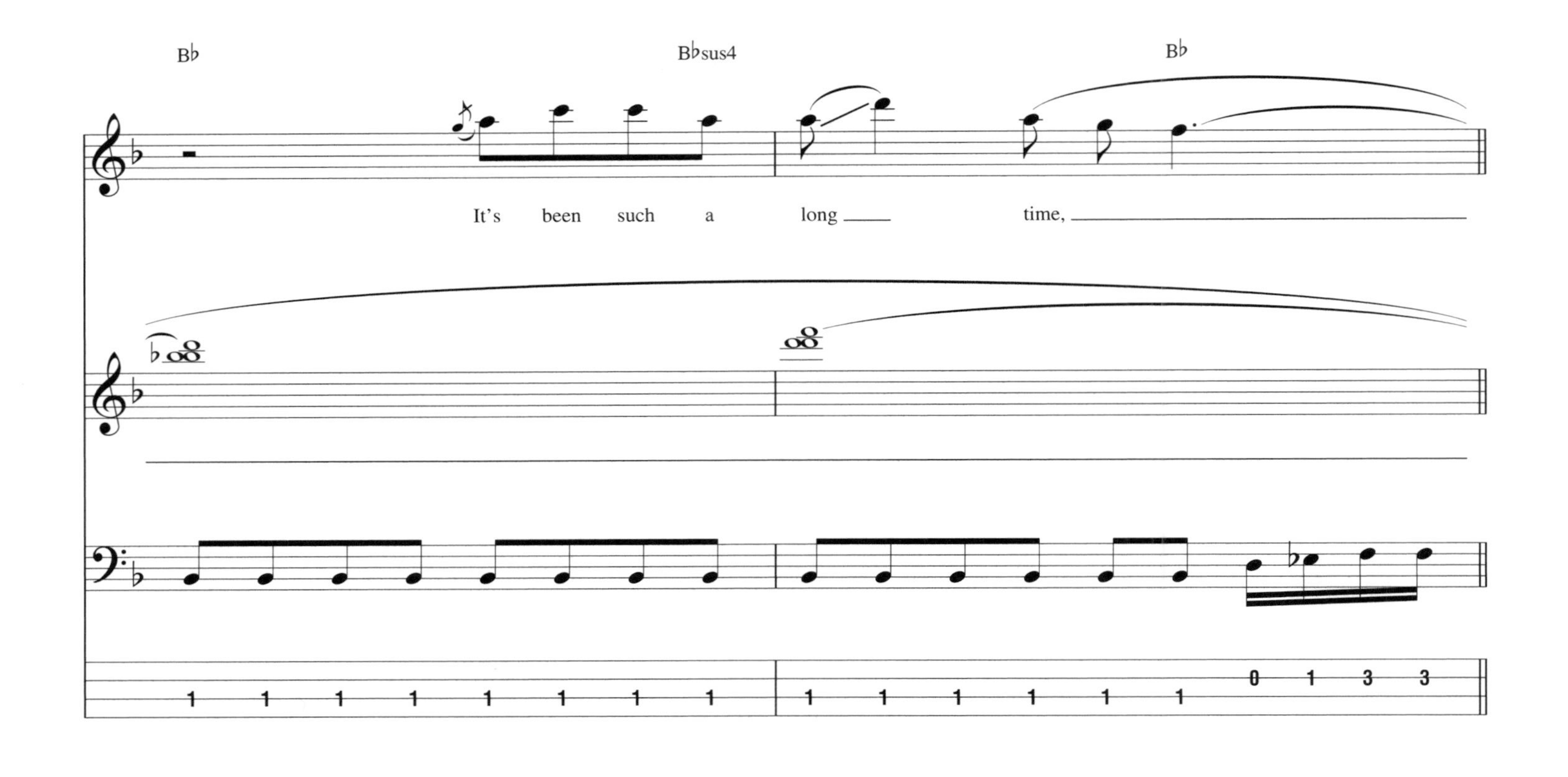
B♭
B♭sus4
B♭
It's been such a long time,
0 1 3 3

Guitar Solo

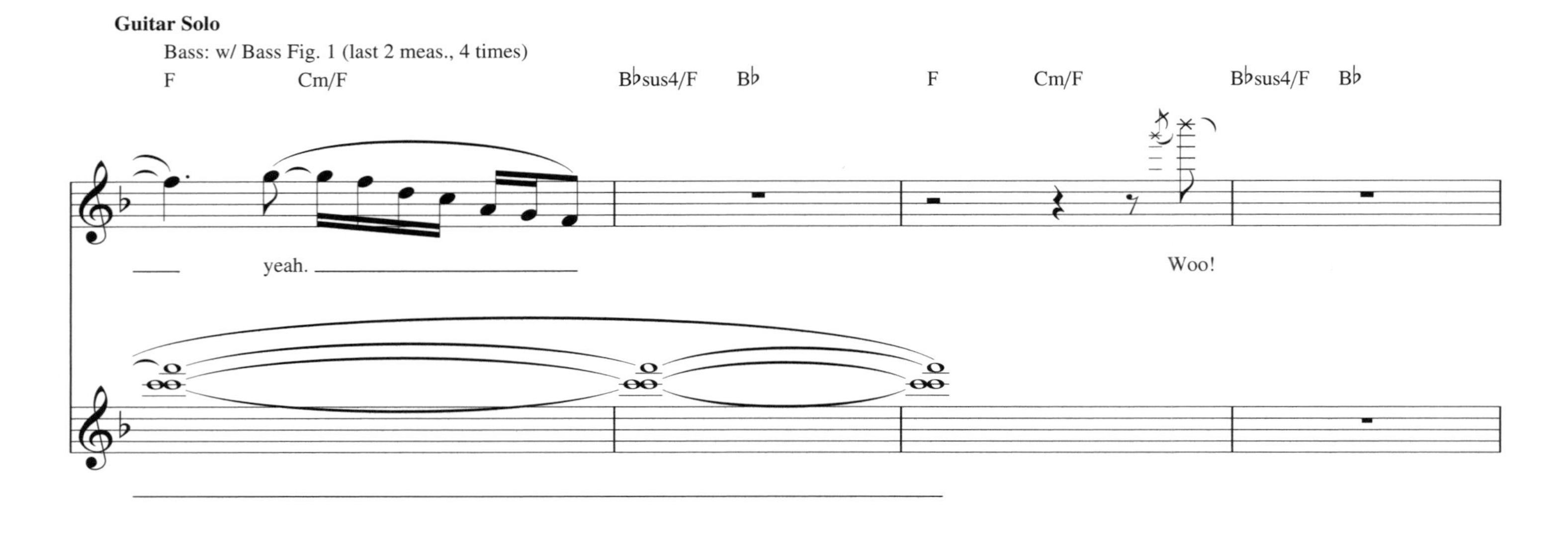
Bass: w/ Bass Fig. 1 (last 2 meas., 4 times)
F Cm/F B♭sus4/F B♭ F Cm/F B♭sus4/F B♭
yeah.
Woo!

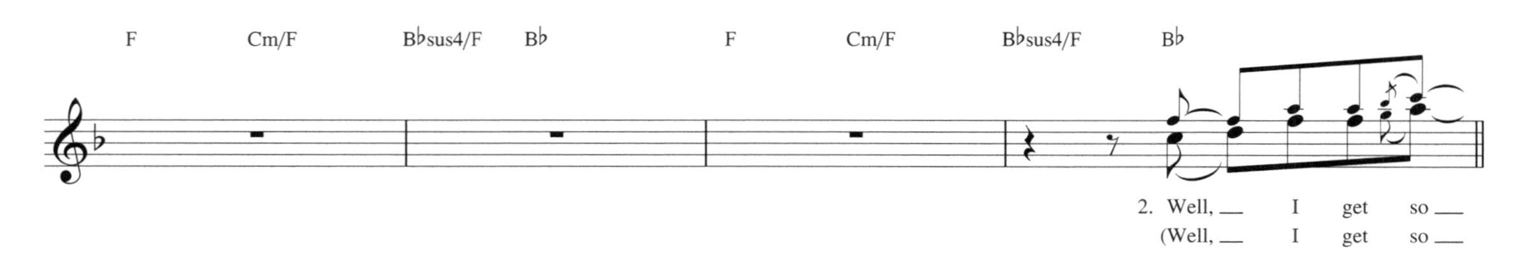
F Cm/F B♭sus4/F B♭ F Cm/F B♭sus4/F B♭
2. Well, I get so
(Well, I get so

Verse

Bass: w/ Bass Fig. 1
F Cm/F B♭sus4/F B♭/F F Cm/F B♭sus4/F B♭/F
lonely when I am with - out you, oo. But in my mind,
lone - ly.)

F Cm/F B♭sus4/F B♭/F F Cm/F B♭sus4/F B♭/D E♭
deep in my mind, I can't for-get a - bout you, whoa.
Good times, and fac-es that re - mind me, yeah. I'm
(Good times.)
C5
try - in' to for-get your name and leave it all be - hind me.
F5/C C5 B♭5
D.S. al Coda
You're com - in' back to find me.

Coda
D5
E5
F5
G
Yeah, yeah, yeah.
B♭
B♭sus4
B♭sus4
B♭
It's been such a long time.
It's been such a long time.
Interlude
F
Cm
E♭
B♭
F
Cm
E♭/G
B♭/F
Guitar Solo
F
Cm
E♭
B♭/D
F
Cm
E♭/B♭
B♭
F
Cm
E♭
B♭/D

F
Cm
E♭
B♭/D
F
Cm
E♭/G
B♭/F
F
Cm/B♭
E♭/A
B♭/F
F
Cm/G
E♭/F
B♭/E♭
F
Interlude
G5
E♭/A♭
B♭/A♭
Cm/A♭
B♭/A♭
E♭/A♭
B♭/A♭
Cm/A♭
B♭/A♭
Csus4
C
Yeah,
yeah!

Csus4 C Csus4 C
3. It's been such a

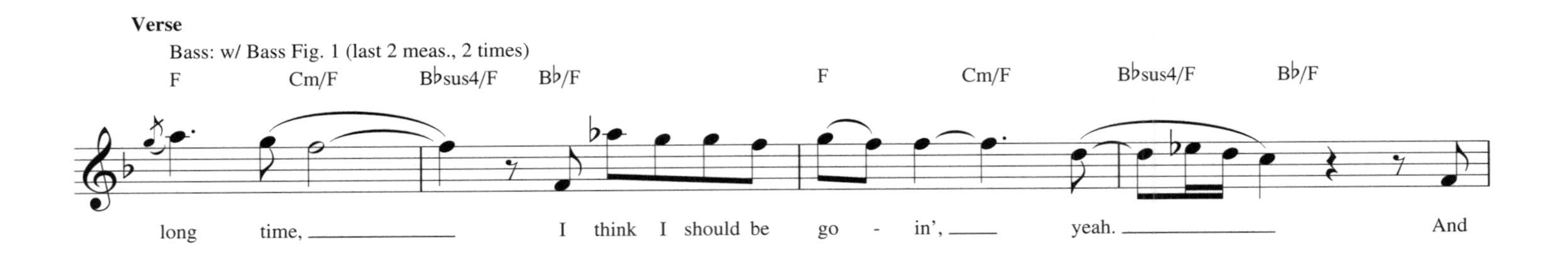
Verse
Bass: w/ Bass Fig. 1 (last 2 meas., 2 times)
F Cm/F B♭sus4/F B♭/F F Cm/F B♭sus4/F B♭/F
long time, I think I should be go - in', yeah. And

F Cm/F B♭sus4/F B♭/F F Cm/F B♭sus4/F B♭/D E♭
time does-n't wait for me, it keeps on roll - in'. There's a
(There's a

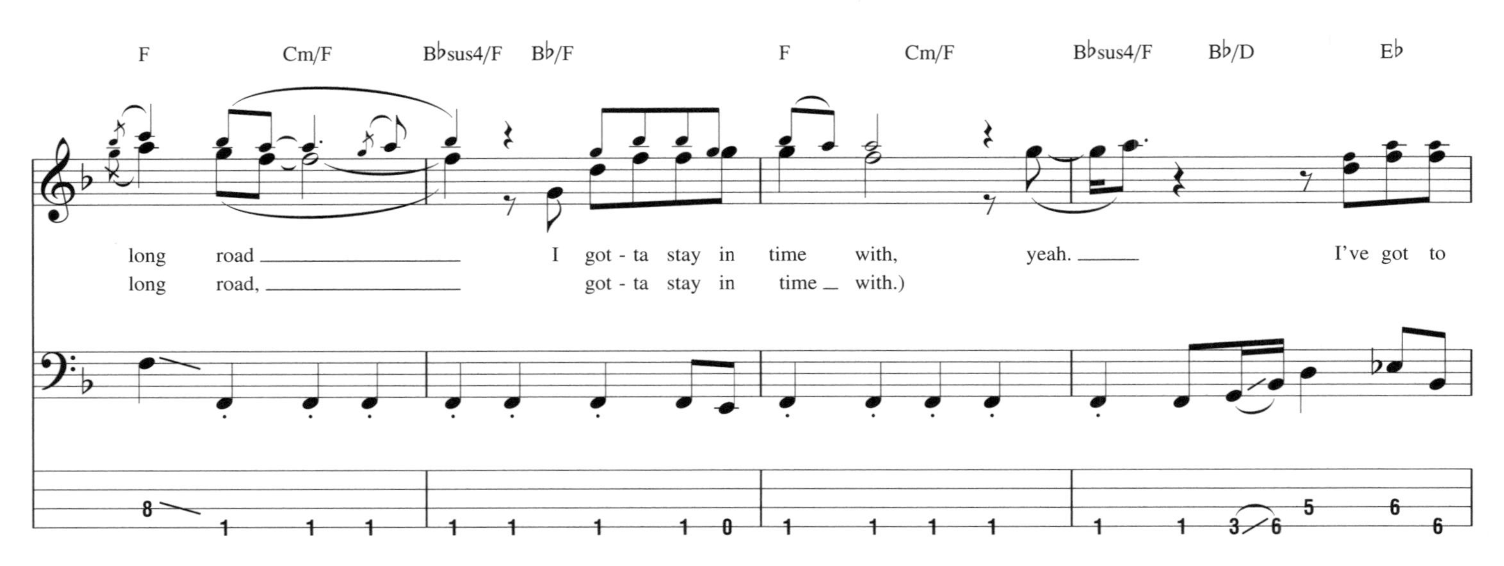
F Cm/F B♭sus4/F B♭/F F Cm/F B♭sus4/F B♭/D E♭
long road I got-ta stay in time with, yeah. I've got to
long road, got-ta stay in time with.)

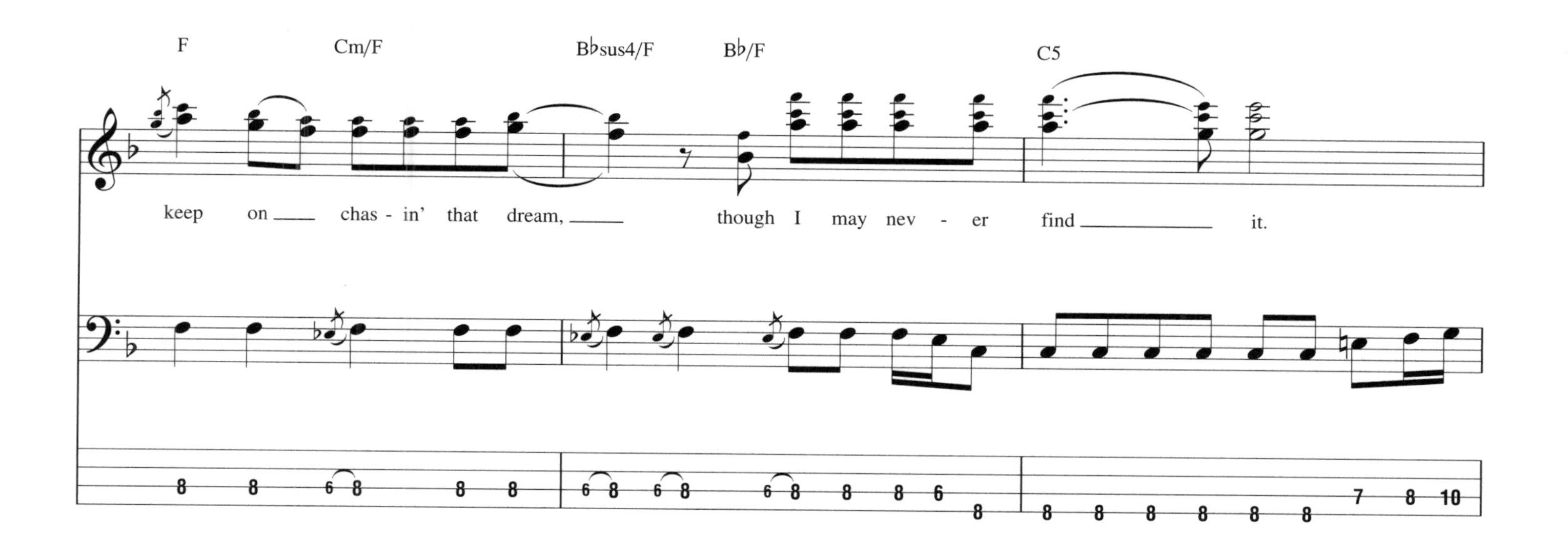
F
Cm/F
B♭sus4/F
B♭/F
C5
keep on chas - in' that dream,
though I may nev - er find it.
8 8 6 8 8 8
6 8 6 8 6 8 8 8 6 8
8 8 8 8 8 8 7 8 10

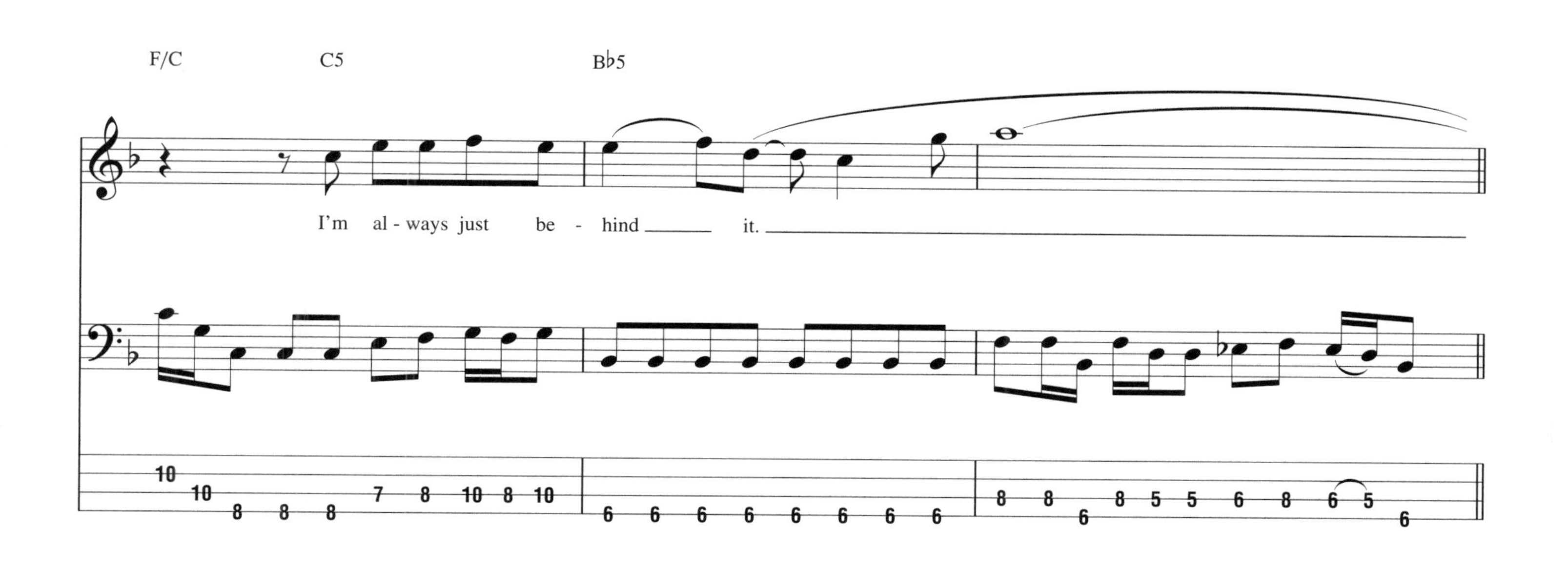
F/C
C5
B♭5
I'm al - ways just be - hind it.
10 10 8 8 8 7 8 10 8 10
6 6 6 6 6 6 6 6
8 8 6 8 5 5 6 8 6 5 6

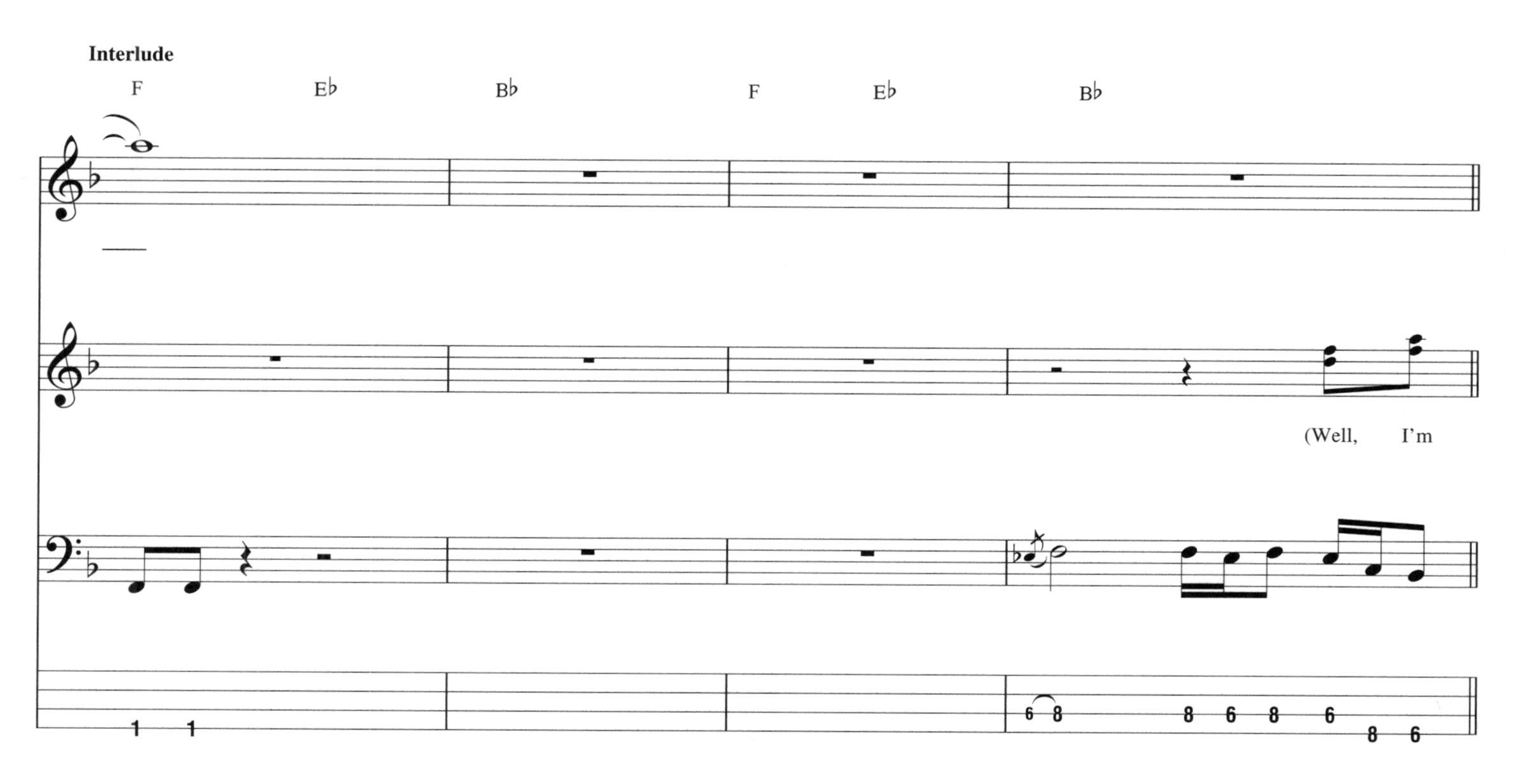
Interlude
F
E♭
B♭
F
E♭
B♭
(Well, I'm
1 1
6 8 8 6 8 6 8 6

Outro
F Eb Bb Eb/Bb F Eb
I'm just mov - in' a - long. Oh,
tak - in' my time. oo. Tak - in' my time,
Bb Eb/Bb F Eb Bb Eb/Bb
just mov - in' a - long. Ah, just tak - in' my time.
oo. Tak - in' my time, oo.
Lead Voc.: ad lib. (till fade)
F Eb Bb Eb/Bb F Eb
Yeah.
Tak - in' my time. oo. Tak - in' my time,

B♭
E♭/B♭
F
E♭
oo.
Tak - in' my time,
Begin fade
E♭/F
Fade out
B♭/F
1 1 8 6 8 6 8

Mr. Brightside

Words and Music by Brandon Flowers, Dave Keuning, Mark Stoermer and Ronnie Vannucci

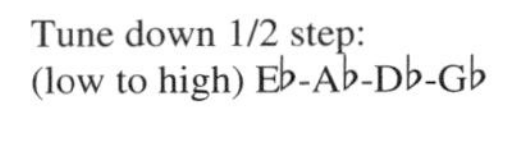
Tune down 1/2 step:
(low to high) E♭-A♭-D♭-G♭

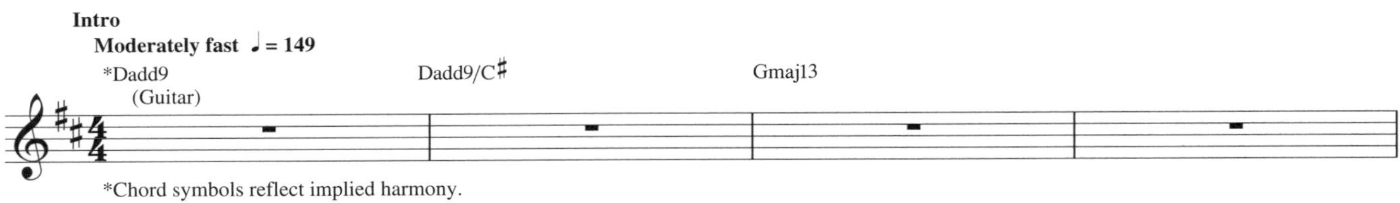
Intro
Moderately fast ♩ = 149
*Dadd9
(Guitar)
Dadd9/C♯
Gmaj13
*Chord symbols reflect implied harmony.

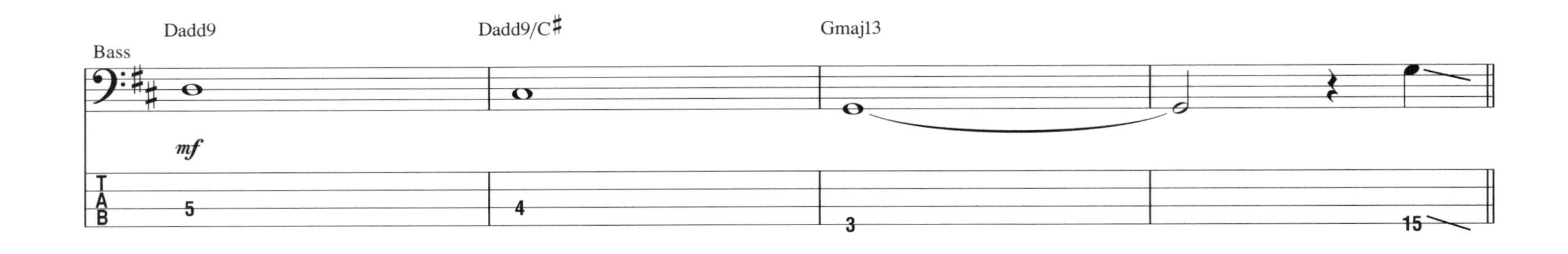
Dadd9
Dadd9/C♯
Gmaj13
Bass
mf

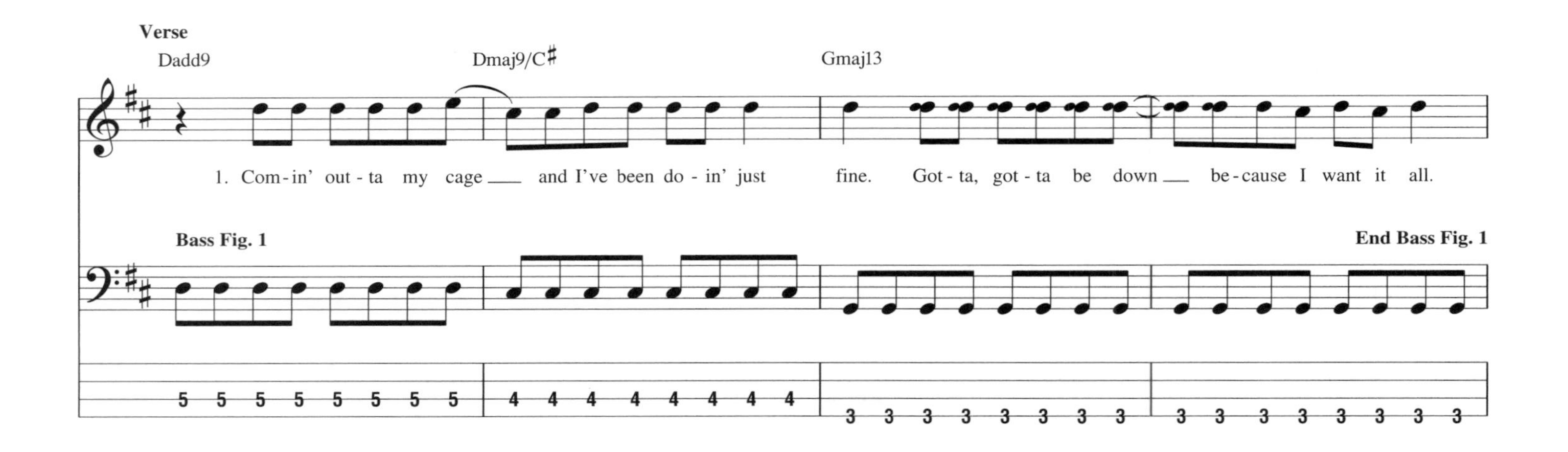
Verse
Dadd9
Dmaj9/C♯
Gmaj13
1. Com-in' out-ta my cage and I've been do-in' just fine. Got-ta, got-ta be down be-cause I want it all.
Bass Fig. 1
End Bass Fig. 1

Bass: w/ Bass Fig. 1 (2 times)
Dadd9
Dmaj9/C♯
Gmaj13
It start-ed out with a kiss. How did it end up like this? It was on-ly a kiss, it was on-ly a kiss.
Now I'm fall-ing a-sleep, and she's call-ing a cab while he's hav-in' a smoke and she's tak-in' a drag.

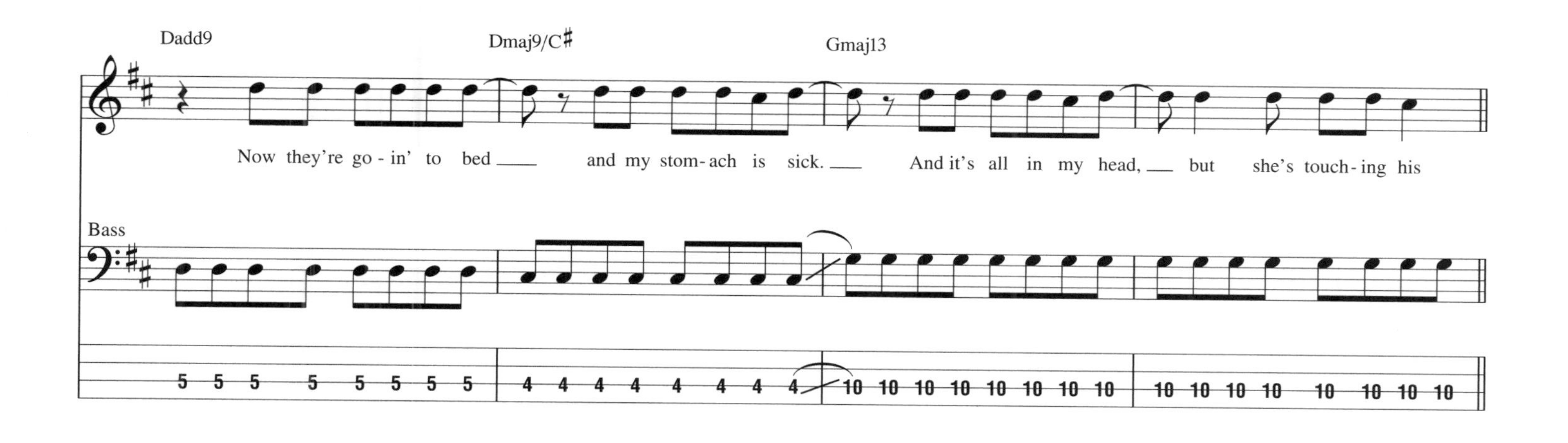
Dadd9
Dmaj9/C♯
Gmaj13
Now they're go - in' to bed ___ and my stom - ach is sick. ___ And it's all in my head, ___ but she's touch - ing his
Bass
5 5 5 5 5 5 5 5
4 4 4 4 4 4 4 4
10 10 10 10 10 10 10 10
10 10 10 10 10 10 10 10

Pre-Chorus
Bm7add4
Bm7add4/A
chest. Now he takes off her dress. Now let me
7 7 7 7 7
7 9 7 5 5
5 5 5 5 5
7 9 7 5 5

G6/9
go.
3 3 3 3
5 7 5 4
3 3 3 3
2 4 5

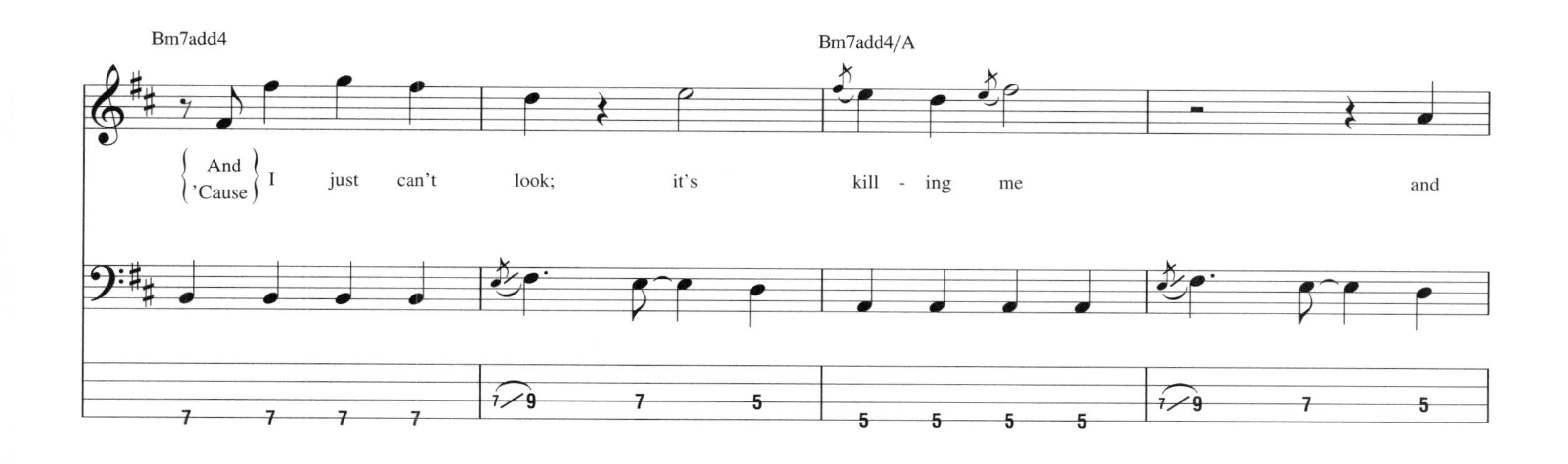
Bm7add4
Bm7add4/A
And
'Cause
I just can't look; it's kill - ing me and
7 7 7 7
7 9 7 5
5 5 5 5
7 9 7 5

G6/9
tak - ing con - trol.
2 3 3 3 3
2 3 3 3 3 3 3 3 3
2 3 3 3 3 3 3
3 15 15 15 15 15 15 15

Chorus
D5 G5 Bm A5
Jeal - ous - y, turn - ing saints in - to the sea. Swim - ming through sick
5 5 5 5 5 5 5 5 5 5 5 5 5 5 5 5 7 7 7 7 7 7 7 7 5 5 5 5 5 5 5 5

D5 G5 Bm A5
lull - a - bies, chok - ing on your al - i - bis, but it's just the
5 5 5 5 5 5 5 5 5 5 5 5 5 5 5 5 7 7 7 7 7 7 7 7 5 5 5 5 5 5 5 5

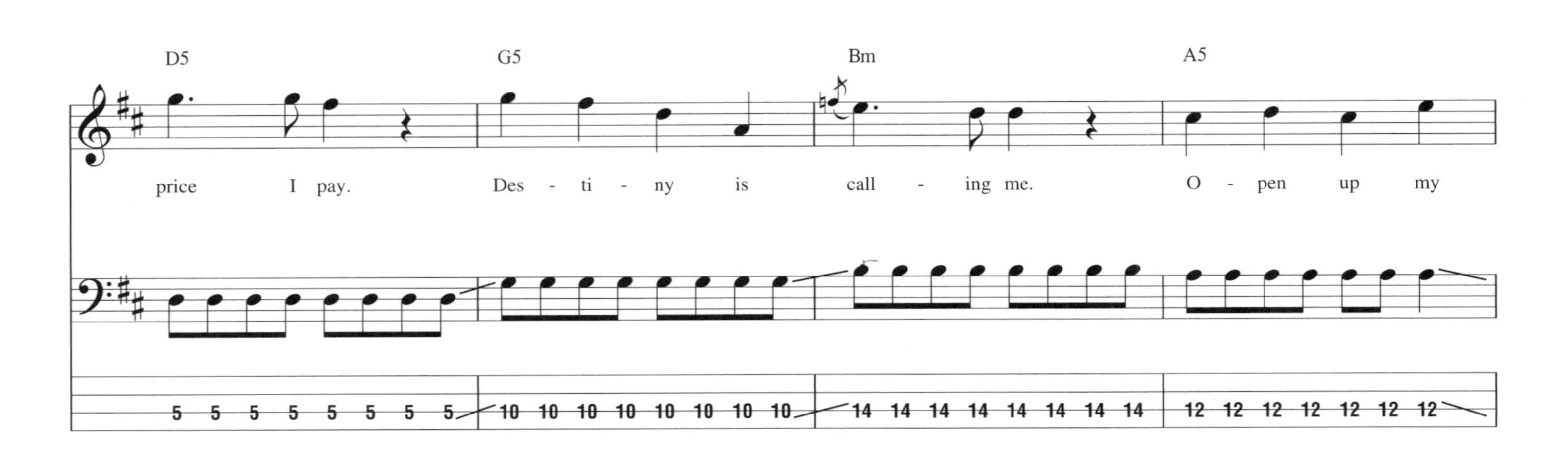
D5 G5 Bm A5
price I pay. Des - ti - ny is call - ing me. O - pen up my
5 5 5 5 5 5 5 5 10 10 10 10 10 10 10 10 14 14 14 14 14 14 14 14 12 12 12 12 12 12 12

To Coda
D5
G5
Bm
A5
ea - ger eyes 'cause I'm Mis - ter Bright - side.
Interlude
D5
Bass Fig. 2
G5
Bm
A5
End Bass Fig. 2
Verse
Bass: w/ Bass Fig. 1
Dadd9
Dmaj9/C♯
Gmaj13
2. I'm com - in' out - ta my cage and I've been do - in' just fine. Got - ta, got - ta be down be - cause I want it all.
Dadd9
Dmaj9/C♯
Gmaj13
It start - ed out with a kiss. How did it end up like this? It was on - ly a kiss.
Spoken: (It was on - ly a kiss.)
Bass
Bass: w/ Bass Fig. 1
Dadd9
Dmaj9/C♯
Gmaj13
Now I'm fall - ing a - sleep, and she's call - ing a cab while he's hav - in' a smoke and she's tak - in' a drag.
D.S. al Coda
Dadd9
Dmaj9/C♯
Gmaj13
Now they're go - in' to bed and my stom - ach is sick. And it's all in my head, but she's touch - ing his
Bass

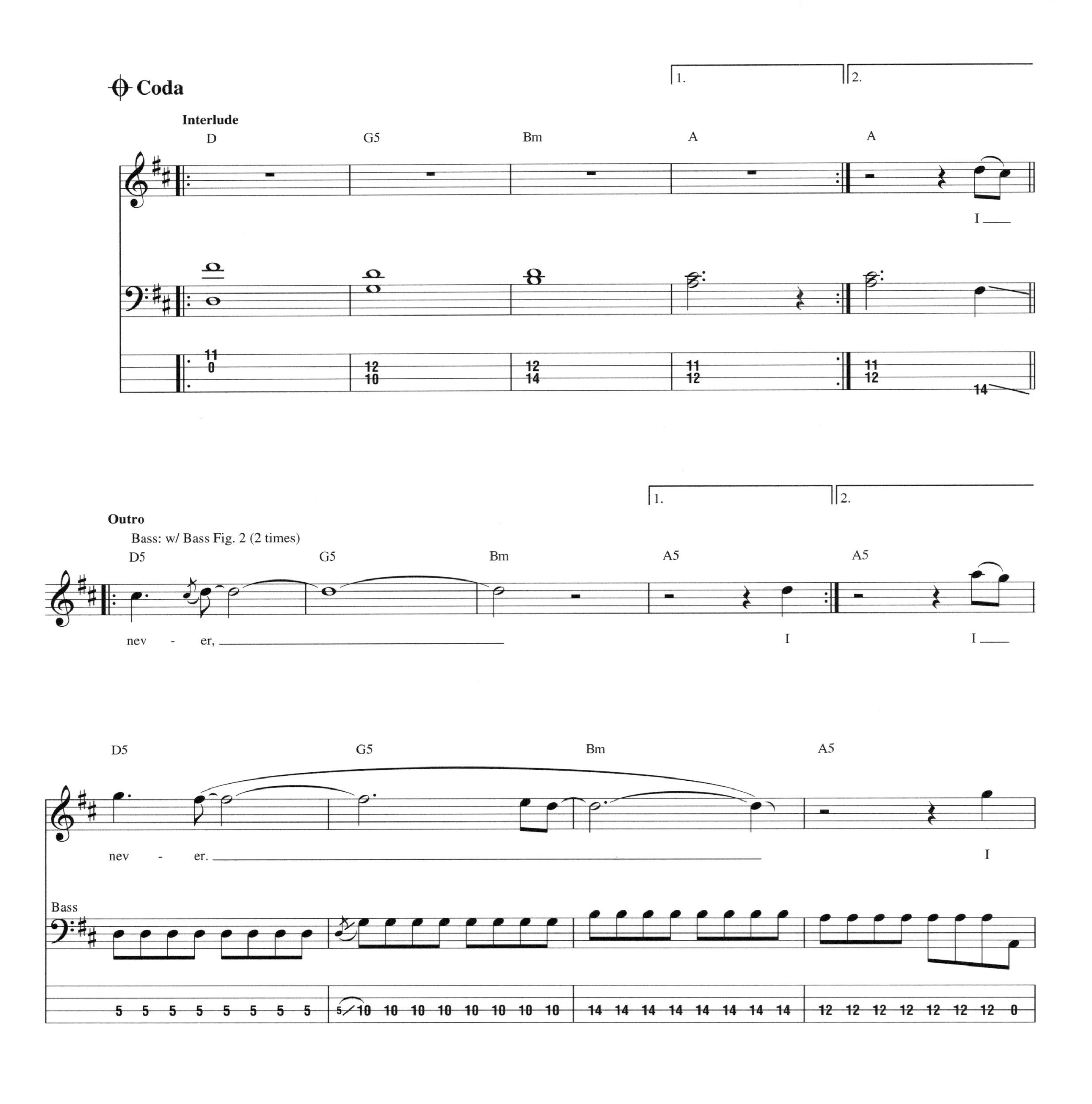
Coda
1.
2.
Interlude
D
G5
Bm
A
A
I
11
0
12
10
12
14
11
12
11
12
14
1.
2.
Outro
Bass: w/ Bass Fig. 2 (2 times)
D5
G5
Bm
A5
A5
nev - er,
I
I
D5
G5
Bm
A5
nev - er.
I
Bass
5 5 5 5 5 5 5 5
5 10 10 10 10 10 10 10 10
14 14 14 14 14 14 14 14
12 12 12 12 12 12 12 0

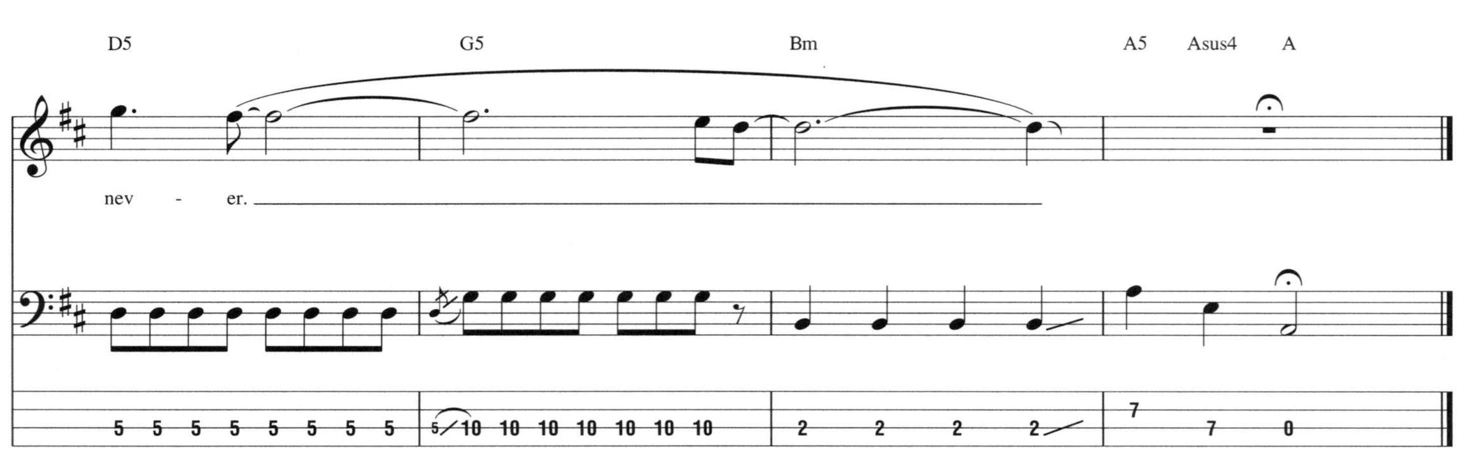
D5
G5
Bm
A5
Asus4
A
nev - er.
5 5 5 5 5 5 5 5
5 10 10 10 10 10 10 10
2 2 2 2
7 7 0

Money

Words and Music by Roger Waters

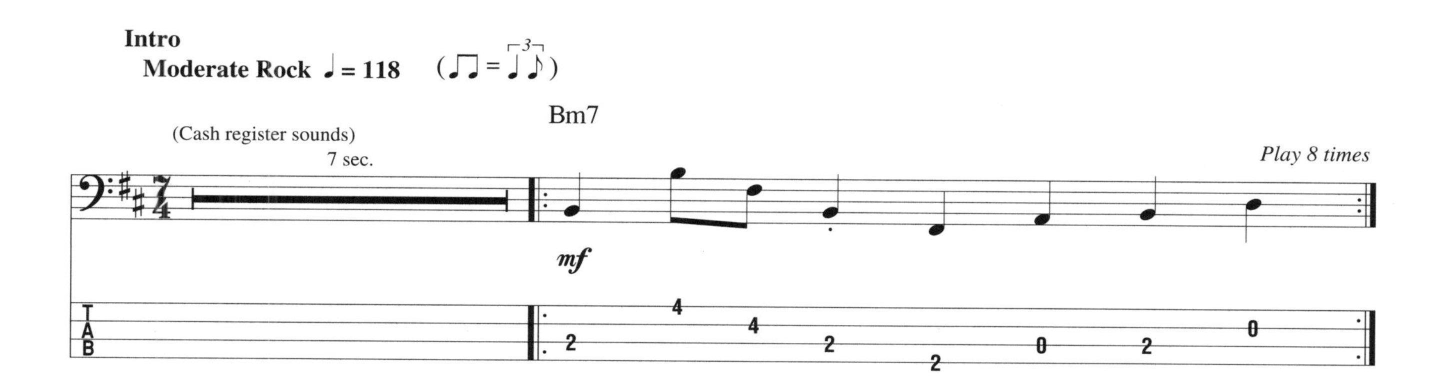

Intro
Moderate Rock ♩ = 118
Bm7
(Cash register sounds)
7 sec.
Play 8 times
mf
T
A
B

Verse
Bm7
1. Mon - ey, ah, get a - way. You get a
2., 3. See additional lyrics

good job with more pay and you're o - kay. Mon -

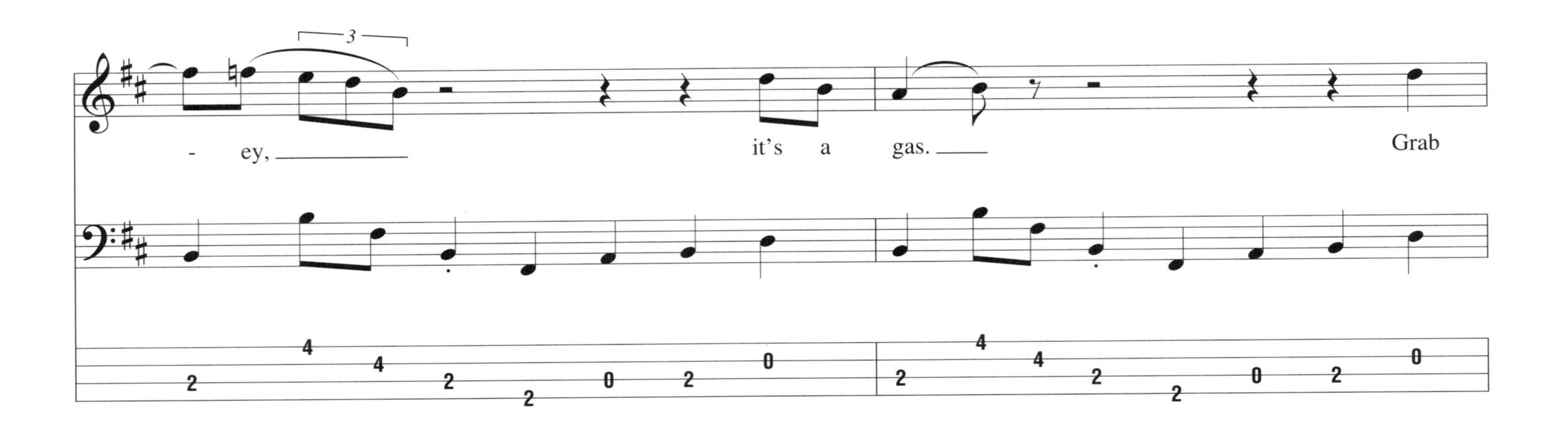
3
- ey, it's a gas. Grab
4 4 2 2 0 2 0 4 4 2 2 0 2 0
2 2 2 2

that cash with both hands and make a stash.
2 0 2 2 0 2 0 2 4 4 2 2 0 2 0
4/4

To Coda
F♯m
Em7
New car, cav - i - ar, four star day - dream. Think I'll buy me a foot - ball
4 4 4 2 0 4 4 3 2 2 0 3 0 2 0
4/4 6/4 7/4

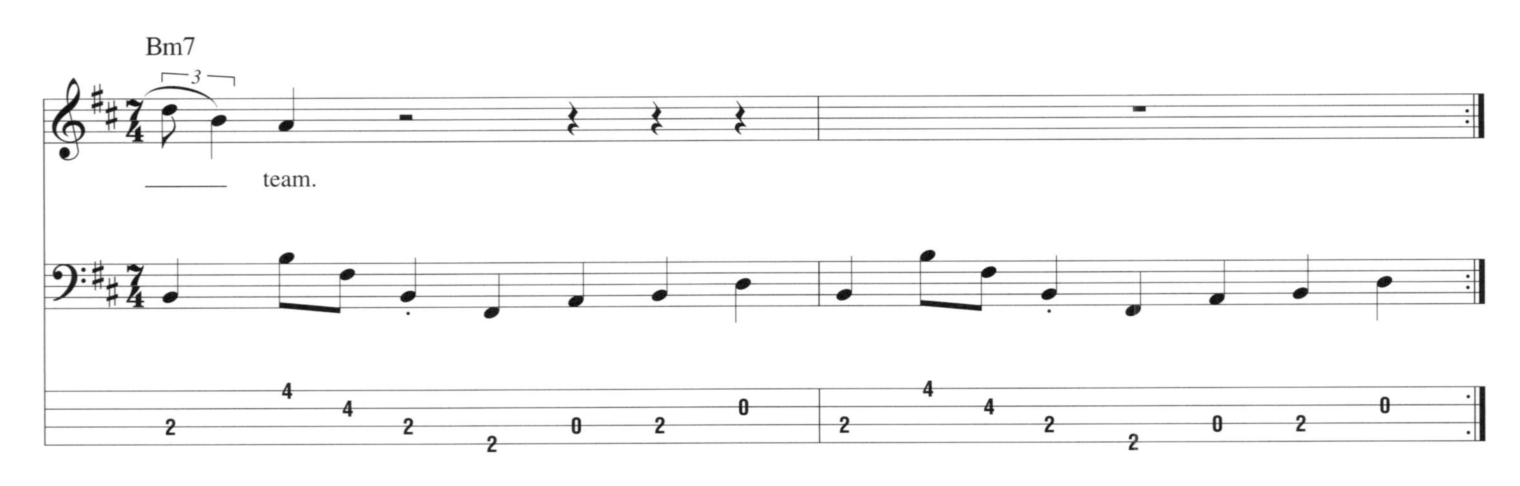
Bm7
3
team.
2 4 4 2 2 0 2 0 2 4 4 2 2 0 2 0
7/4

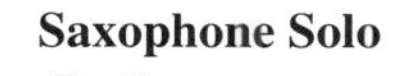
Saxophone Solo

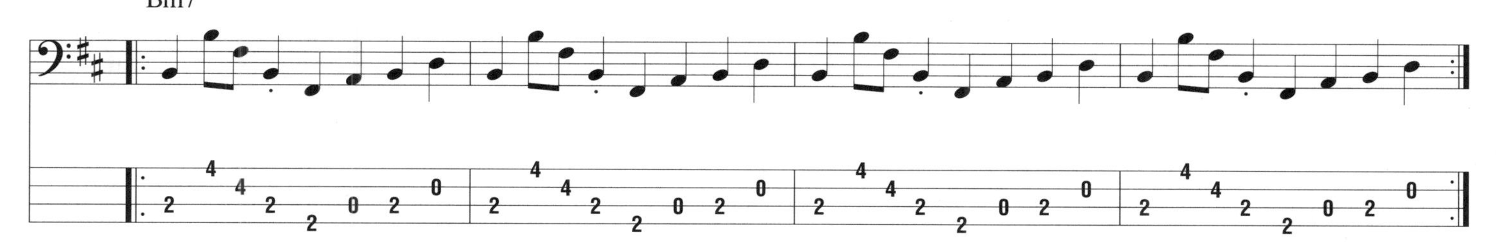
Bm7

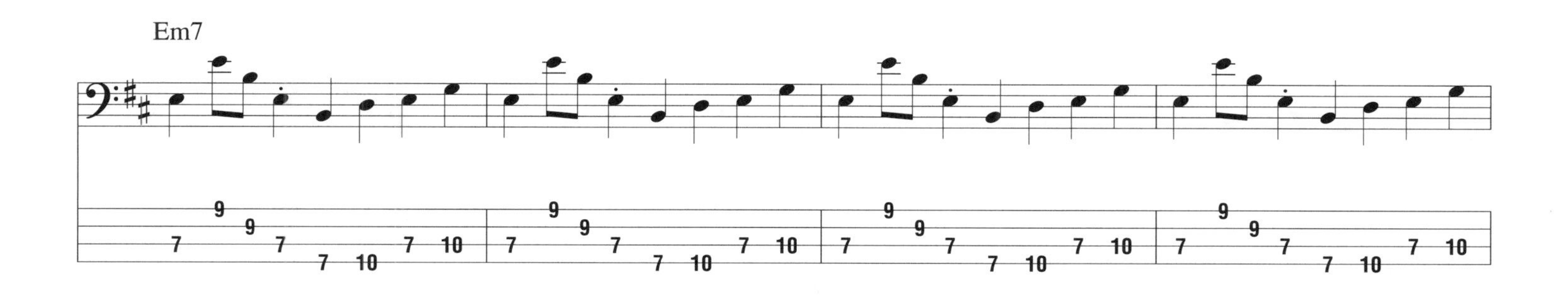
Em7

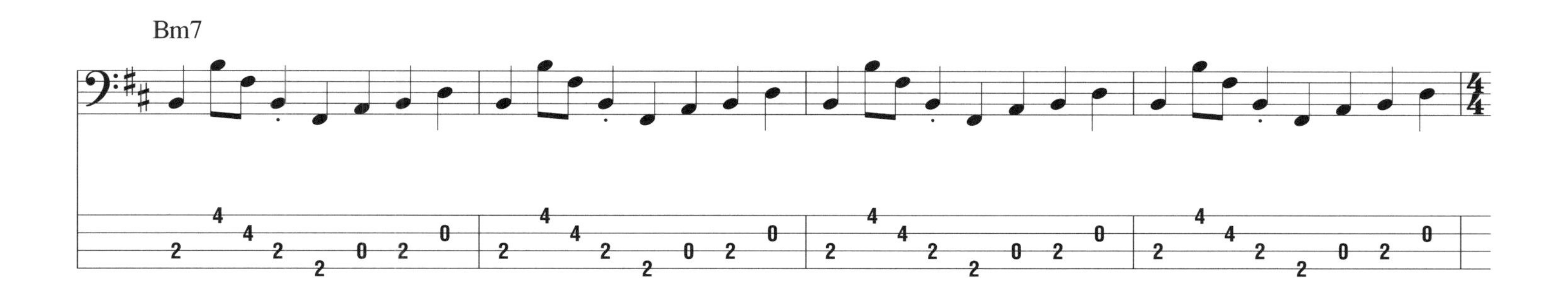
Bm7

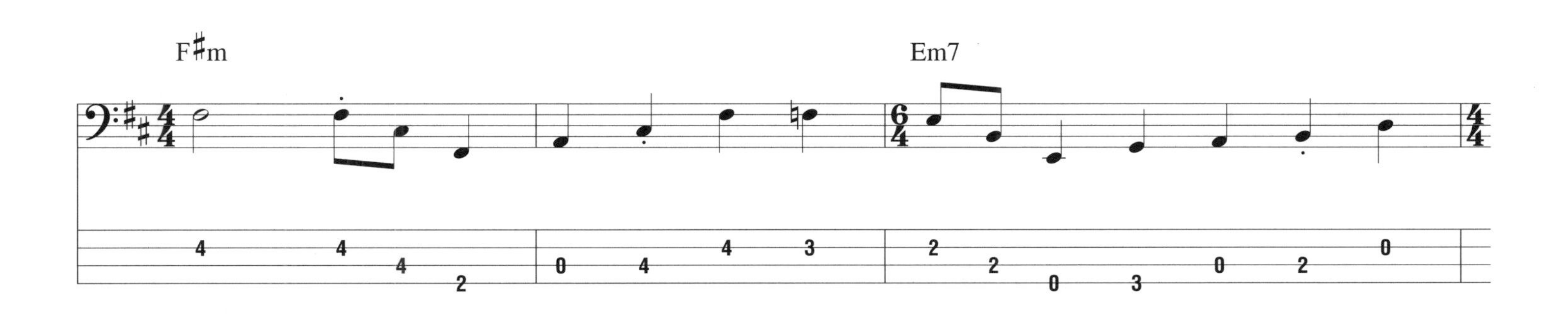
F♯m
Em7

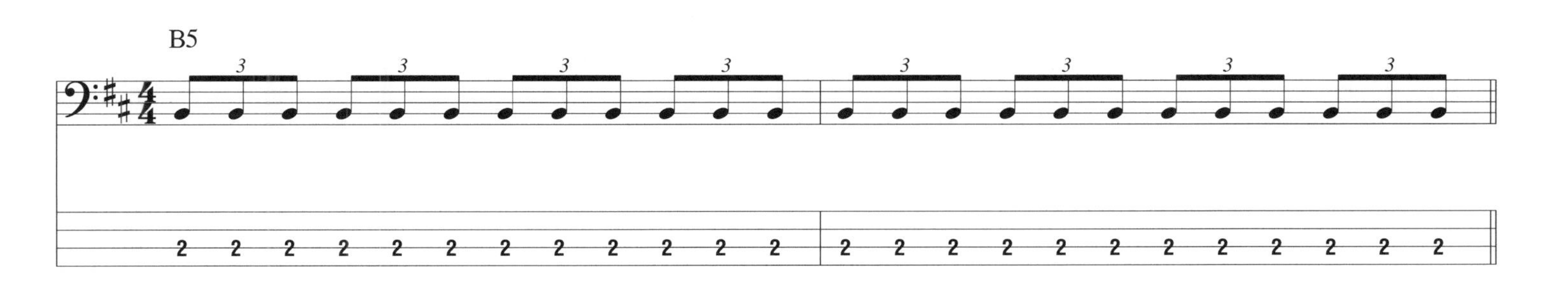
B5

Guitar Solo

Bm7
*
2 2 5 4 3 0 2 2 5 4 3 0 2 2 5 4 3 0 2 2 5 4 3 0

*Slur to 1st B note on repeats.

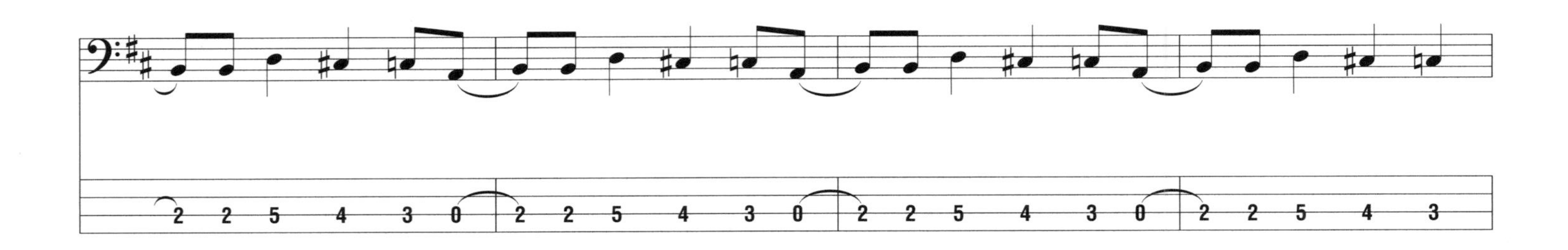
2 2 5 4 3 0 2 2 5 4 3 0 2 2 5 4 3 0 2 2 5 4 3

Em
7 6 5 4 0 7 6 5 4 0 7 6 5 4 0 7 6 5 4 0

Bm
2 2 5 4 3 0 2 2 5 4 3 0 2 2 5 4 3 0 2 2 5 4 3

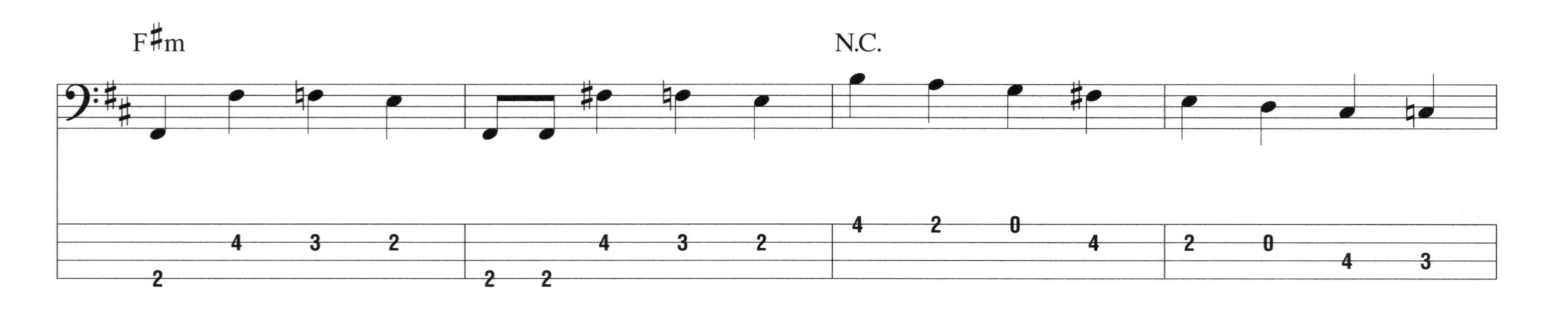
F♯m
N.C.
2 4 3 2 2 2 4 3 2 4 2 0 4 2 0 4 3

1., 2.
Bm7

3.
Bm7
D.S. al Coda

Coda

Outro
w/ Voc. ad lib., till fade
Bm7
Repeat and fade
A - way,
a - way,
'way,
a - way.

Additional Lyrics

2. Money, well, get back.
   I'm all right, Jack, keep your hands off of my stack.
   Money, it's a hit.
   Ah, don't give me that do goody good bullshit.
   I'm in the high fidelity first class traveling
   Set, and I think I need a Lear jet.

3. Money, it's a crime.
   Share it fairly, but don't take a slice of my pie.
   Money, so they say,
   Is the root of all evil today.
   But if you ask for a rise it's no surprise
   That they're giving none away.

My Generation

Words and Music by Peter Townshend

Intro
Very fast ♩ = 192
N.C.(G5)
(G5/F)
(G5)
(G5/F)
Bass
f
Verse
2nd time, Bass: w/ Fill 1 (4 times)
N.C.(G5)
(G5/F)
G5
G/F
*Voc. Fig. 1
End Voc. Fig. 1
1. Peo - ple try to put us d - down,
2. Why don't you all ff - fade a - way,
and
(Talk- in' 'bout my gen - er - a - tion.)
Bass Fig. 1
*Refers to upstemmed vocs. only.
G
N.C.(G5)
(G5/F)
Bkgd. Voc.: w/ Voc. Fig. 1
G5
G/F
just be - cause we get a - round.
don't try and dig what we all s - s - s - say.
I'm
End Bass Fig. 1
Fill 1

Bass: w/ Bass Fig. 1
N.C.(G5)
(G5/F)
Bkgd. Voc.: w/ Voc. Fig. 1
G5
G5/F
Things they ___ do look aw - ful c - c - c - cold. I
not try - in' to cause a big s - s - s - sen - sa - tion, I'm just
G N.C.(G5)
(G5/F)
Bkgd. Voc.: w/ Voc. Fig. 1
G5
G/F
hope I die be - fore ___ I get old. ___ This is my ___ gen - er - a -
talk - in' 'bout my g - g - g - gen - er - a - tion. ___ My gen - er -
Chorus
1.
G
Gsus4
G7
Gsus4
G
Gsus4
G7
G7sus4
- tion. This is my ___ gen - er - a - tion, ba - by. ___
a - tion.
Bass

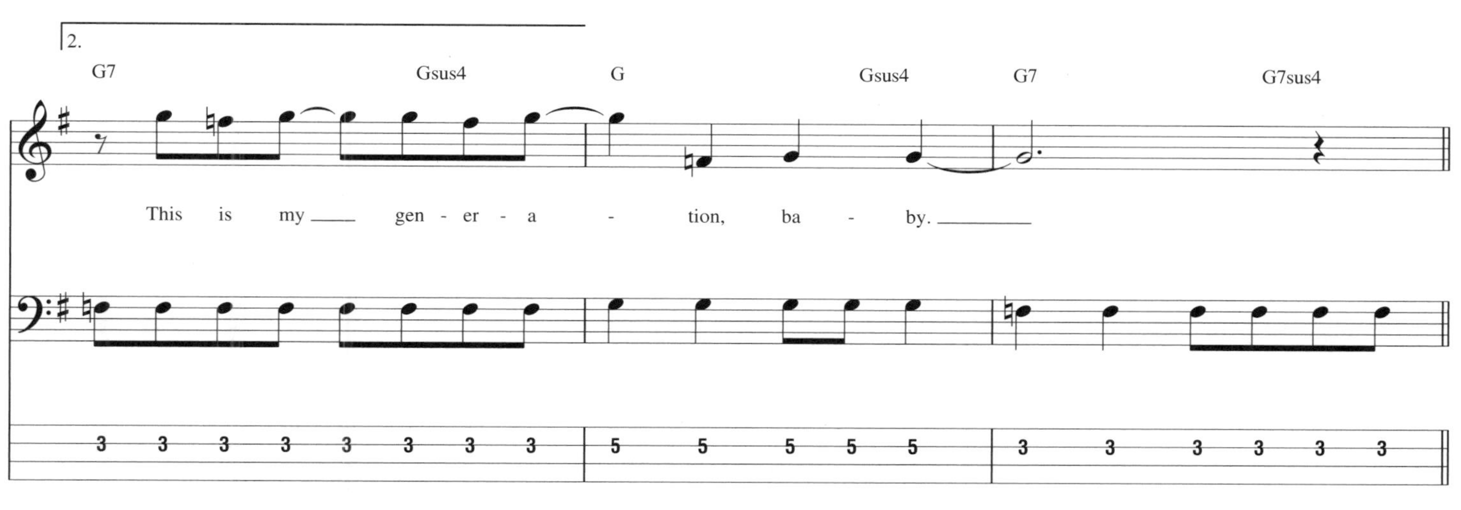
2.
G7
Gsus4
G
Gsus4
G7
G7sus4
This is my ___ gen - er - a - tion, ba - by. ___

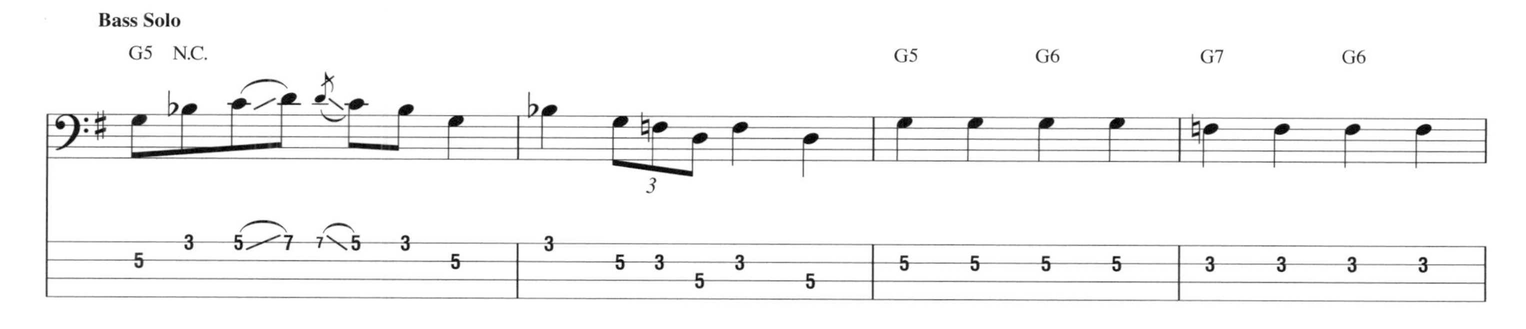
Bass Solo
G5 N.C.
G5
G6
G7
G6

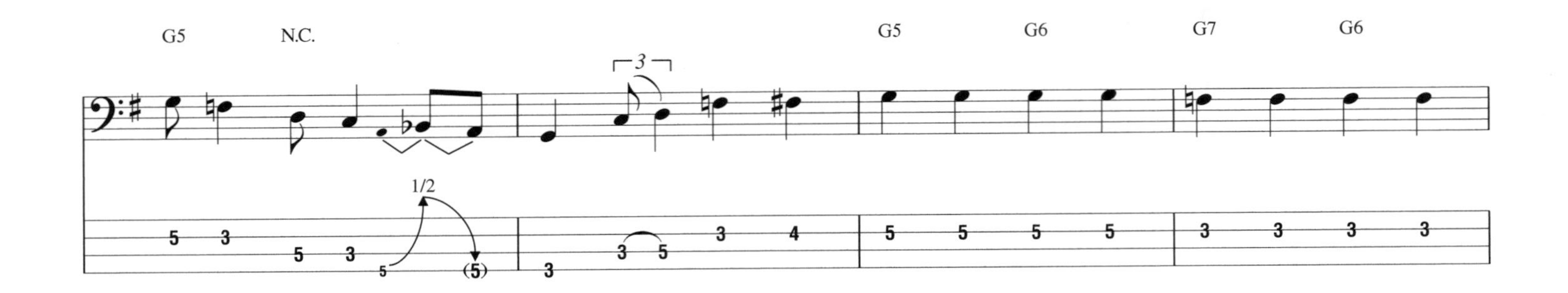
G5 N.C.
G5 G6 G7 G6
1/2

G5 N.C.
G5 G6 G7 G6

G5 N.C.
G6 G7 G6

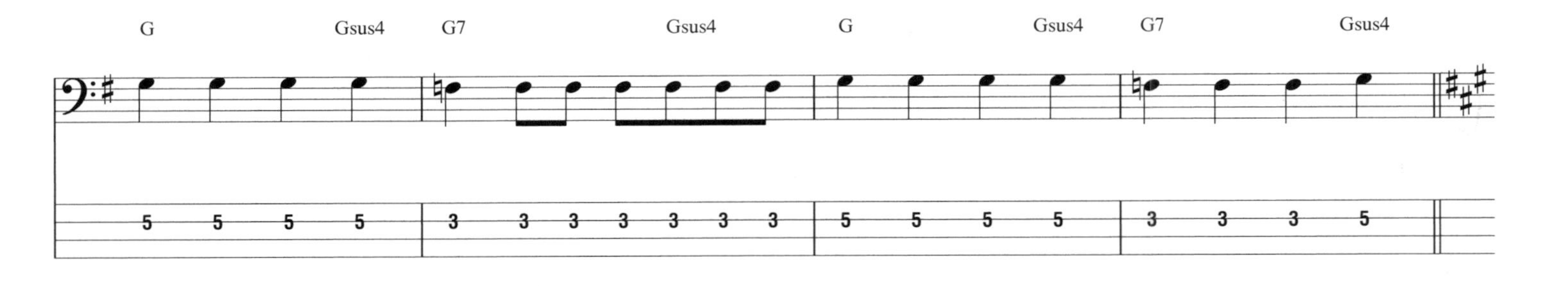
G Gsus4 G7 Gsus4 G Gsus4 G7 Gsus4

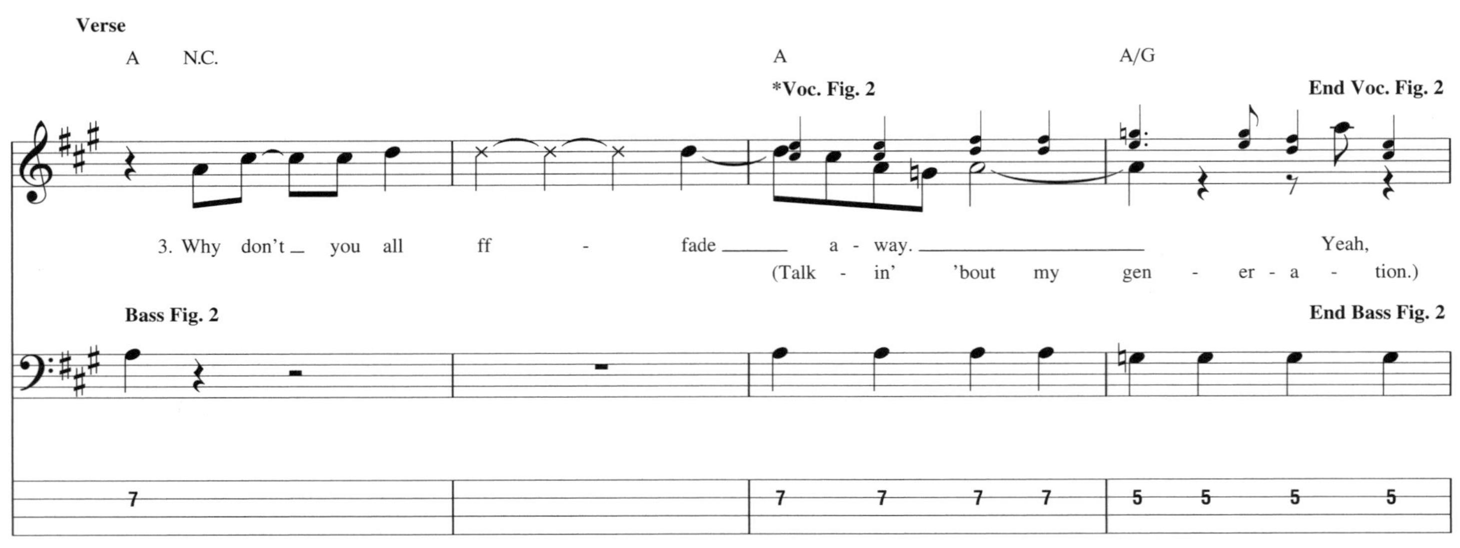
Verse
A N.C.
A A/G
*Voc. Fig. 2
End Voc. Fig. 2
3. Why don't you all ff - fade a - way. Yeah,
(Talk - in' 'bout my gen - er - a - tion.)
Bass Fig. 2
End Bass Fig. 2

*As before

Bass: w/ Bass Fig. 2 (3 times)
A
N.C.
Bkgd. Voc.: w/ Voc. Fig. 2
A
A/G
3
don't try and d - dig what we all s - s - s - s - s - say.

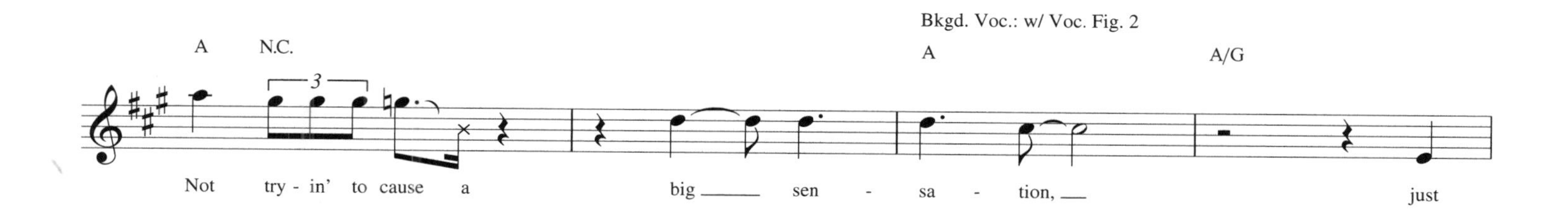
A
N.C.
Bkgd. Voc.: w/ Voc. Fig. 2
A
A/G
3
Not try - in' to cause a big sen - sa - tion, just

A
N.C.
Bkgd. Voc.: w/ Voc. Fig. 2
A
A/G
talk - in' 'bout my g - gen - er - a - tion. Ba - by, my gen - er - a -

Chorus
A
Asus4
A
Asus4
- tion, this is my gen - er - a - tion, ba - by.
Bass
7 7 7 7 7
5 5 5 5
7 7 7 7 7 7
5 5 5 5 5 5 5

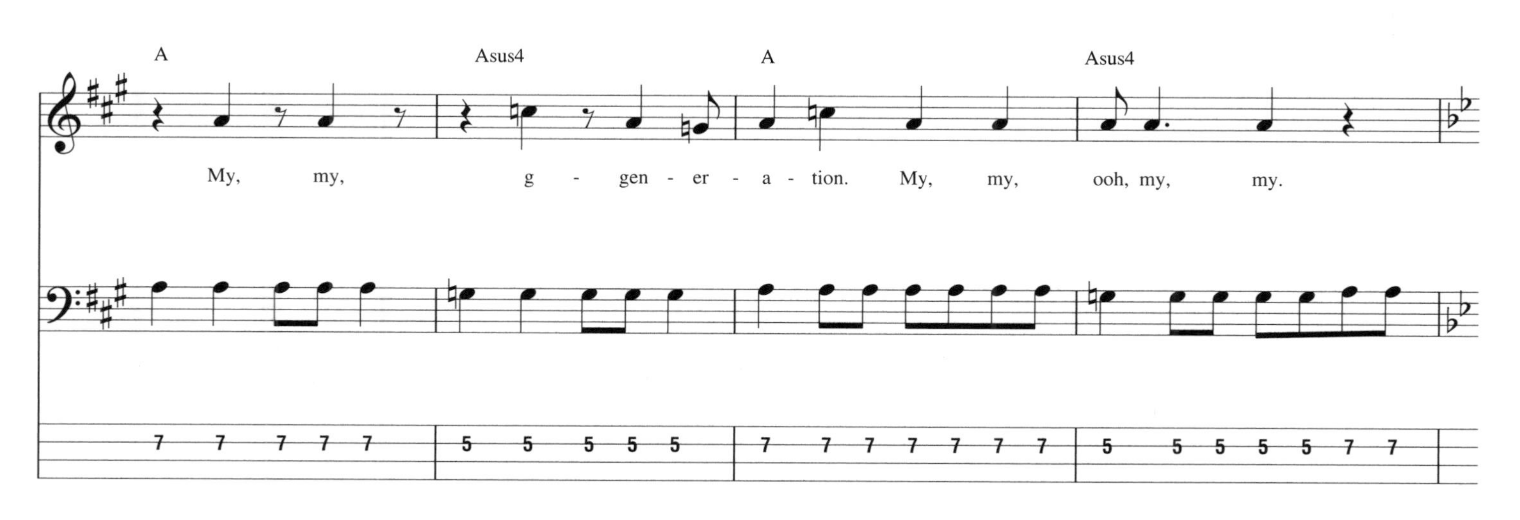
A
Asus4
A
Asus4
My, my, g - gen - er - a - tion. My, my, ooh, my, my.
7 7 7 7 7
5 5 5 5 5
7 7 7 7 7 7 7
5 5 5 5 5 7 7

B♭5
B♭5/A♭
B♭5
B♭5/A♭
My, my, my, my gen - er - a - tion.
8 8 8 8 8 8
6 6 6 6
8 8 8 8 8 8
6 6 6 6
Verse
B♭5 N.C.
B♭5
B♭6
B♭7
B♭6
*Voc. Fig. 3
End Voc. Fig. 3
4. Peo - ple try to put us d - down
(Talk - in' 'bout my gen - er - a - tion.)
Bass Fig. 3
End Bass Fig. 3
8
8 8 8 8
6 6 6 6
*As before
Bass: w/ Bass Fig. 3
B♭5 N.C.
Bkgd. Voc.: w/ Voc. Fig. 3
B♭5
B♭5/A♭
3
3
just be - cause we g - g - g - get a - round.
Bkgd. Voc.: w/ Voc. Fig. 3
B♭5 N.C.
B♭
B♭sus4
B♭
B♭sus4
Things they do look aw - ful c - c - cold,
yeah, I
Bass
8 6
8 8 8 8
6 6 6 6
Bass: w/ Bass Fig. 3
B♭ N.C.
Bkgd. Voc.: w/ Voc. Fig. 3
B♭
B♭sus4
hope I die be - fore I get old.
My gen - er -

Chorus
B♭
B♭sus4
B♭
B♭sus4
a - tion.
This is my gen - er - a - tion, ba - by.
Mm,
Bass
B♭
B♭sus4
B♭
B♭sus4
my, my, my, my, my gen - er - a - tion, gen - er - a - tion.
Guitar Solo
C5
F/C
C
F/C
C
F/C
C
F/C
C
F/C
C
B♭/C
C
B♭/C

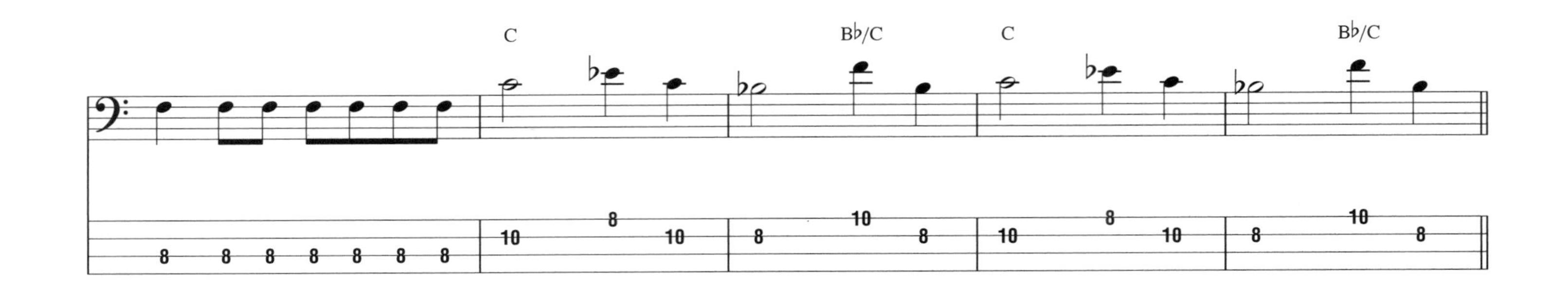
C
B♭/C
C
B♭/C

Outro

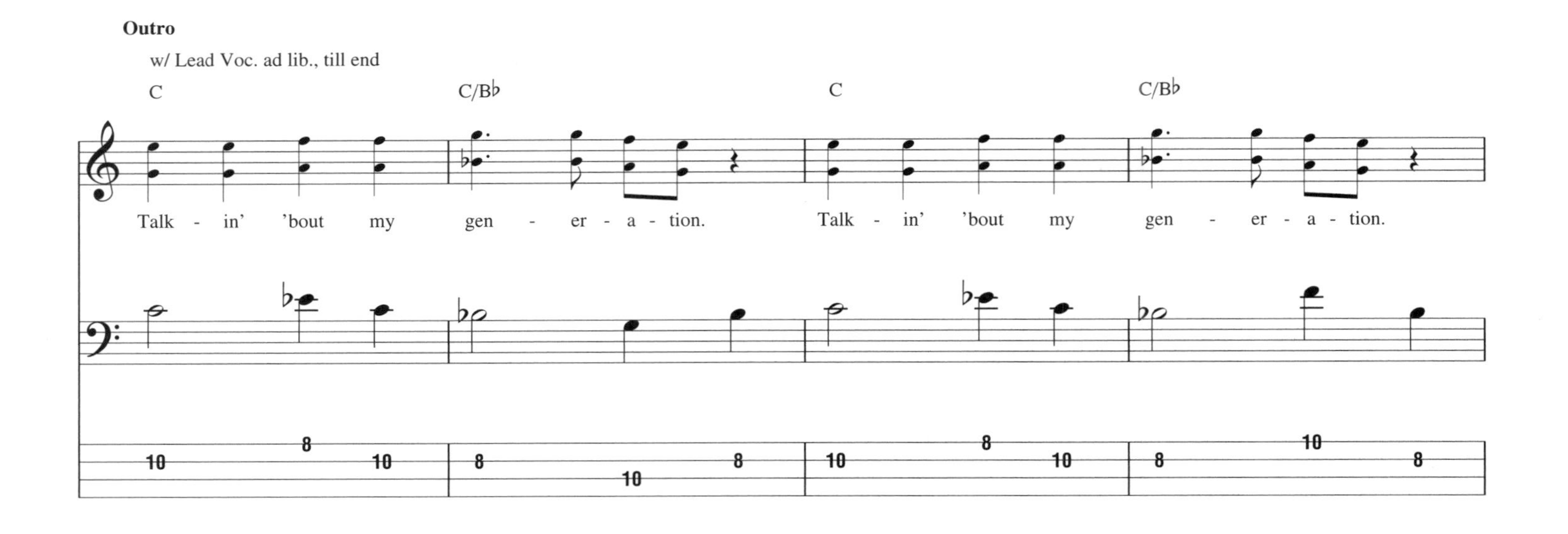
w/ Lead Voc. ad lib., till end
C
C/B♭
C
C/B♭
Talk - in' 'bout my gen - er - a - tion.
Talk - in' 'bout my gen - er - a - tion.

C
C/B♭
C
C/B♭
Talk - in' 'bout my gen - er - a - tion.
Talk - in' 'bout my gen - er - a - tion.

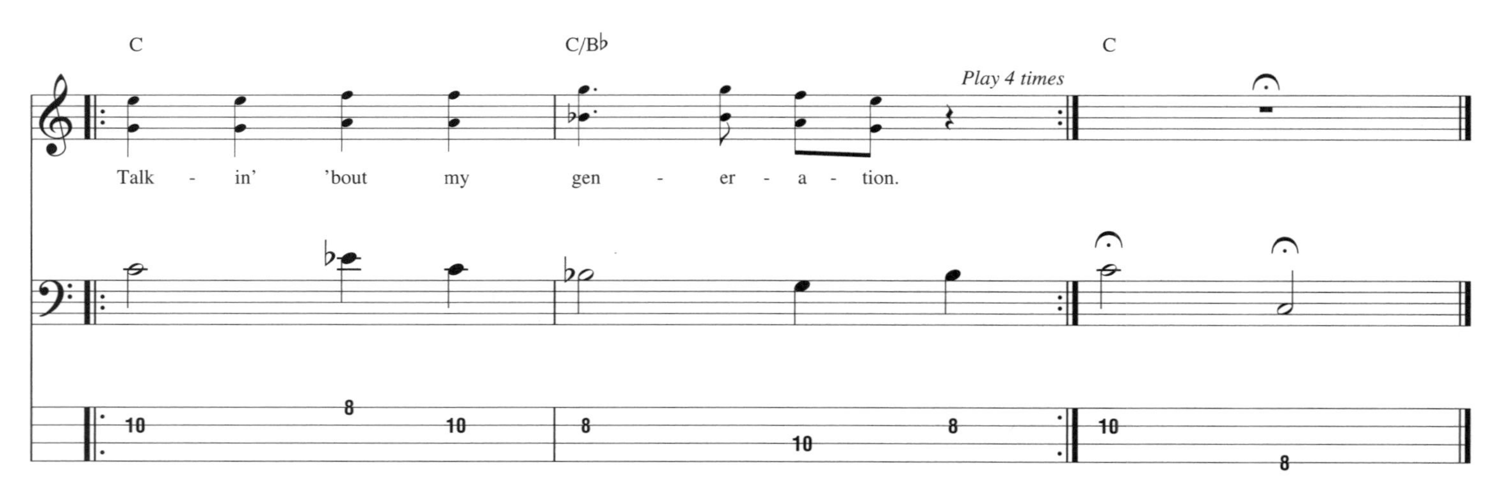
C
C/B♭
Play 4 times
C
Talk - in' 'bout my gen - er - a - tion.

N.I.B.

Words and Music by Frank Iommi, John Osbourne, William Ward and Terence Butler

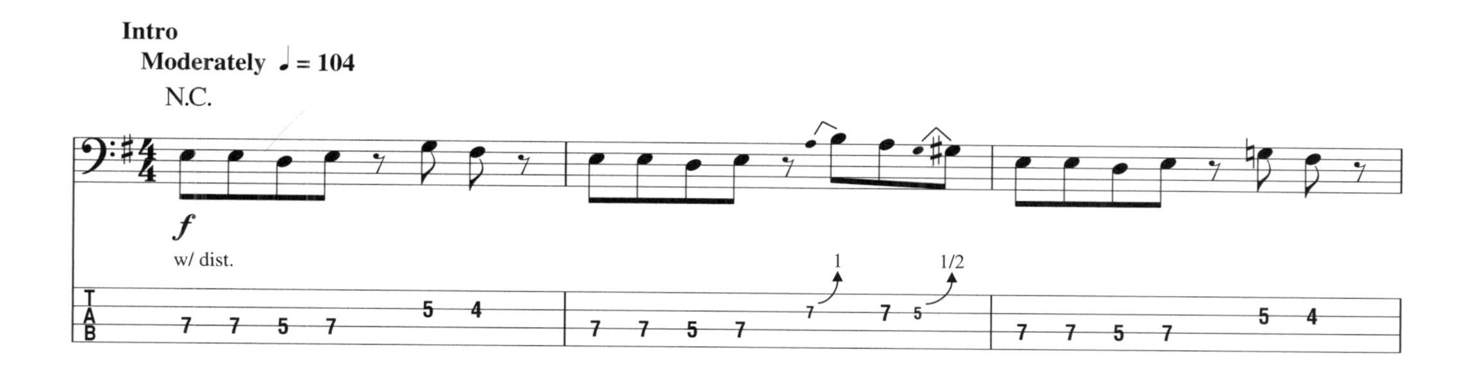

Intro
Moderately ♩ = 104
N.C.
w/ dist.

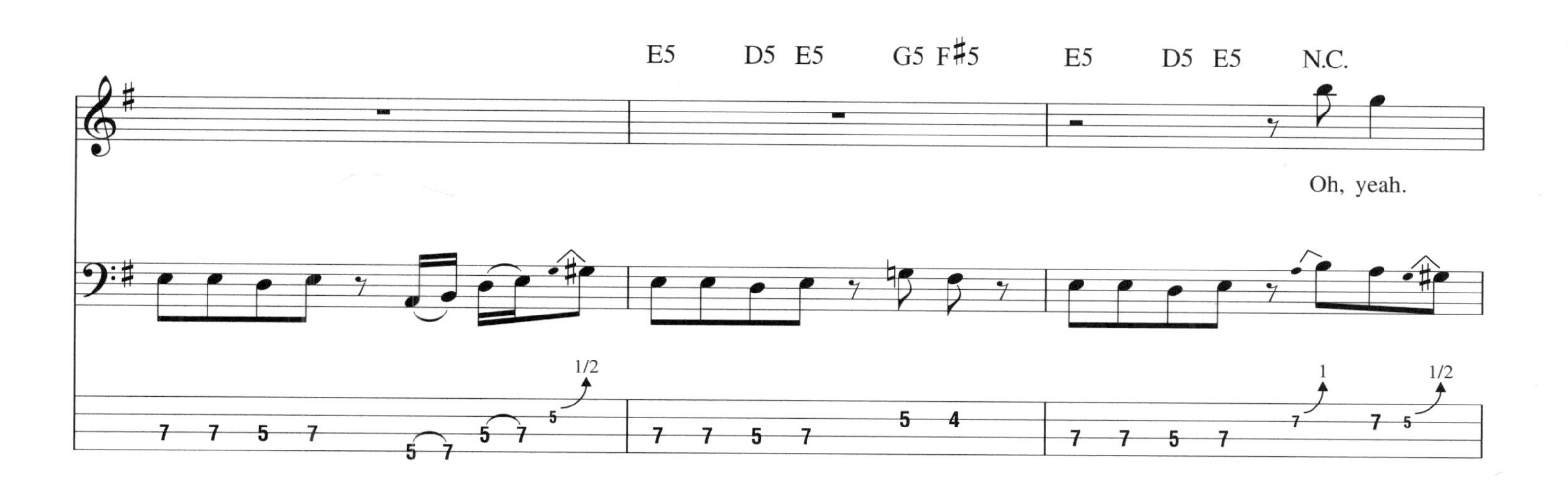

E5 D5 E5 G5 F♯5 E5 D5 E5 N.C.
Oh, yeah.

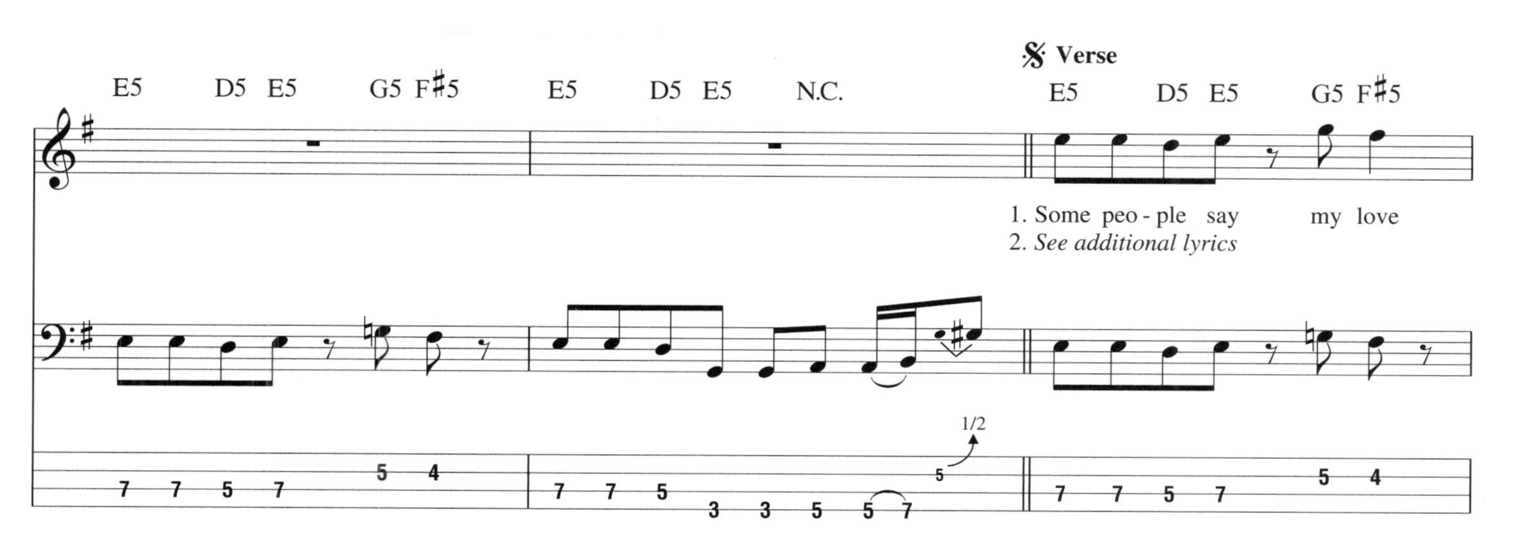

E5 D5 E5 G5 F♯5 E5 D5 E5 N.C.
Verse
E5 D5 E5 G5 F♯5
1. Some peo - ple say my love
2. See additional lyrics

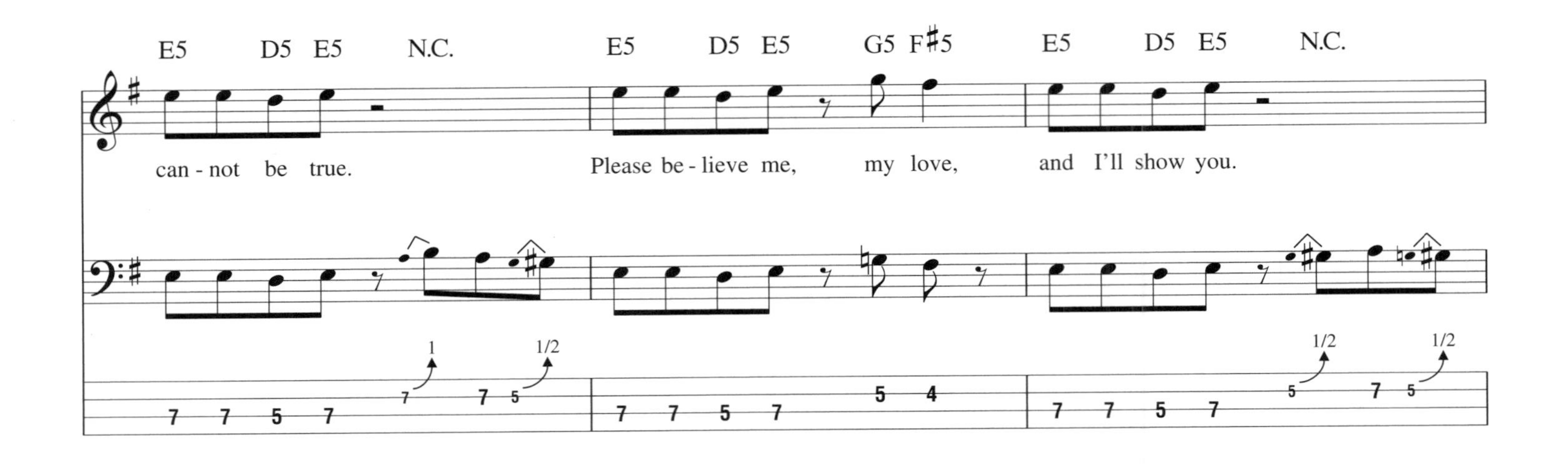
E5 D5 E5 N.C. E5 D5 E5 G5 F#5 E5 D5 E5 N.C.
can - not be true. Please be - lieve me, my love, and I'll show you.

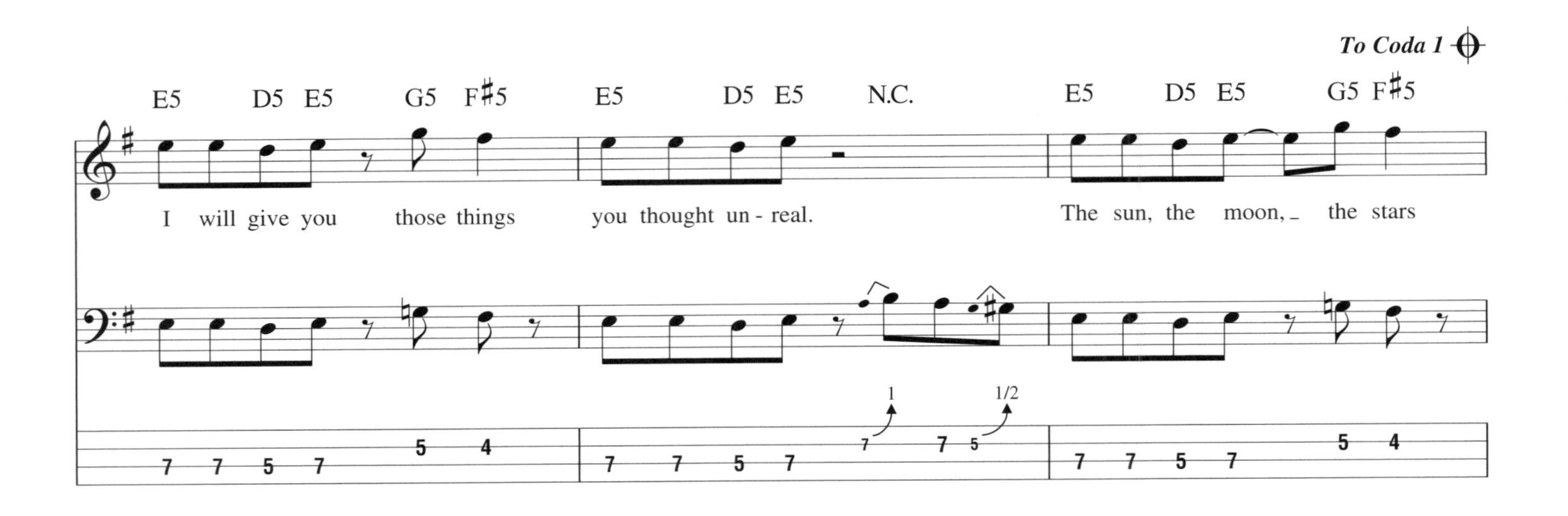
To Coda 1
E5 D5 E5 G5 F#5 E5 D5 E5 N.C. E5 D5 E5 G5 F#5
I will give you those things you thought un - real. The sun, the moon, the stars

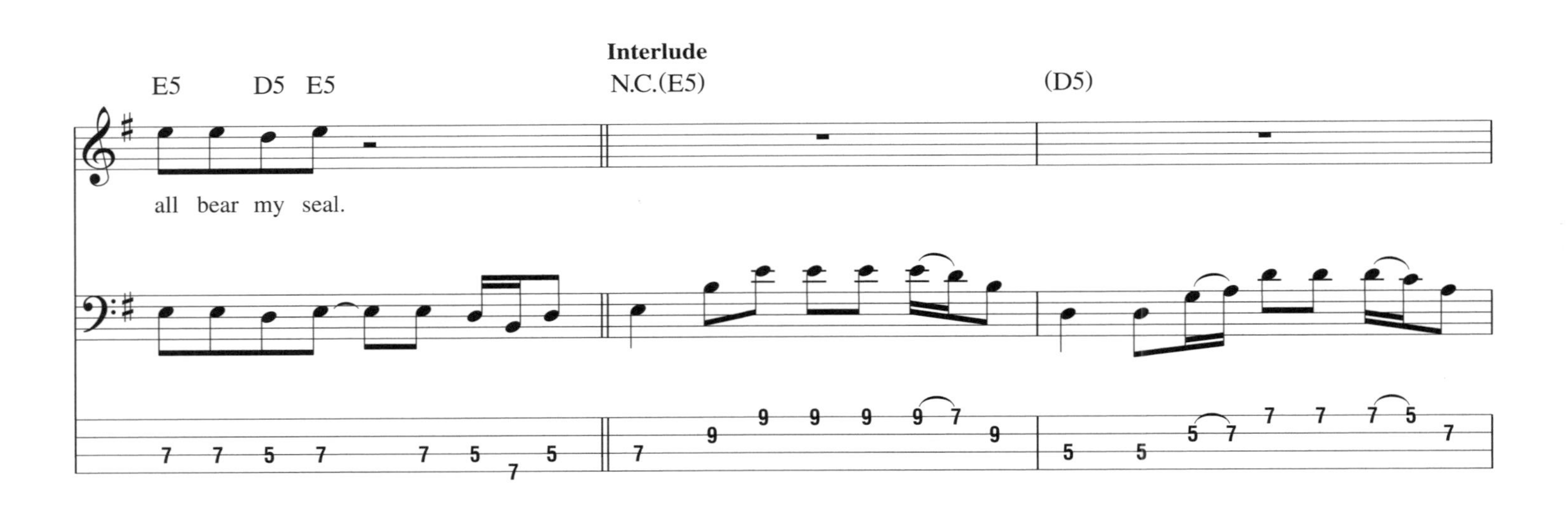
Interlude
E5 D5 E5 N.C.(E5) (D5)
all bear my seal.

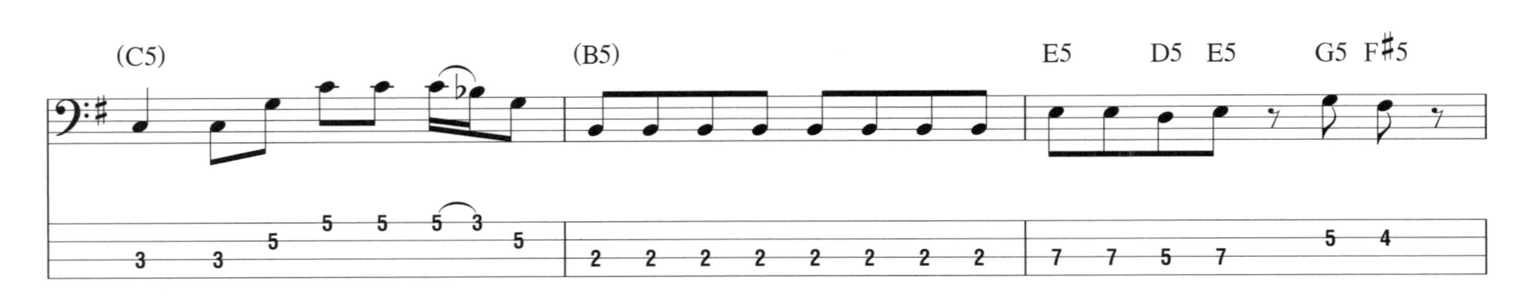
(C5) (B5) E5 D5 E5 G5 F#5

D.S. al Coda 1
E5 D5 E5 N.C. E5 D5 E5 G5 F#5 E5 D5 E5 N.C.
Oh, yeah.
Coda 1
Bridge
E5 D5 E5 E5 D5/E
the end of time. Your love for me has just
mf
dist. off
C5/E B5 E5
got to be real before you know
D5/E C5/E B5
the way I'm go - in' to feel,

C5
B5
C5
I'm go - in' to feel,
I'm go - in' to
B5
Interlude
E5 D5 E5 G5 F♯5
E5 D5 E5 N.C.
feel.
Oh, yeah.
w/ dist.
E5 D5 E5 G5 F♯5
E5 D5 E5 N.C.
Verse
E5 D5 E5 G5 F♯5
3., 5. Now I have you with me
E5 D5 E5 N.C.
E5 D5 E5 G5 F♯5
E5 D5 E5 N.C.
un - der my pow'r.
Our love grows strong - er now
with ev - 'ry hour.

To Coda 2
E5 D5 E5 G5 F#5
E5 D5 E5 N.C.
E5 D5 E5 G5 F#5
Look in - to my — eyes, you'll
see who I am.
My name is Lu - ci - fer,
1/2
E5 D5 E5 N.C.
Interlude
N.C.(E5)
(D5)
please take my hand.
1
1/2
(C5)
(B5)
Guitar Solo
N.C.(E5)
(D5)
(C5)
(B5)
(E5)
(D5)
(C5)

(B5)
(E5)
(D5)

(C5)
(B5)
(E5)

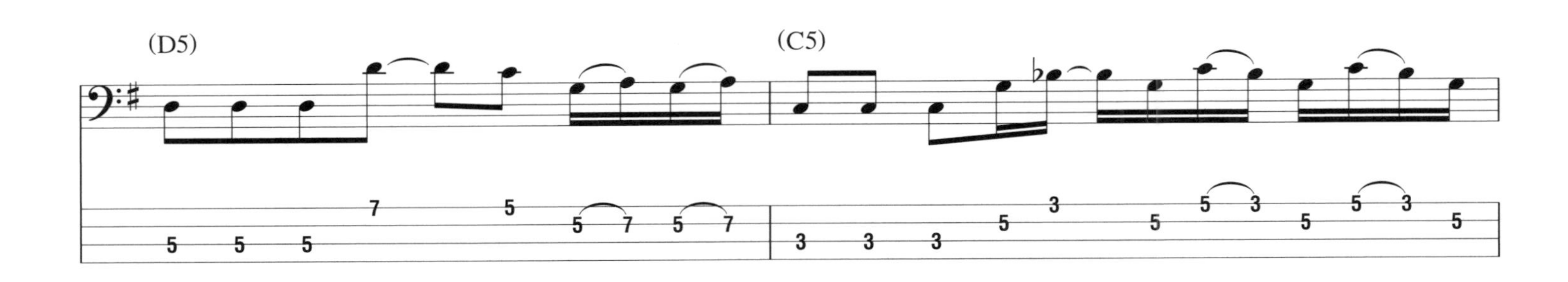

(D5)
(C5)

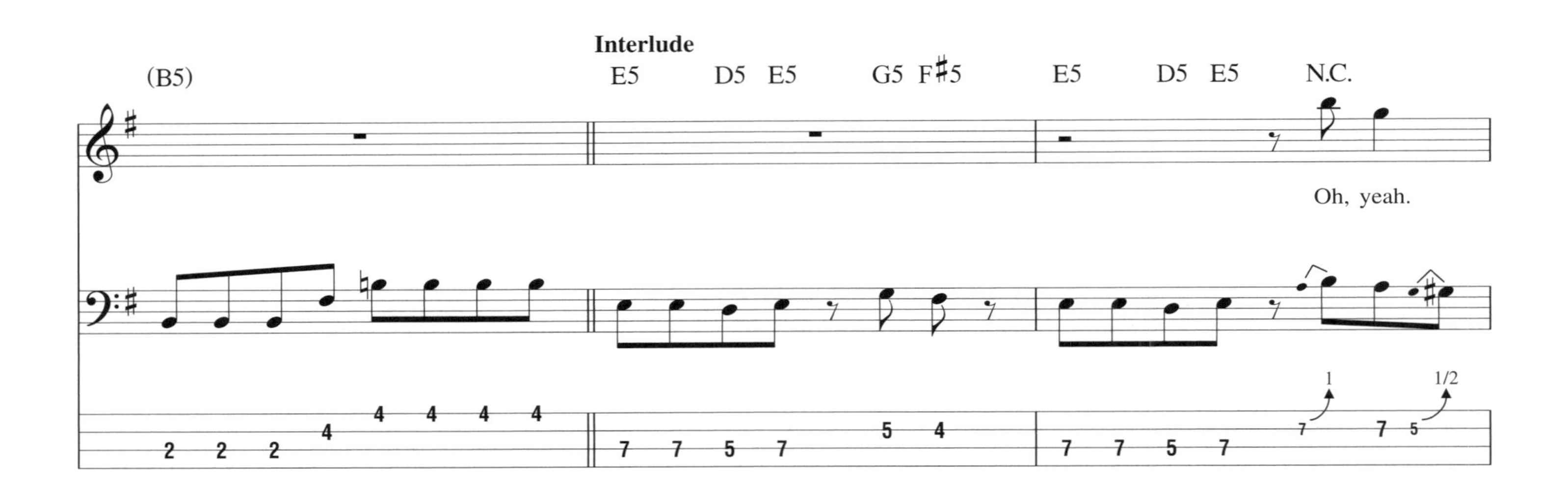

Interlude
(B5)
E5 D5 E5 G5 F♯5
E5 D5 E5 N.C.
Oh, yeah.

E5 D5 E5 G5 F♯5
E5 D5 E5 N.C.
Verse
E5 D5 E5 G5 F♯5
4. Fol-low me now and you

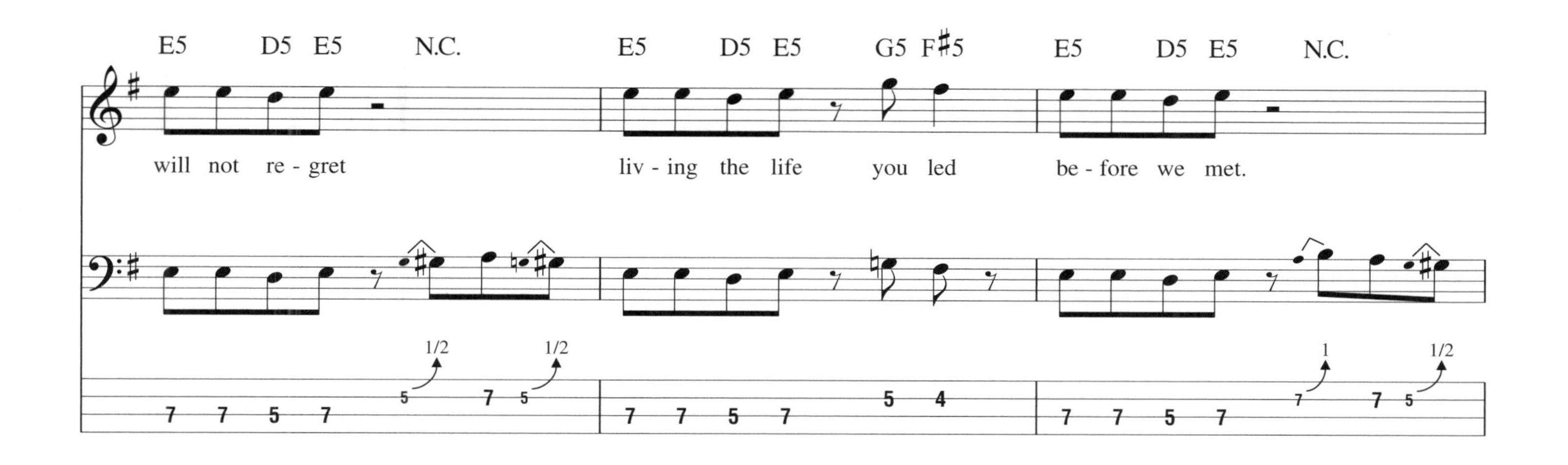
E5 D5 E5 N.C.
E5 D5 E5 G5 F♯5
E5 D5 E5 N.C.
will not re - gret
liv - ing the life you led
be - fore we met.
1/2
1/2
1
1/2

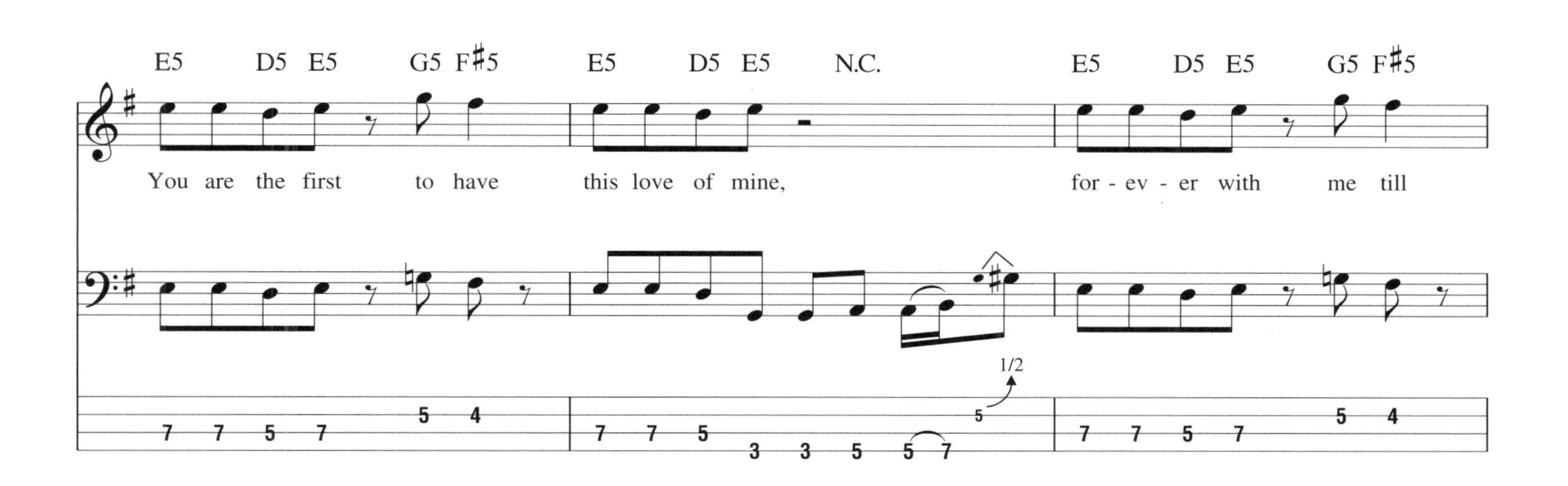
E5 D5 E5 G5 F♯5
E5 D5 E5 N.C.
E5 D5 E5 G5 F♯5
You are the first to have
this love of mine,
for - ev - er with me till
1/2

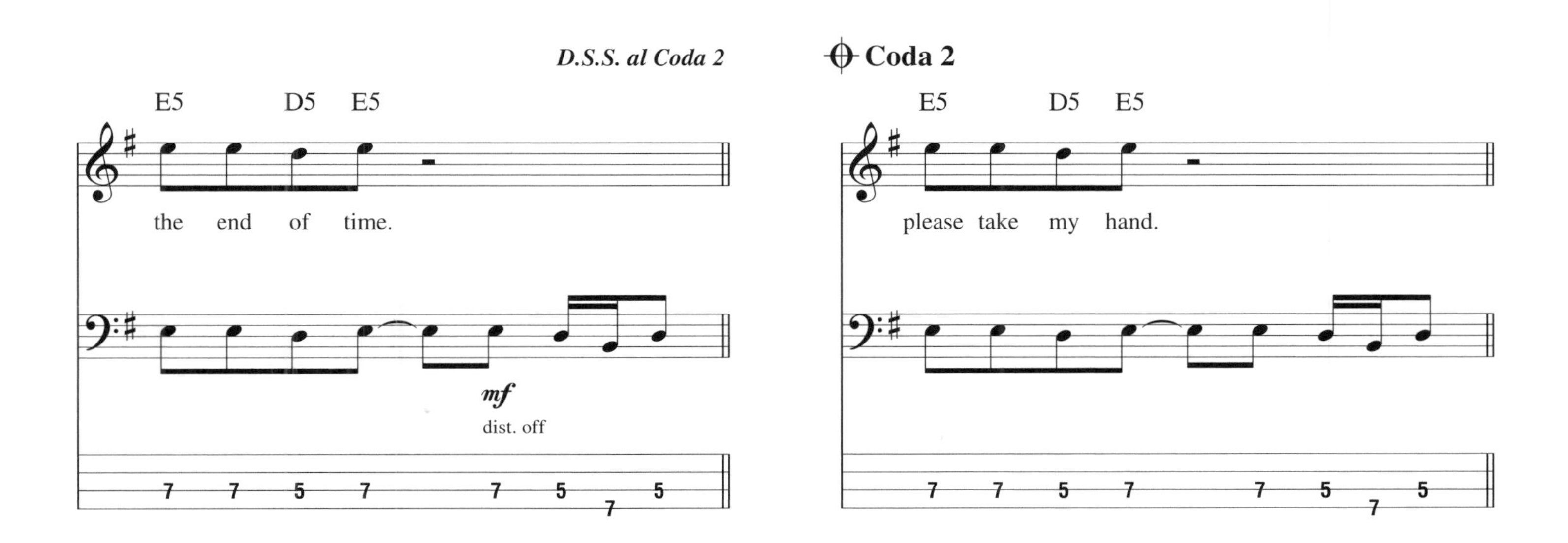
D.S.S. al Coda 2
Coda 2
E5 D5 E5
the end of time.
mf
dist. off
E5 D5 E5
please take my hand.

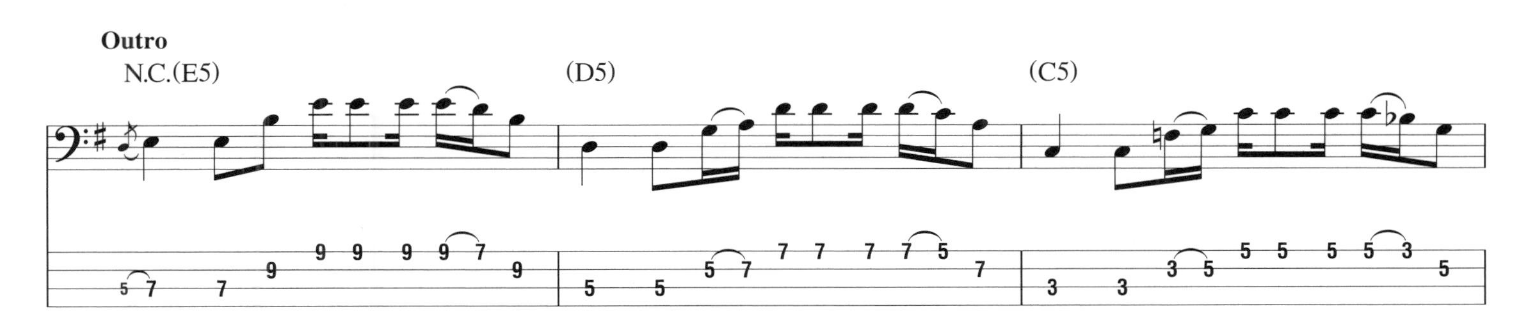
Outro
N.C.(E5)
(D5)
(C5)

(B5)
(E5)
(D5)

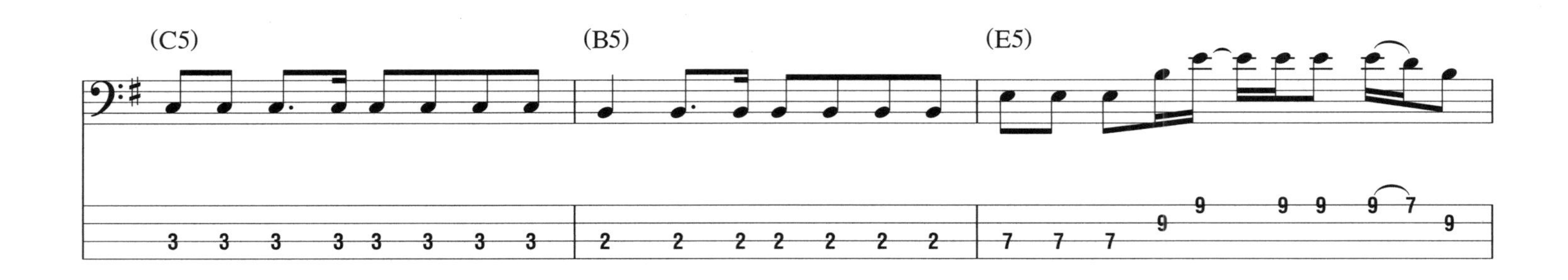
(C5)
(B5)
(E5)

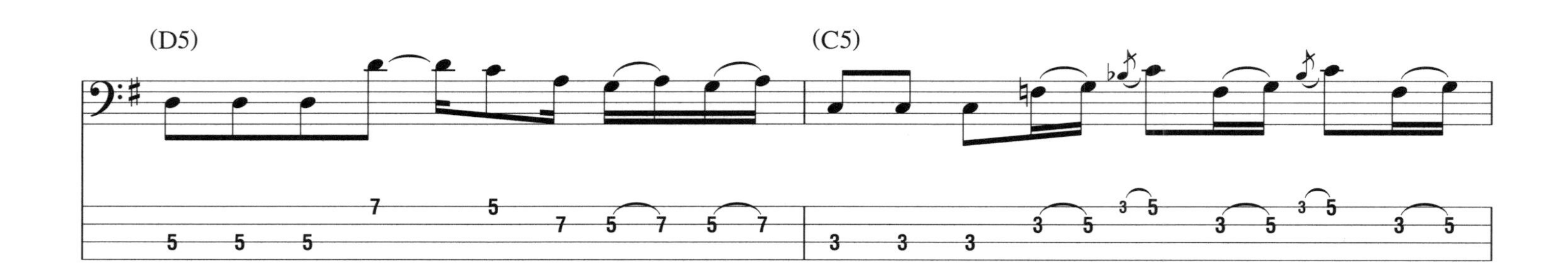
(D5)
(C5)

(B5)
(E5)

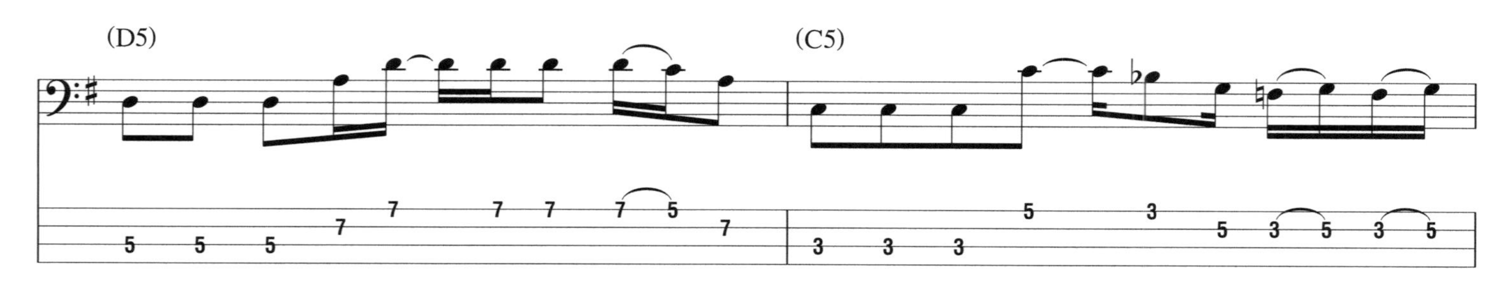
(D5)
(C5)

(B5)
(E5)

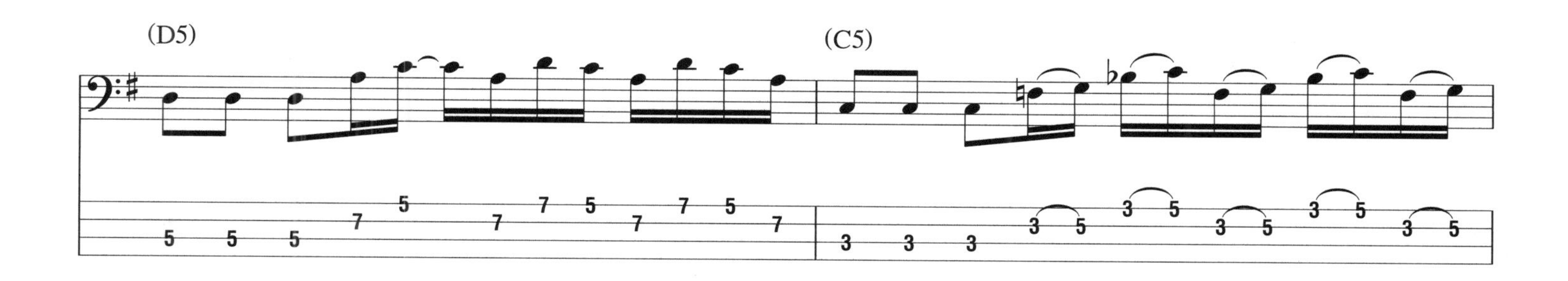
(D5)
(C5)

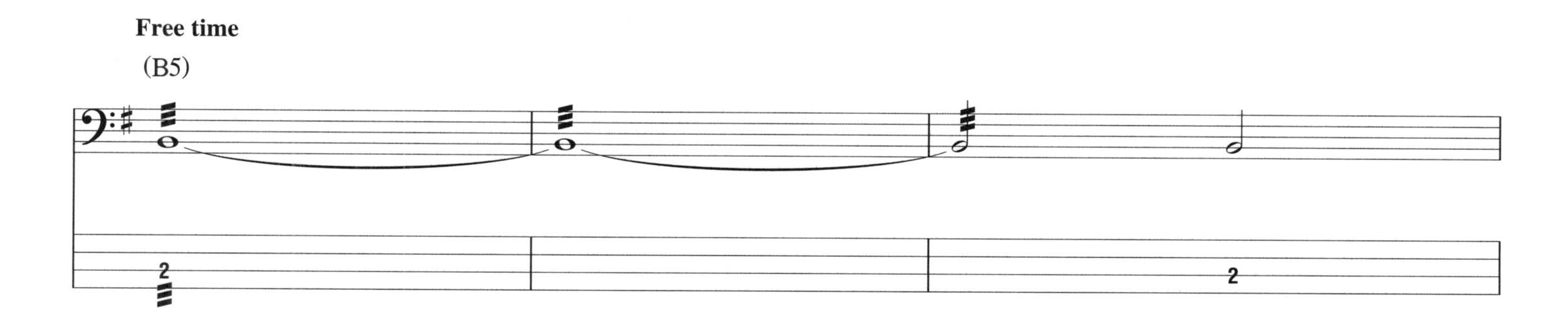
Free time
(B5)

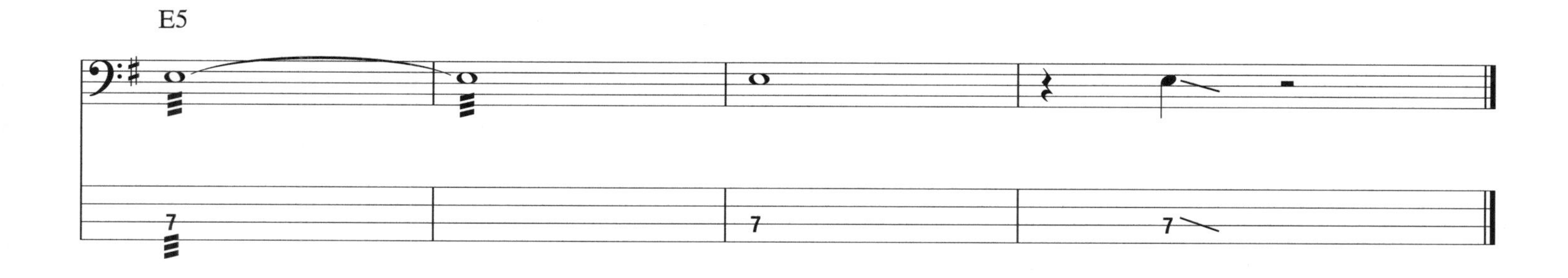
E5

Additional Lyrics

2. Follow me now and you will not regret
   Living the life you led before we met.
   You are the first to have this love of mine,
   Forever with me till the end of time.

No More Tears

Words and Music by Ozzy Osbourne, Zakk Wylde, Randy Castillo, Michael Inez and John Purdell

Drop D tuning, down 1/2 step:
(low to high) D♭-A♭-D♭-G♭

Intro

Moderate Rock ♩ = 104

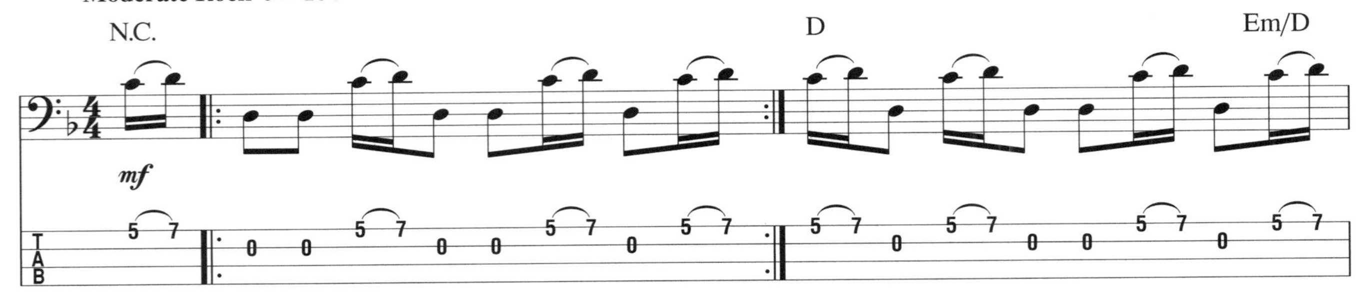
N.C.
D
Em/D
mf
TAB

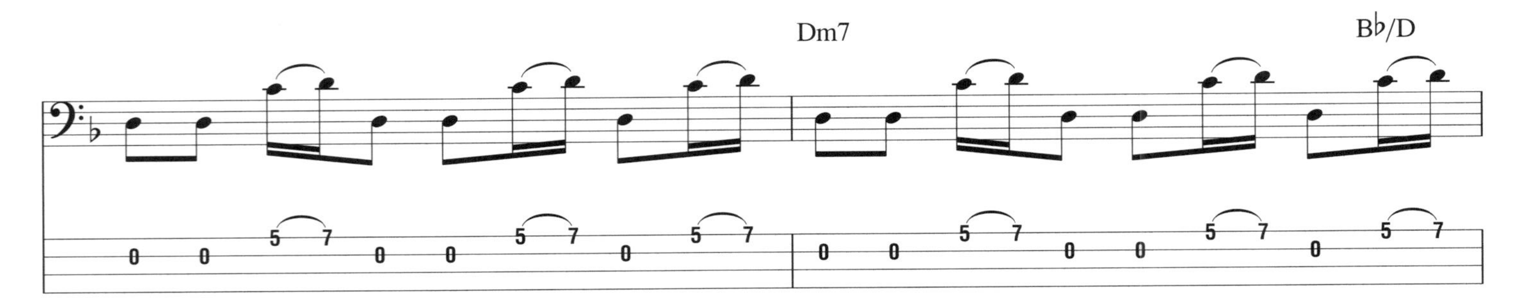
Dm7
B♭/D

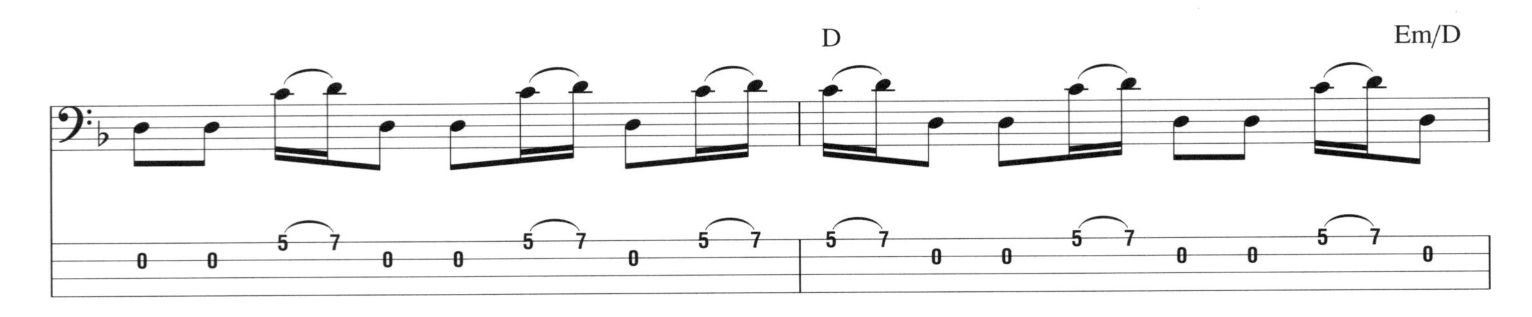
D
Em/D

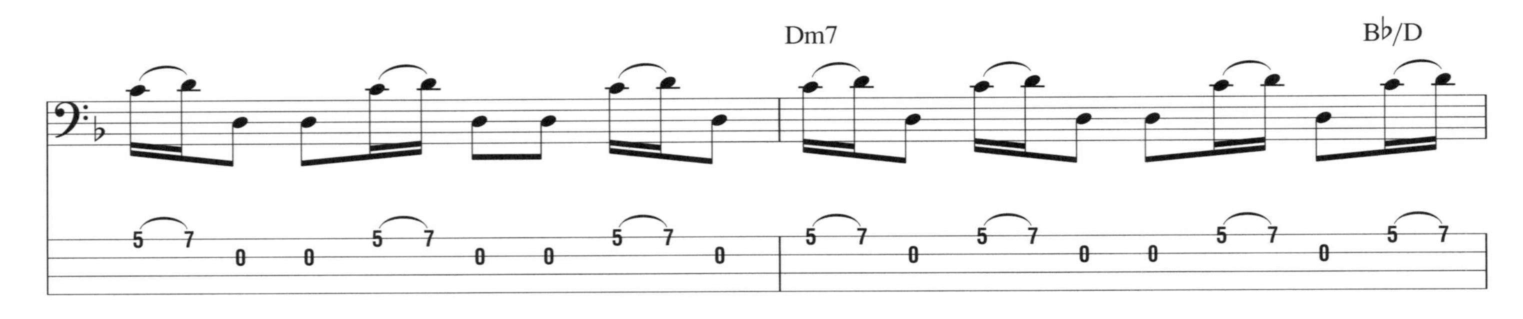
Dm7
B♭/D

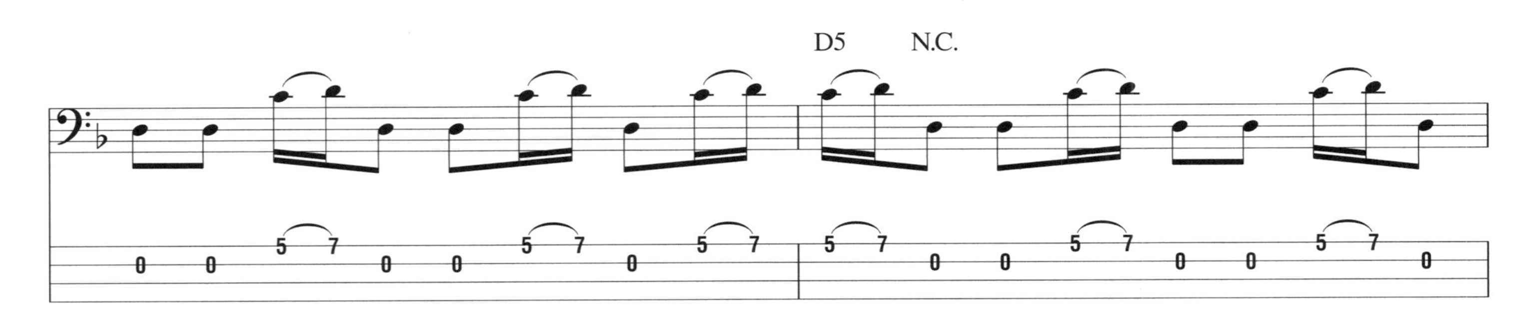
D5
N.C.

Verse
N.C.
1. The light in the win - dow is a
3. See additional lyrics
D5 F5 D5 A♭5 G5 F5 G5 F5 D5 A♭5
crack in the sky.
G5 F5 G5 N.C.
D5 N.C.
A stair - way to dark - ness in the
G5 F5 G5 A♭5 G5 F5 G5 F5 A♭5
blink of an eye.

G5 F5 G5 F5
D5 N.C.
A lev - ee of tears ___ to learn she'll
D5 F5 D5
Ab5 G5 F5 G5 F5 D5 Ab5
nev - er be com - ing back. ___
G5 F5 G5 N.C.
D5 N.C.
The man in the dark ___ will bring an -
G5 F5 G5
Ab5 G5 F5 G5 F5 Ab5
oth - er at - tack. ___

Pre-Chorus

2nd time, substitute Fill 3
G5
F5
G5
F5
D5
E5/D
1. Your mom - ma told
2., 3. See additional lyrics
2nd time, substitute Fill 1
3rd time, substitute Fill 4
F5/D
B♭/D
you that you're not sup - posed to talk to strang - ers.
D5
E5/D
F5/D
B♭/D
Look in the mir - ror, tell me, do you think your life's
Fill 1
Fill 3
Fill 4

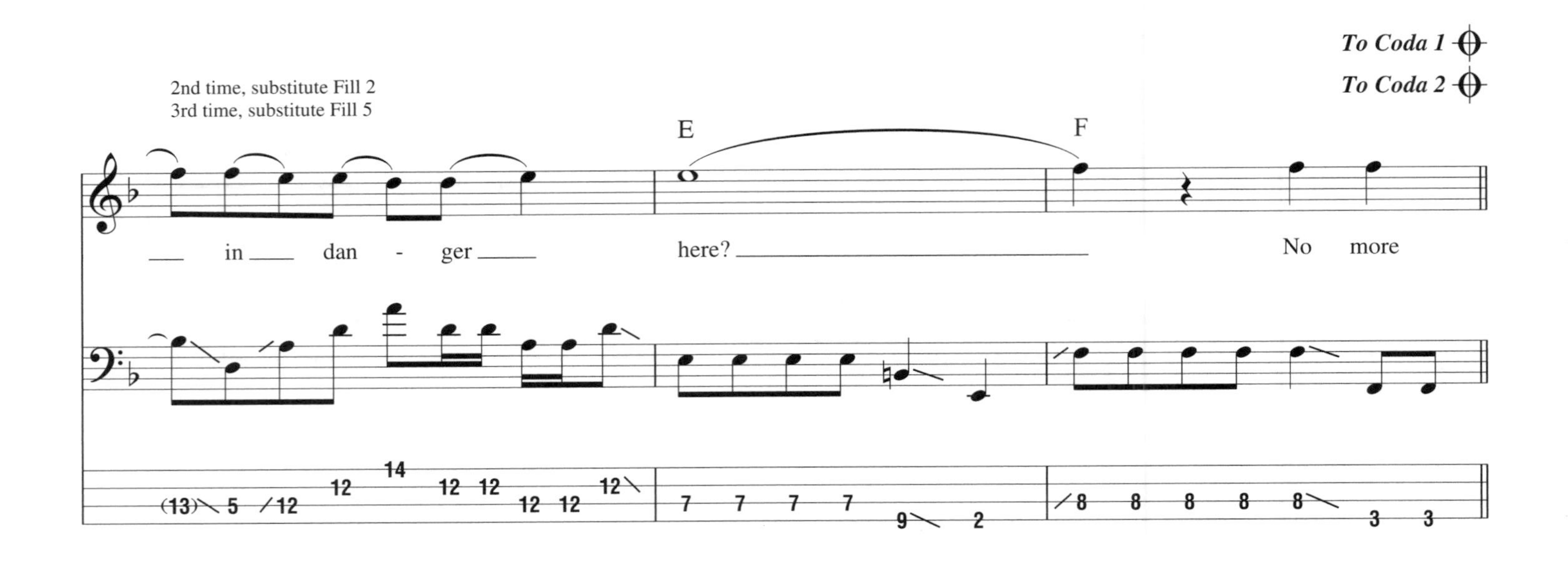
To Coda 1
To Coda 2
2nd time, substitute Fill 2
3rd time, substitute Fill 5
E
F
in dan - ger
here?
No more

Chorus
N.C.
Bb5 G5 Ab5 G5 F5
N.C.
tears.
No more
tears.

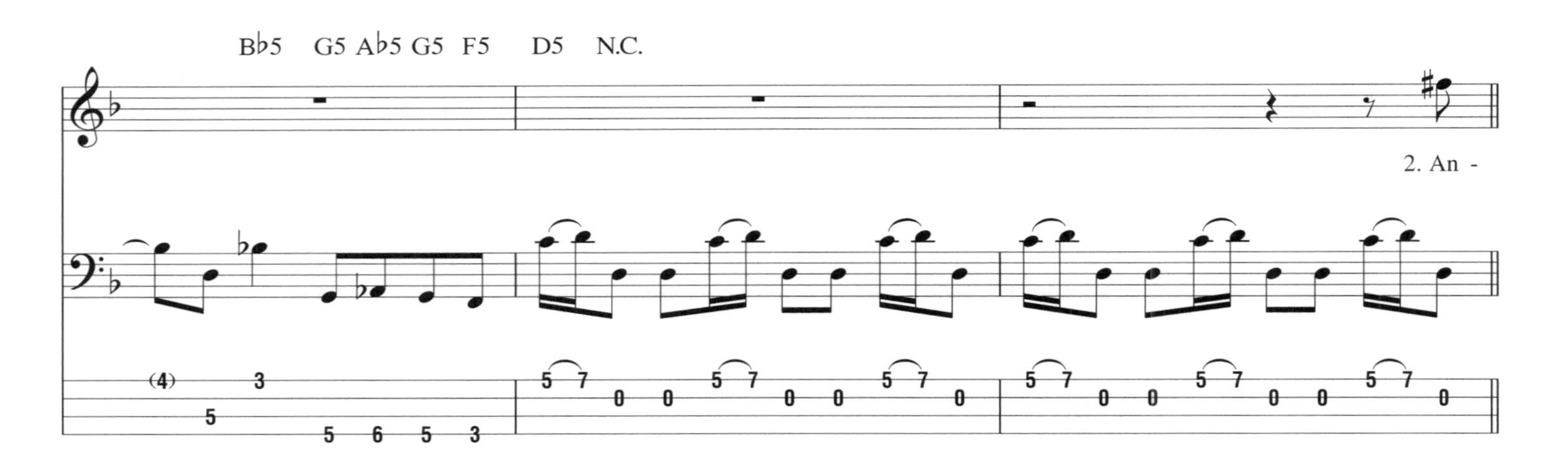
Bb5 G5 Ab5 G5 F5 D5 N.C.
2. An -

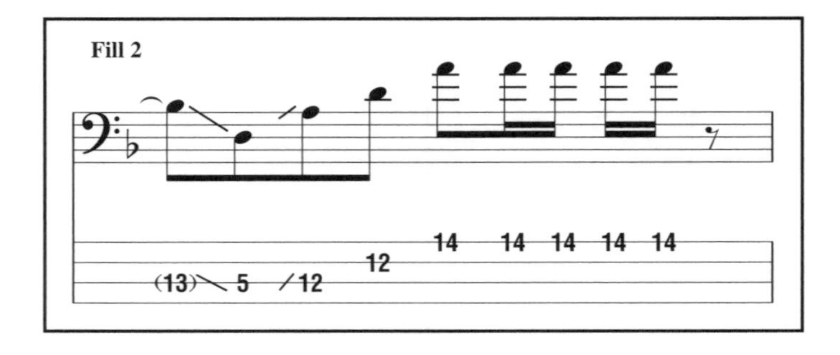
Fill 2

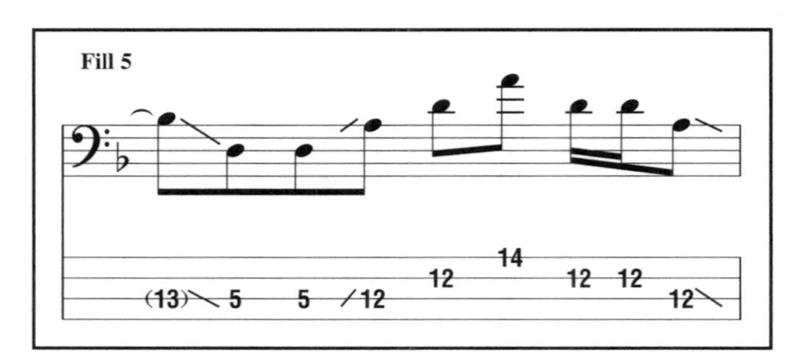
Fill 5

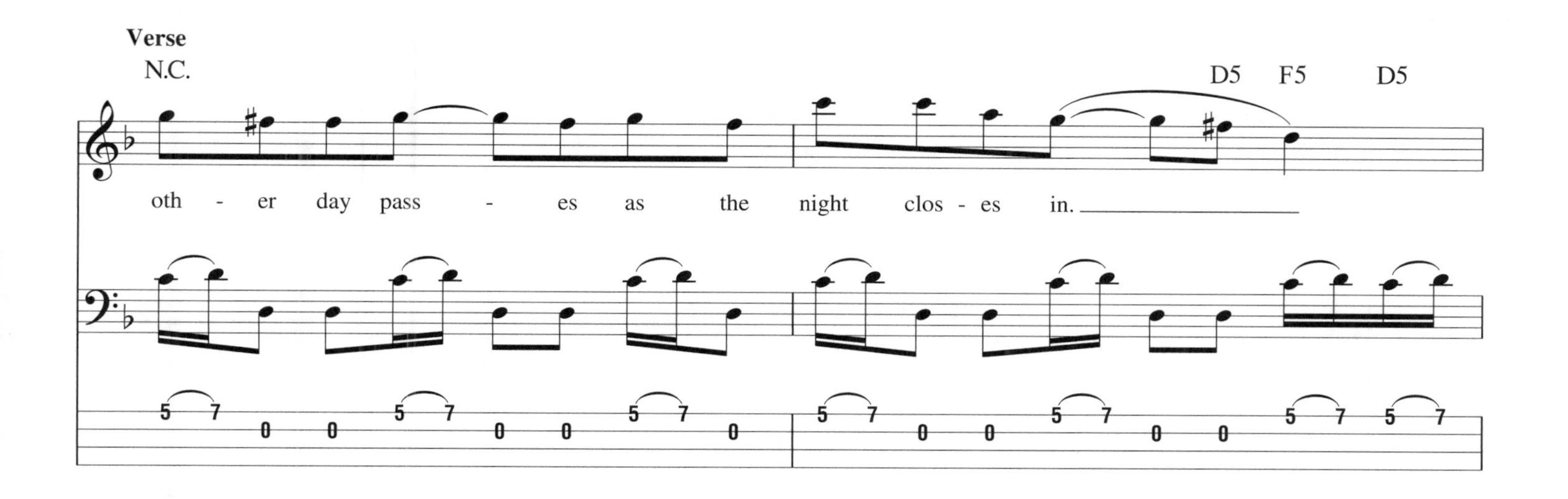
Verse
N.C.
D5 F5 D5
oth - er day pass - es as the night clos - es in.

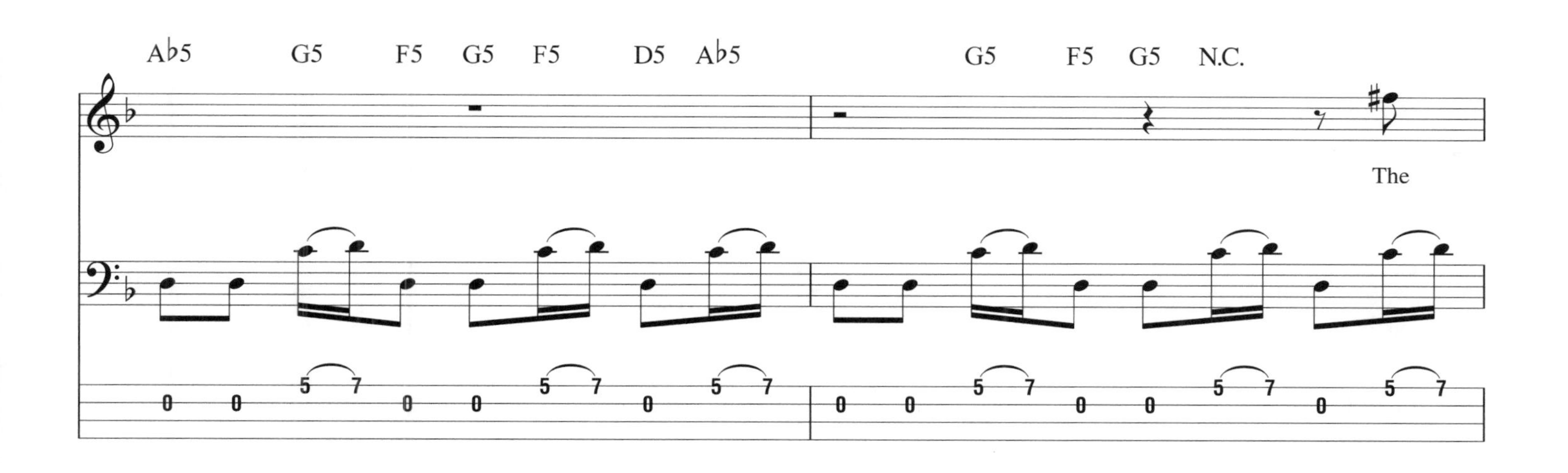
A♭5 G5 F5 G5 F5 D5 A♭5
G5 F5 G5 N.C.
The

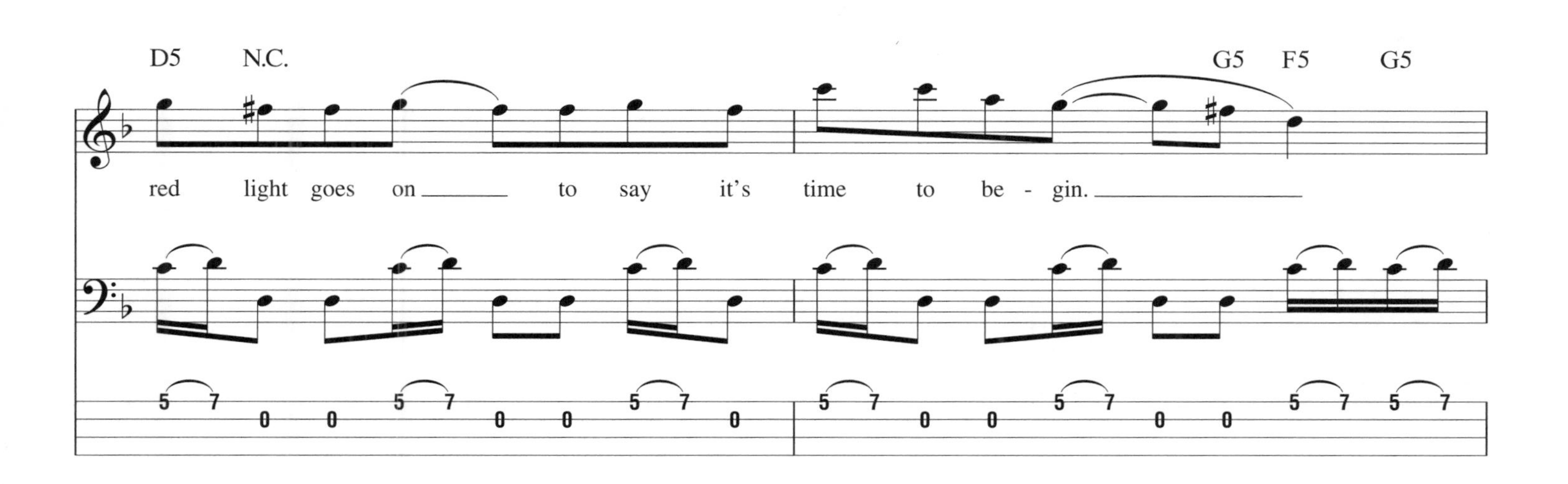
D5 N.C.
G5 F5 G5
red light goes on to say it's time to be - gin.

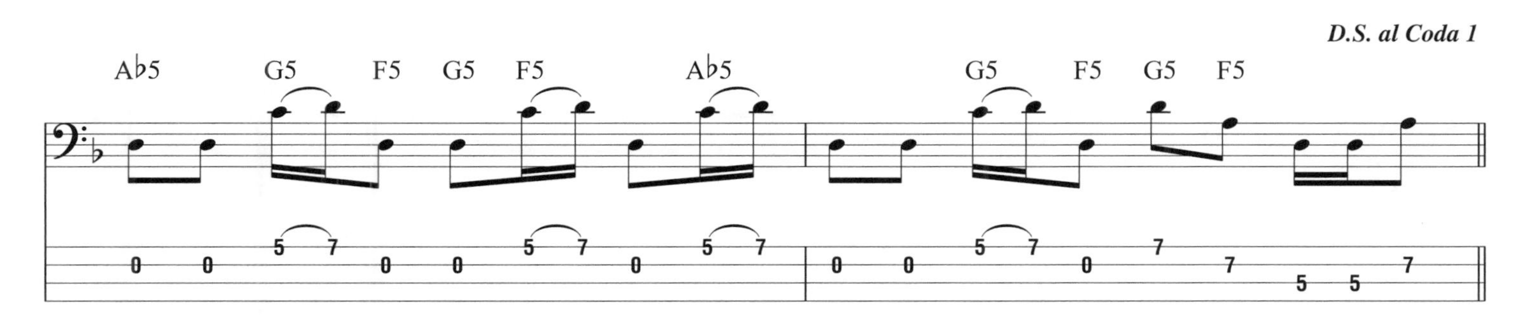
D.S. al Coda 1
A♭5 G5 F5 G5 F5 A♭5
G5 F5 G5 F5

Coda 1
Chorus
N.C.
1., 2., 3.
4.
Bb5 G5 Ab5 G5 F5
Bb5 G5 Ab5 G5 F5
tears. _
No more

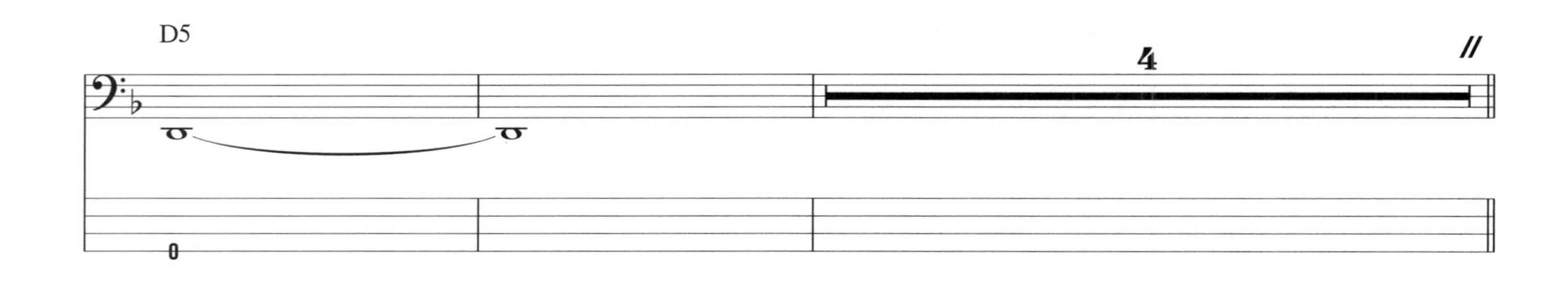

D5
4

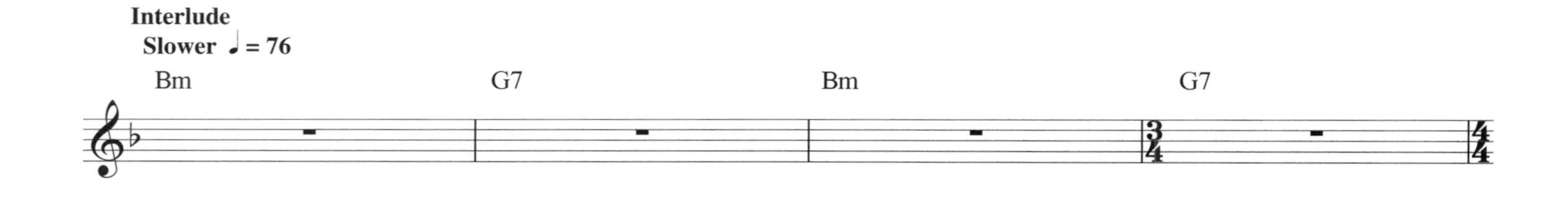

Interlude
Slower ♩ = 76
Bm
G7
Bm
G7

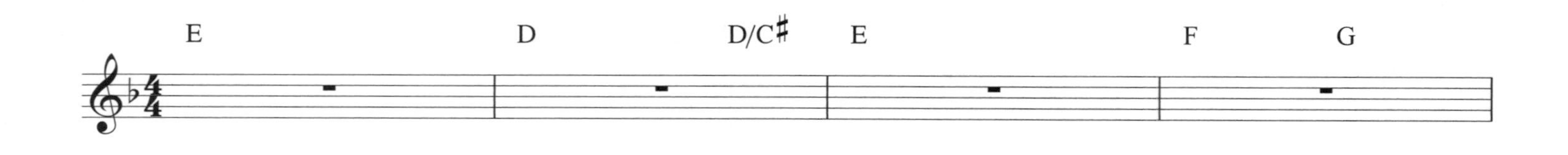

E
D
D/C♯
E
F
G

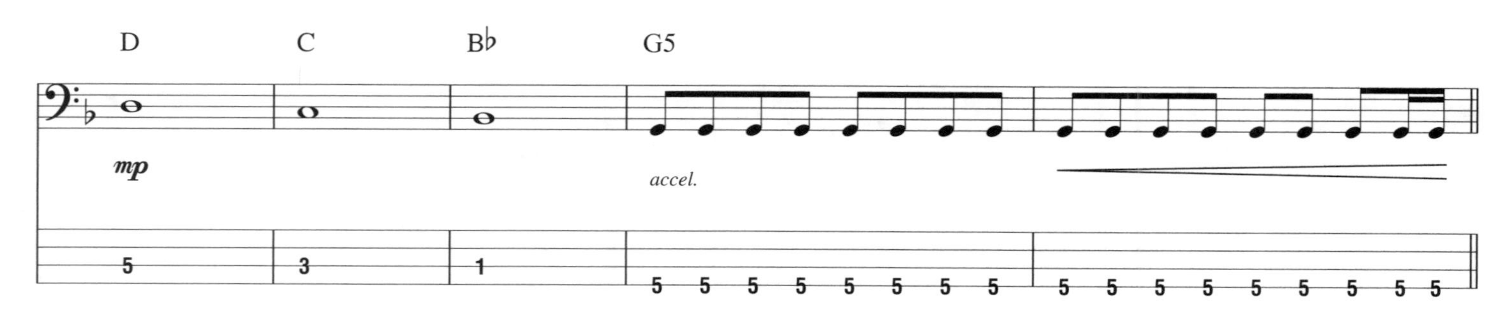

D
C
Bb
G5
mp
accel.

Guitar Solo
Tempo I ♩ = 104

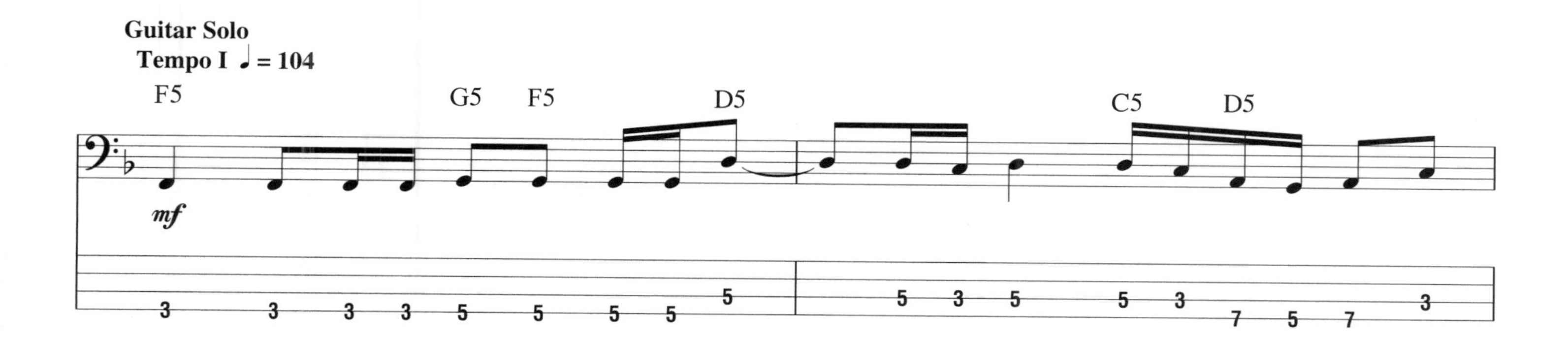
F5
G5
F5
D5
C5
D5
mf

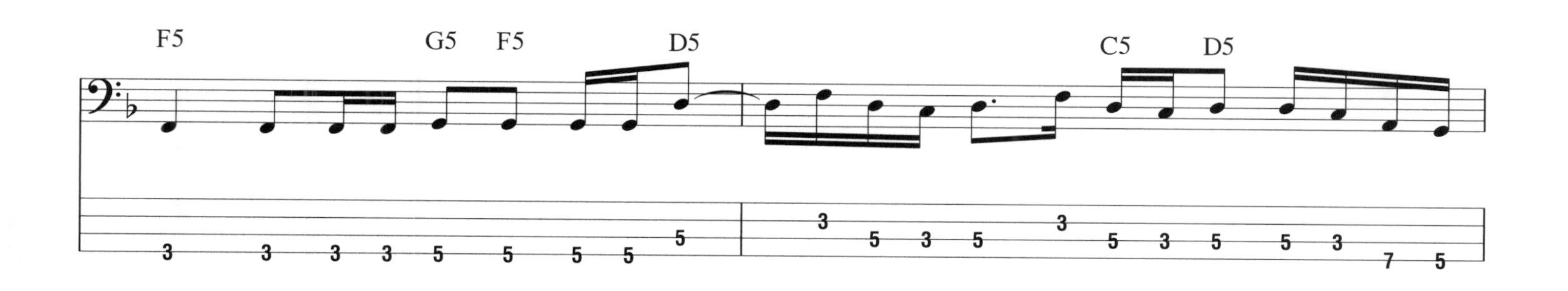
F5
G5
F5
D5
C5
D5

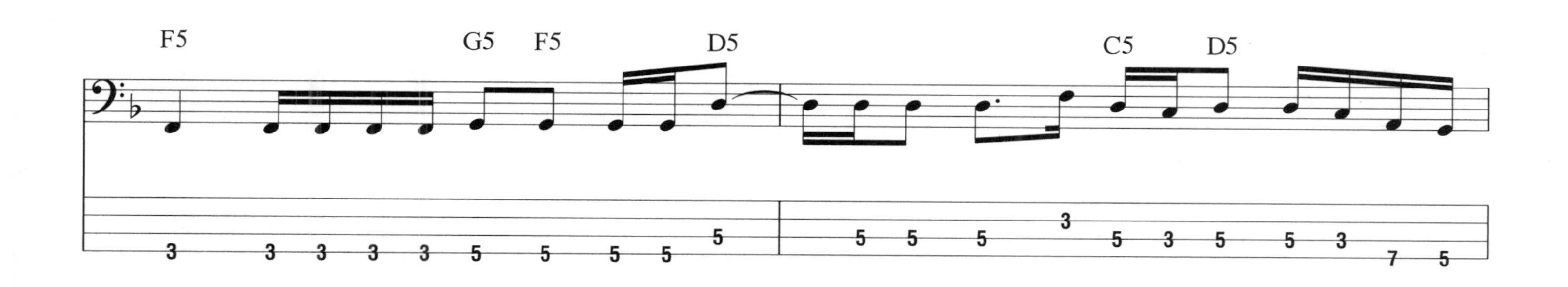
F5
G5
F5
D5
C5
D5

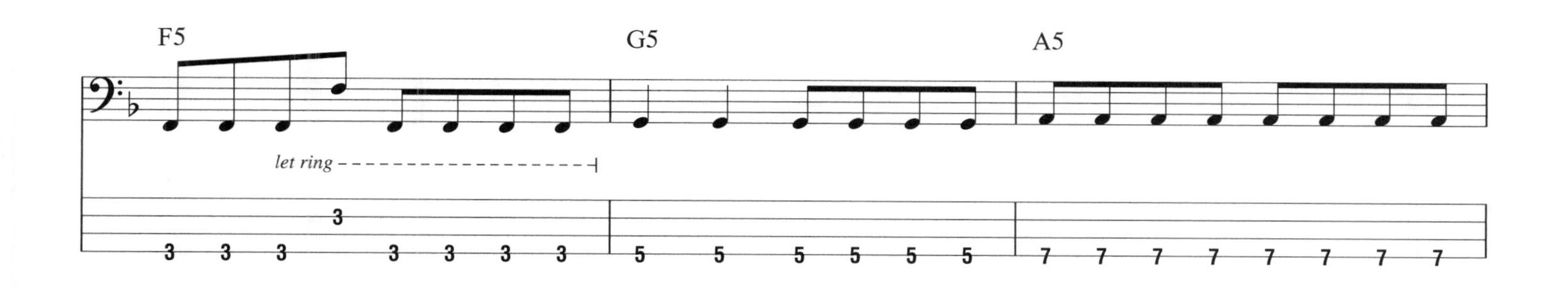
F5
G5
A5
let ring

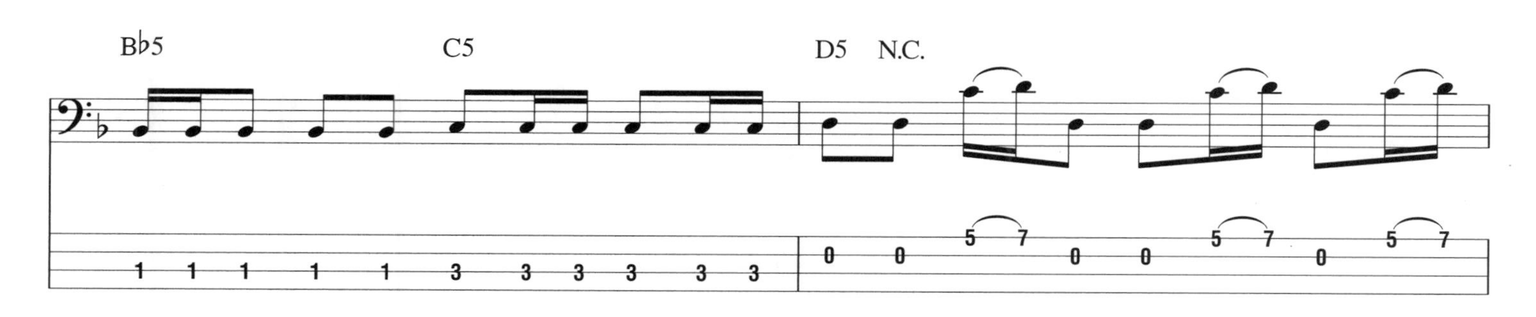
B♭5
C5
D5
N.C.

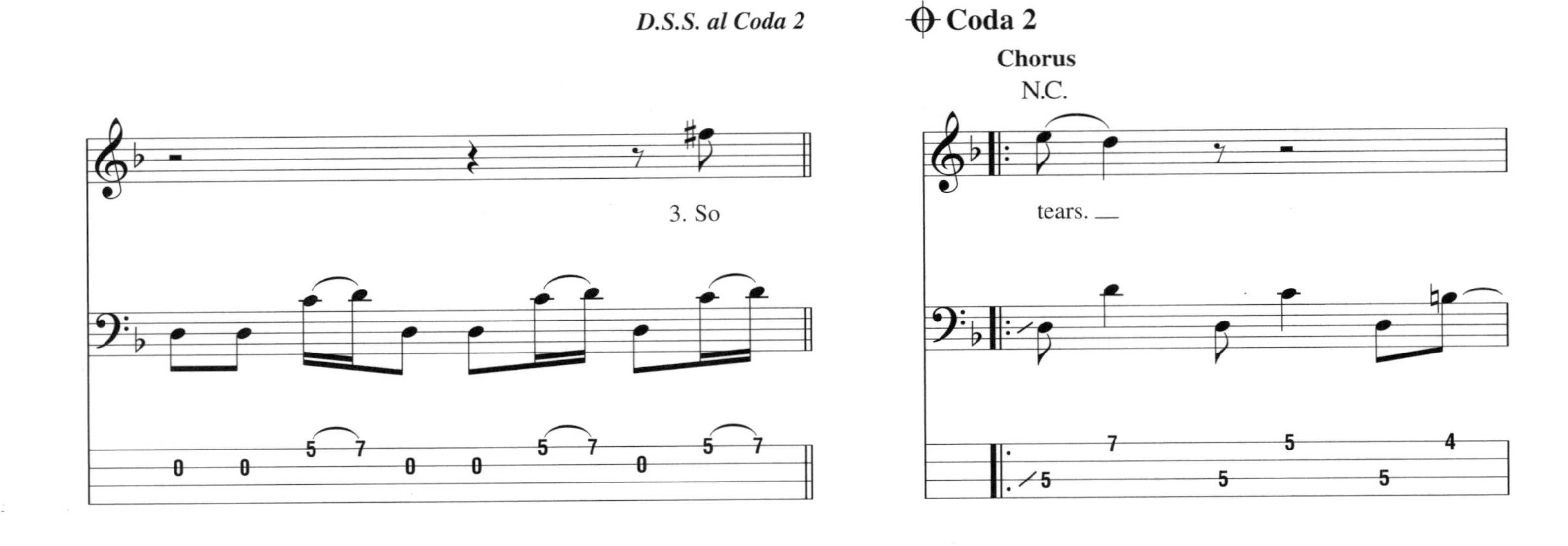
D.S.S. al Coda 2
Coda 2
Chorus
N.C.
3. So
tears. __

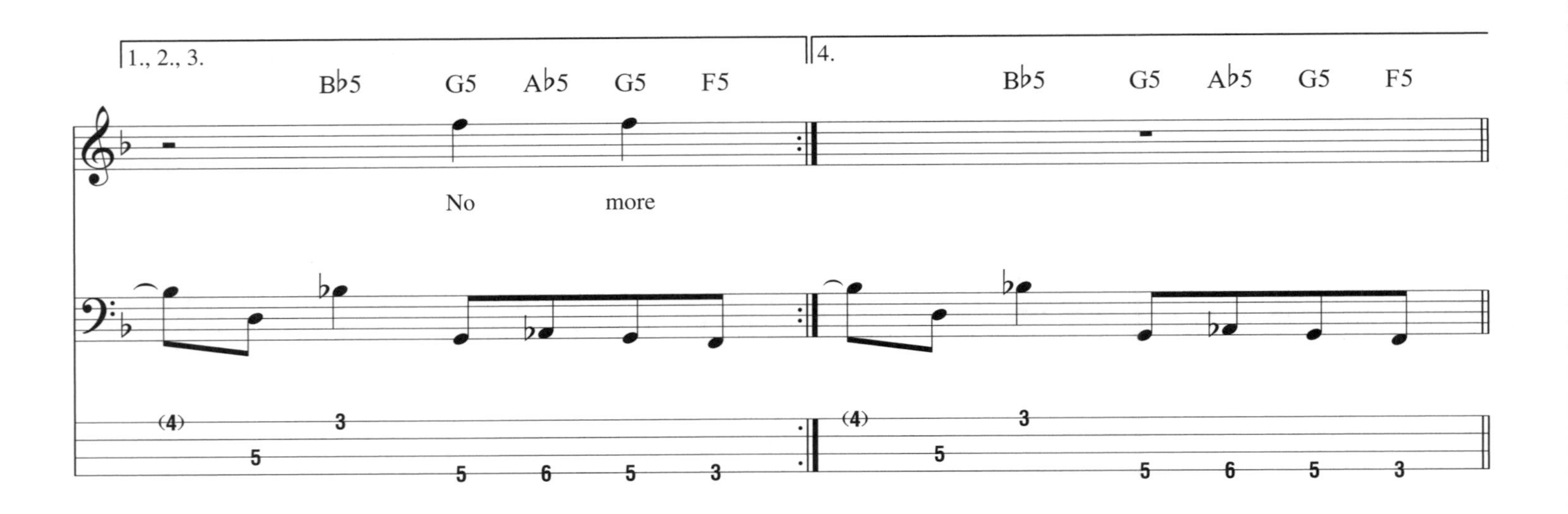
1., 2., 3.
4.
B♭5
G5
A♭5
G5
F5
No
more

Outro
N.C.
B♭5
G5
A♭5
G5
F5
D5

Additional Lyrics

Pre-Chorus 2. I see the man around the corner waiting, can he see me?
I close my eyes and wait to hear the sound of someone screaming here.

3. So now that it's over, can we just say goodbye?
I'd like to move on and make the most of the night.
Maybe a kiss before I leave you this way.
Your lips are so cold, I don't know what else to say.

Pre-Chorus 3. I never wanted it to end this way, my love, my darling.
Believe me when I say to you in love I think I'm falling here.

Peace Sells

Words and Music by Dave Mustaine

Tune down 1/4 step
Intro
Moderate Rock ♩ = 140
N.C. (Em)
Play 4 times
Bass
f
Verse
E5
G♯5
E5
G5
1. What do you mean I don't be - lieve in God?
2. What do you mean I hurt your feel - ings?
Bass Fig. 1
E5
G♯5
E5
B♭5
A5
Talk to Him ev - 'ry day.
I did - n't know you had an - y feel - ings.
End Bass Fig. 1
Bass: w/ Bass Fig. 1 (3 times)
E5
G♯5
E5
G5
E5
G♯5
What do you mean I don't sup - port your sys - tem?
What do you mean I ain't kind?
I go to court when I have
Just not your kind.

E5
Bb5 A5
G#5
G5
to.
What do you mean I can't get to work on time?
What do you mean I could-n't be the Pres - i - dent
Got noth - ing bet-ter to do.
of the U-nit-ed States of A - mer - i - ca?
What do you mean I don't pay
Tell me some - thing,
my bills?
it's still "We
Why do you think I'm broke?
The Peo-ple," right?
Huh?
Chorus
D5
F#5
If there's a new way,
well, I'll be the first in line.
1.
F5 C5
But it bet-ter work this time.
Interlude
Bass: w/ Bass Fig. 1

2.
Interlude
G5
F♯5 F5 C5
E5
But it bet - ter work this time.
*Sing 1st time only.
1.
2.
G♯5 G5
Oh.
Guitar Solo
F♯5
G5
F♯5
G5 F♯5 E5
**Sing 1st time only.
G♯5 G5
F♯5
Play 3 times
G5
F♯5
D5 D♯5

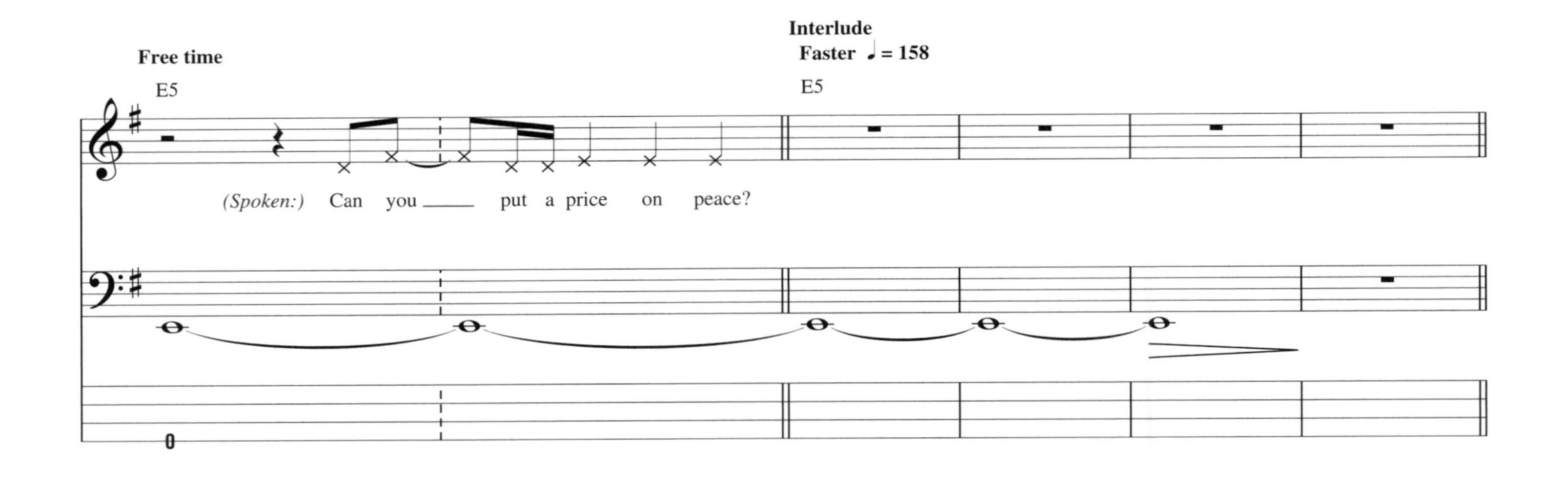
Free time
E5
(Spoken:) Can you put a price on peace?
Interlude
Faster ♩ = 158
E5

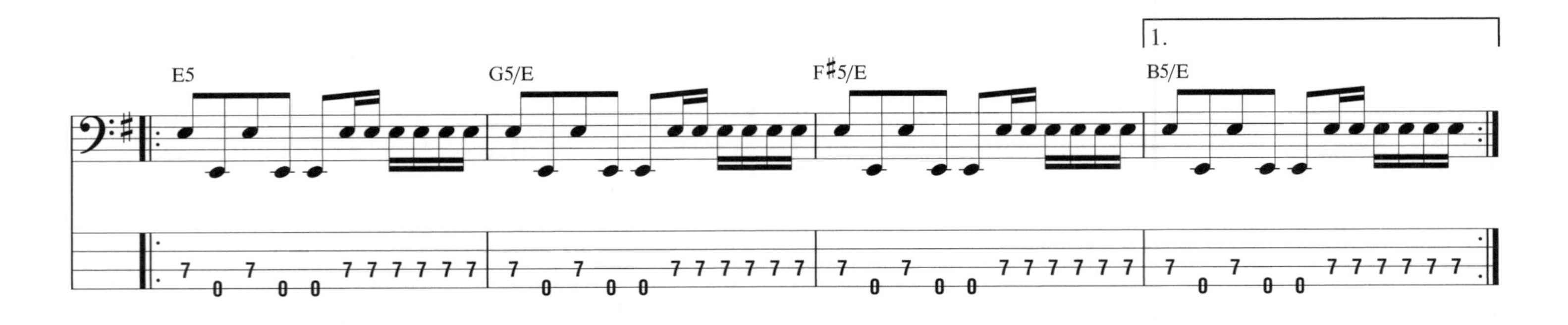
E5
G5/E
F♯5/E
1.
B5/E

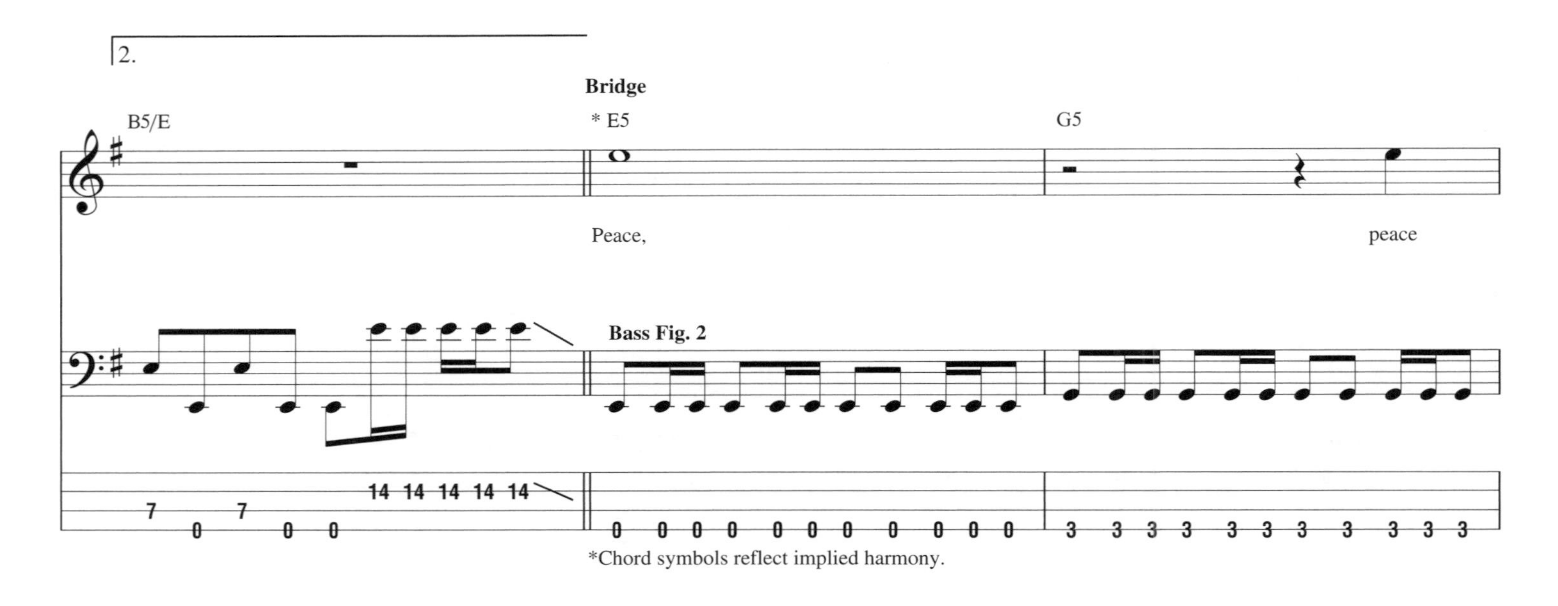
2.
B5/E
Bridge
* E5
G5
Peace,
peace
Bass Fig. 2

*Chord symbols reflect implied harmony.

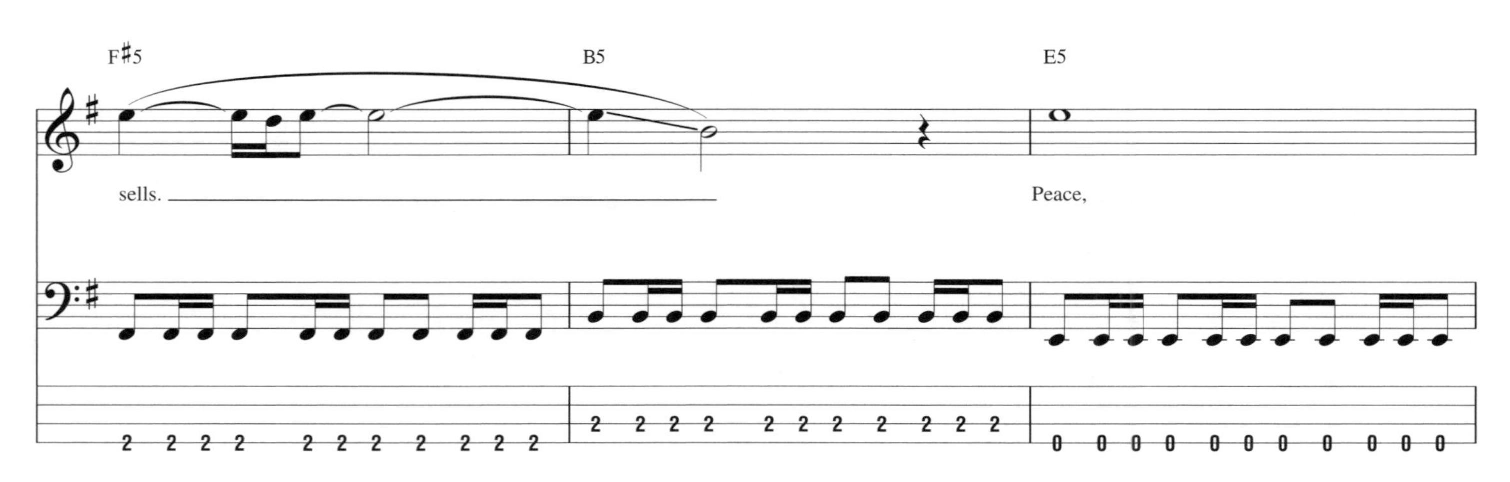
F♯5
B5
E5
sells.
Peace,

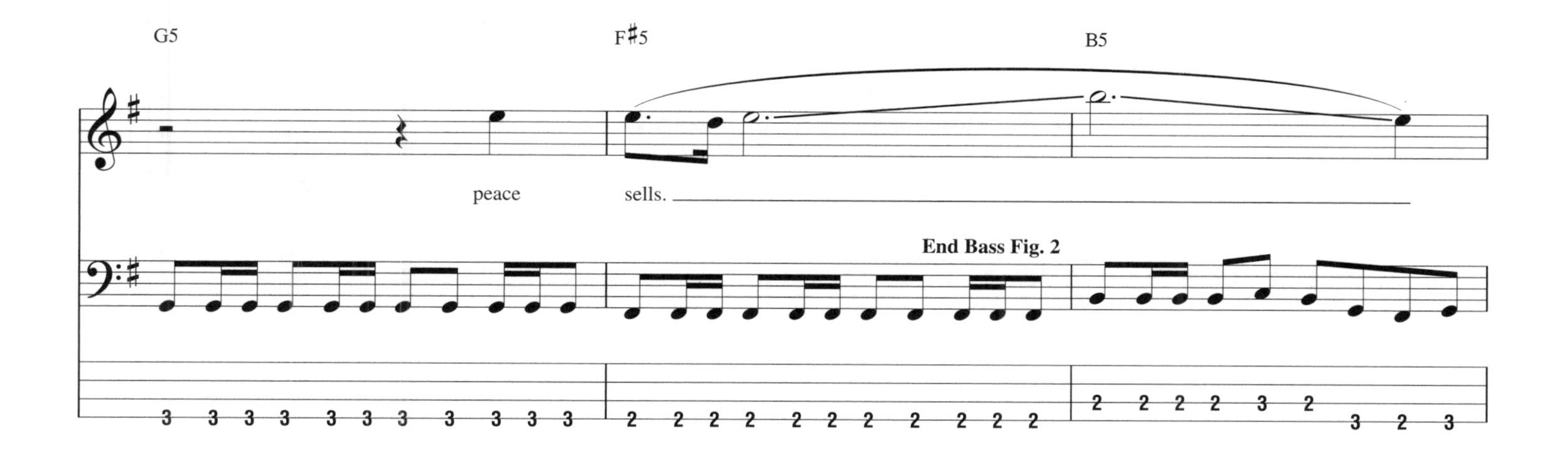
G5
F#5
B5
peace sells.
End Bass Fig. 2
3 3 3 3 3 3 3 3 3 3 3
2 2 2 2 2 2 2 2 2 2 2
2 2 2 2 3 2 3 2 3

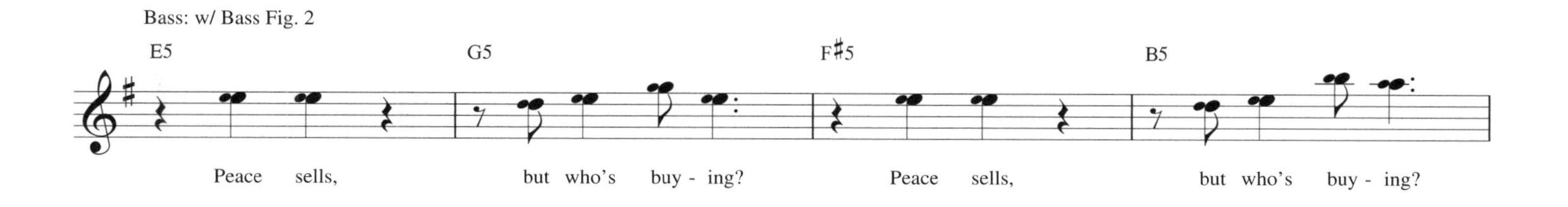
Bass: w/ Bass Fig. 2
E5
G5
F#5
B5
Peace sells, but who's buy - ing? Peace sells, but who's buy - ing?

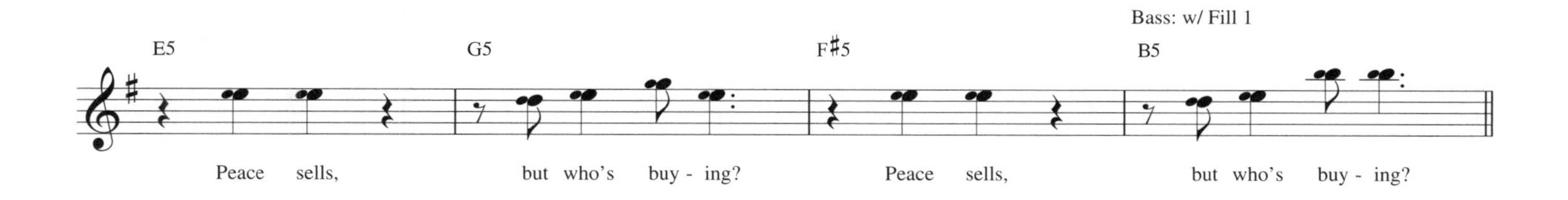
Bass: w/ Fill 1
E5
G5
F#5
B5
Peace sells, but who's buy - ing? Peace sells, but who's buy - ing?

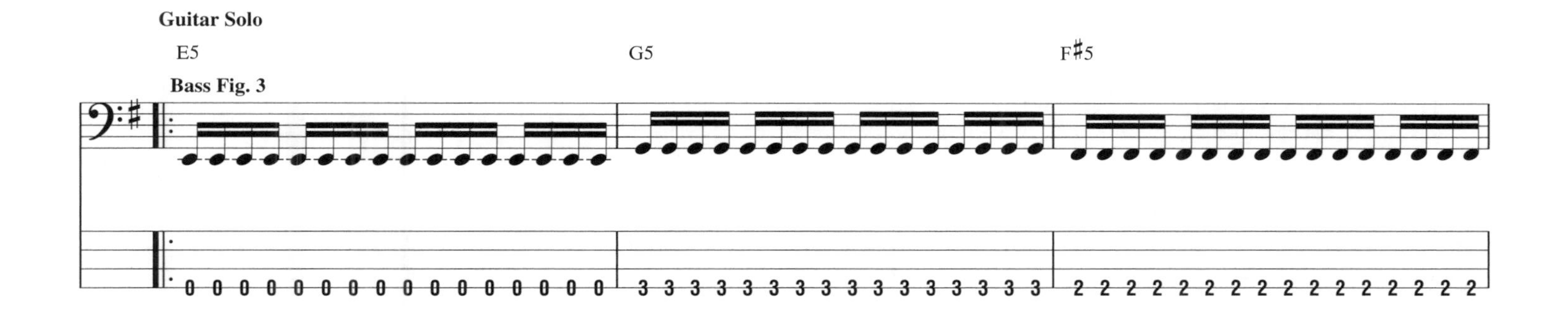
Guitar Solo
E5
G5
F#5
Bass Fig. 3
0 0 0 0 0 0 0 0 0 0 0 0 0 0 0 0
3 3 3 3 3 3 3 3 3 3 3 3 3 3 3 3
2 2 2 2 2 2 2 2 2 2 2 2 2 2 2 2

Fill 1
Bass
2 2 2 2 2 2 2 4 4 4 4 4 4

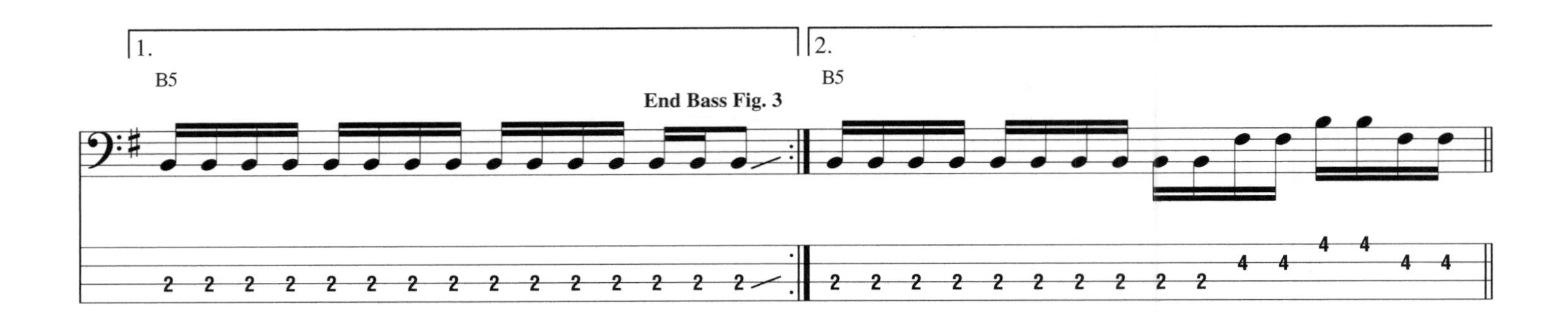
1.
B5
End Bass Fig. 3
2.
B5

Bridge

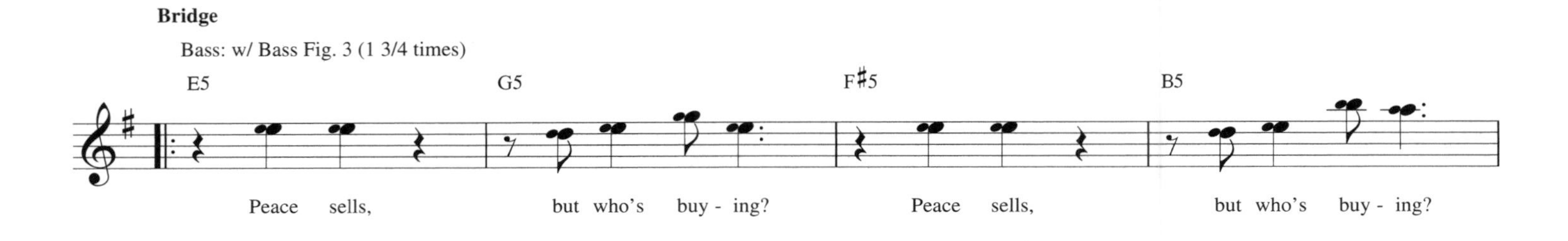
Bass: w/ Bass Fig. 3 (1 3/4 times)
E5
G5
F♯5
B5
Peace sells, but who's buy - ing? Peace sells, but who's buy - ing?

E5
G5
F♯5
Peace sells, but who's buy - ing? Peace sells,

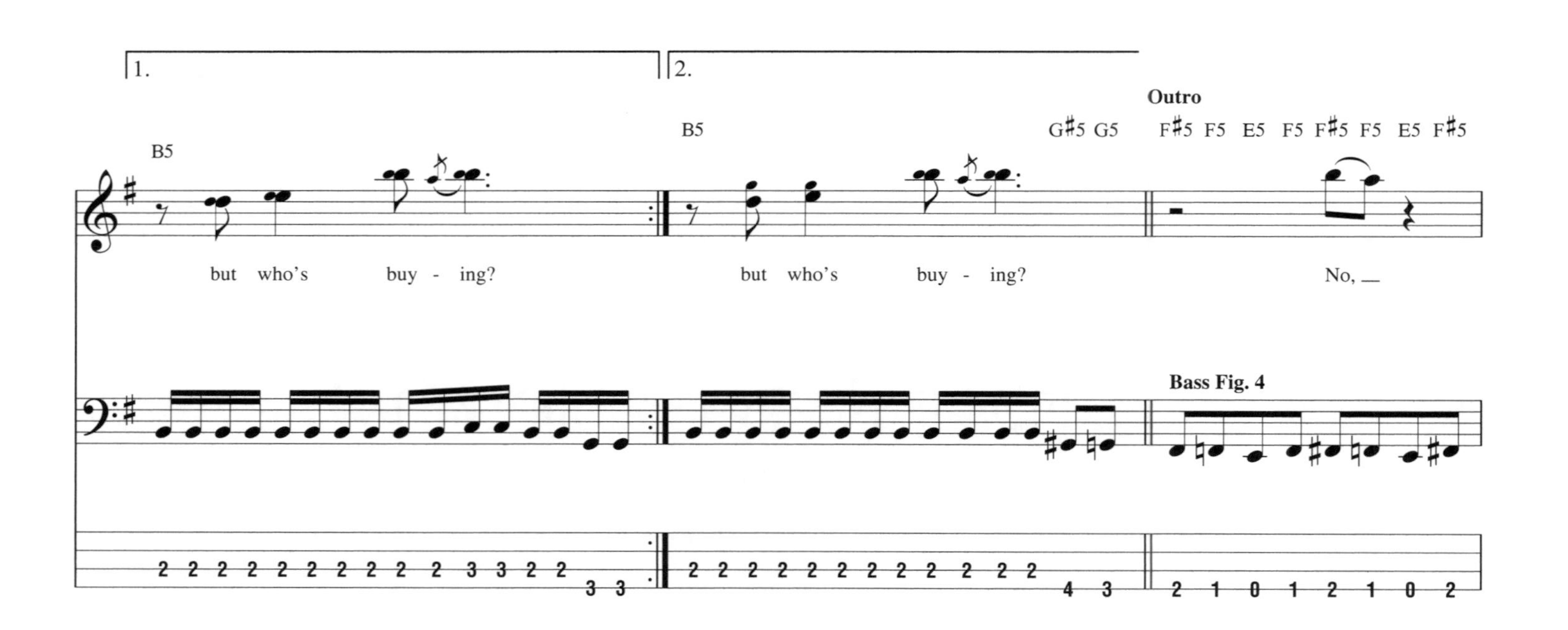
1.
2.
Outro
B5
B5
G♯5 G5
F♯5 F5 E5 F5 F♯5 F5 E5 F♯5
but who's buy - ing? but who's buy - ing? No,
Bass Fig. 4

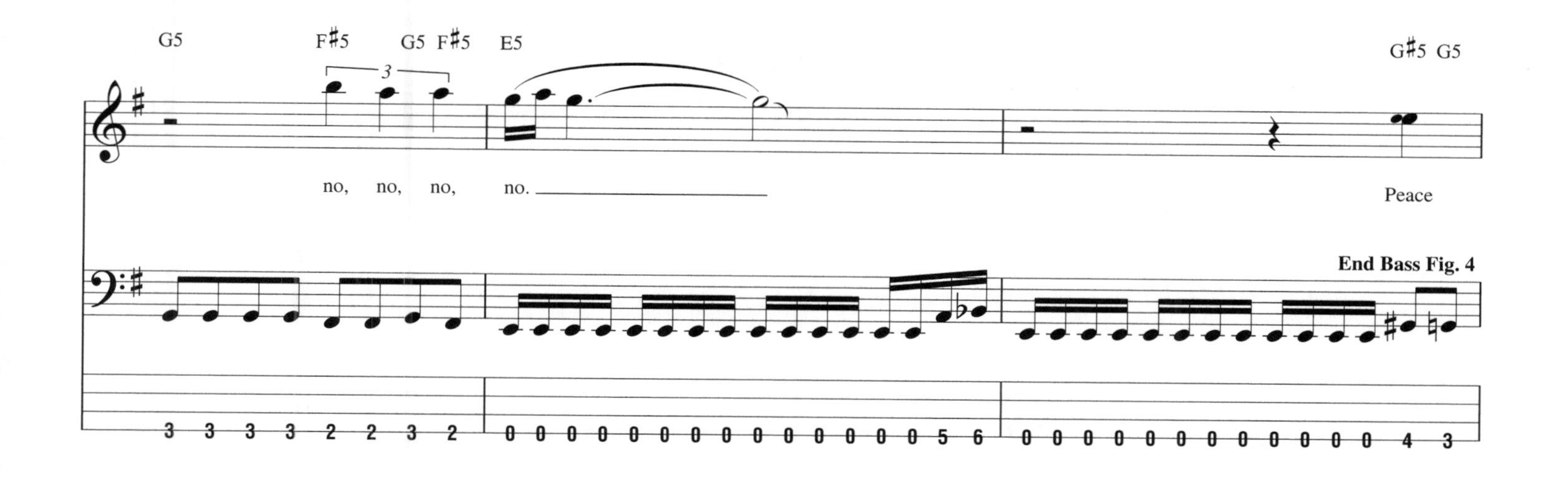
G5 F#5 G5 F#5 E5 G#5 G5
3
no, no, no, no.
Peace
End Bass Fig. 4
3 3 3 3 2 2 3 2
0 0 0 0 0 0 0 0 0 0 0 0 0 0 5 6
0 0 0 0 0 0 0 0 0 0 0 0 4 3

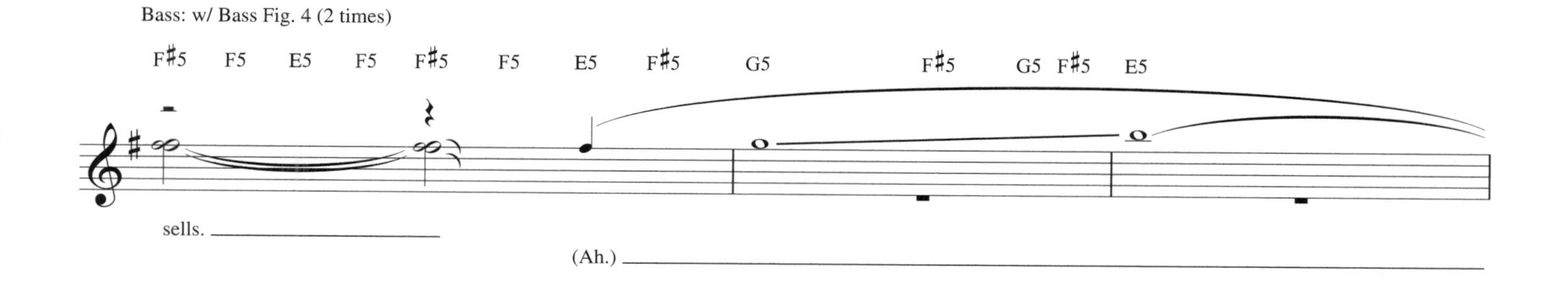
Bass: w/ Bass Fig. 4 (2 times)
F#5 F5 E5 F5 F#5 F5 E5 F#5 G5 F#5 G5 F#5 E5
sells.
(Ah.)

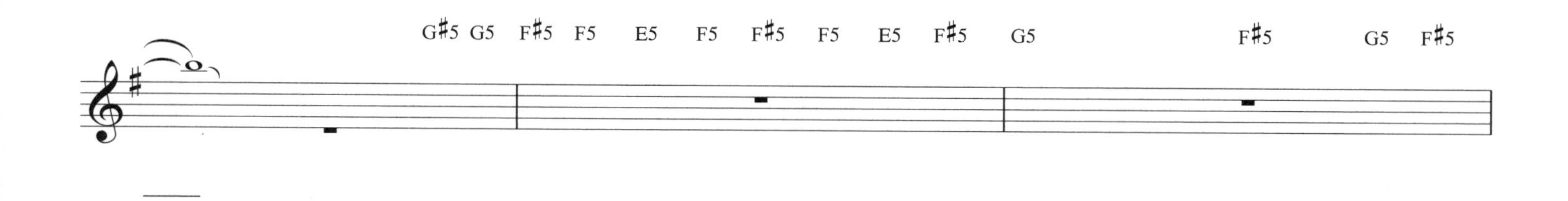
G#5 G5 F#5 F5 E5 F5 F#5 F5 E5 F#5 G5 F#5 G5 F#5

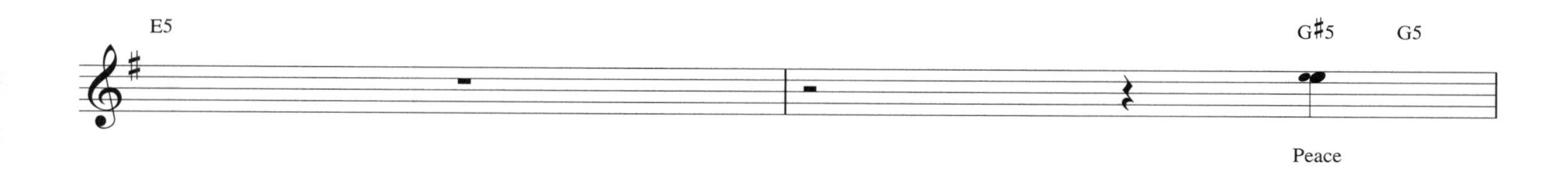
E5 G#5 G5
Peace

F#5 F5 E5 F5 F#5 F5 E5 F#5 G5 F#5 G5 F#5 E5
sells.
Ah!
2 1 0 1 2 1 0 2
3 3 3 3 2 2 3 2
0

Plush

Words and Music by Scott Weiland, Dean DeLeo, Robert DeLeo and Eric Kretz

Intro
Moderately slow ♩ = 72
G5
B♭°7
Gsus4/C
G
G5
B♭°7
Bass
mf
T
A
B

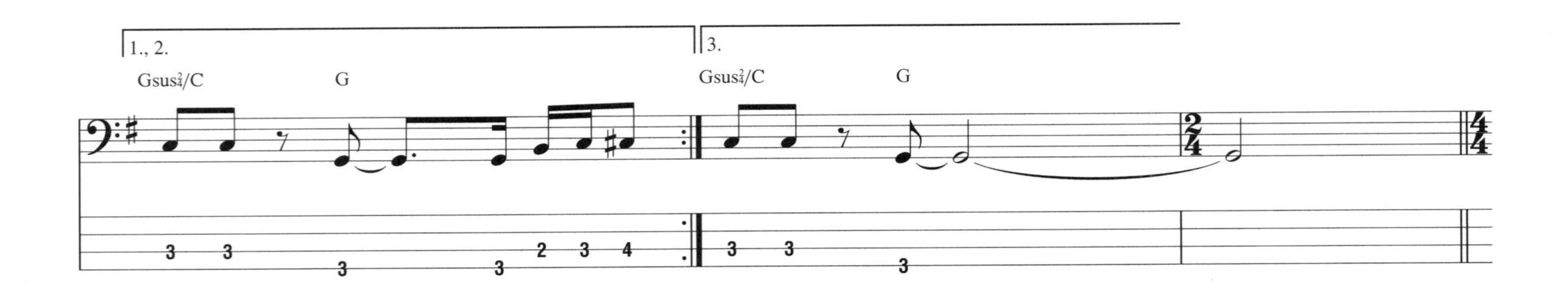
1., 2.
3.
Gsus4/C
G
Gsus4/C
G

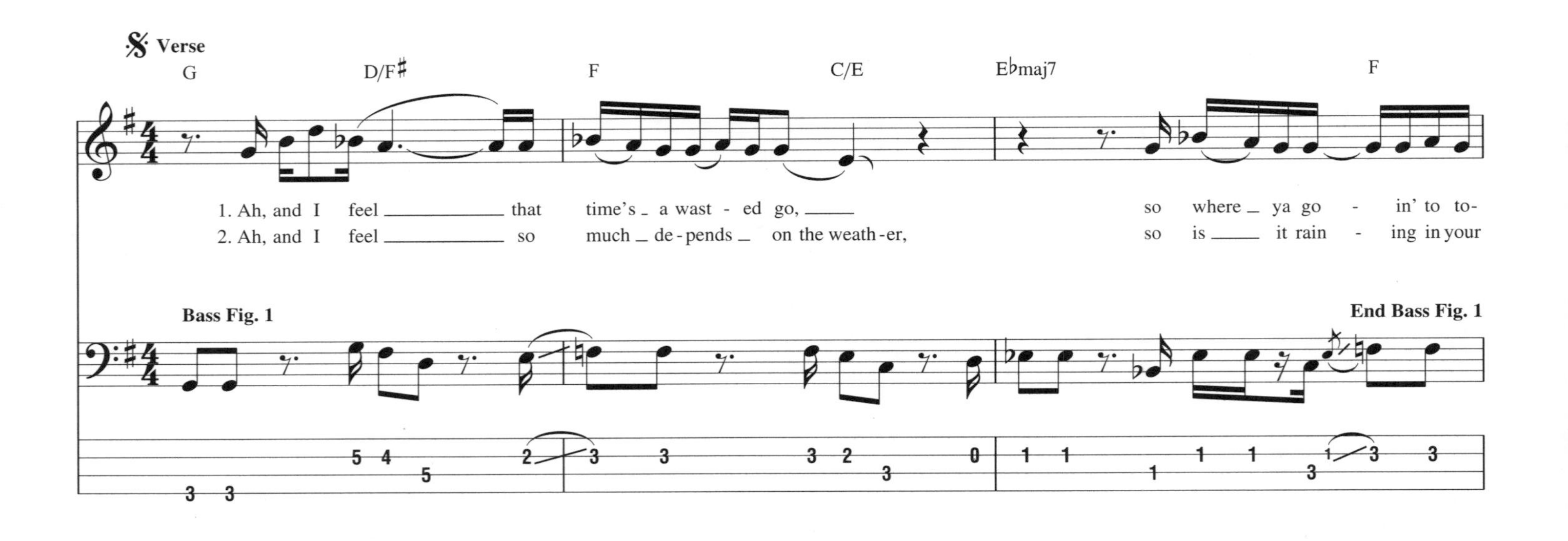
Verse
G
D/F♯
F
C/E
E♭maj7
F
1. Ah, and I feel that time's a wast - ed go,
so where ya go - in' to to-
2. Ah, and I feel so much de-pends on the weath-er,
so is it rain - ing in your
Bass Fig. 1
End Bass Fig. 1

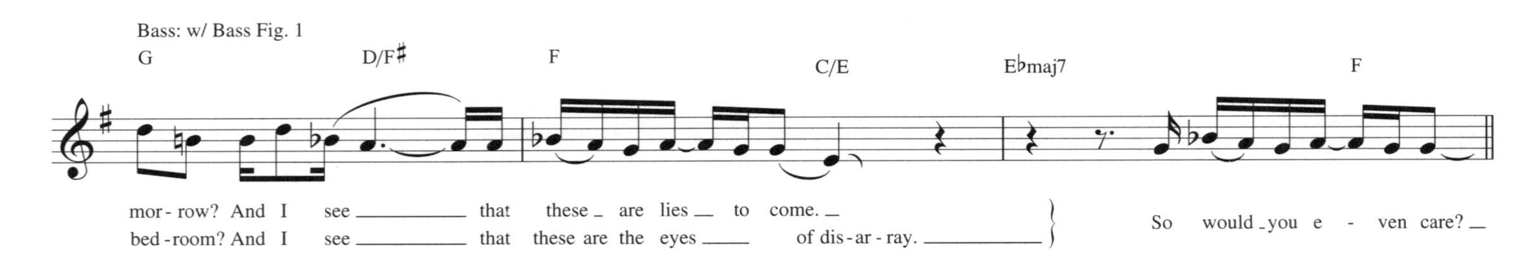
Bass: w/ Bass Fig. 1
G
D/F♯
F
C/E
E♭maj7
F
mor-row? And I see that these are lies to come.
bed-room? And I see that these are the eyes of dis-ar-ray.
So would you e - ven care?

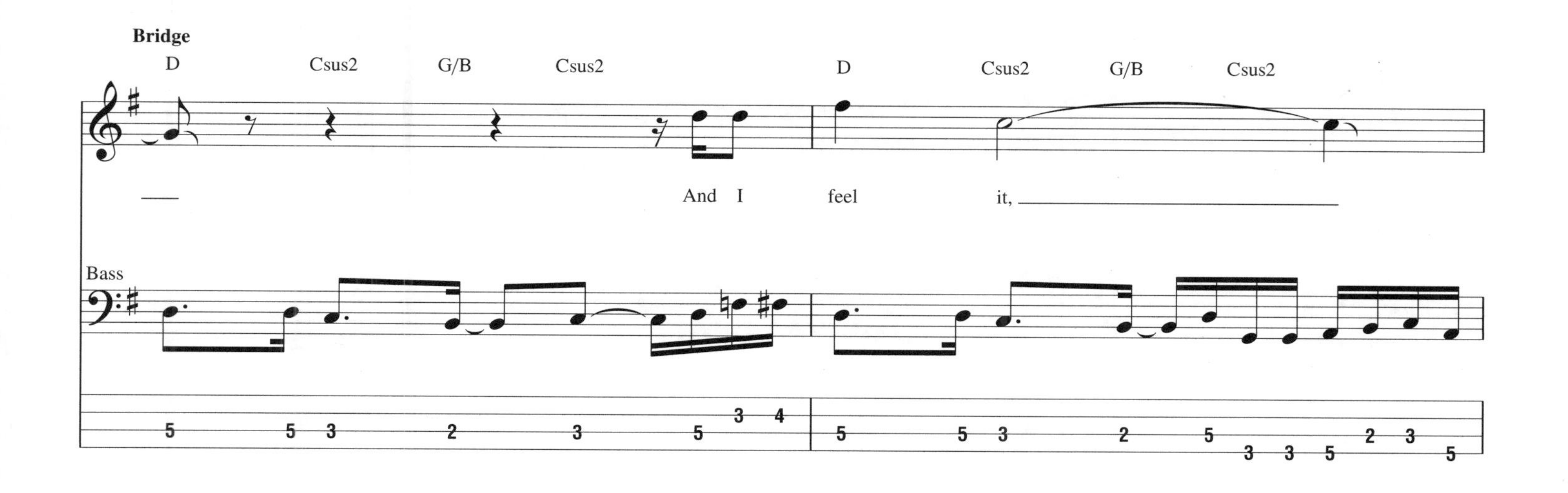
Bridge
D
Csus2
G/B
Csus2
D
Csus2
G/B
Csus2
And I feel it,
Bass

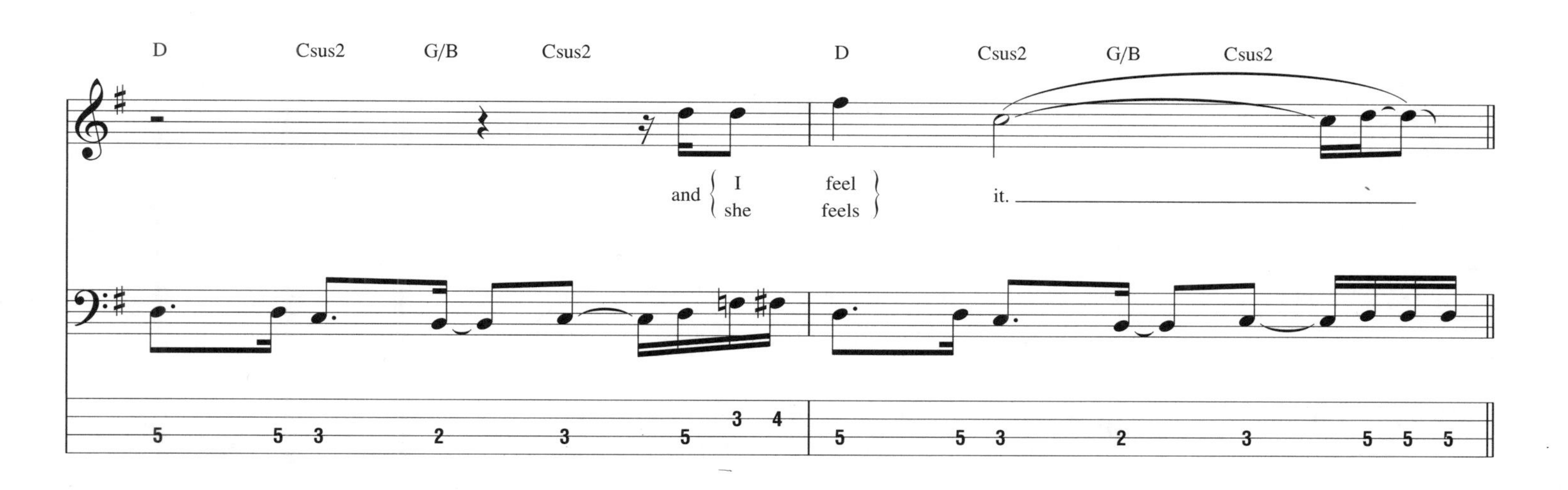
D
Csus2
G/B
Csus2
D
Csus2
G/B
Csus2
and I she feel feels it.

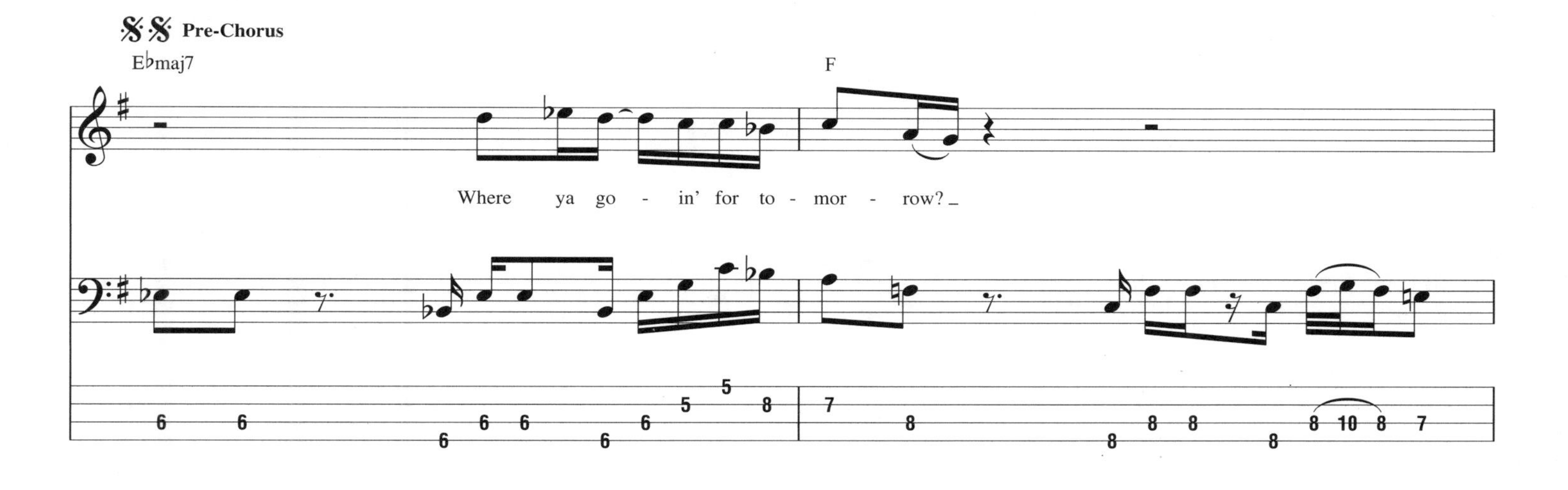
Pre-Chorus
E♭maj7
F
Where ya go - in' for to - mor - row?

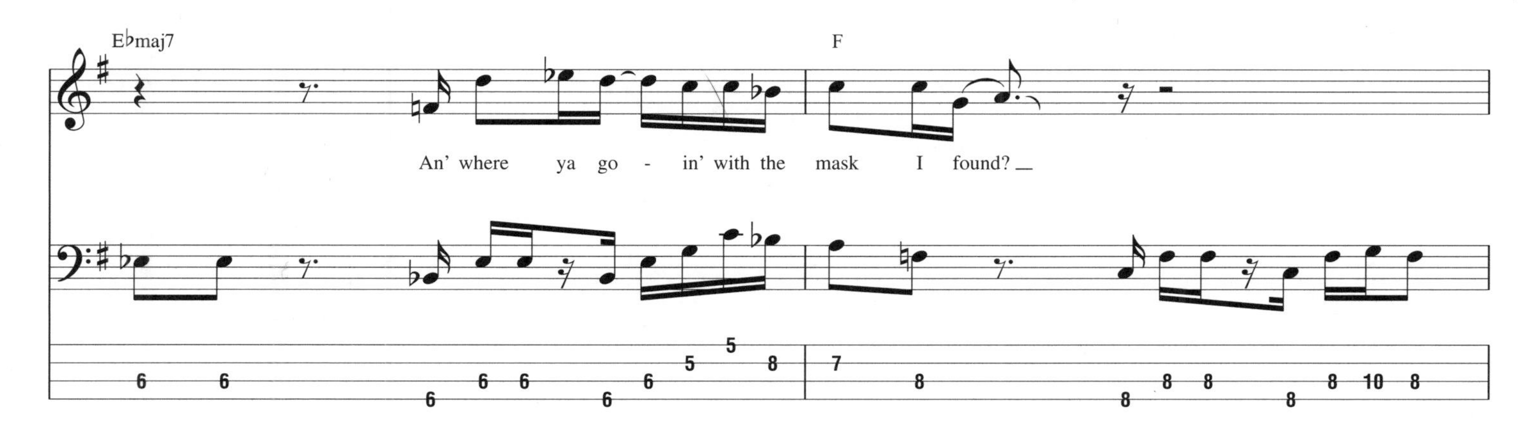
E♭maj7
F
An' where ya go - in' with the mask I found?

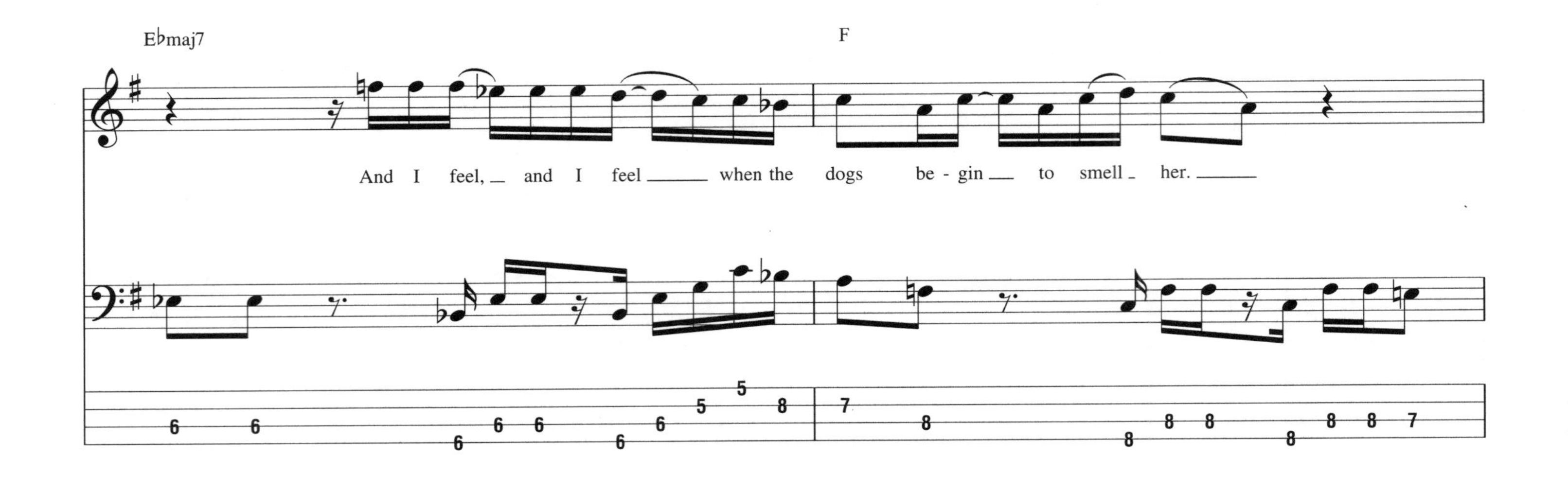
E♭maj7
F
And I feel, and I feel when the dogs be - gin to smell her.
6 6 6 6 6 6 6 5 5 8
7 8 8 8 8 8 8 8 7

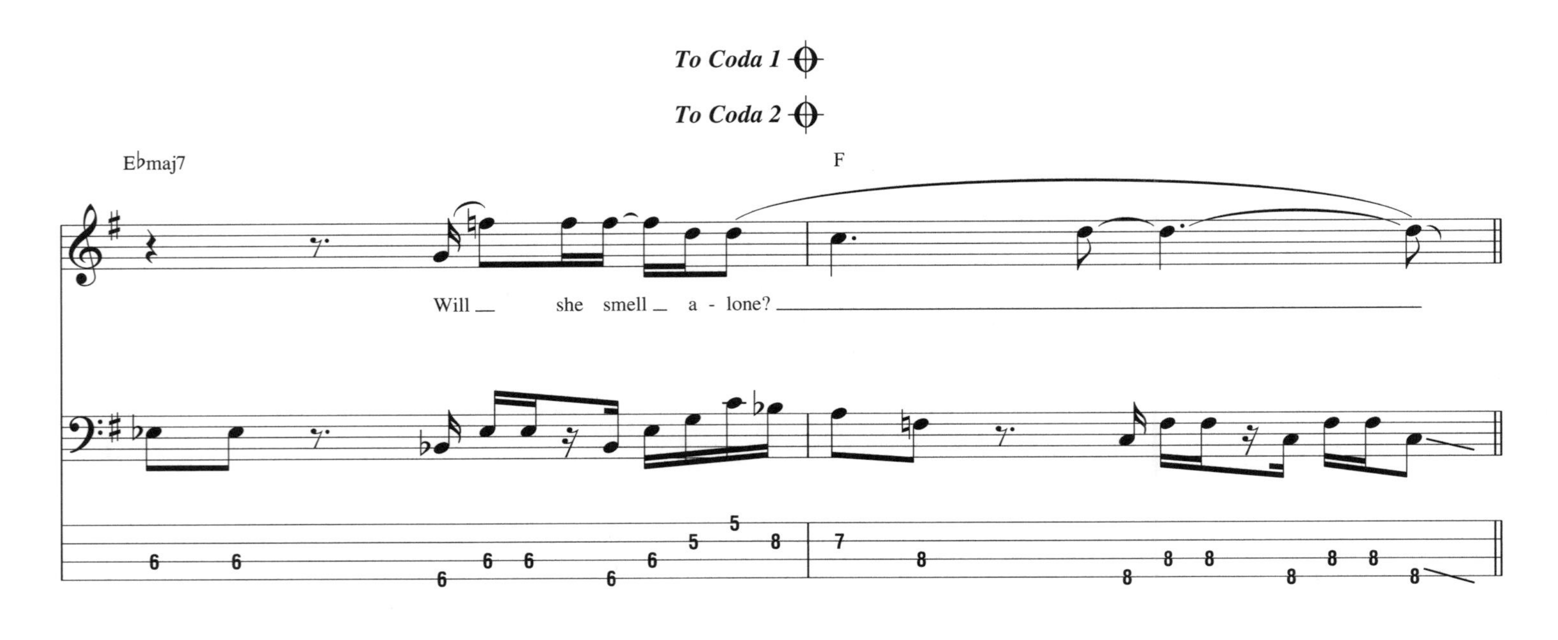
To Coda 1
To Coda 2
E♭maj7
F
Will she smell a - lone?
6 6 6 6 6 6 6 5 5 8
7 8 8 8 8 8 8 8 8

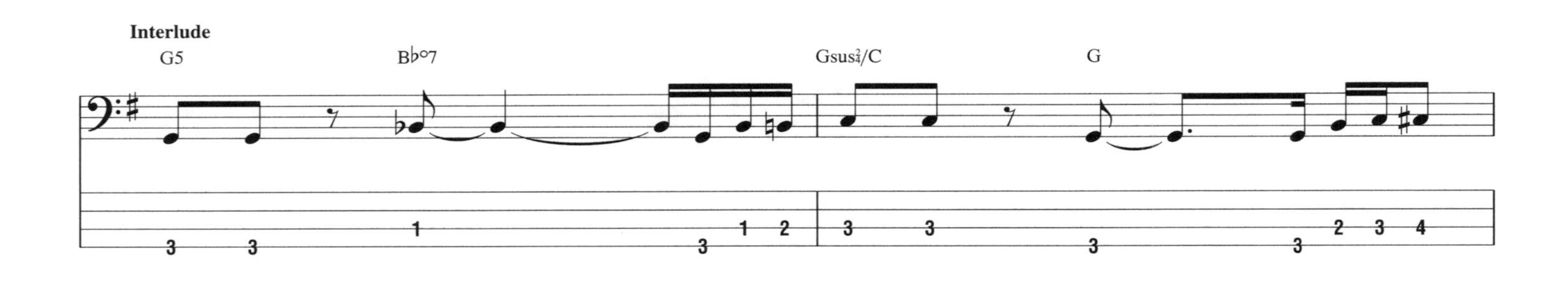
Interlude
G5
B♭°7
Gsus4/C
G
3 3 1 3 1 2
3 3 3 3 2 3 4

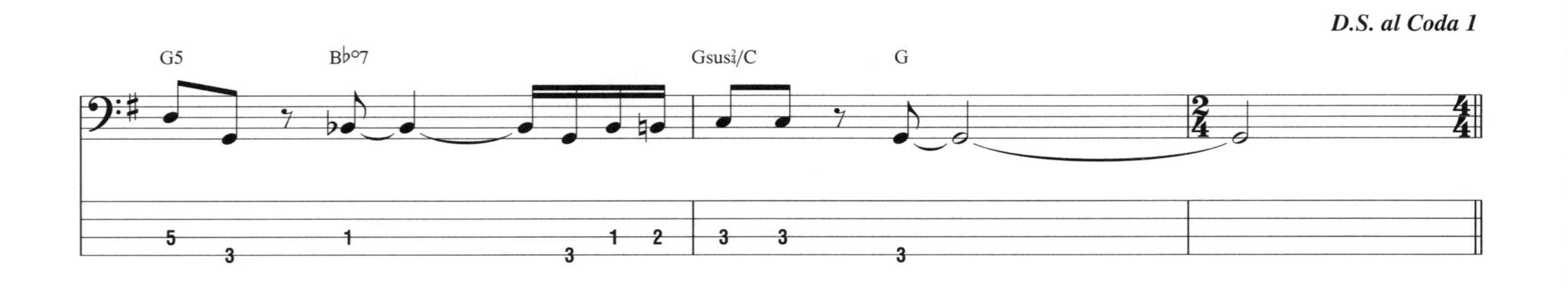
D.S. al Coda 1
G5
B♭°7
Gsus4/C
G
5 3 1 3 1 2
3 3 3

Coda 1

Chorus
F
G5
F5
C/E
D5 E♭5
D5
When the dogs do find her, we got time, time (to) wait for to-
Bass Fig. 2
End Bass Fig. 2
7
8
8 8 8 8 8 8 8
3 3 3 3 3 3 1 1 1 1 1
0 0 0 0 0 5 6 6 6 6 5 5 5

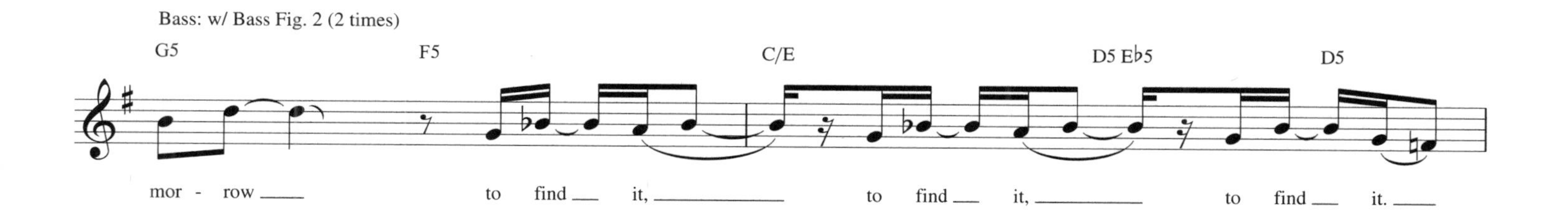
Bass: w/ Bass Fig. 2 (2 times)
G5
F5
C/E
D5 E♭5
D5
mor - row to find it, to find it, to find it.

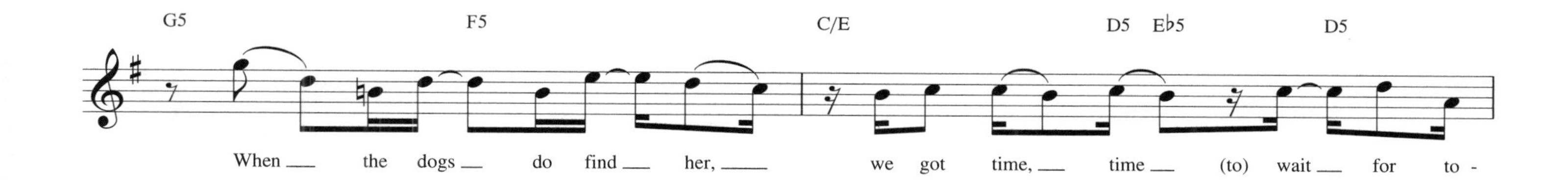
G5
F5
C/E
D5 E♭5
D5
When the dogs do find her, we got time, time (to) wait for to -

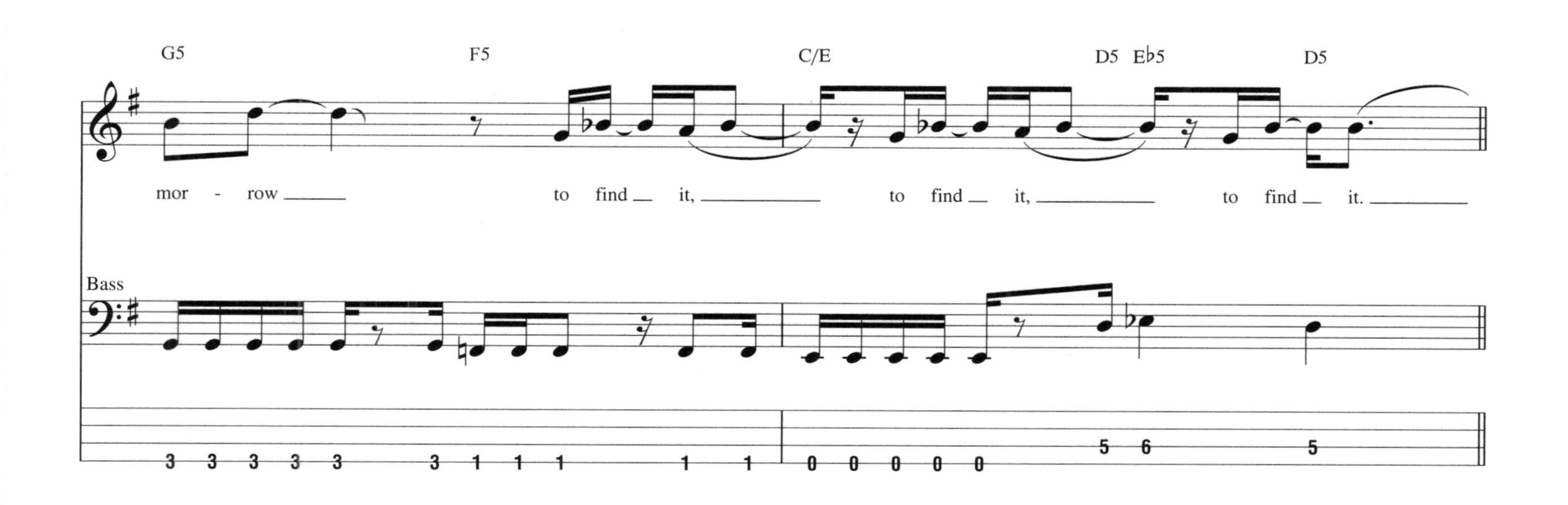
G5
F5
C/E
D5 E♭5
D5
mor - row to find it, to find it, to find it.
Bass
3 3 3 3 3 3 1 1 1 1 1
0 0 0 0 0 5 6 5

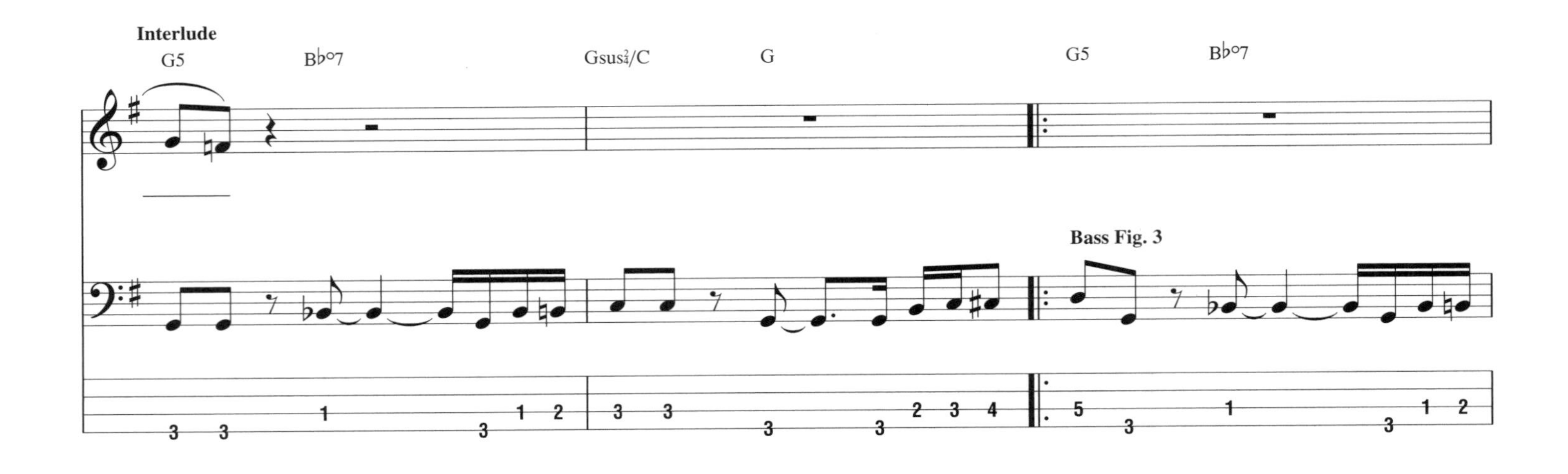
Interlude
G5
B♭°7
Gsus4/C
G
G5
B♭°7
Bass Fig. 3

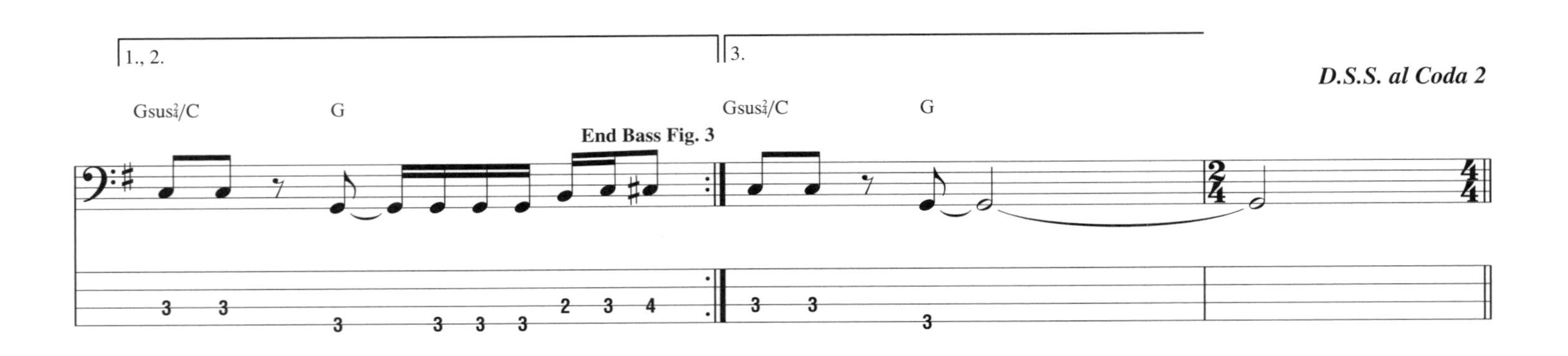
1., 2.
3.
D.S.S. al Coda 2
Gsus4/C
G
End Bass Fig. 3
Gsus4/C
G

Coda 2
Chorus
F
G5
F5
C/E
D5 E♭5
D5
When the dogs do find her, we got time, time to wait for to-

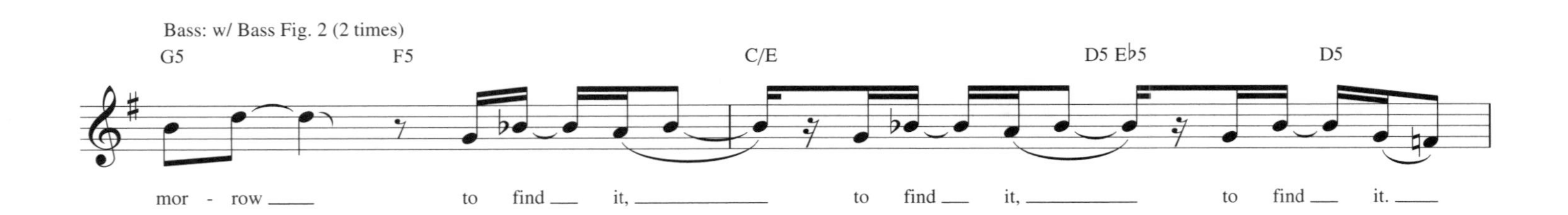
Bass: w/ Bass Fig. 2 (2 times)
G5
F5
C/E
D5 E♭5
D5
mor - row to find it, to find it, to find it.

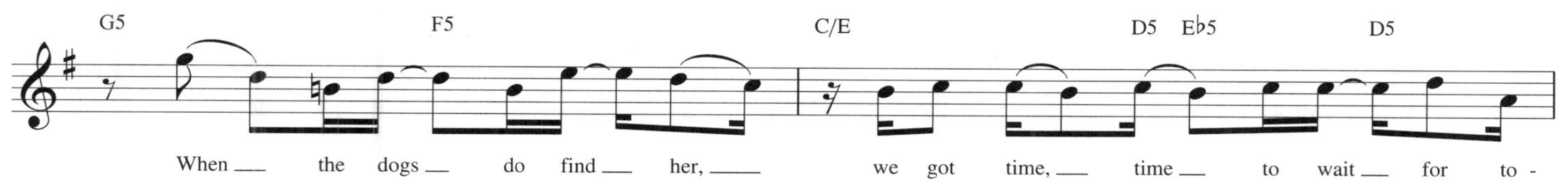
G5
F5
C/E
D5 E♭5
D5
When the dogs do find her, we got time, time to wait for to -

G5
F5
C/E
D5 E♭maj7
D7sus4
mor - row to find it, to find it, to find it.
Bass
3 3 3 3 3 3 1 1 1 1 1
0 0 0 0 0 5 6 5
Outro
G5
B♭°7
Gsus4/C
G
To find it,
3 3 1 3 1 2
3 3 3 2 3 4

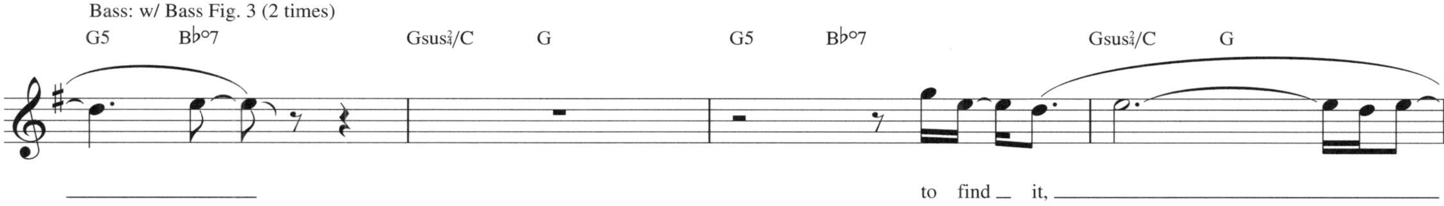
Bass: w/ Bass Fig. 3 (2 times)
G5
B♭°7
Gsus4/C
G
G5
B♭°7
Gsus4/C
G
to find it,

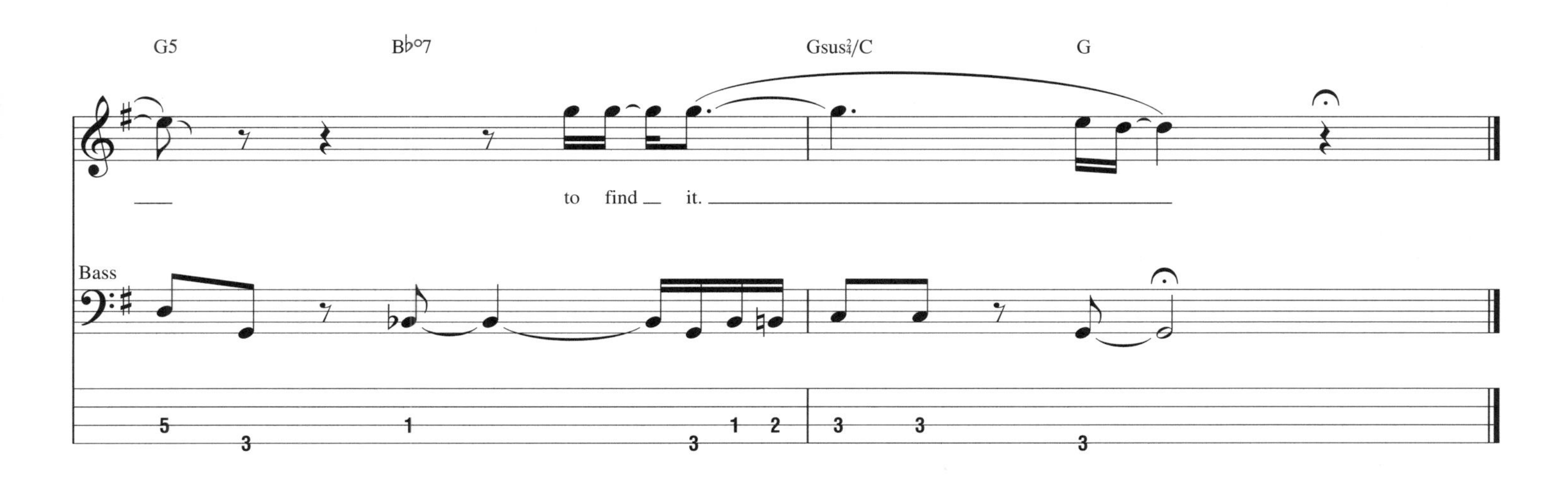
G5
B♭°7
Gsus4/C
G
to find it.
Bass
5 3 1 3 1 2
3 3 3

The Pretender

Words and Music by Dave Grohl, Taylor Hawkins, Christopher Shiflett and Nate Mendel

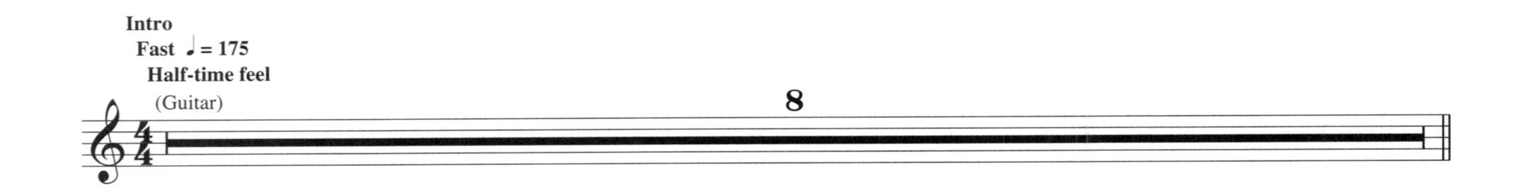
Intro
Fast ♩ = 175
Half-time feel
(Guitar)
8

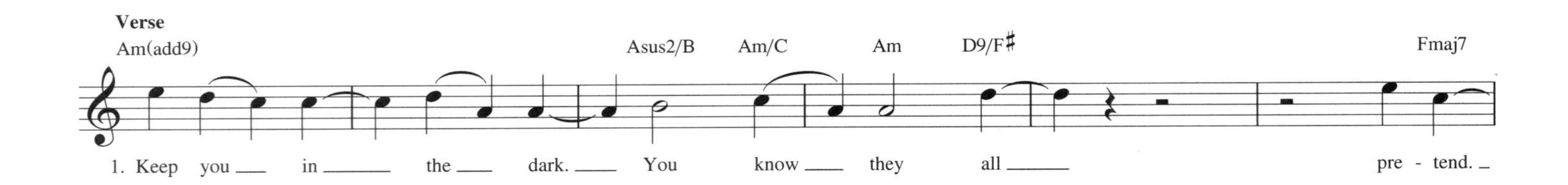
Verse
Am(add9)
Asus2/B
Am/C
Am
D9/F♯
Fmaj7
1. Keep you in the dark. You know they all pre - tend.

Am(add9)
Asus2/B
Am/C
Am
D9/F♯
Keep you in the dark, and so it all

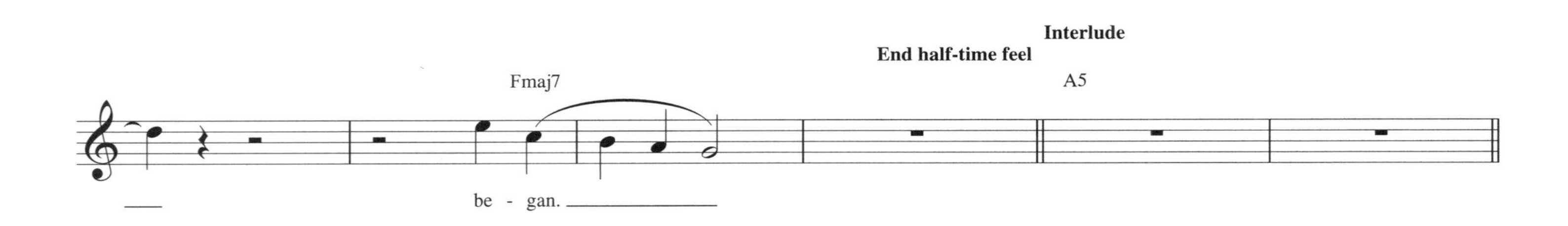
Fmaj7
End half-time feel
Interlude
A5
be - gan.

Verse
Am
2. Send in your skel - e - tons. Sing as their bones come march - ing in
Bass Fig. 1
End Bass Fig. 1
Bass
mf
T
A
B
5 5 5 5 5 5 5 5 5 5 5 5

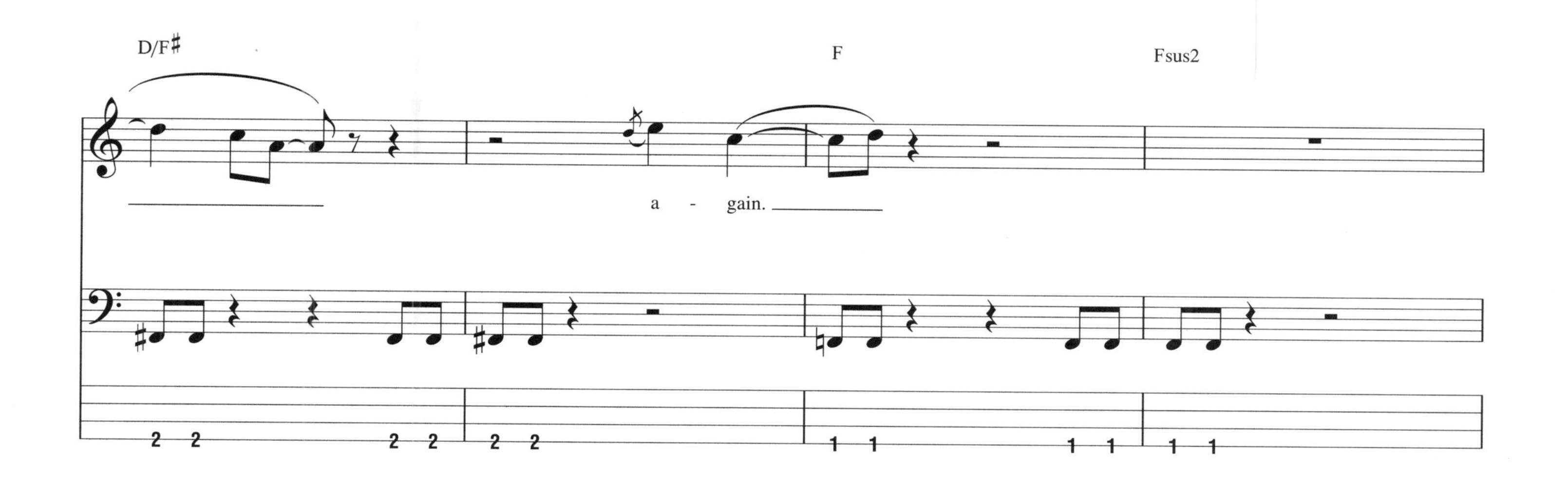
D/F♯
F
Fsus2
a - gain.

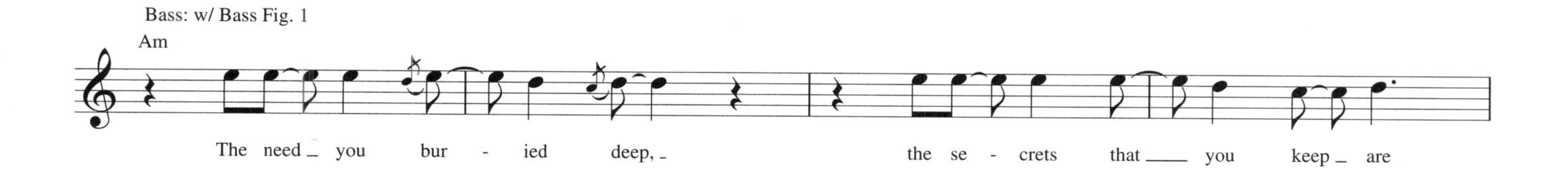
Bass: w/ Bass Fig. 1
Am
The need you bur - ied deep, the se - crets that you keep are

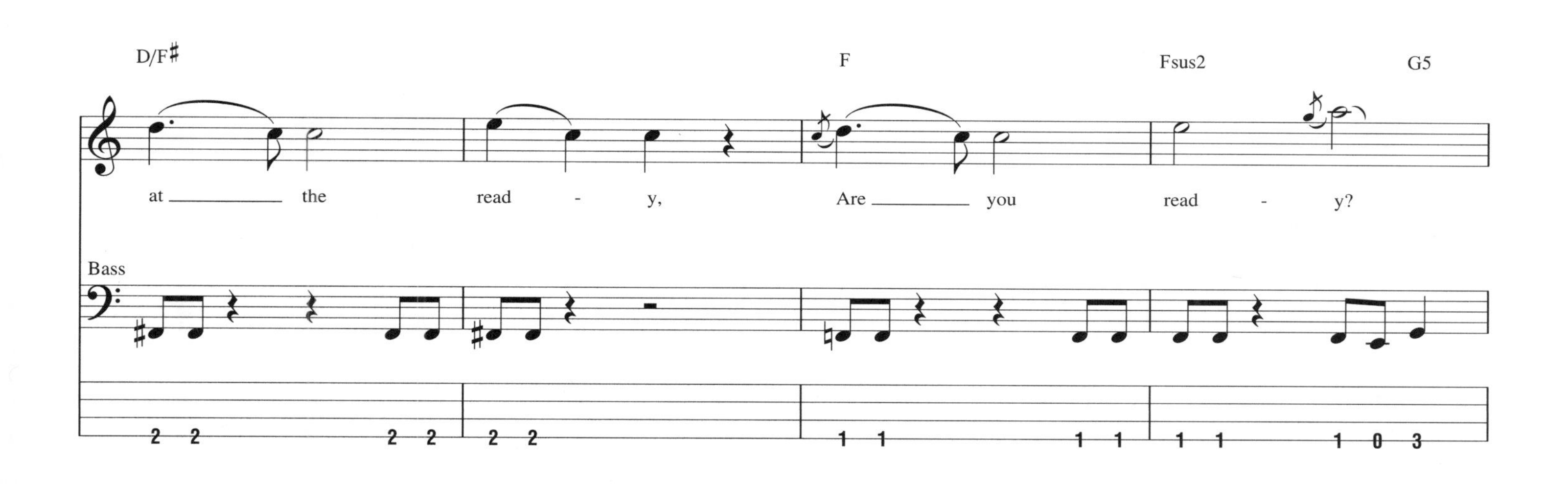
D/F♯
F
Fsus2
G5
at the read - y, Are you read - y?
Bass

Am
I'm fin-ished mak - ing sense, done plead - ing ig - no - rance, that old

D/F#
F
Fsus2
G5
de - fense.
Am
Spin - ning in - fin - i - ty, but the wheel is spin - ning me. It's
Bass Fig. 2
D/F#
F
Fsus2
G5
nev - er - end - ing, nev - er - end - ing.
Chorus
D5
D/E
D
Dsus4/G
Am
Same old sto - ry. What if I say I'm not like the oth - ers?
End Bass Fig. 2

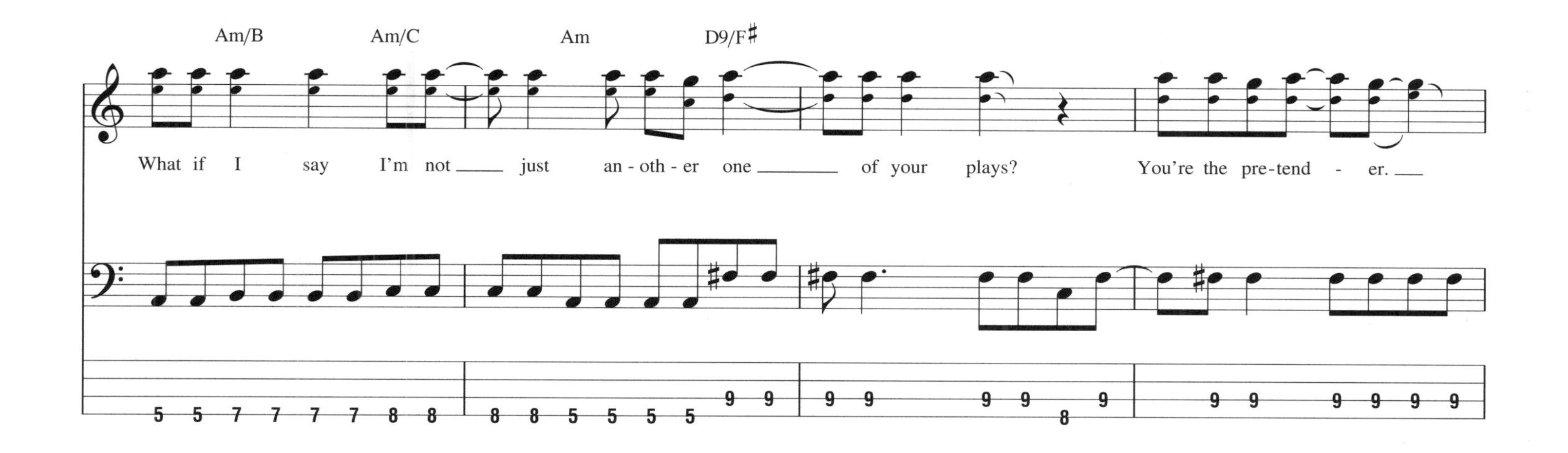
Am/B
Am/C
Am
D9/F♯
What if I say I'm not just an-oth-er one of your plays? You're the pre-tend-er.
5 5 7 7 7 7 8 8
8 8 5 5 5 5 9 9
9 9 9 9 8 9
9 9 9 9 9 9

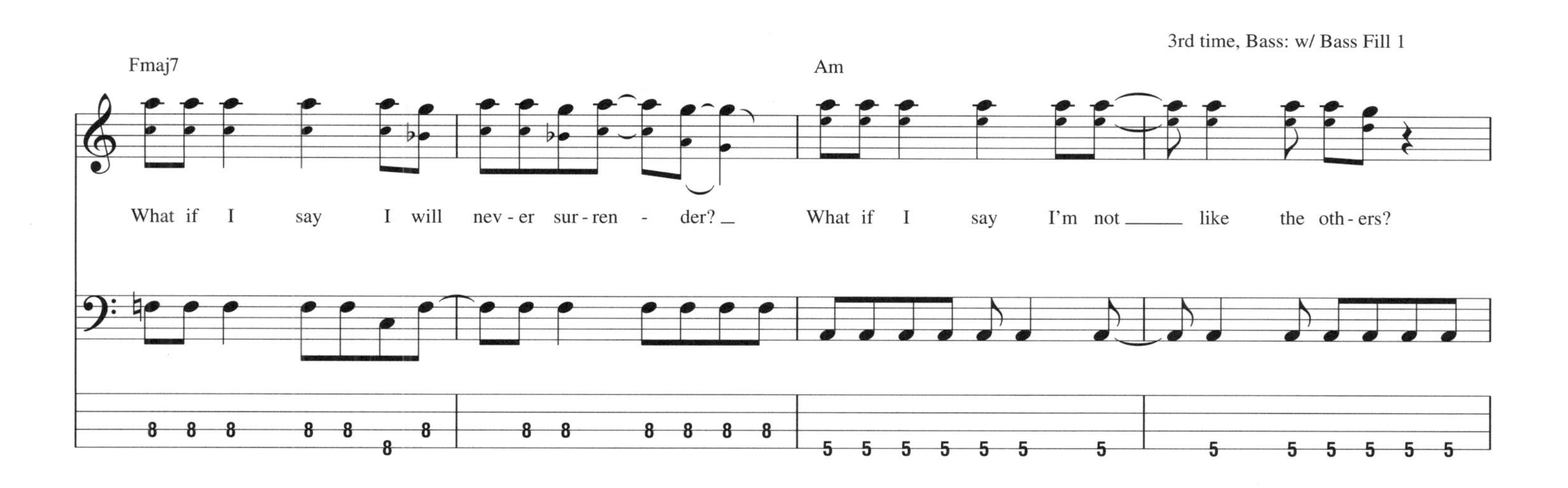
3rd time, Bass: w/ Bass Fill 1
Fmaj7
Am
What if I say I will nev-er sur-ren-der? What if I say I'm not like the oth-ers?
8 8 8 8 8 8 8
8 8 8 8 8 8
5 5 5 5 5 5 5
5 5 5 5 5 5

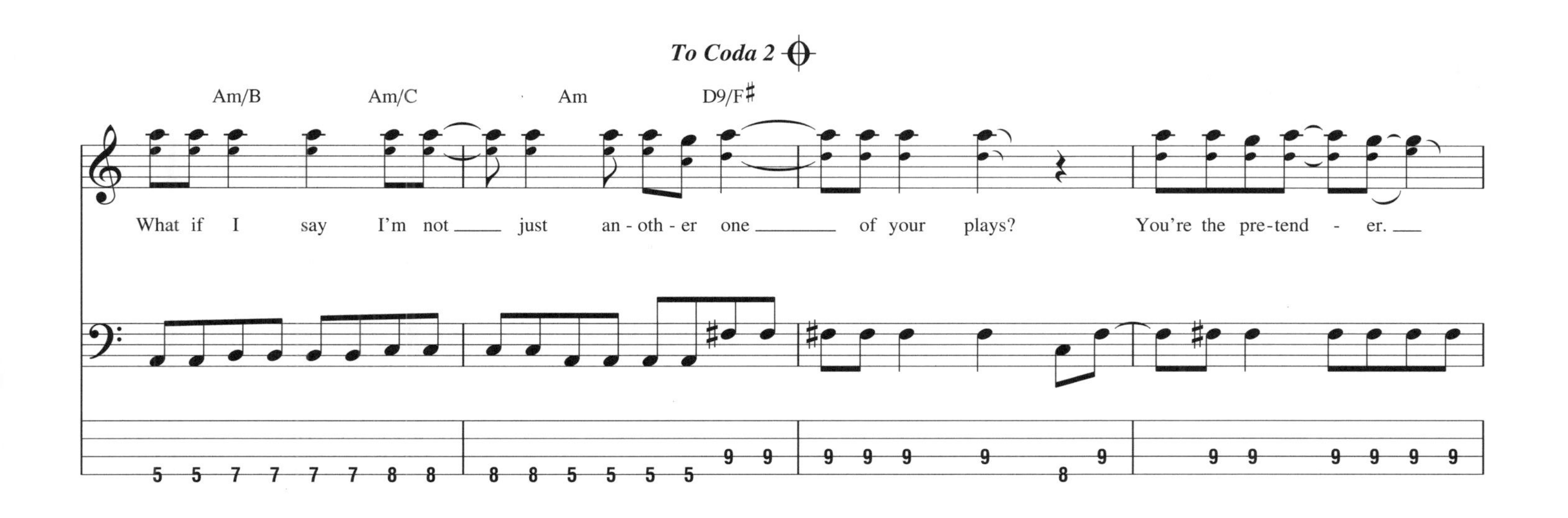
To Coda 2
Am/B
Am/C
Am
D9/F♯
What if I say I'm not just an-oth-er one of your plays? You're the pre-tend-er.
5 5 7 7 7 7 8 8
8 8 5 5 5 5 9 9
9 9 9 9 8 9
9 9 9 9 9 9

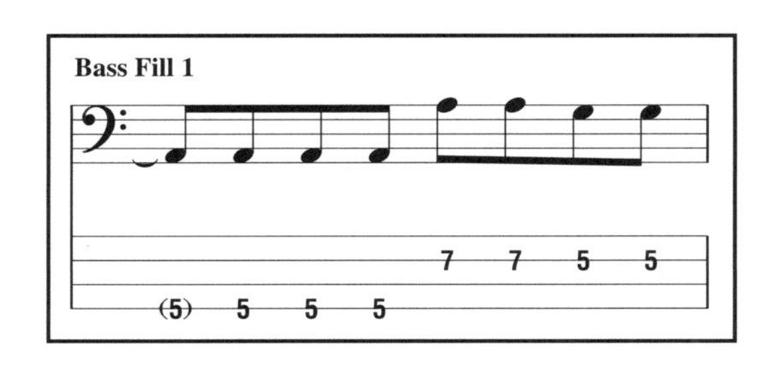
Bass Fill 1
(5) 5 5 5 7 7 5 5

To Coda 1

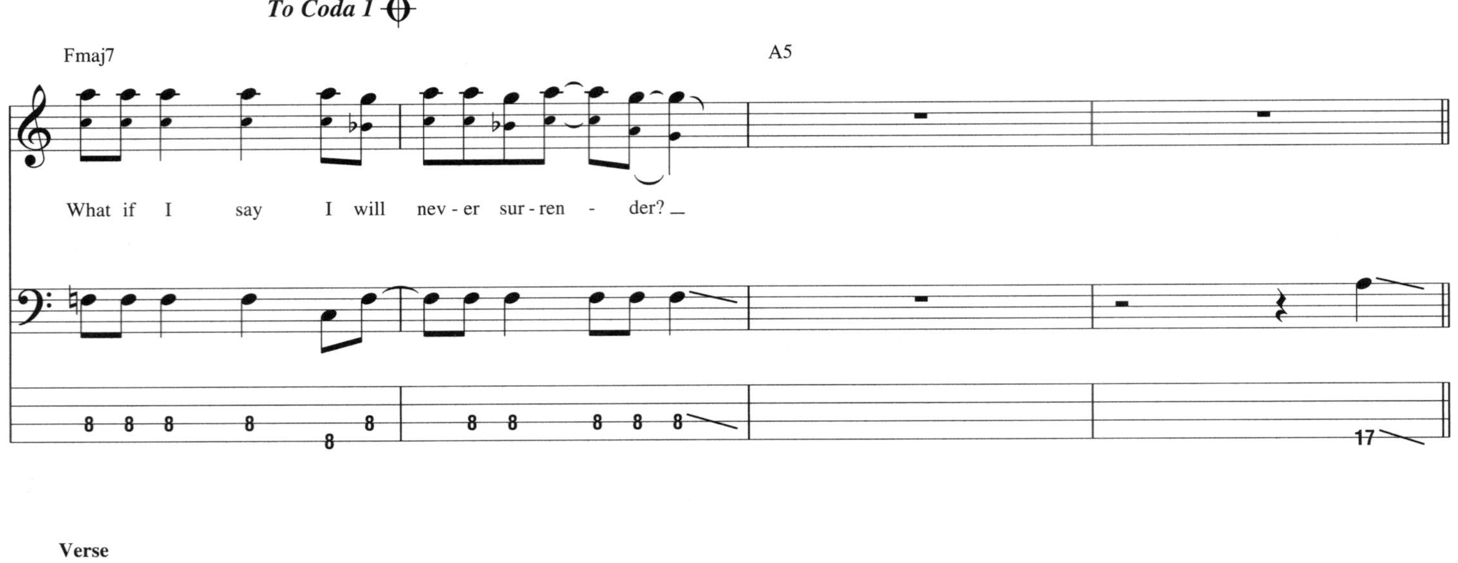
Fmaj7
A5
What if I say I will nev - er sur - ren - der?
8 8 8 8 8 8
8 8 8 8 8
17

Verse
Am
3. In time, or so I'm told,
I'm just an - oth - er soul for sale.
5 5 5 5 5 5 5 5 5 5 5 5

D/F♯
F
Fsus2
G5
Oh, well.
2 2 2 2 2 2 2 0 8 1 1 1 1 1 1 1 0 3

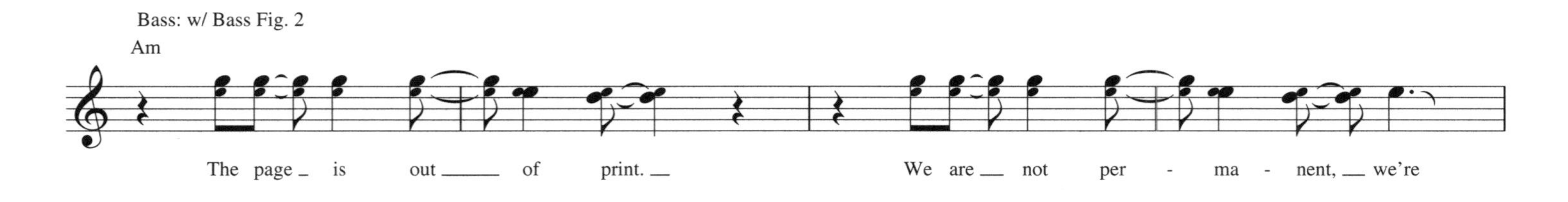
Bass: w/ Bass Fig. 2
Am
The page is out of print.
We are not per - ma - nent, we're

D/F♯
F
tem - po - rar - y, tem - po -

D.S. al Coda 1

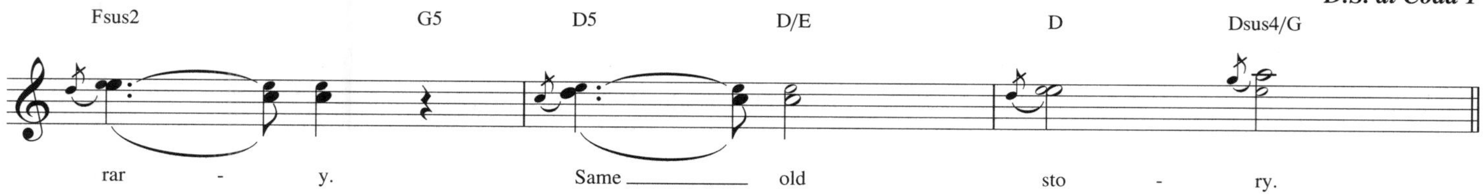
Fsus2
G5
D5
D/E
D
Dsus4/G
rar - y.
Same old
sto - ry.

Coda 1

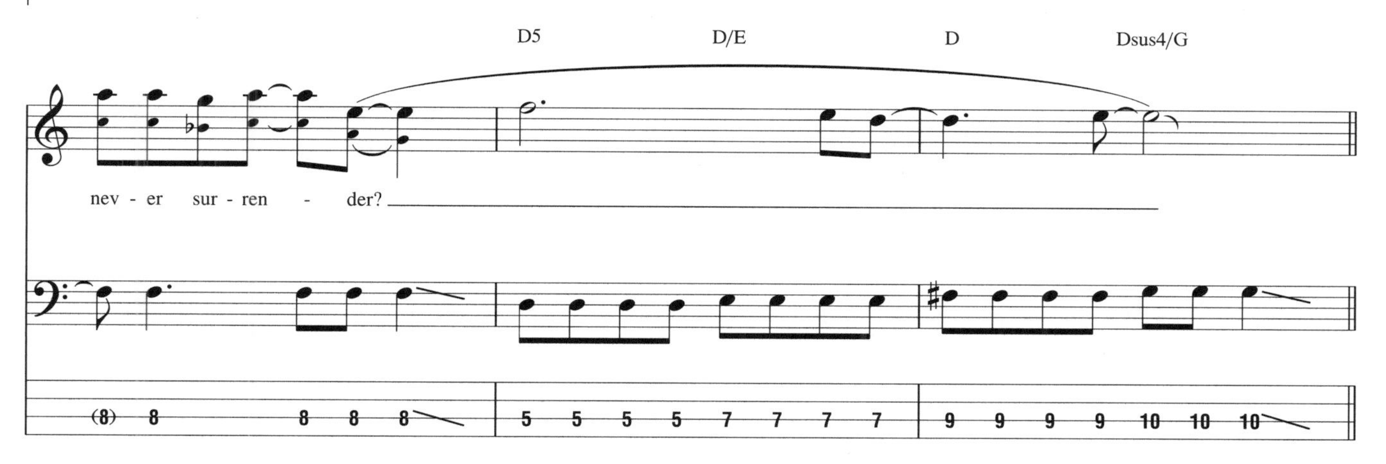
D5
D/E
D
Dsus4/G
nev - er sur - ren - der?
(8) 8 8 8 8
5 5 5 5 7 7 7 7
9 9 9 9 10 10 10

Interlude

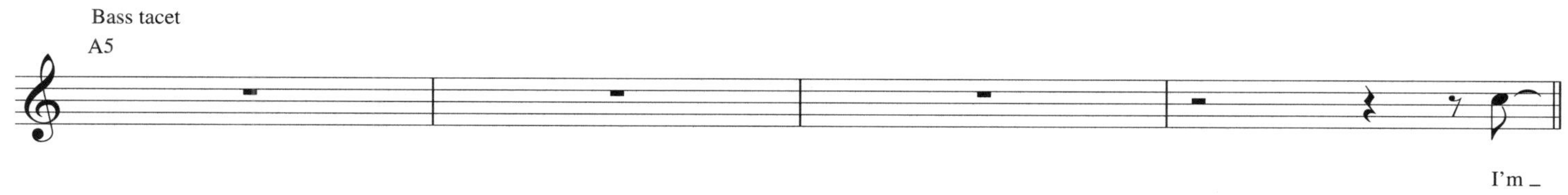
Bass tacet
A5
I'm

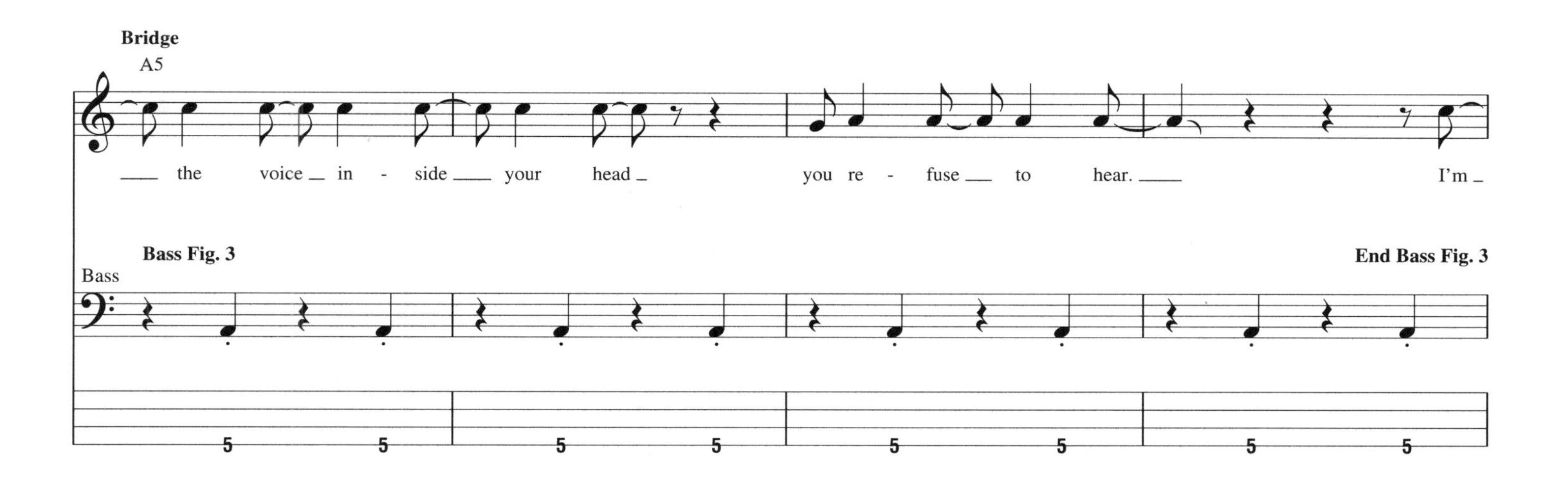
Bridge
A5
the voice in - side your head
you re - fuse to hear.
I'm
Bass Fig. 3
End Bass Fig. 3
Bass
5 5 5 5 5 5 5 5

Bass: w/ Bass Fig. 3
the face that you have to face,
mir - rored in your stare.
I'm

___ what's left. ___ I'm ___ what's right. ___ I'm ___ the en - e - my. I'm ___
Bass Fig. 4
End Bass Fig. 4
Bass
5 5 5 5 5 5 5 5 5 5 5 5 5 5 5 5 5 5 5 5 5 5 5 5 5 5 5 5 5 5 5 5

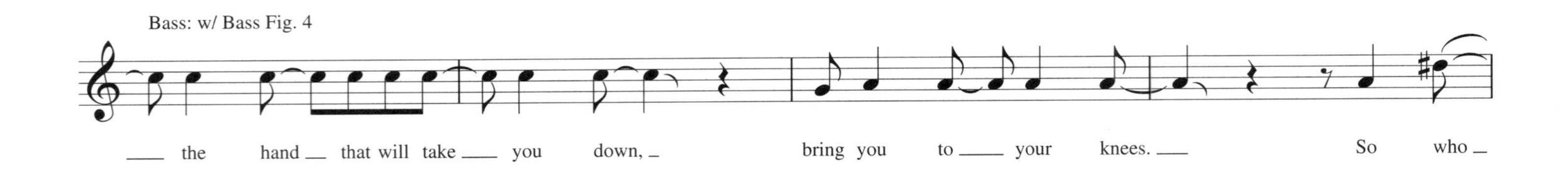

Bass: w/ Bass Fig. 4
___ the hand ___ that will take ___ you down, ___ bring you to ___ your knees. ___ So who ___

___ are you? ___ Yeah, who ___ are you? ___ Yeah, who ___
Bass
5 5 5 5 5 5 2 3 5 5 5 5 5 5 2 3 5 5 5 5 5 5 2 3 5 5 5 5 5 5 2 3

___ are you? ___ Yeah, who ___ are you? ___
5 5 3 4 5 2 3 5 5 5 3 4 5 2 3 5 5 5 3 4 5 2 3 5 5 5 3 4 5 2 3 5

Verse

Half-time feel

Bass tacet

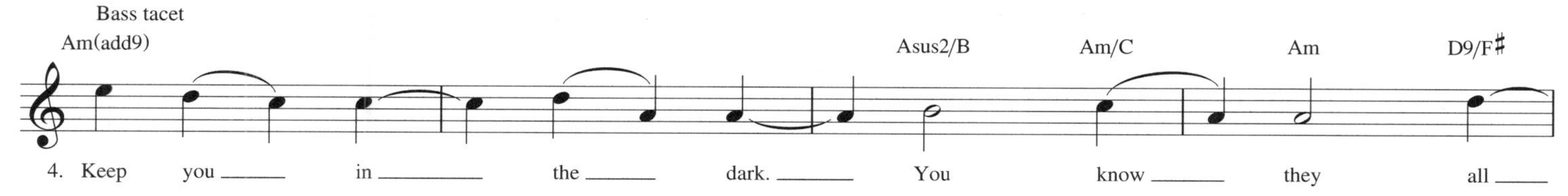
Am(add9)
Asus2/B
Am/C
Am
D9/F♯
4. Keep you ___ in ___ the ___ dark. ___ You know ___ they all ___

D.S. al Coda 2

End half-time feel

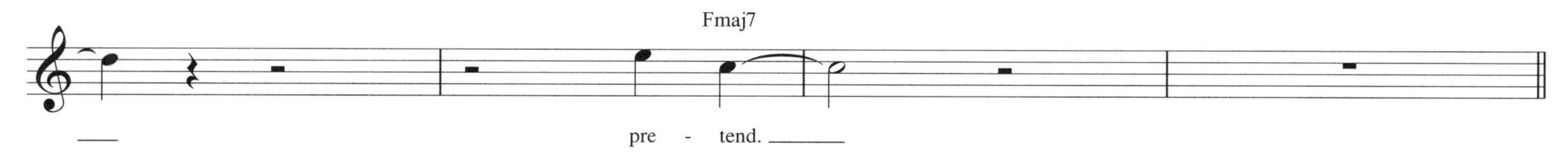
Fmaj7
___ pre - tend. ___

Coda 2

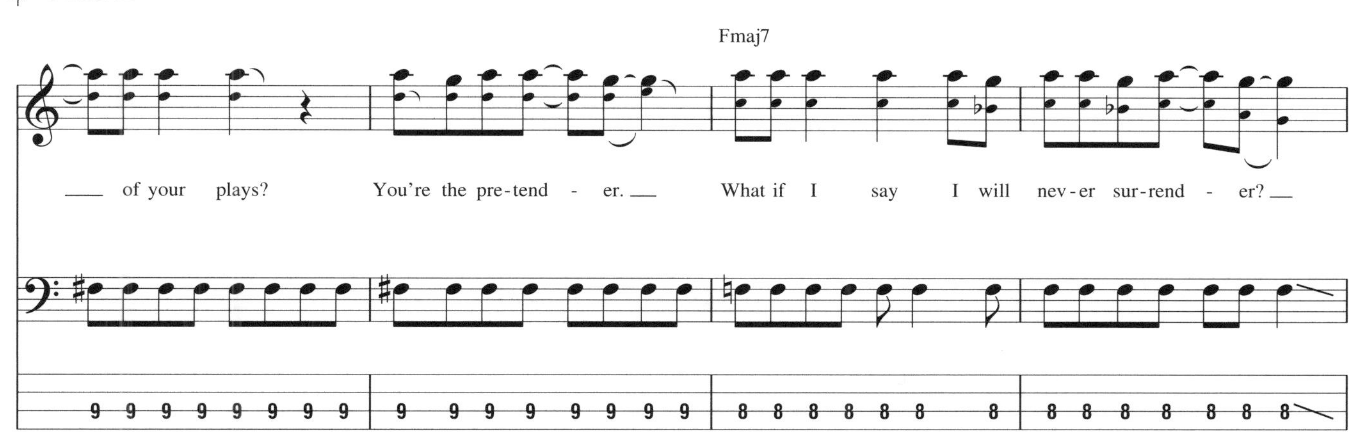
Fmaj7
___ of your plays? You're the pre-tend - er. ___ What if I say I will nev-er sur-rend - er? ___
9 9 9 9 9 9 9 9
9 9 9 9 9 9 9 9
8 8 8 8 8 8 8
8 8 8 8 8 8 8

Am
Am/B
Am/C
Am
D9/F♯
What if I say I'm not ___ like the oth-ers? What if I say I'm not ___ just an-oth-er one ___
Voc. Fig. 1
(Keep you ___ in ___ the dark. ___ You know ___ they all ___
5 5 5 5 5 5 5 5
5 5 5 5 7 7 5 5
5 5 7 7 7 7 8 8
8 8 5 5 5 5 9 9

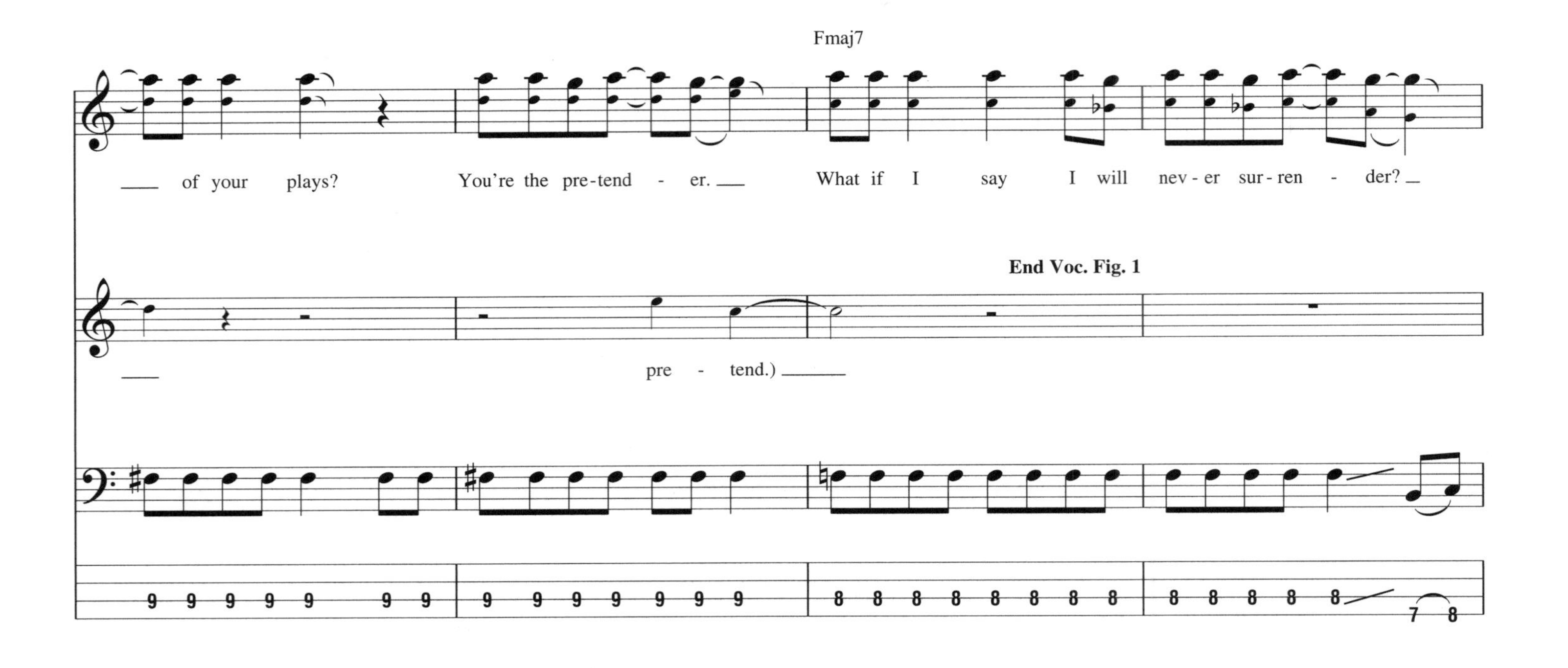
Fmaj7
of your plays? You're the pre-tend - er. What if I say I will nev-er sur-ren - der?
End Voc. Fig. 1
pre - tend.)
9 9 9 9 9 9 9
9 9 9 9 9 9 9
8 8 8 8 8 8 8 8
8 8 8 8 8 7 8
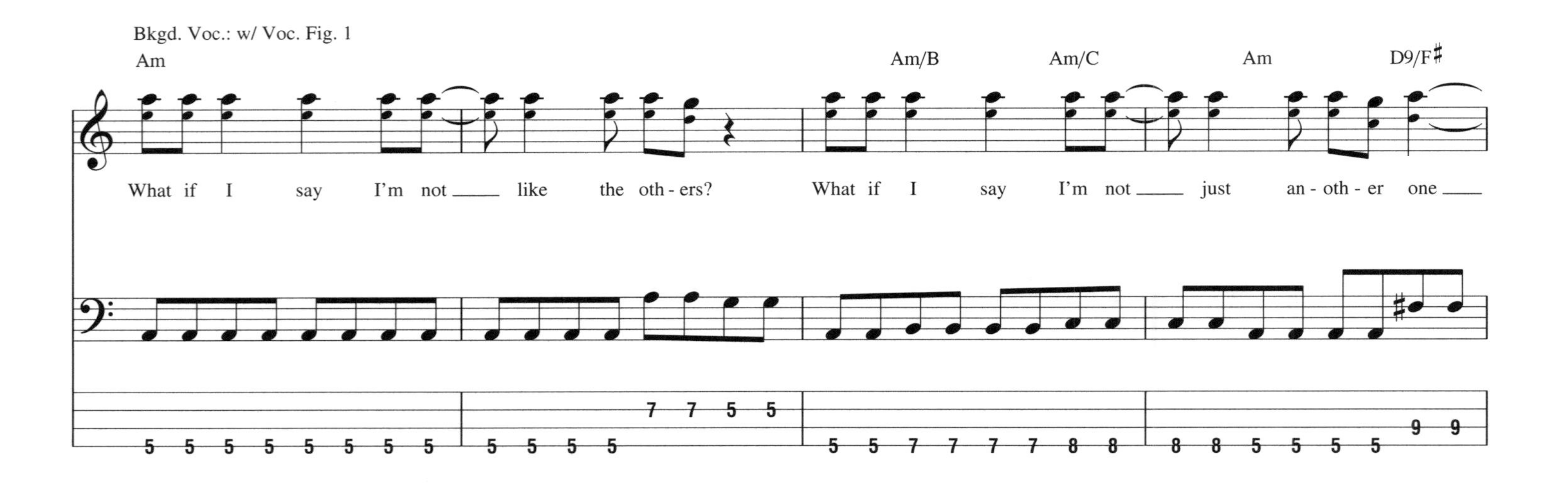
Bkgd. Voc.: w/ Voc. Fig. 1
Am
Am/B
Am/C
Am
D9/F♯
What if I say I'm not like the oth-ers? What if I say I'm not just an-oth-er one
5 5 5 5 5 5 5 5
5 5 5 5 7 7 5 5
5 5 7 7 7 7 8 8
8 8 5 5 5 5 9 9

Fmaj7
of your plays? You're the pre-tend - er. What if I say I will
9 9 9 9 9 9 9
9 9 9 9 9 9 9
8 8 8 8 8 8 8

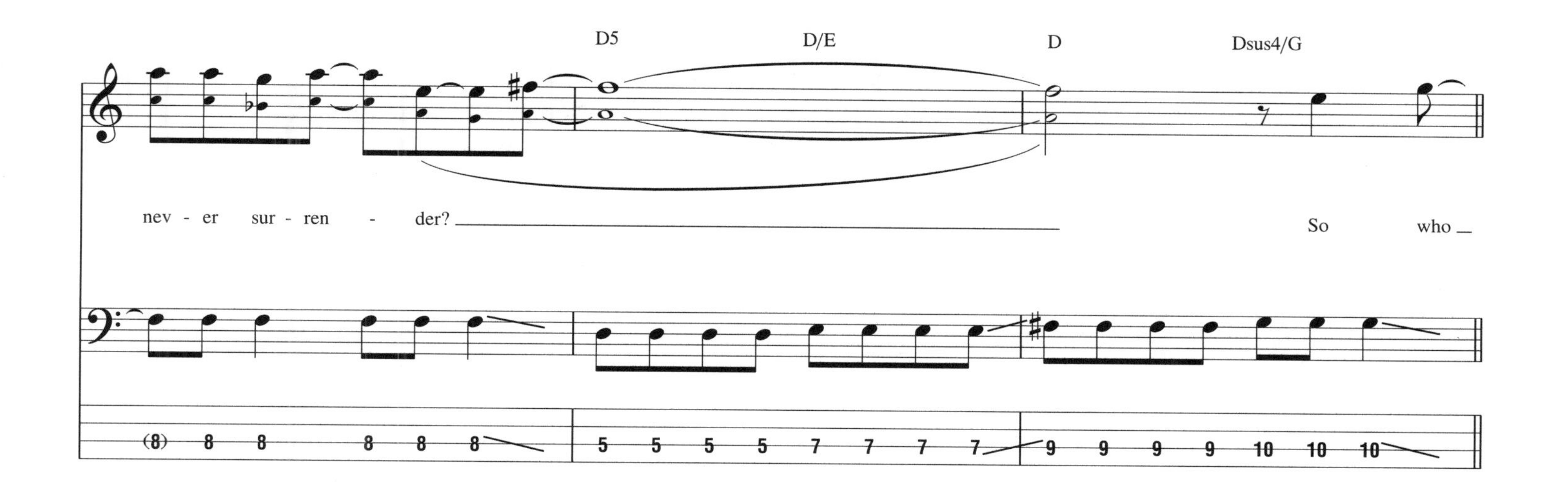
D5
D/E
D
Dsus4/G
nev - er sur - ren - der?
So who
(8) 8 8 8 8 8
5 5 5 5 7 7 7 7
9 9 9 9 10 10 10

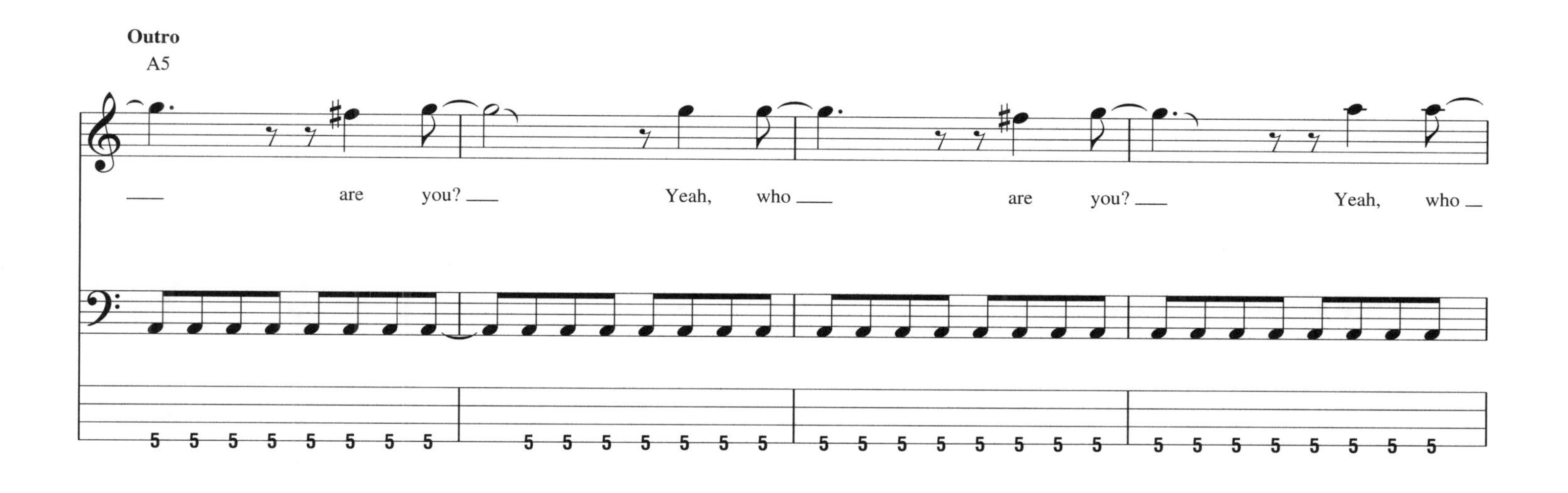
Outro
A5
are you?
Yeah, who
are you?
Yeah, who
5 5 5 5 5 5 5 5

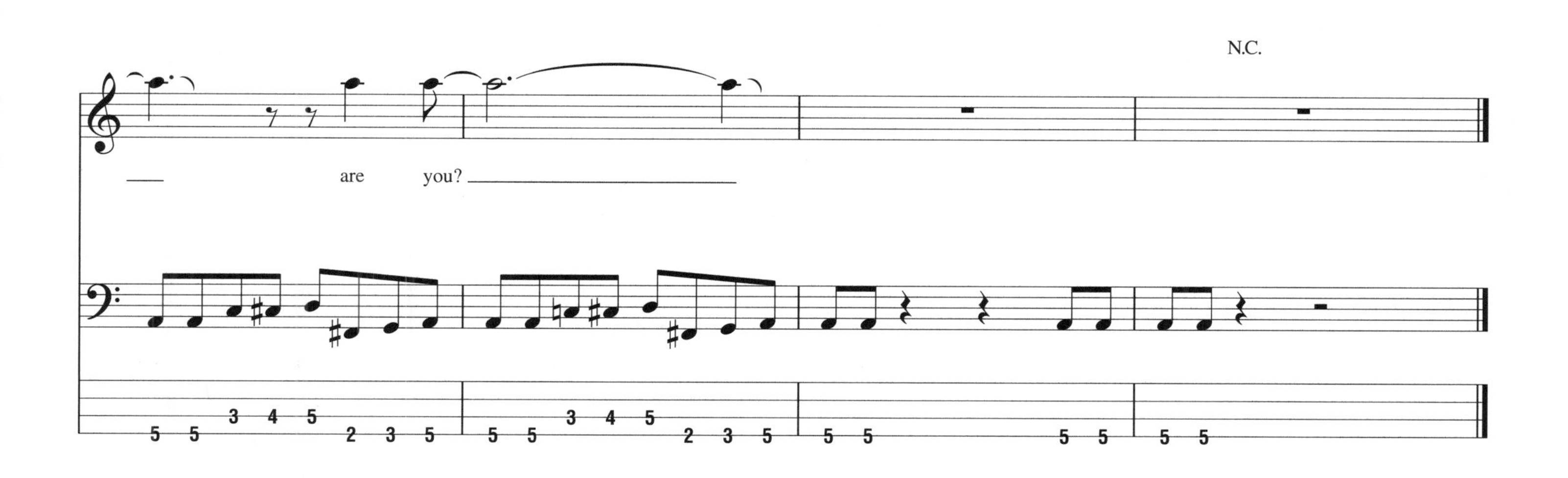
N.C.
are you?
5 5 3 4 5 2 3 5

Psychosocial

Words and Music by M. Shawn Crahan, Paul Gray, Nathan Jordison, Corey Taylor, Chris Fehn, Mic Thomson, Sid Wilson, James Root and Craig Jones

Drop D tuning, down 2 1/2 steps:
(low to high) A-E-A-D

Intro

Moderately fast ♩ = 135

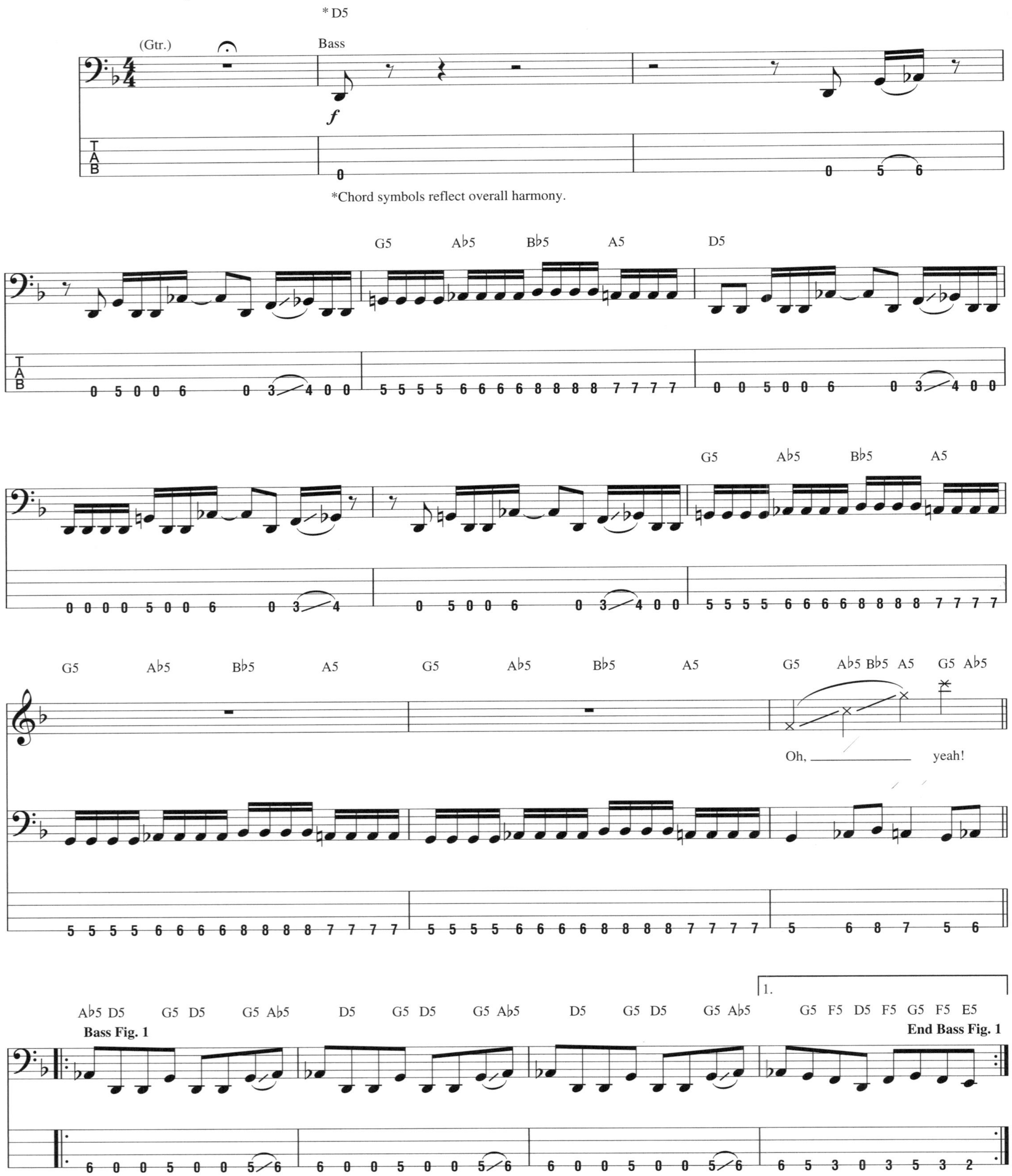

*D5

(Gtr.) Bass

f

T A B
0 | 0 5 6

*Chord symbols reflect overall harmony.

G5 Ab5 Bb5 A5 D5

0 5 0 0 6 0 3 4 0 0 | 5 5 5 5 6 6 6 6 8 8 8 8 7 7 7 7 | 0 0 5 0 0 6 0 3 4 0 0

G5 Ab5 Bb5 A5

0 0 0 0 5 0 0 6 0 3 4 | 0 5 0 0 6 0 3 4 0 0 | 5 5 5 5 6 6 6 6 8 8 8 8 7 7 7 7

G5 Ab5 Bb5 A5 G5 Ab5 Bb5 A5 G5 Ab5 Bb5 A5 G5 Ab5

Oh, ________ yeah!

5 5 5 5 6 6 6 6 8 8 8 8 7 7 7 7 | 5 5 5 5 6 6 6 6 8 8 8 8 7 7 7 7 | 5 6 8 7 5 6

Ab5 D5 G5 D5 G5 Ab5 D5 G5 D5 G5 Ab5 D5 G5 D5 G5 Ab5 | 1. G5 F5 D5 F5 G5 F5 E5

Bass Fig. 1 **End Bass Fig. 1**

6 0 0 5 0 0 5 6 | 6 0 0 5 0 0 5 6 | 6 0 0 5 0 0 5 6 | 6 5 3 0 3 5 3 2

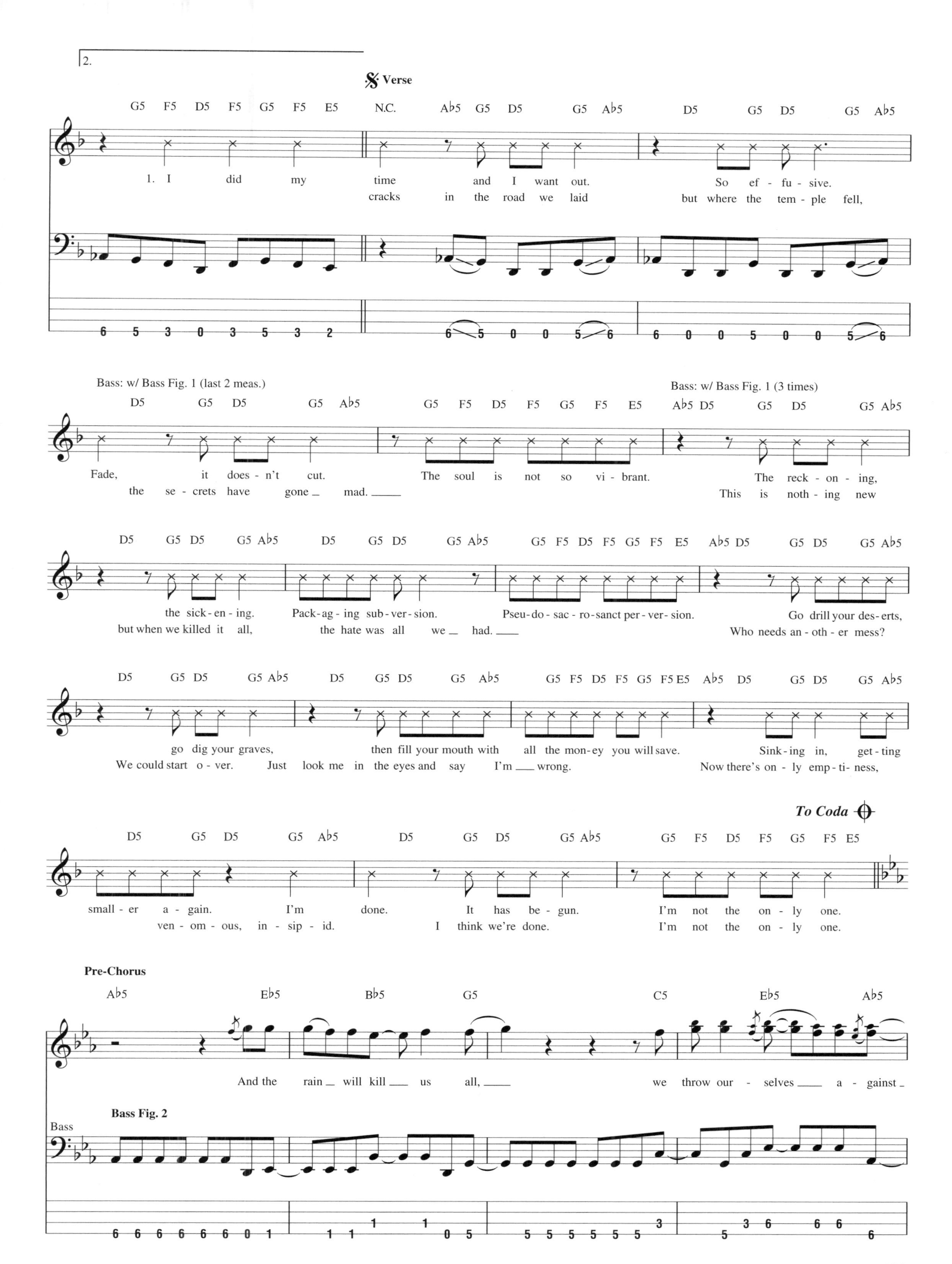
2.
Verse
G5 F5 D5 F5 G5 F5 E5 N.C. A♭5 G5 D5 G5 A♭5 D5 G5 D5 G5 A♭5
1. I did my time and I want out. So ef - fu - sive.
cracks in the road we laid but where the tem - ple fell,
Bass: w/ Bass Fig. 1 (last 2 meas.)
Bass: w/ Bass Fig. 1 (3 times)
Fade, it does - n't cut. The soul is not so vi - brant. The reck - on - ing,
the se - crets have gone mad. This is noth - ing new
the sick - en - ing. Pack - ag - ing sub - ver - sion. Pseu - do - sac - ro - sanct per - ver - sion. Go drill your des - erts,
but when we killed it all, the hate was all we had. Who needs an - oth - er mess?
go dig your graves, then fill your mouth with all the mon - ey you will save. Sink - ing in, get - ting
We could start o - ver. Just look me in the eyes and say I'm wrong. Now there's on - ly emp - ti - ness,
To Coda
small - er a - gain. I'm done. It has be - gun. I'm not the on - ly one.
ven - om - ous, in - sip - id. I think we're done. I'm not the on - ly one.
Pre-Chorus
A♭5 E♭5 B♭5 G5 C5 E♭5 A♭5
And the rain will kill us all, we throw our - selves a - gainst
Bass Fig. 2
Bass

Eb5
Bb5
G5
F5 Ab5
G5 N.C.
D5 G5 Ab5
the wall. But no one else can see the pres-er - va-tion of the mar-tyr in
End Bass Fig. 2
(6) 6 6 6 6 6 0 1
1 0 1 1 5
5 5 5 5 5 3 6
5 0 5 6
Chorus
Bass: w/ Bass Fig. 1 (2 times)
Ab5 D5 G5 D5 G5 Ab5 D5 G5 D5 G5 Ab5 D5 G5 D5 G5 Ab5 G5 F5 D5 F5 G5 F5 E5
me. Psy-cho - so-cial. Psy-cho - so-cial. Psy-cho - so-cial.
D.S. al Coda
Ab5 D5 G5 D5 G5 Ab5 D5 G5 D5 G5 Ab5 D5 G5 D5 G5 Ab5 G5 F5 D5 F5 G5 F5 E5
Psy-cho - so-cial. Psy-cho - so-cial. Psy-cho - so-cial. 2. Oh, there are
Coda
Pre-Chorus
Bass: w/ Bass Fig. 2
Ab5 Eb5 Bb5 G5 C5 Eb5 Ab5
And the rain will kill us all, we throw our - selves a - gainst
Eb5 Bb5 G5 F5 Ab5 G5 N.C. D5 F5Ab5
the wall. But no one else can see the pres - er - va - tion of the mar - tyr in
Guitar Solo
Bass: w/ Bass. Fig. 1 (1st 2 meas., 2 times)
Ab5 D5 G5 D5 G5 Ab5 D5 G5 D5 G5 Ab5 D5 G5 D5 G5 Ab5 D5 G5 D5 G5Ab5
me. Psy - cho - so - cial. Psy - cho - so - cial. Psy - cho - so - cial.

D5 G5 D5 G5 A♭5 D5 G5 D5 G5 A♭5 D5 G5 D5 G5 A♭5 D5 G5 D5 F5 E5
Voc. Fig. 1
End Voc. Fig. 1
Psy cho - so - cial. Psy cho - so - cial. Psy cho - so - cial.
Bass
6 0 0 5 0 0 5 6 6 0 0 5 0 0 5 6 6 0 0 5 0 0 5 6 6 0 0 5 0 0 3 2
A♭5 E♭5 B♭5 G5 C5 E♭5 A♭5
6 6 6 6 6 6 0 1 1 1 1 1 0 5 5 5 5 5 5 5 3 3 0 6 6 0 6
E♭5 B♭5 G5
(6) 6 6 6 6 6 0 1 1 0 1 1 0 5 5 5 5 5 5 5 5 5 5 5 5 5 5 5 5 5
Bridge
D5
7
The lim - its of the dead.
Bass Fig. 3
End Bass Fig. 3
0 0 0 0 0 0 0 0 0 0 0 0 0 0
Bass: w/ Bass Fig. 3 (3 times)
The lim - its of the dead.

The lim-its of the
Ab5 F5 D5
G5 E5 D5 Ab5 F5 D5
dead.
Bass
F#5 E5 D5 Ab5 F5 D5
F#5 E5
The lim-its of the dead.
D5 Ab5 F5 D5
E5 F5
Verse
Bkgd. Voc.: w/ Voc. Fig. 1 (2 times)
Bass: w/ Bass Fig. 1 (2 times)
3. Fake an-ti-fas-cist lie. I tried to tell you, but your pur-ple hearts are giv-ing out.
Can't stop a kill-ing i-de-a if it's hunt-ing sea-son. Is this what you want? I'm not the on-ly one.

Pre-Chorus

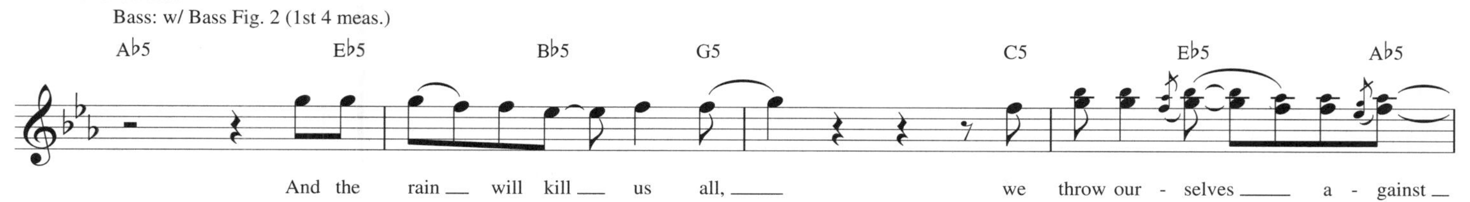
Bass: w/ Bass Fig. 2 (1st 4 meas.)
A♭5 E♭5 B♭5 G5 C5 E♭5 A♭5
And the rain will kill us all, we throw our - selves a - gainst

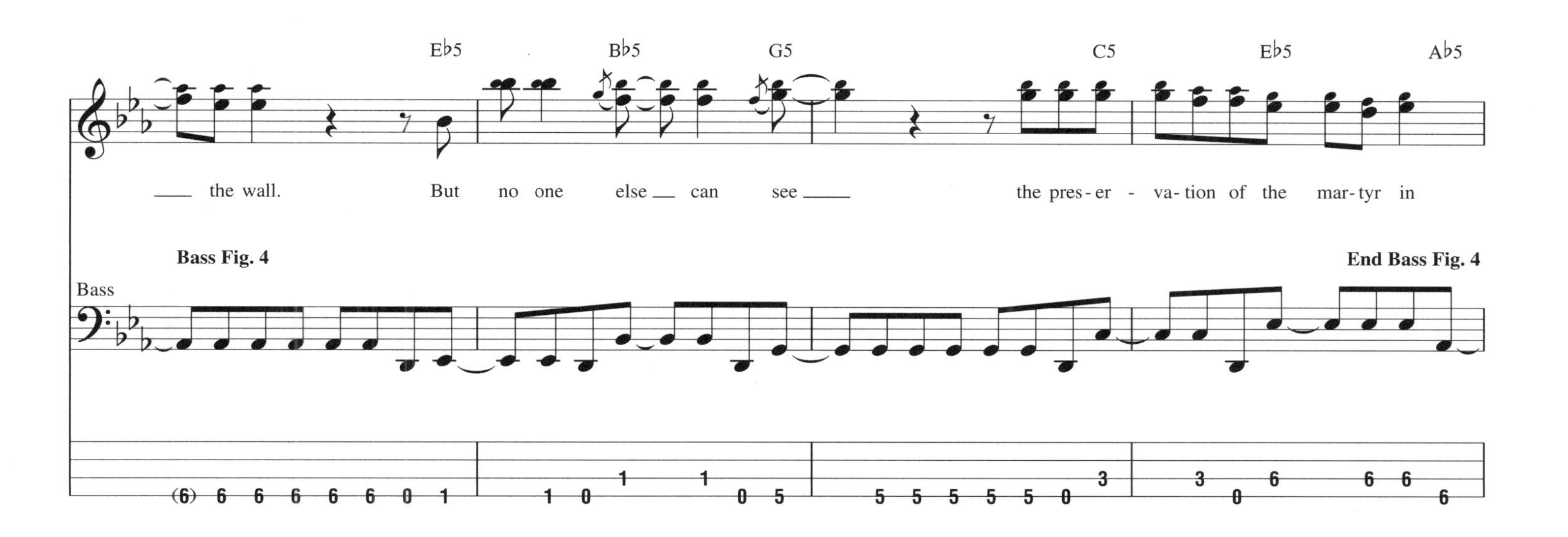
E♭5 B♭5 G5 C5 E♭5 A♭5
the wall. But no one else can see the pres - er - va - tion of the mar - tyr in
Bass Fig. 4
End Bass Fig. 4
Bass

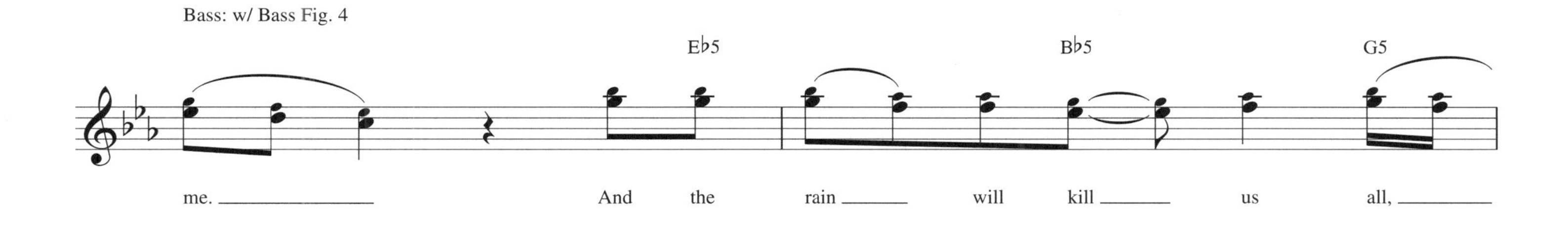
Bass: w/ Bass Fig. 4
E♭5 B♭5 G5
me. And the rain will kill us all,

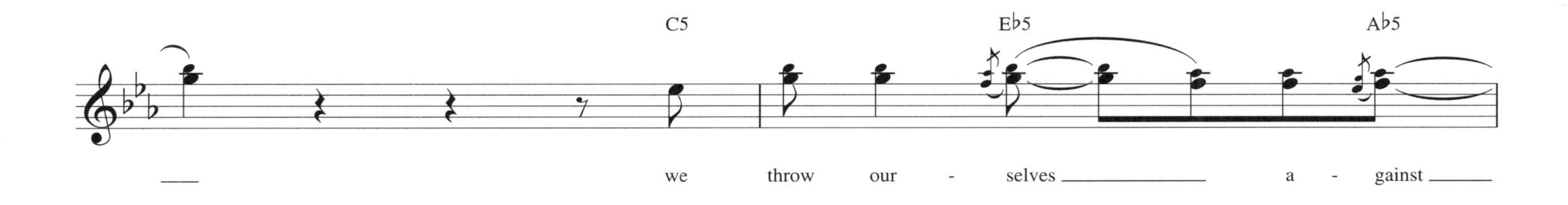
C5 E♭5 A♭5
we throw our - selves a - gainst

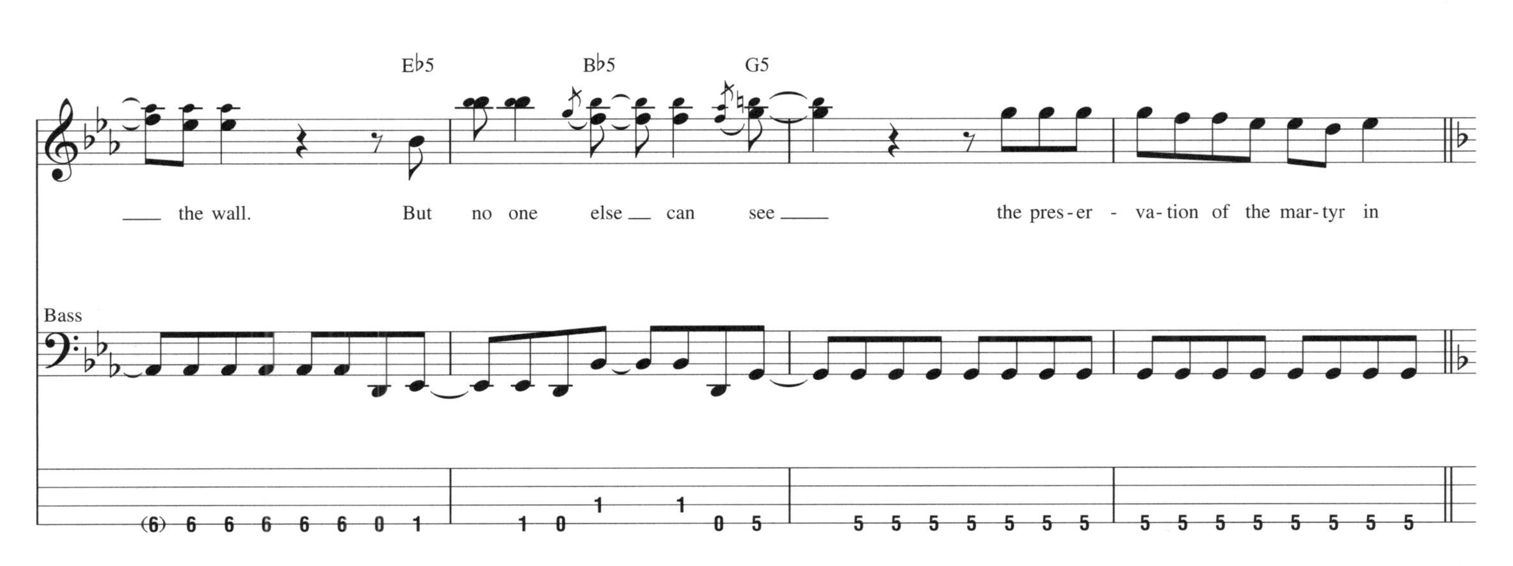
E♭5 B♭5 G5
the wall. But no one else can see the pres - er - va - tion of the mar - tyr in
Bass

Outro
D5
Play 3 times
me.
*Sing 1st time only.
The lim - its of the
dead.
Bass Fig. 5
End Bass Fig. 5
F5
E5
Bass: w/ Bass Fig. 5 (2 times)
D5
F5
E5
D5
F5
E5
The lim - its of the dead.
D5
Bass

Pump It Up

Words and Music by Elvis Costello

Intro
Moderately fast ♩ = 140
N.C.(F♯7)
Bass
Play 3 times
f
T
A
B
1 2 1 0 1 2
2 2 0 2 0 2 0
1 2 1 0 1 2
2 2 4 4 0 0 1 1

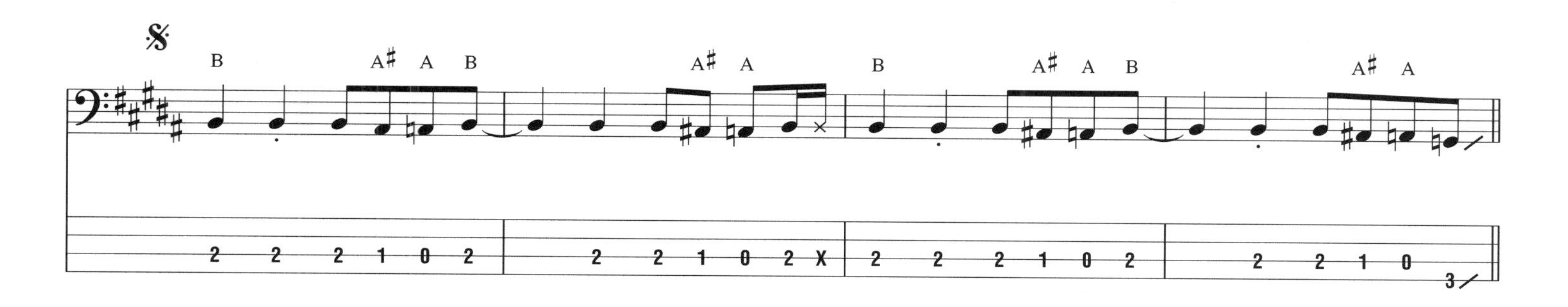
B A♯ A B A♯ A B A♯ A B A♯ A
2 2 2 1 0 2 2 2 1 0 2 X 2 2 2 1 0 2 2 2 1 0 3

Verse
B7
1. I've been on ten - ter - hooks end - ing in dirt - y looks,
3. She's been a bad girl, she's like a chem - i - cal.
Bass Fig. 1
End Bass Fig. 1
7 6 7 6 5 6
7 7 5 7 5 7 5

Bass: w/ Bass Fig. 1 (2 times)
lis - t'ning to the Mu - zak, think - ing 'bout this and that.
Though you try to stop it, she's like a nar - cot - ic.

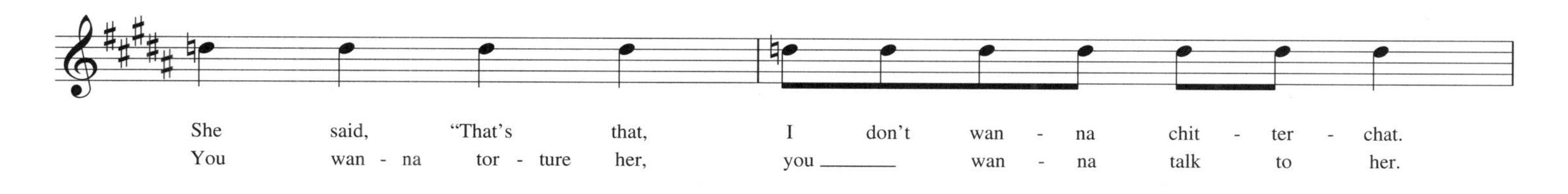
She said, "That's that, I don't wan - na chit - ter - chat.
You wan - na tor - ture her, you wan - na talk to her.

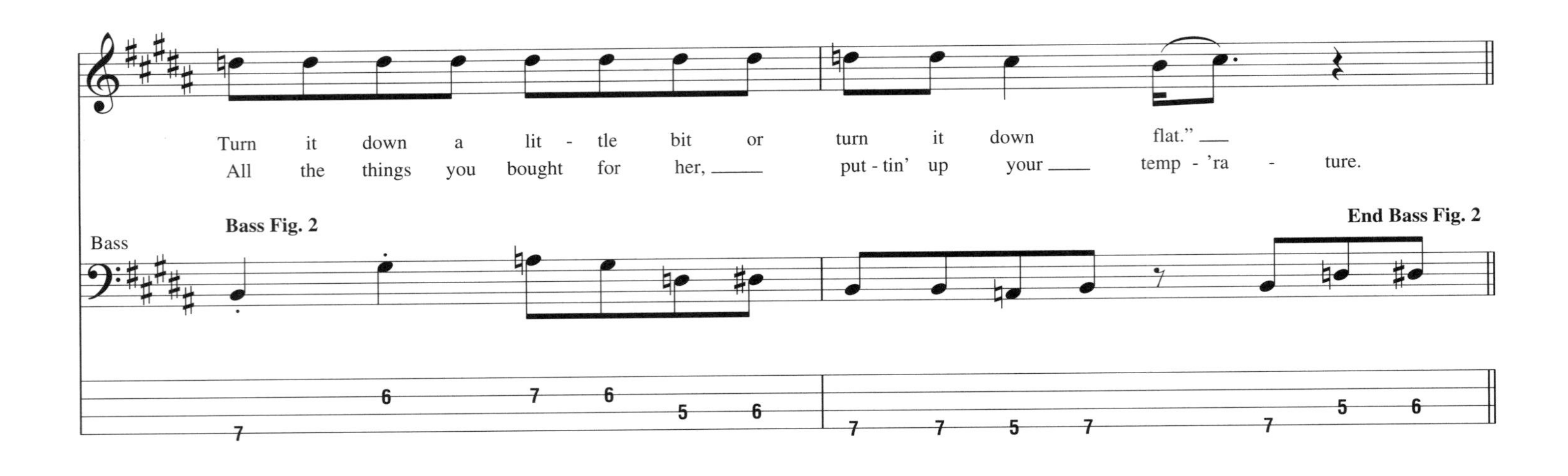
Turn it down a lit - tle bit or turn it down flat."
All the things you bought for her, put - tin' up your temp - 'ra - ture.
Bass Fig. 2
Bass
End Bass Fig. 2

Chorus
E7
Pump it up when you don't real - ly need it.
Pump it up a un - til you can feel it.
Bass Fill 1
End Bass Fill 1

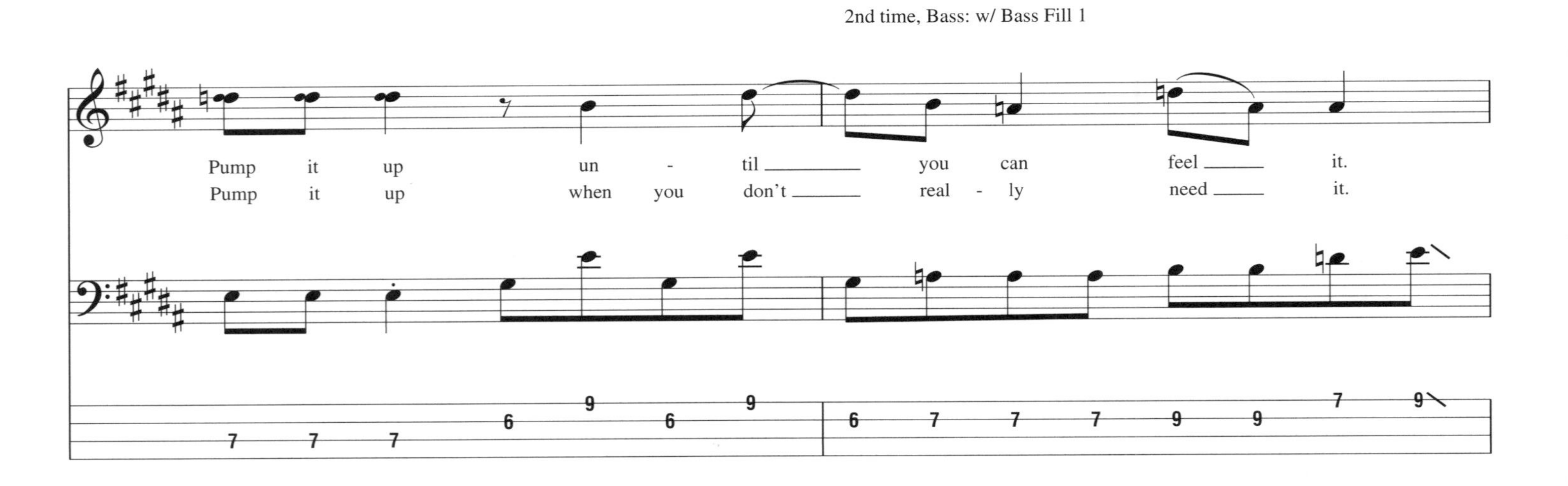
2nd time, Bass: w/ Bass Fill 1
Pump it up un - til you can feel it.
Pump it up when you don't real - ly need it.

To Coda
B A# A B A# A B A# A B A# A

Verse
Bass: w/ Bass Fig. 1 (2 times)
B7
2. Down in the pleas - ure cen - ter, hell - bent or heav - en sent,
list - ten to the prop - a - gan - da, lis - ten to the lat - est slan - der.
Bass: w/ Bass Fig. 2
There's noth - ing un - der - hand that she would - n't un - der - stand.
Chorus
E7
Pump it up un - til you can feel it. Pump it up when you don't
Bass
really need it.
Interlude
B
A♯
A
B
A♯
A
1., 2. 3.
4.
A♯
A
E
D.S. al Coda
Hey!

Coda

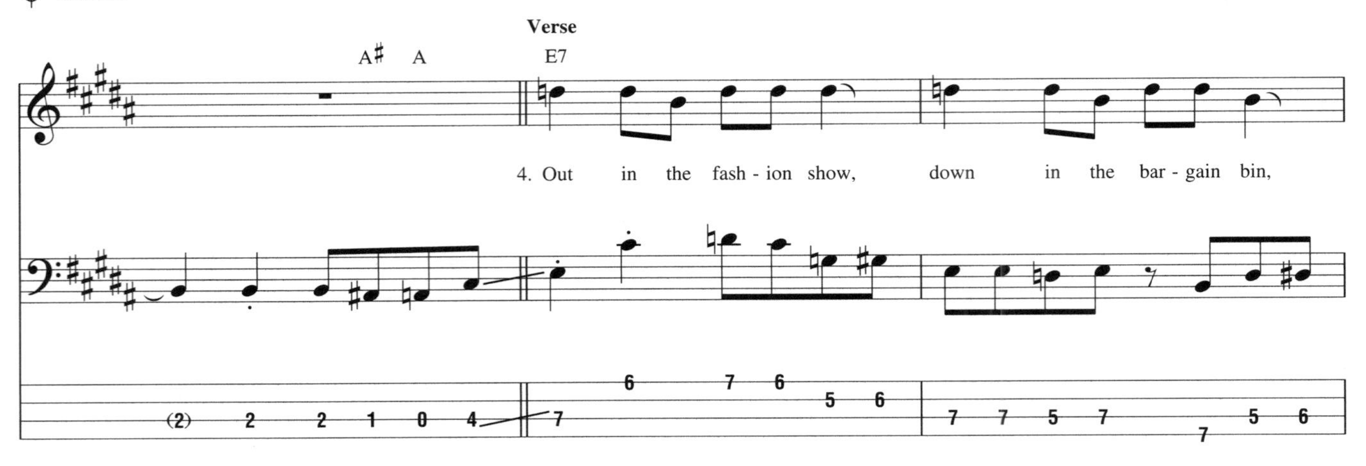
Verse
A♯ A
E7
4. Out in the fash - ion show, down in the bar - gain bin,

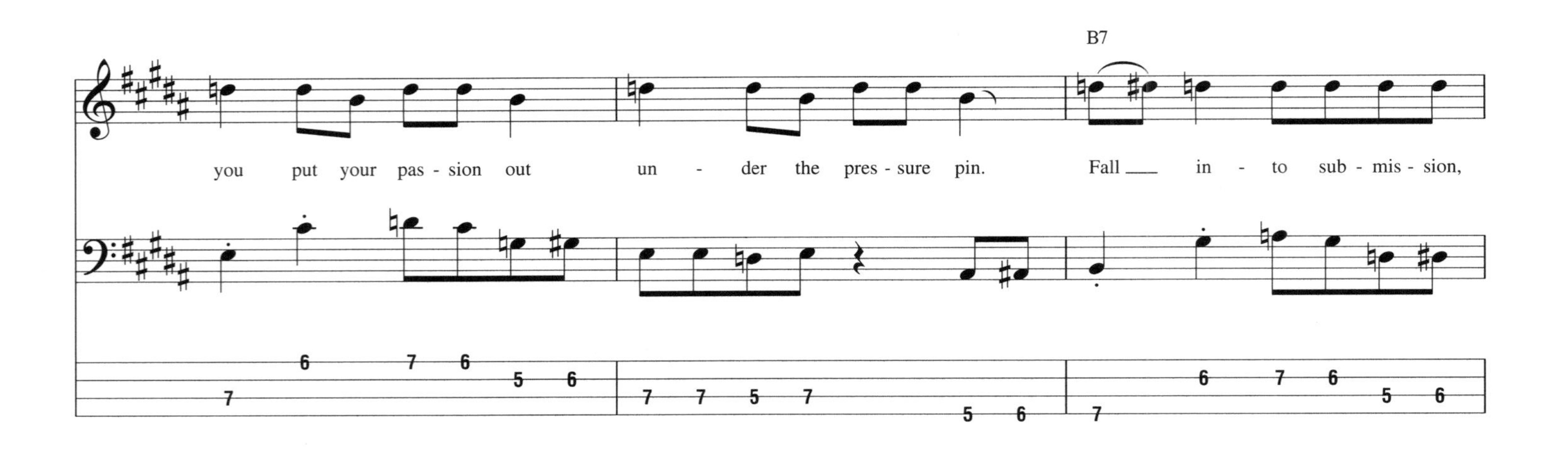
B7
you put your pas - sion out un - der the pres - sure pin. Fall in - to sub - mis - sion,

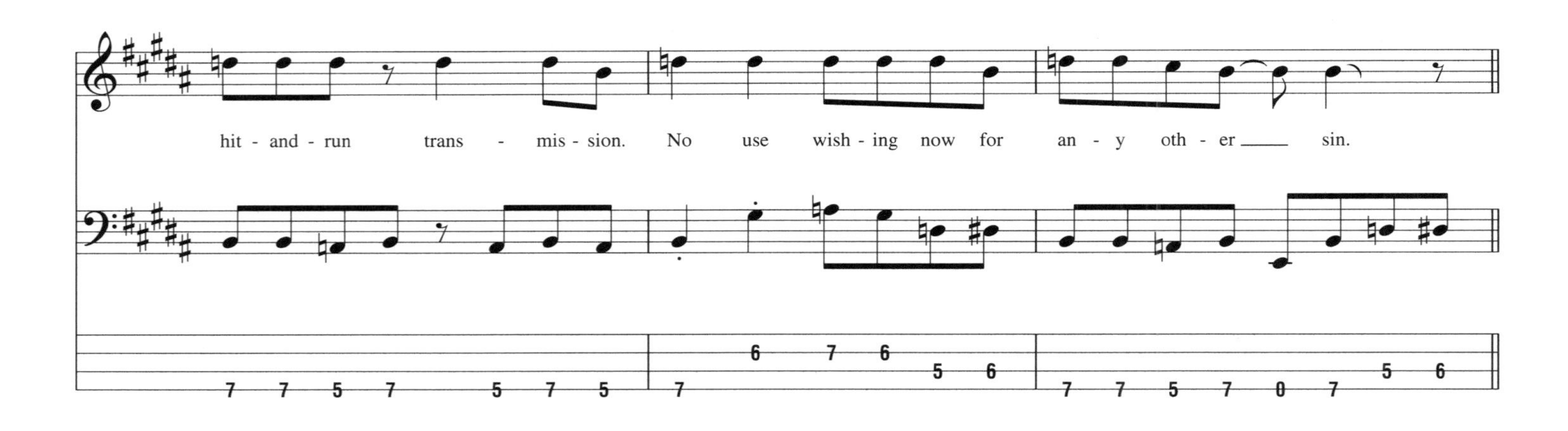
hit - and - run trans - mis - sion. No use wish - ing now for an - y oth - er sin.

Chorus
E7
Pump it up un - til you can feel it. Pump it up when you don't

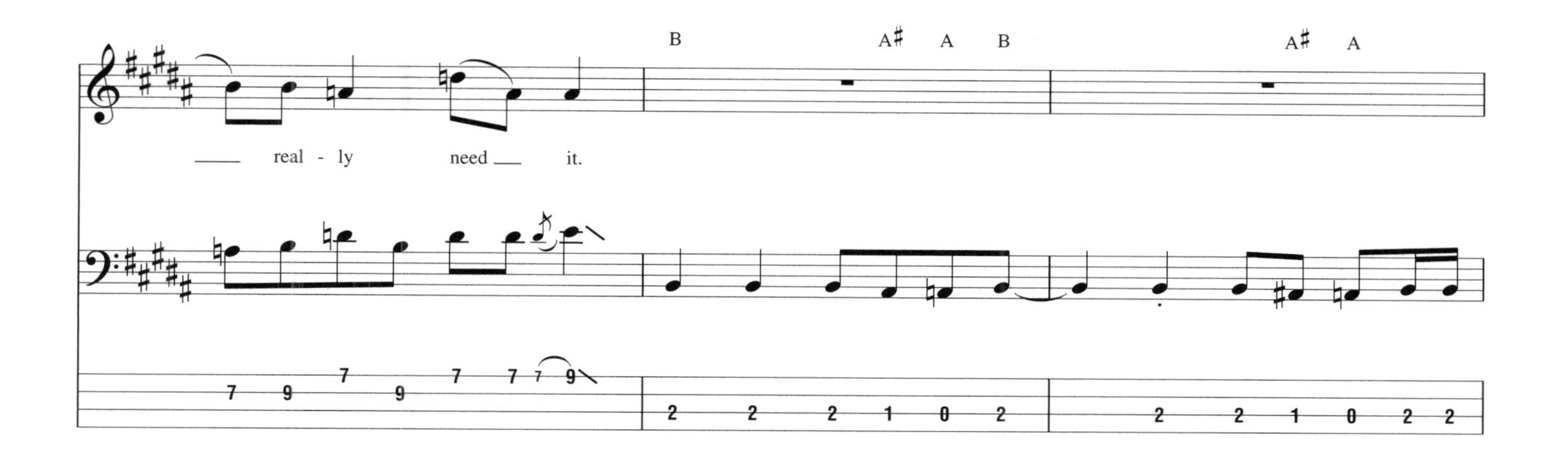
B
A♯
A
B
A♯
A
really need it.
7 9 7 9 7 7 7 9
2 2 2 1 0 2
2 2 1 0 2 2

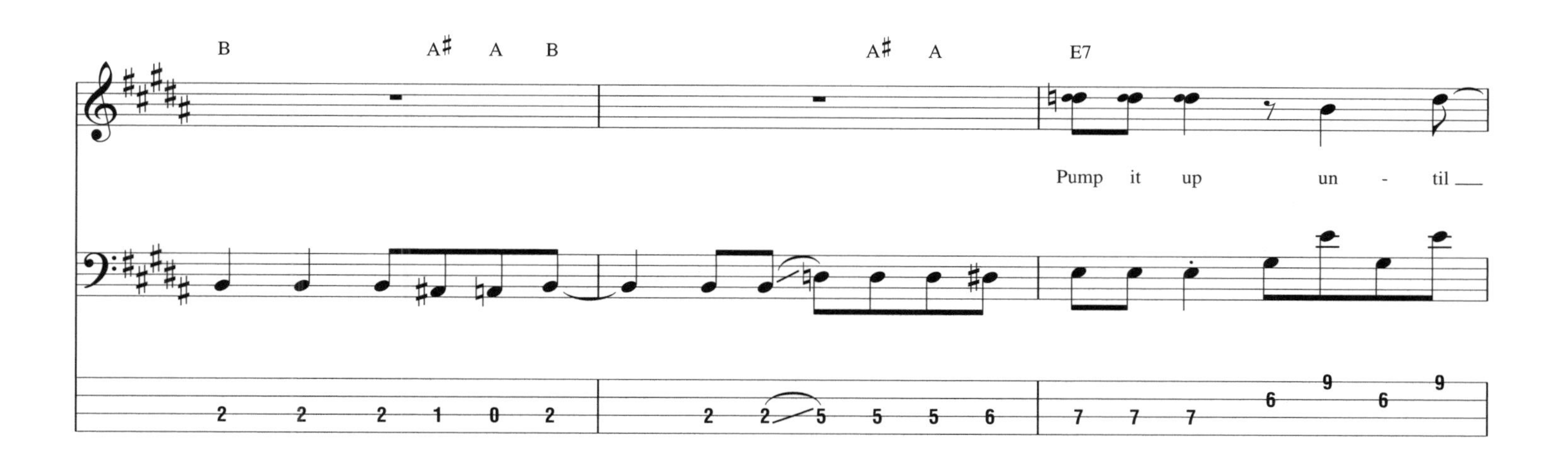
B
A♯
A
B
A♯
A
E7
Pump it up until
2 2 2 1 0 2
2 2 5 5 5 6
7 7 7 6 9 6 9

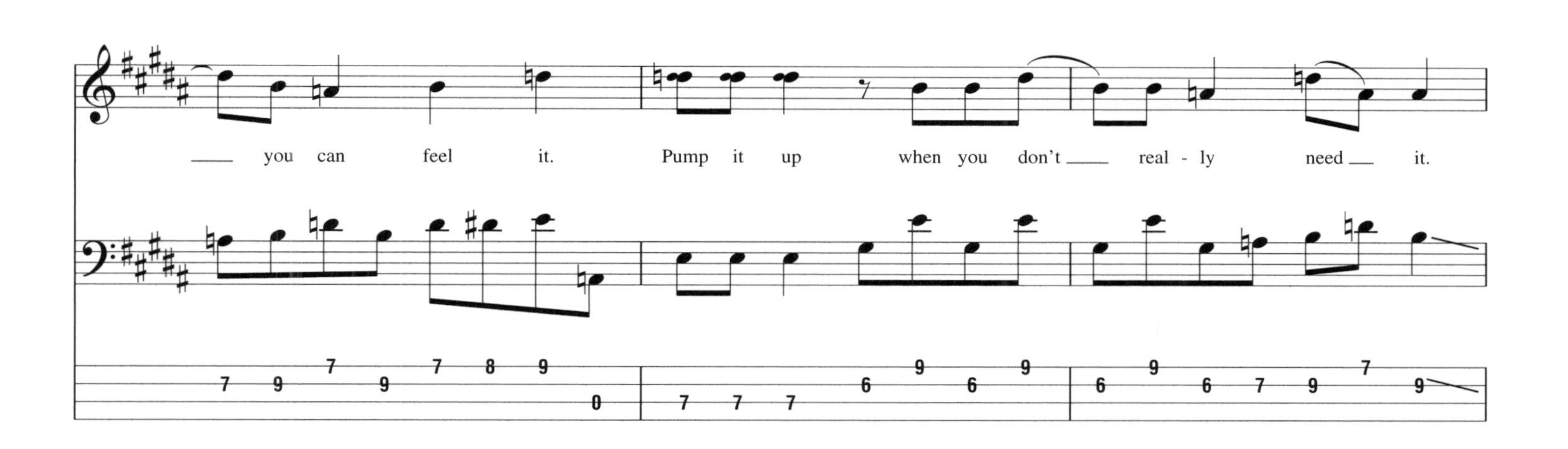
you can feel it. Pump it up when you don't really need it.
7 9 7 9 7 8 9 0
7 7 7 6 9 6 9
6 9 6 7 9 7 9

B
A♯
A
B
A♯
A
B
A♯
A
B
2 2 2 1 0 2
2 2 1 0 0 1
2 2 2 1 0 1 1

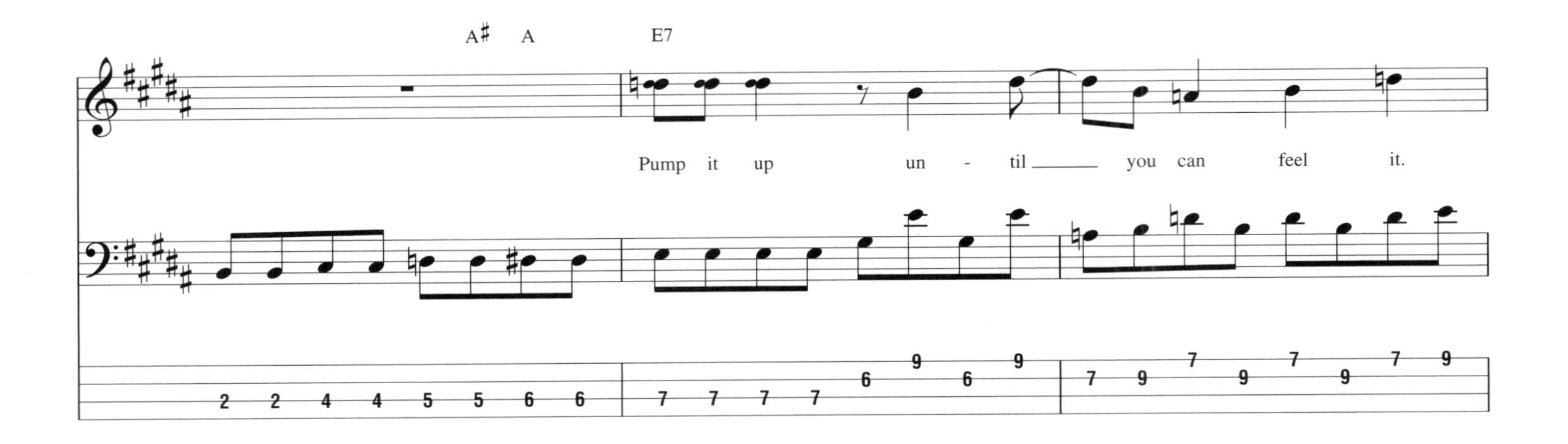
A♯ A E7
Pump it up un - til you can feel it.

Outro
B A♯ A B
Pump it up when you don't real - ly need it. Don't

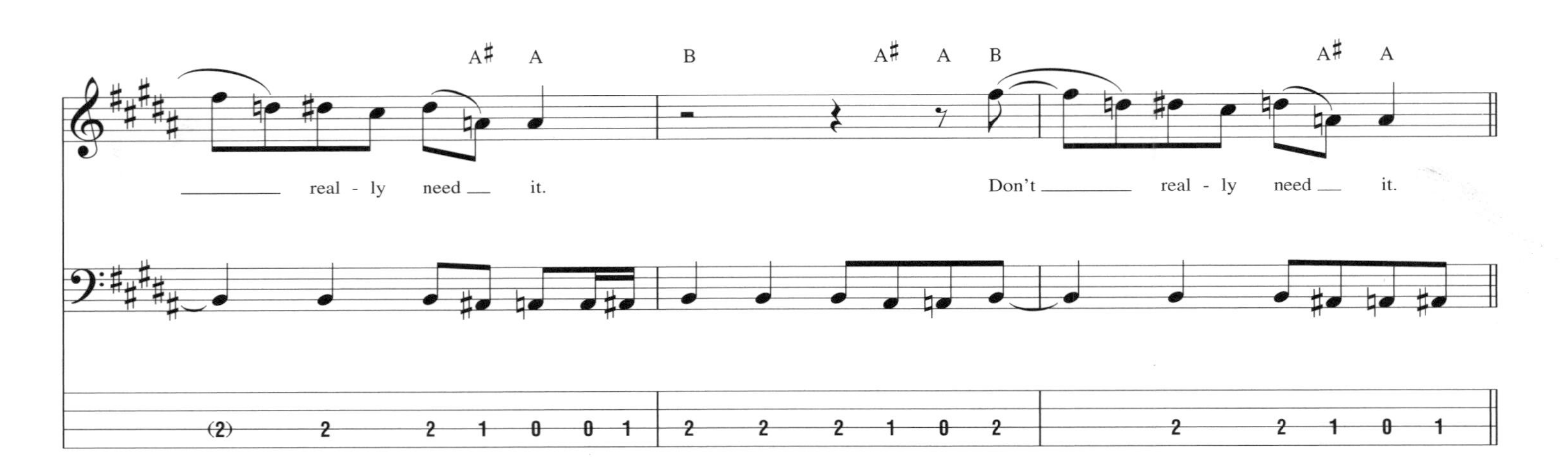
A♯ A B A♯ A B A♯ A
real - ly need it. Don't real - ly need it.

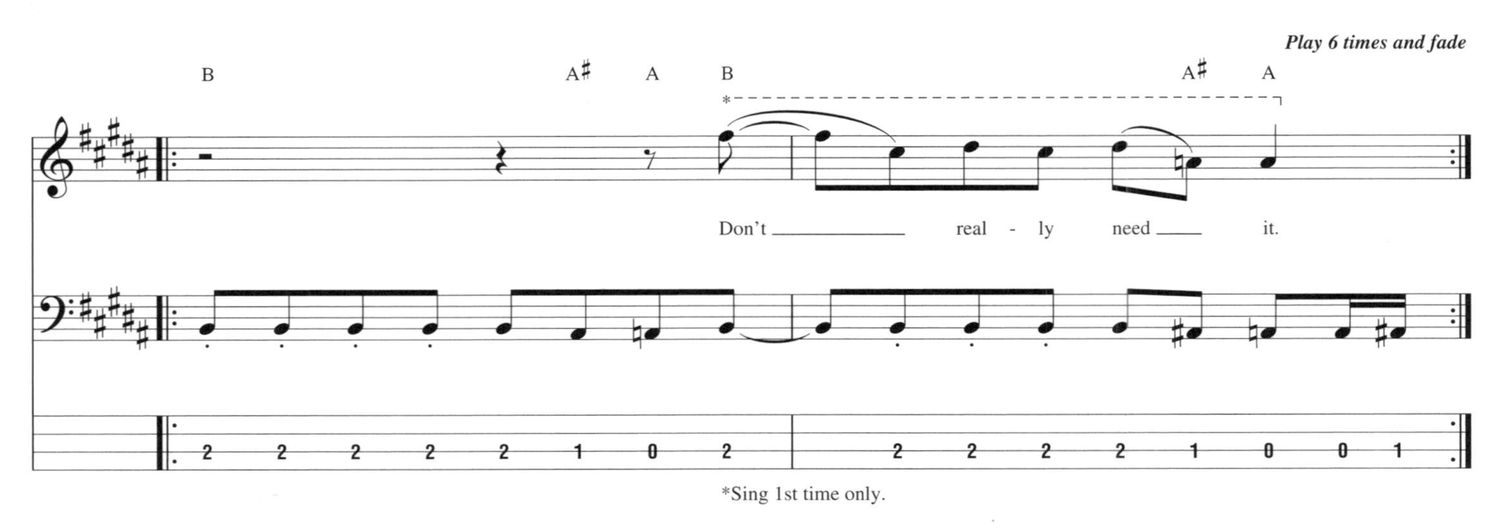
Play 6 times and fade
B A♯ A B A♯ A
Don't real - ly need it.

*Sing 1st time only.

Santeria

Words and Music by Brad Nowell, Eric Wilson and Floyd Gaugh

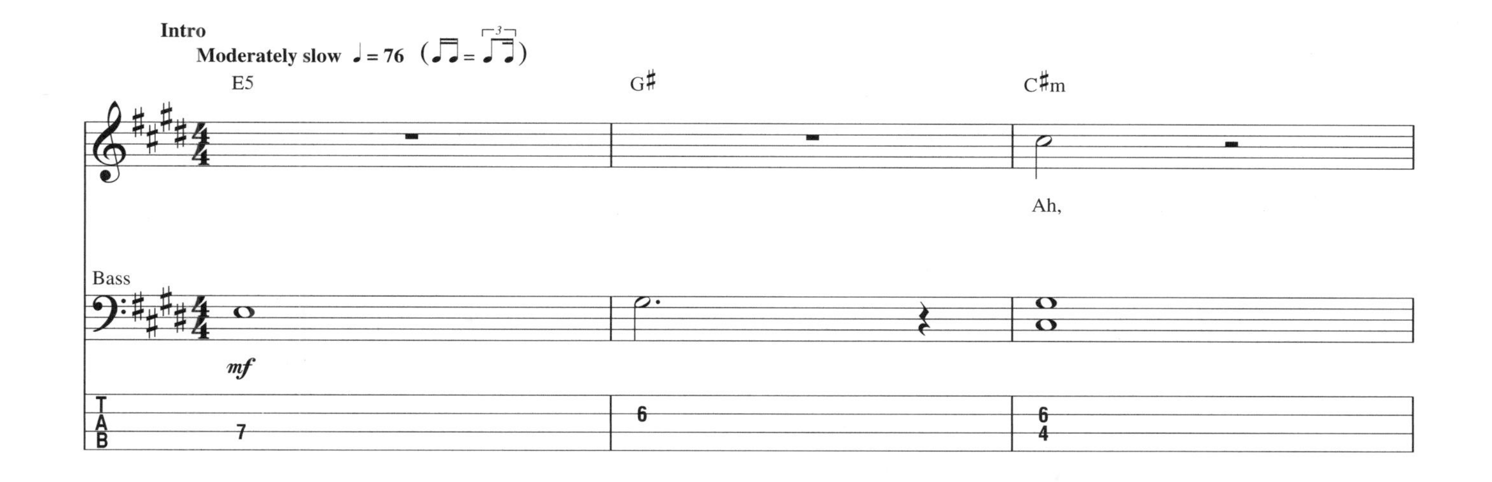

Intro
Moderately slow ♩ = 76
E5
G♯
C♯m
Ah,
Bass
mf

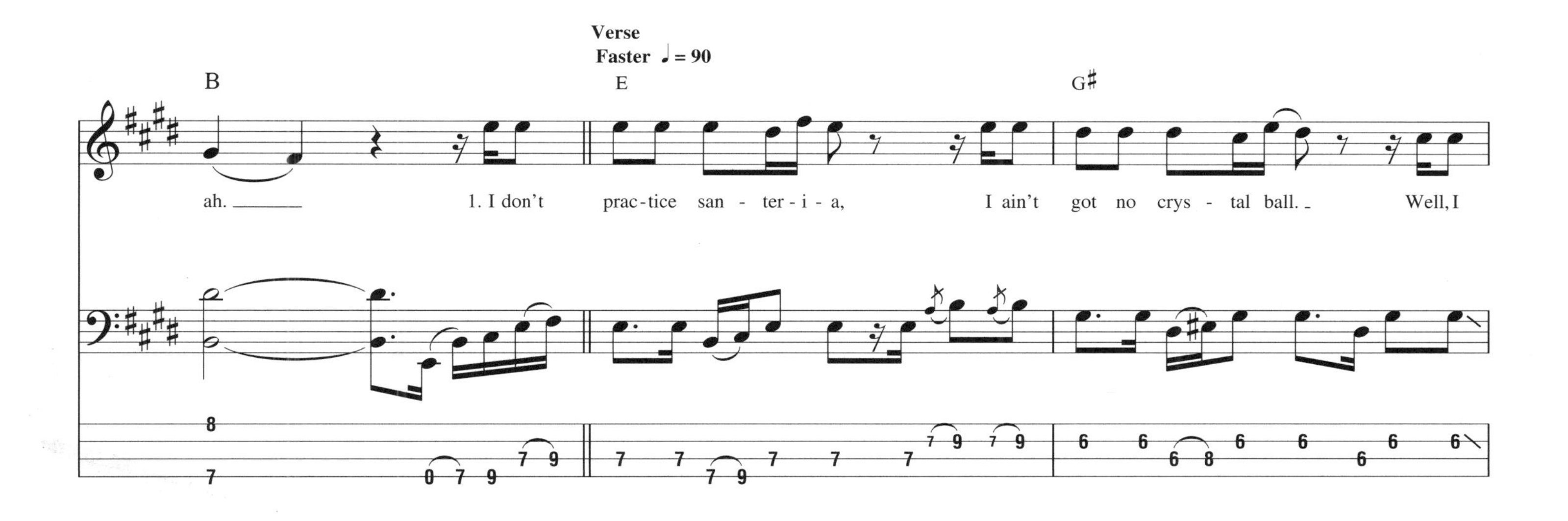

Verse
Faster ♩ = 90
B
E
G♯
ah. 1. I don't prac-tice san-ter-i-a, I ain't got no crys-tal ball. Well, I

C♯m
B
E
had a mil-lion dol-lars but I, I'd spend it all. If I could find that hei-na and that

G♯
C♯m
B
San-cho that _ she's found, _ well, I'd pop a cap in San-cho and I'd slap her down. ______
Chorus
A
B
E
D♯m
C♯m
A
B
___ What I real - ly wan-na know, _____ my ba - by, mm. _____ What I real - ly wan-na say _
E
D♯m
C♯m
A
B
E
D♯m
C♯m
___ I can't de - fine. _____ Well, it's love _ that I need. __________ 2. Oh, _
Verse
A
B
E
G♯
___ my soul _ will have _ to wait 'til I ___ get back, _ find a hei-na of ___ my own. ____

C♯m
B
E
Dad-dy's gon - na love one and all.
I feel the break, feel the break, feel
G♯
C♯m
B
the break and I got to live it up,
oh, yeah, huh.
Well, I swear that I,
Chorus
A
B
E
D♯m
C♯m
A
B
what I real - ly wan-na know,
my ba - by.
What I real - ly wan-na say
E
D♯m
C♯m
A
B
I can't de - fine.
Got love, make it

E
D♯m
C♯m
A
B
go.
Well, my soul will have to...
Guitar Solo
E
G♯
C♯m
B
E
G♯
C♯m
B
Chorus
A
B
Oo,
what I real - ly wan - na say,

E
D♯m
C♯m
A
B
ah, ba - by.
What I real - ly wan - na say
is I've got mine and I'll make it. Oo, yes, I'm com - ing up.
Verse
G♯
3. Tell San - chi - to that if he knows what is good for him he best go run and hide.
Dad - dy's got a new for - ty five.
And I won't think twice to stick that bar - rel

G♯ C♯m B
straight down San - cho's throat. Be - lieve me when I say that I got some-thing for his punk ass.
Chorus
A B E D♯m C♯m A B
What I real - ly wan-na know, my ba - by. Oo, what I real - ly wan-na say
E D♯m C♯m A B E D♯m C♯m
is there's just one way back and I'll make it, yeah.
A B E5 D♯5 C♯5 B5 A5 B5 E7
rit.
My soul will have to wait. Yeah, yeah, yeah.
rit.

Sex on Fire

Words and Music by Caleb Followill, Nathan Followill, Jared Followill and Matthew Followill

Intro
Moderately fast ♩ = 150
*E5
(Guitar)
4
C♯m
Bass
mf
*Chord symbols reflect overall harmony.
E5
C♯m
Verse
E5
1. Lay where you're lay - ing.
Don't make a sound.
I know they're watch -
C♯m
- ing,
they're watch - ing.
All the com-mo-

E
- tion, the kid-die-like play
has peo-ple talk-
7 7 7 7 7 7 7 7

C♯m7
- ing, talk - ing.
9 9 9 9 9 9 9 9
11 11

Chorus

E
You,
your sex is on fire.
7 7 7 7 7 7 7 7
11 11 11
9 11

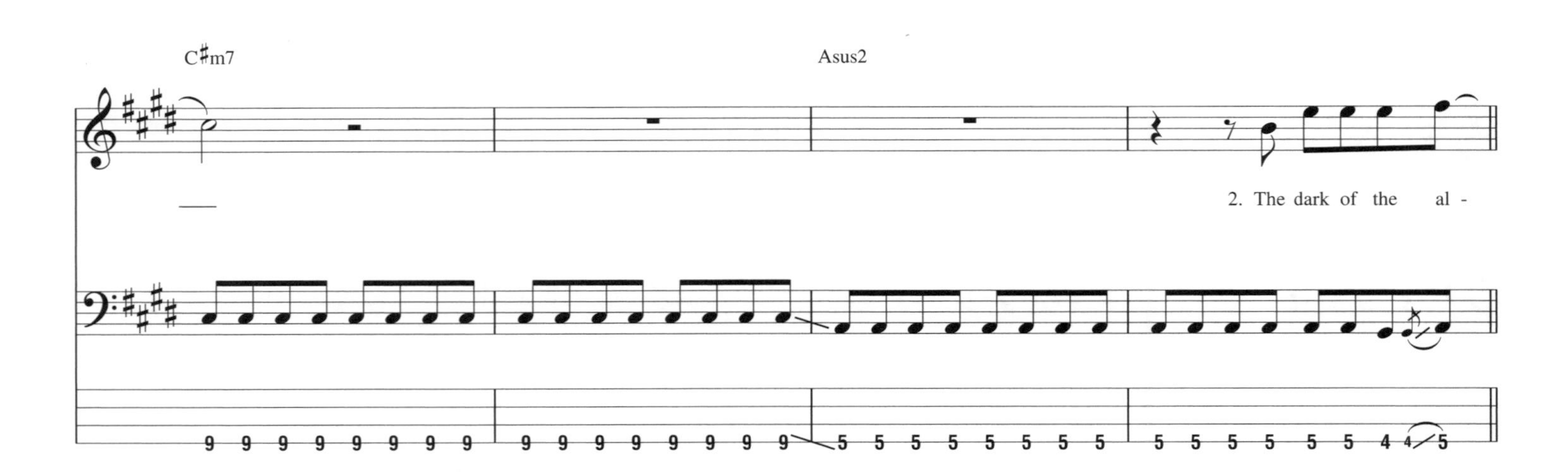
C♯m7
Asus2
2. The dark of the al -
9 9 9 9 9 9 9 9
5 5 5 5 5 5 5 5
4 5

Verse
E
- ley.
The break - ing of day.
The head while I'm driv -
- ver.
Rat - tl - ing bones.
I could just taste
7 7
7 7
7 7
7 7 11 11

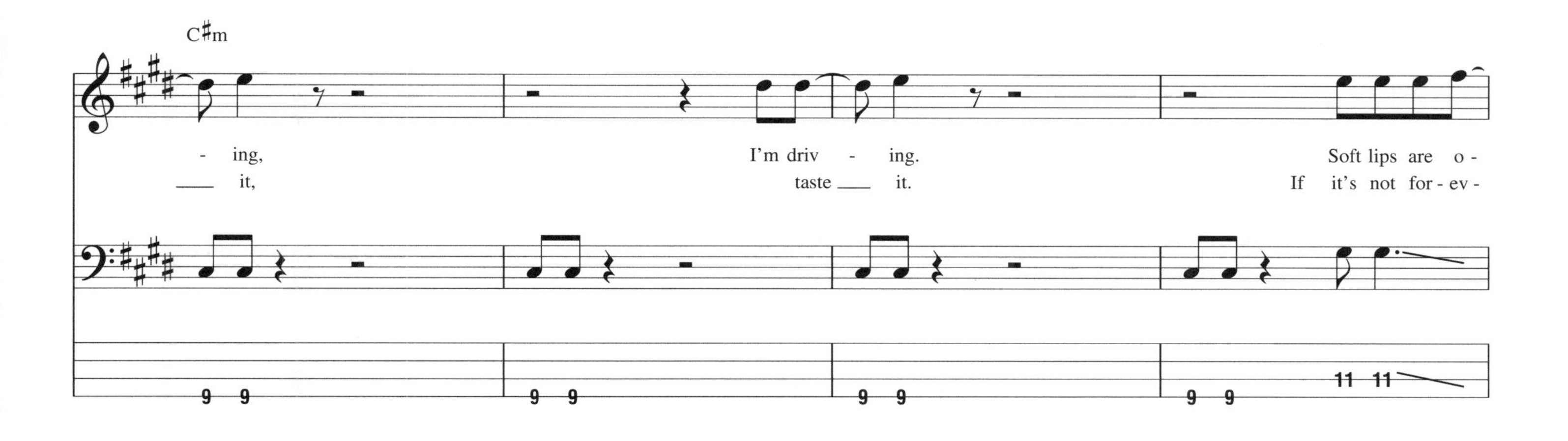
C♯m
- ing,
I'm driv - ing.
Soft lips are o -
it,
taste it.
If it's not for - ev -
9 9
9 9
9 9
9 9 11 11

E
- pen.
The knuck - les are pale.
Feels like you're dy -
- er,
if it's just to - night,
oh, it's still the great -
5 7 7 7 7 7 7 7 7
7 7 7 7 7 7 7 7
7 7 7 7 7 7 7 7
7 7 7 7 7 7 11 11

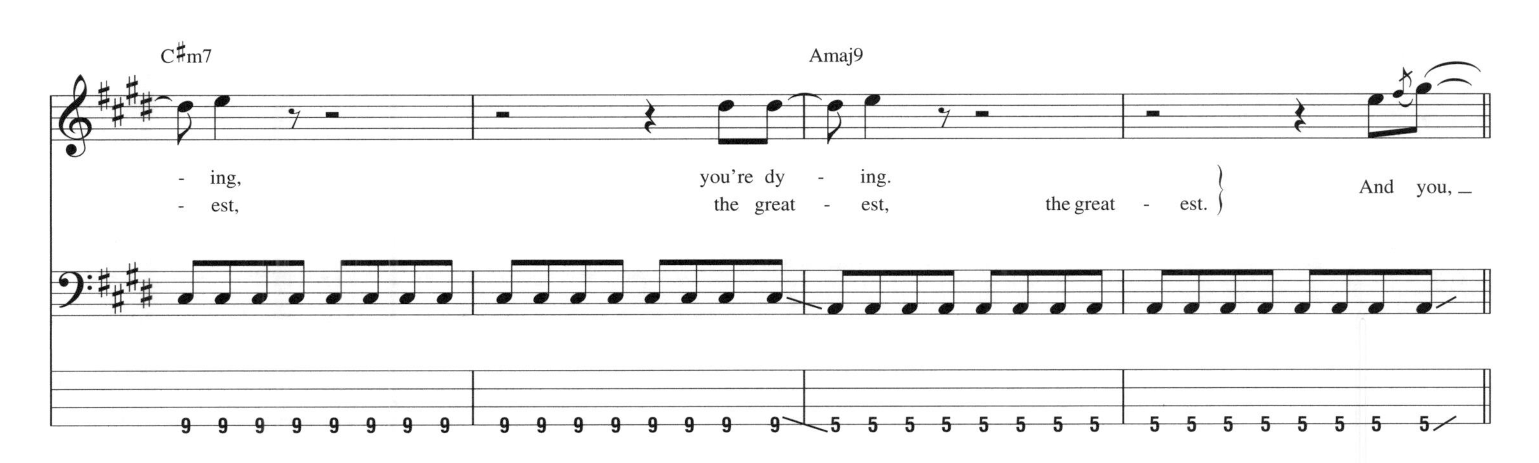
C♯m7
Amaj9
- ing,
you're dy - ing.
- est,
the great - est,
the great - est.
And you,
9 9 9 9 9 9 9 9
9 9 9 9 9 9 9 9
5 5 5 5 5 5 5 5
5 5 5 5 5 5 5 5

Chorus
E
your sex is on fire.

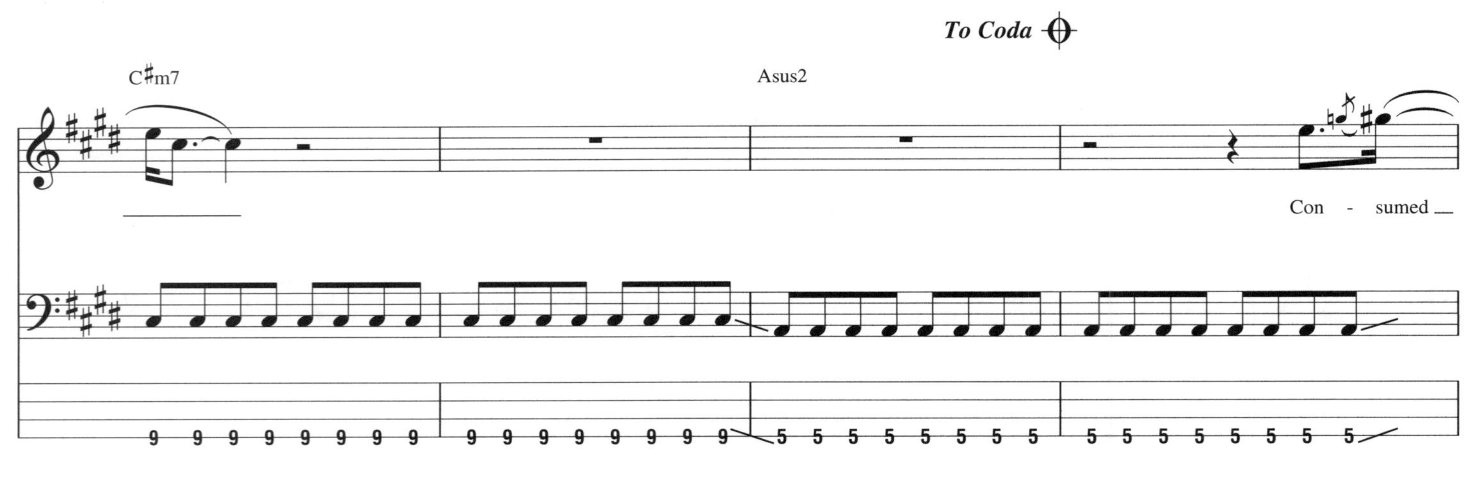

To Coda
C♯m7
Asus2
Con - sumed

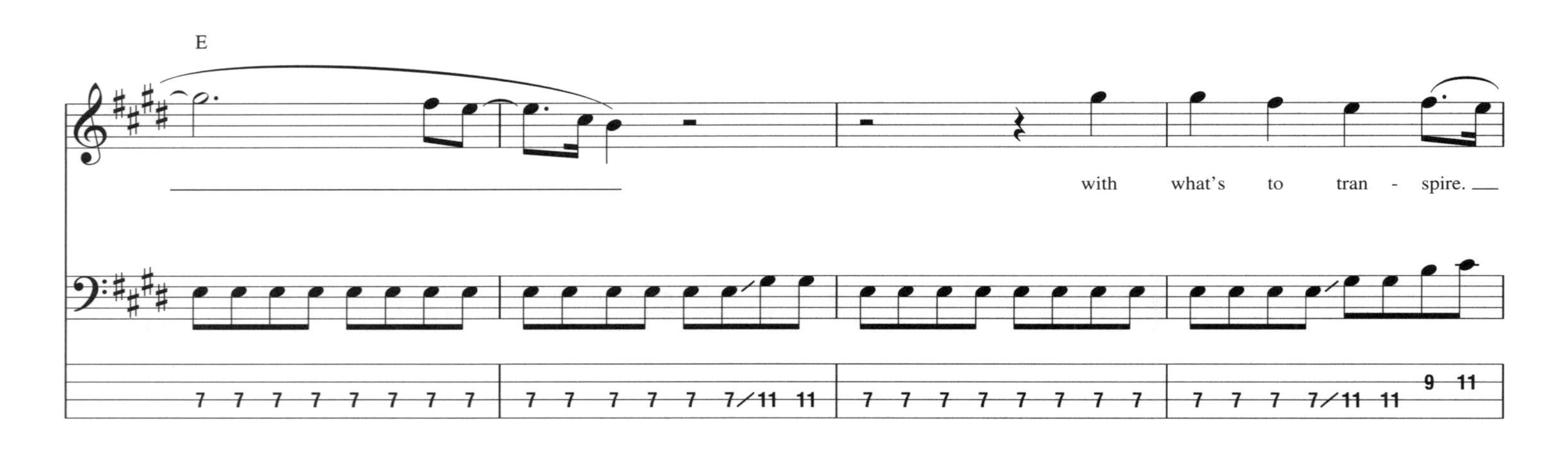

E
with what's to tran - spire.

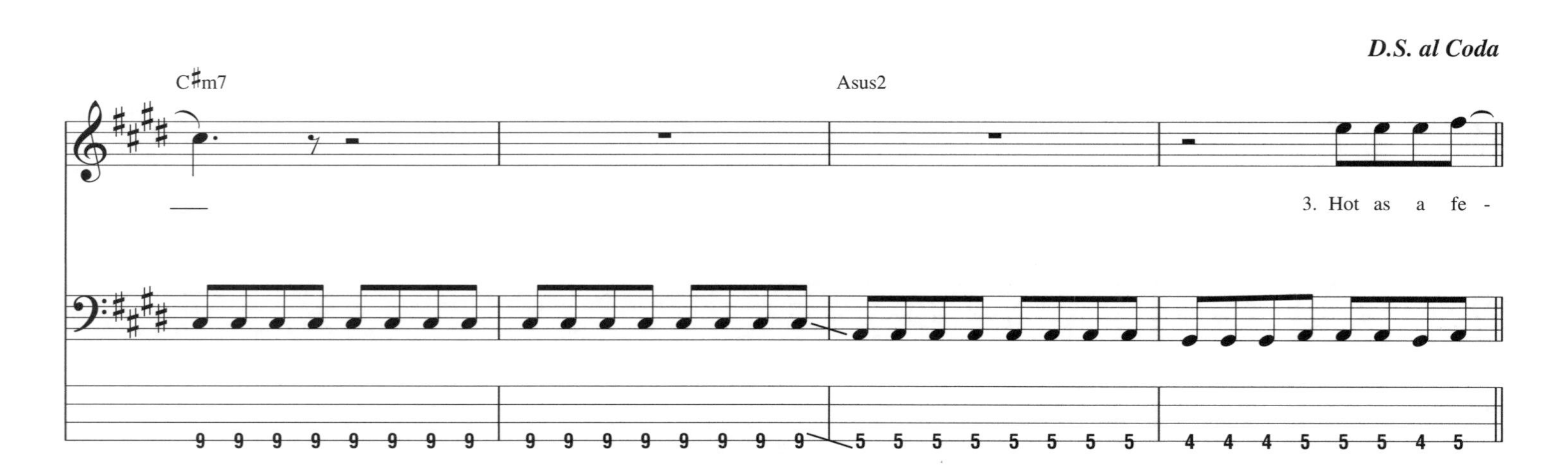

D.S. al Coda
C♯m7
Asus2
3. Hot as a fe -

Coda
E N.C.
E N.C.
E N.C.
And you,
your
E N.C. E6sus2 N.C. C♯m7
Eadd9
sex is on fire.
Ah.
Con - sumed
E
with what's to tran - spire.
C♯m7
Asus2
And you,

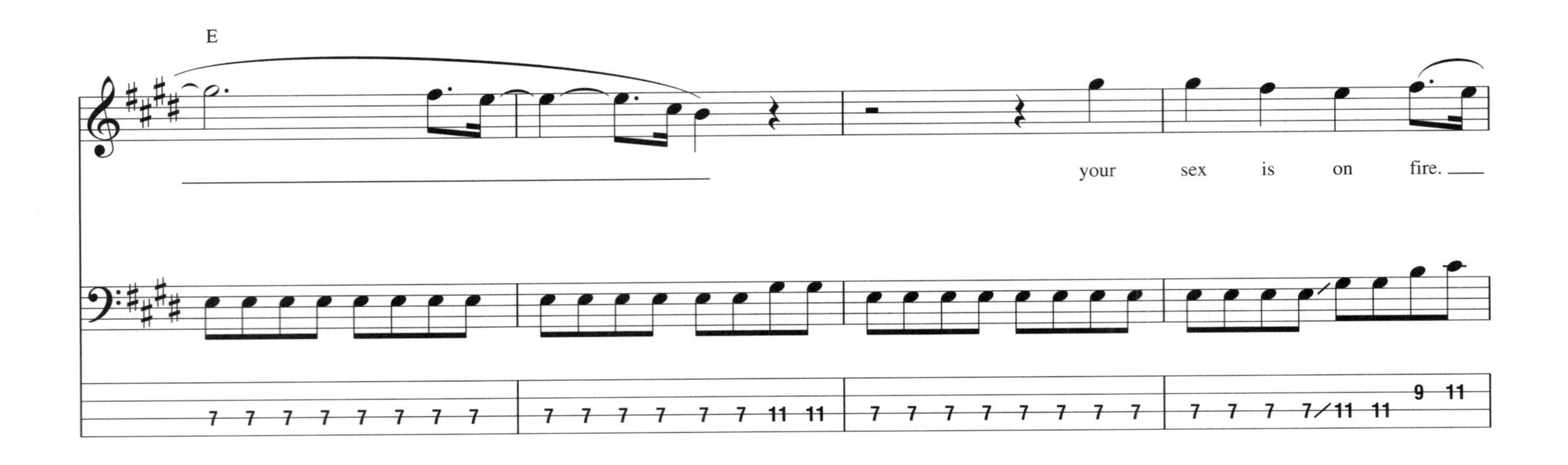
E
your sex is on fire.

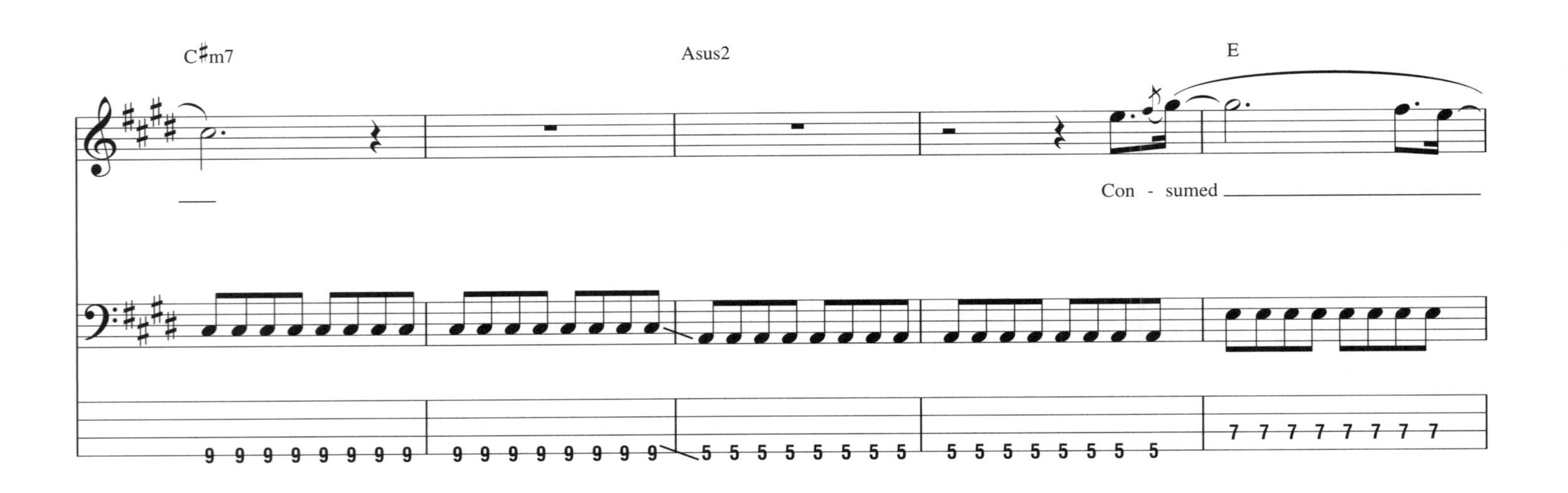
C♯m7
Asus2
E
Con - sumed

C♯m7
with what's to tran - spire.

Asus2
E N.C.

Smells Like Teen Spirit

Words and Music by Kurt Cobain, Krist Novoselic and Dave Grohl

Intro
Moderate Rock ♩ = 114
(Guitar)
F5
B♭
1., 2., 3.
4.
A♭5
D♭
N.C. (F5)
(B♭5)
(A♭5)
(D♭5)
(F5)
Verse
1. Load up on guns and bring your friends. It's fun to lose
2., 3. See additional lyrics

(Ab5) (Db5) (F5) (Bb5) (Ab5) (Db5)
and to pre - tend. She's o - ver bored and self - as - sured.
(F5) (Bb5) (Ab5) (Db5)
Pre-Chorus
F5 Bb5
Oh no, I know a dirt - y word. Hel - lo, hel - lo,
Ab5 Db5 F5 Bb5 Ab5 Db5
hel - lo, how low? Hel - lo, hel - lo, hel - lo, how low?
F5 Bb5 Ab5 Db5 F5 Bb5
Hel - lo, hel - lo, hel - lo, how low? Hel - lo, hel - lo,

Chorus
Ab5 Db5 F5 Bb5 Ab5 Db
hel - lo. With the lights out it's less dan - g'rous. Here we are
F5 Bb Ab5 Db F5 Bb
now, en - ter - tain us. I feel stu - pid and con - ta -
Ab5 Db F5 Bb Ab5 Db
- gious. Here we are now, en - ter - tain us. A mu - lat -
To Coda
F5 Bb Ab5 Db F5 Bb
- to, an al - bi - no, a mos - qui - to, my li - bi -

Bridge

A♭5
D♭
F5
E5
F5
G♭5
N.C.
F5/C
E5/C
F5/C
B♭5
A♭5
G5
- do.
Yay,
yay,
4 4 4 4 4 4 3
1 1 0 1 2 2
3 3 3 1 1 4 3

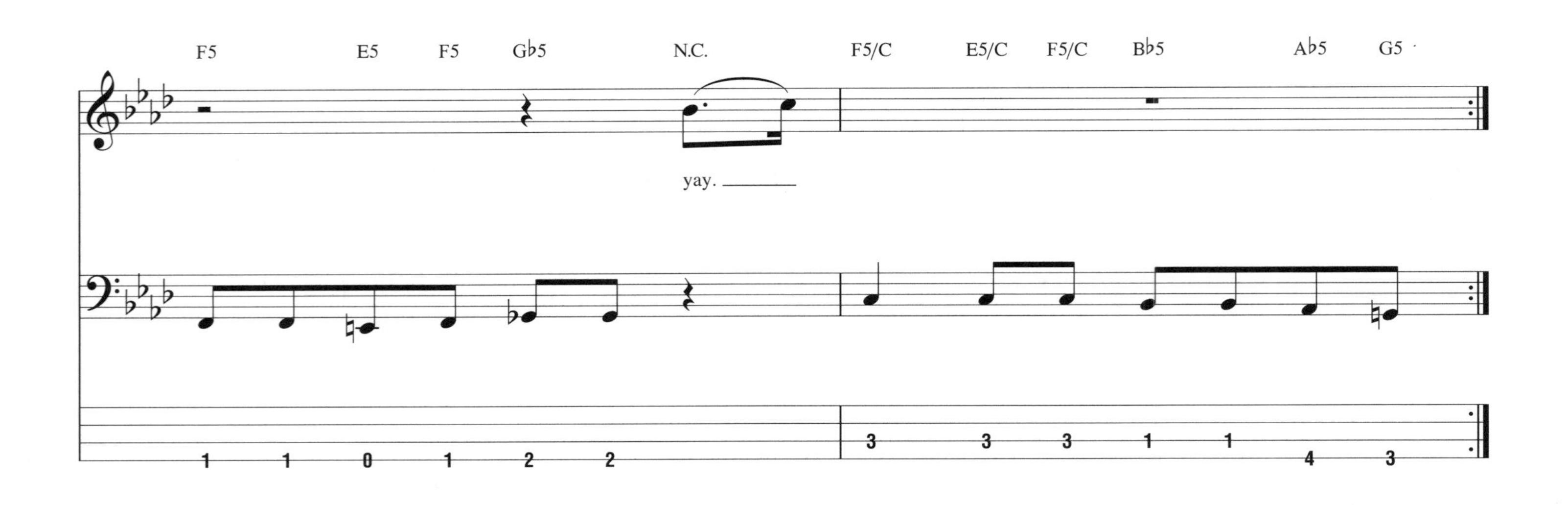

F5
E5
F5
G♭5
N.C.
F5/C
E5/C
F5/C
B♭5
A♭5
G5
yay.
1 1 0 1 2 2
3 3 3 1 1 4 3

Guitar Solo

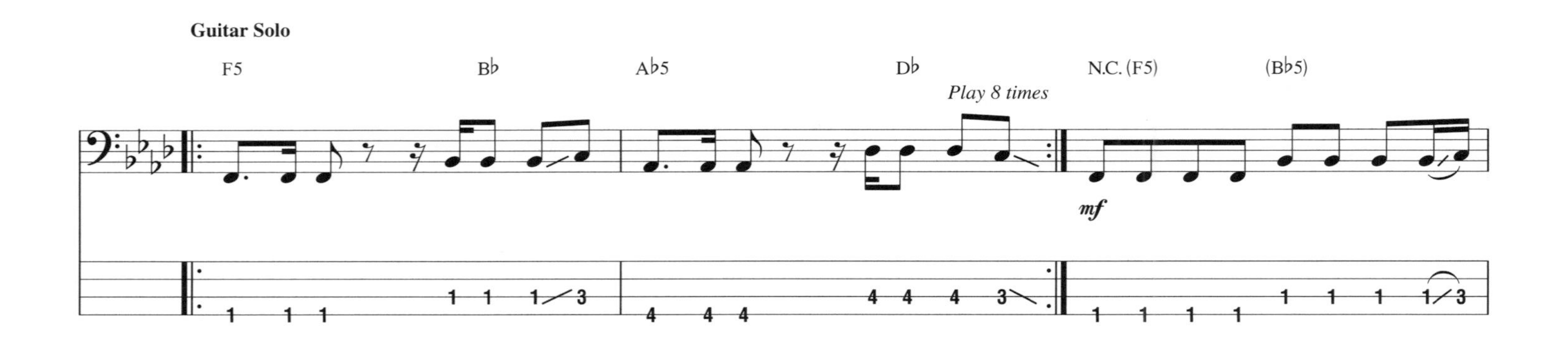

F5
B♭
A♭5
D♭
N.C. (F5)
(B♭5)
Play 8 times
mf
1 1 1 1 1 1 3
4 4 4 4 4 4 3
1 1 1 1 1 1 1 1 3

D.S. al Coda

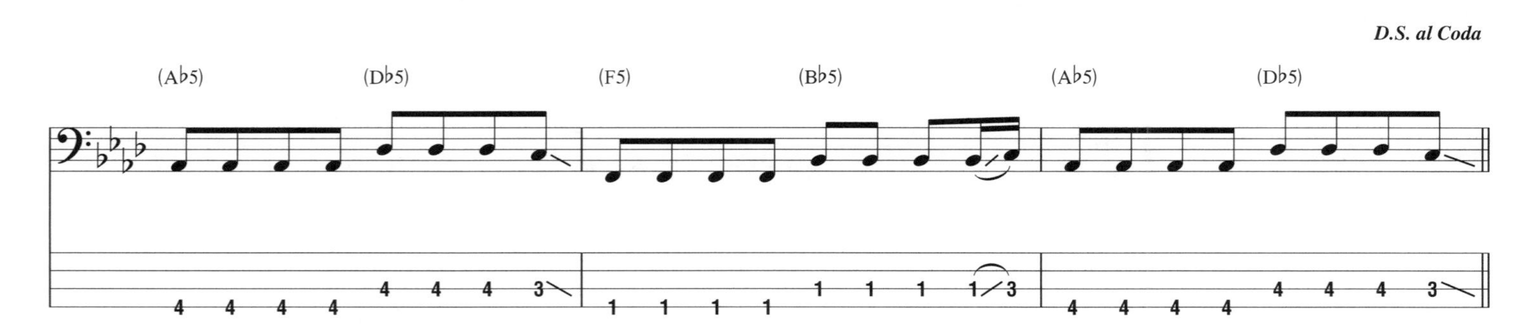

(A♭5)
(D♭5)
(F5)
(B♭5)
(A♭5)
(D♭5)
4 4 4 4 4 4 4 3
1 1 1 1 1 1 1 1 3
4 4 4 4 4 4 4 3

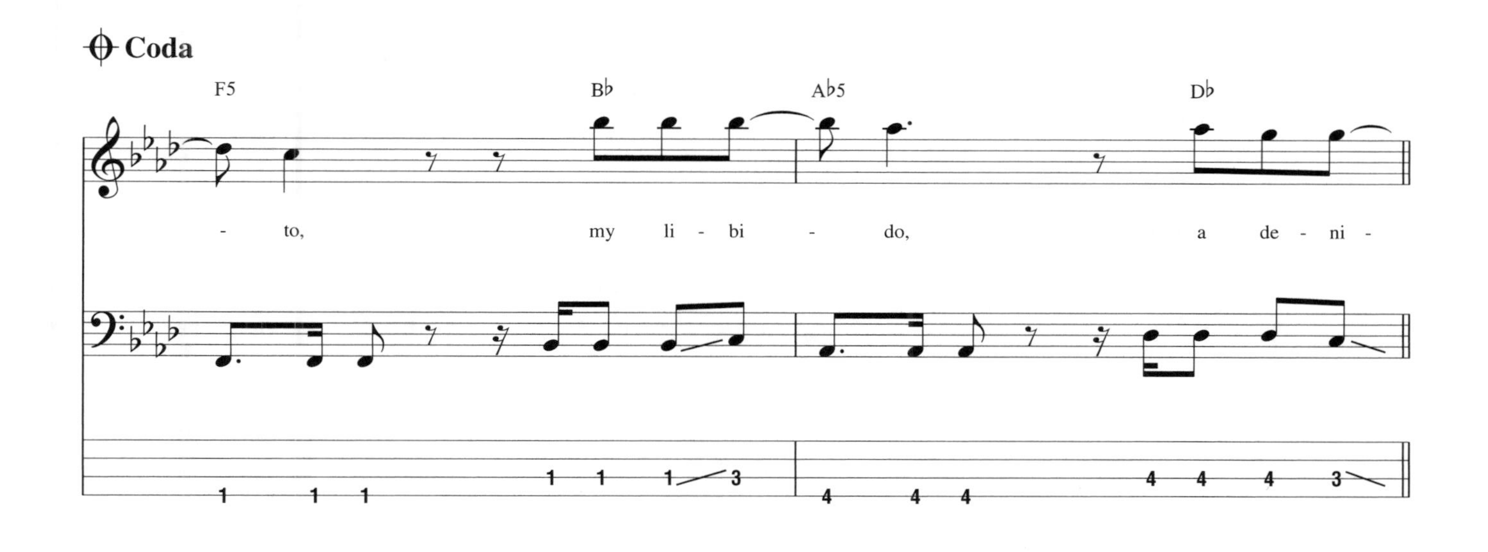
Coda
F5
B♭
A♭5
D♭
- to, my li - bi - do, a de - ni -

Outro
F5
B♭
A♭5
D♭
F5
B♭
- al, a de - ni - al, a de - ni - al, a de - ni -

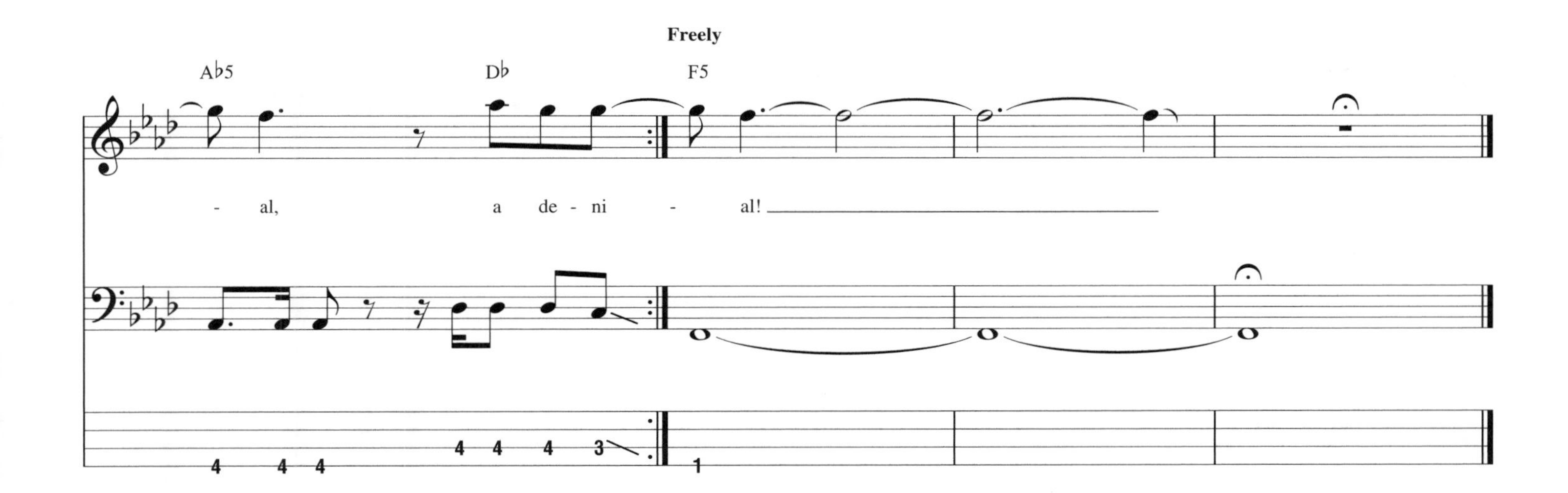
Freely
A♭5
D♭
F5
- al, a de - ni - al!

Additional Lyrics

2. I'm worse at what I do best,
And for this gift I feel blessed.
Our little group has always been
And always will until the end.

3. And I forget just why I taste.
Oo, yeah, I guess it makes you smile,
I found it hard, it's hard to find.
Oh well, whatever, never mind.

Smoke on the Water

Words and Music by Ritchie Blackmore, Ian Gillan, Roger Glover, Jon Lord and Ian Paice

Intro
Moderate Rock ♩ = 112
(Guitar) 15
G5
Bb5 C5 G5 Bb Db5 C5
f

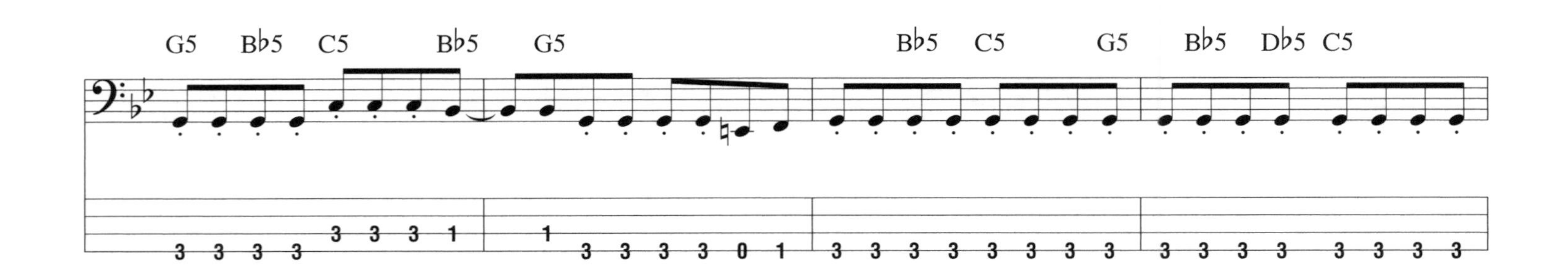
G5 Bb5 C5 Bb5 G5
Bb5 C5 G5 Bb5 Db5 C5

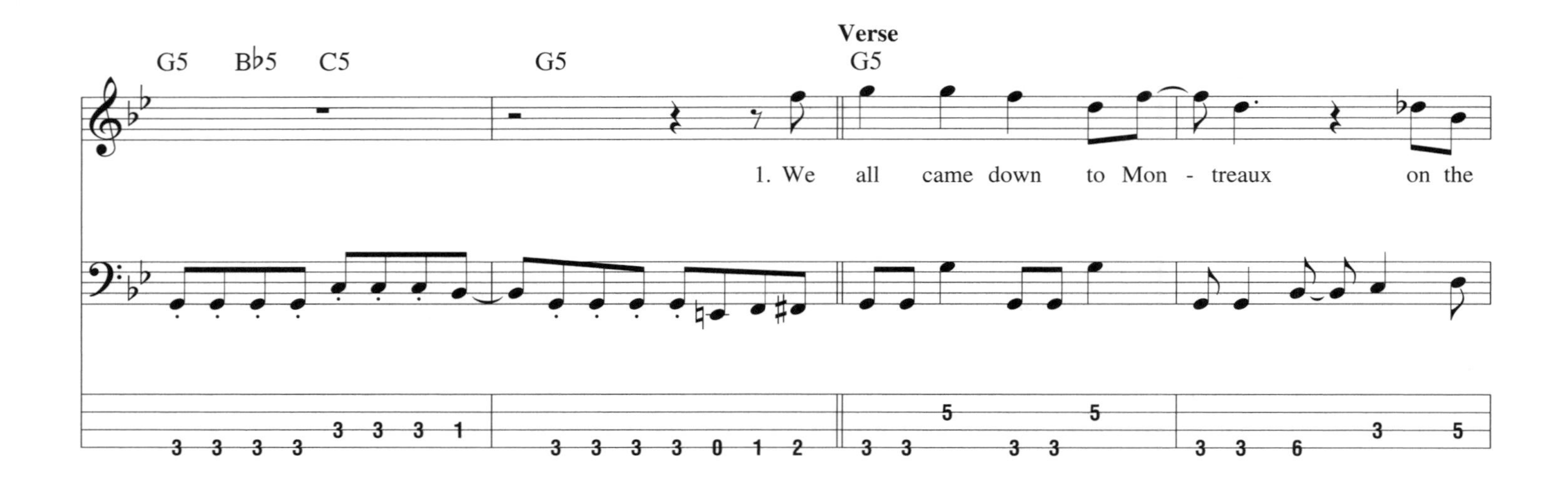
G5 Bb5 C5 G5
Verse
G5
1. We all came down to Mon - treaux on the

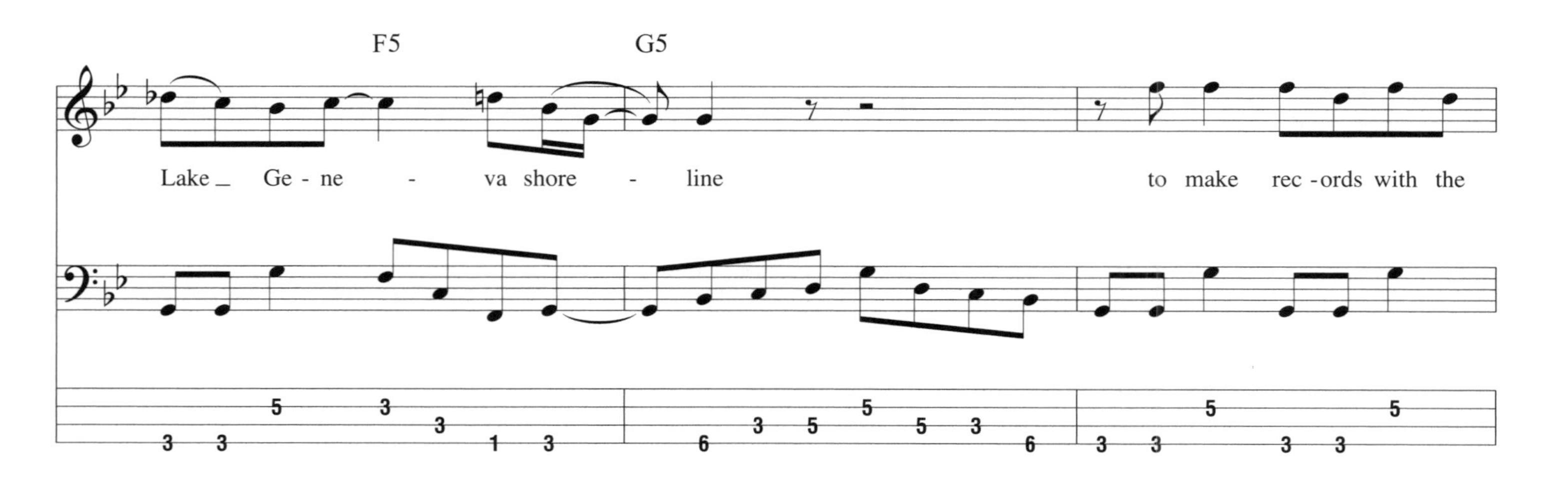
F5 G5
Lake Ge - ne - va shore - line to make rec - ords with the

F5
mo - bile,
we did - n't have much time.
But Frank Zap - pa and the Moth - ers
were at the best place a - round.
G5
But some stu - pid with a flare gun
F5
G5
burned the place to the ground.
Chorus
C5
A♭5
Smoke on the wa - ter,

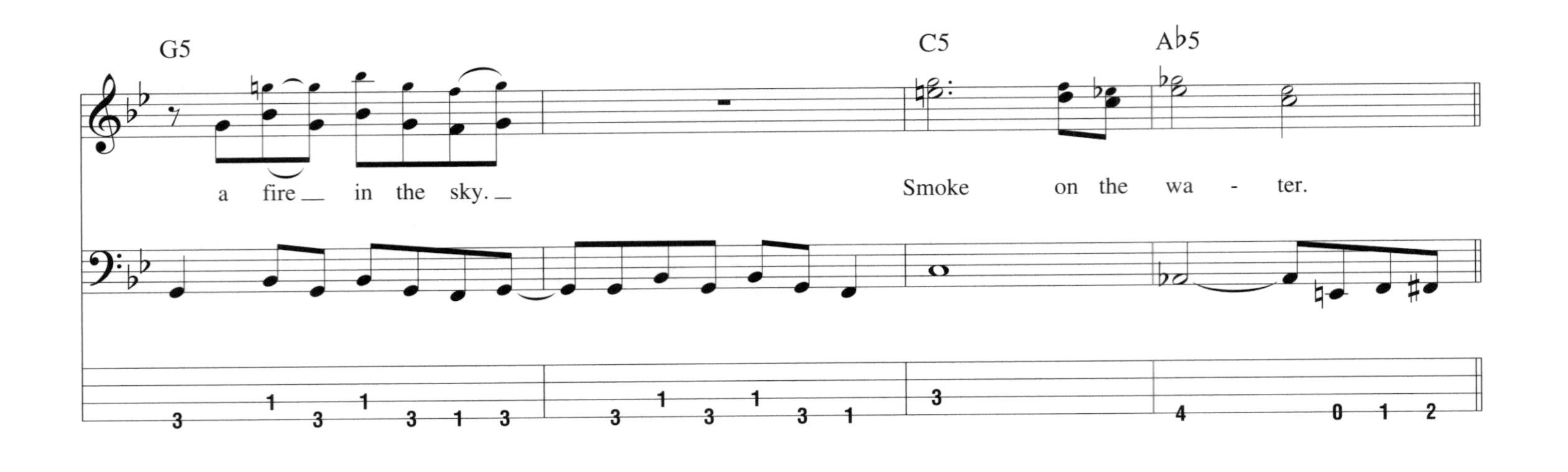
G5
C5
A♭5
a fire in the sky.
Smoke on the wa - ter.

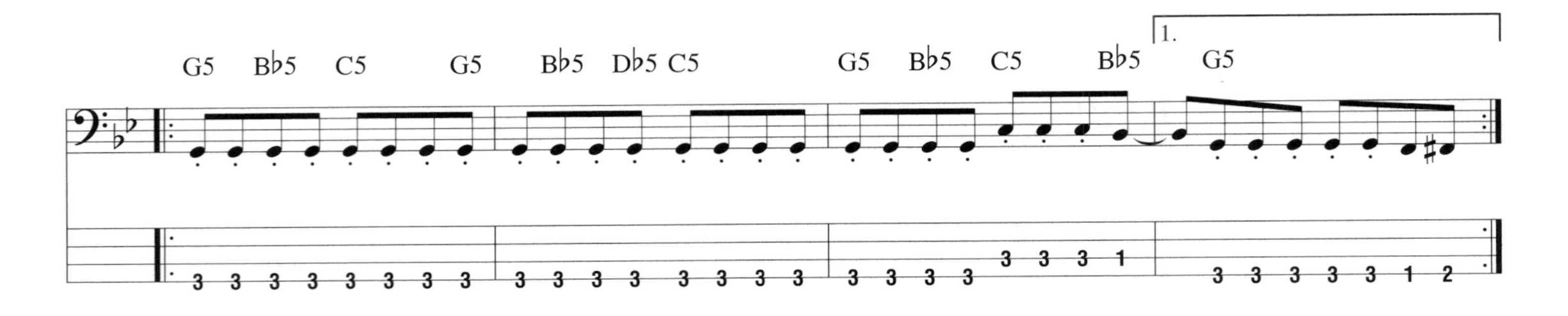
G5 B♭5 C5 G5 B♭5 D♭5 C5 G5 B♭5 C5 B♭5
1. G5

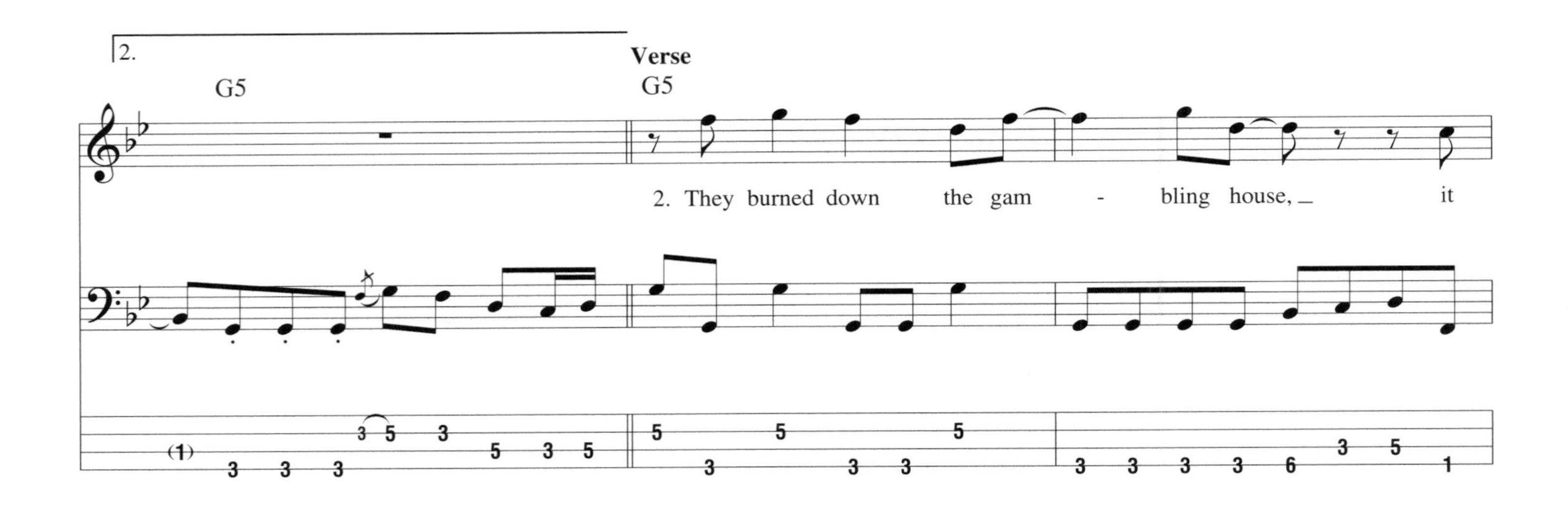
2. G5
Verse
G5
2. They burned down the gam - bling house, it

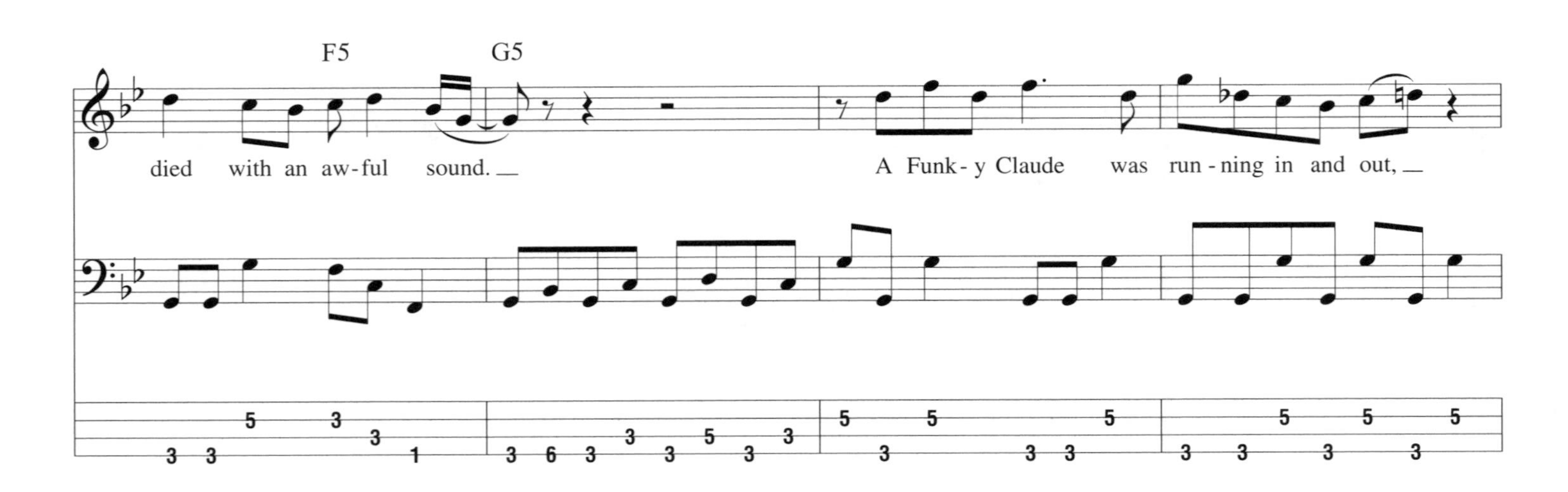
F5 G5
died with an aw-ful sound.
A Funk-y Claude was run-ning in and out,

F5
G5
pull - ing kids out the ground. __
When it all was o -
- ver, ______
F5
G5
we had to find an - oth - er place. _
F5
G5
But Swiss time was run - ning out;
it seemed that we would lose the race. ___
Chorus
C5
A♭5
G5
Smoke on the wa - ter,
a fire ___ in the sky. ___

C5
A♭5
Smoke on the wa - ter.
G5 B♭5 C5 G5 B♭5 D♭5 C5 G5 B♭5 C5 B♭5 G5
B♭5 C5 G5 B♭5 D♭5 C5 G5 B♭5 C5 B♭5 G5
Guitar Solo
G5
C5
G5
C5
G5
C5
G5

C5
G5
C5
F5
G5 B♭5 C5 G5 B♭5 D♭5 C5
G5 B♭5 C5 B♭5 G5
B♭5 C5 G5 B♭5 D♭5 C5
G5 B♭5 C5 G5
Verse
G5
3. We end - ed up at the Grand
Ho - tel, it was emp - ty, cold and bare. But with the
F5
G5

F5
Roll - ing truck Stones thing just __ out - side, __ mak - ing our
5 5 5 5 3 3 5 3 6 3 5 5 3 3 3 3 3 3 3 3

G5
mu - sic there. __ With a few red lights, __ a few old beds __

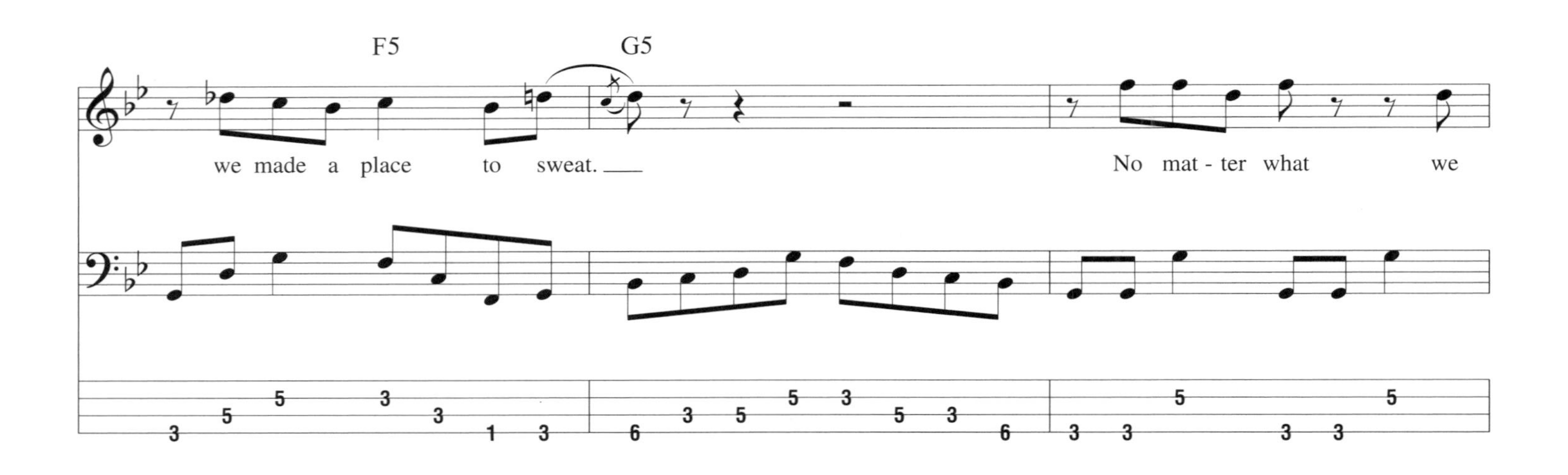
F5
G5
we made a place to sweat. ___ No mat - ter what we

F5
G5
get out of this, __ I know, I know we'll nev - er for - get. __

Chorus
C5
Ab5
G5
Smoke on the wa - ter,
a fire in the sky.
C5
Ab5
Smoke on the wa - ter.
G5 Bb5 C5 G5 Bb5 Db5 C5 G5 Bb5 C5 Bb5 G5
1.
2.
G5
Outro-Organ Solo
Repeat and fade

So Far Away

Words and Music by Matthew Sanders, Jonathan Seward, James Sullivan, Brian Haner, Jr. and Zachary Baker

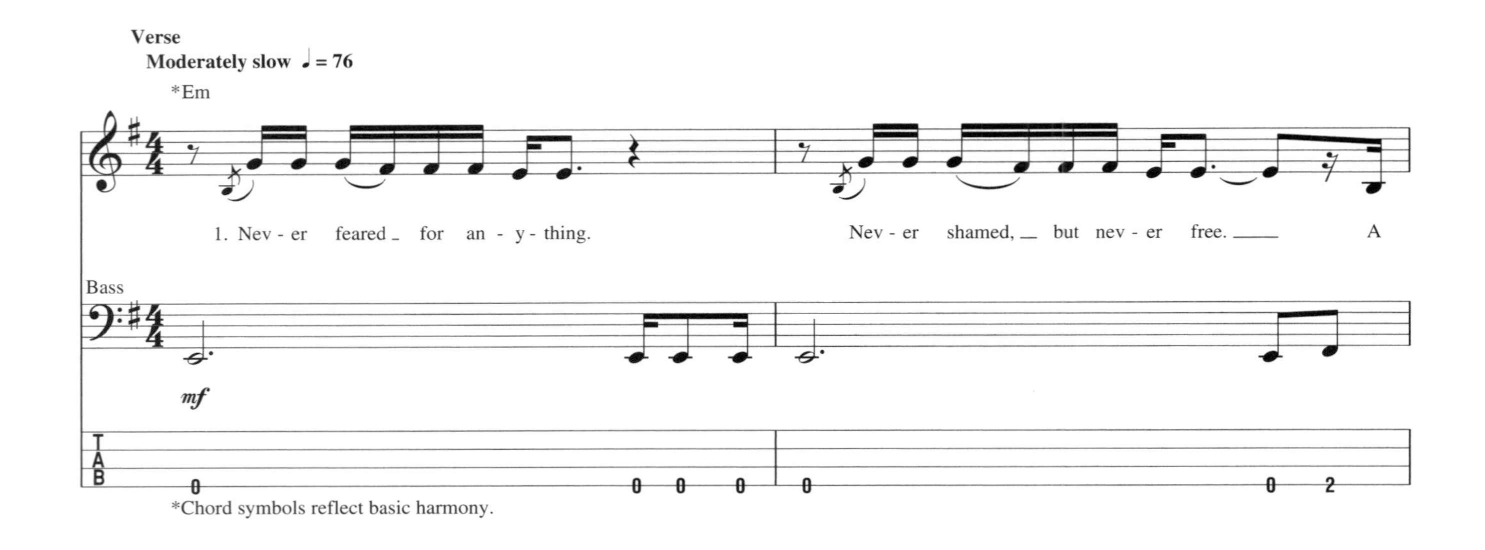

Verse
Moderately slow ♩ = 76
*Em
1. Nev - er feared for an - y - thing. Nev - er shamed, but nev - er free. A
Bass
mf
T
A
B
0 0 0 0 0 0 2
*Chord symbols reflect basic harmony.

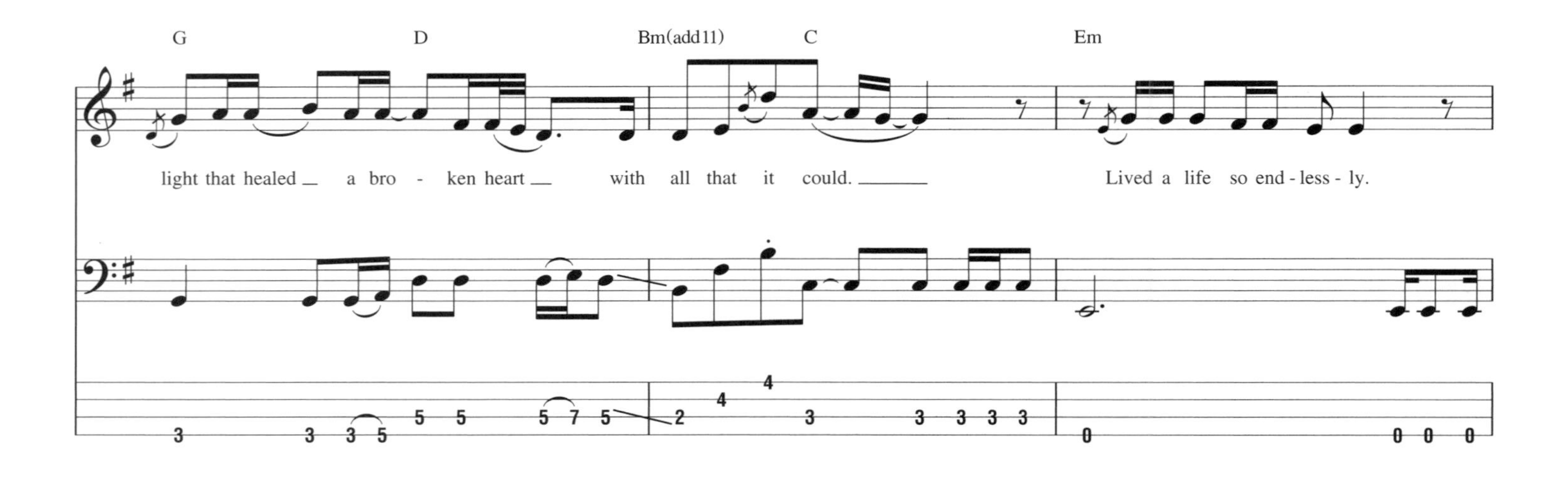

G D Bm(add11) C Em
light that healed a bro - ken heart with all that it could. Lived a life so end - less - ly.
3 3 3 5 5 5 5 7 5 2 4 4 3 3 3 3 3 0 0 0 0

G D Bm(add11) C
Saw be - yond what oth - ers see. I tried to heal your bro - ken heart with all that I could.
0 5 7 7 2 3 5 5 7 7 7 4 5 2 2 3 3 3 3 3

Chorus
D
Em
Will you stay, will you stay a-way forever? How do I live without the
G
Am
*Voc. Fig. 1
**Em/G
D
End Voc. Fig. 1
ones I love? Time still turns the pag-es of the book it's burned.
(Ah.)
*Refers to upstemmed voc. only.
**Bass plays G.
Em
G
Bkgd. Voc.: w/ Voc. Fig. 1
Am
Place and time al-ways on my mind. I have so much to say but you're so
C
D
Verse
Em
far a-way. 2. Plans of what our fu-tures hold, fool-ish lies of grow-ing old. It

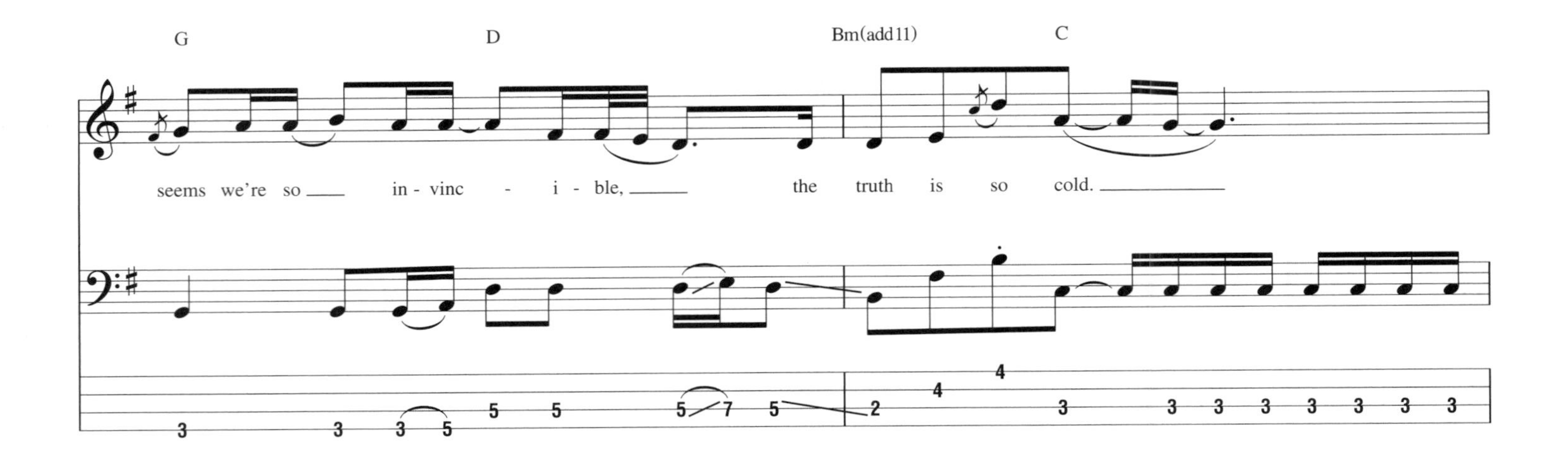
G
D
Bm(add11)
C
seems we're so in - vinc - i - ble, the truth is so cold.

Em
G
D
A fi-nal song, a last re-quest. A per-fect chap-ter laid to rest. Now and then I try to find a

Bm(add11)
C
D
place in my mind where you can stay, you can stay a - wake for-ev-er.

Chorus
Em
G
Bkgd. Voc.: w/ Voc. Fig. 1
Am
How do I live with-out the ones I love? Time still turns the pag - es of the

Em/G
D
Em
G
book it's burned.
Place and time
al-ways on my mind.
I have
3 3 3 5 5 5 5 5 7 5
0 0 0 0 0 0 0 2
3 3 3 3 3 3 5 3 2 3

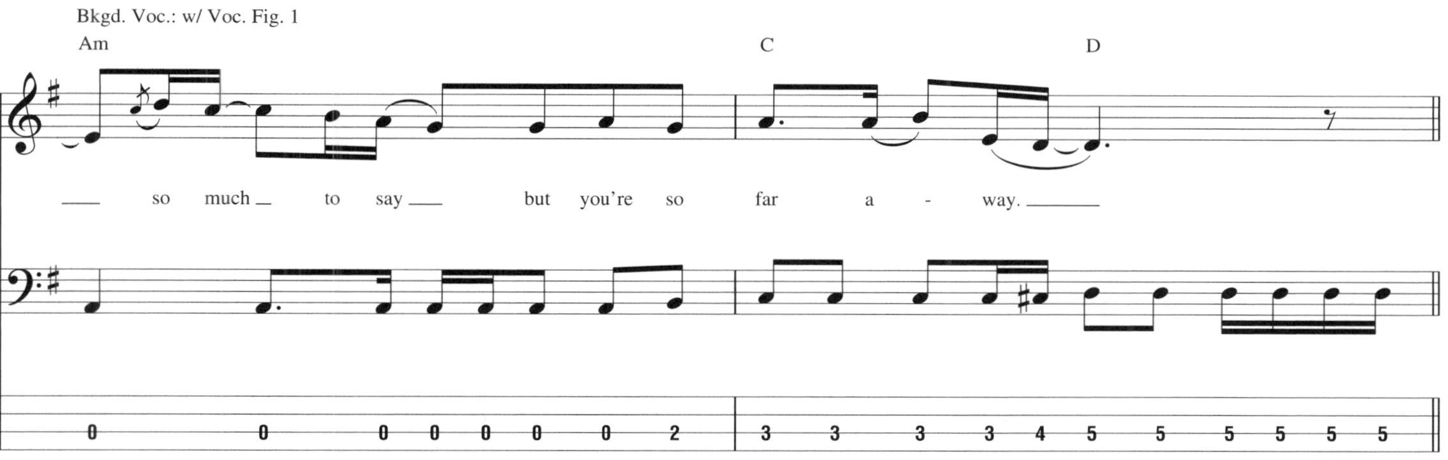
Bkgd. Voc.: w/ Voc. Fig. 1
Am
C
D
so much to say but you're so far a - way.
0 0 0 0 0 0 0 2
3 3 3 3 4 5 5 5 5 5 5

Bridge
E
C
Am
Sleep tight, I'm not a-fraid.
(Not a-fraid.)
The ones that we love are here
7 7 7 9 9 9 7 7
3 3 3 5 5 5 3 3
5 5 5 7 7 5 7 5

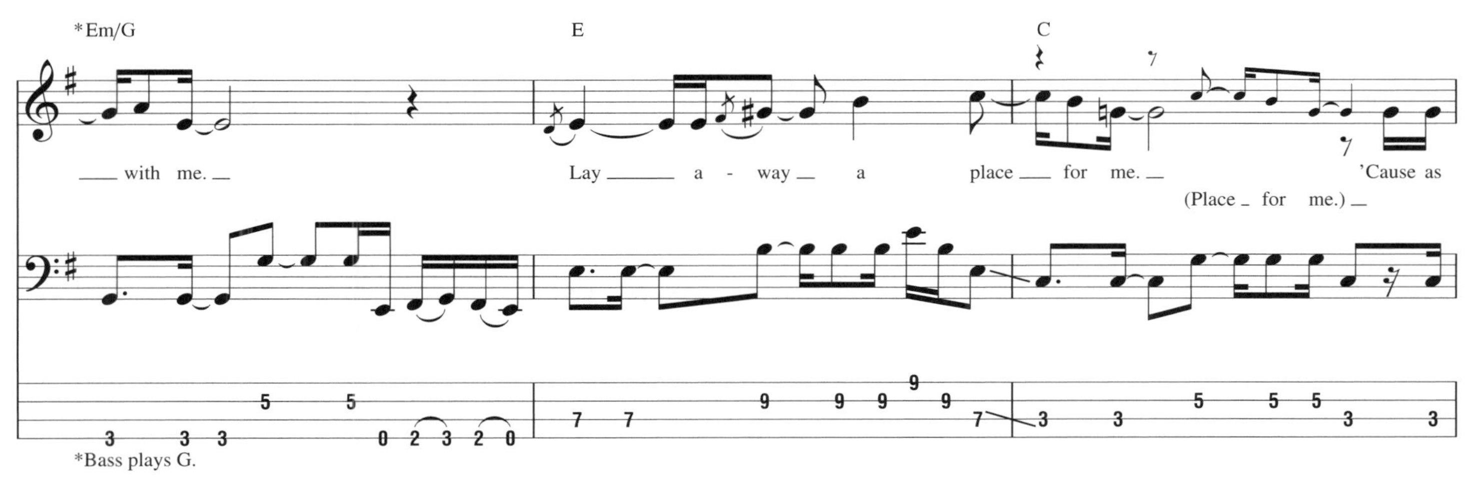
*Em/G
E
C
with me.
Lay a-way a place for me.
(Place for me.)
'Cause as
3 3 3 5 5 0 2 3 2 0
7 7 9 9 9 9 9 7
3 3 5 5 5 3 3
*Bass plays G.

D
Cadd9
D
soon as I'm done I'll be on my way to live e - ter - nal - ly.
(On my way.)
Guitar Solo
E
C
Am

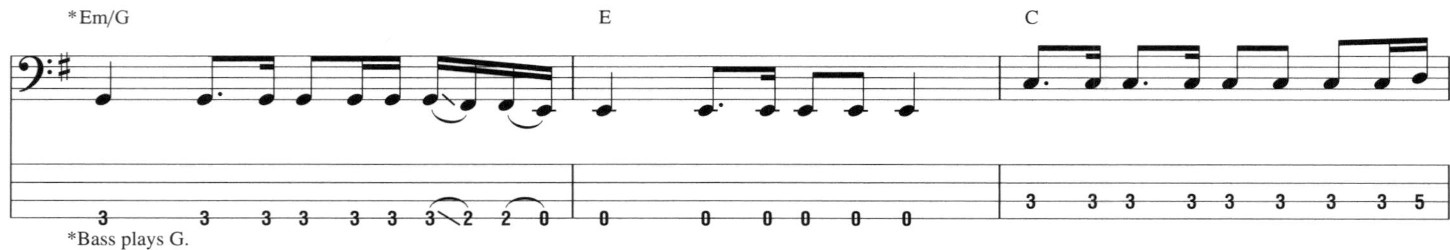
*Em/G
E
C
*Bass plays G.

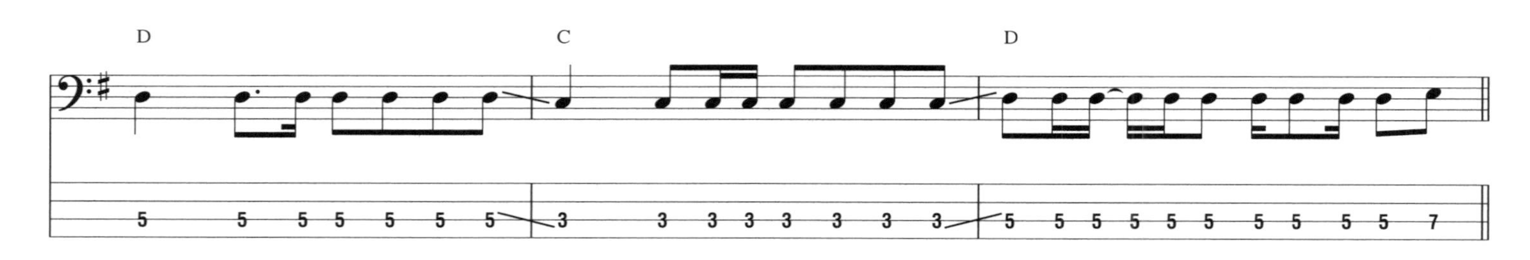
D
C
D

Chorus
Em
G
Bkgd. Voc.: w/ Voc. Fig. 1
Am
How do I live with - out the ones I love?
Time still turns the pag - es of the

Em/G D Em G
book it's burned. Place and time always on my mind. And the light
Bkgd. Voc.: w/ Voc. Fig. 1 (2 times)
Am C D Am
you left remains but it's so hard to stay when I have so much to say and you're so
C D Em
far away.
Interlude
Bass tacet
Em D Am G D/F♯ Em D/A Cmaj7
Em D Am G D/F♯ Em D Cmaj7
Bass

Em
D
Am
G
D/F♯
Em
D
Cmaj7
Em
D
Cmaj7
Outro
Em
D
Am
G
D/F♯
Em
D
I love you, you were read - y. The pain is strong and urg - es rise.
Cmaj7
Em
D
Am
G
D/F♯
But I see you when it lets me. Your pain is gone, your hands un-tied.
Em
D
Cmaj7

Em
D
Cmaj7
Em
D
So
far
a - way.
And I need you to know.
(So
far
a - way.
So
far
a - way.
Cmaj7
Em
D
Cmaj7
So
far
a - way.
So
far
a - way.
So
Em
rit.
D
Cmaj7
And I need you to, need you to know.
rit.
far.)
rit.

Stand by Me

Words and Music by Jerry Leiber, Mike Stoller and Ben E. King

Intro
Moderately
A
F♯m
E
F♯m
Bass Fig. 1
*Bass
mf
T
A
B
2 2 2 1
2 2 2 1
4 4 2
4 4 4 2

*Upright bass arr. for bass gtr.

D
E
A
1. When the night
End Bass Fig. 1
0 0 0 4
2 2 2 1
2 2 2 1
2 2 2 1

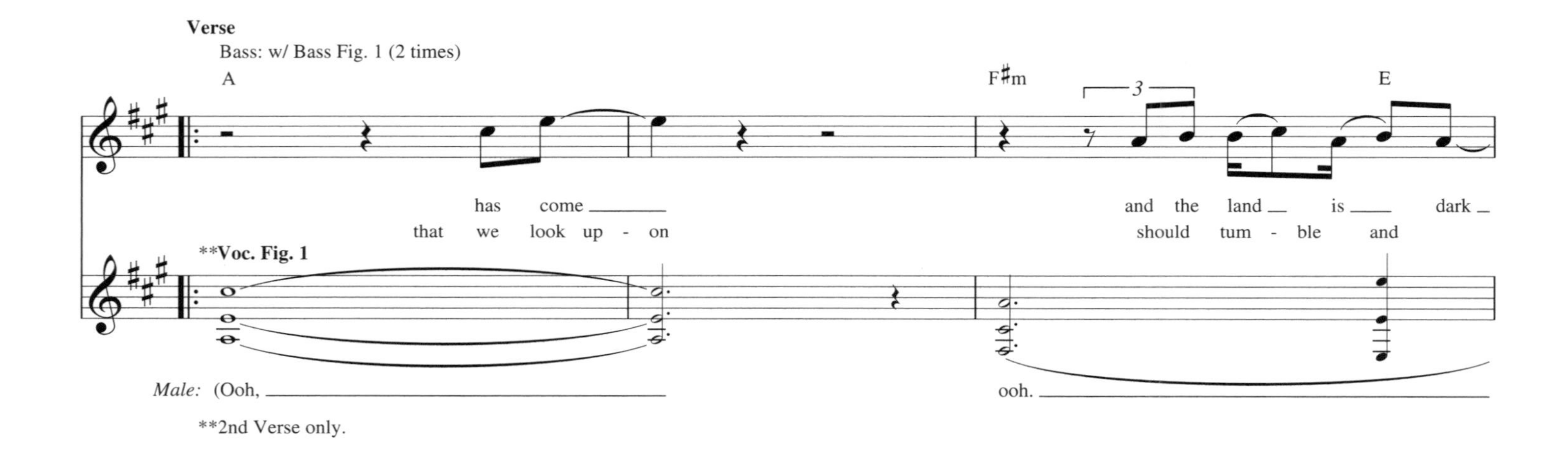

Verse
Bass: w/ Bass Fig. 1 (2 times)
A
F♯m
E
3
has come
that we look up - on
and the land is dark
should tum - ble and
**Voc. Fig. 1
Male: (Ooh,
ooh.

**2nd Verse only.

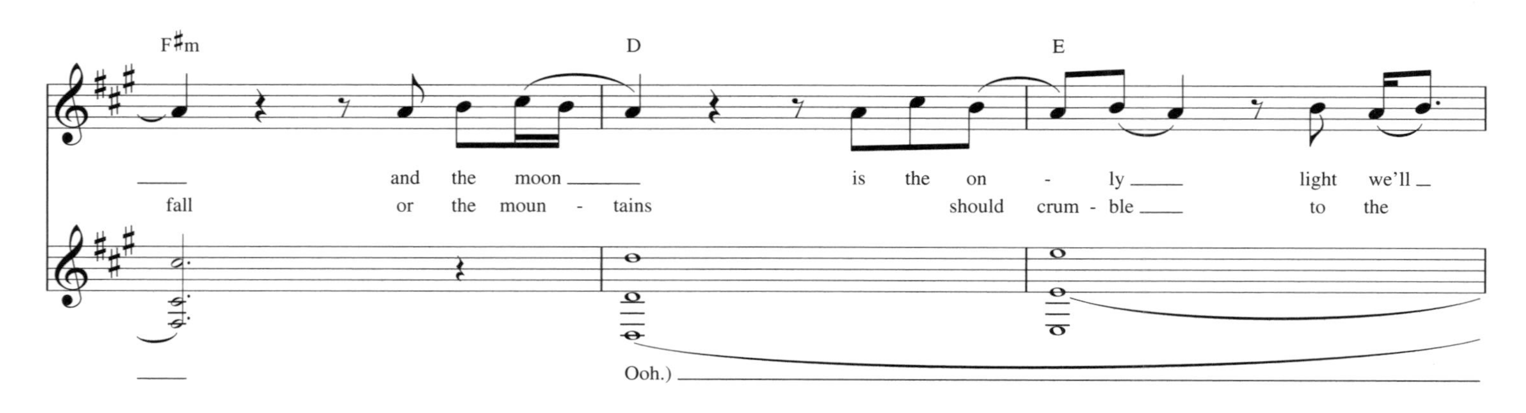

F♯m
D
E
and the moon
is the on - ly
light we'll
fall
or the moun - tains
should crum - ble
to the
Ooh.)

2nd time, Bkgd. Voc.: w/ Voc. Fig. 1
A
see,
sea,
no, I won't
I won't cry,
be a - fraid,
I won't cry,
End Voc. Fig. 1
F♯m
E
F♯m
oh, I won't be a - fraid just as long
no, I won't shed a tear just as long
D
E
A
as you stand, stand by me. So
as you stand, stand by me. And
Chorus
Bass: w/ Bass Fig. 1
A
dar - ling, dar - ling,
dar - ling, dar - ling,
stand by me, oh, stand
F♯m
E
F♯m
D
by me. Oh, stand,
E
A
1.
2.
stand by me, stand by me. 2. If the sky
Interlude
Bass: w/ Bass Fig. 1 (2 times)
A
F♯m
E
F♯m
D
E
A
Female: (Ah.
Ah.

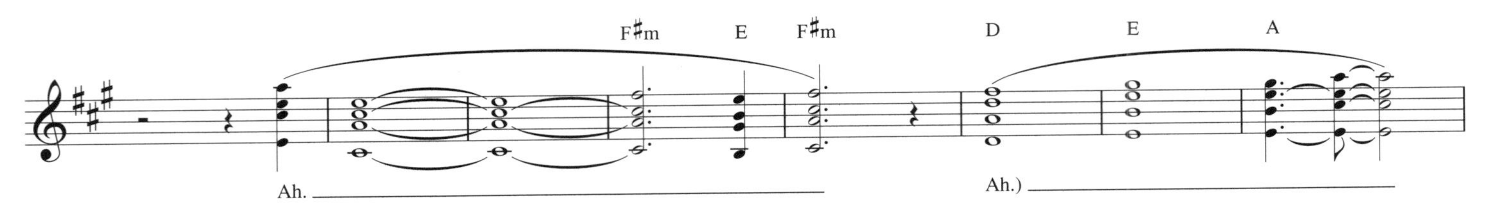
F♯m E F♯m D E A
Ah. Ah.)

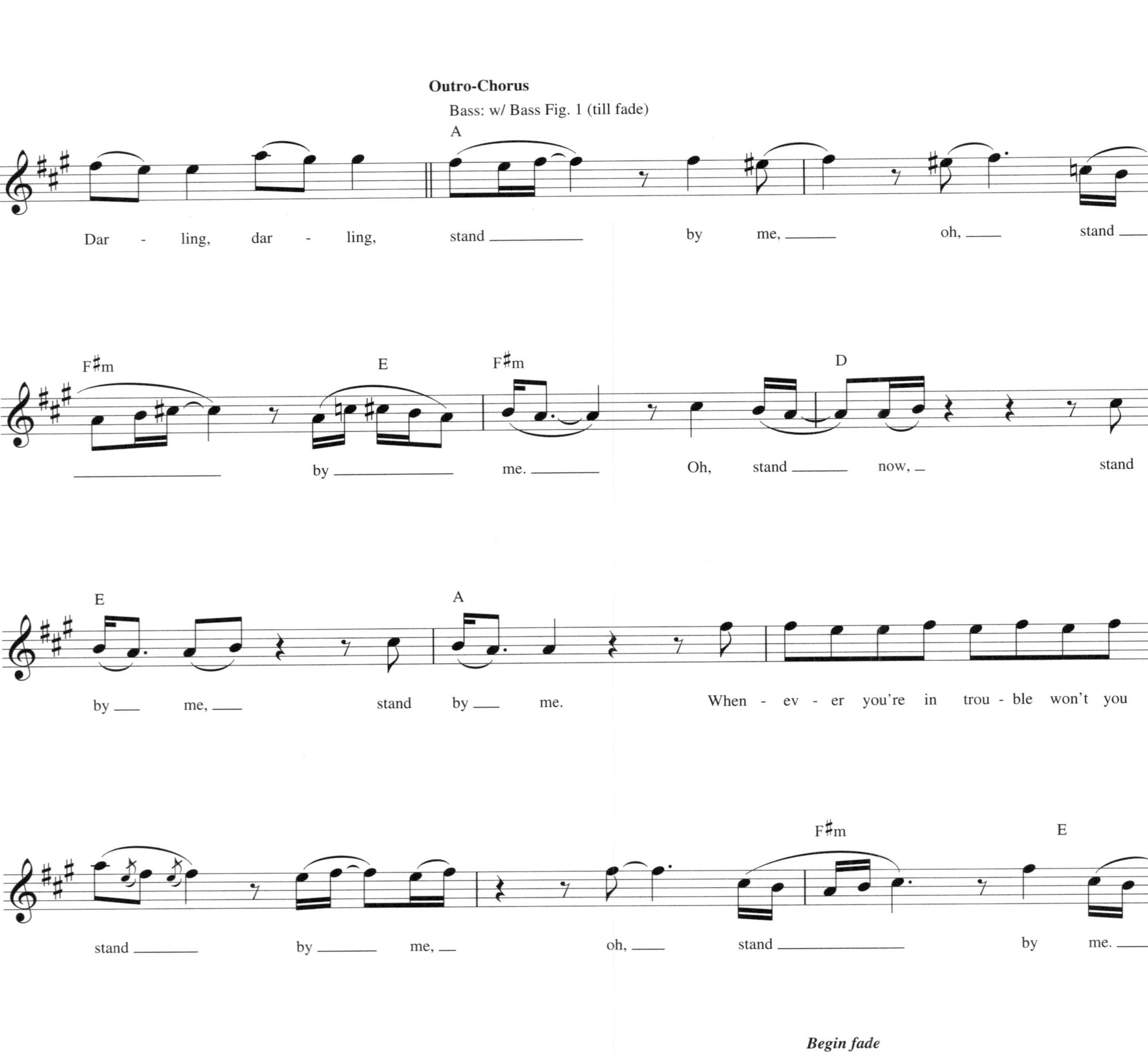
Outro-Chorus
Bass: w/ Bass Fig. 1 (till fade)
A F♯m E F♯m D E A F♯m E
Dar - ling, dar - ling, stand by me, oh, stand by me. Oh, stand now, stand by me, stand by me. When - ev - er you're in trou - ble won't you stand by me, oh, stand by me.

Begin fade
F♯m D E
Whoa, just stand now, oh, stand stand by

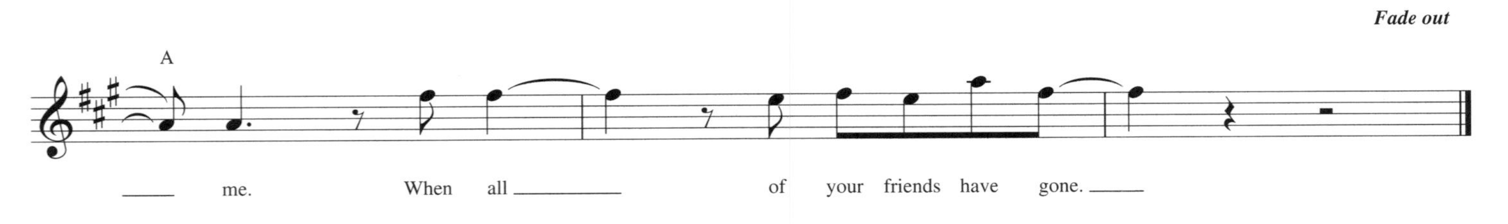
Fade out
A
me. When all of your friends have gone.

Super Freak

Words and Music by Rick James and Alonzo Miller

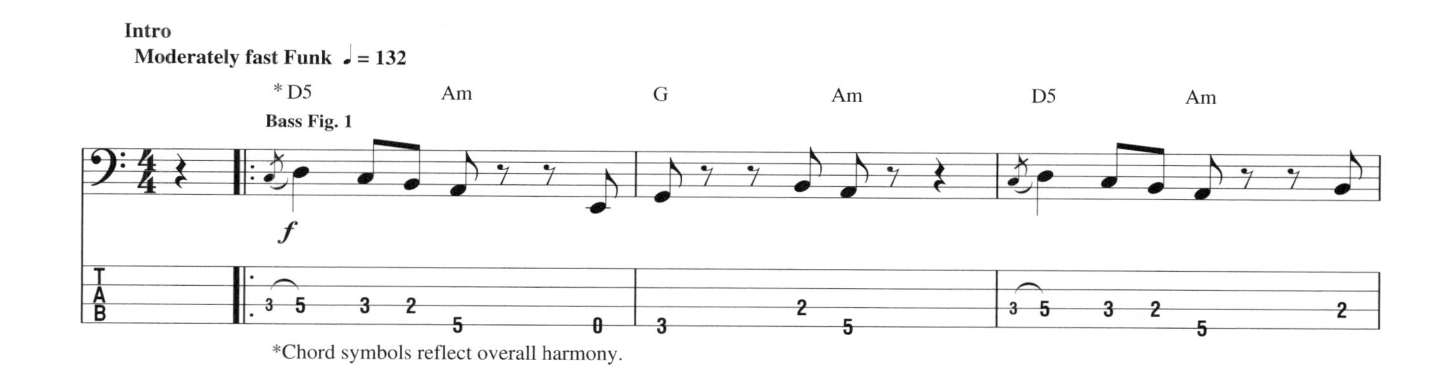
Intro
Moderately fast Funk ♩ = 132
*D5
Am
G
Am
D5
Am
Bass Fig. 1
f
T
A
B

*Chord symbols reflect overall harmony.

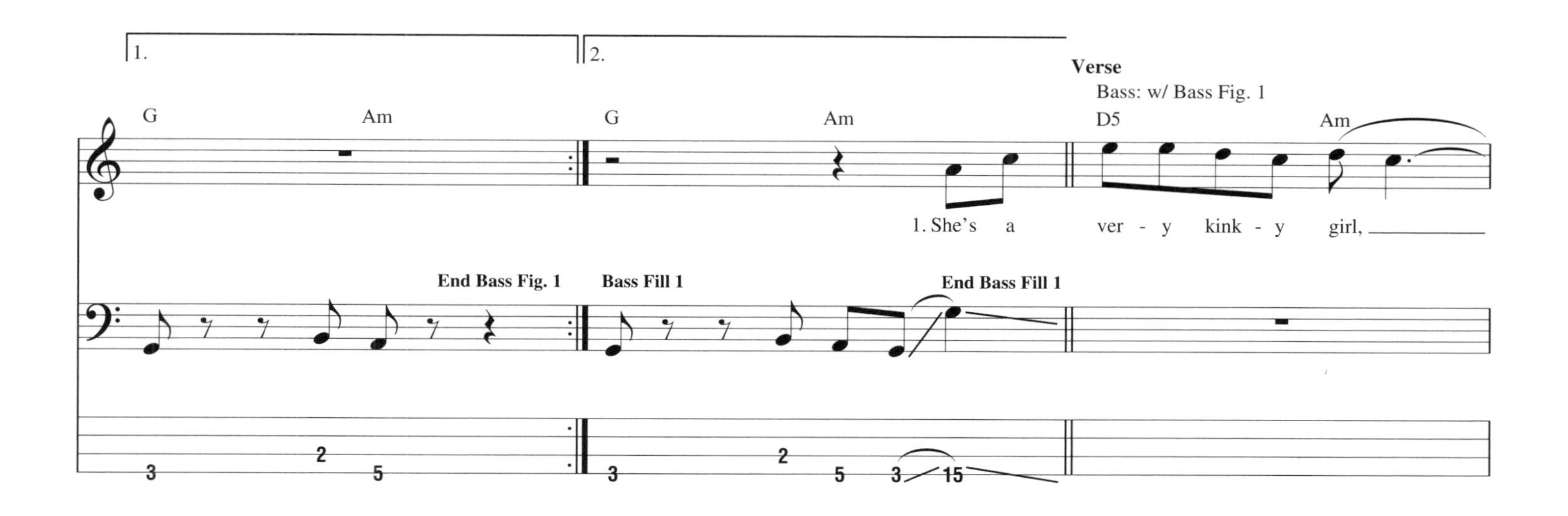
1.
2.
Verse
Bass: w/ Bass Fig. 1
G
Am
G
Am
D5
Am
1. She's a ver - y kink - y girl,
End Bass Fig. 1
Bass Fill 1
End Bass Fill 1

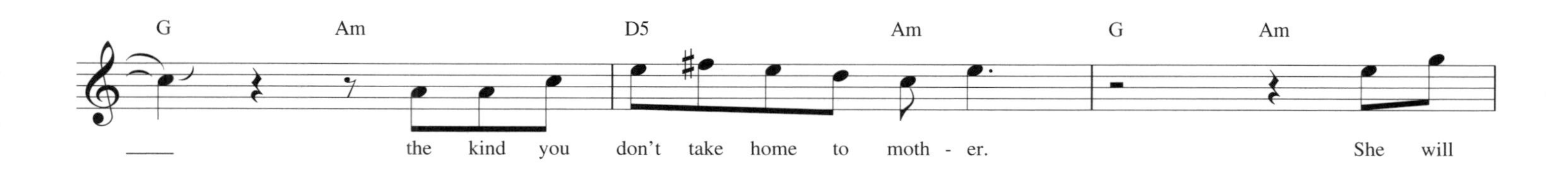
G
Am
D5
Am
G
Am
the kind you don't take home to moth - er.
She will

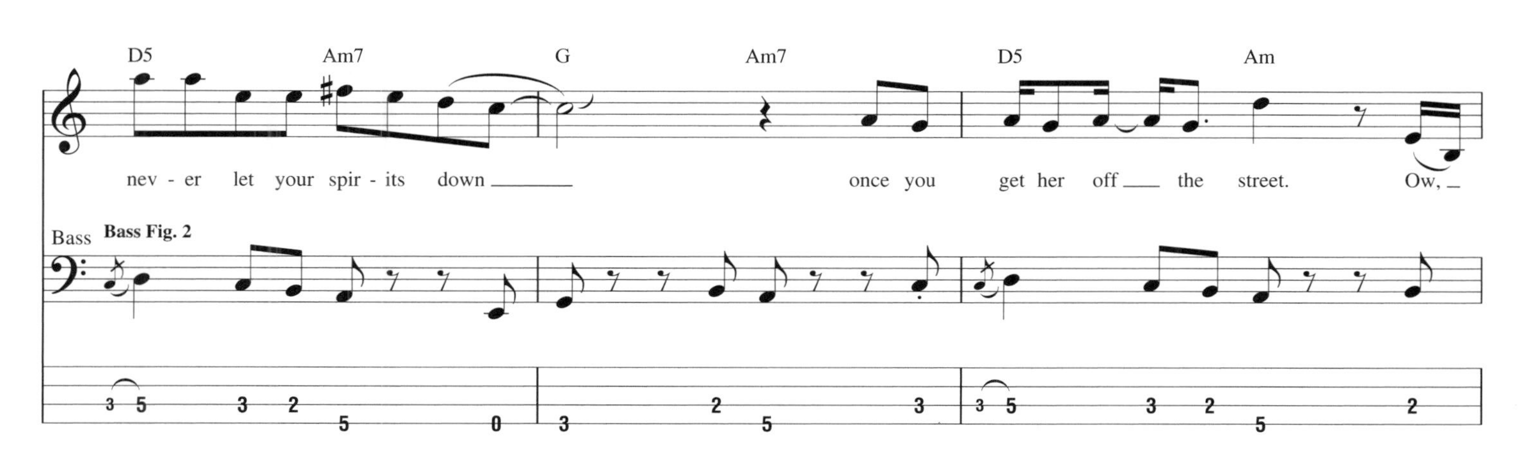
D5
Am7
G
Am7
D5
Am
nev - er let your spir - its down
once you
get her off the street.
Ow,
Bass
Bass Fig. 2

Bass: w/ Bass Fig. 1 (2 times)
G
Am
D5
Am7
G
Am7
girl.
She likes the boys in the band.
She says that
End Bass Fig. 2
D5
Am
G
Am
D5
Am7
I'm her all - time fa - v'rite.
When I make my move to her room it's the
G
Am7
D5
Am
G
Am
right time.
She's nev - er hard to please.
Oh, no.
That
Pre-Chorus
D5
Am
F
G
Am
girl is pret - ty
wild now.
kink - y.
The
(The girl's a su - per freak.
Bass
Bass Fig. 3
D5
Am
F
G
Am
kind of girl you read a - bout...
That
...in new wave mag - a - zines.
End Bass Fig. 3

Bass: w/ Bass Fig. 3
D5
Am
F G
Am
girl is pret - ty { kink - y. / wild ___ now. }
I'd
The girl's a su - per freak.
D5
Am
F G
Am
real - ly { love / like } to taste ___ her...
...ev - 'ry time we meet.)
Chorus
F G Am
F G Am
She's all right. ___
(She's all right.
She's all right. ___
She's all right.
That
The
Bass
3 5 0
1 3 0
Asus4
girl's ___ all ___ right ___ with ___ me, ___
girl's all right.)
yeah. ___
Hey, hey, hey, hey!
To Coda

Interlude

Bass: w/ Bass Fig. 2 (1 3/4 times)
D5
Am
G
Am
D5
Am7
She's a su - per freak, su - per freak.

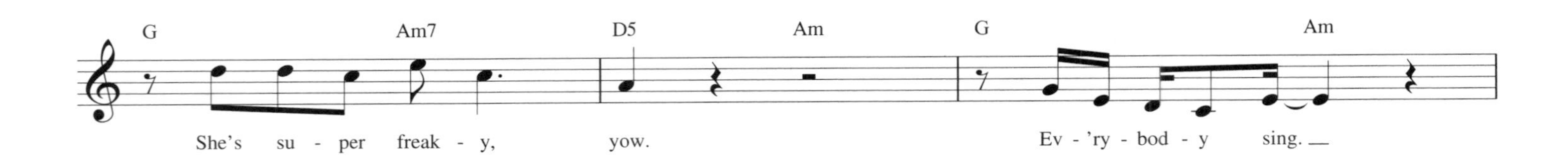
G
Am7
D5
Am
G
Am
She's su - per freak - y, yow. Ev - 'ry - bod - y sing.

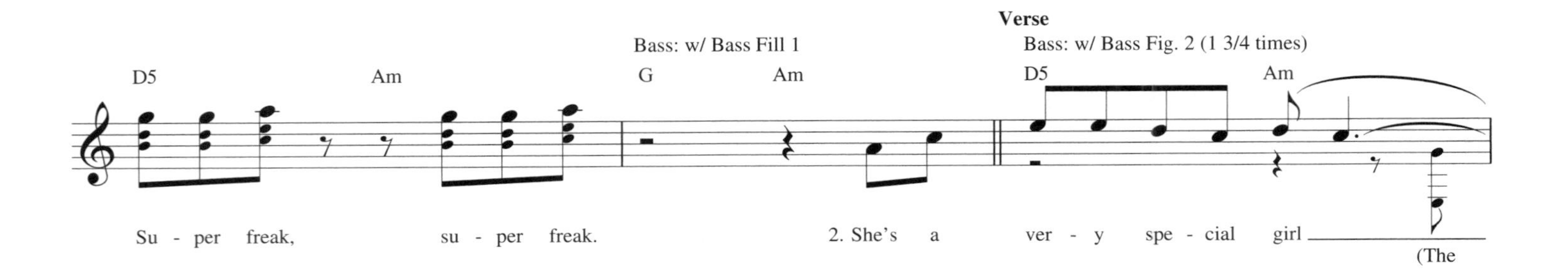
Bass: w/ Bass Fill 1
Verse
Bass: w/ Bass Fig. 2 (1 3/4 times)
D5
Am
G
Am
D5
Am
Su - per freak, su - per freak. 2. She's a ver - y spe - cial girl
(The

G
Am
D5
Am7
G
Am7
from her head down to her toe - nails. And she'll
kind of girl you want to love. Down to her feet, yeah.)

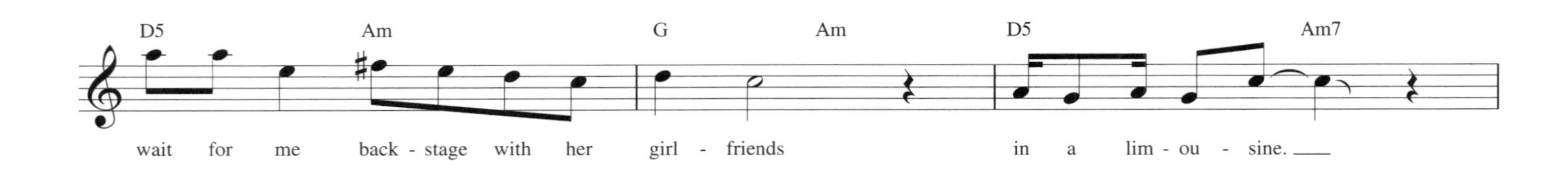
D5
Am
G
Am
D5
Am7
wait for me back - stage with her girl - friends in a lim - ou - sine.

G
Am7
D5
Am
G
Am
Three's not a crowd to her. She says, "Room sev - en
(Long and black and shin - ing bright. Mé - nage à trois, we love you.
Bass

Bass: w/ Bass Fig. 2
D5 Am7 G Am7 D5 Am
four - teen, I'll be wait - ing." __
When I get there she's got in - cense, wine, and
Ow.) ________
3 5 3 2 5 2
3 2 5 3

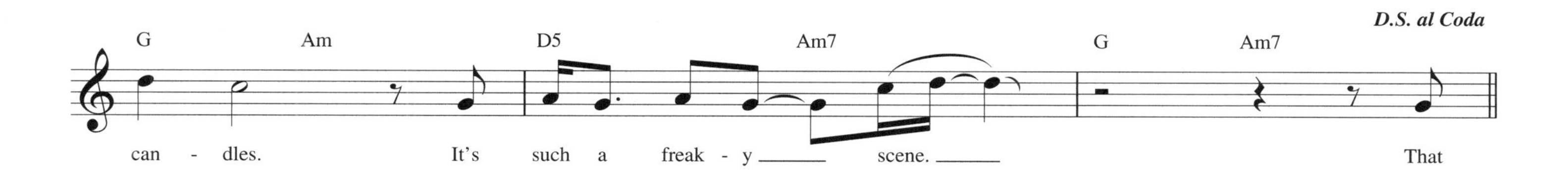
D.S. al Coda
G Am D5 Am7 G Am7
can - dles. It's such a freak - y ____ scene. ____ That

Coda
Interlude
Bass: w/ Bass Fig. 2 (1st 3 meas.)
D5 Am G Am D5 Am7
She's a su - per freak, su - per freak.

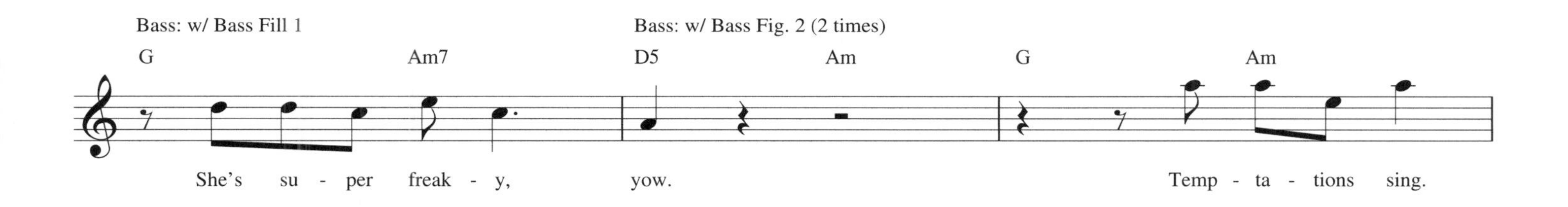
Bass: w/ Bass Fill 1
Bass: w/ Bass Fig. 2 (2 times)
G Am7 D5 Am G Am
She's su - per freak - y, yow. Temp - ta - tions sing.

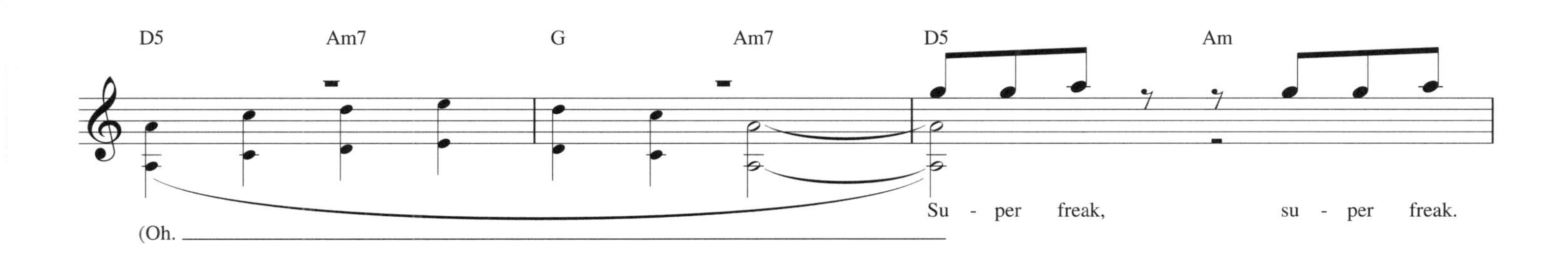
D5 Am7 G Am7 D5 Am
(Oh. ____
Su - per freak, su - per freak.

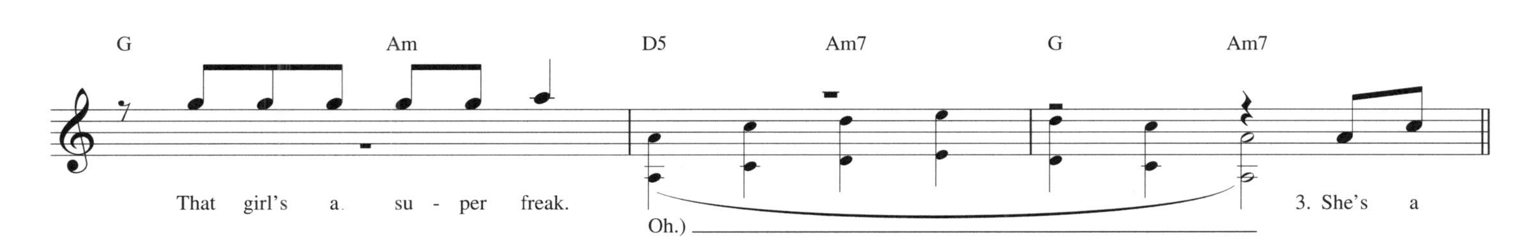
G Am D5 Am7 G Am7
That girl's a su - per freak.
Oh.) ____
3. She's a

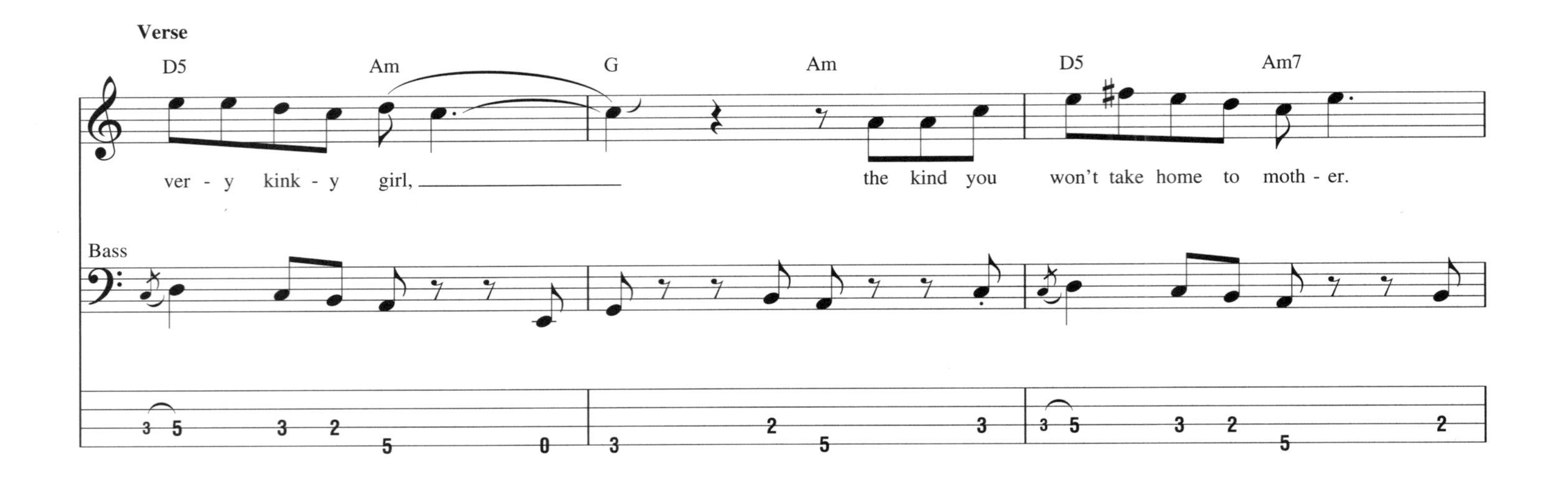
Verse
D5
Am
G
Am
D5
Am7
ver - y kink - y girl,
the kind you
won't take home to moth - er.
Bass

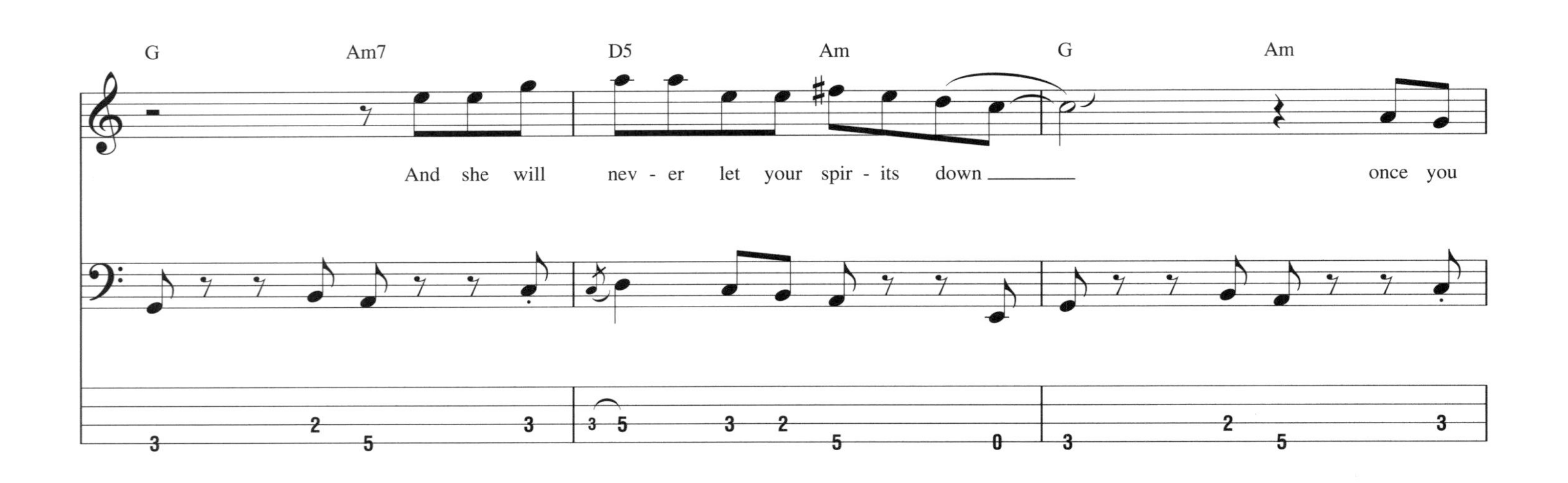
G
Am7
D5
Am
G
Am
And she will
nev - er let your spir - its down
once you

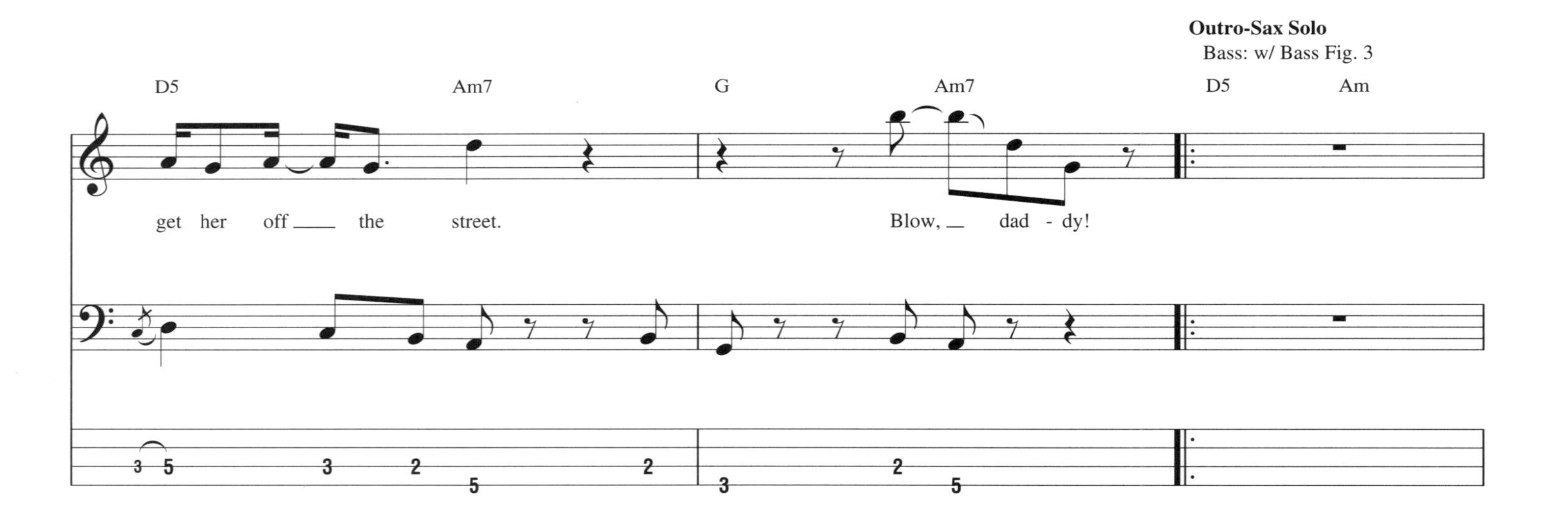
Outro-Sax Solo
Bass: w/ Bass Fig. 3
D5
Am7
G
Am7
D5
Am
get her off the street.
Blow, dad - dy!

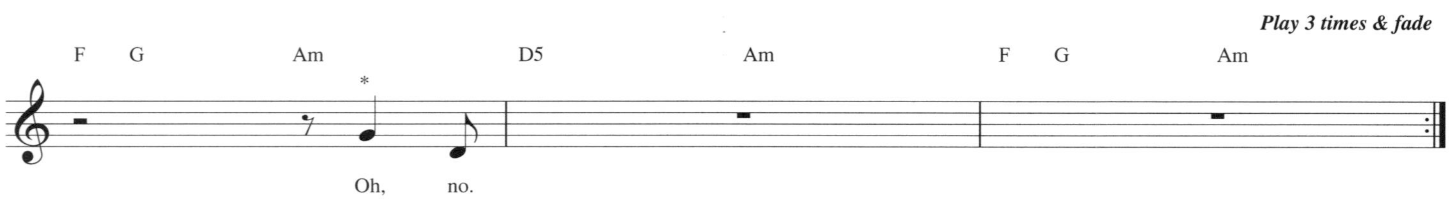
Play 3 times & fade
F G
Am
D5
Am
F G
Am
Oh, no.

*Sung 1st & 3rd times.

Sweet Child o' Mine

Words and Music by W. Axl Rose, Slash, Izzy Stradlin', Duff McKagan and Steven Adler

Tune down 1/2 step:
(low to high) E♭-A♭-D♭-G♭

Intro
Moderately ♩ = 122
N.C.(D)
(Guitar)
(C)
(G)
(D)

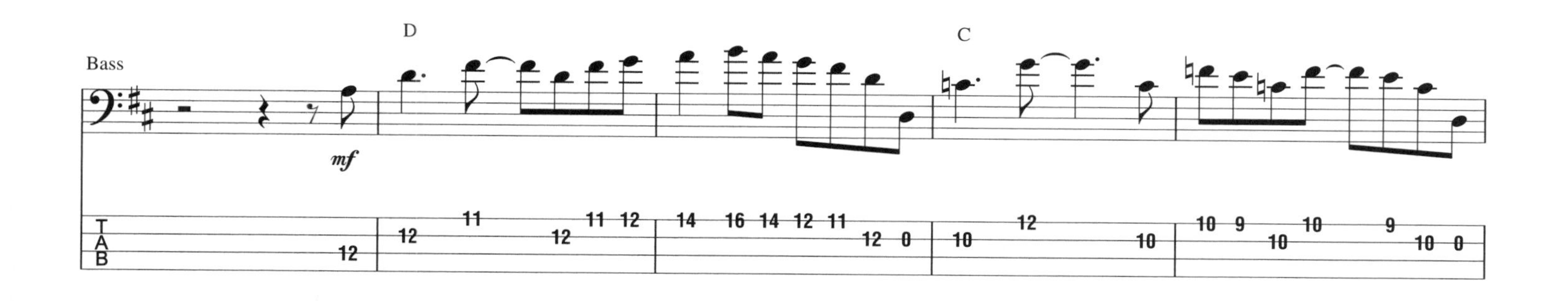
Bass
D
C
mf
T
A
B

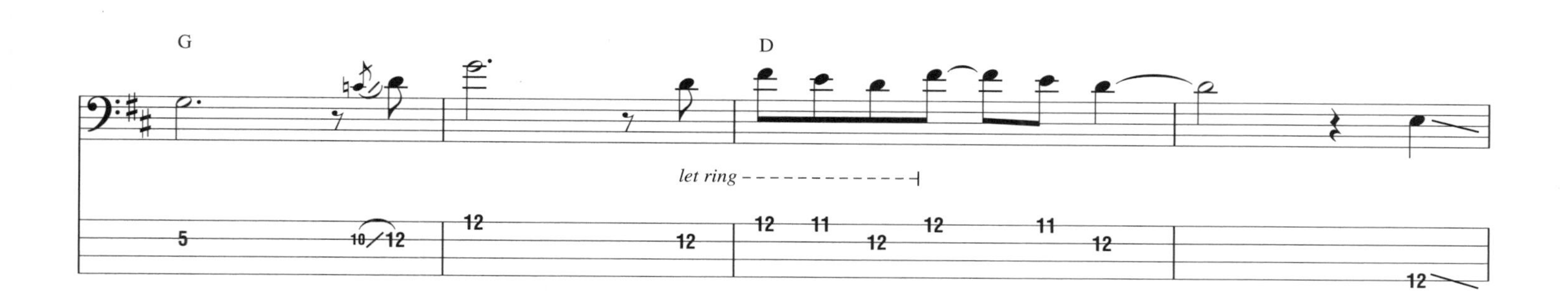
G
D
let ring

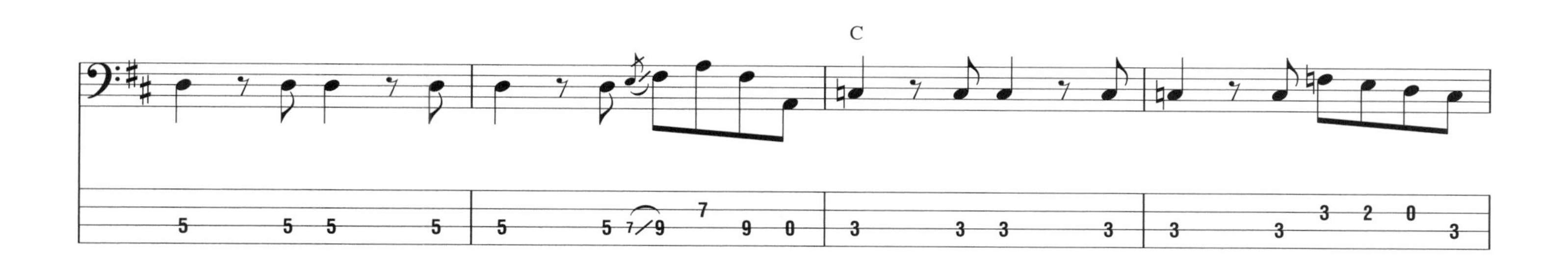
C

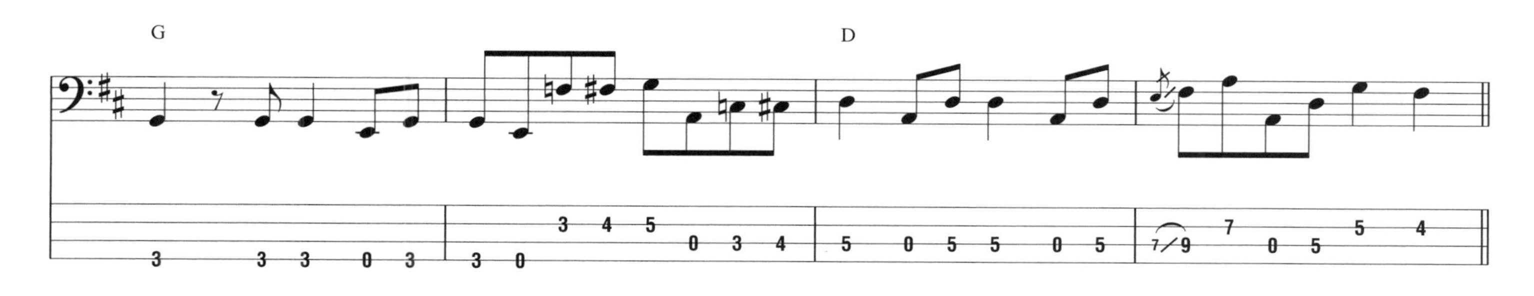
G
D

Verse
D
Cadd9
1. She's got a smile _ that it seems to me _ re - minds _ me of child - hood mem - o - ries, _ where ev -

G
D
- 'ry - thing _ was as fresh _ as the bright _ blue sky. _
*w/ echo set for half-note regeneration w/ 2 repeats.

Now and then _ when I see her face _ she

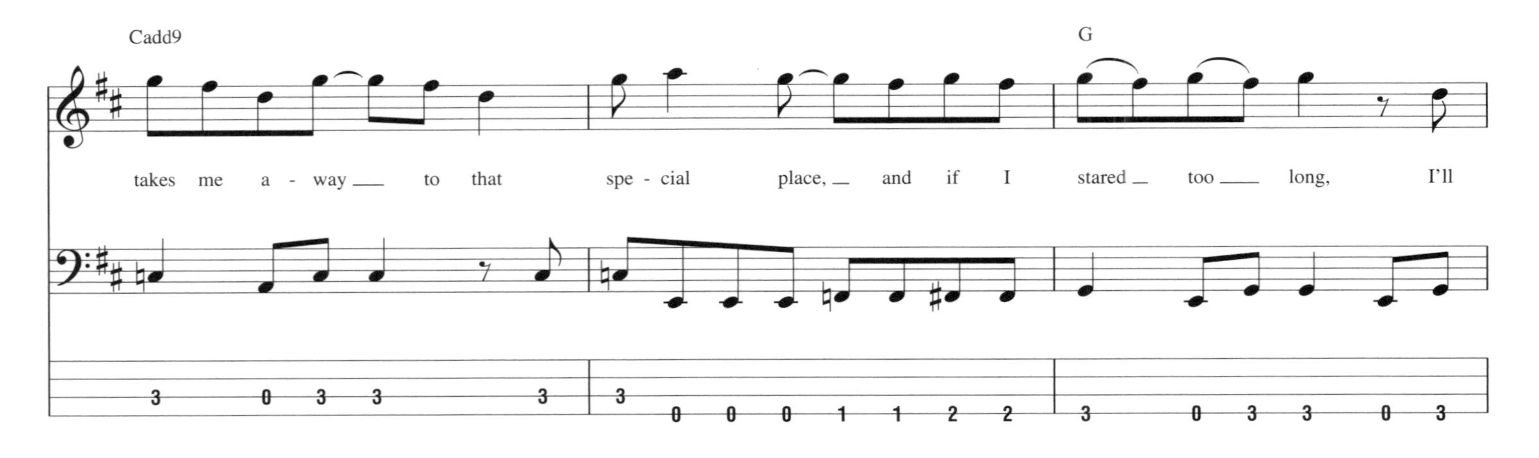
Cadd9
G
takes me a - way _ to that spe - cial place, _ and if I stared _ too _ long, I'll

D
prob - 'ly break down and cry.
Chorus
A5
B5
C5
D
Whoa, whoa, whoa, sweet child o' mine.
A5
B5
Whoa, oh, oh, oh,
C5
D
sweet love of mine.

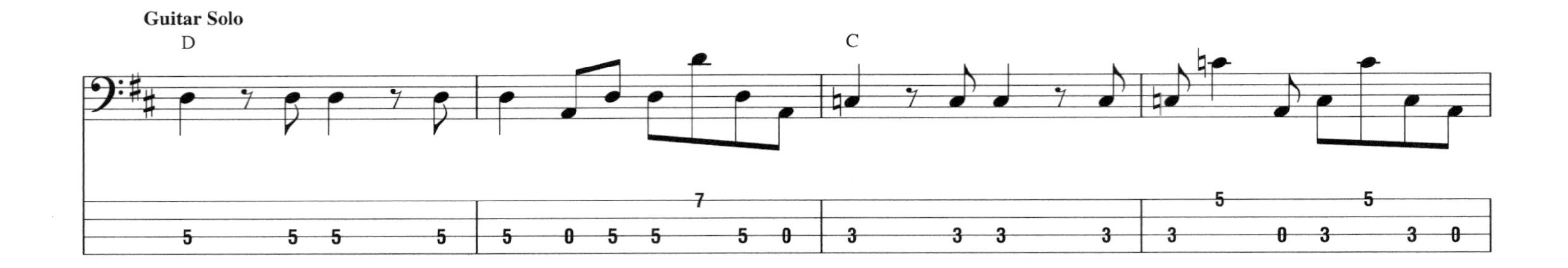
Guitar Solo
D
C

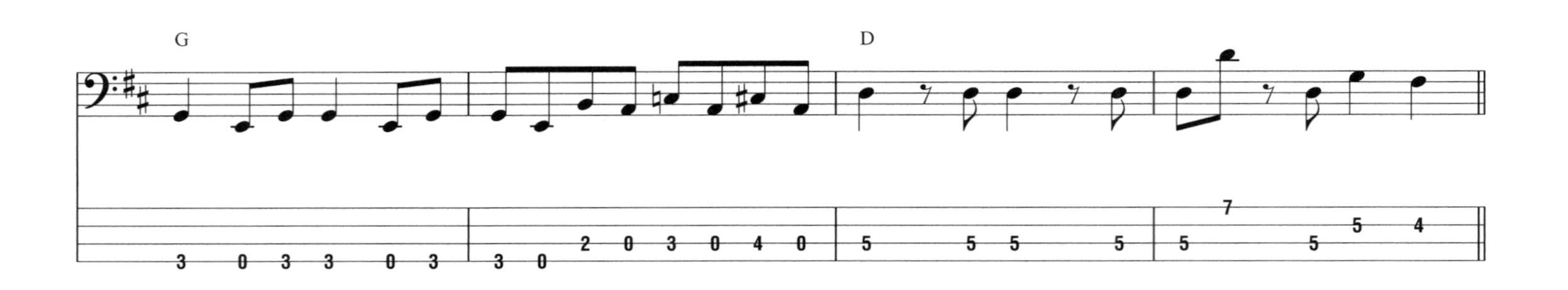
G
D

Verse
D
Cadd9
2. She's got eyes ___ of the blu - est skies, ___ as if they thought of rain. ___

G
I'd hate to look in - to those eyes ___ and

D
see an ounce of pain.
Her hair re - minds me of a
C
warm, safe place where as a child I'd hide.
And
G
pray for the thun - der and the rain
D
to qui - et - ly pass me by.
Chorus
A5
B5
C5
D
Whoa, whoa, whoa, sweet child o' mine.
Whoa,

A5
B5
C5
D
whoa, oh, oh, oh, sweet love of mine.
let ring
Guitar Solo
D
C
G
D
D
C
Oo.
G
D
Whoa, yeah!

Chorus
A5
C5
D
Whoa, oh, oh, oh, sweet child o' mine.
Oo,
A5
C5
D
oo, whoa, oh, sweet love of mine.
A5
B5
C5
Oh, oh, oh, oh, sweet child o' mine.
D
A5
B5
Woo, yeah, yeah!
Ooh,
let ring

C5
D5
D♯5
sweet love of mine.

Guitar Solo

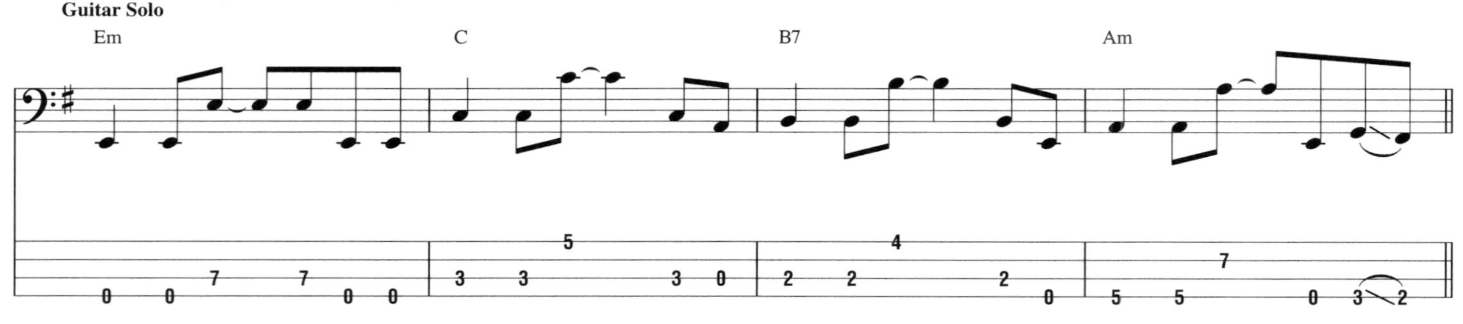
Em
C
B7
Am

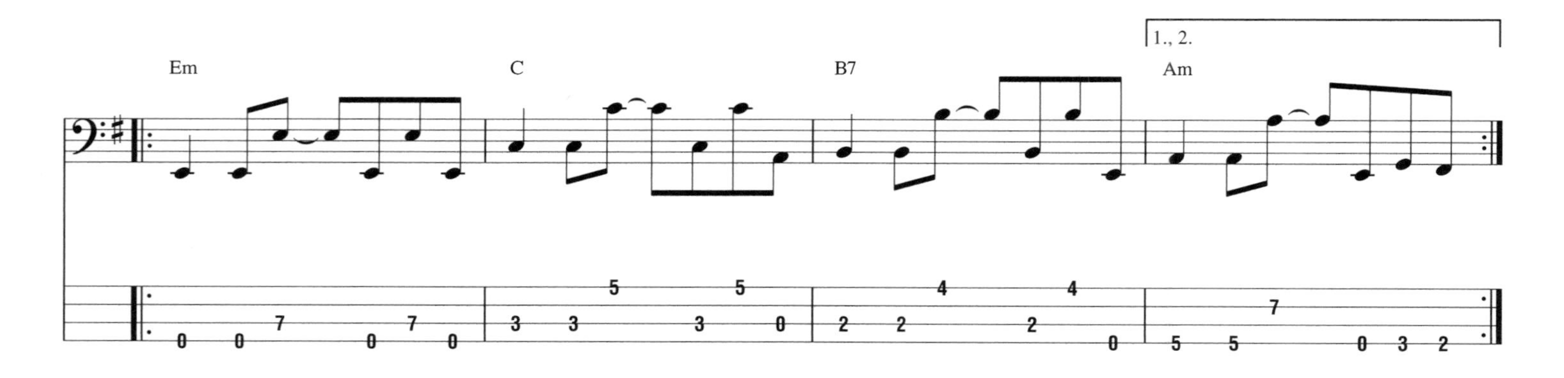
1., 2.
Em
C
B7
Am

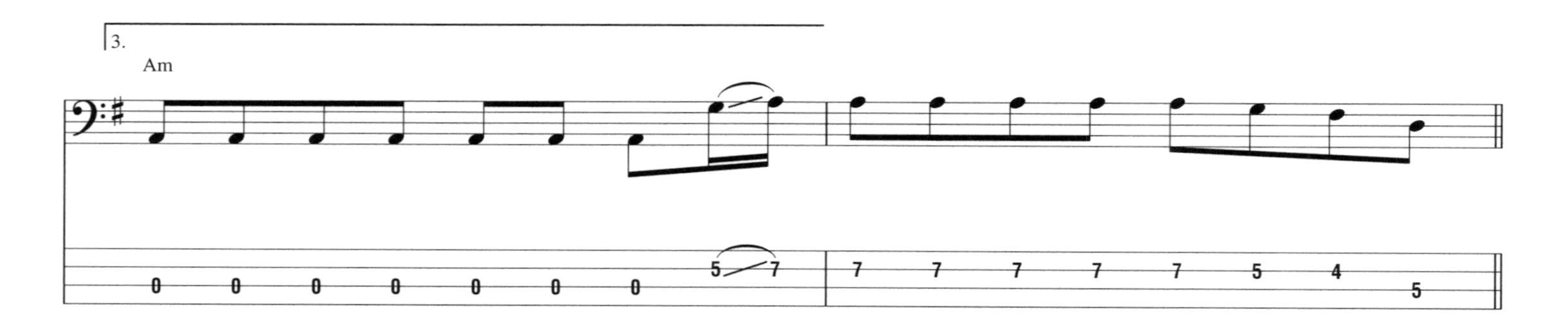
3.
Am

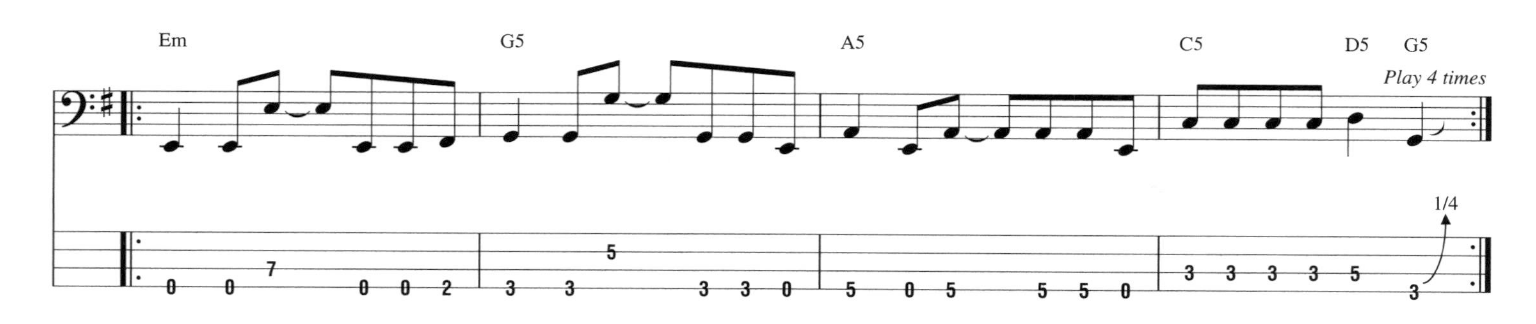
Em
G5
A5
C5
D5
G5
Play 4 times
1/4

Outro
E5
G5
A5
Where do we go?
Where do we go now?
Where do we go?
C5
D5
G5
E5
G5
Mm, mm, oh, where do we go?
(Where do we go?
Oh,
Where do we go now?
A5
C5
D5
G5
E5
Where do we go, now?
Where do we go?)
Where do we go?
G5
A5
C5
D5
G5
Oh,
Whispered: (Sweet Child!)
where do we go now?

E5
G5
A5
I, I, I, I, I, I, I, I, where do we go now? Oh,
(Where do we go? Where do we? Where do we go now?)
C5
D5
G5
E5
G5
ah. Where do we go? Ah.
A5
B5
C5
D5
G5
E5
Where do we go now? Oh, where do we go?
1/4
G5
A5
Where do we go now?

C5
D5
G5
E5
Where do we go?
1/4
G5
A5
B5
E5
D5
B5
B♭5
A5
G
Whoa,
where do we go now?
No, no, no, no, no, no,
E5
G5
A5
no.
Sweet child,
sweet
child
C5
D5
grad rit.
E5
of mine.
grad rit.

21 Guns

Words and Music by David Bowie, John Phillips, Billie Joe Armstrong, Mike Pritchard and Frank Wright

Intro
Free time
Dm Bb F C Dm Bb F C
(Guitar)
Verse
Moderately ♩ = 79
2nd time, Bass: w/ Bass Fig. 1
Dm Bb F C Dm Bb F C
1. Do you know what's worth fight - ing for when it's not worth dy - ing for?
2. When you're at the end of the road and you lost all sense of con - trol.
2nd time, Bass: w/ Bass Fill 1
Dm Bb F C Bb C
Does it take your breath a - way and you feel your - self suf - fo - cat - ing?
And your thoughts have tak - en their toll when your mind breaks the spir - it of your soul.
Dm Bb F C Dm Bb F C
Does the pain weigh out the pride and you look for a place to hide?
Your faith walks on bro - ken glass and the hang - o - ver does - n't pass.
Bass Fig. 1
Bass
mf
Bass Fill 1

- contains samples of "All The Young Dudes" by David Bowie and "San Francisco (Be Sure To Wear Some Flowers In Your Hair)" by John Phillips

Dm
B♭
F
C
B♭
Did some-one break your heart in - side?
Noth - ing's ev - er built to last.
You're in ru - ins.
End Bass Fig. 1
Chorus
F5 N.C. C/E N.C. D5 N.C. C5 B♭5 F5 C5
*Voc. Fig. 1
End Voc. Fig. 1
One, twen-ty-one guns. Lay down your arms. Give up the fight.
(Aye.)
*Refers to upstemmed voc. only.
To Coda
Bkgd. Voc.: w/ Voc. Fig. 1
F5 N.C. C/E N.C. D5 N.C. C5 B♭5 F5 C5
One, twen-ty-one guns. Throw up your arms in-to the sky, you and I.
B♭5 F5
1.
C5
2.
C5

Bridge
D5 B♭5 F5 C5 D5 B♭5 F5 A5
Did you try to live on your own when you burned down the house and home?
D5 B♭5 F5 A5 B♭5 C5
Did you stand too close to the fire like a li - ar look ing for for - give - ness from a stone?
Interlude
F5 C/E D5 C5 A B♭5 F5 C5
F5 C/E D5 C5 B♭5 F5
C5 B♭5 F5 A5

Interlude
Bass tacet
Dm Bb F C Dm Bb F C
Verse
Dm Bb F C Dm Bb F C
3. When it's time to live and let die and you can't get an-oth-er try,
Dm Bb F C Bb
D.S. al Coda
some-thing in-side this heart has died. You're in ru-ins.
Coda
C5 F5 N.C. C/E N.C. D5 N.C. C5
One, twen-ty-one guns. Lay down your arms.
Bkgd. Voc.: w/ Voc. Fig. 1
Bb5 F5 C5 F5 N.C. C/E N.C. D5 N.C. C5
Give up the fight. One, twen-ty-one guns. Throw up your arms
Bkgd. Voc.: w/ Voc. Fig. 1 (2 times)
Bb5 F5 C5 Bb5 F5 C5
in-to the sky, you and I.

Two Minutes to Midnight

Words and Music by Bruce Dickinson and Adrian Smith

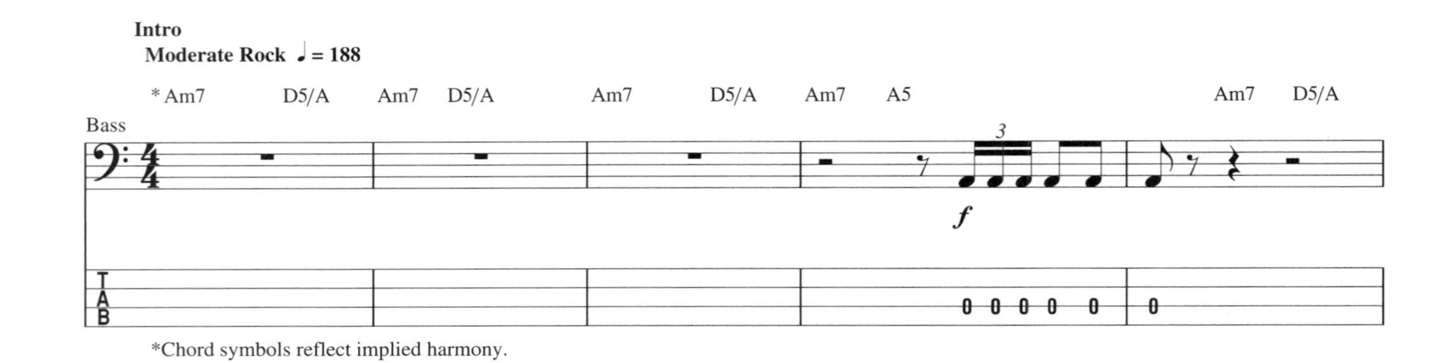

Intro
Moderate Rock ♩ = 188
*Am7 D5/A Am7 D5/A Am7 D5/A Am7 A5 Am7 D5/A
Bass
3
f
T
A
B
0 0 0 0 0
0

*Chord symbols reflect implied harmony.

Am7 D5/A Am7 D5/A Am7 A5 Am7 D5/A Am7 D5/A Am7 D5/A
0 0 7 7 5 7 5 7
0

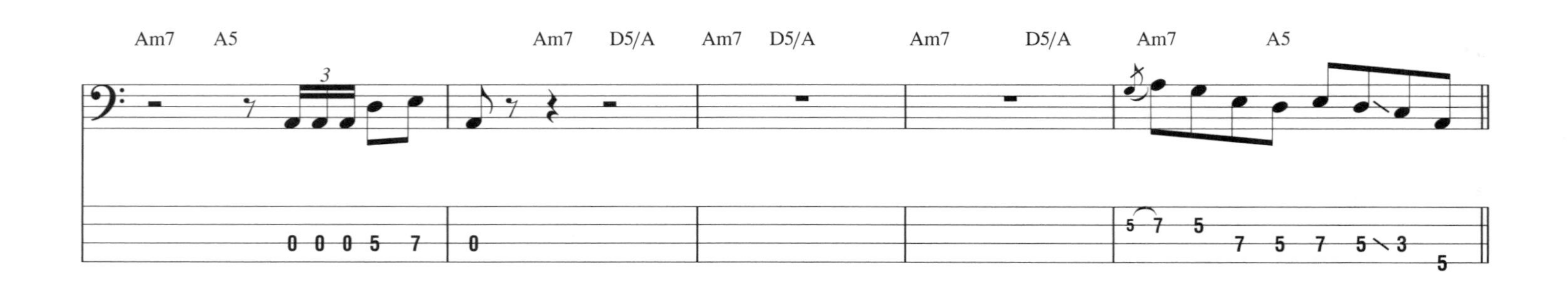

Am7 A5 Am7 D5/A Am7 D5/A Am7 D5/A Am7 A5
3
0 0 0 5 7
0
5 7 5 7 5 7 5 3 5

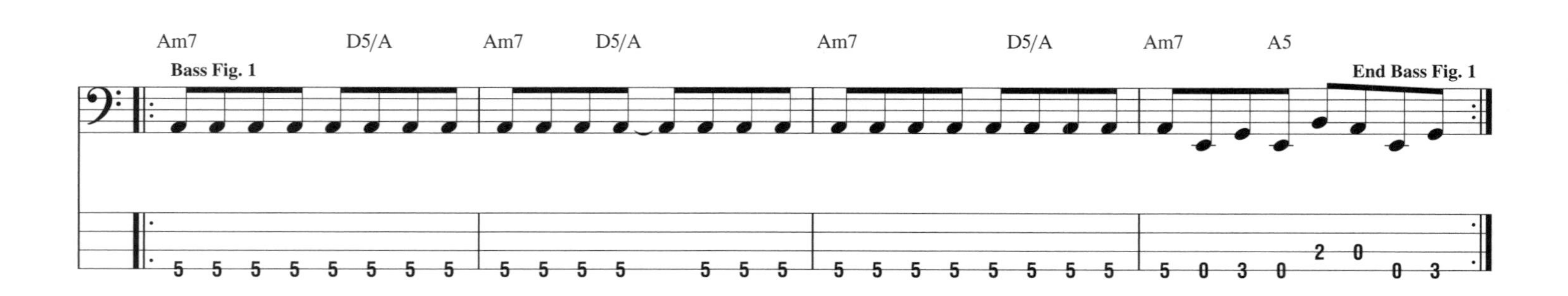

Am7 D5/A Am7 D5/A Am7 D5/A Am7 A5
Bass Fig. 1
End Bass Fig. 1
5 5 5 5 5 5 5 5
5 5 5 5 5 5 5
5 5 5 5 5 5 5 5
5 0 3 0 2 0 0 3

Verse
Bass: w/ Bass Fig. 1 (1 1/2 times)
Am7 D5/A Am7 D5/A Am7 D5/A
1. Kill for gain or shoot to maim, but we don't need a
Am7 A5 Am7 D5/A Am7 D5/A
rea - son. The Gold - en Goose is on the loose and
Am7 D5/A Am7 A5 Am7 D5/A
nev - er out of sea - son. Black - ened pride still
Am7 D5/A D7sus4 D5 D7sus4 Am7
burns in - side this shell of blood - y trea - son.
D5/A Am7 D5/A D7sus4 D5 D7sus4 Am7
Here's my gun for a bar - rel of fun, for the love of liv - ing death. The

Pre-Chorus
Half-time feel
Am
F/A
G/A
Gsus4/A
kill - er's breed or the de - mon's seed. The

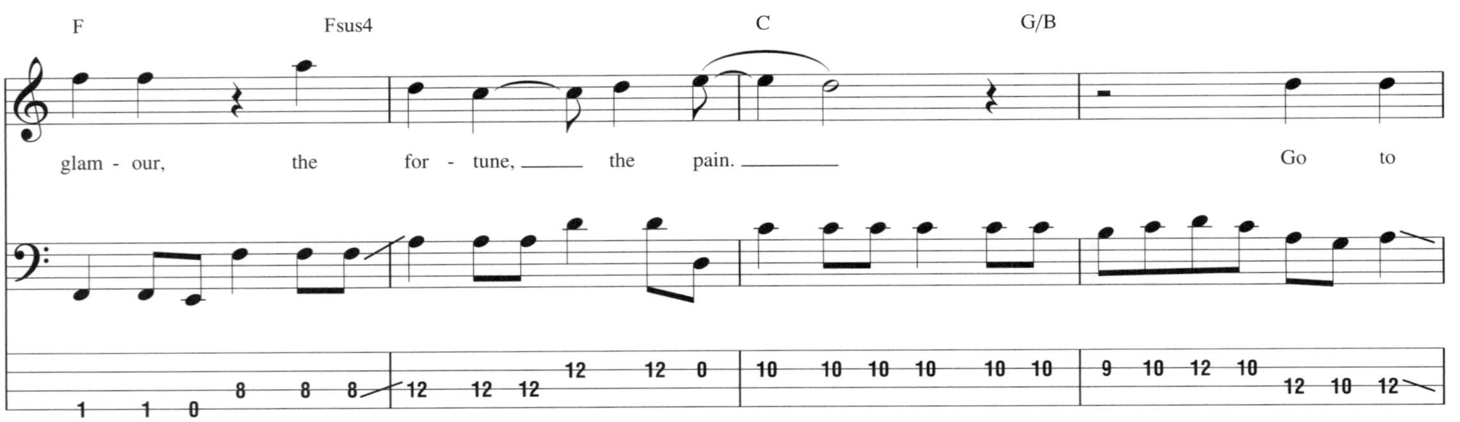

F
Fsus4
C
G/B
glam - our, the for - tune, the pain. Go to

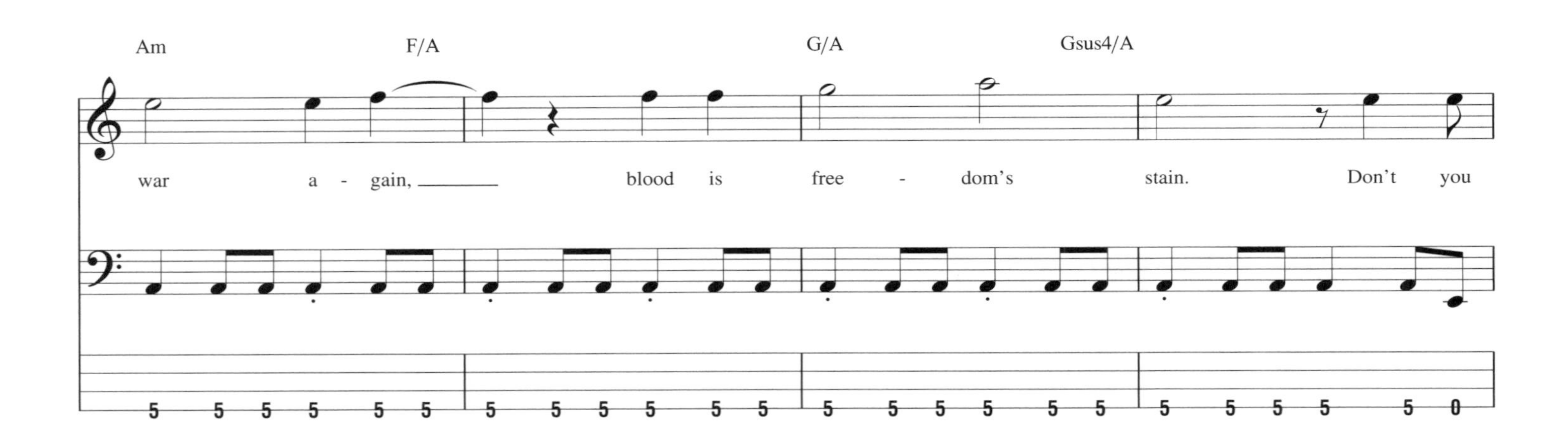

Am
F/A
G/A
Gsus4/A
war a - gain, blood is free - dom's stain. Don't you

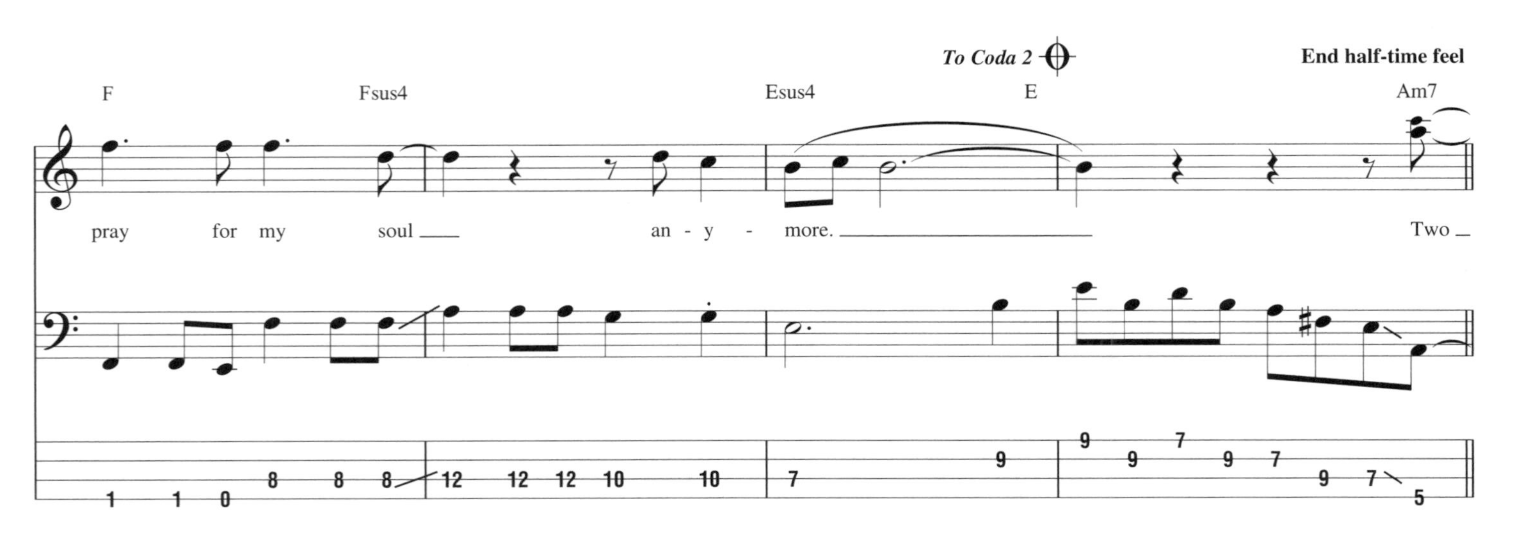

To Coda 2
End half-time feel
F
Fsus4
Esus4
E
Am7
pray for my soul an - y - more. Two

Chorus

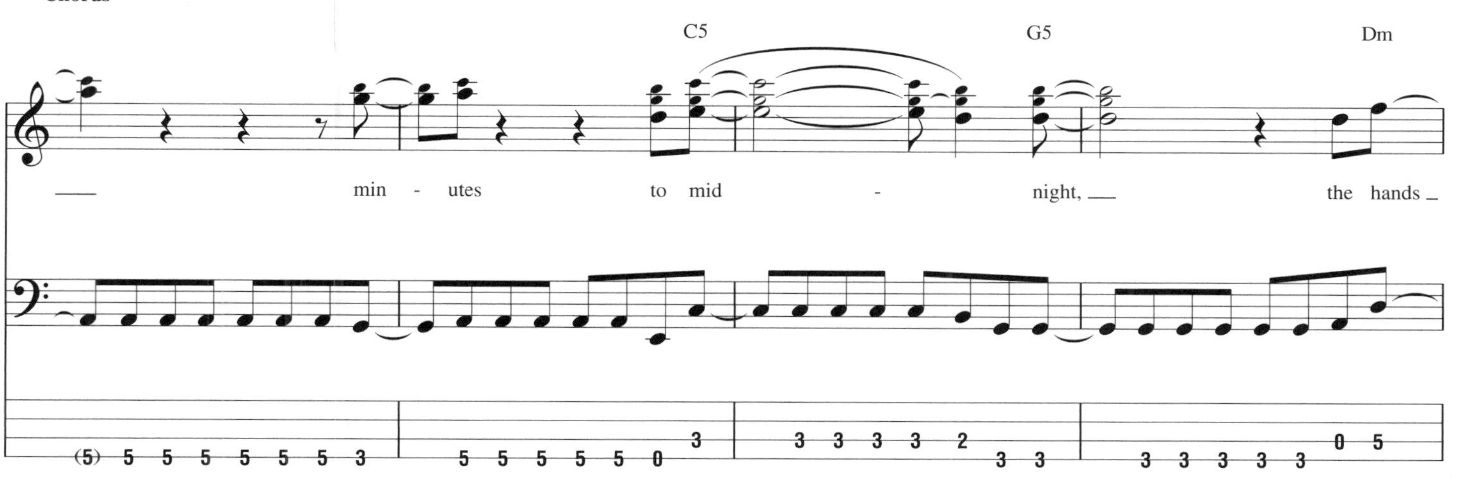
C5
G5
Dm
min - utes
to mid - night,
the hands
(5) 5 5 5 5 5 5 3
5 5 5 5 5 0 3
3 3 3 3 2 3 3
3 3 3 3 3 0 5

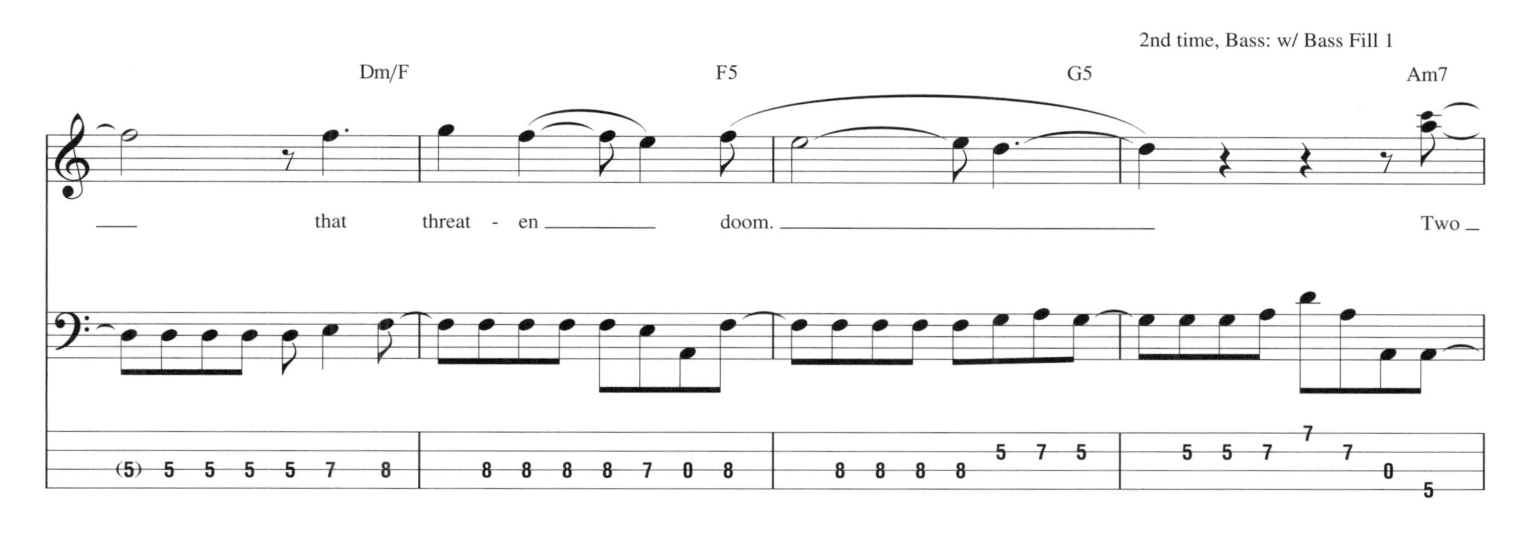
2nd time, Bass: w/ Bass Fill 1
Dm/F
F5
G5
Am7
that threat - en doom.
Two
(5) 5 5 5 5 7 8
8 8 8 8 7 0 8
8 8 8 8 5 7 5
5 5 7 7 7 0 5

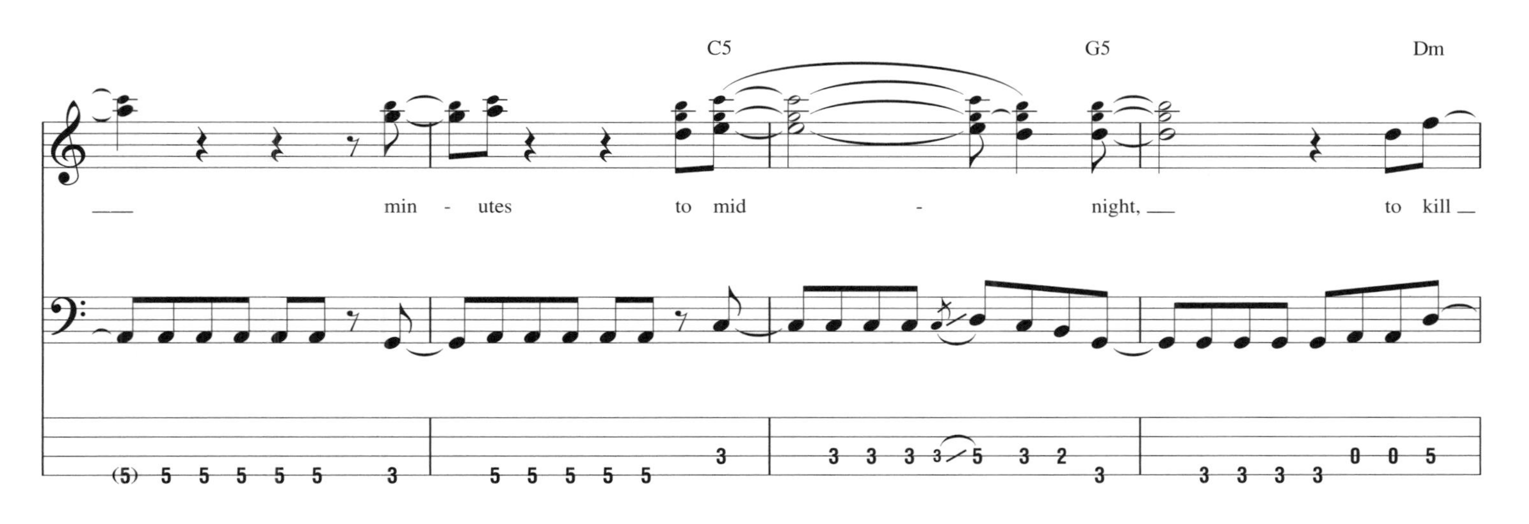
C5
G5
Dm
min - utes
to mid - night,
to kill
(5) 5 5 5 5 5 3
5 5 5 5 5 3
3 3 3 3 5 3 2 3
3 3 3 3 0 0 5

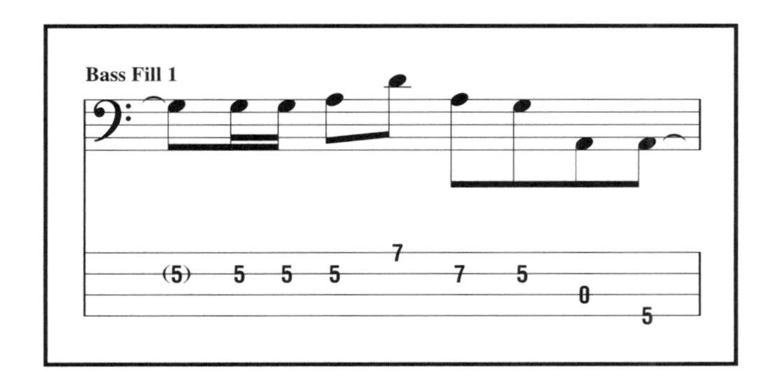
Bass Fill 1
(5) 5 5 5 7 7 5 0 5

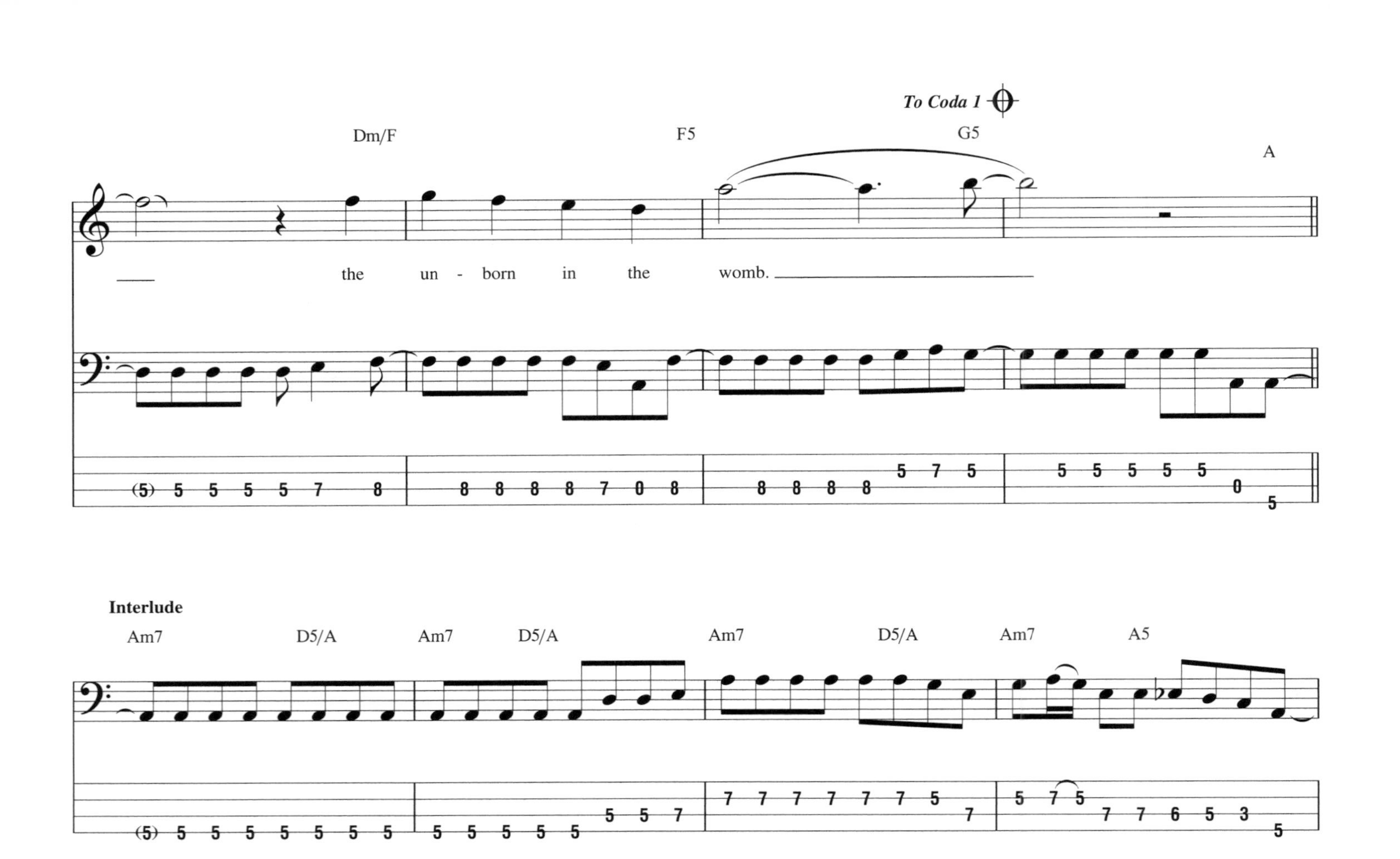
To Coda 1
Dm/F F5 G5 A
the un - born in the womb.
Interlude
Am7 D5/A Am7 D5/A Am7 D5/A Am7 A5

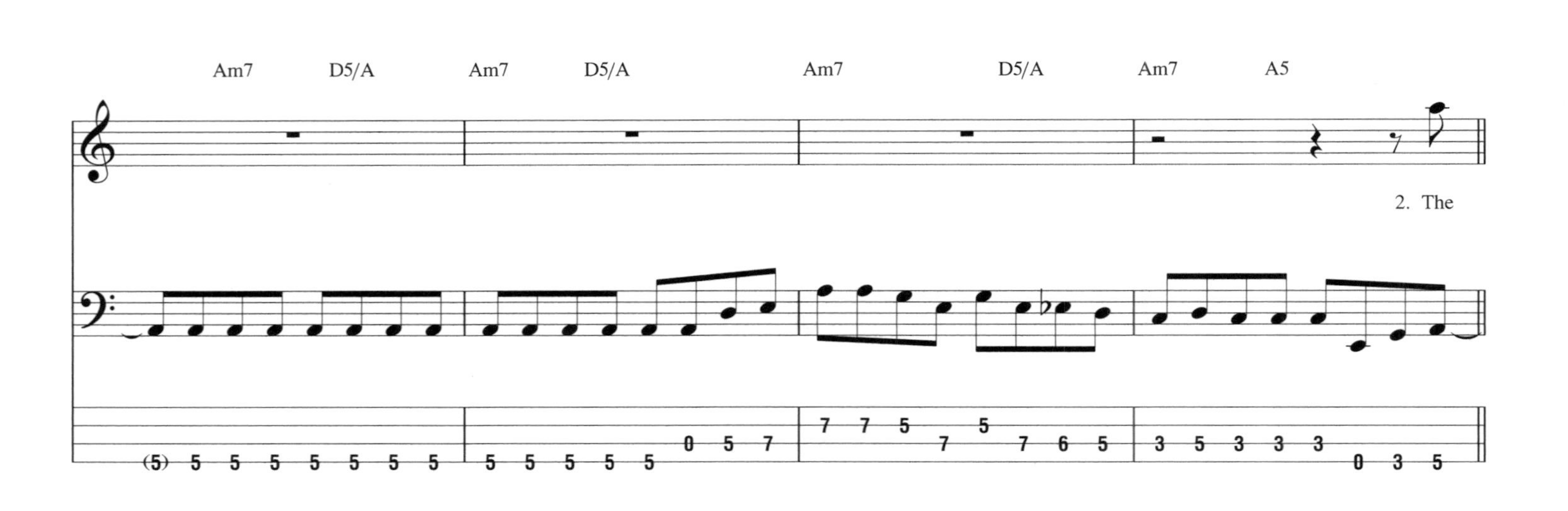
Am7 D5/A Am7 D5/A Am7 D5/A Am7 A5
2. The

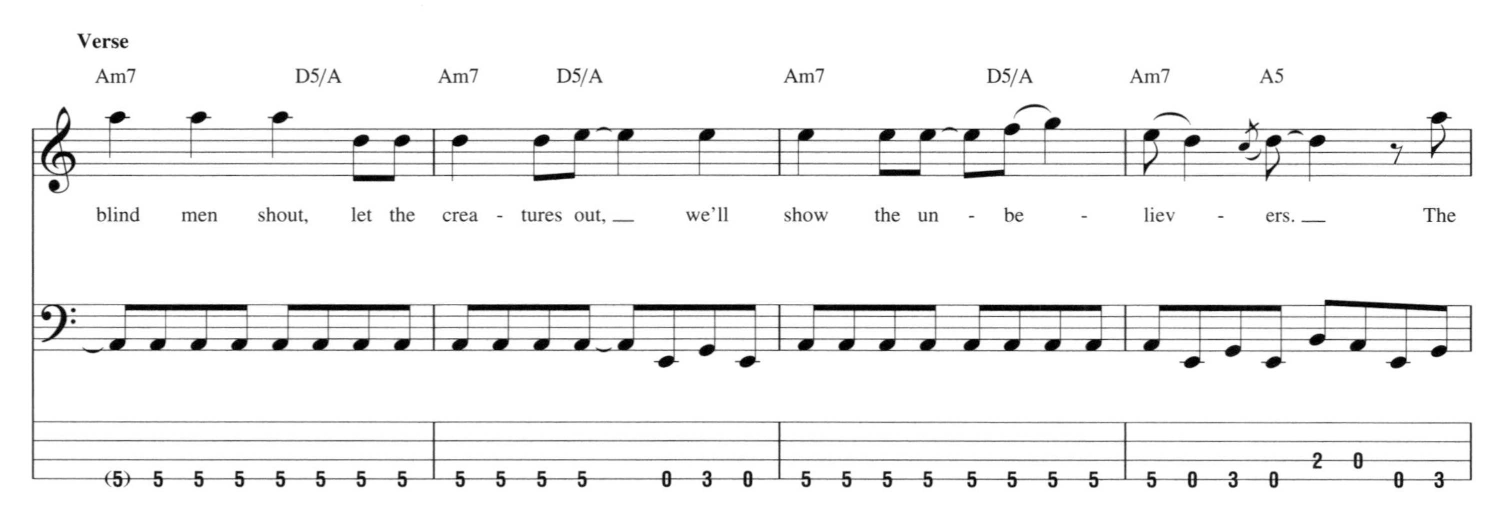
Verse
Am7 D5/A Am7 D5/A Am7 D5/A Am7 A5
blind men shout, let the crea - tures out, we'll show the un - be - liev - ers. The

Am7 D5/A Am7 D5/A Am7 D5/A Am7 A5
na - palm screams of hu - man flames, of a prime time Bel - sen feast, yeah. As the
Am7 D5/A Am7 D5/A D7sus4 D5 D7sus4 Am7
rea - sons for the car - nage cut their meat and lick the gra - vy. We oil
D.S. al Coda 1
D5/A Am7 D5/A D7sus4 D5 D7sus4 Am7
the jaws of the war ma - chine and feed it with our ba - bies. The
Coda 1
Guitar Solo
A5 A5 E5/A G5/A

F5 C/E Dadd4
A5 E5/A G5/A

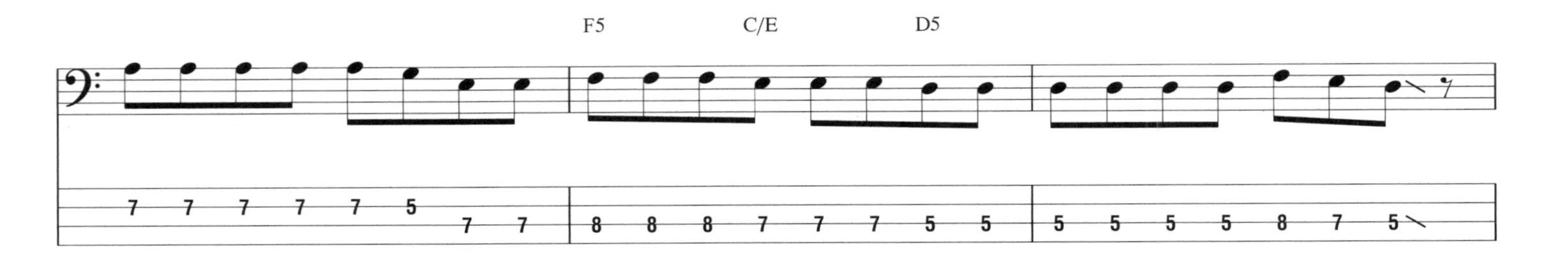
F5 C/E D5

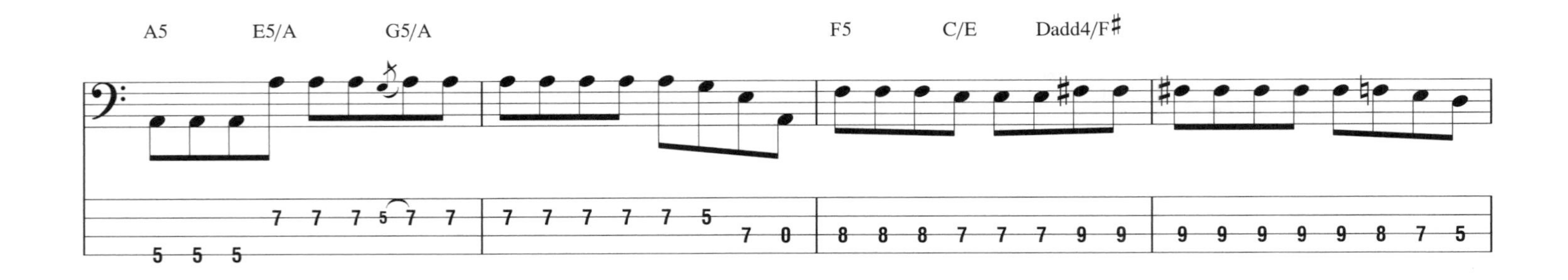
A5 E5/A G5/A
F5 C/E Dadd4/F♯

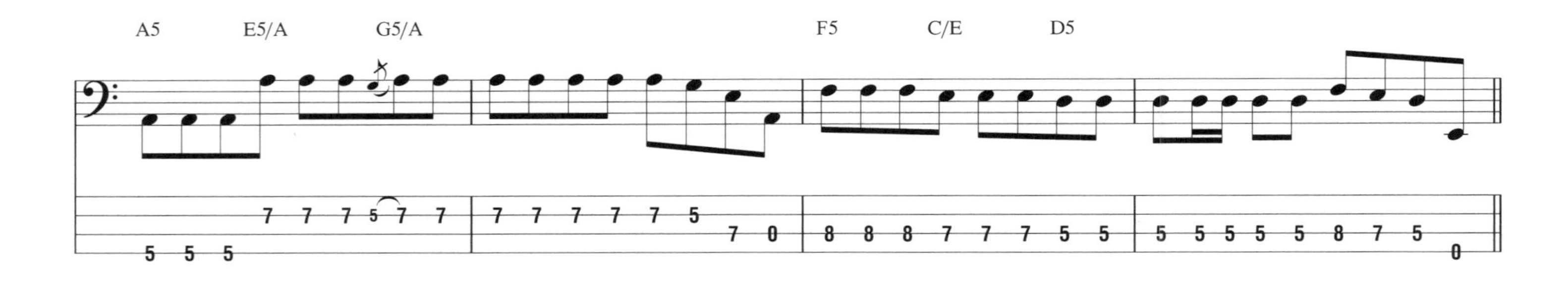
A5 E5/A G5/A
F5 C/E D5

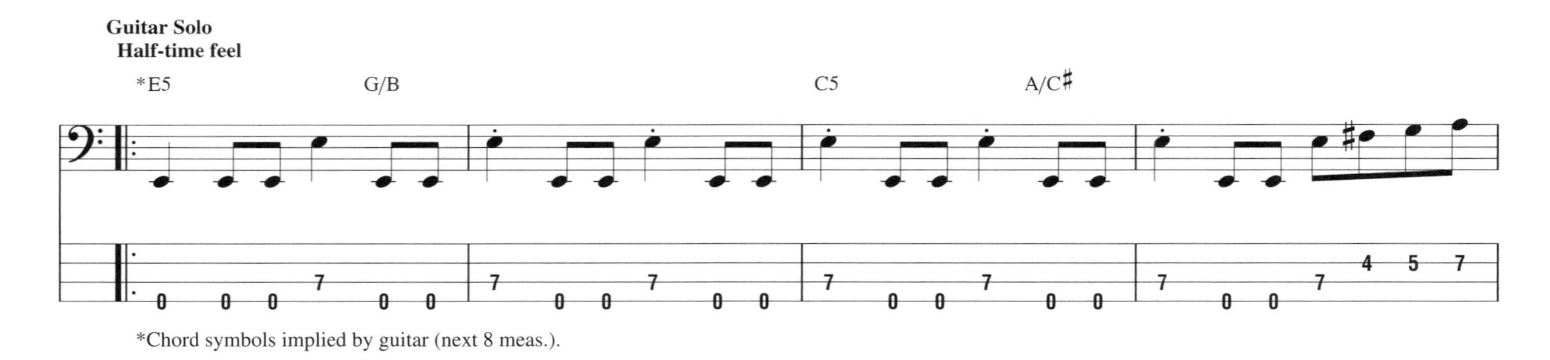
Guitar Solo
Half-time feel
*E5 G/B
C5 A/C♯

*Chord symbols implied by guitar (next 8 meas.).

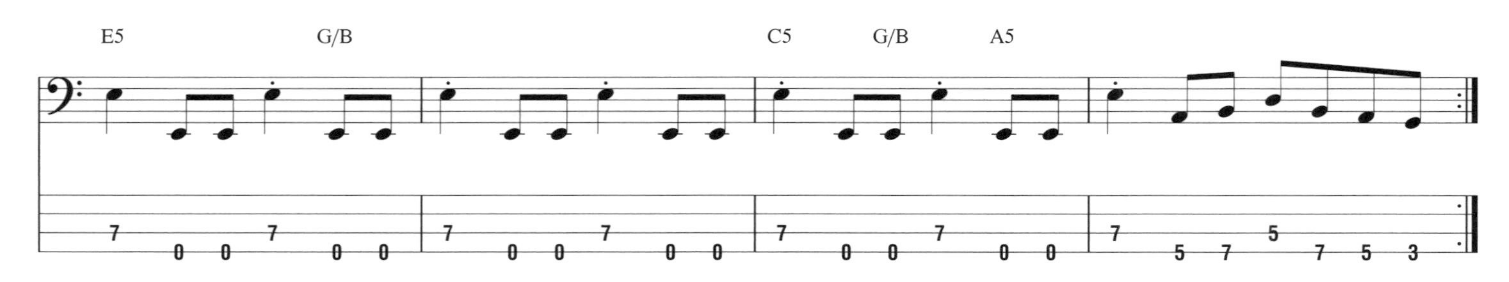
E5 G/B
C5 G/B A5

Interlude
C/E
D5/E
E5
D5/E
E5
G5
D5
E5
1.
2.
C/E
D/E
Em
C/E
D5/E
E5
End half-time feel
C5
D5

Interlude
Am7 D5/A Am7 D5/A Am7 D5/A Am7 A5
Am7 D5/A Am7 D5/A Am7 D5/A Am7 A5
3. The
Verse
Am7 D5/A Am7 D5/A Am7 D5/A Am7 A5
bod - y bags and lit - tle rags of chil - dren torn in two. And the
Bass Fig. 2
End Bass Fig. 2
Bass: w/ Bass Fig. 2
Am7 D5/A Am7 D5/A Am7 D5/A Am7 A5
jel - lied brains of those who re - main to put the fin - ger right on you. As the
Am7 D5/A Am7 D5/A D7sus4 D5 D7sus4 Am7
mad men play on words and make us all dance to their song. To the

D.S. al Coda 2
D5/A
Am7
D5/A
D7sus4
D5
D7sus4
Am7
tune of starv - ing mil - lions to make a better kind of gun. The
Coda 2
Chorus
End Half-time feel
Am7
C5
G5
Two min - utes to mid - night,
Dm
Dm/F
F5
G5
the hands that threat - en doom.
Am7
C5
G5
Two min - utes to mid - night,

Dm
Dm/F
F5
G5
A
to kill the un - born in the womb.
G5/A
A5
F5/A
G5/A
Mid - night,
mid - night,
C5/A
D5/A
C5/A
A5
mid - night
is all night.
G5/A
A5
F5/A
G5/A
Mid - night,
mid - night,

C5/A
D5/A
C5/A
A5
mid - night
is all
night.
G5/A
A5
F5/A
G5/A
C5/A
D5/A
C5/A
A5
G5/A
A5
F5/A
G5/A
C5/A
D5/A
C5
A5
N.C.
Mid - night
all
night!

Walk This Way

Words and Music by Steven Tyler and Joe Perry

Intro
Moderate Rock ♩ = 120
N.C.
(Drums)
(Drums & gr.)
Bass
A5
Verse
N.C. (C7)
1. Back - stroke lov - er al - ways hid - in' 'neath the cov - ers, "Gon - na talk to you," my dad - dy say, said, "You
2. School girl skin - ny with a class - y kind - a sas - sy lit - tle skirt's climb - in' way up her knee, there was
Bass Fig. 1
End Bass Fig. 1
Bass: w/ Bass Fig. 1 (2 times)
ain't seen noth - in' till you're down on a muf - fin and you're sure to be a - chang - in' your ways." I met a
three young lad - ies in the school gym lock - er when I no - ticed they was look - in' at me. I was a
cheer - lead - er, was a real young bleed - er all the times I cound rem - i - nisce, 'cause the
high school los - er, nev - er made it with a la - dy 'til the boys told me some - thin' I missed, then my
A5
best things in lov - in' with a sis - ter and a cou - sin on - ly start - ed with a lit - tle kiss, a - like this!
next door neigh - bor with a daugh - ter had a fav - or so I gave her just a lit - tle kiss a - like this!

Interlude
N.C. (E5)
Bass Fig. 2
5 6 7 7 5 6 7 7 0
5 6 7 7 5 6 7 7 0
5 6 7 7 5 6 7 7 0
A5
End Bass Fig. 2
5 6 7 7 5 6 7 7 0
Verse
Bass: w/ Bass Fig. 1 (3 times)
N.C. (C7)
2., 4. See - saw swing - in' with the boys in the school and your feet fly - 'in' up in the air, I sing,
"Hey did - dle did - dle" with your kit - ty in the mid - dle of the swing like you did - n't care. So I
took a big chance at the high school dance with a mis - sy who was read - y to play, was a
*Sing harmony 1st time only.
me she was fool - in' 'cause she knew what she was do - in'
and I know'd love was here to stay when she told me to...
when she told me how to walk this way. She told me to...
3 3 1 3 0 1 3 0 3
3 3 1 3 1 3 1 2

Chorus
C7
F7
(Walk this way,
talk this way,
Bass Fig. 3
End Bass Fig. 3
1st time, Bass: w/ Bass Fig. 3 (3 times)
2nd time, Bass: w/ Bass Fig. 3 (2 times)
C7
F7
C7
walk this way,
talk this way,
walk this way,
To Coda
F7
C7
F7
talk this way,
walk this way,
talk this way.)
Uh, just gim - me a kiss.
Guitar Solo
N.C. (C7)
Interlude
Bass: w/ Bass Fig. 2
D.S. al Coda
A5
N.C. (E5)
A5
A - like this!
Oo,
Uh.

Coda
C7
F7
walk this ___ way, ___
talk this ___ way.) ___
Uh, just gim - me a kiss. _

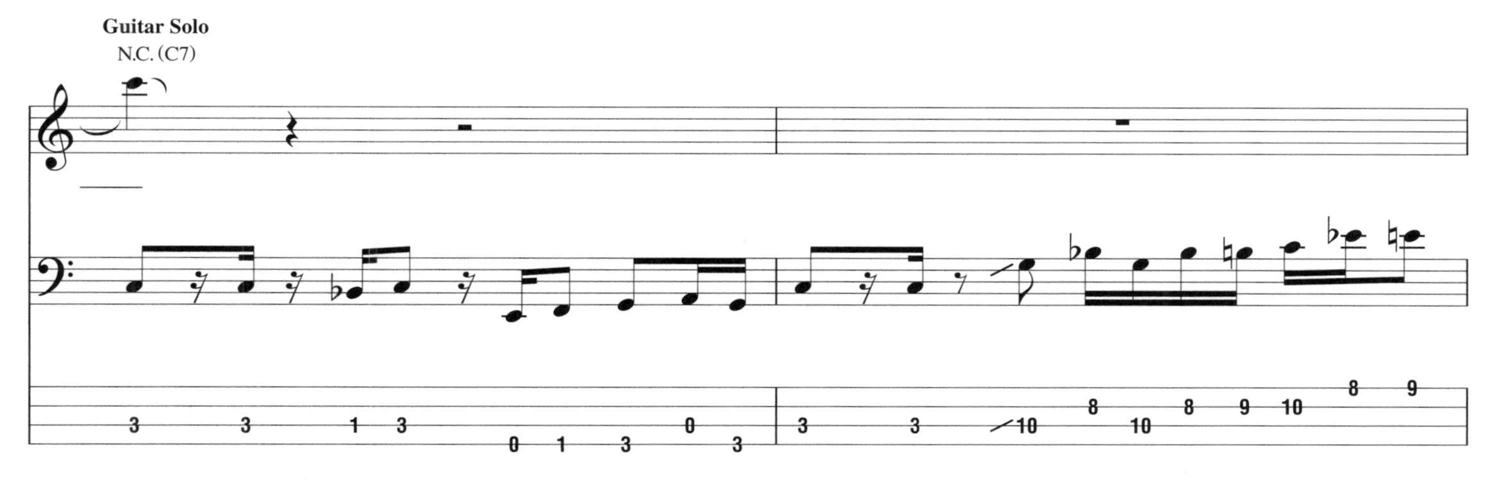
Guitar Solo
N.C. (C7)

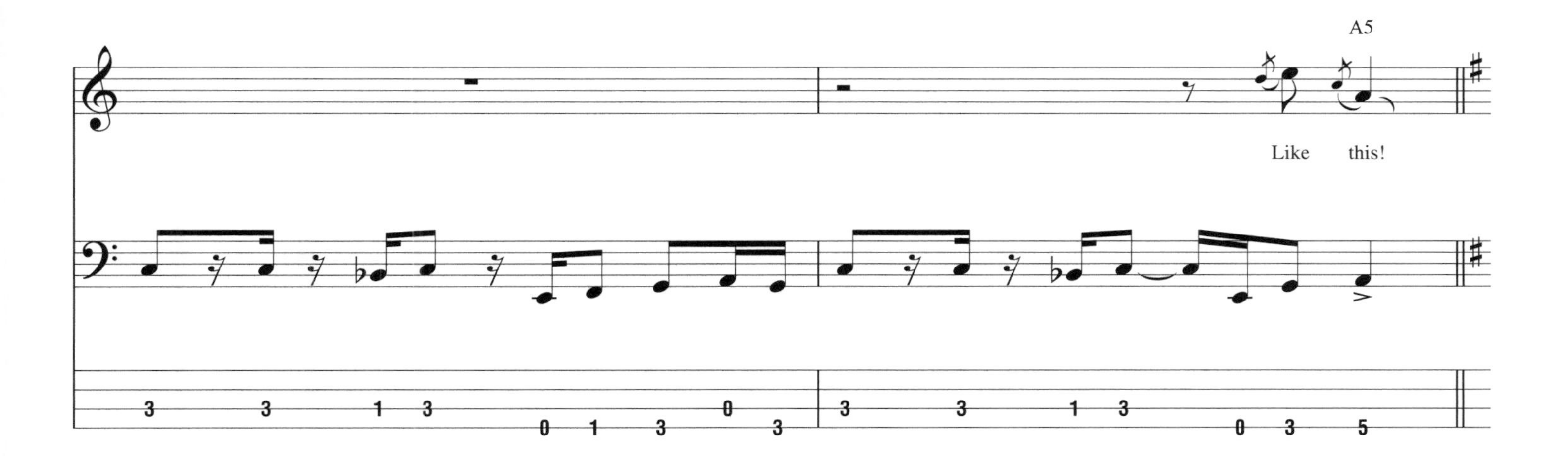
A5
Like this!

Play 12 times and fade

N.C.

Walking on the Moon

Music and Lyrics by Sting

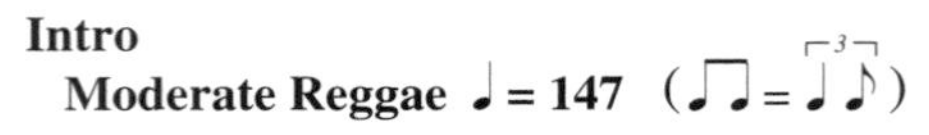

Intro
Moderate Reggae ♩ = 147

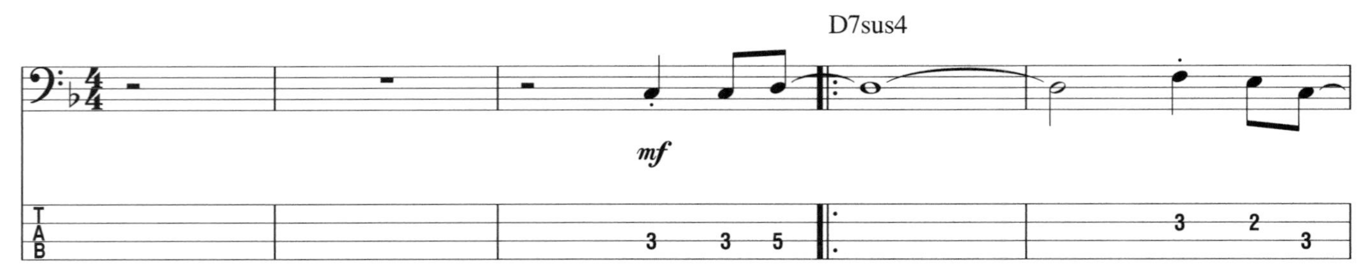

D7sus4
mf

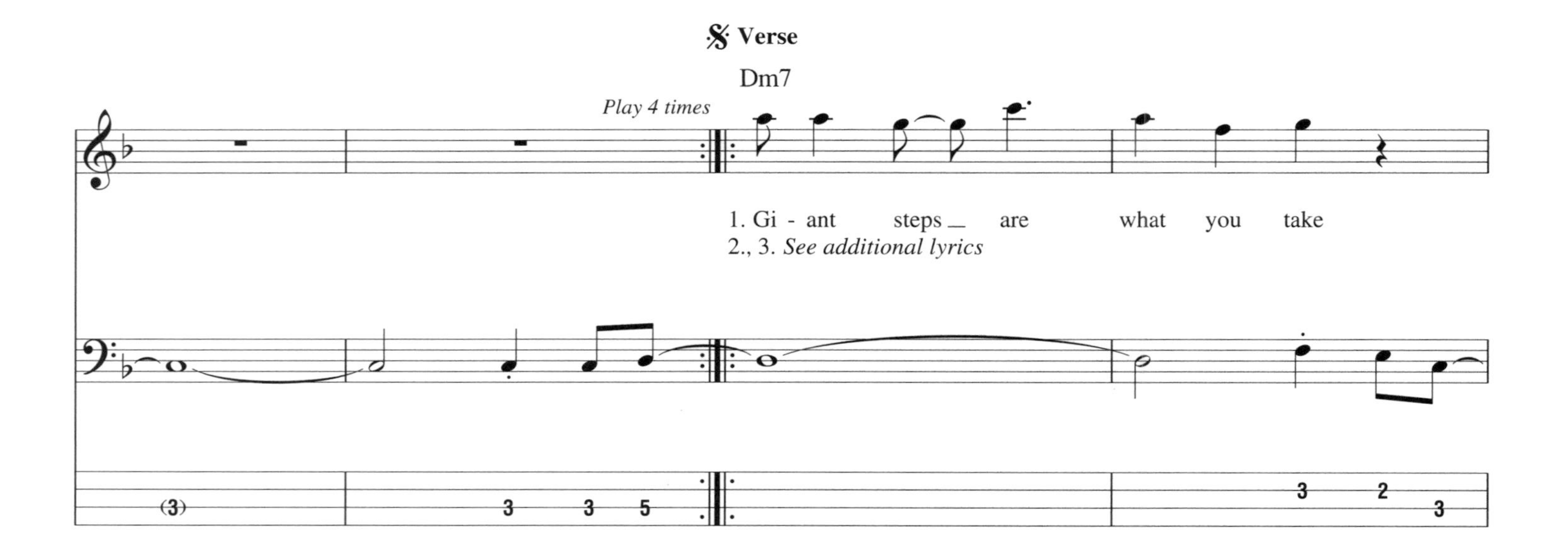

Verse
Dm7
Play 4 times
1. Gi - ant steps are what you take
2., 3. See additional lyrics

B♭/C
C
Dm7
walk - ing on the moon.
I hope my leg don't break

B♭/C
C
Dm7
3
walk - ing on the moon.
We could walk for - ev - er

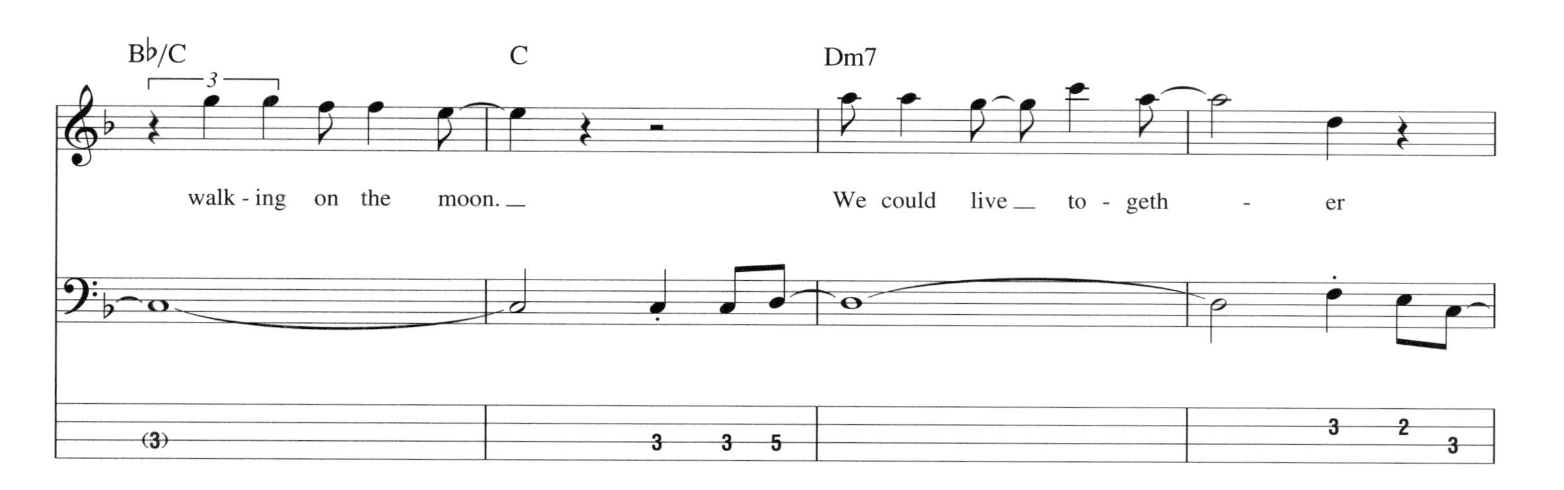
B♭/C
C
Dm7
3
walk - ing on the moon.
We could live to - geth - er

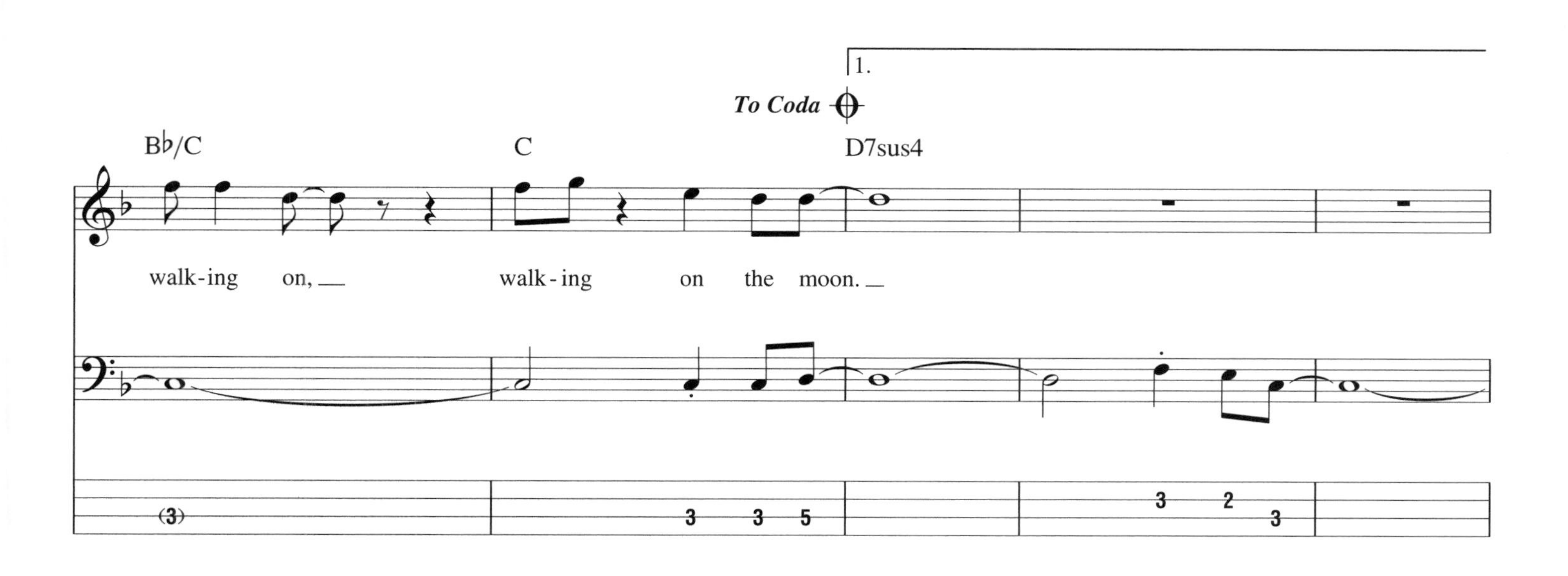
1.
To Coda
B♭/C
C
D7sus4
walk - ing on,
walk - ing on the moon.

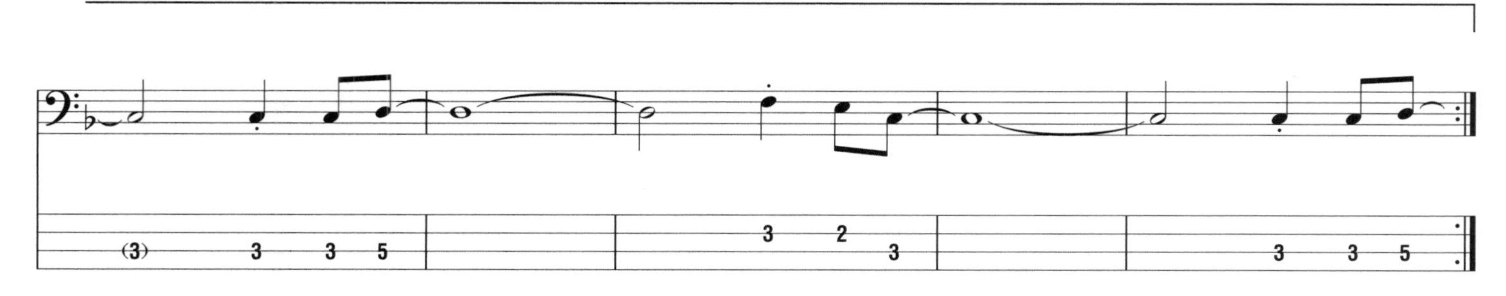

2.
Chorus
Dm7
B♭
F
Some may say
C
Gm
B♭
F
I'm wish-ing my days a - way; no way.
C
Gm
B♭
F
And, if it's a price I pay, some say,
C
Gm
B♭
F
"To-mor-row's an - oth - er day; you'll stay." I

Interlude
C
D7sus4
may as well play.
D.S. al Coda
Coda
Dm7
Chorus
B♭
F
C
Gm
Some may say I'm wish-ing my days a - way;
no way. And, if it's a price I pay,

Bb
F
C
Gm
some say, "To-mor-row's an - oth - er day;
Bb
F
C
you'll stay." I may as well play.
Interlude
D7sus4
Outro
Dm7
Bb/C
C
Repeat and fade
Keep it up. Keep it up.

Additional Lyrics

2. Walking back from your house,
   Walking on the moon.
   Walking back from your house,
   Walking on the moon.
   Feet, they hardly touch the ground,
   Walking on the moon.
   My feet don't hardly make no sound,
   Walking on, walking on the moon.

3. Giant steps are what you take
   Walking on the moon.
   I hope my leg don't break
   Walking on the moon.
   We could walk forever
   Walking on the moon.
   We could live together
   Walking on, walking on the moon.

We Gotta Get Out of This Place

Words and Music by Barry Mann and Cynthia Weil

Intro
Moderately ♩ = 121
C7
Bass Fig. 1
End Bass Fig. 1
Bass
f
T
A
B
3 5 3 3 2 5 3 3 5 3 3 2 5 3

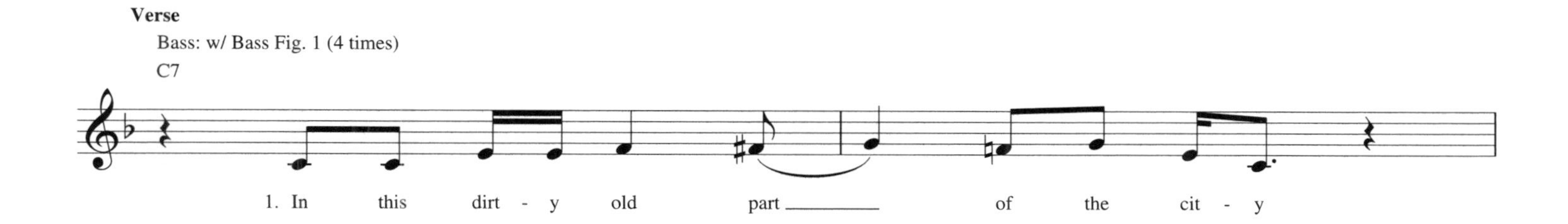
Verse
Bass: w/ Bass Fig. 1 (4 times)
C7
1. In this dirt - y old part of the cit - y

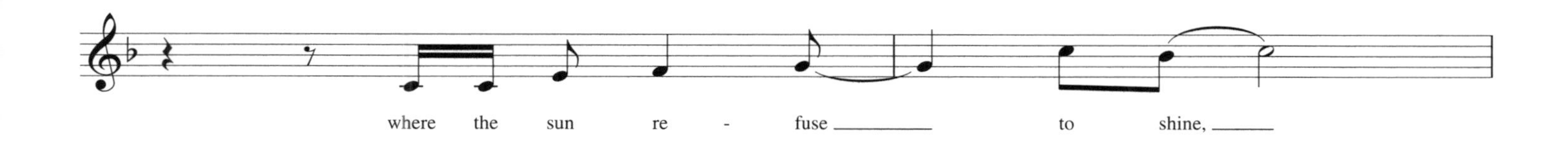
where the sun re - fuse to shine,

peo - ple tell me there ain't no use in try -

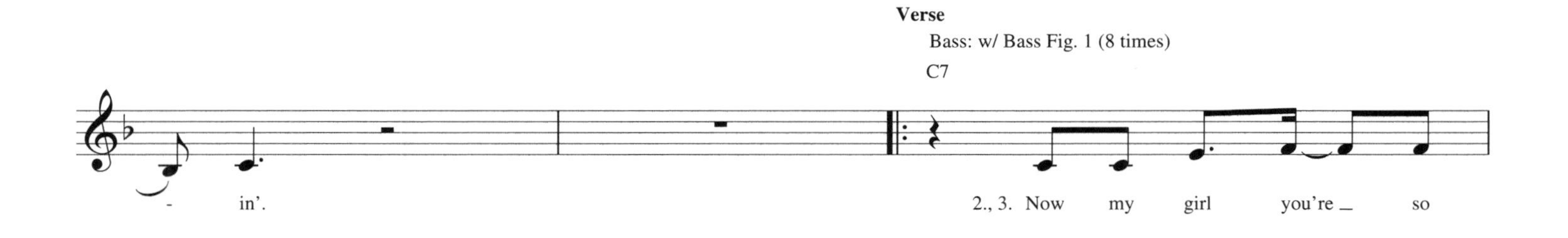
Verse
Bass: w/ Bass Fig. 1 (8 times)
C7
- in'.
2., 3. Now my girl you're so

young and pret - ty and one thing I know is true,

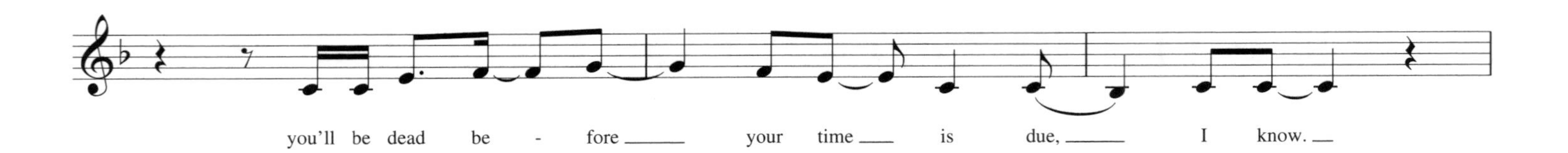
you'll be dead be - fore your time is due, I know.

Watch my dad - dy in bed a - dy - in',

watch his hair been turn - in' gray, yeah. He's been work - in' and slav -

- in' his life a - way,
oh yes, I know it.
I know he's been work - in' so hard.

Pre-Chorus

Bass: w/ Bass Fig. 1 (3 1/2 times)

C7
He's been work - in' so hard.
I've been work - in' too, babe.
Yeah.
Yeah.

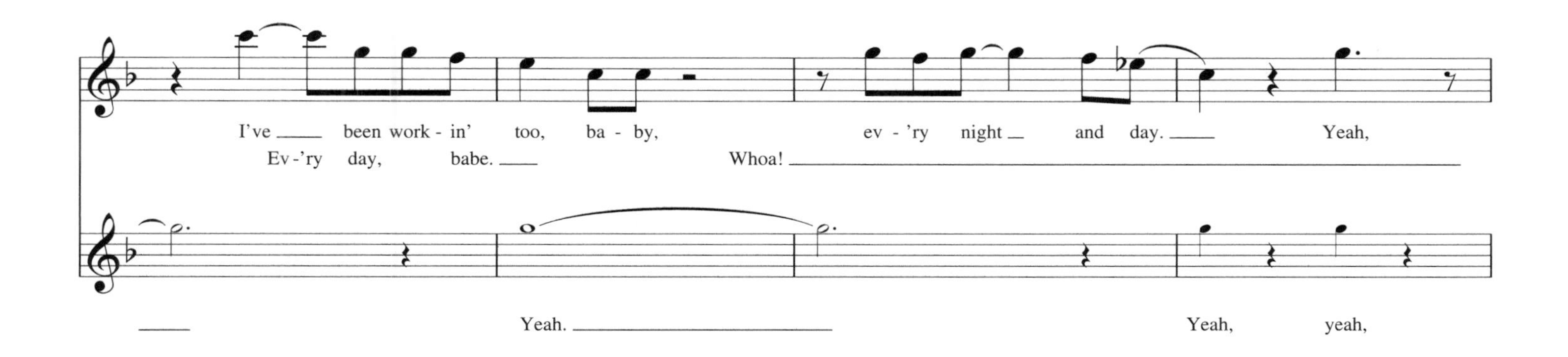
I've been work - in' too, ba - by, ev - 'ry night and day. Yeah,
Ev-'ry day, babe. Whoa!
Yeah. Yeah, yeah,

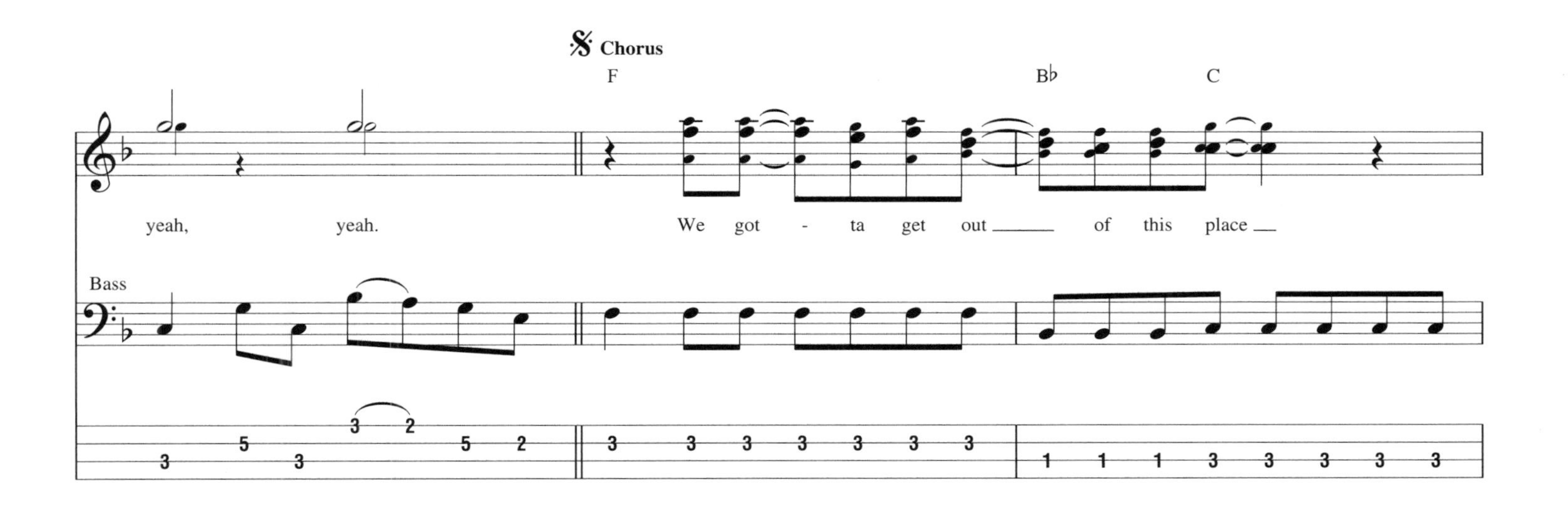
Chorus
F
B♭
C
yeah, yeah. We got - ta get out of this place
Bass

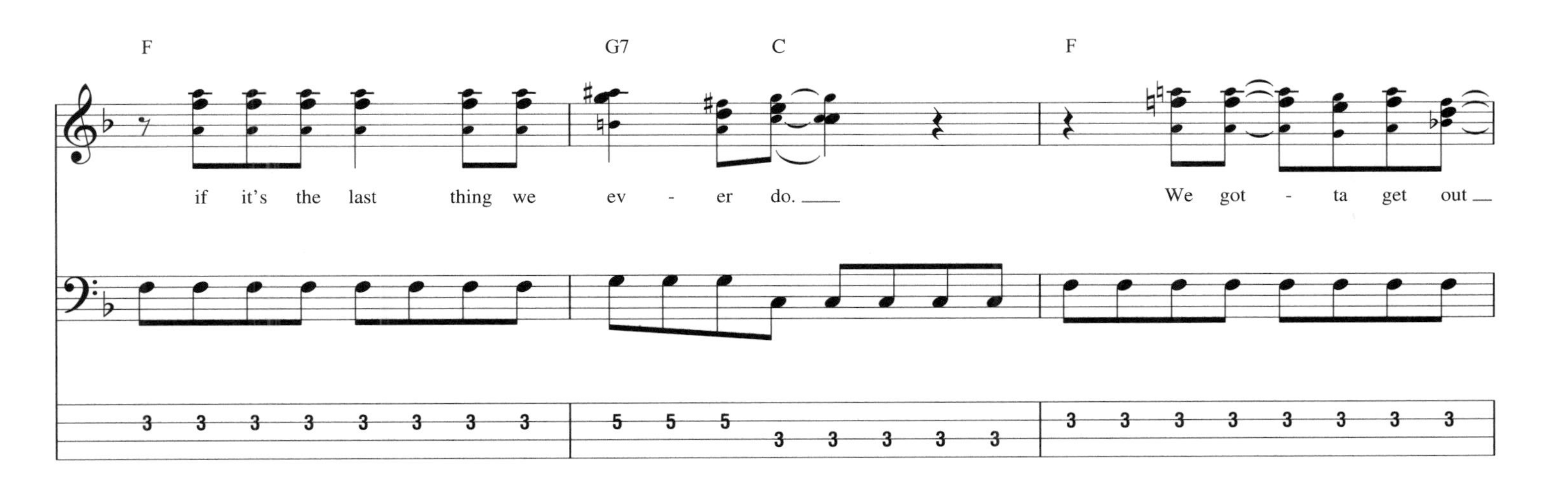
F
G7
C
F
if it's the last thing we ev - er do. We got - ta get out

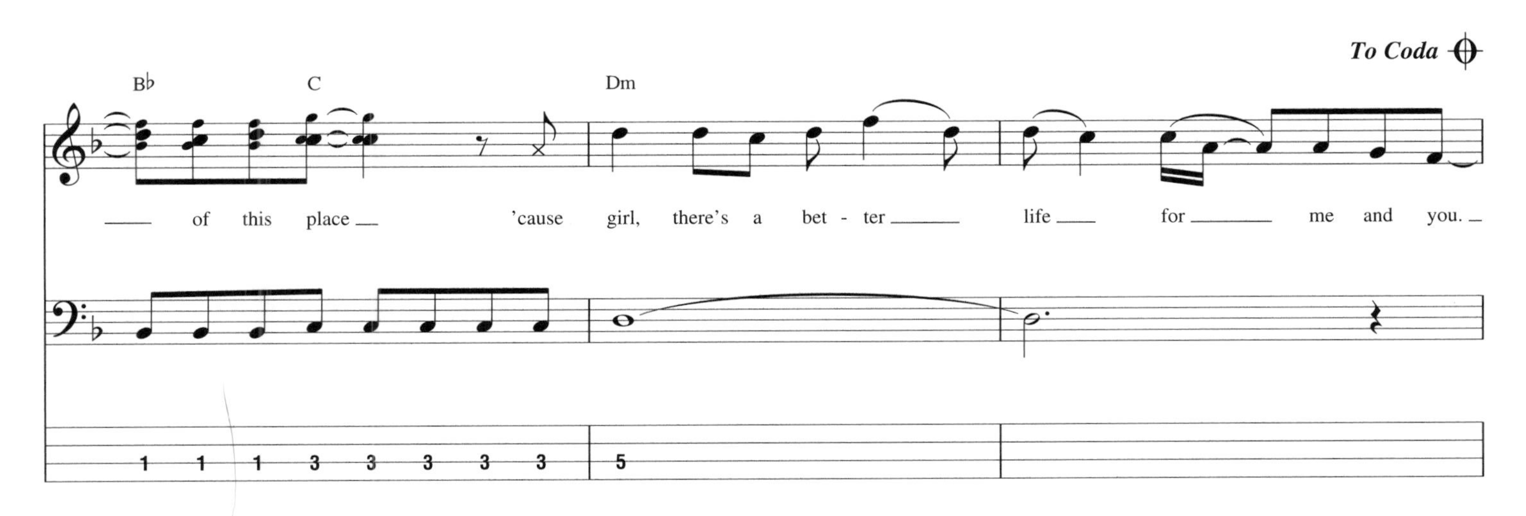
To Coda
B♭
C
Dm
of this place 'cause girl, there's a bet - ter life for me and you.

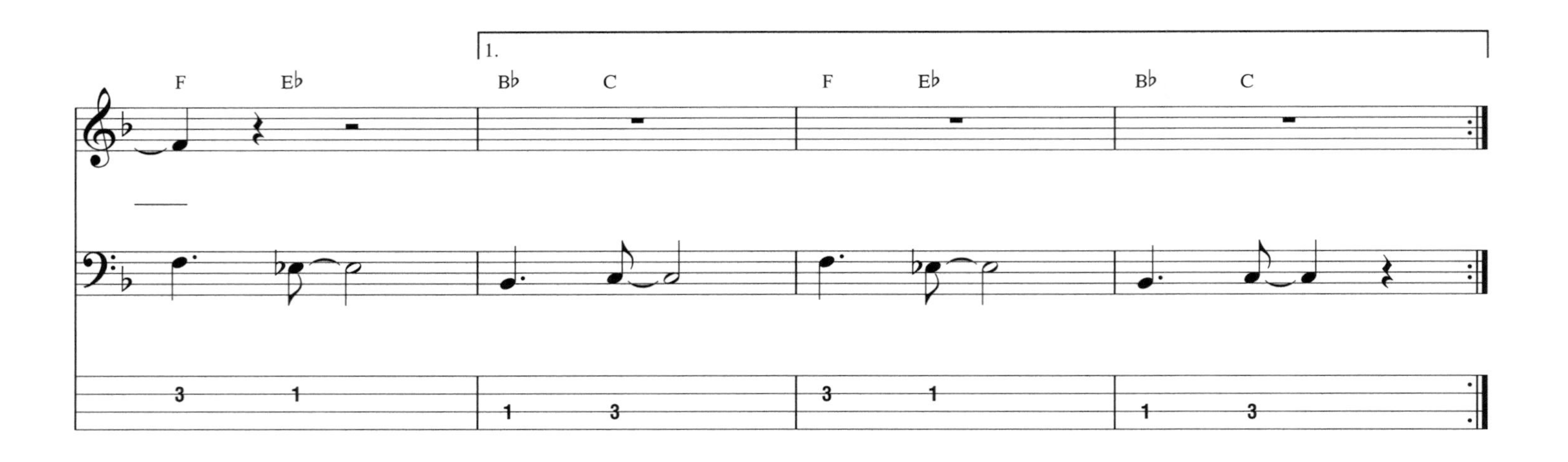
1.
F Eb Bb C F Eb Bb C
3 1 1 3 3 1 1 3

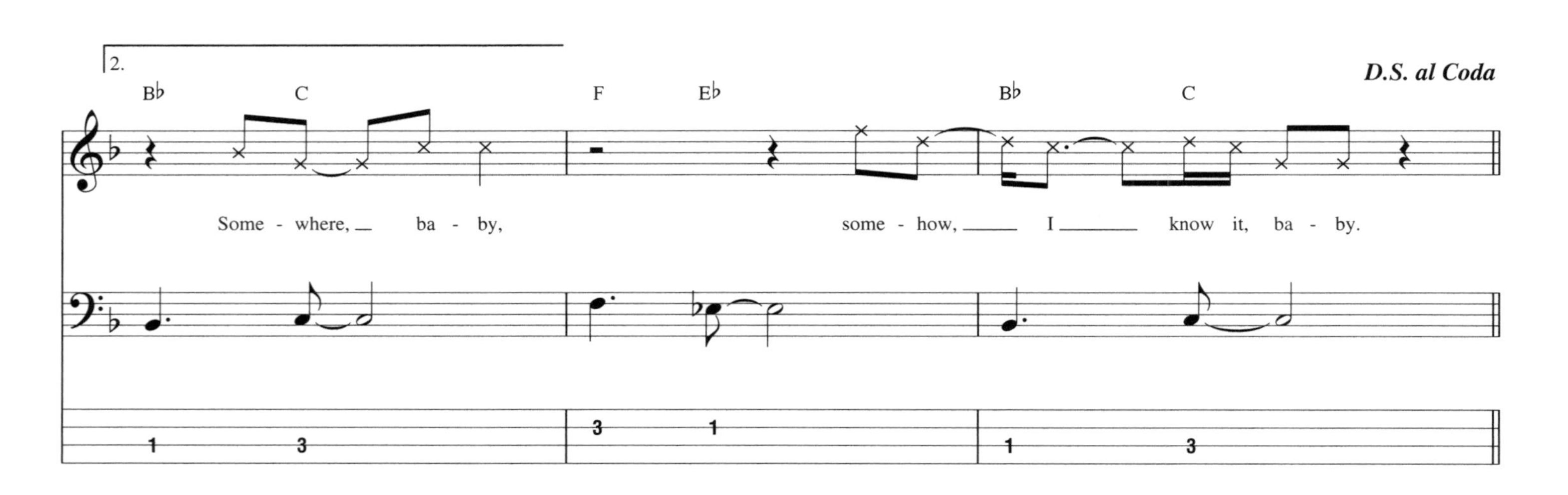
2.
D.S. al Coda
Bb C F Eb Bb C
Some - where, ba - by, some - how, I know it, ba - by.
1 3 3 1 1 3

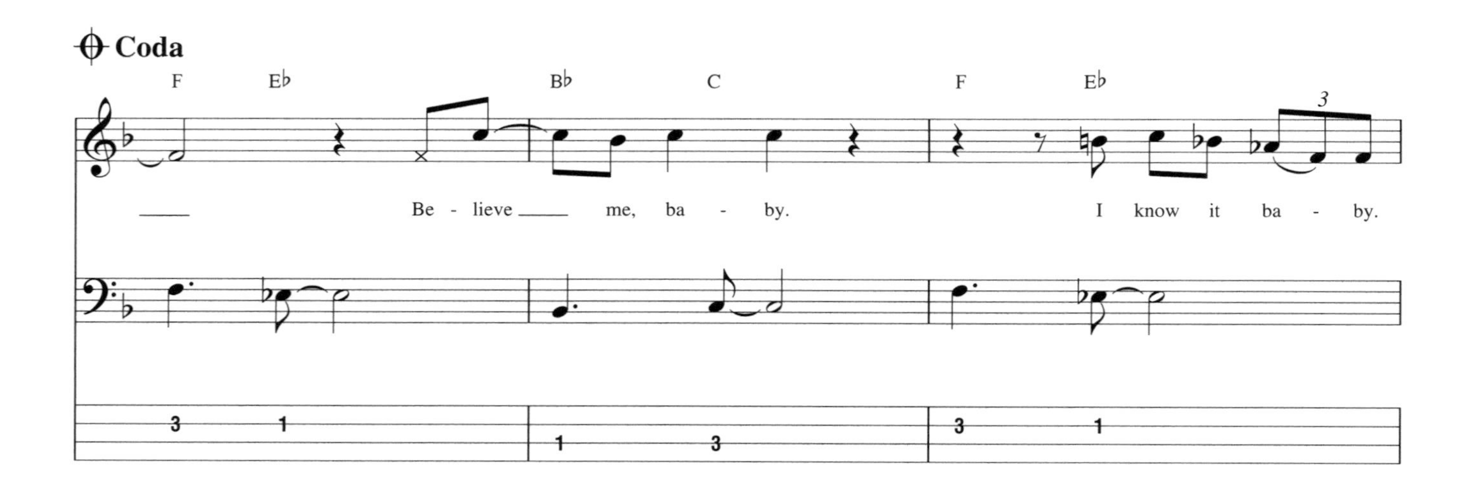
Coda
F Eb Bb C F Eb
Be - lieve me, ba - by. I know it ba - by.
3
3 1 1 3 3 1

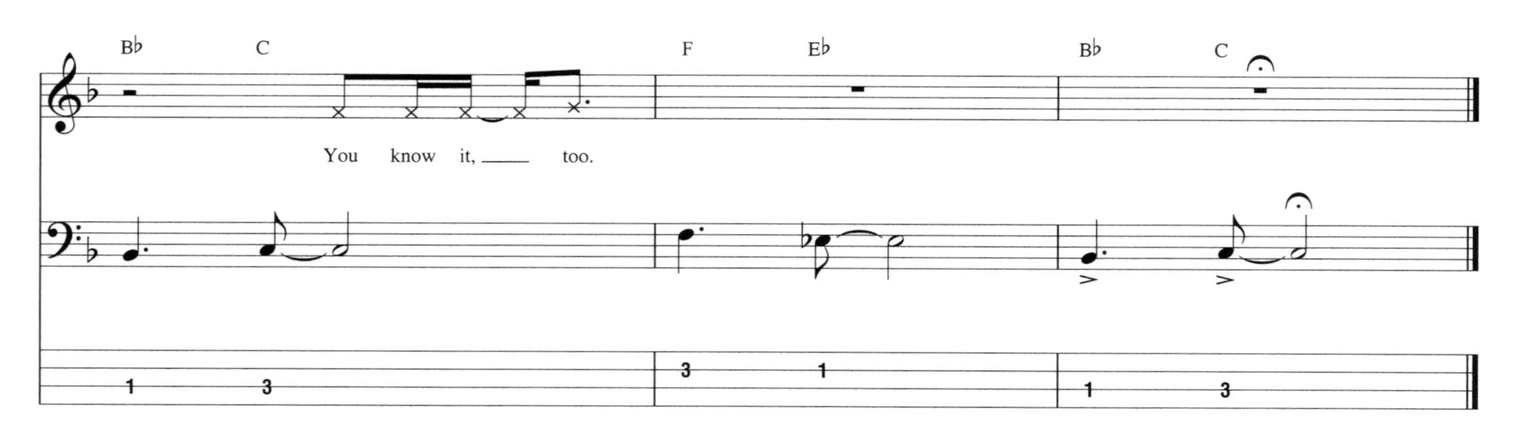
Bb C F Eb Bb C
You know it, too.
1 3 3 1 1 3

We're an American Band

Words and Music by Donald Brewer

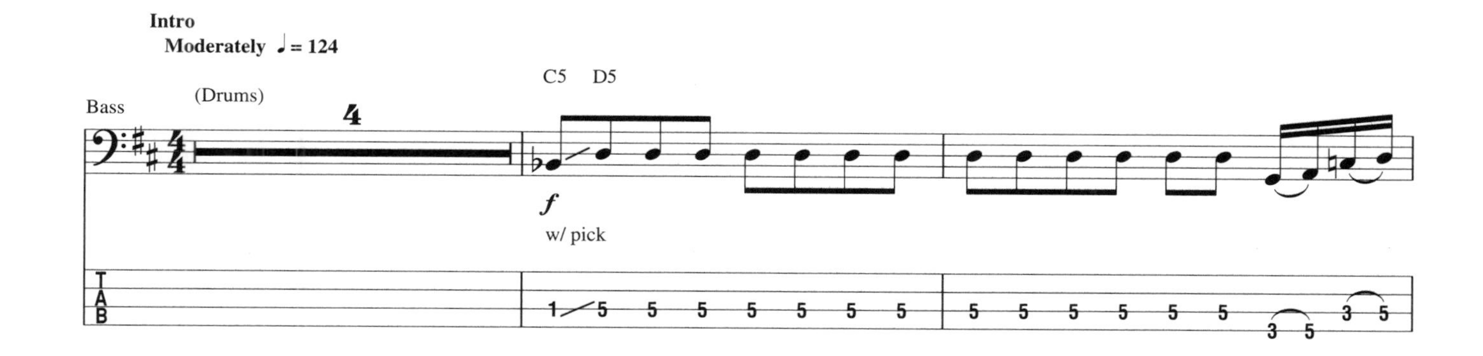
Intro
Moderately ♩ = 124
Bass
(Drums)
4
C5 D5
f
w/ pick
T
A
B

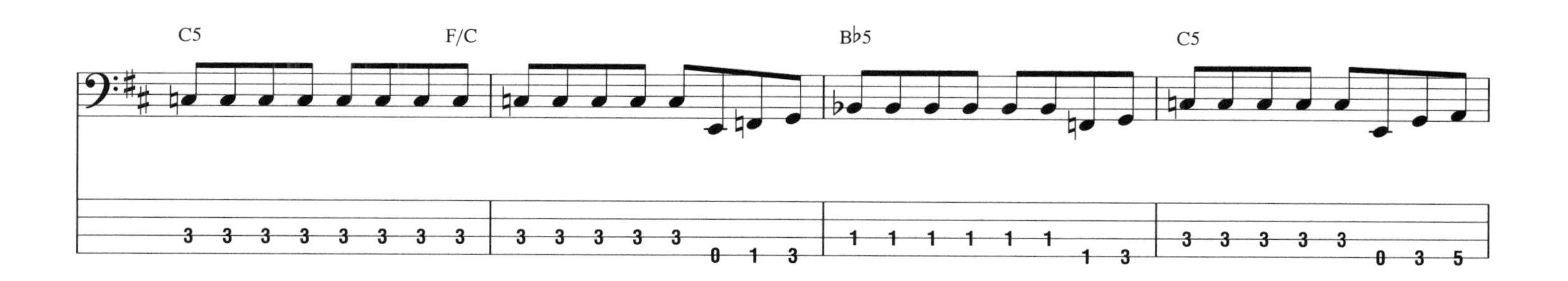
C5
F/C
B♭5
C5

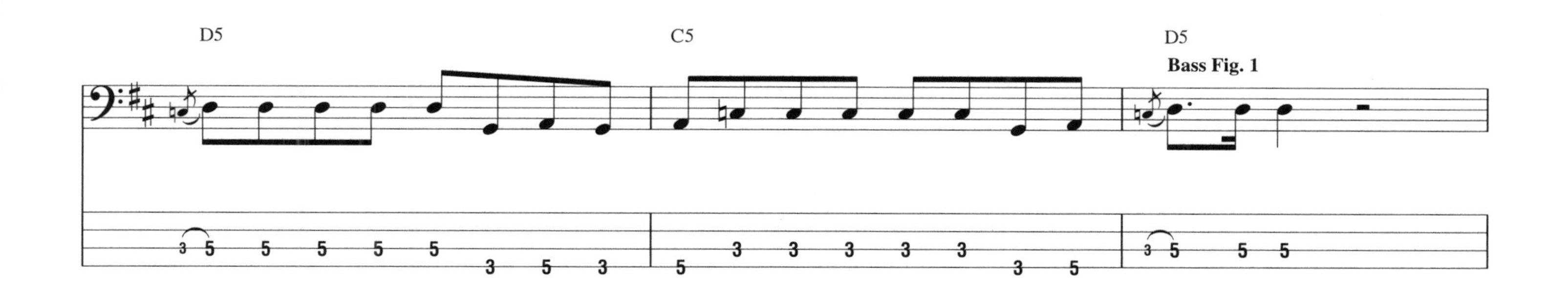
D5
C5
D5
Bass Fig. 1

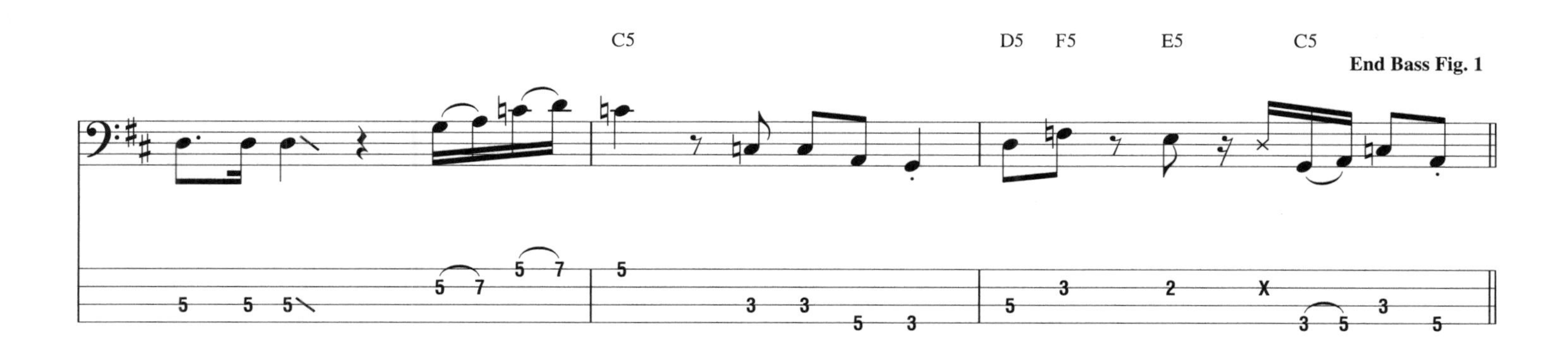
C5
D5 F5
E5
C5
End Bass Fig. 1

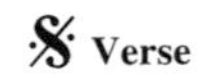

Verse

Bass: w/ Bass Fig. 1 (1 1/2 times)

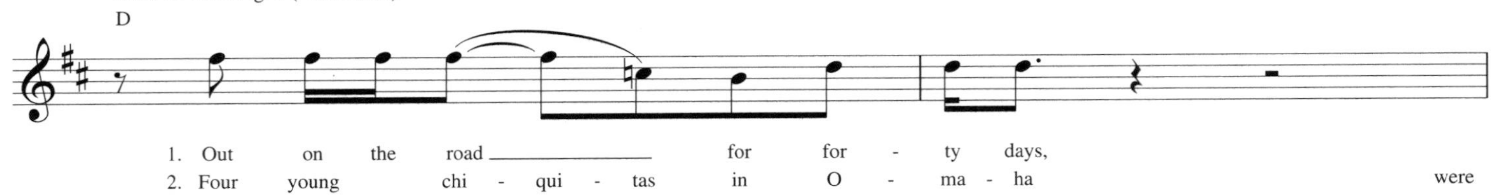
D
1. Out on the road ___ for for - ty days,
2. Four young chi - qui - tas in O - ma - ha were

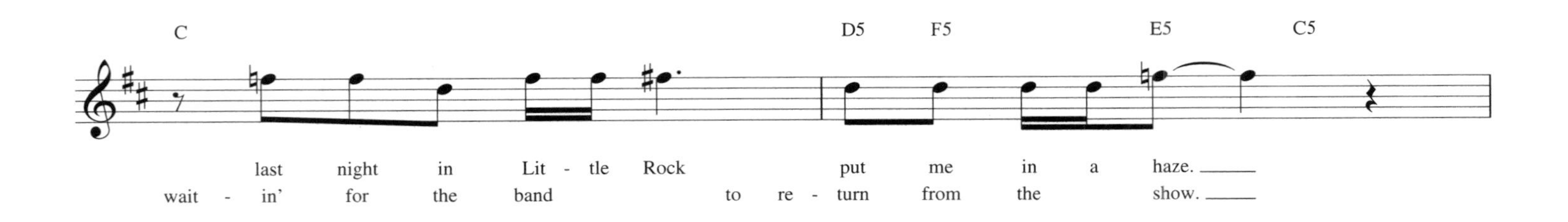
C D5 F5 E5 C5
last night in Lit - tle Rock put me in a haze. ___
wait - in' for the band to re - turn from the show. ___

D
Sweet, ___ sweet Con - nie was do - in' her act; she
Feel - in' good, feel - in' right, it's Sat - ur - day night. The

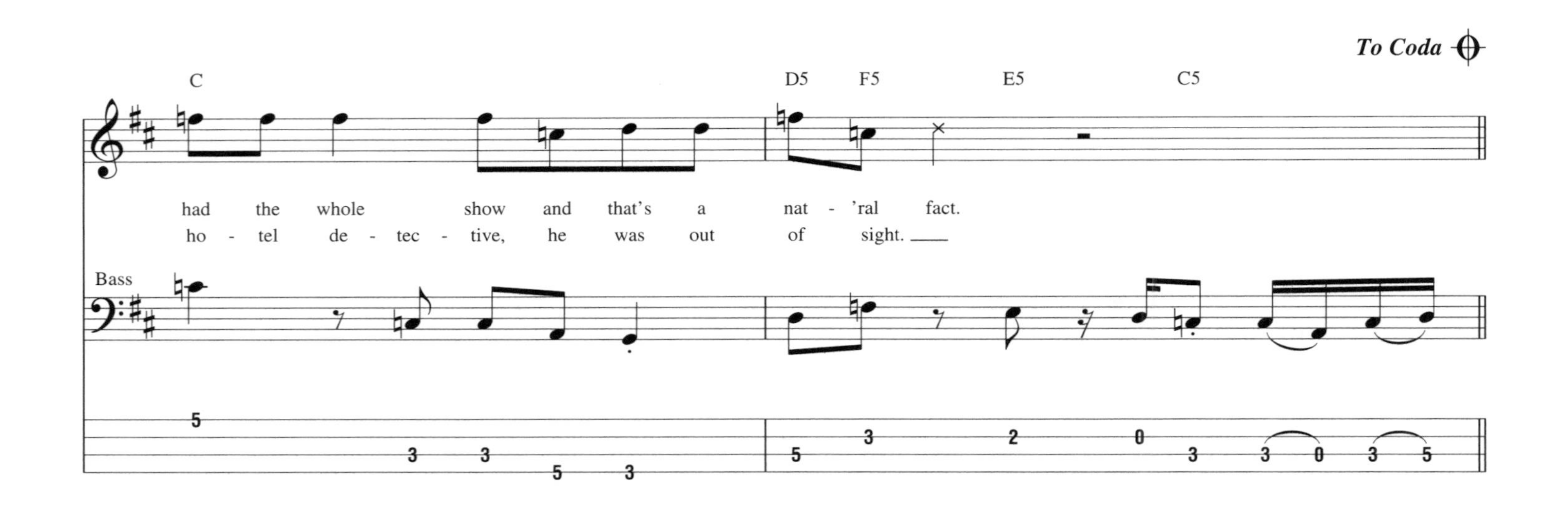
To Coda
C D5 F5 E5 C5
had the whole show and that's a nat - 'ral fact.
ho - tel de - tec - tive, he was out of sight. ___
Bass

Pre-Chorus

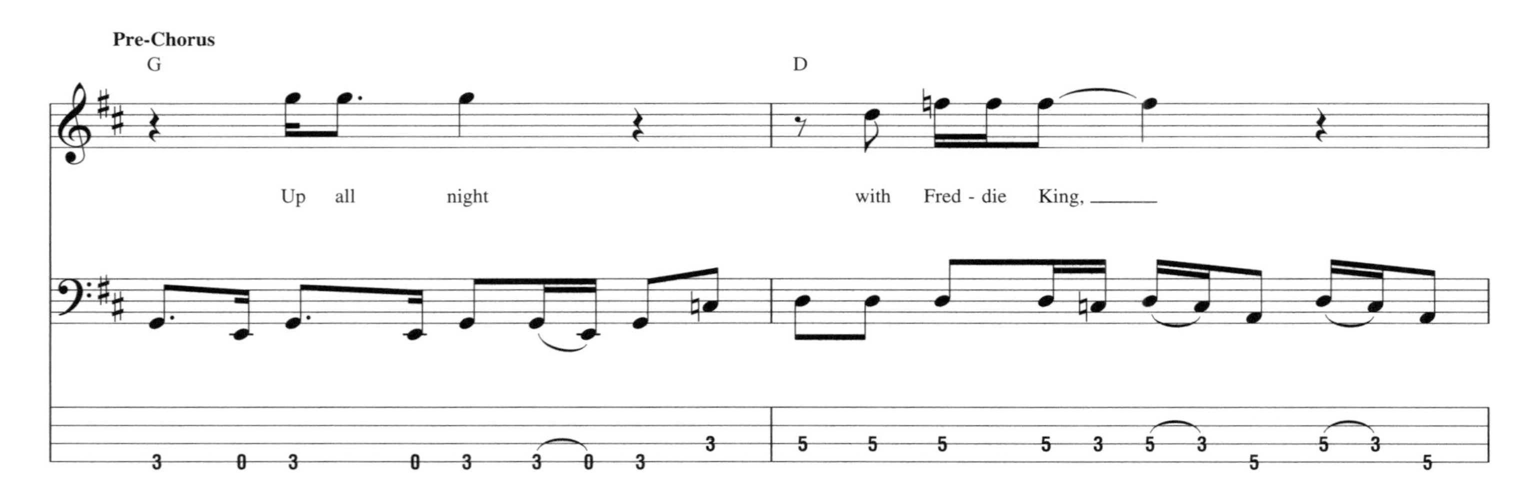
G D
Up all night with Fred - die King, ___

C
D
I got to tell you, po - ker's his thing.
G
D
Uh, booze and la - dies keep me right as
To Coda
F
G
long as we can make it to the show to - night. We're an A -
Chorus
D5
C
F/C
mer - i - can band.
We're an A - mer - i - can band.
Bass Fig. 2

B♭5
We're com - in' to your town, we'll help you
3 3 3 1 3 3 1 3 1
1 1 1 1 1 1 3 1

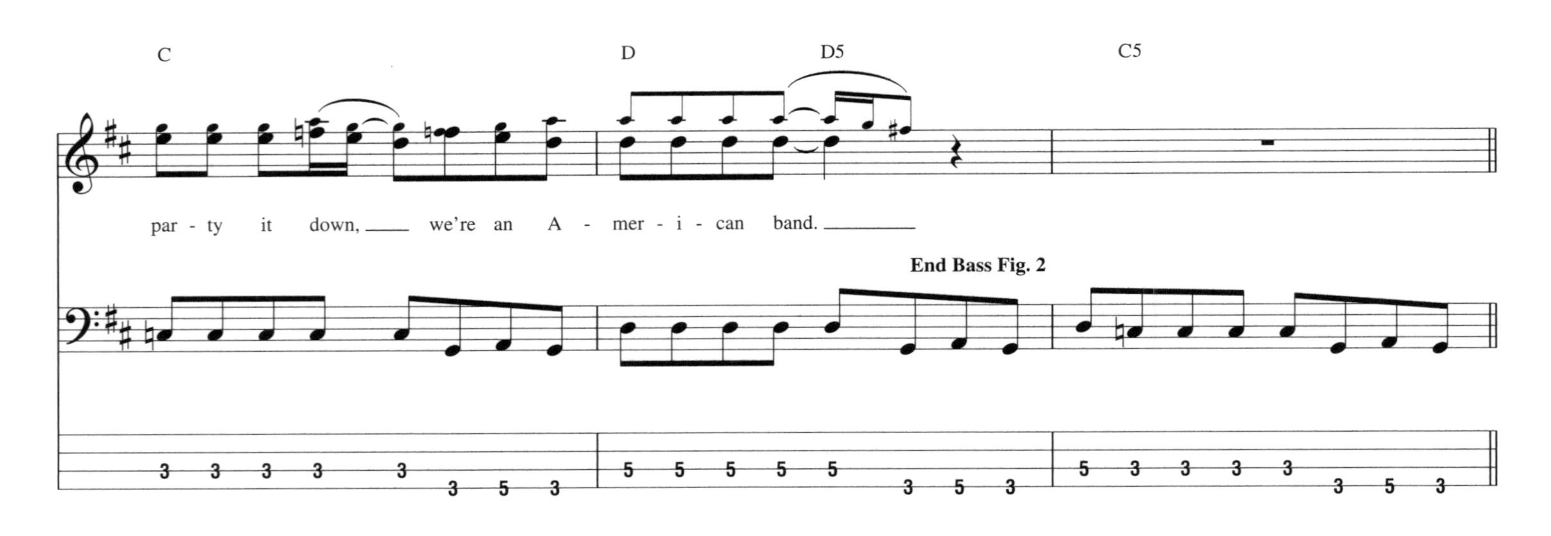
C
D
D5
C5
par - ty it down, we're an A - mer - i - can band.
End Bass Fig. 2
3 3 3 3 3 3 5 3
5 5 5 5 5 3 5 3
5 3 3 3 3 3 5 3

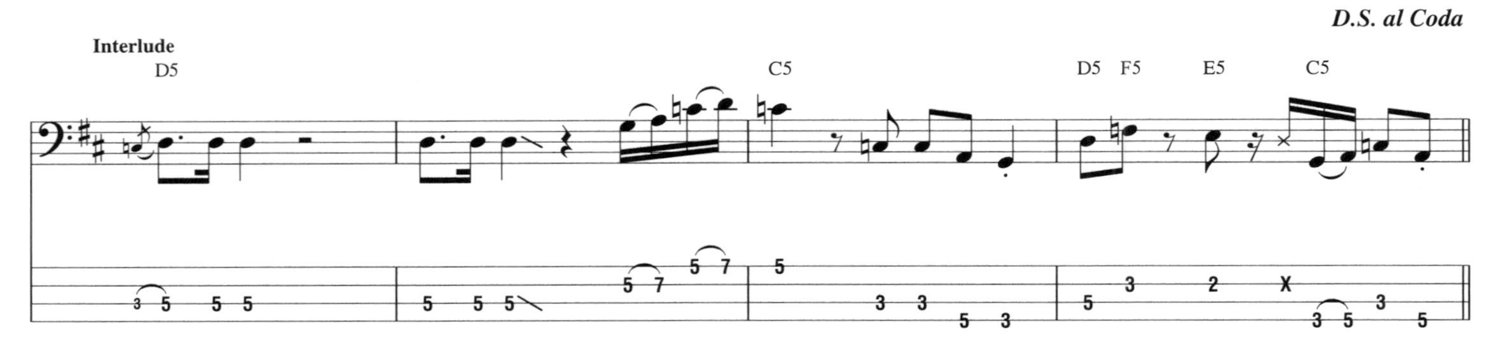
D.S. al Coda
Interlude
D5
C5
D5 F5 E5 C5

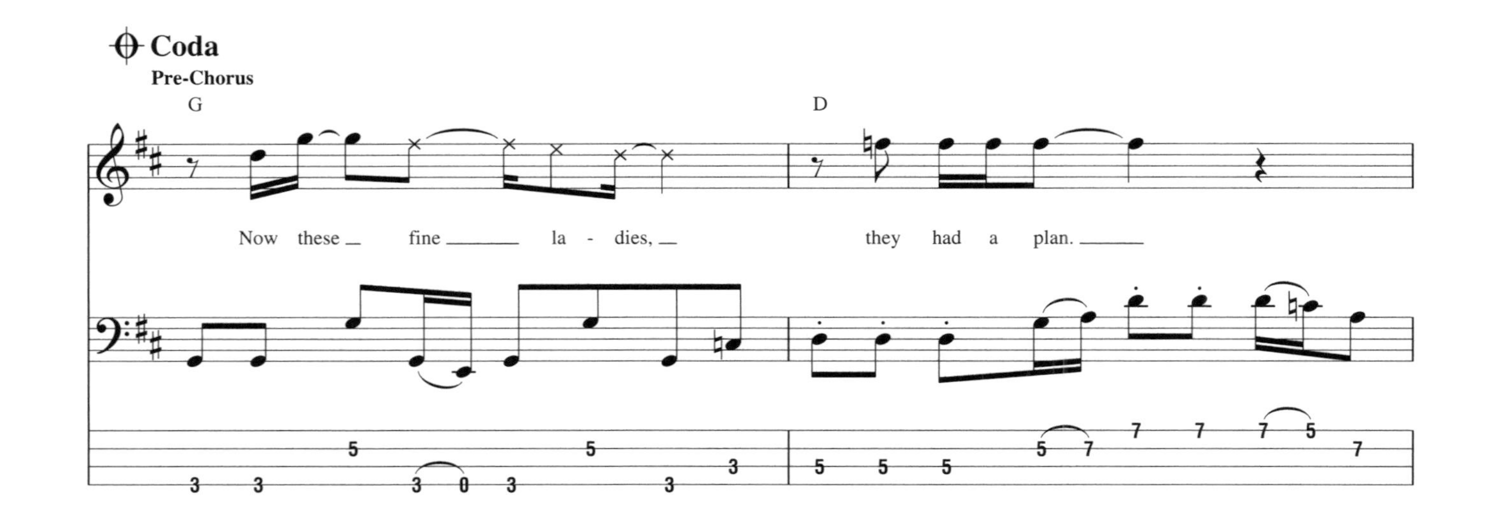
Coda
Pre-Chorus
G
D
Now these fine la - dies, they had a plan.

C
D
They was out to meet the boys in the band. They said,
G
D
"Come on, dudes, let's get it on," and we pro-
F
G
ceed-ed to tear that ho-tel down. We're an A-
Chorus
Bass: w/ Bass Fig. 2
D5
C
F/C
mer-i-can band. We're an A-mer-i-can band.
B♭5
C
We're com-in' to your town, we'll help you par-ty it down, we're an A-

1.
2.
Bass: w/ Bass Fill 1
D
D5
C5
Bass: w/ Bass Fill 1
D
D5
C5
mer - i - can band.
Hey! We're an A -
mer - i - can band. Hey, hey, hey, go!

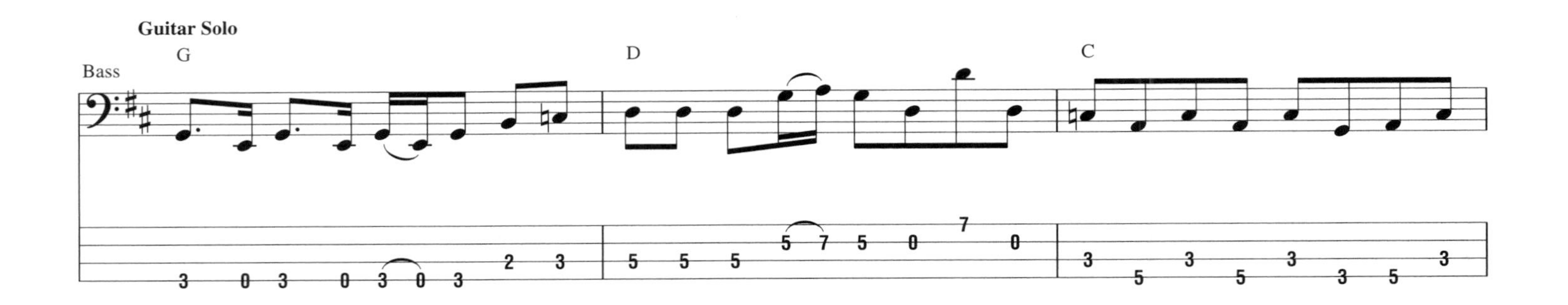
Guitar Solo
Bass
G
D
C

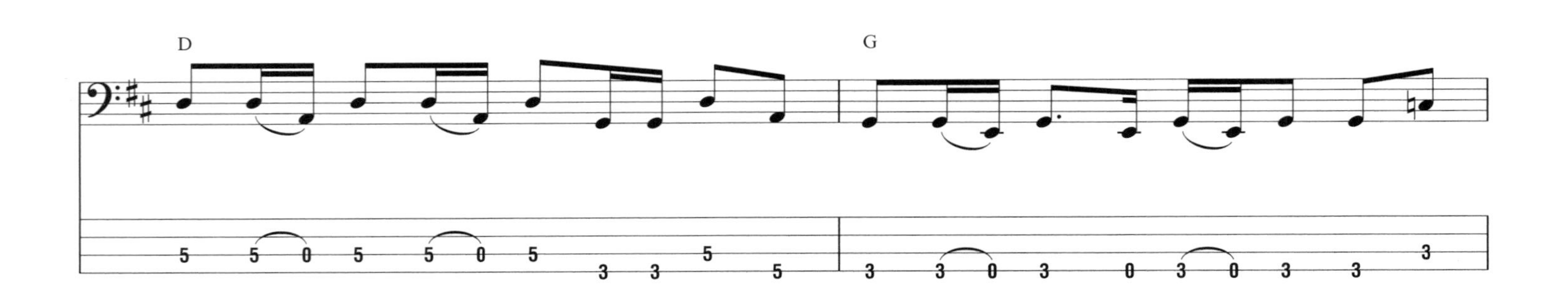
D
G

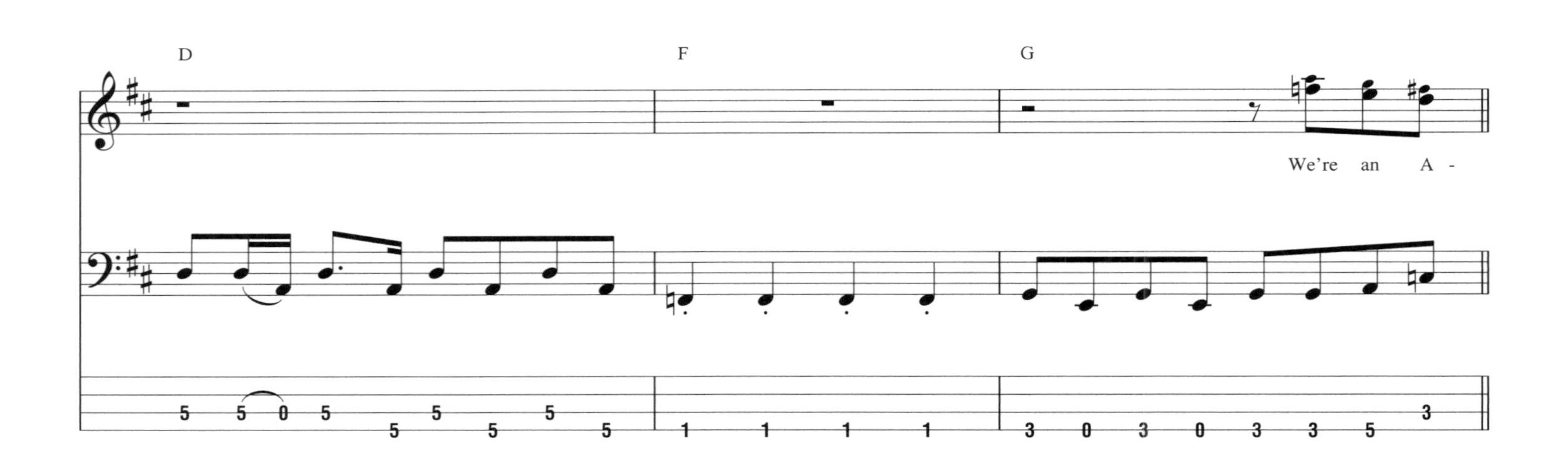
D
F
G
We're an A -

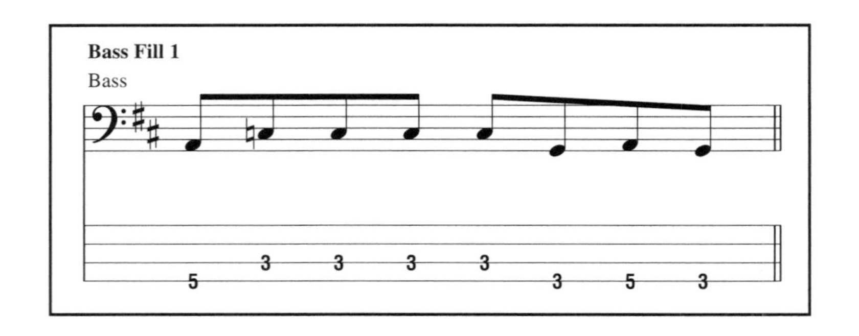
Bass Fill 1
Bass

Outro-Chorus
Bass: w/ Bass Fig. 2
D5
C
F/C
mer - i - can band.
We're an A - mer - i - can band.
We're com - in'
B♭5
C
1.
D
D5
to your town, we'll help you par - ty it down, we're an A - mer - i - can band. Hey, hey,
Bass: w/ Bass Fill 1
C5
2.
D
D5
Bass: w/ Bass Fill 1
C5
hey, hey. We're an A - mer - i - can band.
We're an A -
D
C
D
mer - i - can band, woo. We're an A - mer - i - can band, woo.
Bass
C
D
C
We're an A - mer - i - can band, woo.
D

Wishing Well

Words and Music by Paul Rodgers, Simon Kirke, Tetsu Yamauchi, Paul Kossoff and John Bundrick

Intro
Moderately ♩ = 120
N.C.(E5)
(A5)
(B5)
(E5)
(A5)
Mm.
Bass Fig. 1
Bass
f
1
7 5 7 5
7 5 3 0
5 5 7 5

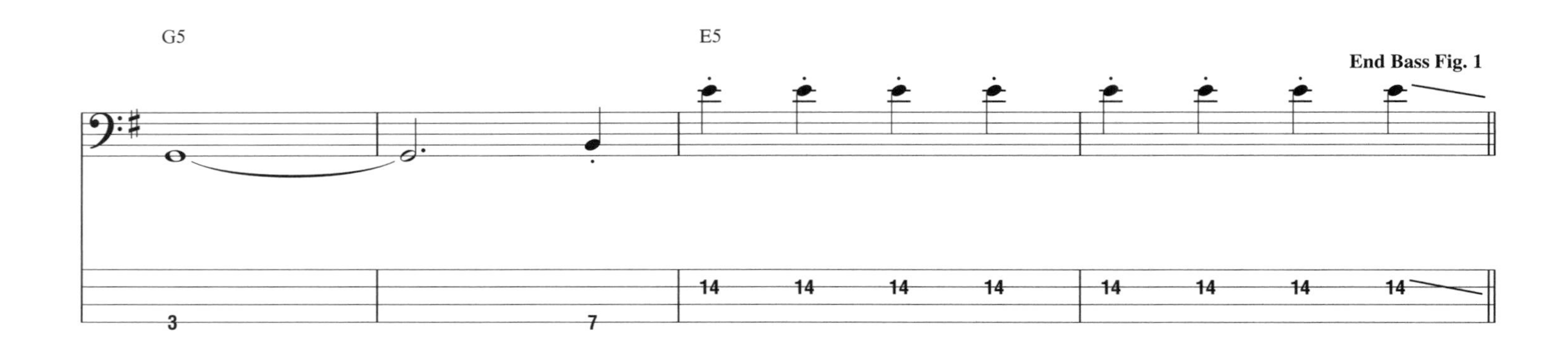
G5
E5
End Bass Fig. 1
3
7
14 14 14 14
14 14 14 14

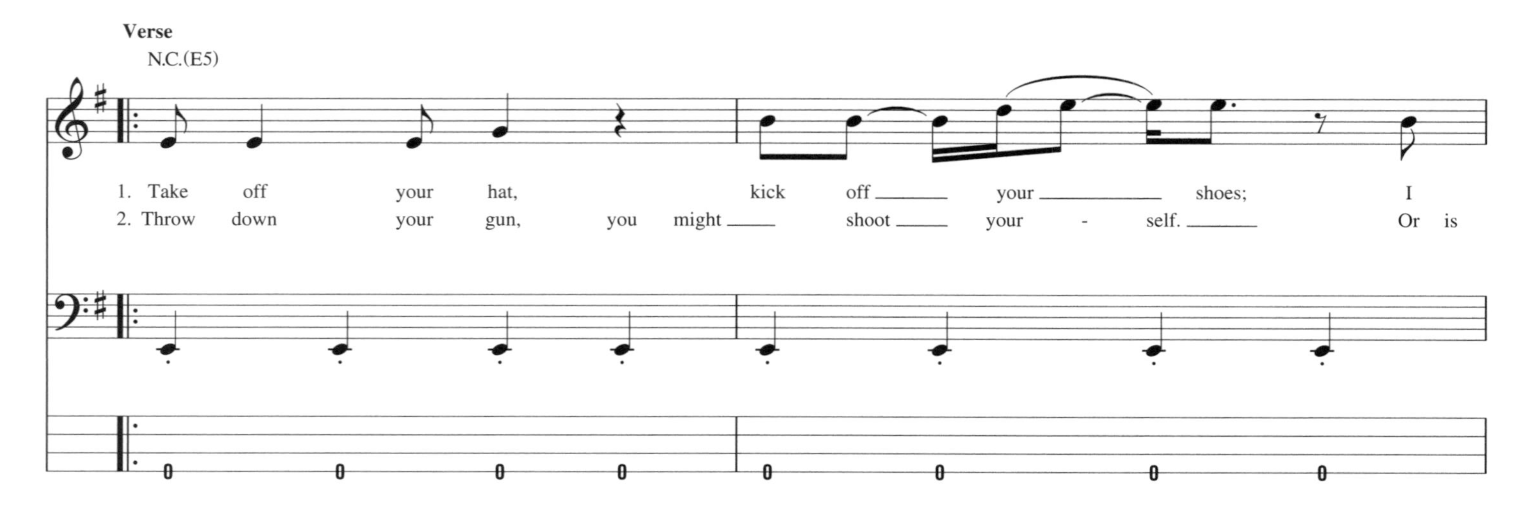
Verse
N.C.(E5)
1. Take off your hat, kick off your shoes; I
2. Throw down your gun, you might shoot your - self. Or is
0 0 0 0
0 0 0 0

C
D
Em
3
know you ain't go - in' an - y - where.
that what you're try - in' to do?
3 2 5 3 5 4 7 5
7 7 7 7

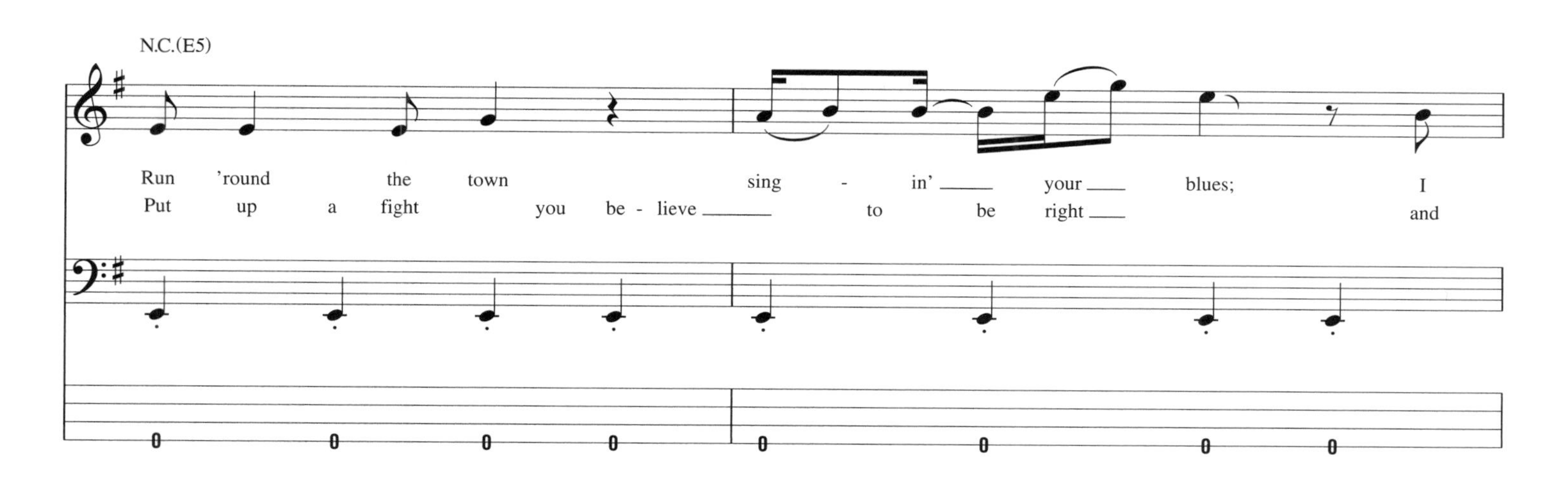
N.C.(E5)
Run 'round the town sing - in' your blues; I
Put up a fight you be - lieve to be right and
0 0 0 0
0 0 0 0

Chorus
2nd time, Bass: w/ Bass Fill 1
C
D
Em
C
D
3
know you ain't go - in' an - y - where.
some - day the sun will shine through
You've al - ways been a
You've al - ways got
3 2 5 3 5 4 7 5
7 7 7 7
3 5 5 5 7 7

Bass Fill 1
7 7 7 7 7

Em
C
D
good friend of mine,
but you're al - ways say - in' fare - well.
some - thing to hide,
some - thing you just can't tell.
2nd time, Bass: w/ Bass Fill 2
Em
C
D
And the on - ly time that you're
Em
C
D
sat - is - fied is with your feet in the wish - ing well.
Interlude
1st time, Bass: w/ Bass Fill 2
2nd time, Bass: w/ Bass Fig. 1 (1st 3 meas.)
N.C.(E5)
(A5)
(B5)
(E5)
(A5)
Oh.
Bass Fill 2

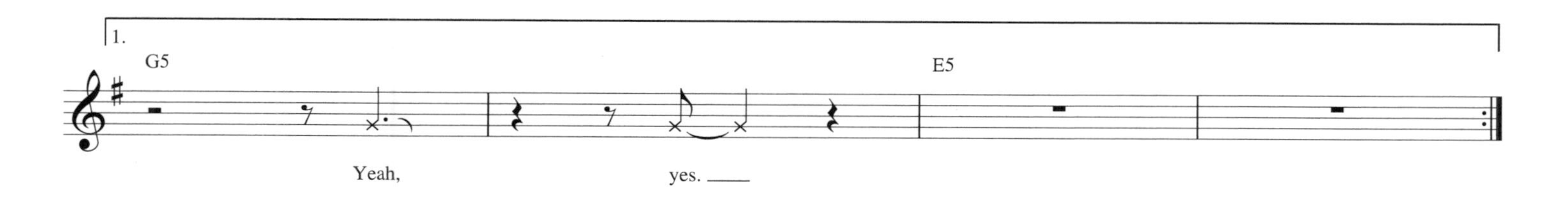
1.
G5
E5
Yeah,
yes.

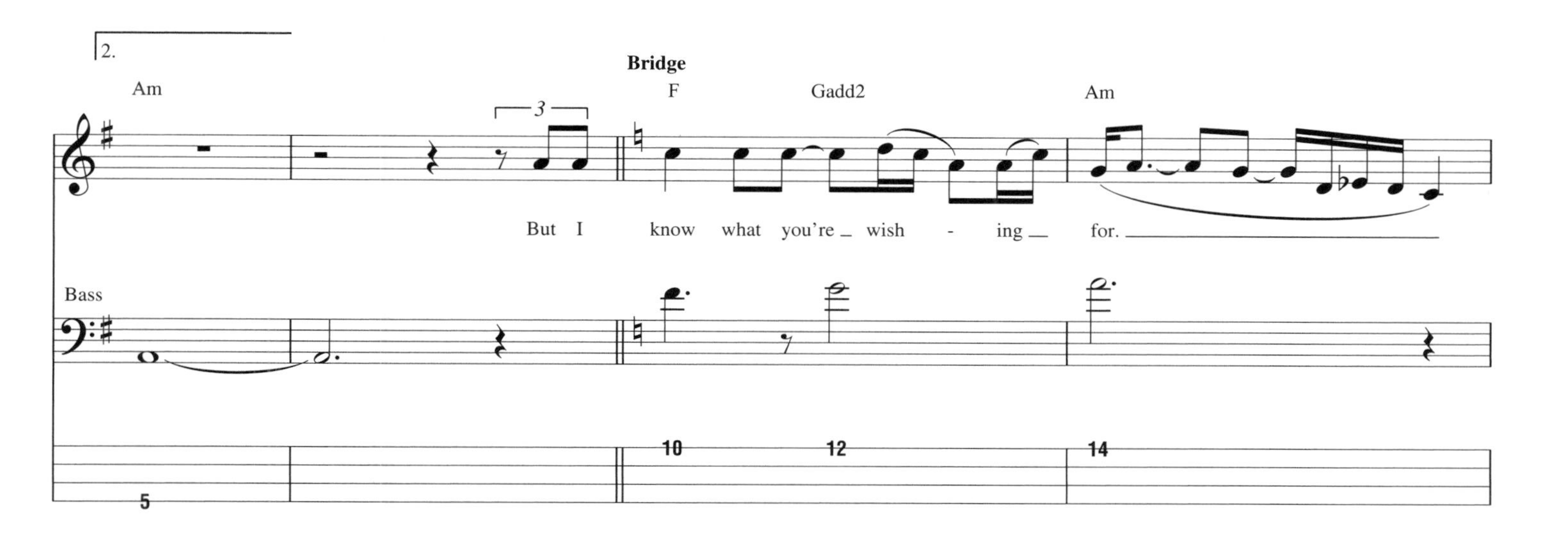
2.
Bridge
Am
F
Gadd2
Am
But I know what you're wish - ing for.
Bass
10
12
14
5

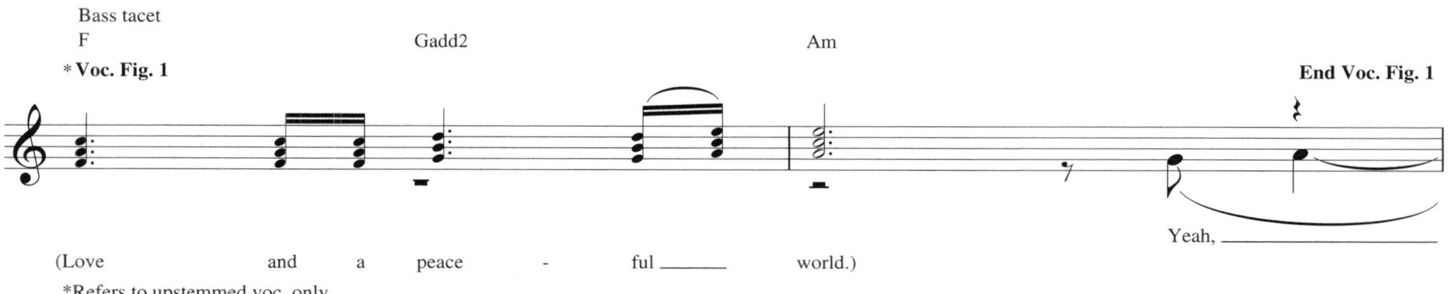
Bass tacet
F
Gadd2
Am
*Voc. Fig. 1
End Voc. Fig. 1
Yeah,
(Love and a peace - ful world.)
*Refers to upstemmed voc. only.

Bkgd. Voc.: w/ Voc. Fig. 1 (2 times)
F
Gadd2
Am
F
Gadd2
Am
oh,
yeah.
Mm,
mm,

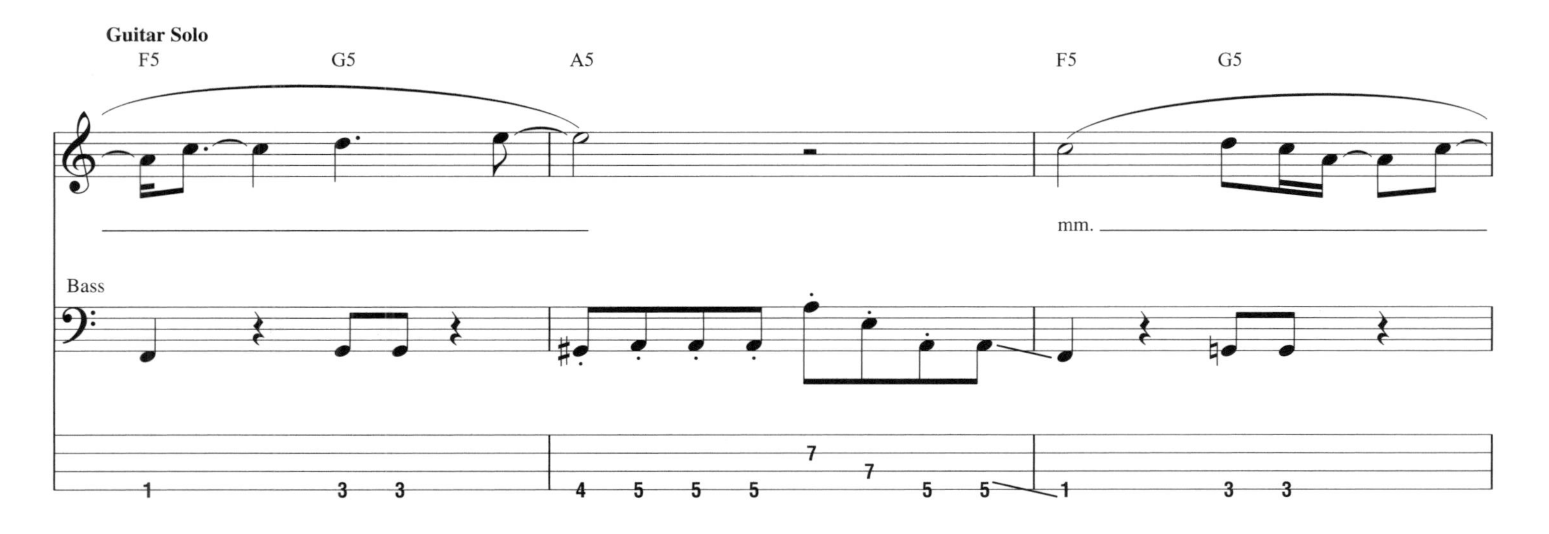
Guitar Solo
F5
G5
A5
F5
G5
mm.
Bass
1 3 3
4 5 5 5 7 7 5 5
1 3 3

A5
F5
G5
A5
3
3
Na, na, na. na, na, na, na, na. Na,

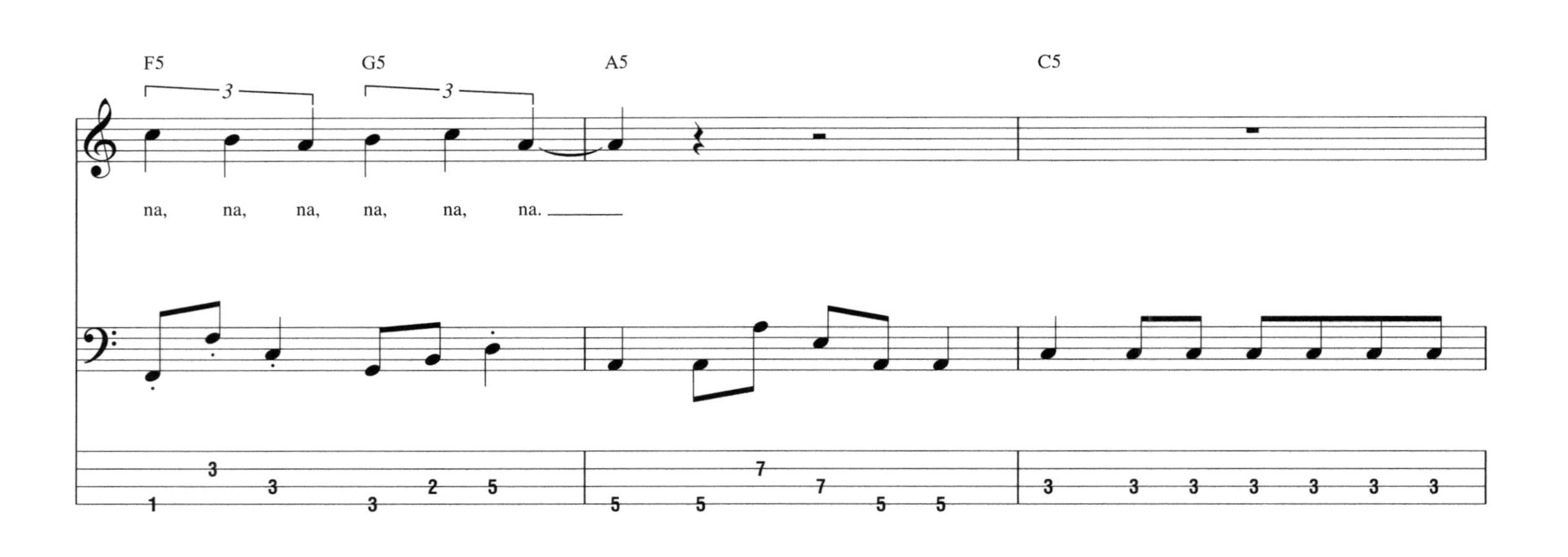
F5
G5
A5
C5
3
3
na, na, na, na, na, na.

D5

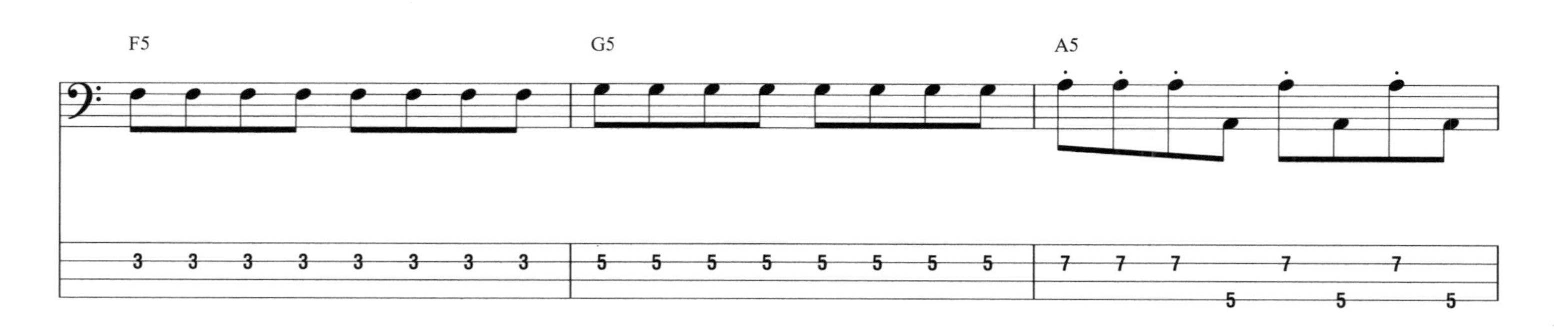
F5
G5
A5

Chorus
F5 G5 A5
You've always been a good friend of mine, but you're
F5 G5 A5
always sayin' farewell And the
F5 G5 A5
only time that you're satisfied is with your
F5 G5
feet in the wishing well.
Outro
N.C.(A5) (D5) (E5) (A5)
Bass Fig. 2
End Bass Fig. 2

Bass: w/ Bass Fig. 2 (2 times)
(D5) (E5) (A5) (D5) (E5) (A5)
Oh, yes, but, uh. Ow! I wish you well.

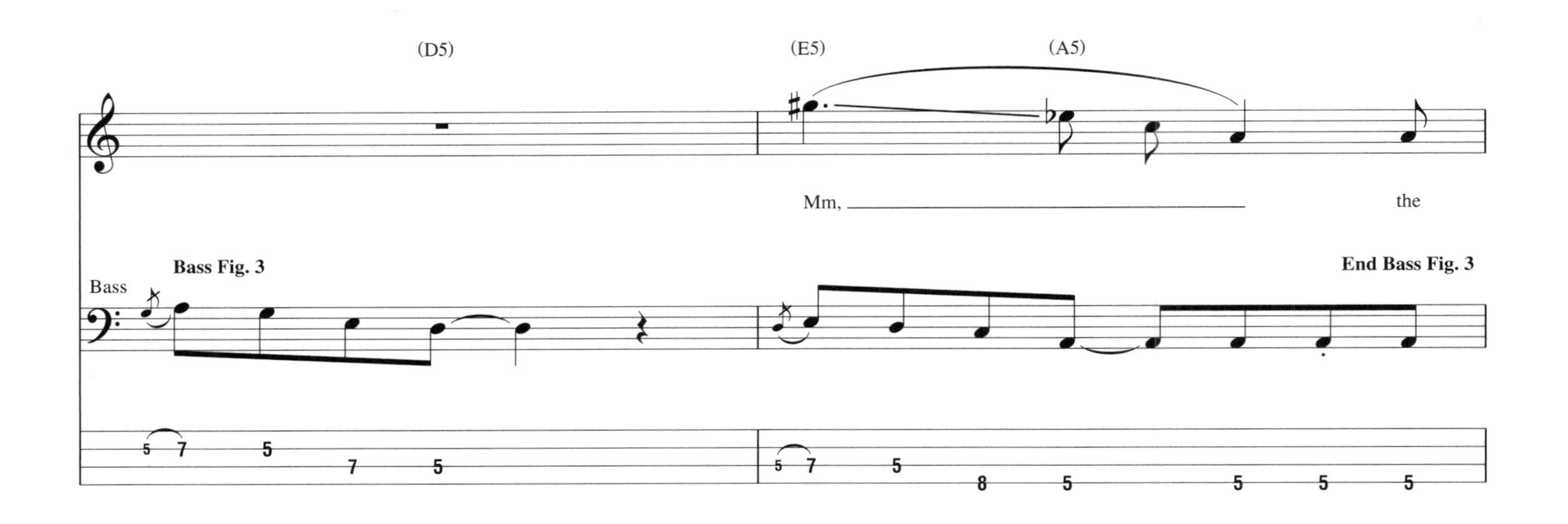
(D5) (E5) (A5)
Mm, the
Bass Fig. 3
Bass
End Bass Fig. 3

Bass: w/ Bass Fig. 3 (3 times)
(D5) (E5) (A5) (D5)
wish - ing well, ow! Yeah, ev - 'ry - bod - y has a wish,

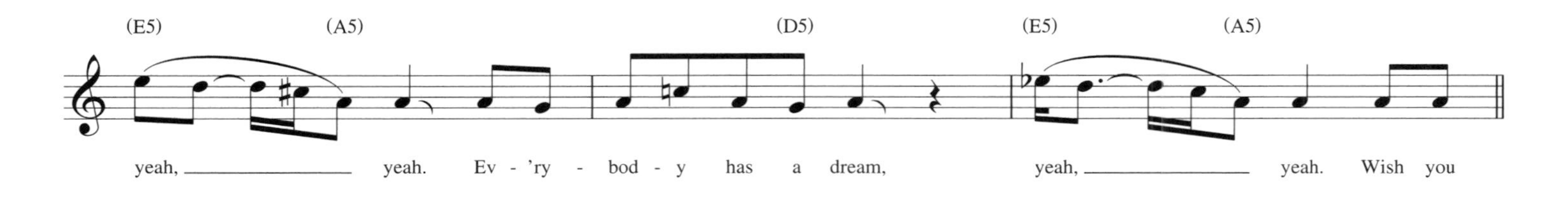
(E5) (A5) (D5) (E5) (A5)
yeah, yeah. Ev - 'ry - bod - y has a dream, yeah, yeah. Wish you

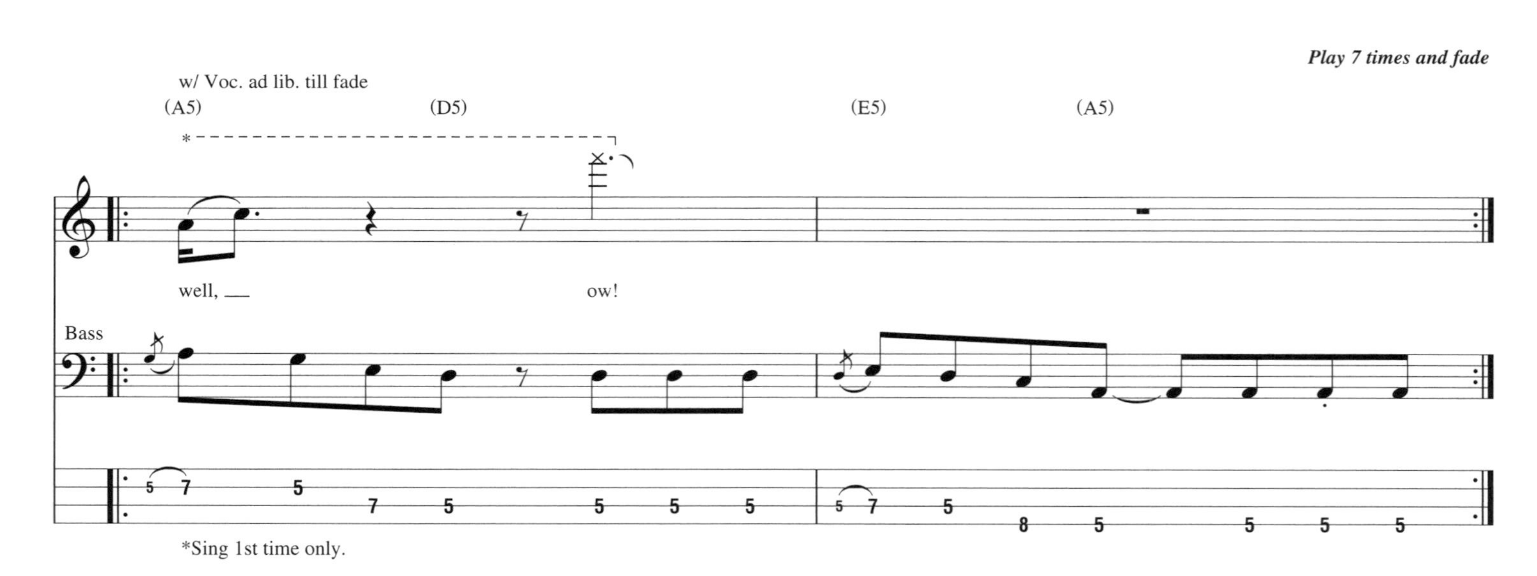
Play 7 times and fade
w/ Voc. ad lib. till fade
(A5) (D5) (E5) (A5)
well, ow!
Bass
*Sing 1st time only.

Wonderwall

Words and Music by Noel Gallagher

Intro
Moderately slow ♩ = 87
F#m7 A Esus4 B7sus4
(Guitar)
Play 4 times
Verse
F#m7 A
1. To - day is gon - na be the day that they're
Esus4 B7sus4 F#m7 A
gon - na throw it back to you. By now you should have some - how re - al -
Esus4 B7sus4 F#m7 A
ized what you got - ta do. I don't be - lieve that an - y - bod - y
Esus4 B7sus4 Dadd9 Esus4 B7sus4
feels the way I do a - bout you now.
Verse
2nd time, Bass: w/ Bass Fig. 1
F#m7 A Esus4 B7sus4
2. Back - beat, the word is on the street that the fire in your heart is out.
3. To - day was gon - na be the day, but they'll nev - er throw it back to you.
Bass
mf
T
A
B
F#m7 A Esus4 B7sus4
I'm sure you've heard it all be - fore, but you nev - er real - ly had a doubt.
By now you should have some - how re - al - ized what you're not to do.
Bass Fig. 1
End Bass Fig. 1

F♯m7
A
Esus4
B7sus4
I don't be - lieve that an - y - bod - y feels the way I do about you now.
F♯m7
A
Esus4
B7sus4
And all
Pre-Chorus
D
E
F♯m7
the roads we have to walk are wind - ing, and all
that lead you there were wind - ing, and all
D
E
F♯m7
the lights that lead us there are blind - ing.
the lights that light the way are blind - ing.

D
E
A
E/G♯
F♯m7
A
There are man - y things that I would like to say to you, but I don't know how.
B7sus4
Be - cause
I said
Chorus
Dadd9
F♯m7
A
F♯m7
may - be
you're gon - na be the one that
Bass Fig. 2
End Bass Fig. 2
Bass: w/ Bass Fig. 2 (2 1/2 times)
Dadd9
F♯m7
A
F♯m7
Dadd9
F♯m7
A
F♯m7
Dadd9
F♯m7
saves me.
And af - ter all
you're my won - der - wall,
1.
A
F♯m7
2.
A
F♯m7
I said

Chorus

Bass: w/ Bass Fig. 2 (8 times)
Dadd9
F#m7
A
F#m7
Dadd9
F#m7
may - be
(I said may - be.)
you're gon - na be the one that saves me.

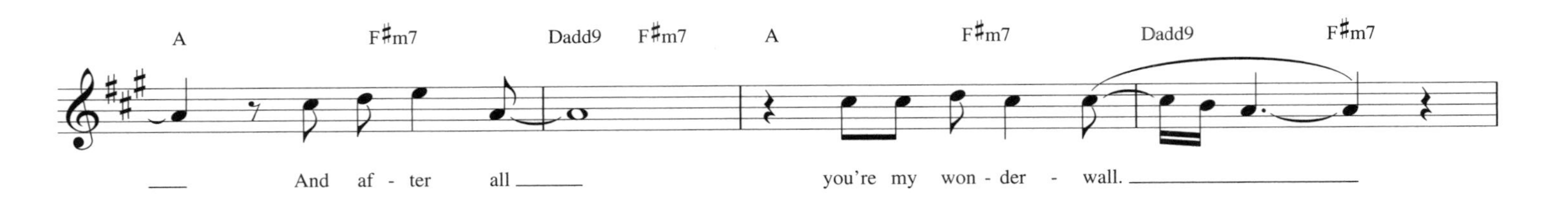
A
F#m7
Dadd9
F#m7
A
F#m7
Dadd9
F#m7
And af - ter all
you're my won - der - wall.

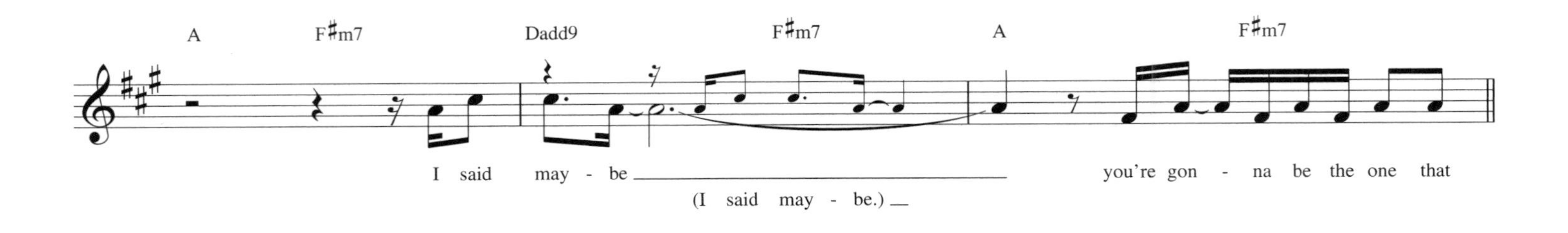
A
F#m7
Dadd9
F#m7
A
F#m7
I said may - be
(I said may - be.)
you're gon - na be the one that

1., 2.
3.
Dadd9
F#m7
A
F#m7
A
F#m7
saves me.
(Saves me.)
You're gon - na be the one that

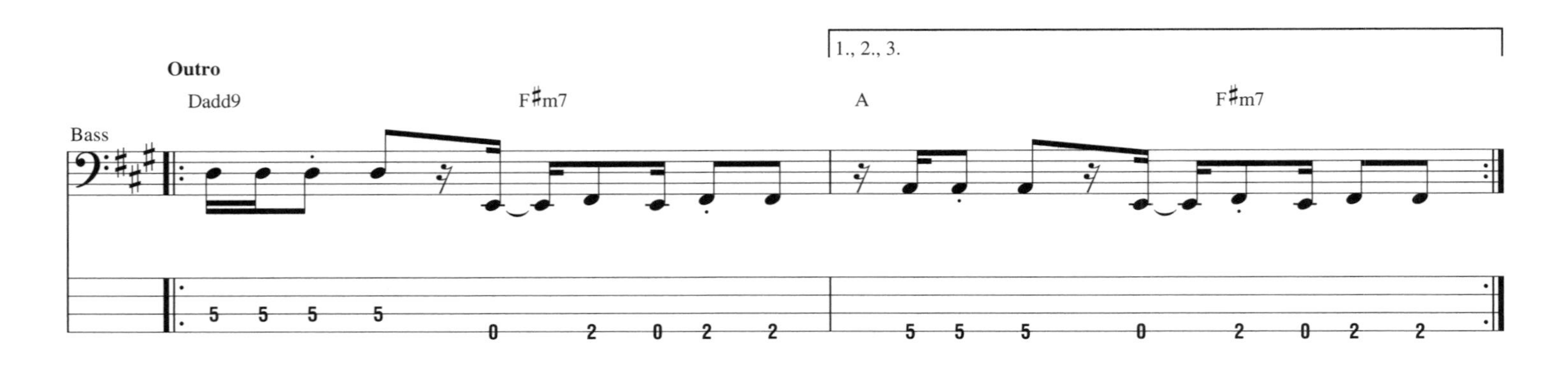
Outro
1., 2., 3.
Dadd9
F#m7
A
F#m7
Bass

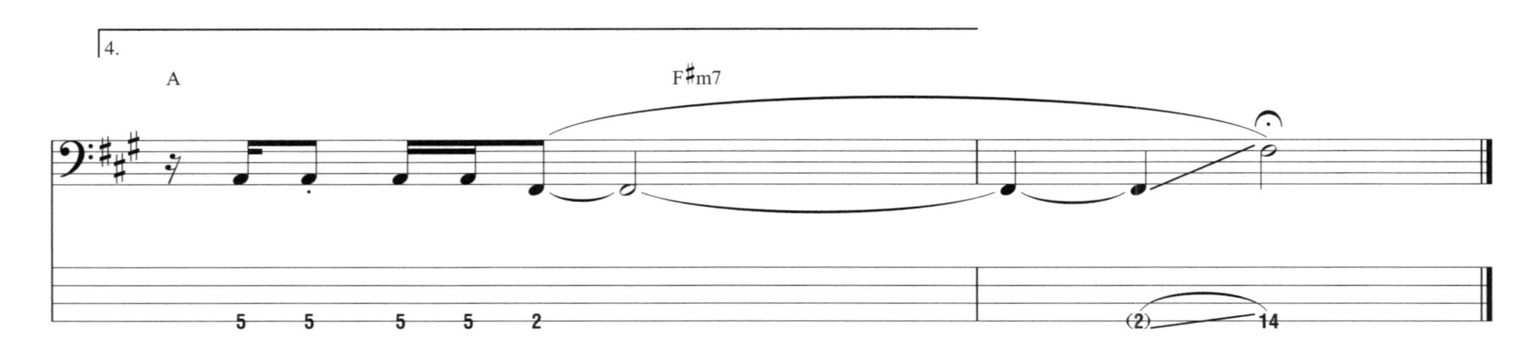
4.
A
F#m7

BASS NOTATION LEGEND

Bass music can be notated two different ways: on a *musical staff*, and in *tablature*.

THE MUSICAL STAFF shows pitches and rhythms and is divided by bar lines into measures. Pitches are named after the first seven letters of the alphabet.

TABLATURE graphically represents the bass fingerboard. Each horizontal line represents a string, and each number represents a fret.

Notes: G E C A / A F D B G

Strings: high G D A low E

3rd string, open — 2nd string, 2nd fret — 1st & 2nd strings open, played together

HAMMER-ON: Strike the first (lower) note with one finger, then sound the higher note (on the same string) with another finger by fretting it without picking.

T A B
3 5

PULL-OFF: Place both fingers on the notes to be sounded. Strike the first note and without picking, pull the finger off to sound the second (lower) note.

T A B
5 3

LEGATO SLIDE: Strike the first note and then slide the same fret-hand finger up or down to the second note. The second note is not struck.

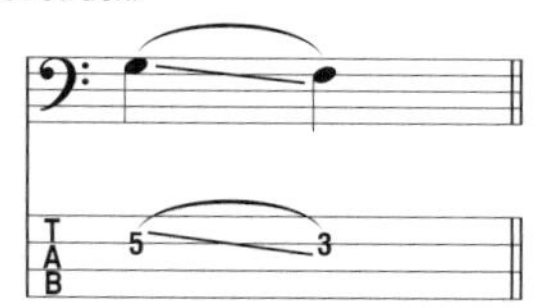

T A B
5 3

SHIFT SLIDE: Same as legato slide, except the second note is struck.

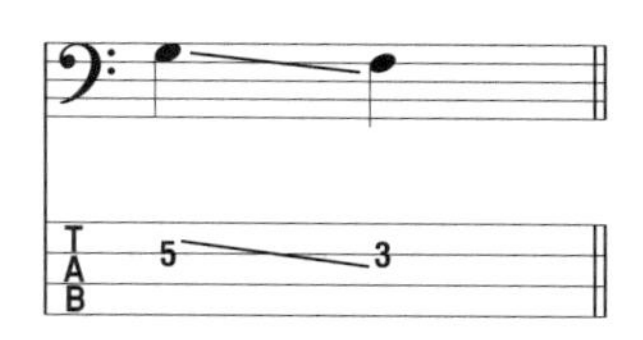

T A B
5 3

TRILL: Very rapidly alternate between the notes indicated by continuously hammering on and pulling off.

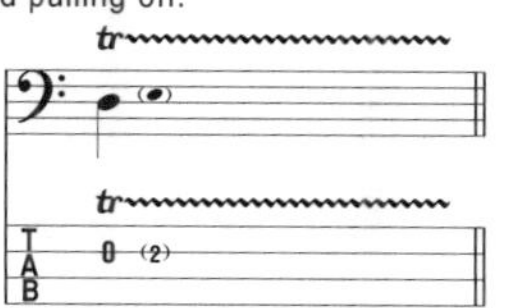

tr
T A B
0 (2)

TREMOLO PICKING: The note is picked as rapidly and continuously as possible.

T A B
5 7

VIBRATO: The string is vibrated by rapidly bending and releasing the note with the fretting hand.

T A B
5

SHAKE: Using one finger, rapidly alternate between two notes on one string by sliding either a half-step above or below.

T A B
7

NATURAL HARMONIC: Strike the note while the fret hand lightly touches the string directly over the fret indicated.

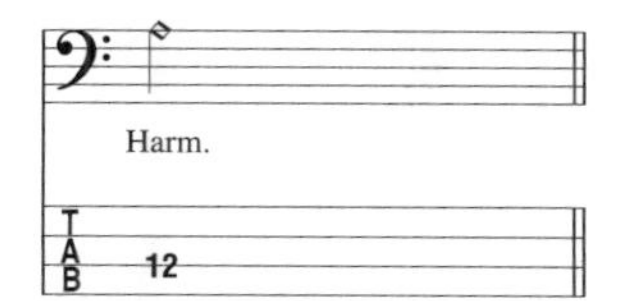

Harm.
T A B
12

MUFFLED STRINGS: A percussive sound is produced by laying the fret hand across the string(s) without depressing them and striking them with the pick hand.

T A B
X X

BEND: Strike the note and bend up the interval shown.

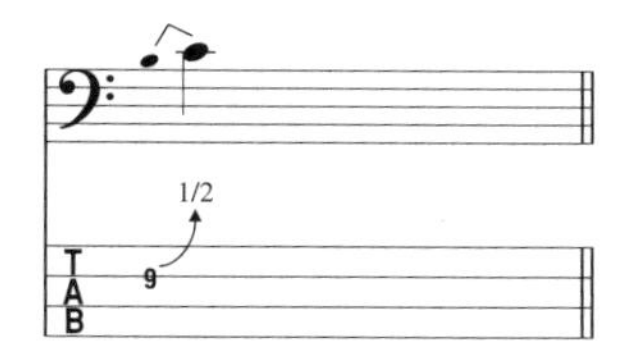

1/2
T A B
9

BEND AND RELEASE: Strike the note and bend up as indicated, then release back to the original note. Only the first note is struck.

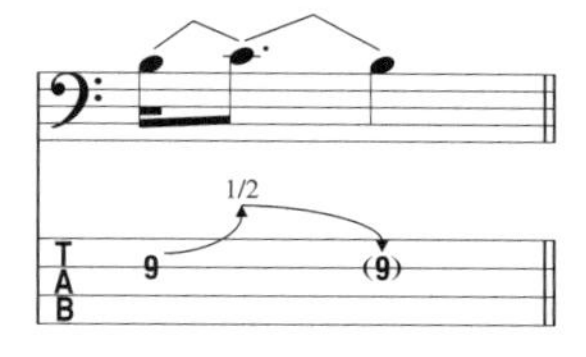

1/2
T A B
9 (9)

RIGHT-HAND TAP: Hammer ("tap") the fret indicated with the "pick-hand" index or middle finger and pull off to the note fretted by the fret hand.

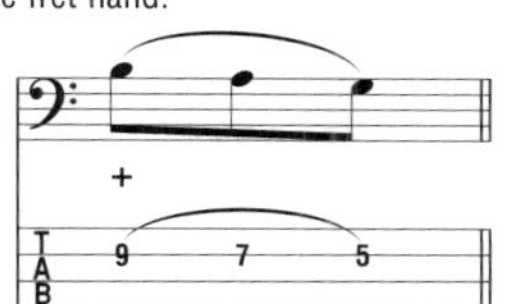

+
T A B
9 7 5

LEFT-HAND TAP: Hammer ("tap") the fret indicated with the "fret-hand" index or middle finger.

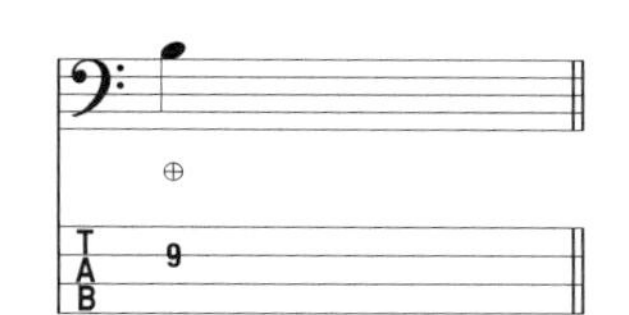

T A B
9

SLAP: Strike ("slap") string with right-hand thumb.

T
T A B
0

POP: Snap ("pop") string with right-hand index or middle finger.

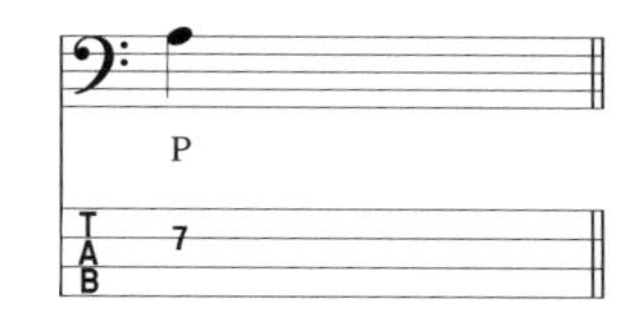

P
T A B
7

Additional Musical Definitions

(accent) • Accentuate note (play it louder).

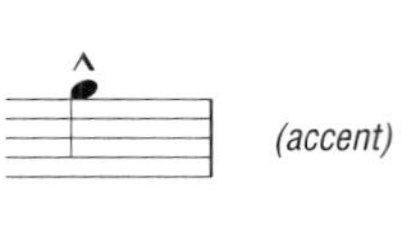

(accent) • Accentuate note with great intensity.

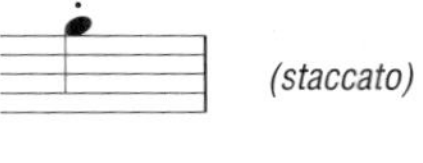
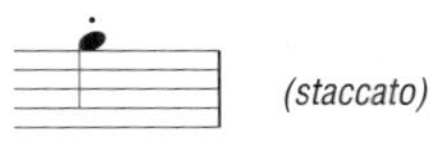
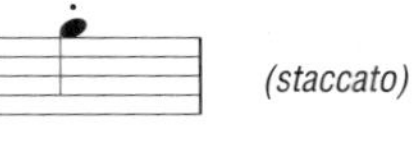

(staccato) • Play the note short.

⊓ • Downstroke

V • Upstroke

D.S. al Coda • Go back to the sign (𝄋), then play until the measure marked "***To Coda***," then skip to the section labelled "**Coda**."

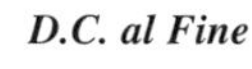

D.C. al Fine

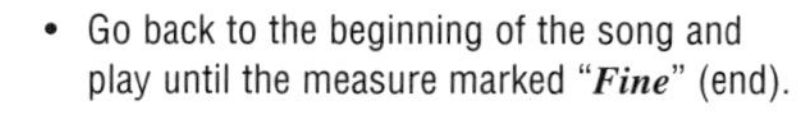

• Go back to the beginning of the song and play until the measure marked "***Fine***" (end).

Bass Fig. • Label used to recall a recurring pattern.

Fill

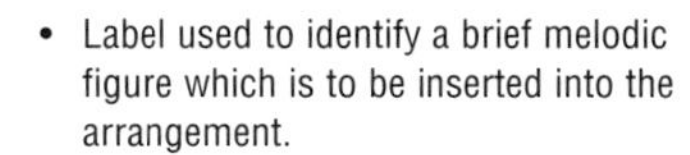

• Label used to identify a brief melodic figure which is to be inserted into the arrangement.

tacet • Instrument is silent (drops out).

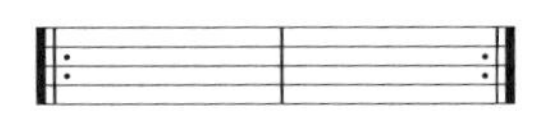

• Repeat measures between signs.

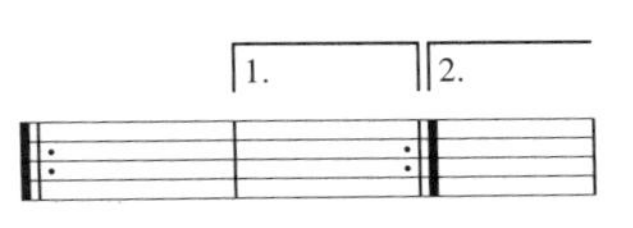

1.
2.

• When a repeated section has different endings, play the first ending only the first time and the second ending only the second time.

NOTE: Tablature numbers in parentheses mean:

1. The note is being sustained over a system (note in standard notation is tied), or
2. The note is sustained, but a new articulation (such as a hammer-on, pull-off, slide or vibrato) begins.

HAL•LEONARD
BASS
PLAY•ALONG

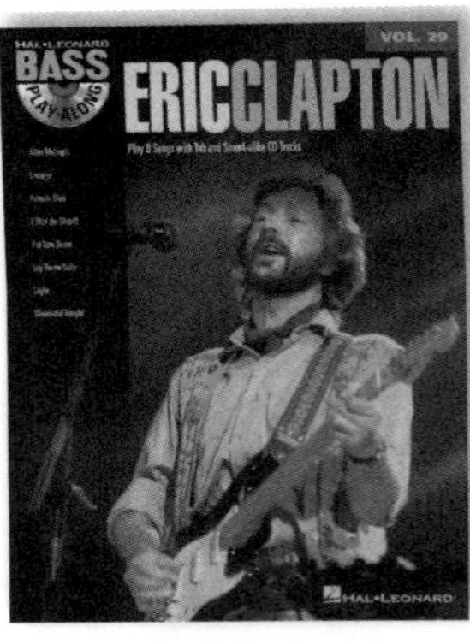
BASS PLAY-ALONG
VOL. 29
ERIC CLAPTON

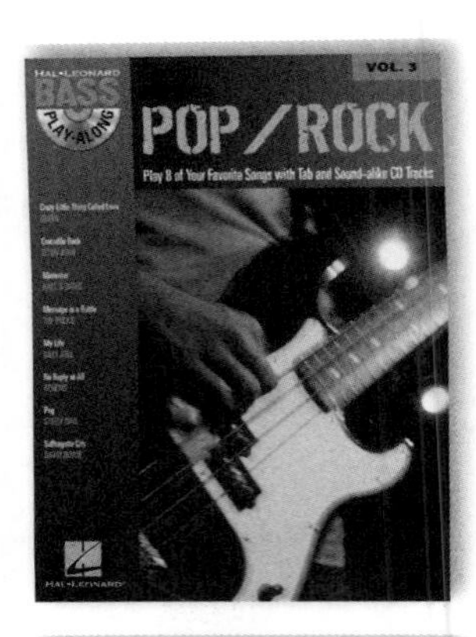
BASS PLAY-ALONG
VOL. 3
POP/ROCK

BASS PLAY-ALONG
VOL. 35
Bob Marley

The Bass Play-Along™ Series will help you play your favorite songs quickly and easily! Just follow the tab, listen to the CD to hear how the bass should sound, and then play along using the separate backing tracks. The melody and lyrics are also included in the book in case you want to sing, or to simply help you follow along. The CD is enhanced so you can use your computer to adjust the recording to any tempo without changing pitch!

BASS PLAY-ALONG
VOL. 27
KISS

BASS PLAY-ALONG
VOL. 11
Country

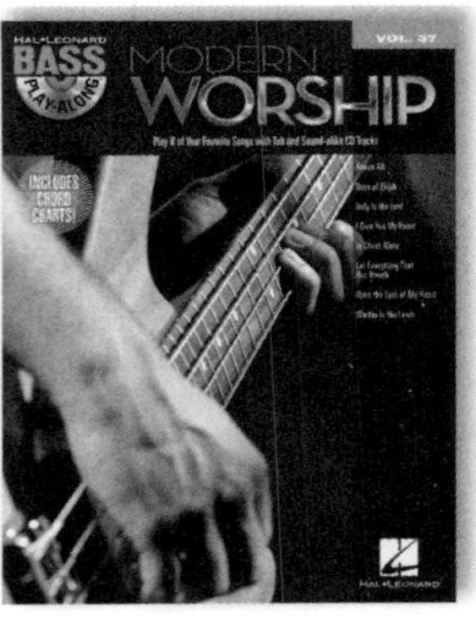
BASS PLAY-ALONG
VOL. 37
MODERN WORSHIP

BASS PLAY-ALONG
VOL. 38
AVENGED SEVENFOLD

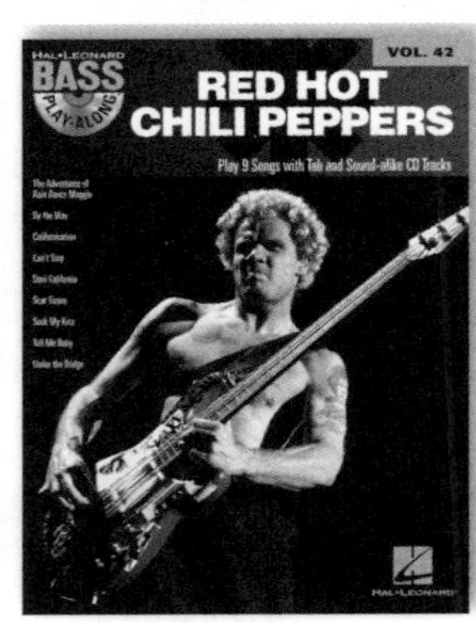
BASS PLAY-ALONG
VOL. 42
RED HOT CHILI PEPPERS

BASS PLAY-ALONG
VOL. 34
EASY SONGS

1. Rock
00699674 Book/CD Pack $12.95

2. R&B
00699675 Book/CD Pack $14.99

3. Pop/Rock
00699677 Book/CD Pack $12.95

4. '90s Rock
00699679 Book/CD Pack $12.95

5. Funk
00699680 Book/CD Pack $12.95

6. Classic Rock
00699678 Book/CD Pack $12.95

7. Hard Rock
00699676 Book/CD Pack $14.95

8. Punk Rock
00699813 Book/CD Pack $12.95

9. Blues
00699817 Book/CD Pack $14.99

10. Jimi Hendrix Smash Hits
00699815 Book/CD Pack $16.95

11. Country
00699818 Book/CD Pack $12.95

12. Punk Classics
00699814 Book/CD Pack $12.99

13. Lennon & McCartney
00699816 Book/CD Pack $14.99

14. Modern Rock
00699821 Book/CD Pack $14.99

15. Mainstream Rock
00699822 Book/CD Pack $14.99

16. '80s Metal
00699825 Book/CD Pack $16.99

17. Pop Metal
00699826 Book/CD Pack $14.99

18. Blues Rock
00699828 Book/CD Pack $14.99

19. Steely Dan
00700203 Book/CD Pack $16.99

20. The Police
00700270 Book/CD Pack $14.99

21. Rock Band – Modern Rock
00700705 Book/CD Pack $14.95

22. Rock Band – Classic Rock
00700706 Book/CD Pack $14.95

23. Pink Floyd – Dark Side of The Moon
00700847 Book/CD Pack $14.99

24. Weezer
00700960 Book/CD Pack $14.99

25. Nirvana
00701047 Book/CD Pack $14.99

26. Black Sabbath
00701180 Book/CD Pack $16.99

27. Kiss
00701181 Book/CD Pack $14.99

28. The Who
00701182 Book/CD Pack $14.99

29. Eric Clapton
00701183 Book/CD Pack $14.99

30. Early Rock
00701184 Book/CD Pack $15.99

31. The 1970s
00701185 Book/CD Pack $14.99

32. Disco
00701186 Book/CD Pack $14.99

33. Christmas Hits
00701197 Book/CD Pack $12.99

34. Easy Songs
00701480 Book/CD Pack $12.99

35. Bob Marley
00701702 Book/CD Pack $14.99

36. Aerosmith
00701886 Book/CD Pack $14.99

37. Modern Worship
00701920 Book/CD Pack $12.99

38. Avenged Sevenfold
00702386 Book/CD Pack $16.99

40. AC/DC
14041594 Book/CD Pack $16.99

41. U2
00702582 Book/CD Pack $16.99

42. Red Hot Chili Peppers
00702991 Book/CD Pack $19.99

45. Slipknot
00703201 Book/CD Pack $16.99

For More Information, See Your Local Music Dealer,
Or Write To:

HAL•LEONARD®
CORPORATION

7777 W. Bluemound Rd. P.O. Box 13819 Milwaukee, WI 53213

Visit Hal Leonard Online at **www.halleonard.com**
Prices, contents, and availability subject to change without notice.

0712